KV-510-434

Flash™ 4 Bible

Flash™ 4 Bible

Robert Reinhardt and Jon Warren Lentz

IDG Books Worldwide, Inc.
An International Data Group Company

Foster City, CA ✦ Chicago, IL ✦ Indianapolis, IN ✦ New York, NY

Flash™ 4 Bible

Published by
IDG Books Worldwide, Inc.
An International Data Group Company
919 E. Hillsdale Blvd., Suite 400
Foster City, CA 94404
www.idgbooks.com (IDG Books Worldwide Web site)

Copyright © 2000 IDG Books Worldwide, Inc. All rights reserved. No part of this book, including interior design, cover design, and icons, may be reproduced or transmitted in any form, by any means (electronic, photocopying, recording, or otherwise) without the prior written permission of the publisher.

ISBN: 0-7645-3356-8

Printed in the United States of America

10 9 8 7 6 5 4

1B/QW/QR/QQ/FC

Distributed in the United States by IDG Books Worldwide, Inc.

Distributed by CDG Books Canada Inc. for Canada; by Transworld Publishers Limited in the United Kingdom; by IDG Norge Books for Norway; by IDG Sweden Books for Sweden; by IDG Books Australia Publishing Corporation Pty. Ltd. for Australia and New Zealand; by TransQuest Publishers Pte Ltd. for Singapore, Malaysia, Thailand, Indonesia, and Hong Kong; by Gotop Information Inc. for Taiwan; by ICG Muse, Inc. for Japan; by Intersoft for South Africa; by Eyrolles for France; by International Thomson Publishing for Germany, Austria and Switzerland; by Distribuidora Cuspide for Argentina; by LR International for Brazil; by Galileo Libros for Chile; by Ediciones ZETA S.C.R. Ltda. for Peru; by WS Computer Publishing Corporation, Inc., for the Philippines; by Contemporanea de Ediciones for Venezuela; by Express Computer Distributors for the Caribbean and West Indies; by Micronesia Media Distributor, Inc. for Micronesia; by Chips Computadoras S.A. de C.V. for Mexico; by Editorial Norma de Panama S.A. for Panama; by American Bookshops for Finland.

For general information on IDG Books Worldwide's books in the U.S., please call our Consumer Customer Service department at 800-762-2974. For reseller information, including discounts and premium sales, please call our Reseller Customer Service department at 800-434-3422.

For information on where to purchase IDG Books Worldwide's books outside the U.S., please contact our International Sales department at 317-596-5530 or fax 317-572-4002.

For consumer information on foreign language translations, please contact our Customer Service department at 1-800-434-3422, fax 317-572-4002, or e-mail rights@idgbooks.com.

For information on licensing foreign or domestic rights, please phone +1-650-653-7098.

For sales inquiries and special prices for bulk quantities, please contact our Sales department at 800-762-2974 or write to the address above.

For information on using IDG Books Worldwide's books in the classroom or for ordering examination copies, please contact our Educational Sales department at 800-434-2086 or fax 317-572-4005.

For press review copies, author interviews, or other publicity information, please contact our Public Relations department at 650-653-7000 or fax 650-653-7500.

For authorization to photocopy items for corporate, personal, or educational use, please contact Copyright Clearance Center, 222 Rosewood Drive, Danvers, MA 01923, or fax 978-750-4470.

Library of Congress Cataloging-in-Publication Data
Reinhardt, Robert, 1973-
    Flash 4 bible / Robert Reinhardt and Jon Warren Lentz.
        p. cm.
    ISBN 0-7645-3356-8 (alk. paper)
    1. Computer animation. 2. Flash (Computer file)
3. Interactive multimedia. I. Lentz, Jon Warren. II. Title.
TR897.7 .R45 1999
006.6'96—dc21   99-047389

LIMIT OF LIABILITY/DISCLAIMER OF WARRANTY: THE PUBLISHER AND AUTHOR HAVE USED THEIR BEST EFFORTS IN PREPARING THIS BOOK. THE PUBLISHER AND AUTHOR MAKE NO REPRESENTATIONS OR WARRANTIES WITH RESPECT TO THE ACCURACY OR COMPLETENESS OF THE CONTENTS OF THIS BOOK AND SPECIFICALLY DISCLAIM ANY IMPLIED WARRANTIES OF MERCHANTABILITY OR FITNESS FOR A PARTICULAR PURPOSE. THERE ARE NO WARRANTIES WHICH EXTEND BEYOND THE DESCRIPTIONS CONTAINED IN THIS PARAGRAPH. NO WARRANTY MAY BE CREATED OR EXTENDED BY SALES REPRESENTATIVES OR WRITTEN SALES MATERIALS. THE ACCURACY AND COMPLETENESS OF THE INFORMATION PROVIDED HEREIN AND THE OPINIONS STATED HEREIN ARE NOT GUARANTEED OR WARRANTED TO PRODUCE ANY PARTICULAR RESULTS, AND THE ADVICE AND STRATEGIES CONTAINED HEREIN MAY NOT BE SUITABLE FOR EVERY INDIVIDUAL. NEITHER THE PUBLISHER NOR AUTHOR SHALL BE LIABLE FOR ANY LOSS OF PROFIT OR ANY OTHER COMMERCIAL DAMAGES, INCLUDING BUT NOT LIMITED TO SPECIAL, INCIDENTAL, CONSEQUENTIAL, OR OTHER DAMAGES.

Trademarks: For Dummies, Dummies Man, A Reference for the Rest of Us!, The Dummies Way, Dummies Daily, and related trade dress are registered trademarks or trademarks of IDG Books Worldwide, Inc. in the United States and other countries, and may not be used without written permission. All other trademarks are the property of their respective owners. IDG Books Worldwide is not associated with any product or vendor mentioned in this book.

is a registered trademark under exclusive license to IDG Books Worldwide, Inc. from International Data Group, Inc.

ABOUT IDG BOOKS WORLDWIDE

Welcome to the world of IDG Books Worldwide.

IDG Books Worldwide, Inc., is a subsidiary of International Data Group, the world's largest publisher of computer-related information and the leading global provider of information services on information technology. IDG was founded more than 30 years ago by Patrick J. McGovern and now employs more than 9,000 people worldwide. IDG publishes more than 290 computer publications in over 75 countries. More than 90 million people read one or more IDG publications each month.

Launched in 1990, IDG Books Worldwide is today the #1 publisher of best-selling computer books in the United States. We are proud to have received eight awards from the Computer Press Association in recognition of editorial excellence and three from Computer Currents' First Annual Readers' Choice Awards. Our best-selling ...*For Dummies*® series has more than 50 million copies in print with translations in 31 languages. IDG Books Worldwide, through a joint venture with IDG's Hi-Tech Beijing, became the first U.S. publisher to publish a computer book in the People's Republic of China. In record time, IDG Books Worldwide has become the first choice for millions of readers around the world who want to learn how to better manage their businesses.

Our mission is simple: Every one of our books is designed to bring extra value and skill-building instructions to the reader. Our books are written by experts who understand and care about our readers. The knowledge base of our editorial staff comes from years of experience in publishing, education, and journalism — experience we use to produce books to carry us into the new millennium. In short, we care about books, so we attract the best people. We devote special attention to details such as audience, interior design, use of icons, and illustrations. And because we use an efficient process of authoring, editing, and desktop publishing our books electronically, we can spend more time ensuring superior content and less time on the technicalities of making books.

You can count on our commitment to deliver high-quality books at competitive prices on topics you want to read about. At IDG Books Worldwide, we continue in the IDG tradition of delivering quality for more than 30 years. You'll find no better book on a subject than one from IDG Books Worldwide.

John Kilcullen
Chairman and CEO
IDG Books Worldwide, Inc.

Steven Berkowitz
President and Publisher
IDG Books Worldwide, Inc.

VIII WINNER

*Eighth Annual
Computer Press
Awards 1992*

IX WINNER

*Ninth Annual
Computer Press
Awards 1993*

WINNER

WINNER

X WINNER

*Tenth Annual
Computer Press
Awards 1994*

XI WINNER

*Eleventh Annual
Computer Press
Awards 1995*

IDG is the world's leading IT media, research and exposition company. Founded in 1964, IDG had 1997 revenues of $2.05 billion and has more than 9,000 employees worldwide. IDG offers the widest range of media options that reach IT buyers in 75 countries representing 95% of worldwide IT spending. IDG's diverse product and services portfolio spans six key areas including print publishing, online publishing, expositions and conferences, market research, education and training, and global marketing services. More than 90 million people read one or more of IDG's 290 magazines and newspapers, including IDG's leading global brands — Computerworld, PC World, Network World, Macworld and the Channel World family of publications. IDG Books Worldwide is one of the fastest-growing computer book publishers in the world, with more than 700 titles in 36 languages. The "...For Dummies®" series alone has more than 50 million copies in print. IDG offers online users the largest network of technology-specific Web sites around the world through IDG.net (http://www.idg.net), which comprises more than 225 targeted Web sites in 55 countries worldwide. International Data Corporation (IDC) is the world's largest provider of information technology data, analysis and consulting, with research centers in over 41 countries and more than 400 research analysts worldwide. IDG World Expo is a leading producer of more than 168 globally branded conferences and expositions in 35 countries including E3 (Electronic Entertainment Expo), Macworld Expo, ComNet, Windows World Expo, ICE (Internet Commerce Expo), Agenda, DEMO, and Spotlight. IDG's training subsidiary, ExecuTrain, is the world's largest computer training company, with more than 230 locations worldwide and 785 training courses. IDG Marketing Services helps industry-leading IT companies build international brand recognition by developing global integrated marketing programs via IDG's print, online and exposition products worldwide. Further information about the company can be found at www.idg.com.

1/24/99

Credits

Acquisitions Editor
Kathy Yankton

Development Editor
Colleen Dowling

Technical Editors
Paul Mendigochea
Bill Turner
Chrissy Rey

Copy Editors
Michael D. Welch
Publication Services

Project Coordinator
Linda Marousek

Quality Control Specialists
Chris Weisbart
Laura Taflinger

Graphics and Production Specialists
Mario Amador
Michael Lewis
Jude Levinson
Dina Quan
Victor Varella

Book Designer
Drew R. Moore

Illustrators
Mary Jo Richards
Angie Hunckler
Clint Lahnen

Proofreading and Indexing
York Production Services

Cover Illustration
Evan Deerfield

About the Authors

Robert Reinhardt has developed multimedia courses for educational facilities in Canada and the United States, delivered conference seminars on Web design, and served as technical editor for several Photoshop and Web books. With a degree in photographic arts, Robert takes a holistic approach to computer applications for the creation of provocative multimedia. Recently, he created installation and digital art for the Warner Bros. feature film *Gossip*. Now based in Los Angeles, he continues his work through "The Makers" (www.theMakers.com) as a multimedia artist, programmer, and instructor with his partner Snow and his creatively inclined dog, Stella.

Jon Warren Lentz is a graduate of the Classical Studies program at UCSC, and a freelance artist and author. He is the lead co-author of a popular Web design book, <*deconstructing web graphics.2*>, co-authored with Lynda Weinman. He's also an associate editor and columnist for *EFX Art and Design* magazine, formerly known as *Mac Art & Design*. Prior to entering the photodigital frontier, Lentz achieved notice as a sculptor working with sand-carved glass — a process that he helped to define as a fine art medium. Jon's images have been featured in the 1997 Graphis Poster Annual,

Mac Art & Design magazine (Sweden), *IdN* — the International Designer's Network magazine (Hong Kong), and other magazines. In July 1998, *Shutterbug* magazine explored connections between his fine art abstractions and commercial works. His work may be viewed online at www.uncom.com. Jon has lectured on digital art, design, and technology at many venues, including the Maine Photographic Workshops, and the Thunder Lizard Photoshop Conference. In 1998, Jon was the visiting artist at Bradford College in Bradford, Massachusetts. In 1999, he joined the faculty at Palomar College, where he now teaches Photoshop, Flash, and Web design. Jon's personal interests are board surfing, photography, fine art, and the study of classical Latin and Greek poetry. He lives with his wife and son in Carlsbad, a beach community near San Diego, California.

Contributors and Technical Editors

Justin Jamieson (justin@mediumLarge.com) started using his first computer when he was eight years old. Years later, after studying design and cinematography, he combined his training with his computing knowledge to co-found mediumLarge (www.mediumLarge.com), a new media design firm in Toronto. In 1997, while developing a Web site for a local Toronto rap group, Justin began his research into the use of sound on the Internet and there's been no turning back. He recently began an online record company for unsigned Canadian acts that will distribute CDs and MP3s to listeners around the world.

One of the first true Flashmasters, **Paul Mendigochea** has been working with the program since the release of FutureSplash. He's renowned as the architect of the award-winning FlashPad Web site (www.flasher.net/flashpad.html), which was the first community forum for like-minded Flashers. FlashPad is built entirely in Flash 4, with exemplary use of the new features. According to Paul, "Flash 4's robust forms and client/server features make Flash 4 a viable alternative to HTML-based Web sites." Paul predicts that these new features will propel "the great Internet facelift era," meaning that clunky HTML interfaces will soon be replaced with easy-to-use Flash front ends. To kick-start this era, he also maintains the Flashcgi Web site (www.flashcgi.com), which delivers support to developers who build Flash-based client/server applications.

Having originally studied fine arts (BA, University of Waterloo) and literature, language, and computer-mediated-communication (MA, University of Waterloo), **Colin Moock** now explores theoretical and practical creativity on the Web. During the mid '90s, Colin produced SoftQuad Inc's corporate Web site, when SoftQuad's HoTMetaL PRO ruled the Web-authoring software world. He's now a Web designer at Toronto-based new media firm ICE (www.iceinc.com), creating Web sites and interactive experiences for companies such as Levi's, Sony, The Movie Network, and McClelland & Stewart. Colin's personal exploration of the Web occurs at www.moock.org, where he maintains online artwork, Web experiments, and collections of essays and tutorials for Web developers.

An advocate of Web accessibility, Colin volunteers as an illustrator and Web designer for the Yuri Rubinsky Insight Foundation (www.yuri.org), which works closely with the World Wide Web Consortium (W3C), Microsoft, SoftQuad, and the NCSA to establish accessible standards for the Web's disabled community. Colin has contributed to such books as *Teach Yourself the Internet, SGML on the Web*, and to *Toronto Computes*. His Web sites have appeared in magazines ranging from *Gardening Life* and *Windows Magazine* to *Web Week* and *Blues Review*. His Flash animations have been featured in *Flash 3 Web Animation* and *Applied Arts* magazine, and on Macromedia's *Shocked Site of the Day* Web site.

Chrissey Rey is an energetic young woman from the suburbs of Washington, D.C. She graduated from the University of Maryland in 1995, with a degree in zoology. During her final year of study, she discovered the Web. After a couple of brief stints in her field of study (as a zookeeper aide and an animal technician) she veered away from zoology to pursue the Web full time, working as both a freelance contractor (evenings) and as a full-time developer (days). In her spare time she runs FlashLite (www.flashlite.net), which she established to post tutorials and tips on the use of Flash. She's also the founder of the FlashCorps (www.flashcorps.org). Recently, she changed her day job in order to teach Flash, Fireworks, Dreamweaver, and other software in association with Fig Leaf Software (www.figleaf.com).

Since the age of five, **Bill Turner's** mission has been to create an entertaining cartoon show. A self-taught artist, at age 15 he sold his first cartoons to an underground college radio station for their logo T-shirts. Since then, his still cartoon work has appeared during the '80s in various national magazines and editorial pages of newspapers. In the late '80s, computers entered Billl's picture, providing tools to apply his talent to the animated cartoon. He's created numerous animations in 2D and 3D for commercial broadcast. When he discovered Flash (then FutureSplash), Bill knew this was the ticket to realizing a dream. He created an interactive animated cartoon Web site, "Dubes," that made its way to Macromedia's Cutting Edge Gallery. Dubes was also featured in a chapter on Shockwave in the book *HTML Publishing for Netscape*. Most recently, Bill created the cartoon show *Weber* about a web-footed, snorkel-sporting, mischief-making pelican in the vein of the cartoons that influenced his childhood. He resides on Florida's Space Coast with wife Julia, son Trent, and daughter Majenta—his favorite audience and creative advisors. Bill can be reached through turnertoons productions' Web site at www.turnertoons.com.

To my father, Joseph Reinhardt, who once said,
"Robert, I don't care what they say about you — you're alright by me."

RJR

My efforts on this book are dedicated to my wife and soul mate, Roanne.
Thank you for understanding and supporting me while I "wrote the Bible."

Love, Jon

Preface

About two years ago Macromedia acquired a small Web graphics program, FutureSplash. This was a quirky little program with the astounding ability to generate compact, vector-based graphics and animations for delivery over the Web. With Macromedia's embrace, Flash blossomed. Now, Flash has obtained ubiquity. The Flash Player plug-in ships with most major browsers and operating systems. Now Flash graphics appear all over the Web and the number of Flash users continues to increase at an astounding pace.

Flash 4 has greatly expanded the feature set of Flash movies. Once the domain of Flash's dynamic server component, Generator, Flash movies can now communicate directly with server-side scripts and programs. Sounds can be encoded as MP3 audio, for high-quality music on the Web at the smallest file sizes. The Flash interface now looks and feels like other Macromedia products, with more tool options and docking windows. Third-party developers are creating applications that output to the Flash movie format, .SWF files. Flash is poised to be the central application for generating hot, low-bandwidth, interactive content for delivery over the Web.

This is the first edition

We wrote this book because we couldn't find a book that does the program justice. In the early stages, when we'd only began to talk about this project, we were greatly encouraged to write the book because so many Flash users informed us that they were "desperate" to have this book.

We wrote this book to fill the need for a user-friendly, in-depth book that will serve both the Web novice and the accomplished Webmaster and will endure as their guide to the minute workings and higher capabilities of this powerful program.

It's fitting that this mature version of Flash should finally have a *Bible* to document both the features of the program and the many ways that Flash can be used in concert with other programs to create high-quality multimedia—everything from 3D animations to complex interactivity between Flash and Director movies. Because Flash is rarely used as the complete content creator for interactive presentations, we thought readers would be interested in how Flash fits into a workflow for interactive multimedia development. Furthermore, in the transition between Versions 3 and 4, Flash has gone through some pretty major changes. So, even if you already know Flash, we're pretty sure that this book will be able to show you more than a thing or two.

Is there any other Flash book for you?

Before we started this project, we went to the bookstores. There weren't any Flash books available. We went online. We ordered both of the books that were in print at the time. Neither of them afforded much of an alternative to the manual that ships with the program.

The *Flash 4 Bible* is the most comprehensive and exhaustive reference on Flash. It will help you get started on your first day with the program and will still be a valuable resource when you've attained mastery of the program. When you are looking for clues on how to integrate Flash with other programs so that you can deliver unique and compelling content in the Flash format, you'll know where to turn.

- ✦ **Exhaustive coverage of Flash.** We spent a great deal of time covering every aspect of Flash functionality. The first part of the book is entirely dedicated to the Flash interface, and Parts II and III explain how to integrate animations and sound into your Flash movies.

- ✦ **Flash isn't a simple program anymore.** You can think of Flash as a multitasking application: it's an illustration program, an image and sound editor, an animation machine, and a scripting engine, all rolled into one. In this book, we dissect Flash into each of these components and explain how each works with the other parts.

- ✦ **This is a real-world book.** We've gone to great lengths to make sure that our lessons, examples, and explanations are based in reality (not that the Web isn't real!). We even recruited some of the top names in the Flash industry to lend us their tips and techniques so that you could benefit their years of expertise.

- ✦ **Foremost technical advisors.** To ensure that this book was as technically accurate as possible, we enlisted the aid of Paul Mendigochea from Flasher.net (a.k.a. *FlashPad*), Chrissy Rey from Flashlite.net, and Bill Turner from Turnertoons.com. Not only did these individuals double-check our work, but they also contributed tutorials to the book.

- ✦ **The CD-ROM.** The CD-ROM that accompanies this book includes many of the source .FLA files and original artwork for the examples and lessons in the book. It also includes trial versions of Flash 4 and other Macromedia products, as well as popular image and multimedia plug-ins for image-editing applications.

- ✦ **The authors' Web site.** In order to create a forum for the delivery of updates, notes, and sample files, we have also established a Web site:

    www.theFlashBible.com

    One of the first things you'll want to go there for is to download Turner's Flash 4 Keyboard Shortcuts and Quick Keys.

How to get the most out of this book

Here are two things to know so you can get the most out of this book.

First, regarding menu and keyboard commands, here's the convention for indicating that you're going to need to select a command from a menu: The menu and command will be separated by an arrow symbol. For example, when told to open the Toolbars Option palette from the Flash menu bar, the instructions will say to choose Window ⇨ Toolbar.

Second, jump in anywhere. Although this book was written to take a beginner by the hand, starting from page one, you can also use it as a reference. Use the index and the table of contents to find what you're looking for, and just go there. If you already know Flash and want to get some details on sound, for example, just go to the sound sections.

Icons: What do they mean?

Although the icons are pretty standard and self-explanatory (they have their names written on them!), here's a brief explanation of what they are and what the mean.

Tips will offer you extra information that further explains a given topic or technique, often suggesting alternatives or workarounds to a listed procedure.

Notes provide supplementary information to the text, shedding light on background processes or miscellaneous options that aren't crucial to the basic understanding of the material.

When you see the Caution icon, make sure you're following along closely to the tips and techniques being discussed. Some external applications may not work exactly the same with Flash on different operating systems.

If you want to find related information to a given topic in another chapter, look for the cross-reference icons.

The New Feature icons point out any differences between Flash 4 and previous versions of Flash.

This icon indicates that the CD-ROM contains a related file in the given folder.

How this book is organized

This book has been written in a format that gives you access to "need to know" information very easily in every section (or Part) of the book. If you are completely new to Flash, then you'll want to read Parts I through IV. After you have developed a familiarity with the Flash interface, then you can proceed to Parts V and VI. However, if you've already used Flash 3, then you may want to jump right into Parts IV, V and VI to learn more about ActionScript, creating artwork and content in other applications, and using the new Publish commands, respectively. Part V is especially useful if you have a favorite application like Dreamweaver or Director in which you want to use Flash movies.

Part I — Mastering Flash Tools

The first part of this book explores the Flash interface, starting with the Flash toolbar (Chapter 1) and moving through the Colors window (Chapter 2) and then explaining the context in which Flash movies interact on the Web (Chapter 3). Each menu command and window in the Flash interface is discussed in Chapter 4, and Chapter 5 shows you how to use help resources that are bundled with the Flash application, as well as online resources and tutorials.

Part II — Creating Flash Graphics

After you've learned how to work your way through the Flash interface, you can start to learn how to draw with Flash (Chapter 6) and incorporate external media files like JPEGs and GIFs (Chapter 7) into your Flash artwork. Chapter 8 shows you how to animate your artwork with motion and shape tweening, while Chapter 9 presents the framework of Flash asset management by using the Library and symbols.

Part III — Sound Planning

Because Parts I and II focus mainly on the visual presentation of a Flash movie, you need to start thinking about the effect of sound within a Flash movie. In Chapter 10, you learn the basics of digital sound and see which file formats can be imported into Flash. Chapter 11 shows you how to control the playback of sounds within a Flash movie, and you'll learn how to create interactive buttons with rollover sounds. Chapter 12 explains how to adjust and optimize audio compression in an exported Flash movie.

Part IV — Flash Interactivity: Making Things *Happen*

Not everyone wants to use Flash to create animating buttons for HTML documents on the Web. In Part IV, you'll learn how to start using Flash to create highly interactive and responsive presentations. Flash 4 has greatly increased the capacity of Flash movies to communicate between its own internal elements like nested movie clips or between the movie and an external program like a CGI script running on your Web server. With this heightened interactivity, you can create Flash movies that accept visitor input or manipulate content that is retrieved from a database.

Part V — Using Flash with Other Programs

Every multimedia designer uses Flash with some other graphics, sound, and authoring application to create a unique workflow that solves the problems of daily interactive project development. Part V shows you how to create content in popular applications like Macromedia Fireworks, Freehand, and Director, as well as Adobe Photoshop and Kinetix 3D Studio Max — just to name a few. We're sure that you'll find our coverage of QuickTime 4 and QuickTime Flash movies particularly interesting.

Part VI — Distributing Flash Movies

Finally, you'll need to learn how to export (or publish) your Flash presentations to the .SWF file format for use on a Web page, or within another presentation like a floppy disk or CD-ROM project. Chapter 25 details every option in the new Publish commands of Flash 4, as well providing tips for optimizing your Flash movies in order to achieve smaller file sizes for faster download performance. If you prefer to hand-code your HTML, then read Chapter 26, which describes how to use the <EMBED> and <OBJECT> tags. If you want to find out how to create a Flash standalone projector, or use the Flash standalone player, then check out Chapter 27.

Appendixes

Among other items, you'll find a listing of our contributors' contact information and directions for using the *Flash 4 Bible* CD-ROM in the appendixes.

Getting in touch with us

Unlike many authors, we aren't going to make any promises about answering every e-mail that comes to us. We already have more mail than we can *possibly* begin to answer. However, if you have a really, really good tip or idea that you want to share with us, we'd like to hear from you. You can also send us comments about the book to:

```
jon@theFlashBible.com
rob@theFlashBible.com
```

Also check Appendix B for more information on contacting this book's various contributors and technical editors.

You can help make Flash better!

The latest version of Flash is more powerful, has more robust capabilities, and is easier to use than any previous version of Flash. It's also the best (Freehand can also export to the .FLA file format) program that's capable of creating highly-compact, vector-based content for transmission over the Web. We're convinced that Flash 4 is a *great* program. (That's why we wrote this book!) But we also know that Macromedia is probably already planning the next version. So, if you have an idea or feature request for the next version, let the folks at Macromedia know. Send them an e-mail to:

```
wish-flash@macromedia.com
```

The simple fact is this: if more users request a specific feature or improvement, it's more likely that Macromedia will implement it.

Acknowledgments

Robert Reinhardt: This book would not have been possible without the help and talent of many people. I haven't physically encountered many of the experts that lent their tips and techniques to this book — most of the people were contacted via e-mail or ICQ, but everyone cooperated at a moment's notice. The generosity and diversity of our contributors built the unique and valuable resource that I hoped the *Flash 4 Bible* would be.

Thanks to everyone at IDG Books Worldwide who put endless hours into the production of this book. As any writer can attest, a great manager can make or break a project. Colleen Dowling, our development editor, was always gracious and effective in her efforts to aid the progress and continuity of this volume. Without her expertise and tireless work, this book wouldn't be in your hands. Also, I'd like to thank Kathy Yankton, our acquisitions editor, for trusting us to undertake the task of writing this book.

Of course, any book on a computer program would not be very useful if it wasn't technically accurate. Many thanks to the developers, engineers and support staff at Macromedia, especially Gary Grossman, Jonathan Gay and Erica Norton, who answered my questions during the development of Flash 4. Also, I am indebted to Colin Moock and Paul Mendigochea for coming to our aid with their insightful comments and contributions.

Finally, I now understand why so many authors thank their significant others in the acknowledgments. The process of writing this book necessarily involved spending entire days and nights — for many months — researching and developing the material. I couldn't have finished this project without the support and understanding of my partner, Snow Dowd.

Jon Warren Lentz: I would like to thank my partner, Robert Reinhardt, for suggesting this project and for his pertinacity in seeing it through to such a marvelous conclusion. Robert, your technical acumen and aesthetic sensibility make you the ideal co-author.

Tremendous thanks are also due our agent, David Fugate, both for placing this title and for counseling us through several daunting challenges. We couldn't have done this without you.

Thanks to Colleen Dowling, our developmental editor, for bringing such good, clear energy to this project at a critical time. Thanks Colleen. I'd also like to thank our acquisitions editor, Kathy Yankton, for her unflagging belief in this title.

Contents at a Glance

Contents

Part II: Creating Flash Graphics   129

Chapter 6: Drawing in Flash 131

Chapter 7: Using Media with Flash Artwork 157

Chapter 8: Animating with Flash 167

Mastering Flash Tools

Y ou probably want to jump right into creating something with Flash, right? The first chapter of Part I will show you every detail of the Flash toolbar so that you'll know where to go when you want to turn your design concept into a tangible piece of Flash artwork. Because Web color limitations still remain a primary concern for many designers and Web surfers, we'll introduce you to Flash color in Chapter 2. In Chapter 3, you'll learn the difference between Flash editor documents (.FLA files) and their exported versions, Flash movies (.SWF files). Chapter 4 will show you to access and use Flash menus and palettes, while Chapter 5 will point in the right direction for Flash support resources within the application interface and on the Web.

Defining the Flash Toolbar

In this chapter, we describe all fourteen tools that appear in the Flash Drawing toolbar. We discuss the uses of each tool and the ways in which they can be modified and controlled. We also cover keyboard shortcuts and menu bar equivalents. In the process of describing the tools and telling you about their functionality, we define, for each tool, the specific terminology that is used throughout the book. So, feel free to return to this chapter anytime that you need quick information on Flash tools.

Flash Tool Basics

A book about a software program must be clear and consistent in the terms and names that are used to describe the various thingamajigs and doohickeys that make the program work. After considerable deliberation and several rewrites of this particular chapter, we settled upon the terminology that has — hopefully — been applied consistently throughout this book. So, here's our logic: Wherever possible, we have attempted to use terms derived from the Flash Interface. For example, although a window might be referred to as a palette, we will refer to it as a window if it is accessible from the Windows menu of the menu bar.

New Feature

Most, if not all, of the individual interface components can now be "undocked" and turned into floating palettes, or vice versa — and floating palettes can be docked. Docking means that a floating palette is dragged to the edge of the program window, where it then melds to the border of the window. It will remain docked there until it is moved to another docked position, is floated off to resume usage as a palette, or is closed. Sadly, this functionality is not fully implemented in the Mac version of Flash 4 — only the Timeline can be undocked from the main Flash workspace window. Disappointed? Write your congressman.

Using the Drawing toolbar

The default location for the Flash Drawing toolbar is in the upper-left corner of the Flash Program window. However, if you haven't just installed Flash, or if someone else has changed the defaults in Flash, you may not be able to find the Drawing toolbar.

Making the Drawing toolbar visible

If the Drawing toolbar is not visible on the PC Flash screen, it can be opened from the Flash menu bar by choosing Window ➪ Toolbar, which opens the Toolbars Option Palette. Then, in the Show area of this palette, check the Drawing check box. Conversely, when the Drawing toolbar is visible, unchecking the Drawing check box will close (or hide) the Drawing toolbar.

Tip   The PC keyboard shortcut to access the Toolbars Option palette is Alt+W; then choose T. (The Mac has no such keyboard shortcut.)

On the Mac, the Drawing toolbar is always a floating palette that can be dragged anywhere in the screen. If the Drawing toolbar isn't visible on the Mac Flash screen, it can be opened from the Flash menu bar by choosing Window ➪ Toolbar. This same process can be used to close (or hide) the Drawing toolbar when it's visible.

Docking the Flash Drawing toolbar on the PC

On the PC, the Drawing toolbar can be deployed either as a floating palette or as a palette that is docked to the edge of the Flash program window. It has the (almost) unique capability to dock either to the menu bar or to the edge of the Flash program window. Docking means that a floating palette is dragged to the edge of the program window, where it then melds to the border of the window. It will remain docked there until it is moved to another docked position, is floated off to resume usage as a palette, or is closed. You can drag the palette anywhere around the screen, or you can drag it to the edge of the Flash program window, where it docks.

Tip   To drag the Drawing toolbar to the edge of the program window, yet prevent it from docking, press the Ctrl key while dragging.

Docking the Flash Drawing toolbar on the Mac

Unfortunately, absolute true cross-platform consistency was not a high priority in the development of Flash 4. Consequently, the Mac toolbar does not have the same docking capability as the PC. This inconsistency extends to the Controller window, the Zoom Control, and other minor details that may lead to confusion—especially for the novice.

Quick work with keyboard shortcuts

All of the tools that are accessed from the Drawing toolbar have keyboard equivalents, or shortcuts, that are single keystrokes. For example, to access the Arrow tool — which is the tool with the arrow icon, located in the upper-left corner of the Drawing Toolbar — you can simply press the A key. *Thus, the A key is the keyboard shortcut for the Arrow tool on both the Mac and the PC.* Using this shortcut is easier than moving the mouse up to the Drawing toolbar to click the Arrow tool, and it saves mouse miles besides. Henceforth, when we mention a new tool, the keyboard shortcut for that tool will follow in parentheses, as follows: Arrow (A). The Drawing toolbar is shown in Figures 1-1 and 1-2. The keyboard shortcut is in parentheses next to the tool name.

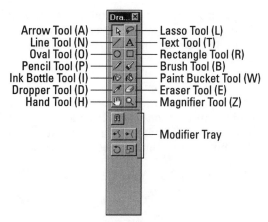

Figure 1-1: The PC Drawing toolbar

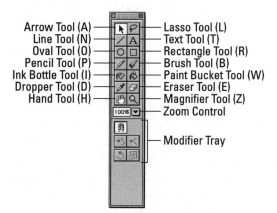

Figure 1-2: The Mac Drawing toolbar

Note A comprehensive chart of all Mac and PC keyboard shortcuts is available for download and printing at our Web site: www.theFlashBible.com.

Using modifiers and options

Each tool in the Flash Drawing toolbar has modifiers and options that control the functionality of the tool. Although these modifiers and options appear within the Modifier tray of the tool palette, most of them can also be accessed from menus on the menu bar, or with keyboard combinations. All modifiers and options for each tool are described in detail in this chapter in the section for that particular tool.

More fun differences between Mac and PC toolbars

Whether you are running Flash on a Mac or PC, the Drawing toolbar is *nearly* the same. To be fair, this version of Flash *is* a considerable improvement over all previous versions — which were inferior in their handling of cross-platform interface consistency.

One nagging difference that remains between the Mac and PC versions of Flash 4 is the manner in which the Drawing toolbar is *nested* within the program interface. Another difference — for a major graphics application now released in its fourth version — is the placement of the Zoom control. Zoom control on the Mac resides on the Drawing toolbar; on the PC, it is buried on a thing called the *Standard toolbar* — even though we rarely use it.

Tooltips

On both PC and Mac platforms, most tools have a cursor icon that resembles the tool's icon in the Drawing toolbar. For example, when you select the Pencil by clicking the Pencil button on the Drawing toolbar, the cursor (or mouse pointer) turns into an icon similar to the Pencil icon in the Drawing toolbar. The brush and Eraser tool display the tip size and shape in use. The Oval, Rectangle, and Line tools display a crosshair. In most other programs, these cursor icons are commonly referred to as *tooltips*. When you are working with a particular tool, the cursor icon for that tool appears on screen. In Flash, this kind of tooltip cannot be turned off. That's because Flash uses the term *tooltip* to refer to a text label that appears onscreen, adjacent to the cursor, when the cursor is paused over a tool button in the Drawing toolbar. These text labels — Flash tooltips — tell you the name of the tool and its keyboard shortcut. You can personalize Flash so that these Flash tooltips are either visible or hidden.

- ✦ To change the tooltips setting on the PC, choose Window ➪ Toolbar to open the Toolbars dialog box; then either check or uncheck Show Tooltips.

- ✦ To change the tooltips setting on the Mac, choose File ➪ Preferences to open the Toolbars Options palette, and then either check or uncheck Show Tooltips.

Note

Tooltips display information only about the tools that are part of the actual Flash program itself, and not about buttons that are part of a scene in a Flash movie. (If you are familiar with Macromedia Director, then you know that sprites — which can be similar to buttons in Flash — can show or hide information about their properties. Flash does not offer this type of *tip*.) Flash movies and buttons are introduced in Chapter 3.

The Flash Drawing Toolbar (a.k.a. The Toolbar)

In this section we discuss all of the Flash tools by name and explain the contents and use of the modifier tray for each tool. But first, let's start with a quick tour of the Drawing toolbar and Modifier tray.

The Drawing toolbar (as seen in Figure 1-3) consists of two main sections. The top half contains all fourteen of Flash's tools, from left to right and top to bottom: Arrow, Lasso, Line, Text tool, Oval, Rectangle, Pencil, Brush, Ink Bottle, Paint Bucket, Dropper, Eraser, Hand, and Magnifier. The lower half consists of the Modifier tray.

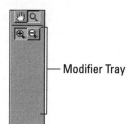

— Modifier Tray

Figure 1-3: Here's the Drawing toolbar with the Magnifier tool active. This tool has two modifiers in the Modifier tray.

Depending on the tool selected, the Modifier tray changes appearance to display the particular modifiers, or properties, that are associated with, or adjustable for, each tool. (These modifiers are similar in nature to the options that appear in the Photoshop Options palette, which also changes depending on the currently active tool.) Some modifiers are menus with additional options — either pop-up menus or drop-down menus. Other modifiers are simple buttons that are used to toggle a property on or off.

✦ If a modifier turns a property on or off, then it will be represented by a button. For example, if Lasso is selected, the Magic Wand option can be turned on or off by clicking its button in the modifier tray.

✦ If a modifier has more than two options, then it will appear as a pop-up or drop-down menu. See the section on line styles for an example of a drop-down menu for a modifier.

Color and Flash tools

 The Color chip, the Current Colors pop-up, and other colorful matters are discussed in depth in Chapter 2.

Navigation and viewing tools

Before you embark on a project in Flash, you need to know how to get to the action—in a scene, a symbol, or any other element in the movie. You need to know how to change the size of your viewing area (not everyone has a 21" monitor). You also need to know how to move efficiently and quickly to areas of the scene that might be off-screen. That's because (surprise!) scrollbars aren't necessarily the easiest way to shift around the contents of the screen! Flash offers familiar controls for changing the viewable area of a scene and for moving to different areas of a scene; these are the navigation and viewing tools.

The Magnifier tool

The Flash Magnifier tool (Z) is similar to the zoom tool of many other programs. It has two modifiers, Zoom In and Zoom Out. The Z key is the keyboard shortcut for the Magnifier tool on both the Mac and the PC. Although this may seem counterintuitive, the Magnifier is nearly synonymous with the Zoom tool. Furthermore, this keyboard shortcut brings Flash into alignment with usage established in other major software. Keyboard shortcuts for tools located in the Drawing toolbar are single keystrokes, remember? For example, simply press the Z key to activate the Magnifier tool.

Zoom In/Zoom Out

Zoom In brings you closer into the drawing so that you're viewing it at a greater level of magnification, while *Zoom Out* pulls you away from the drawing by showing it at a lesser level of magnification. Each level of *Zoom In* brings you in twice as close while each level of *Zoom Out* pulls you away in increments of one half.

To toggle the Magnifier tool (see Figure 1-4) between the Zoom In and the Zoom Out modifiers on the PC, press Alt and click. On the Mac, press Option and click.

Figure 1-4: The Magnifier tool's modifiers are Zoom In and Zoom Out.

When you want to zoom in on a specific area of your work, activate the Magnifier tool either by clicking it in the Drawing toolbar or by pressing the (Z) key, and then drag out a rectangle with the Magnifier tool in the Flash workspace. Flash will open the rectangular area at the highest level of magnification that includes the entire area of the rectangle.

The Hand tool

When you're zoomed in close on the screen, you can easily navigate the Flash workspace contents by using the Hand tool (H). This tool is used by clicking and dragging (while holding down the mouse) in the direction you want to move the screen. It's important to note that the Hand tool does not move objects in a scene to a new location — which is what the Arrow tool does. Rather, the Hand tool shifts the viewable portion of a scene to reveal another section that may be positioned awkwardly or somewhere off-screen.

> **Tip**　The Hand tool can also be activated temporarily by pressing the space bar. this is a toggle that causes the Hand tool mouse pointer to appear, regardless of what tool is currently selected in the Tool Palette.

Zoom Control

In addition to the use of the Magnifier tool, similar operations of magnification can also be accomplished with either the Zoom Control or the View Command. The only real differences between these tools and the Magnifier tool are where they are located within the program and the manner in which they are used to control the level of magnification.

The Zoom Control

On the Mac, the Zoom Control is a numerical entry box with an adjacent pop-up menu, located on the Drawing toolbar between the tools and the modifiers. On the PC, the Zoom Control is also a numerical entry box with pop-up menu, except that it is located on the Standard toolbar (which the Mac version doesn't have). On both Mac and PC, the Zoom Control (see Figures 1-5 and 1-6) can be used as either a pop-up menu or a numerical entry box. Click the pop-up to display a series of preset zoom levels, or enter a number in the numerical entry box to view the Flash workspace at any other Zoom percentage that you desire.

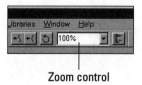

Figure 1-5: The Zoom Control on the PC

Zoom control

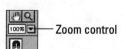

Figure 1-6: The Zoom Control on the Mac

Zoom control

The View Menu commands

On both Mac and PC, the View menu is accessed from the menu bar and contains four commands that enable you to adjust your screen view. Three of these view commands are equivalent to settings available through the Zoom Control drop-down menu. On the PC, pressing Alt+V will also access the View menu. The Mac has no shortcut for the View menu.

The four view commands also have corresponding keyboard shortcuts:

✦ **100% — Command+1 (Ctrl+1).** Depending on your monitor resolution and video card, this setting shows your work at "actual size." For example, if your movie size is 500 pixels × 400 pixels and your screen size is 800 × 600, then your movie will occupy roughly 40 percent of your total screen area in Flash.

✦ **Show All — Command+2 (Ctrl+2).** This setting adjusts the zoom to fit the contents of the current frame. If the frame is empty, the entire scene is displayed.

✦ **Show Frame — Command+3 (Ctrl+3).** This setting adjusts the zoom to show everything within the frame boundary, as defined by the movie properties.

✦ **Work Area — Shift+W (Ctrl+Shift+W).** This setting adjusts the view to include the entire work area. It's useful when you are working with items that are completely or partially out of the scene. This setting enables you to position items off screen and then have them move into view.

Tip

In order to see the broadest possible Work Area and Stage, choose View ➪ Work Area, and then select either 50% or 100%, depending on your screen size and movie size.

How Zoom Affects Tool Size

Zoom has a counter-intuitive effect on brush sizes and other tools. For example, identical brush sizes will draw at different sizes, depending on the zoom level that you're working with! Similarly, the Paint Bucket's interpretation of gap (meaning, is that a big gap or a small gap?) is entirely dependent upon the zoom setting. It's best to think of brush size and gap size as a fixed *screen* image size. (Caution: This is *unlike* Photoshop and many other programs with fixed *image* pixel size.) In Flash, whatever size the brush appears to be on the screen or work area *is the effective size of that brush*. Its size is not measured in fixed pixels.

Other tools and functions that are affected by the zoom setting are those that modify shapes, such as the Smooth Modifier and the functions available by choosing Modify ➪ Curves.

Flash Selection Tools

Flash has a pair of tools — the Arrow tool and the Lasso tool — that can be used to select lines, shapes, groups, symbols, buttons, objects, and other items. The Flash Lasso tool is used primarily to select odd-shaped sections of a drawing. The Flash Arrow tool is used primarily to select discrete lines, shapes, groups, symbols, buttons, objects, and other items. In combination with the Magnet Modifier and the Shape Recognition modifiers, the Flash Arrow tool has many unique capabilities not found in any other program.

The Arrow Tool

Unlike other vector-based programs, Flash uses no Bézier curves or Bézier handles. Instead, it uses the Arrow tool to reshape a line by pulling on the line itself or on its end points, curves, or corners. The Arrow tool is also used to select, move, and reshape Flash elements, including lines, shapes, groups, symbols, buttons, objects, and other items.

Five modifiers (or options) for the Arrow tool appear in the Modifier tray when the Arrow tool (A) is selected: Magnet (or Snap), Smooth, Straighten, Rotate, and Scale, as seen in Figure 1-7.

Figure 1-7: The Arrow tool's five modifiers

Tip   When you are busy with another tool, you can temporarily toggle to the Arrow tool by pressing the Command (Mac) or Ctrl (PC) key.

Using the Magnet Modifier of the Arrow tool

The Magnet (or Snap) Modifier button is a toggle that causes items being drawn or moved on screen to snap to an invisible, user-defined grid. Click the modifier button to toggle snapping on or off, or choose View ➪ Snap. The Magnet (Snap) Modifier button also has a keyboard shortcut: Option+Command+G on the Mac and Ctrl+Alt+G on the PC.

Note that, even if the Magnet modifier is turned on, you can temporarily override the Snap function by holding down the "G" key as you drag or move an item.

You can tell that an item is snapping to the grid by the presence of an "o" icon beside the arrow mouse pointer. For some shapes, the Icon or Snap function will not work unless, in clicking to grab the shape prior to moving, you click the shape at the center, corner, or side. Although the grid itself does not need to be shown in order for the Magnet or Snap function to work, you can turn the grid on by choosing View ⇨ Grid, or Option+Shift+Command+G (Alt+Shift+Ctrl+G).

The functionality and degree of precision of the Magnet (or Snap) button are controlled by settings that can be customized in the Grid field of the Movie Properties dialog box, which can be accessed by choosing Modify ⇨ Movie. The settings are measured in pixels, relative to the movie size (*not* the screen size). Further adjustments are made in the File ⇨ Assistants dialog box for setting how close to the grid snapping will occur.

Understanding shape recognition

So, what's the meaning of *shape recognition?* Shape recognition is the general term for a class of modifiers that can be set to assist accurate drawing and manipulation of basic shapes. These modifiers are the Smooth and Straighten modifiers, which are used in conjunction with the Arrow tool (by clicking their respective buttons to invoke their smoothing or straightening action) to clean up drawings. This is fully explained in the sections that follow.

When used in conjunction with the Pencil tool, more powerful shape recognition can be invoked — the only real difference is that, with respect to the Pencil tool, shape recognition automatically processes the lines. For example, a crude lumpy oval is automatically recognized and processed into a true oval. More specific details of using shape recognition with the Pencil tool are explained here in this chapter in the section about the Pencil tool.

For the Arrow and the Pencil tools, both the degree to which shape recognition processes your drawings and the strength with which the Smooth and Straighten modifiers will interact with your drawings can be adjusted with the Assistant dialog box, File ⇨ Assistant.

Cross-Reference   In addition to the treatment here in this chapter, shape recognition is detailed elsewhere in the book. The settings that control shape recognition are explained in Chapter 4. Shape recognition is also discussed in context with actual drawing processes in Chapter 6.

Using the Smooth Modifier with the Arrow tool

The Smooth Modifier is a button used to simplify selected curves. Smoothing reduces the number of bumps and variations (or points of transition) along the span of a complex curve so that the curve spans the same distance with fewer points. Repeated use of the Smooth button on a line results in a curve with only two points, one at either end. To use this modifier, you must first select a line with the Arrow tool; then the Smooth button can be used to reduce the points in the selected line (or line segment). The action of the Smooth button can also be accessed by choosing Modify ➪ Curves ➪ Smooth.

Using the Straighten Modifier with the Arrow tool

The Straighten Modifier is a button used to make selected line segments less curved. The Straighten button operates on the same principle as the Smooth button, except that it's used for straightening instead of smoothing a selected line segment. Repeated use of the Straighten button will turn a curvy line into a series of angled lines. The Straighten Modifier button can also be accessed by choosing Modify ➪ Curves ➪ Straighten.

Note

The degree of the Smoothing or Straightening adjustments that can be made with the Smooth or Straighten button is regulated by the number of times the button is clicked. Although it may appear that the degree of automatic, Smoothing or Straightening can be adjusted by choosing File ➪ Assistant and then selecting one of the four choices (Off, Rough, Normal, or Smooth). These options affect only smoothing or straightening done *during* the drawing process and not adjustments made with the Smooth or Straighten buttons.

Using the Rotate Modifier with the Arrow tool

The Rotate Modifier button is used to initiate the rotation of a selected line, item, group, symbol, or object. When the Rotate button is clicked, the item is put into rotation mode, and handles appear for rotation of the item. The Rotation Modifier can also be accessed by choosing Modify ➪ Transform ➪ Rotate.

Using the Scale Modifier with the Arrow tool

The Scale Modifier button is used to initiate scaling of a selected line, shape, group, symbol, button, object, or other item. When the Scale button is clicked, the item is put into scale mode, and handles appear for scaling of the item. The Scale Modifier is also available by choosing Modify ➪ Transform ➪ Scale.

Using the Scale and Rotate dialog box

Choosing Modify ➪ Transform ➪ Scale and Rotate elicits a dialog box that combines the properties of both the Rotate and Scale Modifier buttons into one tool. This dialog box enables you to input numeric values for the amount of scale and transformation. (It's very much like the Photoshop Numeric Transform tool.) The keyboard shortcut for this hybrid is Option+Command+S (Ctrl+Alt+S). Unfortunately, using a numeric transform dialog box is rather unintuitive, and it is hard to use unless you already know what you want to accomplish. This dialog box is fully described in Chapter 6.

New Feature

Flash 4 adds a Transform Inspector, which should not be confused with the Scale and Rotate dialog box. It can be accessed by choosing Window ⇨ Inspectors ⇨ Transform. The primary advantage of this inspector is that it permits numeric input for three types of transformations: both uniform and nonuniform scaling, rotation, and skew. It affords other advantages as well. Although an improvement over the Scale and Rotate dialog box, the Transform Inspector suffers from the same disadvantages (that numerically applied transformations are unintuitive, and difficult to control) unless you already have the numeric values for a desired effect. Thus, a good bit of trial and error may be involved in effective use of this Inspector. This Inspector is further described in Chapter 6.

Using arrow states to reshape and reposition drawings

In addition to the actions accomplished by selecting a line (or line section) and clicking a modifier, three arrow states — Move Selected Element, Reshape Curve or Line, and Reshape Endpoint or Corner — enable you to reshape and move parts of your drawings. It works like this: As you move the Arrow tool over a Flash scene, the Arrow pointer changes the visual state to indicate the particular action that can be done on the line or fill closest to the Arrow tool's current position.

1. Start with a line that has been drawn with the Line tool.

2. Single-clicking the line activates the Move Selected Element State of the Arrow Tool, indicated by the compass-style arrow adjacent to the Arrow cursor. The line is then click-dragged to a new location.

3. The line is deselected by clicking anywhere away from the line. Then the line is reshaped — with the Reshape Curve or Line State of the Arrow tool — by clicking and dragging anywhere between the endpoints of the line.

4. The line is has been deselected again. Now clicking an endpoint activates the Reshape Endpoint or Corner State of the Arrow tool. Then the endpoint is click-dragged to a new location.

To make your reshaping go even more easily, try the following techniques:

✦ Press the Option (Alt) key, click near an unselected line or segment of a line, and drag to create a new corner point.

✦ Selected lines cannot be reshaped. Click anywhere (outside all selected objects) to deselect, and then reshape the line by clicking it with the one of the different states of the Arrow tool.

✦ Smooth complex lines to make reshaping easier.

✦ Increase magnification to make your reshaping easier and more accurate.

Using the Arrow tool to select items

The Arrow tool is the primary selection tool in Flash. When you click a line, a checkered pattern appears, surrounding the line, to indicate that the line has been selected.

In addition to clicking a line to select it, you can also select one or more items by dragging a marquee over them using the Arrow tool. This operation is called *drag-select*. Additional items can be added to a current selection by pressing the shift key and clicking the items.

New Feature

Previously, the implementation of Shift Select in Flash was completely unlike other graphics applications — in Flash only, additional lines were added to a selection simply by clicking them. *This is no longer the default setting for making selections in Flash.* Now, the Shift key must be pressed in order to add to the current selection. To change this *new* default setting for Shift Select, go to File ➪ Preferences; then, in the ensuing Preferences dialog box, uncheck the check box for Shift Select.

Tip

When you drag-select to make a selection, previously selected items are deselected and excluded from the selection. In order to include previously selected items, press the Shift key as you drag-select.

Deselect one or more objects by using any of the following methods:

✦ Pressing the Escape key

✦ Using the keyboard shortcut Command+Shift+A (Ctrl+Shift+A)

✦ Choosing Edit ➪ Deselect All

✦ Clicking anywhere outside all the selected objects

Moving grouped and ungrouped elements with the Arrow tool

Text and groups are selected as single elements and will move as a single unit. After you create text in a given frame (text functions are discussed later in this chapter), Flash treats the text as one block, or group, meaning that all the individual letters within a box will move together when the box is selected. Similarly, a collection of graphic elements — such as lines, outlines, fills, or shapes — can be grouped and moved or manipulated as a single element. When you move an item that is not grouped, however, only the selected part is moved. This can be tricky when you have ungrouped fills and outlines, because selecting one without the other could result in detaching the fill from the outline or vice versa.

To move separate elements (such as a rectangular line and its colored fill area) in the same direction simultaneously, group them first. In order to group separate elements, select them all; then group them with Modify ➪ Group. They can be ungrouped later, if necessary. Grouping is further discussed in Chapter 6 and again in Chapter 8.

Reshaping items with the Arrow tool

The Arrow tool can be used in conjunction with either or both of two modifiers—the Scale Modifier and the Rotate Modifier—to reshape parts of a graphic.

The Scale Modifier button

The Scale Modifier button enables you to scale or stretch graphic elements. With the graphic element selected, click the Scale Modifier button. Eight rectangular handles appear around the selected graphic element. Click and drag a corner handle to scale the object. Click and drag either a middle or side handle to stretch the object.

Tip   When reshaping brush strokes and similar items with the Arrow tool, make sure that you don't select the entire brush stroke before trying to reshape the outline: If you do, you'll only be able to move the entire brush stroke—and won't be able to reshape it.

The Rotate Modifier

The Rotate Modifier enables you to rotate, skew, or slant graphic elements. With the graphic element selected, click the Rotate Modifier. The Rotate Modifier also has eight rectangular handles. Drag a corner handle to rotate the object. Drag either a middle or side handle to skew or slant.

Tip   When you're reshaping, scaling, or rotating a solid object with fills, Flash handles the filled area as if it were enclosed by a line of zero thickness. As you readjust such an item to a new shape, the fill will either expand or contract accordingly.

Shape recognition with the Arrow tool

The Straighten Modifier of the Arrow tool can be used for shape recognition. Here's how that works: Sketch something spontaneously (but not too wildly!). Then, you can use *shape recognition* to transform your sketch into precise geometric forms. Start by sketching a rough circle, square, or rectangle. Then click the Arrow tool and select the object you've just sketched. Then click the Straighten Modifier button to begin shape recognition.

✦ For hard-edged items such as a polygon, click the Straighten Modifier button repeatedly until your rough sketch is a recognizable and precise geometric form. At odds with its name, the Straighten Modifier will also recognize a roughly drawn circle and make it perfect oval. Using the Straighten Modifier button is equivalent to the menu sequence Modify ⇨ Curves ⇨ Straighten, or, on the PC, Alt+O-C-T.

✦ For smooth-edged items, click the Smooth Modifier button repeatedly until your rough sketch becomes as smooth as possible. Using the Smooth Modifier button is equivalent to the menu sequence, Modify ⇨ Curves ⇨ Smooth, or, on the PC, Alt+O-C-S.

Duplicating items with the Arrow tool

The Arrow tool can also be used for duplicating items. Simply press the Option (on the PC, either Ctrl or Alt) key while dragging with the Arrow tool. The original item will remain in place, while a new item is deposited at the end of your drag stroke.

The Lasso Tool

The Lasso tool (L) is used to group-select odd or irregular shaped areas of your drawing. After the areas are selected, they can be moved, scaled, rotated, or reshaped as a single unit. The Lasso tool can also be used to split shapes or select portions of a line or shape. It has three modifiers, as seen in Figure 1-8: the Polygon Lasso, the Magic Wand, and the Magic Wand properties.

Figure 1-8: The Lasso Tool Modifiers

The Lasso Tool works best if you drag a loop around the area you wish to select. (Hence the tool name, Lasso!) But if you slip, or if you don't end the loop near where you started, Flash will close the loop with a straight line between your starting point and the end point. Because you can use the Lasso tool to define an area of *any* shape (limited only by your ability to draw and use the multiple selection capabilities of Flash), the Lasso tool gives you far more control over selections than does the Arrow tool.

Tip

To add to a previously selected area, hold down the Shift key prior to initiating additional selections.

New
Feature

The Polygon Lasso is a significant enhancement that brings Flash into closer alignment with other major graphics programs. It delivers greater precision when making straight-edge selections, or — in mixed mode — selections that combine freeform areas with straight edges.

Using the Polygon Modifier with the Lasso tool

In order to describe a simple polygon selection, click the Polygon Modifier to toggle the Lasso tool *on* and commence Polygon selection mode. In Polygon mode, selection points are created by a mouse click, causing a straight selection line to extend between mouse clicks. To complete the selection, double-click.

Mixed mode usage, which includes Polygon functionality, is available when the Lasso tool is in Freeform Mode. To work in Freeform Mode, the Polygon Modifier must be in the *off* position. While drawing with the Freeform Lasso, press the Alt [Option] key to temporarily invoke Polygon mode. (Polygon mode continues only as long as the Alt [Option] key is pressed.) Now, straight polygonal lines can be described between selection points that are created by a mouse click. That is, *as long as the Alt [Option] key is pressed, a straight selection line will extend between mouse clicks*. To return to Freeform Mode, simply sneeze — or release the Alt [Option] key. Release the mouse to close the selection.

Note

Sometimes aberrant selections — selections that seem inside out, or that have a weird, unwanted straight line bisecting the intended selection — result from Lasso selections. That's usually because the point of origination of a Lasso selection is the point to which the Lasso will snap when the selection is closed. It usually takes a little practice to learn how to *plan* the point of origin so that the desired selection will be obtained when the selection is closed.

Using the Magic Wand Modifier with the Lasso tool

The Magic Wand Modifier of the Lasso tool is used to select ranges of a similar color in a bitmap that has been broken apart. After you select areas of the bitmap, you can change their fill color or delete them.

Breaking apart a bitmap means that the bitmap image is subsequently seen by Flash as a collection of individual areas of color. (This is not the same as *tracing* a bitmap, which reduces the vast number of colors in a continuous tone bitmap to areas of solid color.) After an image is broken apart, you can select individual areas of the image with any of the selection tools, including the Magic Wand modifier of the Lasso tool. You can *unbreak* a broken bitmap by selecting the entire image (this will cause it to look like a negative relief) and then choosing Modify ➪ Group from the menu bar (the equivalent shortcut is Command+G (Ctrl+G).

Using Magic Wand properties

The Magic Wand Properties Modifier has two settings that can be modified: Threshold and Smoothing.

The Threshold Setting of the Magic Wand Modifier

The Threshold Setting defines the breadth of adjacent color values that the Magic Wand Modifier will include in a selection. The higher the setting, the broader the selection of adjacent colors, and, conversely, a smaller number results in the Magic Wand, making a narrower selection of adjacent colors.

Note   A value of zero results in a selection of contiguous pixels that are all of the same color as the target pixel. With a value of 20, clicking a red target pixel with a value of 55 will select all contiguous pixels in a range of values extending from red 35 to red 75. (For those of you who are familiar with Photoshop, it is important to note that the Flash Threshold is unlike Photoshop, where a Threshold setting of 20 will select all contiguous pixels in a range of values extending from red 45 to red 65.)

The Smoothing Setting of the Magic Wand Modifier

The Smoothing Setting of the Magic Wand Modifier determines to what degree the edge of the selection should be smoothed. This is similar to *antialiasing*. The options are Smooth, Pixels, Rough, and Normal. *Antialiasing* is defined, together with the discussion of movie sizes, in Chapter 3.

The Flash Drawing and Painting Tools

In previous versions of Flash, many of the drawing tools were subordinated under the Pencil tool as modifiers and were not separate tools on the Tool palette. Flash 4 has three new tool icons. These are for the Oval, Rectangle, and Line tools. These tools are similar in that they draw perfect geometric shapes and, with the exception of the Line tool, these shapes are filled with a solid color that may be different from the color of the outline that describes the shape. Each of these tools has similar modifiers that interact with the tool in unique ways. The Pencil, Brush, Ink Bottle, and Paint Bucket tools have remained nearly the same as they were in Flash 3. In this section, we'll take a look at how to use all of these tools and see what's changed with each of them from the last version.

Choosing colors

Whenever any of the Flash Drawing or Painting tools is selected, the Flash toolbar displays one or two color chips in the Modifier Tray. These color chips do two things: They indicate the current color that will be applied to the stroke or the fill by any drawing or painting tool. The chips are also buttons: Click the Color Chip button to open the Current Colors pop-up. Most tools will have only one color chip. Only the Oval and Rectangle tools have two color chips: one to describe the line color (which, depending on the tool may be either the line or the outline color), and one to describe the fill (which is the color within the outline).

If you're already feeling a little discolored by the double-agent nature of these color chip/icon/button/pop-ups — just take a deep breath and relax. Although the handling of colors in Flash may seem a bit like one of those Russian dolls where one opens to reveal yet another, it will become second nature to you in *no* time. That's because we've devoted an entire chapter to the explanation of Flash Color. It includes not only the details of working with Flash Color on the Web, but also a little primer on color theory, computer color, and Web color.

Color Focus Buttons

Both line/outline color chips and fill color chips have a small button adjacent to them on the right. These are the new Color Focus buttons. For the line color chip, the Color Focus button looks like a little squiggle, while the Color Focus button for the fill color chip looks like a small white-to-black gradient. These buttons change the focus of the Color window (Window ➪ Colors) so that colors may be selected for either line or fill, regardless of which color chip was active when the Color window was originally opened.

This is a smart new addition to Flash that makes working with color much easier. How does it work? Suppose the Color window is opened while the fill color chip has focus (is active, meaning that any palette changes are currently reflected in the fill chip) and you want to change the line color. With this new feature you can simply click the line color's squiggly Color Focus button. This now gives the line color focus, meaning that subsequent palette changes will appear in the line color chip.

Note that, for tools with a single color, although the Color Focus button appears on the tool-bar, *it does nothing*.

Both the Line and Fill color chips, their associated Color Focus buttons, the Current Colors pop-ups, The Solid and Gradient Color palettes, and other color matters are discussed (in depth!) in Chapter 2.

Clicking the Color Chip button accesses the Current Colors pop-up for the Pencil tool. It's both a pop-up and also the palette containing the current colors as seen in Figure 1-9. The colors that are displayed in this palette can be changed in the Color window, which may be accessed by clicking the button located at the top of this pop-up. (Hint: It resembles a tiny color palette.) Note the new Color Focus button, which has the squiggly line, to the right of the Color Chip button.

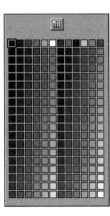

Figure 1-9: This is the Current Colors pop-up menu for the Pencil tool.

The Pencil Tool

The Pencil tool is used to draw lines and shapes in any given frame of a scene and — at first glance — operates much like a real pencil. (A frame is the basic unit of a Flash creation. Frames and scenes are described in Chapter 3. But a deeper examination reveals that — unlike a real pencil — the Flash Pencil tool can be set to straighten lines and smooth curves as you draw. It can also be set to recognize or correct basic geometric shapes. In addition, you can use the Pencil tool modifiers to create specific shapes. You can also modify lines and shapes manually.

When the Pencil tool is active, five modifiers appear in the modifier tray as shown in Figure 1-10. The first modifier (from the top) is the Pencil Mode pop-up menu. It is used to set the Pencil tool's current drawing mode. The second modifier is the Line Color modifier. This is the Flash color chip's appearance among the Pencil Modifiers. To the right of the color chip is the Line Color Focus modifier. Note, however, that Line Color Focus does nothing here, because no fill color exists to compete with the line color for focus. (Refer to the previous section, "Choosing Colors," for an explanation of this new feature, which is dormant here in its relationship with the Pencil tool.) The remaining modifiers for the Pencil tool are two drop-down menus: Line Thickness and Line Style. The Line Thickness pop-up menu and Line Style pop-up menu are used for setting line attributes.

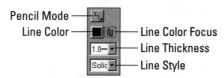

Figure 1-10: The Pencil tool's Modifiers

Using the Pencil Mode pop-up modifiers

The Pencil Mode pop-up menu has options that control how Flash processes the lines you draw. That's right, unlike any other program we know of, Flash can *p-r-o-c-e-s-s* the lines that you draw, as you draw them! We call this *line processing* — it's a kind of Shape Recognition specific to the Pencil tool that may make drawing easier for artists who are draftsmanship-challenged. It also has the benefit of generating drawings that are less complex. As a result, the drawings transmit across the Web at greater speed, because they require less data (which means a smaller file size) to describe them. The Pencil tool has three processing options as shown in Figure 1-11. Two are Straighten and Smooth; the third, for those who prefer the characteristics of hand drawing, is Ink Mode. By working in Ink Mode you turn off all line processing.

Figure 1-11: The Pencil Mode Modifier pop-up reveals the Straighten, Smooth, and Ink processing options.

Understanding line processing

So, what is meant by, "processing the lines?" Processing differs from shape recognition in that it is automatic and occurs while the line is in the process of being drawn. This differs from shape recognition with the Arrow tool because that occurs after the line has been drawn — in fact, it can be done at any time after the line has been drawn. (For more information on *shape recognition,* refer to the section on the Arrow tool, earlier in this chapter.) The degree to which processing occurs automatically by the Pencil tool is controlled the Straighten, Smooth, and Ink Processing Modifiers. Each of these modifiers is detailed here in this chapter, in subsequent sections of this discussion of the Pencil tool. These modifiers are also affected by the settings in the Assistant dialog box, File ➪ Assistant.

Cross-Reference

In addition to the treatment here, *line processing* and *shape recognition* are discussed elsewhere in the book. The settings that control line processing and shape recognition are explained in Chapter 4. Line processing is discussed again, in context with actual drawing processes, in Chapter 6.

Straighten option

Drawing with the Straighten Option processes your drawings while taking into account line and shape recognition. This means that separate lines are automatically connected, lines that approximate straight are straightened, and wobbly curves are smoothed — in short, approximate shapes are recognized and automatically adjusted.

Smooth option

Drawing with the Smooth Option reduces the zeal with which Flash automatically processes your drawings. With Smooth Option, line straightening and shape recognition are disabled. You can draw curved lines and they will be smoothed slightly, and a line that ends near another line will be joined to it.

Ink option

Drawing with the Ink Option turns off all Flash processing. You're left with the lines as you've drawn them. Your lines are *not* smoothed, straightened, or joined.

Lines that are drawn with the Ink Option can become unnecessarily complex. In that case, these lines can be selected with the Arrow tool and then slightly optimized by choosing Modify ➪ Curves from the menu bar.

You can also choose to smooth, straighten, or join lines and shapes that have been drawn with the Ink Option simply by using the Arrow tool to select what you've drawn and then using either the Arrow tool's Smooth or Straighten modifiers.

Using the Pencil tool Line Color Modifier

The Line Color Modifier is the Flash color chip's appearance among the Pencil tool modifiers. This color chip does two things: It indicates the current color and is also a button—click the color chip to open the Current Colors pop-up. The basic concepts of working with color are explained earlier in this chapter, in the section titled, "Choosing Colors." For a more exhaustive discussion of color, please refer to Chapter 2. The current line color can be changed in two simple steps. Click the color chip (or Line Color Modifier) to open the Current Colors pop-up and select a new color from the Current Colors palette by clicking the desired color.

Using the Pencil tool Line Thickness Modifier

The Line Thickness Modifier drop-down menu (see Figure 1-12) offers eight options. Six of them are lines of preset thickness, measured in points that range from hairline to 8 points. The seventh option is merely a convenient holder for the most recent entry in the Line Settings dialog box (which is accessed from the eighth, or *Custom,* option of the Line Thickness Modifier). Whenever you change the setting in the Custom option of the Line Thickness Modifier (see Figure 1-13), the value of this seventh option changes accordingly.

Figure 1-12: The Pencil tool Line Thickness Modifier drop-down menu

Figure 1-13: The Line Settings dialog box appears when the Custom option is selected from the Line Thickness drop-down menu.

The eighth option, Custom, is used for creating a custom line thickness. Select this option to open the Line Settings dialog box, which has a numeric entry field in which to enter the desired custom line thickness. Permissible values range from 0 to 10, with fractions expressed in decimals.

✦ Hairline always draws a line that is one pixel wide. Use Hairline for lines that won't change their thickness when you scale a shape.

✦ Depending on the level of zoom, some lines may not be visible on screen — even though they will print correctly on a high-resolution printer.

✦ Line thickness may also be adjusted in the Line Style dialog box, which is accessible from the Custom option of the Line Style pop-up menu.

Using the Pencil tool Line Style Modifier

The Line Style Modifier drop-down menu (see Figure 1-14) offers seven line styles, six of which are preset, and one of which is custom. The Custom option doesn't really generate custom lines. Instead, through various options, which vary depending on the type of line that is being customized, it controls the properties of the six preset lines. The six preset lines are Solid, Dashed, Dotted, Ragged, Stippled, and Hatched.

Figure 1-14: The Line Style Modifier drop-down menu

 Of the six preset line styles, *Solid* is the least complex. As such, use of the Solid line style will result in Flash movies that can play back more efficiently on slower computers. If possible, limit the use of the other line styles within your Flash movies.

Using the Custom Line Style

The Custom Line Style dialog box is used to change the properties of each preset line. The basic options include Line Thickness and Sharp Corners. Depending on the preset line style, additional options are available for each specific line style. You have two possible routes for customizing a preset line. All preset lines may be customized in either of these two ways:

✦ If you select a preset line style and subsequently return to the Line Style pop-up menu to choose the Custom line style, the previously selected preset will appear as the current Line Type in the Line Style dialog box.

✦ Select the Custom line style from the Line Style pop-up to open the Line Style dialog box (see Figure 1-15). Use the Line Type drop-down menu in the Line Style dialog box to choose a preset line style for customization.

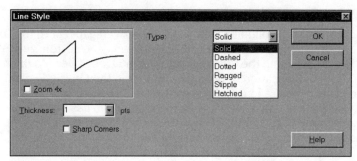

Figure 1-15: The Line Style dialog box appears when the Custom option is selected from the Line Style drop-down menu.

Note Points are the default unit of measurement for determining lengths in the Line Style dialog box.

To closely examine a custom line before you begin drawing with it, click the Zoom 4x check box under the preview area of the Line Style dialog box. Note the Sharp Corners check box, which toggles this Line Style feature on or off — check the box to turn Sharp Corners on.

Cross-Reference If you want to make more extensive use of Custom Line Styles, you can apply these styles quite easily to other lines by using the Dropper tool in conjunction with the Ink Bottle tool. See the sections on both the Dropper tool and the Ink Bottle tool in this chapter.

The Solid Line Style

The Solid Line Style draws a solid, unbroken line. This is the optimal line style for Web viewing. Settings for this line style may be customized in the Line Style dialog box by selecting the Custom option of the Line Styles Modifier drop-down menu. The customization options that appear in the Line Style dialog box for the Solid Line Style are limited to Line Thickness and Sharp Corners.

The only variables for the Solid Line style are Line Thickness and Sharp Corners — which is obscured here by the drop-down menu. These two variables, Thickness and Sharp Corners, are always available in the Line Style dialog box, regardless of which Line Style is being customized.

Note The Solid Line Style creates smaller file sizes than other line styles, which theoretically translates into faster download times when the artwork is transmitted over the Web. However, the difference in file size may be so nominal that the difference in download time that it saves is negligible.

The Dashed Line Style

The Dashed Line Style draws a solid line with regularly spaced gaps. Both the Dash and Gap lengths are adjustable. Settings for this line style may be customized in the Line Style dialog box by selecting the Custom option of the Line Styles Modifier drop-down menu. The customization options that appear in the Line Style dialog box for the Dashed Line Style are Line Thickness, Sharp Corners, Dash Length, and Gap Length. The Line Style dialog box for the Dashed Line Style has two unique variables, Dash Length and Gap Length. Change the numeric entries in these fields to control the dashed quality of the custom dashed line.

Dotted Line Style

The Dotted Line Style draws a dotted line with evenly spaced gaps. The Dot Spacing is adjustable. Settings for this line style may be customized in the Line Style dialog box by selecting the "Custom" option of the Line Styles Modifier drop-down menu. The customization options that appear in the Line Style dialog box for the Dotted Line Style are Dot Thickness, Sharp Corners, and Dot Spacing. At first glance, the Dotted Line Style appears to have only one variable—Dot Spacing. Use this setting to change the numeric entries in these fields to control the quality of the custom dashed line. But don't overlook the Thickness drop-down menu, which offers a range of settings for Dot Thickness.

Ragged Line Style

The Ragged Line Style draws a dotted line with evenly spaced gaps between the dots. The quality of the raggedness is adjustable. In addition to Line Thickness and Sharp Corners customization options, the Ragged Line Style dialog box has three parameters unique to ragged lines: Pattern, Wave Height, and also Wave Length. Settings for this line style may be customized in the Line Style dialog box by selecting the Custom option of the Line Styles Modifier drop-down menu (see Figure 1-16).

Stippled Line Style

The Stipple Line Style draws a stipple line that goes a long way toward mimicking an artist's hand-stippling technique. The qualities of stippling are adjustable. Settings for this line style may be customized in the Line Style dialog box by selecting the Custom option of the Line Styles Modifier drop-down menu. Customization options that appear in the Line Style dialog box for the Stipple Line Style (see Figure 1-17) include Line Thickness, Sharp Corners, and three parameters that are unique to the nature of stippled lines: Dot Size, Dot Variation, and Density.

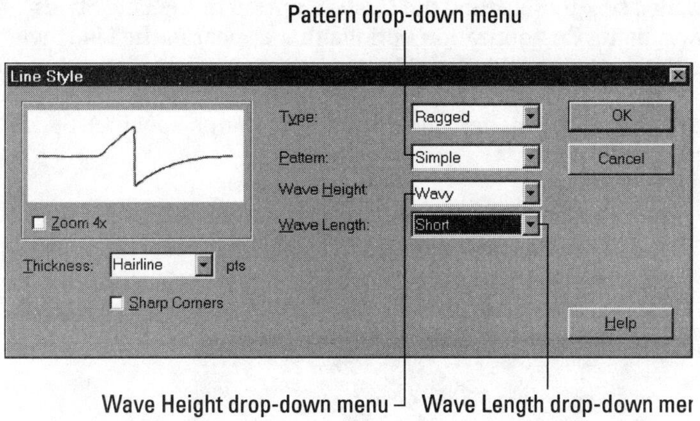
Pattern drop-down menu
Line Style
Type:
Ragged
OK
Pattern:
Simple
Cancel
Wave Height:
Wavy
Wave Length:
Short
Zoom 4x
Thickness:
Hairline
pts
Sharp Corners
Help
Wave Height drop-down menu
Wave Length drop-down mer

Figure 1-16: Customization options for the Ragged Line Style include three drop-down menus which, in combination, afford myriad possibilities.

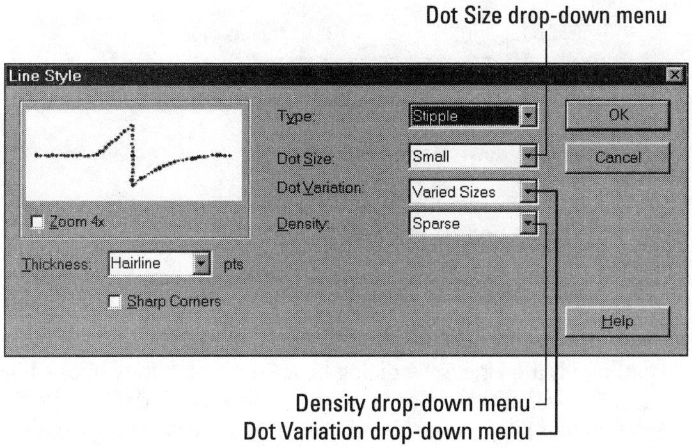
Dot Size drop-down menu
Line Style
Type:
Stipple
OK
Dot Size:
Small
Cancel
Dot Variation:
Varied Sizes
Density:
Sparse
Zoom 4x
Thickness:
Hairline
pts
Sharp Corners
Help
Density drop-down menu
Dot Variation drop-down menu

Figure 1-17: Similar to Ragged, the Stipple Line Style also has three drop-down menus, each with multiple settings that can be combined to generate a staggering array of line effects.

Hatched Line Style

The Hatched Line Style draws a hatched line of amazing complexity, which can be used to accurately mimic an artist's hand-drawn hatched-line technique. The numerous hatching qualities are highly adjustable, making this perhaps the most complex of all the Flash drawing tools. Settings for this line style may be customized in the Line Style dialog box by selecting the Custom option of the Line Styles Modifier drop-down menu. Customization options that appear in the Line Style dialog box for the Hatched Line Style (see Figure 1-18) are the usual adjustments for Line Thickness and Sharp Corners. In addition, the Line Style dialog box has six parameters that are unique to hatched lines: Thickness (hatch-specific), Space, Jiggle, Rotate, Curve, and Length.

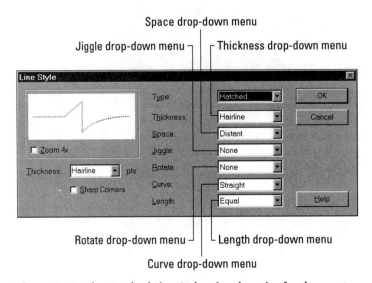

Figure 1-18: The Hatched Line Style wins the prize for the most variables. With these six drop-down menus, a plethora of unique line effects can be hatched.

Note   These thickness settings are in addition to the usual Thickness settings that are available as a default with the Line Style dialog box. Combined, they offer a higher level of adjustment. The default thickness (measured in points) defines the thickness of the overall hatched line, while this additional thickness setting defines the thickness of the individual scrawls that comprise the aggregate hatched line.

New Pencil Tool Functionality

In previous versions of Flash, the Pencil tool had three more modifiers. These were used to access the straight line, oval, and rectangle operations of the Pencil tool. With Flash 4, each of these functions of the Pencil tool has been made into a distinct tool, with new icons appearing on the Drawing toolbar. These *new* tools still behave in much the same way as they did when they were ensconced within the Pencil tool's world — but they've been given some new features too. Some features, such as the color focus buttons, are shared with other tools in the toolbar. The most spectacular new feature is the addition of the Rounded Rectangle Modifier, which is specific to the Rectangle tool.

The Line Tool

Drawing with the Line tool creates a perfectly straight line that extends from the starting point to the end point.

The Line tool has four modifiers (as seen in Figure 1-19), two of which are buttons: the Line Color Modifier button and associated Color Focus button. The remaining modifiers are the drop-down menus for Line Thickness and Line Style. All of these modifiers have the same function and behavior as their counterparts for the Pencil tool. Please refer to the previous section, "The Pencil tool," for the particulars of these modifiers. Note, however, that here, too, the Line Color Focus does nothing, because no fill color exists to compete with the Line Color for Focus.

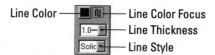

Line Color ——— Line Color Focus
——— Line Thickness
——— Line Style

Figure 1-19: The Line tool's four modifiers

The Oval Tool

Drawing with the Oval tool creates a perfectly smooth oval. Ovals are drawn by dragging from one edge of the shape being drawn to the other. Pressing the Shift key at any time while the shape is being drawn constrains the shape to a perfect circle.

The Oval tool has six modifiers (see Figure 1-20), four of which are buttons: the Line Color Modifier button with its associated Color Focus button, and the Fill Color Modifier with its Color Focus button. The remaining modifiers are the drop-down menus for Line Thickness and Line Style. All of these modifiers have function and behavior similar to that of their counterparts for the Pencil tool. Please refer to the previous section, "The Pencil Tool," for the particulars of these modifiers. The exceptions are the Fill Color Modifier and Color Focus button.

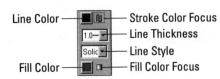

Figure 1-20: The Oval tool's six modifiers

Click the Fill Color Modifier to open the Current Fill Colors pop-up. Then select a new color from the Current Colors palette by clicking the desired color, or click the Color Palette icon to directly access the Color window (Window ➪ Colors). If the Color window is already open, but the line color has focus, use the Fill Color Focus button to switch focus to the fill color. Confused? Color is briefly explained in a prior section of this chapter, "Choosing Color." For a more exhaustive explanation of all aspects of Flash color, refer to Chapter 2.

The Rectangle Tool

Drawing with the Rectangle tool creates a perfect rectangle, which means that all four of the corners are at 90-degree angles. Rectangles are drawn by dragging from one edge of the shape being drawn to the other. Pressing the Shift key at any time while the shape is being drawn creates a perfect square.

The Rectangle tool has seven modifiers (see Figure 1-21), of which five are buttons: the Line Color Modifier button with its associated Color Focus button, and the Fill Color Modifier with its Color Focus button. The final button is the Rounded Rectangle button. Like the other tool from the Pencil realm, the remaining modifiers are drop-down menus for line thickness and line style. These modifiers all have function and behavior similar to that of their counterparts for the Oval tool. Please refer to the earlier section, "The Oval Tool," for the particulars of these modifiers.

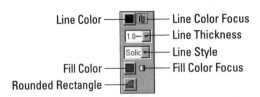

Figure 1-21: The king of the Pencil Family, the Rectangle tool has seven modifiers.

New Feature

One of the most celebrated features of Flash 4 is the addition of rounded rectangle support. It's extremely useful for making rounded rectangles — a.k.a. interactive button shapes. Click this modifier to elicit the Rectangle Settings dialog box, which accepts numeric values from 0 to 999. Subsequent rectangles will be drawn with this value applied to the corner radius, until the value entered in this dialog box is either changed or returned to zero. Note that this button is *not* a toggle — to turn off rounded rectangle drawing, click the modifier and enter a value of zero.

Using the (Paint) Brush Tool

The Brush tool is used to paint with brush-like strokes and to fill enclosed areas. Unlike the Flash Pencil tool, which creates a single, solid line, the Brush tool creates filled shapes with outlines of zero thickness. The fills can be solid colors, gradients, or fills derived from bitmaps. Additionally, the Brush tool modifiers permit you to paint in unusual ways: You can choose to paint in front of or behind an element, or you can apply paint only within a specific filled area or within a selection.

Note Painting with white or the background color is not the same as erasing. When you paint with either, it may appear to accomplish something similar to erasing. But you are in fact creating a filled item that can be selected, moved, deleted, or reshaped. Only erasing erases!

Depending upon whether you have a pressure-sensitive tablet connected to your computer, either six or seven modifiers appear in the modifier tray when the Brush tool is active. The Pressure Modifier — which only appears if you have a pressure-sensitive tablet attached to your computer — and the Brush Mode pop-up are unique to the Brush tool. The Lock Fill Modifier button is common to both the Brush tool and the Ink Bucket (which will be discussed in the next section). Although similar to Line Thickness and Line Style, the Brush Size and Brush Shape drop-down menus are also fairly unique to the Brush tool. The rest of the modifiers — Fill Color and Fill Color Focus — perform the same tasks for the Paint Brush as they do when they are deployed within the modifier tray of the Oval or the Rectangle tools. In the following sections, we'll run through all of the Paint Brush modifiers (see Figure 1-22) — just to make certain that we're clear on all points, even if that requires some review.

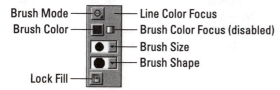

Figure 1-22: The Paint Brush tool's modifiers

Using the Brush Mode Modifier

The Brush Mode Modifier is a drop-down menu (see Figure 1-23) with five modes for applying brush strokes: Paint Normal, Paint Fills, Paint Behind, Paint Selection, and Paint Inside. Used in conjunction with selections, the Brush Modes modifier yields a broad range of sophisticated masking capabilities. Masking is fully described and defined in Chapter 6.

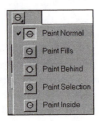

Figure 1-23: The Brush Mode Modifier drop-down reveals five painting modes that are amazingly useful for a wide range of effects when applying brush strokes.

The following paragraphs explain the various ways in which the Paint Brush modes interact with drawn and painted elements. The base image is a solidly gray rounded rectangle drawn with a black hatched outline. Three white lines of various widths are drawn on top of the gray fill of the rectangle.

Paint Normal mode

Paint Normal mode applies brush strokes over the top of any lines or fills. In this mode, a black scrawl covers all elements: background, outline, fill, and drawn lines.

Paint Fills mode

Paint Fills mode applies brush strokes to replace any fills, but leaves lines untouched. In Paint Fills mode, a similar black scrawl covers both the gray fill and the background — which, surprisingly, is considered a fill in this case.

Paint Behind mode

Paint Behind mode applies brush strokes only to blank areas and leaves all fills, lines, and other items untouched. Scrawling again, in Paint Behind mode, the only parts of the stroke that cover are those over the background. Effectively, the scrawl has gone behind the entire shape. If the stroke had originated within the gray fill, it would have covered the fill and gone behind the drawn white lines.

Paint Selection mode

Paint Selection mode applies brush strokes only to selected fills.

Paint Inside mode

Paint Inside mode applies brush strokes only to the fill area where the brush stroke was first initiated. As the name implies, Paint Inside never paints over lines. If you initiate painting from an empty area, the brush strokes won't affect any existing fills or lines, which approximates the same effect as the Paint Behind setting.

Using the Brush Fill Color Modifier

The Brush Fill Color Modifier is the Flash color chip's appearance among the Brush tool modifiers. This color chip does two things: It indicates the current color and it's also a button—click the color chip to open the Current Colors pop-up menu.

Note, however, that the Current Colors pop-up that's associated with the Brush Tool includes an additional function: Gradient color chips. When you're working with the Brush tool, a row of gradient color swatches is located at the bottom of the Current Colors pop-up menu (see Figure 1-24).

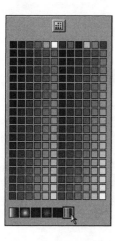

Figure 1-24: This is the Brush Fill Current Colors pop-up menu.

The current fill color (or gradient) can be changed in two simple steps:

1. Click the color chip (or Fill Color Modifier) to open the Current Colors pop-up menu.

2. Select a color (or gradient) from the Current Colors palette by clicking the desired color.

The basic concepts of working with color were explained earlier in this chapter, in the section titled, "Choosing Colors." For a more exhaustive discussion of color, including creating and selecting gradients, please refer to Chapter 2.

Using the Brush Color Focus Modifier

Here again, the Fill Color Focus button does nothing, because no line color exists to compete with the fill color for focus. As with the Line, Pencil, and Ink Bottle Tools, this Fill Color Focus button is vestigial, does nothing, and may even confuse you, so watch out.

Using the Brush Size Modifier

The Brush Size Modifier is a simple drop-down menu (see Figure 1-25) with a range of ten preset available brush sizes. Although the sizes are shown as circles, the diameter size applies to all brush shapes. In the case of an oblong brush, the diameter size refers to the broadest span of the brush. You can combine brush sizes and shapes for a wide variety of custom brush tips.

Figure 1-25: The Brush Size drop-down menu reveals ten well-distributed brush sizes, ranging from pin line to humongous.

Note   In Flash, the apparent brush size is always related to the zoom setting. Therefore, identical brush diameters applied at different zoom settings will result in different sized brush marks.

Using the Brush Shape Modifier

The Brush Shape Modifier is a simple pop-up menu with nine possible brush shapes, based on the circle, ellipse, square, rectangle, and line shapes. The oval, rectangle, and line shapes are available in several angles. Although no custom brush shapes are available, you can combine these stock brush shapes with the range of brush sizes to generate a wide variety of nearly custom brush tips. When using shapes other than circles, the diameter sizes indicated in the Brush Size drop-down menu (see Figure 1-26) will apply to the broadest area of any brush shape.

Figure 1-26: The Brush Shape drop-down menu

Using the Brush Lock Fill Modifier

The Lock Fill Modifier is a toggle button that controls how Flash handles areas filled with gradient color. Once this button is pressed, all subsequent areas (or shapes) that are painted with the same gradient will appear to be part of a single, continuous filled shape. This modifier locks the angle, size, and point of origin of the current gradient so that it remains constant throughout the scene. This capability is useful, for example, if you are creating a gradated sunset sky with gradated clouds, and the clouds must appear to be part of one continuous gradient, while the sky needs to appear to be another.

 Note   When the Dropper tool is used to pick up a fill or gradient from a scene, the Lock Fill button is automatically engaged.

Using the Brush Pressure Modifier

The Brush Pressure Modifier appears only if you have a pressure-sensitive tablet. This modifier button is a simple toggle that is used to enable or disable the finer capabilities of a pressure-sensitive tablet. With pressure-sensitivity enabled, the size of the brush stroke increases with increased drawing pressure.

Difference between the Brush tool and the Pencil tool

To demonstrate the concept of a filled outline of zero thickness, we've made a simple drawing (see Figures 1-27 and 1-28) that shows equal sized pencil and brush strokes — each viewed via regular (View ➪ Antialias) and then as outlines (View ➪ Outlines). The pencil line is on top in both drawings.

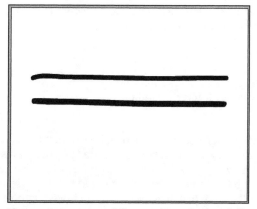

Figure 1-27: A pencil line and a paint brush line

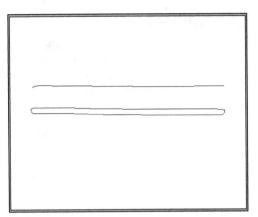

Figure 1-28: The same lines as in Figure 1-27, displayed as outlines

To view lines as outlines, select View ➪ Outlines. When viewed like this, the paint brush line appears as a filled outline of zero thickness, while the pencil line is a vector of zero thickness. Regardless of the width of the pencil line, when it is viewed as an outline, it will *always* appear as a single vector. Conversely, paint brush lines of various thicknesses, when viewed as outlines, will be exhibited as various outlines whose breadth will vary according to the thickness of the stroke — yet the paint brush outlines will be outlines (or vectors) of zero thickness.

The Dropper Tool

The Dropper tool is used to acquire (or copy) the color and style information from existing pencil lines, brush strokes, and fills. The Dropper tool has no modifiers, but then it doesn't need modifiers. That's because the Flash Dropper tool (see Figure 1-29) performs a function entirely unlike any dropper tool in any other program that we know of.

🖊—Dropper Tool   **Figure 1-29:** The Dropper is an amazingly useful "one trick pony." It has no modifiers.

When the Dropper tool isn't hovering over a line, fill, or brush stroke, its cursor is similar to the Dropper icon in the Drawing toolbar. However, the Dropper tool's cursor changes as follows to indicate when it is over a line or a fill: When the cursor is over a line, a tiny pencil appears to the lower right of the standard Dropper tool cursor. When the cursor is over a fill, a tiny brush appears to the lower right of the standard Dropper tool cursor.

With the Shift key pressed when the Dropper tool is over a line, fill, or brush stroke, the cursor changes to an inverted U shape. In this mode, (that is, when you press Shift+click) use of the Dropper tool changes the attributes for all editing tools in Flash (for instance, the Pencil, Brush, Ink Bottle, and Text tools) to match the attributes of the area clicked. That's right! Shift-clicking with the Dropper tool acquires the attributes of the clicked item and simultaneously changes the color and style settings for the Ink Bottle tool, as well as for the Pencil tool and Text tool. It also changes the fill color of all tools to match the color of the line that's clicked. The same is true if a fill color is clicked; all line tools then have the same color as the fill.

Clicking with the Dropper tool acquires all of the attributes (including color, gradient, style, and thickness) of the line or fill that has been clicked. However, the attributes of a group cannot be acquired unless the contents are being edited.

When the clicked item is a line, the Dropper tool is automatically swapped for the Ink Bottle tool, which facilitates the application of the acquired attributes to another line. Similarly, when the clicked item is a fill, the Dropper tool is automatically swapped for the Paint Bucket tool. This facilitates the application of acquired fill attributes to another fill.

When the Dropper tool is used to acquire a fill that is a bitmap, the Dropper tool is automatically swapped for the Paint Bucket tool, and a thumbnail of the bitmap image appears in place of the Fill Color modifier's Current color chip.

Note   The Dropper tool can be extremely helpful when changing the attributes of multiple lines. However, the Ink Bottle cannot apply acquired attributes to lines that are grouped. In order to work around this limitation, first ungroup the lines, and then apply the attributes to the lines (either individually or as a multiple selection), and then regroup the lines.

The Ink Bottle Tool

The Ink Bottle tool is used to change the color, style, and thickness of existing lines. It is most often used in conjunction with the Dropper tool. When the Ink Bottle tool is active, four modifiers appear in the modifier tray. Two are the Line Color and Line Color Focus buttons, while the other two are the Line Thickness, and Line Style drop-down menus. These Ink Bottle modifiers (see Figure 1-30) function just like their equivalent Pencil tool modifiers.

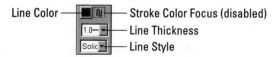

Line Color ———— Stroke Color Focus (disabled)
———— Line Thickness
———— Line Style

Figure 1-30: The Ink Bottle tool's four modifiers

Tip   The Ink Bottle is especially useful for applying custom line styles to multiple lines. You can build a collection of custom line styles either off screen or in a special custom line palette saved as a single-frame Flash movie, and then acquire these line styles whenever necessary.

Caution   When you click a selected line with the Ink Bottle tool, all other selected lines (if any) are changed simultaneously.

Using the Ink Bottle Line Color Modifier

If you've been reading about the Flash toolbar from the beginning of this chapter, it should be no surprise to you that the Ink Bottle's Line Color Modifier pop-up is both a button and a color chip. Nor will you be surprised to hear that it performs in a nearly identical manner to Pencil Tool Line Color Modifier. Similarly, you'll probably already know that the Line Color Focus is disabled here (despite the fact that it appears in the toolbar), because no other color chip exists to compete for focus. But for those of you who jumped in right here, this color chip does two things: It indicates the current color and is also a button—click the color chip to open the Current Colors pop-up menu. Color is briefly explained in a prior section of this chapter, "Choosing Color." Or, for a more exhaustive explanation of all aspects of Flash color, refer to Chapter 2.

Using the Ink Bottle Line Thickness Modifier

The Ink Bottle Line Thickness Modifier drop-down menu (see Figure 1-31) is essentially the same menu as the Pencil Tool Line Thickness Modifier. (So if you've already got that from reading about the Pencil tool, here's your hall pass to skip out while we explain the material to the newcomers.) The Line Thickness Modifier drop-down offers eight options for changing the characteristics of the Ink Bottle's lines. The first six options are preset line thicknesses, measured in points that range from hairline to 8 points.

Figure 1-31: The Ink Bottle Line Thickness Modifier drop-down menu is the same as for the Pencil tool.

The final Line Thickness option of the Line Thickness Modifier drop-down menu is Custom—which is used for setting a custom line width. Select this option to open the Line Settings dialog box, which has one entry field for the desired custom line thickness. Permissible values range from zero to ten, with fractions expressed in decimals. The seventh option of the Line Thickness Modifier pop-up is a holder for the most recent entry in the Line Settings dialog box of the Custom option. For a more detailed explanation, together with complete diagrams of the all Custom drop-down menus, please refer to the Line Thickness Modifier section of the Pencil Tool, earlier in this chapter.

Tip

Lines of hairline thickness are always drawn one pixel wide. Use Hairline for lines that will not change thickness when you scale the shape.

Caution

Depending on the level of zoom, some lines may not appear on the screen — although they will print correctly on a high-resolution printer. Line Thickness may also be adjusted in the Line Style dialog box that is accessible from the Custom option of the Line Style Modifier drop-down.

Using the Ink Bottle Line Style Modifier

Like the Line Thickness Modifier, the Ink Bottle's Line Style Modifier is essentially the same drop-down menu you'll find with the Pencil Tool Line Style Modifier (see Figure 1-32). The Line Style Modifier pop-up offers seven line styles, six of which are preset, while the seventh is Custom. The six preset lines are Solid, Dashed, Dotted, Ragged, Stippled, and Hatched. For more information on preset styles available in the Line Style Modifier, please refer to Line Thickness Modifier section of the Pencil Tool, earlier in this chapter.

Figure 1-32: The Line Style Modifier of the Ink Bottle is practically the same drop-down menu as for the Pencil tool.

The final custom style option of the Line Style Modifier drop-down menu is Custom — which is used for setting a custom line style. Select this option to open the Custom Line Style dialog box, which has numerous controls to describe the custom drawing parameters of the six basic preset lines. For a more detailed explanation, together with complete diagrams of all the Custom drop-down menus, please refer to the Line Style Modifier section of the Pencil Tool, earlier in this chapter.

The Paint Bucket Tool

The Paint Bucket tool is used to fill enclosed areas with color, gradients, or bitmap fills. Although the Paint Bucket tool is a more robust tool than the Ink Bottle, and can be used independently of the Dropper tool, it's often used in conjunction with the Dropper tool. That's because, as was discussed previously in this chapter in the section on the Dropper tool, when the Dropper tool is clicked on a fill, it acquires the fill attributes of the fill that has been clicked and then automatically swaps to the Paint Bucket tool. Because this *acquire and swap* function of the Dropper tool readily facilitates the application of acquired fill attributes to another fill, the Bucket tool is frequently used in tandem with the Dropper.

When the Paint Bucket tool is active, five modifiers appear in the modifier tray as seen in Figure 1-33. Two modifiers are buttons and two are pop-up menus. The button modifiers are the Lock Fill, Transform Fill, and Fill Color Focus modifiers. The pop-up menus are the Fill Color and Gap Size Modifiers. As is the case with other single-color tools, Fill Color Focus does nothing here (despite the fact that it appears in the toolbar) because no other color chip exists to compete for focus.

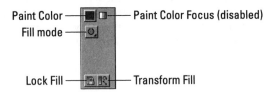

Figure 1-33: The Paint Bucket tool's five modifiers

 Using the Paint Bucket to paint with white (or the background color) is not the same as erasing. When you paint with white (or the background color) it may appear to accomplish something similar to erasing. In fact, you are, however, creating a filled item that can be selected, moved, deleted or reshaped. Only erasing erases!

 If you click with the Paint Bucket tool on one of several selected fills, *all* of the selected fills will be changed with the new fill.

 Like the Ink Bottle, the Paint Bucket can be especially useful for applying custom fill styles to multiple objects. You can build a collection of custom fill styles either off screen or in a special, saved, *custom fills palette* single-frame Flash movie, and acquire these fills whenever necessary.

Using the Paint Bucket Fill Color Modifier

Would you kick the bucket if we told you that the Paint Bucket's Fill Color Modifier is nearly the same pop-up as the Brush Fill Color Modifier? Well, if this repetition makes you pale, skip this section. But for those of you who started reading here let me fill you in: The Fill Color Modifier is the Flash color chip's appearance among the Paint Bucket Tool modifiers. Just like all the others, this color chip both indicates the current color and also behaves like a button — click the color chip to open the Current Colors pop-up. The specifics of this Fill Color Modifier, together with the basic concepts of working with color are explained in Chapter 2.

The current color can be changed by clicking the color chip (or Line Color Modifier) to open the Current Colors pop-up and selecting a new color from the Current Colors Palette. Note, however, that the Current Colors palette associated with the Paint Bucket tool includes Gradient Color Chips. While you are working with the Paint Bucket tool, Gradient color chips are located at the bottom of the Current Colors palette. All of the gradients that have been previously defined appear in rows there. To see what this looks like, refer back to Figure 1-24. Working with gradients is explained in Chapter 2.

Using the Paint Bucket Gap Size Modifier

The Gap Size Modifier pop-up offers four settings that control how the Paint Bucket tool will treat gaps when filling (see Figure 1-34). These settings are Don't Close Gaps, Close Small Gaps, Close Medium Gaps, and Close Large Gaps. If gaps are too large, you may have to close them manually.

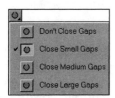

Figure 1-34: The Paint Bucket Gap Size Modifier offers four settings to control how gaps will be handled when filling.

Note   The level of zoom changes the apparent size of gaps. Although the actual size of gaps is unaffected by zoom, the Paint Bucket's interpretation of the gap is dependent upon the current zoom setting. Thus, the Paint Bucket's behavior in relation to gap size will be liable to change with the zoom setting.

Using the Paint Bucket Lock Fill Modifier

The Paint Bucket's Lock Fill Modifier is the same button as the Brush Lock Fill Modifier. The Lock Fill Modifier button controls how Flash handles areas filled with gradient color. When this button is turned on, all areas (or shapes) that are painted with the same gradient will appear to be part of a single, continuous filled shape. The Lock Fill Modifier locks the angle, size, and point of origin of the current gradient so that it remains constant throughout the scene. This unique capability is useful, for example, if you are creating a gradated sunset sky with gradated clouds. The clouds need to appear to be part of one continuous gradient, while the sky needs to appear to be another. The Lock Fill modifier behaves identically with the Paint Bucket tool as it does with the Paint Brush tool. For further information, please refer to the discussion of the Paint Brush Tool earlier in this chapter.

Tip   When the Dropper tool is used to pick up a fill or gradient from the scene, this Lock Fill button is automatically engaged.

Using the Paint Bucket Transform Fill Modifier (a.k.a. The Reshape Arrow cursor)

The Transform Tool Modifier button is used to adjust the size, angle, and center of a gradient or fill, including bitmap fills. When the Transform Tool Modifier is selected, the Paint Bucket tool automatically becomes a *Reshape Arrow cursor*. (This Reshape Arrow cursor is different from either of the Arrow tool's Rotate or Scale modifiers.)

To use the Reshape Arrow to transform a fill, first select the Transform Tool Modifier, and then simply click an existing gradient or fill. A set of three adjustment handles will appear, together with two perpendicular hatched lines. Three transformations can be performed on a fill with this modifier: adjusting the fill's center point, rotating the fill, and scaling the fill.

Adjusting the center point with the Reshape Arrow

To adjust the center point, find the small circular handle that is at the center, between the hatched lines. This circular handle is used for transforming the center point of the gradient or fill. When the Reshape Arrow cursor is brought near the center handle and four arrows appear, pointing left and right, up and down — like a compass — indicating that this handle can now be used to move the center point in any direction.

Rotating a fill with the Reshape Arrow

For a bitmap fill, rotate the fill and find the small circular handle that is at the upper-right of the hatched line. This circular handle is used for rotating a bitmap fill around the center point. Click the handle and four circular arrows appear (as seen in Figure 1-35), indicating that this handle rotates the fill around the center point.

   Figure 1-35: The Reshape Arrow cursor becomes a Rotate cursor when it is brought near the circular handle at the upper-right corner of a bitmap fill.

Reshape Arrow Anomalies

When using the Reshape Arrow, you will find that fills can differ in their characteristics — primarily in the placement of their handles, subject to a number of variables, including whether they are applied horizontally or vertically:

✦ For a horizontally applied fill: To rotate the fill, find the small circular handle that is at the *upper-right* of the hatched line. This circular handle is used for rotating a horizontally applied gradient or fill around the center point. Click the handle and four circular arrows appear, indicating that this handle will rotate the fill about the center point.

✦ For a vertically applied fill: To rotate the fill, find the small circular handle that is at the *upper-left*, at the end of the hatched line. This circular handle is used for rotating a vertically applied gradient or fill around the center point. Click the handle and four circular arrows appear, indicating that this handle will rotate the fill about the center point.

✦ These general characteristics may differ if a fill (or bitmap fill) has been variously copied, rotated, or pasted in any number of ways. The fundamental rule is this: The round center handle moves the center point, round corner handles rotate, round edge handles skew either vertically or horizontally, square edge handles scale either vertically or horizontally, and the square corner handle scales symmetrically.

✦ Some fills may not have the full complement of reshape cursors available.

✦ Skewing and Scaling of bitmap fills may have a counterintuitive effect: If the bitmap fill is scaled *smaller,* it will tile to fill the space of the original fill.

Skewing the fill with the Reshape Arrow

To skew the fill horizontally, find the small round handle at the middle of the right-hand hatched line. This round handle is used to skew the gradient or fill. Click the handle and arrows will appear, parallel to the edge of the fill, indicating the directions in which this handle will skew the fill. Click and drag the round horizontal skew handle with the Skew Arrow cursor (see Figure 1-36) to skew the bitmap fill. Release the skew handle to view the result. Note that the skew procedure is still active, meaning that the skew may be further modified.

To skew a bitmap fill vertically, locate the vertical skew handle. Skewing horizontally is functionally equivalent to skewing vertically.

Figure 1-36: The Reshape Arrow cursor changes to the Skew Arrow cursor when it is brought near a small round horizontal skew handle.

Symmetrically adjusting the scale with the Reshape Arrow

To resize a fill symmetrically, find the small square corner handle, which is usually located at the lower-left corner of the fill. This square handle is used to resize the gradient or fill while retaining the aspect ratio. The Symmetrical Resize cursor (see Figure 1-37), which has diagonal arrows, appears when the Reshape Arrow cursor is brought into proximity of the square corner handle, indicating the direction in which this handle will resize the fill. Click and drag the corner handle to scale the fill symmetrically.

 Figure 1-37: The Symmetrical Resize cursor appears when the Reshape Arrow cursor is brought into proximity with the square corner handle.

Asymmetrically adjusting the scale with the Reshape Arrow

To resize a fill asymmetrically, find a small square handle on either a vertical or a horizontal edge, depending whether you want to affect the width or height of the fill. The Asymmetrical Resize cursor, which has arrows that appear perpendicular to the edge, appears when the Reshape Arrow cursor (see Figure 1-38) is brought into proximity of a square edge handle, indicating the direction in which this handle will resize the fill. Click and drag a handle to reshape the fill.

 Figure 1-38: The Asymmetrical Resize cursor appears when the Reshape Arrow cursor is brought into proximity with the square edge handle.

The Eraser Tool

Although the Eraser tool isn't exactly either a Drawing or Painting tool, we feel that it belongs together with the Drawing and Painting tools rather than orphaned in a category of its own. After all, without the Eraser tool to compliment the Drawing and Painting tools, the process of Drawing and Painting might get impossibly complex—one mistake and you'd have to start over.

The Eraser tool is used in concert with the Drawing and Painting tools to obtain final, useable art. As the name implies, the Eraser tool (see Figure 1-39) is primarily used for erasing. When the Eraser tool is active, three modifiers appear in the modifier tray. Two of these modifiers, the Erase Mode Modifier and the Eraser Shape Modifier, are pop-ups. The third modifier, the Faucet button, is used to clear enclosed areas of fill.

 Figure 1-39: The Eraser tool has three modifiers.

The only alternative to using the Eraser tool to remove graphic elements or areas of drawings is to select them and then delete them — by pressing either the Delete or the Backspace key.

As has been mentioned previously, in context with various Drawing and Painting tools, Drawing or Painting with white (or the current background color) is *not* the equivalent of erasing. Only the Eraser tool erases! Use the simple Eraser tool, or harness the power of the Faucet modifier to take away filled areas and lines. Of all the things that we have repeated about the Flash tools, if you don't get this one, it can really come back to bite you!

The Eraser tool only erases lines and fills that are in the current frame of the scene. It won't erase groups, symbols, or text. When you need to erase a part of a group, you have two options: Either select the group and choose Edit⇨Edit Selected from the menu bar, or select the group and choose Modify⇨Break Apart from the menu bar.

Using the Erase Mode Modifier

The Erase Mode Modifier both controls and limits what and how the Eraser tool erases. The Erase Mode Modifier has five options (as seen in Figure 1-40).

Figure 1-40: The five options of the Erase Mode Modifier pop-up

✦ **Erase Normal.** In Erase Normal Mode the Eraser tool functions like a normal eraser. It erases all lines and fills that it passes over, as long as they are on the active layer.

✦ **Erase Fills.** In Erase Fills Mode the Eraser tool becomes a specialty eraser, erasing only fills and leaving lines unaffected.

✦ **Erase Lines.** When in Erase Lines Mode, the Eraser tool changes specialties; it works by erasing lines only and leaving fills unaffected.

✦ **Erase Selected Fills.** In Erase Selected Fills Mode the Eraser tool becomes even more specialized. In this mode it only erases fills that are currently selected, leaving unselected fills and all lines unaffected.

✦ **Erase Inside.** With Erase Inside Mode, the Eraser tool only erases the area of fill on which you initiate erasing. This is much like the Erase Selected Fills mode, with the exception that the selection is accomplished with the initial erasure. In this mode, the eraser leaves all other fills and all lines unaffected.

Tip   To quickly erase everything in a scene, double-click the Eraser tool in the Drawing toolbar. (Don't click in the scene! You have to double-click the Eraser tool button in the Drawing toolbar, okay?)

Using the Eraser Shape Modifier

The Eraser Shape Modifier defines both the size and shape of the eraser. It's a simple drop-down menu (as seen in Figure 1-41) with ten brushes available in two shapes, circular and square. These are arrayed in two banks of five sizes each, ranging from small to large.

Figure 1-41: The Eraser Shape Modifier drop-down menu with ten eraser sizes in two shapes, round and square

Using the Eraser's Faucet Modifier

The Eraser Tool's Faucet Modifier is Flash's version of selective annihilation — kind of like a neutron bomb. The Faucet modifier deletes an entire line segment or area of fill with a single click. Using the Faucet modifier is the equivalent of selecting and deleting an entire line or fill in a single step. Select the Eraser tool, and then choose the Faucet Modifier button. Click the offending item to say goodbye. Clicking a selected line or fill will erase all selected lines or fills.

The Text Tool

The Text tool is used to create and edit text. Although Flash is neither a drawing program, like Freehand or Illustrator, nor a page-layout program, such as QuarkXPress or PageMaker, its text-handling capabilities are well thought out and implemented. The Text tool delivers a broad range of control for generating, positioning, tuning, and also editing text. When the Text Tool is active, nine modifiers appear in the modifier tray (see Figure 1-42). Two of these modifiers are drop-down menus: Font and Font Size. Two are pop-up menus: Text Color and Text Alignment. Three modifiers are toggle buttons: Bold, Italic, and Editable Text (it's the "ab" button at the bottom of the Modifier Tray). A fourth button, the Paragraph Modifier, launches a dialog box that controls margin, indent, and line-spacing options. The last modifier, which looks like a small, blue *A* next to the color chip, is the Text Color Focus.

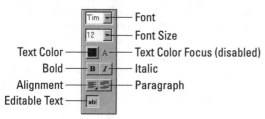

Figure 1-42: When the Text tool is active, nine modifiers appear in the Modifier Tray.

New Feature

With Flash 4 come the welcome addition of Editable Text fields, meaning that the content is variable. The person viewing the Flash movie can change the content of an Editable Text field in a password entry box or a form field. Also, you can use Editable Text fields for nonchangeable *but selectable* text so that the viewer can copy and paste text into another application. Regular text can not be selected or pasted.

Tip

Use Modify ➪ Font from the menu bar to edit selected text font, size, and style — this method has a terrific advantage, because it lets you preview fonts before changing.

New Feature

More "native" font support: Flash 4 now supports sans serif, serif, and typewriter fonts. (These translate, depending on the fonts installed on the player machine, to an Arial style, a Times style, and a Courier style.) Characteristics of these "native" Flash fonts are that they are always available, always fast, never rotate, and may vary in the metrics from player to player.

Tip

Use the Eyedropper tool to acquire text with all of the formatting and attributes of extant text blocks and apply these settings to subsequently applied text.

Cross-Reference

If your handling of text demands a more robust and thorough environment, you can generate your text in Freehand or Illustrator and import that more refined text into Flash. For more information on this type of workflow, refer to Chapter 18.

When you create type, you can edit the individual letters or words inside the text area at any time. But because Flash also treats text as a group, if you click once anywhere on the text, the entire text block will be selected.

Working with Flash text boxes

Flash now generates three flavors of text in three kinds of text boxes: Label Text, Block Text, and Editable Text.

✦ **Label Text.** With Label text, Flash creates text blocks that continue to widen as you continue to add text. Create a Label Text box by clicking once in the movie area with the Text tool. Then commence typing. A Label Text box has a round handle at the upper-right corner. In Label Text mode, if you keep typing without making line breaks, the Label Text box will continue beyond the right edge of the movie area. When this happens, the text is not lost. To regain view of this off-movie text, add line breaks, move the label box, or select View ⇨ Work Area from the menu bar to make the off-movie area Label Text box entirely visible.

✦ **Block Text.** Flash 4 now creates Block Text when a text box is *dragged out* in the movie area. Block Text Box has a fixed width and will wrap words automatically. Create a Block Text box by simply selecting the Text tool, clicking and then dragging out a box of the desired width in the movie area. When you commence typing, the text will wrap automatically and the box will extend downward as you add more lines of text. A Block Text box has a square handle at the upper-right corner.

✦ **Editable Text:** With Editable Text fields, the content is variable. This means that the contents of an Editable Text field can be changed by the page viewer, as, for example, when used in a password entry box or a form field. Create editable text by clicking the Editable Text Modifier; then click in the movie area to drag out and define the text box. An Editable Text box has a square handle at the lower-right corner, which can be dragged in or out to resize it. Because the use of editable text involves interactivity and is rather complex, further discussion of editable text is deferred to the final chapter in the section of this book that is devoted to interactivity. Please refer to Chapter 14 for more information on editable text.

Note   A Label Text box can be converted into a Block Text box. Place the cursor over the round text handle at the upper-right corner of the Label Text box. A double-ended arrow will appear, indicating that you can modify the Label Text box's width. Drag to reshape the Label Text box. When you release the mouse, the text handle at the upper-right corner will now be square (formerly, it was round), indicating that this is now a Block Text box.

Tip   Can't tell if it's label or block text? That's because it's not in Edit Mode. To return the text object to Edit Mode, either Double-click the object with the Arrow tool, or click it once with the Type tool.

Using the Text Tool Font Modifier

The Text Tool's Font Modifier is a simple drop-down menu as seen in Figure 1-43. When the Text tool is active, it displays the current font. If you click the arrow to the immediate right of the text entry box, a pop-up appears, displaying a scrolling menu of available fonts. Choose a font from this scrolling menu to set the font for the next text element that you create. To change the font of existing text, first select the text in the movie area, and then choose a different font from the scrolling menu.

Figure 1-43: The Font Modifier drop-down menu

The font of existing text can also be changed from the menu bar with Modify ➪ Font. For more information on this method refer to the section in this chapter titled, "Using Modify ➪ Font."

Using the Text Tool Font Size Modifier

The Text Tool's Font Size Modifier is both a drop-down menu and a text entry box (see Figure 1-44). When the Text tool is active, it displays the current font size in a text entry box. You can change the font size by entering a specific font size in this text entry box. If you click the arrow to the immediate right of the text entry box, a pop-up displays a scrolling menu of available font sizes.

Figure 1-44: The Font Size Modifier drop-down menu

Using the Text Tool Text Color Modifier

For those of you who have just turned to this section about the text tool, the Text Color Modifier is where the Flash color chip shows up among the Text Tool modifiers. This color chip does two things: It indicates the current color and is also a button — click the color chip to open the Current Colors Pop-up. The current text color can be changed easily by (1) clicking the color chip (or Line Color Modifier) to open the Current Colors pop-up and (2) selecting a new color from the Current Colors palette by clicking the desired color. The specifics of the Text Color Modifier, together with the basic concepts of working with color, are explained in Chapter 2, "Flash Color."

Using the Text Tool's Text Alignment Modifier

The Text Tool's Alignment Modifier is a simple drop-down menu (see Figure 1-45) that displays four options for the arrangement of text: Left, Center, Right, and Full Justification. Alignment affects the currently selected paragraph *only*.

Figure 1-45: The Text Tool Alignment Modifier drop-down menu

Using the Text Tool Bold and Italic Modifiers

The Text tool's Bold Modifier is a simple button that toggles selected text between normal and bold. The Text tool's Italic Modifier is another simple button. It toggles selected text between normal and italic.

Using the Text Tool Paragraph Modifier

The Text tool's Paragraph Modifier is a button that opens the Paragraph Properties dialog box. The Paragraph Properties dialog box has entry fields to change the current settings of the Text tool, including Margins, Indentation, and Line Spacing. It can also be used to adjust the Margins, Indentation, and Line Spacing of selected text.

✦ **Margins.** The Margins Fields of the Paragraph dialog box define the space between the text and the borders of the text box. By default, this space is described in pixels.

✦ **Indentation.** The Indentation Field of the Paragraph dialog box defines the indent (also described by default in pixels) of the first line of a paragraph. This indent is relative to the left margin.

✦ **Line Spacing.** The Line Spacing Field of the Paragraph dialog box defines the space between lines of text. Line spacing is described by default in points. Regardless of line spacing settings for individual fonts, the largest font on a line will always determine line spacing for that line.

Note The default units of measurement for both the Margin and Indentation entries of the Paragraph Properties dialog box are determined by the Ruler Units for the movie. Ruler Units can be reset in the Movie Properties dialog box, which is accessed from the menu bar with Modify ⇨ Movie or from the keyboard by pressing Command+M (Ctrl+M).

Using the Flash Kerning Controls

In addition to all of the other controls that Flash affords for the arrangement and adjustment of text, text can be manually kerned. *Kerning* is the process of adjusting the space between two text characters. Manual kerning can be applied either: (1) to selected (highlighted) text characters or (2) to the pair of text characters on either side of the cursor. The full compliment of Kerning commands is available from the Modify menu:

✦ **Decrease Spacing by One-Half Pixel.** To decrease text character spacing by one-half pixel, select Modify ⇨ Kerning ⇨ Narrower from the menu bar, or press Command+Option+Left Arrow (Ctrl+Alt+Left Arrow).

✦ **Decrease Spacing by Two Pixels.** To decrease text character spacing by two pixels, press Command+Shift+Option+Left Arrow (Ctrl+Shift+Alt+Left Arrow).

✦ **Increase Spacing by One-Half Pixel.** To increase text character spacing by one-half pixel, select Modify ⇨ Kerning ⇨ Wider from the menu bar, or press Command+Option+Right Arrow (Ctrl+Alt+Right Arrow).

✦ **Increase Spacing by Two Pixels.** To increase text character spacing by two pixels, press Command+Shift+Option+Right Arrow (Ctrl+Alt+Right Arrow).

✦ **Reset Spacing to Normal.** To reset text character spacing to normal, select Modify ⇨ Kerning ⇨ Reset from the menu bar, or press Command+Option+Up Arrow (Ctrl+Alt+Up Arrow).

Using Modify ⇨ Font

Selected text can be reworked from the menu bar with Modify ⇨ Font, which opens the Font dialog box. Although most of the controls available in the Font dialog box are available as modifiers while the Text tool is active, this dialog box lets you preview fonts before selecting. You can change the font, size, and style with this dialog box shown in Figure 1-46.

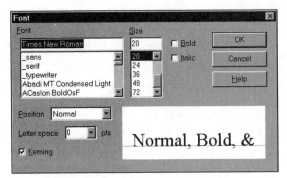

Figure 1-46: The Font dialog box is used to control nearly every aspect of selected text.

Using Modify ➪ Style

Some of the settings of the Modify ➪ Font command are also available from the Style submenu (see Figure 1-47) which appears when you choose Modify ➪ Style from the menu bar.

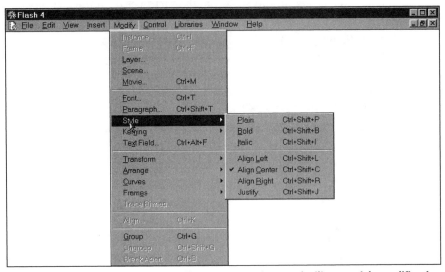

Figure 1-47: The Style submenu offers seven settings to facilitate quick modifications to selected text.

Reshaping and manipulating text characters

In addition to all of the powerful text-handling capabilities previously discussed, Flash also gives you the ability to take standard text and reshape and distort it to suit your taste (or lack thereof). In order to manipulate text, it must first be converted to its component lines and fills. Then it can be reshaped, erased, manipulated, and distorted. Converted text characters can be grouped or changed to symbols. They can also be animated. Once text characters have been converted to lines and fills, however, they can no longer be edited as text. Even if you regroup the text characters or convert them into a symbol, you can no longer apply font, kerning, or paragraph modifiers. For more information on reshaping and manipulating text, refer to Chapter 6. Just to get you started, here are a few tips and guidelines for manipulating text in Flash:

✦ To convert text characters to component lines and fills: First, the text characters that you want to convert must be selected, or highlighted. Then choose Modify ⇨ Break Apart from the menu bar. To undo, choose Edit ⇨ Undo from the menu bar.

✦ Rotation and Break Apart can only be applied to outline fonts such as TrueType.

✦ Bitmap fonts will disappear from the screen if you attempt to break them apart.

✦ PostScript fonts can be broken apart *only* on Macs running ATM (Adobe Type Manager).

✦ Test whether a font is a bitmapped font by choosing View ⇨ Antialias from the menu bar. If the text still appears with ragged edges, it is a bitmapped font and will disappear when broken apart.

✦   ✦   ✦

Flash Color

Computer monitors display color with a method called RGB color. A monitor screen is a tightly packed array of pixels arranged in a grid, where each pixel has an address. The address enables the computer to send a specific color to each pixel. Because each pixel is composed of a single red, green, and blue dot, the colors that the monitor displays can be "mixed" at each pixel by varying the individual intensities of the red, green, and blue color dots. Each individual dot can vary in intensity over a range of 256 values, starting with 0 (which is off) to a maximum value of 255 (which is on). Thus, if red is "half-on" (a value of 127), while green is "off" (a value of 0), and blue is fully "on" (a value of 255), the pixel appears reddish-blue.

This is the description for unlimited, full color — which is sometimes referred to as 24-bit color. However, many computer systems are still incapable of displaying full color. Limited color displays are either 16-bit or 8-bit displays. Although a full discussion of bit-depth is beyond the scope of this book, it is important to note several points:

- ✦ 24-bit color is required to accurately reproduce photographic images.

- ✦ Because 16-bit and 8-bit systems can display a limited number of colors, they must dither down anything that exceeds their gamut, or expanse of possible colors. Dithering means that colors that are missing from the palette will be simulated by placing two colors in close proximity to fool the eye into seeing intermediate colors.

- ✦ Some image formats, such as GIF, utilize a color palette, which limits them to 256 colors total. This is called *indexed color*.

- ✦ Calibration of your monitor is essential for accurate color work. For more information, refer to the calibration area of the ch02 folder at the *Flash 4 Bible* Web site: www.theFlashBible.com/ch02.

Note   For more information about issues pertinent to color on the Web, a concise, thorough resource is the Web color appendix of this book: <*deconstructing web graphics.2*>, by Jon Warren Lentz and Lynda Weinman.

Web Safe Color Issues

Web Safe Color is a complex issue and a discussion of the factors behind it is beyond the scope of this book. What it boils down to is this: The Mac and PC platforms handle their color palettes differently, so the browsers don't have the same colors available to them across platforms. This leads to inconsistent, unreliable color—unless one is careful to choose their colors for Web design from the Web Safe palette. The Web Safe palette is a palette of 216 colors that are consistent on both the Mac and the PC platforms for the Netscape, Explorer, and Mosaic browsers. The Web Safe palette contains only 216 out of 256 possible indexed colors because 40 colors vary between Macs and PCs. Use the Web Safe palette to avoid color shifting and to ensure greater design (color) control. Refer to the color section of this book to see the Web Safe palette, which shows both Hexadecimal and RGB values for all 216 Web Safe colors. It can also be downloaded from `http://www.lynda.com/hex.html`.

Note   The Solid Color Control tab of the Colors window has a check box that toggles the palette to make it "Snap to. Web Safe" colors. It is unclear whether this ensures that both color tweening and alpha transitions will also be snapped to Web Safe Colors.

Hex Defined

Hexadecimal notation is used with HTML code and some scripting languages to specify flat color, which is a continuous area of undifferentiated color, Hex code is used because it describes colors in an efficient manner that HTML and scripting languages can digest. Hexadecimal is used in HTML to specify colored text, lines, background, borders, frame cells, and frame borders. Any RGB color can be described in Hexadecimal. A Hexadecimal color number has six places. It allocates two places for each of the three color channels: R, G, and B. So, in the hexadecimal example, 00FFCC: 00 signifies the red channel, FF signifies the green channel, and CC signifies the blue channel. The following table shows the corresponding values between Hexadecimal and customary integer values.

16 integer values:	0 1 2 3 4 5 6 7 8 9 10 11 12 13 14 15
16 hex values:	0 1 2 3 4 5 6 7 8 9 A B C D E F

ColorSafe and Other Solutions

You can use a couple of valuable tools to create custom-mixed Web Safe colors. They build patterns composed of Web Safe colors that fool the eye into seeing a more desirable color: These are essentially blocks of pre-planned dithers, built out of the Web Safe palette, that augment the useable palette while retaining cross-platform, cross-browser color consistency.

✦ **ColorSafe** is a Photoshop plug-in, which generates hybrid color swatches with this logic. ColorSafe (MAC and Win95) is available directly from BoxTop software at `http://www.boxtopsoft.com/`. Furthermore, the ColorSafe demo is included in the software folder of the *Flash 4 Bible* CD-ROM.

✦ **ColorMix** is an easily used online utility that interactively delivers hybrid color swatches, much like ColorSafe. This is free at `http://www.colormix.com/`.

If you'd like to see the example swatches and associated Flash file for this tutorial open the Hybrid Color Swatches folder located in the ch03 folder of the *Flash 4 Bible* CD-ROM.

To illustrate the principle of hybrid swatches, the images that illustrate this tutorial were created at high zoom levels. In normal practice, the checkered appearance would not be noticeable.

Tutorial: Using hybrid color swatches in Flash

Both ColorSafe (see the figure below) and ColorMix can be teamed up with the Flash Dropper Tool to expand the available palette, yet retain Web Safe Color consistency. It takes a little fussing, but once you've built a set of Flash hybrid color swatches they can be reused from the library, and once you get the knack, new swatches are more easily created.

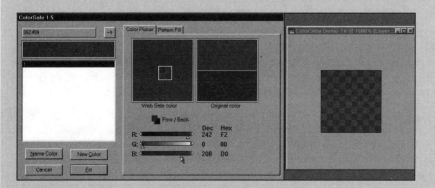

Continued

(continued)

Whether you use ColorMix online or prefer to use the ColorSafe plug-in for Photoshop, the optimal size for your hybrid color swatch is about 10 pixels square. Some swatches for this tutorial were saved as Tiffs, others as GIFs. The optimal workflow is to generate all of your swatches first. Then, before proceeding further, open the Photoshop Preferences dialog box with File ➪ Preferences ➪ General, and make sure that "Export Clipboard" is enabled. Don't close Photoshop.

Next, open a new Flash editor document and name it **HybridSwatches**. Then, turn off Flash's default dithering with View ➪ Fast and then save the document. Return to Photoshop and open all of your hybrid color swatches. Working with the topmost swatch, select and then copy the entire swatch, as follows: Select ➪ All, and then Edit ➪ Copy. Now return to Flash and paste the swatch (that you've just copied) into the HybridSwatches document with Edit ➪ Paste. Use the Arrow Tool to position the swatch. Repeat this procedure for all of your swatches until they've all been pasted into Flash (reference the figure below). Save the HybridSwatches document. Close Photoshop.

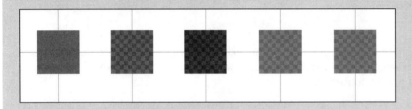

Now for a few examples to show how this works: Add a new layer to your HybridSwatches document and use the Rectangle Tool to drag out a rectangle, filled with any color. Return to the swatches layer and use the Arrow Tool to select a swatch with which to fill the rectangle. When the swatch is selected, break it apart with Modify ➪ Break Apart. (A bitmap that's broken apart is signified by a fine grid pattern that covers the bitmap.) Then use the Dropper Tool to acquire the bitmap fill of this swatch. When you click the swatch, the Dropper Tool is automatically swapped to the Paint Bucket Tool, as shown. Click inside the rectangle with the Paint Bucket — the fill has been replaced with the hybrid bitmap fill!

Follow the same procedure to fill other shapes — either on the same layer or on different layers — with Web Safe hybrid bitmap fills. See the following figure for an example. Note that a swatch layer can be saved with a project and be excluded from the final animation simply by turning off the visibility icon in the layer bar. Regarding the procedure, the most common problem encountered in acquiring the bitmap fill is either forgetting to break apart the bitmap, or failing to do so properly.

To prepare and save the HybridSwatches document so that it can be used as a Library, start by deleting all three layers, including the layer into which the swatches were originally pasted. Add a new layer, leave it blank, and then save the document and close it. Now you can open a new Flash document, and then access the hybrid swatches with File ➪ Open as Library — use the dialog box to locate and open HybridSwatches.fla. As shown in the figure below, now all of the bitmap fills saved in HybridSwatches.fla are available for use within the new Flash document.

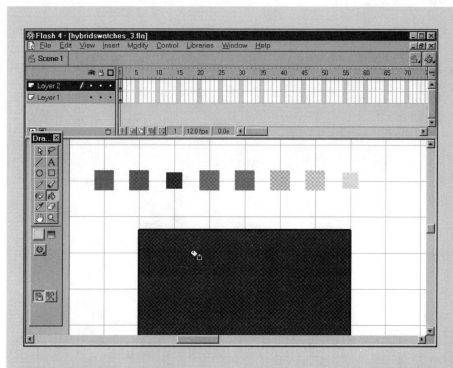

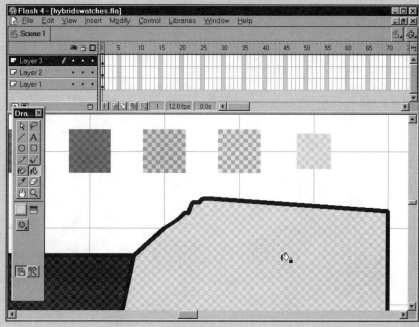

Continued

(continued)

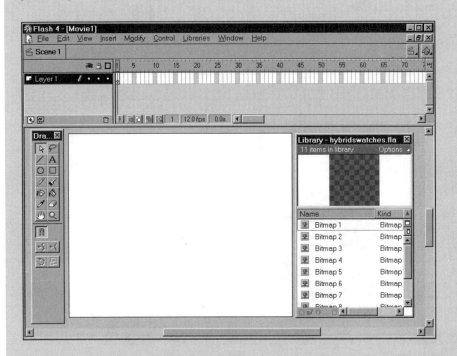

To use a hybrid swatch, select the appropriate swatch from the Library and drag the swatch from the Preview Window onto the active layer—here, the swatch is shown in the upper-left corner. If the swatch is not selected, use the Arrow Tool to select it, then use Modify ⇨ Break Apart, to break it apart. Next, use the Dropper Tool to acquire the bitmap fill, which will load the Paint Bucket Tool. As shown below, the Paint Bucket can now be used to fill any shape with hybrid Web safe color.

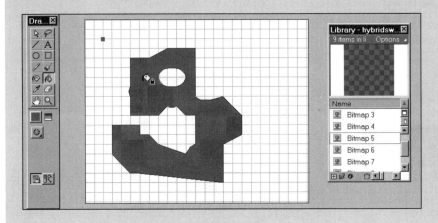

Note As mentioned in Chapter 1, a new feature in Flash 4 is the addition of Color Focus buttons, which are on the toolbar adjacent to both the Color Modifier buttons. Focus for the Line Color Modifier is a button with a squiggle, while that for the Fill Color Modifier has a linear gradation. These buttons change the focus of the Color Window so that colors may be selected for either Line or Fill, regardless of which Color Chip was active when the Color Window was originally opened.

Toolbar Color

Just as you have several ways to approach the subject of color, you can also access the various — but fundamentally similar — color-handling tools in Flash 4 in a number of ways. The quickest, and perhaps most convenient route is to approach color from either of the color buttons located on the toolbar: the Line Color and the Fill Color buttons. As was discussed in Chapter 1, these modifiers serve a double duty. As color chips, they display either the current lines or fill color. Yet they are also buttons: Click the button to launch the Current Color pop-up menu.

Tools that create a line include the Line Tool, Pencil Tool, Ink Bottle Tool, and — because they draw outlines around their fills — both the Oval and Rectangle Tool. Each of these tools is accompanied by the Line Color Modifier, which appears in the Modifier tray of the toolbar. As shown in Figure 2-1, clicking the Line Color Modifier button opens the Current Line Color pop-up menu. The Current Line Color pop-up menu contains all of the colors in the current color set, including any new colors that have been temporarily added to the set. It is identical for any tool that has a Line Color Modifier. It always has two buttons: the Blank Swatch button and the Color Window button. The Blank Swatch button is used for creating a transparent line that only works with the Oval and Rectangle Tools, as any other transparent line (without a fill) is self-deleting. The Color Window button launches the Color window. Working with the Color window (including adding new colors, saving colors, and working with color sets) is fully discussed in the Color Window section of this chapter, so read on.

In addition to tools that create lines, fill tools also exist. The fill tools include the Brush, Paint Bucket, Oval, and Rectangle Tools. Each of these tools is accompanied by the Fill Color Modifier, which also appears in the modifier tray of the toolbar. As shown in Figure 2-2, clicking the Fill Color Modifier button opens the Current Fill Color pop-up menu. Although the Current Fill Colors pop-up menu is similar to the line pop-up, it has one significant difference: In addition to the Blank Swatch and the Color Window buttons, this pop-up menu has another row of buttons at the bottom: These are the Current Gradient buttons. Click a Current Gradient button to fill with that gradient. The Current Fill Color pop-up menu also contains all of the colors in the current color set, including any new colors or gradients that have been temporarily added to the set. It, too, is identical for any tool that has a Fill Color Modifier.

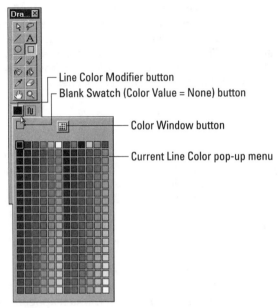

— Line Color Modifier button
— Blank Swatch (Color Value = None) button
— Color Window button
— Current Line Color pop-up menu

Figure 2-1: The Current Line Color pop-up menu

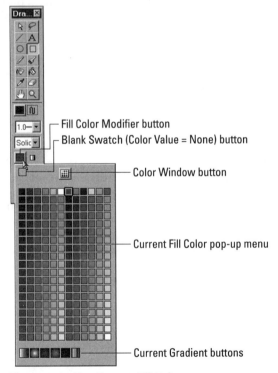

— Fill Color Modifier button
— Blank Swatch (Color Value = None) button
— Color Window button
— Current Fill Color pop-up menu
— Current Gradient buttons

Figure 2-2: The Current Fill Color pop-up menu

Using either the Current Line or Current Fill Color pop-up menu to change the color of a line or fill is quite simple. Just open the pop-up and select a new color from the swatches displayed. If the color you want is not there, click the Color Window button to open the Color window.

Using the Flash Color Window

In addition to opening the Color window from either the Current Line or Current Fill Color pop-up menu, another way to launch it is from the menu bar with Menu ⇨ Colors. The Solid and Gradient tabs delineate the Color window's two primary functions.

Solid colors

The Solid Color tab of the Color window is shown in Figure 2-3. It's used for most operations pertinent to solid colors, including: creating custom colors, adjusting opacity, managing and loading color sets, and controlling Web safe color.

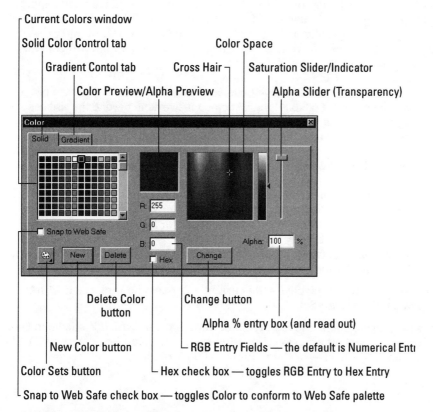

Figure 2-3: The Solid Color tab of the Color window

One of the many celebrated new features of Flash 4 is the ability to load and save Color Sets. These and related Color Set operations occur in the submenus of the Color Sets drop-down menu, which is shown in Figure 2-4. Click the Color Sets button to access the Color Sets drop-down menu.

Figure 2-4: The Color Sets drop-down menu

Colors are now saved *within* your Flash document, rather than as an external file. Flash stores RGB colors and gradients in a proprietary Flash format. Furthermore, Flash can now import and export solid colors from files in the Color Table (.ACT) format — which can be imported by Photoshop and also imported and exported from Fireworks. Flash can also import solid colors from GIF files. If it isn't already obvious, this new capability means greater flexibility for workflow and project management, because now you can save a specific color set for a project and load different color sets as needed.

Caution

Be cautious about creating huge Color Sets! On some systems (for example, a 17-inch monitor set at 800×600) the fill pop-up may extend beyond the visible screen and you'll be forced to use the color window to choose colors that are hidden off-screen. This can get really bad if you add colors from a GIF image.

The Color Sets drop-down menu has eight submenus:

✦ **Add Colors:** opens the Import Color Swatch menu, which is shown in Figure 2-5. Add Colors retains the current color set and appends the color set that is selected from the Import Color Swatch menu.

✦ **Replace Colors:** also opens the Import Color Swatch menu. However, replace Colors drops the current color set when it loads the selected color set.

✦ **Load Default Colors:** clears the current color set and replaces it with the default Flash Color Set.

✦ **Save Colors:** opens the Export Color Swatch menu, which is shown in Figure 2-6. Color Sets may be saved in either the Flash Color Set — on the PC (.CLR), on the MAC (.fclr) — or Color Table (.ACT) format.

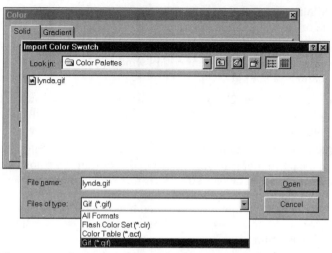

Figure 2-5: The Import Color Swatch menu and File Type drop-down menu. This menu appears when either Add Colors or Replace Colors is selected from the Color Sets drop-down menu, which is accessed by clicking the Color Sets button. The Color Sets drop-down menu is the same for both the Solid Color and Gradient Color tabs.

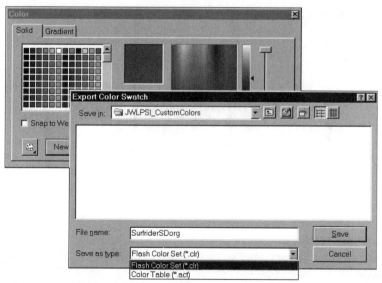

Figure 2-6: The Export Color Swatch menu and File Type drop-down menu

✦ **Save as Default:** saves the current color set as the default — this action will replace the original default Flash Color Set.

✦ **Clear Colors:** when Clear Colors is selected from the Color Sets drop-down menu, the swatches in the current colors window are diminished, leaving only black and white.

✦ **Web 216:** select the Web 216 option to replace the current color set with the Web Safe palette of 216 colors. Upon initial install, this will also be the Flash Default.

✦ **Sort by Color:** click this dandy button to rearrange an accumulation of custom colors into a palette that is freshly re-ordered according to color. Note, however, that sometimes this can deliver strange results when you sort a really large palette. We've found that blacks and grays can get scattered through the "sorted" palette in a random fashion. When it works properly, Sort by Color sorts by hues, with the values of each hue arranged together from light to dark in declining order.

Hex that's easy

As shown in Figure 2-7, you can simply click the Hex check box to display an RGB color in Hex values. Hex values can also be input into the RGB fields to generate a Hex color.

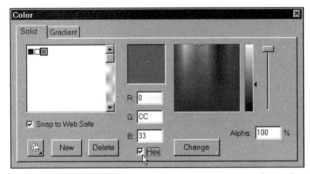

Figure 2-7: Here, the new color that was created previously is now displayed in Hex values.

Alpha transparency

You have two ways to accomplish 50% transparency: You can drag the Alpha slider midway until the Alpha readout says 50%, or you can enter a value of 50 in the Alpha readout. Numeric entry is useful when you already know what level of transparency is required, while the slider is useful for interactive fiddling with transparency to get it "just right."

Gradient colors

The Gradient Color tab of the Color window, shown in Figure 2-8, (which is also included in the color section of the book) is used for most gradient color operations, including: creating custom gradients, opacity adjustments within a gradient, and — like the Solid Color tab — managing and loading color sets

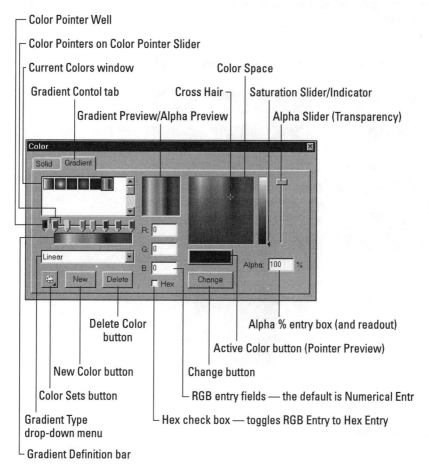

Color Pointer Well

Color Pointers on Color Pointer Slider

Current Colors window

Gradient Contol tab

Gradient Preview/Alpha Preview

Color Space

Cross Hair

Saturation Slider/Indicator

Alpha Slider (Transparency)

Delete Color button

Alpha % entry box (and readout)

Active Color button (Pointer Preview)

New Color button

Change button

Color Sets button

RGB entry fields — the default is Numerical Entr

Gradient Type drop-down menu

Hex check box — toggles RGB Entry to Hex Entry

Gradient Definition bar

Figure 2-8: The Gradient Color tab of the Color window

The Flash 4 Gradient Type drop-down menu has two styles: Linear and Radial.

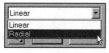

Figure 2-9: The Gradient Type drop-down menu

While creating a custom (or new) gradient, the color of the presently active Color Pointer is displayed by the Active Color button. The color of the pointer can be changed (and the change will be reflected by the Active Color button) by using the RGB entry boxes, the Color Space, and also the Alpha Controls. A color may also be selected from the Current Colors pop-up menu, which is shown in Figure 2-10. When working with gradients, the Current Colors pop-up menu can be accessed by clicking the Active Color button. This pop-up menu contains all of the solid colors in the current color set, including any new colors that have been temporarily added to the set.

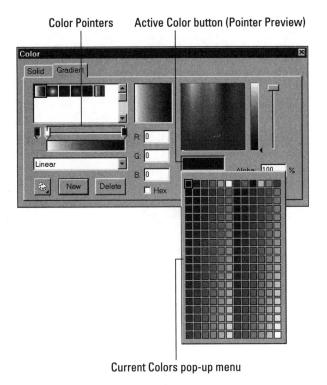

Figure 2-10: The Current Colors pop-up menu

To customize one point of an existing gradient, click a color pointer to give it focus. In this example, the color pointer, which is second from the right, is given focus — which means that it is active and can be edited. Switching from one color pointer to another changes the color displayed by the Active Color button to match that of the color pointer that has focus.

A new color may be selected for the color pointer by clicking in the color space, as shown in Figure 2-11. The Active Color button reflects the color selected, and the Gradient Definition bar updates, too. Click the Change button to update this gradient in the Current Gradients window. Or, click the New button to create a new gradient, without replacing the pre-existing gradient. In addition to selecting from the color space, a new color may also be specified by numeric or Hex entry in the RGB Entry Fields or by selecting a color from the Current Colors pop-up menu.

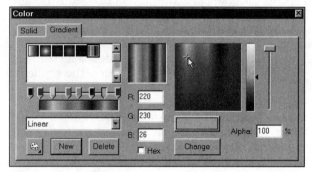

Figure 2-11: A new color is selected for the next-to-last Color Pointer on the right.

It's easy to destroy a valuable gradient by editing it and then clicking the Change button. So, if you're going to make a new gradient based on one that already exists, it's a good idea to get into the habit of starting out by selecting a base gradient and then immediately clicking the New button. In Figure 2-12, the base gradient was the default black and white gradient at the far left of the Current Gradients window. In this example, the new gradient appears, highlighted — indicating that it is the active gradient, subject to editing — to the right. Following this work habit ensures that any changes you make will be to the new gradient. As shown, with the new gradient ready for editing, a new Color Pointer is now being dragged from the color well towards the Color Pointer slider.

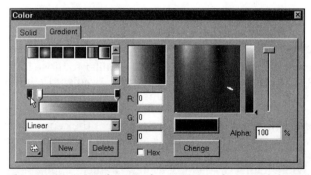

Figure 2-12: First the New button is used to avoid destroying a valuable gradient. Then a new Color Pointer is dragged from the color well towards the Color Pointer slider.

The new color pointer that was acquired in the previous figure is now dragged to the middle of the Color Pointer slider. The color of this pointer can be changed to create a new gradient in several ways. One way to modify the color of a color pointer is to use the Current Colors pop-up menu. Click the Active Color button to invoke the Current Colors pop-up menu, and then select a new color clicking a color chip. Don't forget to click the Change button to update the gradient in the Current Gradients window.

Another way to modify the color of a color pointer is to simply select a color from within the Color Space. Simply click the Crosshair and move it around within the Color Space. As you drag the Crosshair, the Active Color button is instantly updated to display this selected color. Click the Change button to update the gradient in the Current Gradients window.

To adjust the relative opacity or transparency of the active Color Pointer, drag the Alpha slider up or down. When the Alpha slider is used, a visual cue for transparency is the appearance of a faint grid in both the Active Color button and the Gradient Preview/Alpha Preview. The Alpha value is also displayed numerically, as shown in Figure 2-13, in the Alpha % Entry Box.

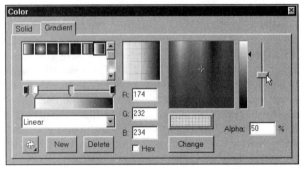

Figure 2-13: Dragging the Alpha slider to adjust the Alpha of the active Color Pointer

Making Radial Gradients

The procedures for making a Radial Gradient are all quite similar to those for creating a linear gradient. The only real difference is that the Gradient Definition bar — when used in conjunction with Radial Gradients — must be considered as a radius, or slice from the center out to the edge, of the circular gradient. Color Pointers at the left end of the Gradient Definition bar represent the center — or inside — of the Radial Gradient, while Color Pointers at the right end represent the outside. As shown in Figure 2-14, a new Gradient has been created based on the default Black and White Radial Gradient. This new Gradient appears, highlighted, at the far right of the Current Gradients window. It looks like a black and white sphere.

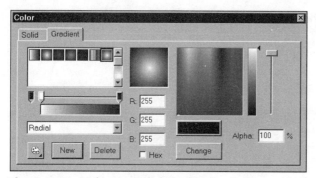

Figure 2-14: Making a Radial Gradient is similar to creating a linear gradient.

Now, to customize the spherical gradient shown in Figure 2-14, in order to make it look like a hoop or halo. As shown in Figure 2-15, the left color pointer — which is responsible for the white color at the center of the sphere — is being dragged to the center of the Gradient Definition bar. When the mouse is released, the Gradient Definition bar will be white from the left edge over to the center, where this Color Pointer is now positioned.

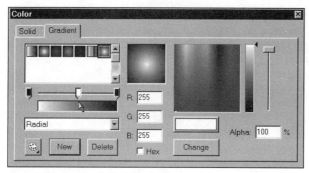

Figure 2-15: The left color pointer, which is responsible for the white color at the center of the sphere, is being dragged to the center of the Gradient Definition bar.

The effect of the previous move appears in the Gradient Preview of Figure 2-16. It looks like a large white disk that gradually changes to black. Now, a new color pointer is dragged from the Color Pointer Well and positioned so that the Gradient Definition bar will change from solid black to a thin diameter of white, and then back to black.

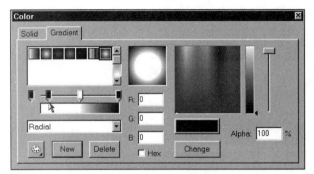

Figure 2-16: The Gradient Preview shows the effect of changes to the Gradient Definition bar.

As shown in Figure 2-17, the previous adjustment now appears in the Gradient Preview. It's a white halo or hoop smoothly appearing from black and then receding back into black. Here, the Color Pointer for the outer black area is being adjusted slightly by moving the far right Color Pointer to tighten the width of the white hoop.

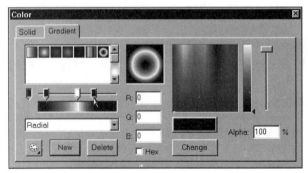

Figure 2-17: Adjusting the Color Pointer for the outer black area to tighten the width of the white hoop

Flash Symbols and tweened color effects

Flash Symbols can be tweened so that they will change color over time. Although this involves color, the selection of colors for the keyframes of the tween is merely a rudimentary application of fill and line color, as described in this chapter. For information regarding the tweening and keyframe aspects of Symbols and Tweened Color Effects, please refer to Chapter 9.

✦   ✦   ✦

Defining the Flash Framework

So far, in the last two chapters, we've seen the Drawing Tools and Color resources of Flash. If you were to look only at those chapters you might get the mistaken impression that Flash is very much like a hybrid between a vector drawing program, such as Freehand or Illustrator, and a photo manipulation program, such as Photoshop. Although Flash truly is such a hybrid, it's so much more. It's also an interactive multimedia-authoring program. It's a sophisticated animation program suitable for creating a range of animations, from simple Web ornaments to broadcast-quality cartoons. Plus, with the implementation of ActionScript with Flash 4 and concurrent development of Generator Studio 2, it's also capable of serving as the front-end and graphics engine for the premiere, robust solution for the delivery of dynamic Web content from databases and other backend resources. In this quick little chapter, we'll take a look at the framework in which all these seemingly disparate functionalities are so seamlessly melded.

What's Flash Capable Of?

So, if Flash is a hybrid animal, what are the components of this hybrid? If they were separated out, how might their capabilities be described?

Vector program

The majority of the Flash animal is a vector-based drawing program, with capabilities similar to either Macromedia Freehand or Adobe Illustrator. A vector-based drawing program doesn't rely upon individual pixels to compose an image. Instead, it draws shapes using individual points, which are described by coordinates. Lines that connect these points are called paths, and vectors at each point describe the curvature of the path. Because this scheme is mathematical, it's both more compact and scaleable without adverse affect.

Vector animation

Another large part of the Flash animal is unlike anything else: the vector animation component. Although Flash is capable of handling bitmaps, its pure file format is vector-based. So, unlike all other animation and media programs, Flash relies on the slim and trim vector format for transmission of your final work. Instead of storing megabytes of pixel information for each frame, Flash stores compact vector descriptions of each frame. Whereas a bitmap-based animation program struggles to display each bitmap in rapid succession, Flash quickly renders the vector descriptions as needed. This is a huge advantage when transmitting Flash animations and Flash content over the Web.

Photo manipulation

In truth, Flash has limited capabilities as a photo manipulation program. It might be more accurate to describe this part of the Flash animal as a bitmap handler. Bitmap images are composed of dots on a grid of individual pixels. Because the location (and color) of each dot must be stored in memory, this is memory intensive, and also leads to large file sizes. However, for photographic quality images, bitmap formats are indispensable. One more drawback to bitmap images is that they cannot be scaled without adversely affecting the quality (clarity and sharpness). The adverse affects of scaling an image up are more pronounced than when scaling down.

Authoring program

You might say that the body of Flash is a multimedia-authoring program, or multimedia-authoring environment. It authors movies, which can contain multiple kinds of media, such as sound, still graphics, and moving graphics. Yet is also an interactive multimedia program because it has the capability to assign viewer action commands to the movies that it authors.

Animation sequencer

There probably isn't a multimedia-authoring program that doesn't have a component that might be called an animation sequencer. Flash is no exception. In fact, the animation sequencer is the backbone of Flash. The organization of sequences, also known as movies, is as follows:

✦ The Movie can have any number of *scenes*, which may be arranged (or rearranged) into a sequence to create a playing order. Scenes play through from first to last (unless actions or scripting dictate otherwise).

✦ Each scene can contain an unlimited number of *layers*, which are viewed from front-to-back in the scene. The stacking order of these layers is arranged in the timeline: the topmost layer in the timeline appears at the front of the scene, while the bottom layer is at the back.

✦ Furthermore, each layer may also have a stacking order of the objects within it. Always at the *bottom* level are ungrouped lines and shapes. Above, in the *overlay* level, are bitmaps, text, groups, grouped items, symbols, and symbol instances. These items may be moved in front or behind others on that layer without moving them to another layer.

✦ The units that are responsible for the illusion of time in the animation are *frames*. Each layer may be composed of a sequence of one or more frames that are controlled by the timeline.

✦ Finally, two basic kinds of frames exist: *static frames* and *keyframes*. Each layer must begin with a keyframe, which may be empty. Static frames simply repeat the content of the prior frame. Keyframes are where content (or emptiness) is either placed or changed. Animation is achieved either by changing the contents on a frame-by-frame basis — which is called *frame-by-frame animation* — or by establishing two keyframes and instructing Flash to interpolate the change in between them — which is called *tweening*.

Programming interface and database front-end

With the release of Flash 4 and the implementation of ActionScript as part of Flash, Macromedia has expanded the capabilities of Flash to include limited — but powerful — programming capabilities that can be used to control the nature and quality of Flash's interactivity. Furthermore, these capabilities — augmented with Generator 2 — give Flash the functionality to work as the database front-end for sophisticated interactive applications such as online shopping, forms, and other activities not normally associated with an animation program.

Viewing Flash movies

Generally, Flash movies are played back in one of three ways. The most common implementation is for Flash Movies to be played back within Web browsers — either as part of an HTML page, or as a self-contained 100% Flash Web page. Flash movies can also be played through a separate application called the Flash Player. In addition to the Flash Player, Flash movies can also be created as Standalone Projectors, which facilitate playback without the need for either the player or the browser.

In addition, Flash Movies, or their parts, can be played back or displayed in several other ways. The Publish feature of Flash 4 has provisions for exporting movies, or sections of movies, to either the QuickTime digital video format, the new QuickTime Flash layer vector format, or to the Animated GIF format. Furthermore, parts of movies can be exported as a series of individual bitmaps, or vector files. Single frames can also be exported to these formats.

What Can a Flash Movie Be?

A Flash movie can be many things, depending on the function and design of a project. Because Flash is only approaching its adolescence, things are starting to get a bit rowdy. If you were to compare the functionality of a Flash 2 movie to that of a Flash 4 movie, you'd agree that FLAs have come a long way in a short time. There's going to be a long trail of Flash movies in the future, the following list below is just the trailhead of possibilities for Flash:

   ✦ A splash page animation for a Web site.

   ✦ Interactive map — just check out Macromedia's main page at `www.macromedia.com`.

   ✦ An interactive form on a Web page — *new* with Flash 4! Learn how to create a form in Chapter 15.

   ✦ An interactive database that sends and retrieves information with CGI scripts — *new* standalone function with Flash 4! No Generator Server required!

   ✦ Standalone Web applications — check out the calculator sample in the Flash samples menu.

   ✦ Entire Web sites, without *any* HTML-based graphics or textual content — which means absolute control over scaling and placement of items, including fonts.

   ✦ Interactive art/Web installation art.

✦ Standalone Presentations or Slide Shows on either CD-ROM or Floppy Disk.

✦ Web cartoons — Check out the *South Park* cartoons at www.shockwave.com.

✦ Broadcast quality cartoons — Learn the basics of cartoon animation with Flash 4 in Chapter 23, "Creating Broadcast Quality Cartoons," which features Bill Turner's *Weber* cartoon, also included on the *Flash 4 Bible* CD-ROM!

✦ Web games.

✦ As a platform for QuickTime enhancements — In Chapter 21, "Working with QuickTime," you'll discover a new world of possibilities in the synergy of QuickTime and Flash 4. (We've developed workflows that even Macromedia said couldn't be done.)

✦ As a portion of a larger Director movie — you'll learn about this in Chapter 24.

As you can see, if you can imagine a use for Flash, it can probably be accomplished. Read the sections that we've mentioned above to get a better idea of what's possible with Flash now.

Components of the Flash Environment

Before you attempt to construct interactive projects in Flash, you should be familiar with the structure of the authoring environment. Flash 4 has added many new features to the interface, some of which you have already seen in Chapters 1 and 2. It's now easier than ever to organize your Timeline separately from the Stage, Library, and Toolbar.

Moreover, you need to proactively plan your interactive projects before you attempt to author them in Flash. An ounce of pre-planning will go a long way during the production process. Don't fool yourself — the better your plan looks on paper, the better it will perform when it comes to the final execution. While it's beyond the scope of this book to teach interactive planning in general, you can teach yourself how to organize interactive elements by creating simple flowcharts, like the one in Figure 3-1 that describes the Flash-authoring environment:

In Figure 3-1, you can see how Flash movies are made up of individual scenes, which, in turn, contain keyframes to describe changes on the Stage. What you can't see in the table is the efficiency created (or time saved) by being able to share Flash Libraries between Flash projects (.FLA files) and by linking other Flash movies to a parent Flash movie using the Load Movie action, which is discussed at length in Chapter 14. Before you start to try doing that level of interactivity, though, you need to know the difference between Flash movies and SWF movies.

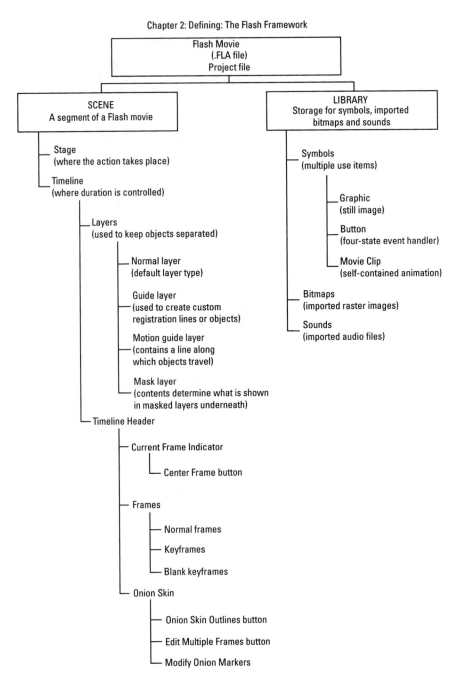

Figure 3-1: Elements of the Flash environment

Contrast: Flash Movie File versus a Shockwave File

As you've already learned, Flash movie (.FLA) files are geared to work in an efficient authoring environment. Within this environment, content can be organized into scenes, and the ordering of scenes can be rearranged throughout the production cycle. Layers provide easy separation of graphics within each scene, and, as guide or mask layers, they can also aid drawing or even provide special effects. The Timeline shows keyframes, motion and shape tweens, labels, and comments. All imported bitmaps and sounds are stored in the Flash Library (which can be shared with other Flash movie files). The quality of these Library files (or symbols) is identical to that of the originals.

However, when a Flash movie (.FLA) is exported to a Shockwave Flash movie (.SWF), much of this information is discarded in order to create small SWF files (or as small as possible) for network delivery (such as on the Internet or on intranets). In fact, just about everything that's stored in the original FLA file will be transformed in some way. The elements in the Library are loaded and stored on the first frame of their use—while unused Library elements are simply discarded (they are *not* exported to the SWF file). Thus, for maximum efficiency, elements that are reused are saved only once because they are referenced from one location in the SWF file. Layers and scenes are "flattened" in the order that is laid out in the FLA file. Meaning, the SWF file contains all the elements from the original .FLA in one layer, controlled by a single timeline. Oddly enough, Shockwave Flash (.SWF) files are not compressed like ZIP or SIT/HQX files—only the individual bitmaps and sounds are compressed according to the settings specified for each element in the Library and/or during the export process.

Note   Flash movie (.FLA) files are also referred to as *Flash editor documents* by some documentation included with the software. Also, the term *Shockwave Flash* no longer exists in the Macromedia Flash 4 literature—Flash movies for the Web are simply called "SWF files," even though SWF stands for Shockwave Flash. (Because "Shockwave" originally referred to Shockwave Director movies, perhaps Macromedia is trying to avoid confusion between the two Shockwaves?) Still, Flash movies are considered "Shockwave" movies—check out the www.shockwave.com Web site, and you'll see plenty of SWF movies.

See Figure 3-2 for a graphic explanation of the characteristics of the Shockwave Flash Movie (.SWF) Format.

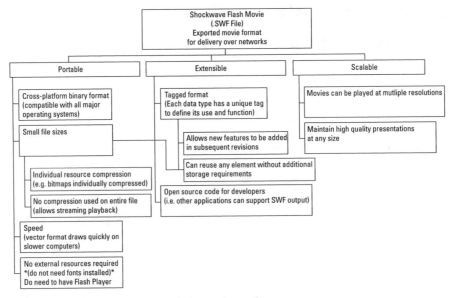

Figure 3-2: How a Shockwave Flash movie works

As you've learned in this chapter, Flash is a hybrid program that has combined many of the most powerful features of various other types of programs, and then mixed them together with some unique capabilities. Consequently, Flash is recognized as one of the most robust and capable programs available for the creation of content for the Web. You've also learned that Flash is not limited to the Web. In fact, Flash is the software of choice in numerous other niches.

Now that we've given you a taste of the capabilities and distinctions of the Flash Authoring environment, and shown you how some of the larger pieces fit together; it's time for you to look at some of the particulars. In Chapter 4, you'll tour the menus, palettes, settings, and preferences — which will prepare you for productive and knowledgeable use of Flash.

✦   ✦   ✦

Menus, Palettes, Settings, and Preferences

In this chapter we tour through all Flash menus and palettes. In some cases, the basic function of a palette or menu item is discussed, while the deeper explanation is deferred to another chapter or area of the book that's dedicated to that particular function or group of functions. In most cases, however, we've tried to deliver a full explanation right here in this chapter. We hope you'll use it as both a learning device and as a reference tool.

Fundamental Flash Palettes

Before discussing all the Flash menu items, dialog boxes, and palettes, we're going to take a look at the default array of palettes and toolbars — the way the program looks when first opened after installation, and the basic possibilities for arranging these and other fundamental palettes and toolbars.

Cross-platform consistency

Unfortunately, although there's much to celebrate in this new version, it is lamentable that Flash 4 didn't attain true cross-platform consistency. Despite vehement protests from many Flash beta users, a number of quirky inconsistencies still linger between the Mac and the PC. (You've already had a glimpse of this with the divergent implementations of the Zoom Control, as discussed in Chapter 1.) For the most part, these are not *really* problematic — unless you use Flash on dual platforms or, worse yet, if you are attempting to either teach the program or write about it. (The big problem is that minute interface differences can make a huge difference if Flash happens to be your first experience with digital art programs.) So, if you find an undocumented platform inconsistency, please let us know. We'll post them in the ERRATA area of our Web site, www.theFlashBible.com.

As shown in Figures 4-1 and 4-2, both the Mac and PC versions of Flash consist of seven major components: menu bar, Controller window, Inspector window, Work Area, Stage, Drawing toolbar, and Timeline. In setting up these figures, an effort was made to minimize the differences between platforms. (In fact, this is pretty much the default look of both the Mac and PC versions, upon installation.) However, the PC version differs in the options for rearranging the interface. Also, note the Zoom Control on the Mac Drawing toolbar.

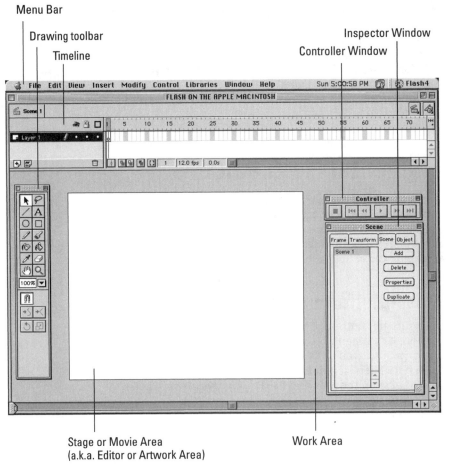

Figure 4-1: Flash on the Mac

Drawing Tool Bar

Timeline

Menu Bar   Application Window Bar (PC only)

Inspector Window

Controller Window

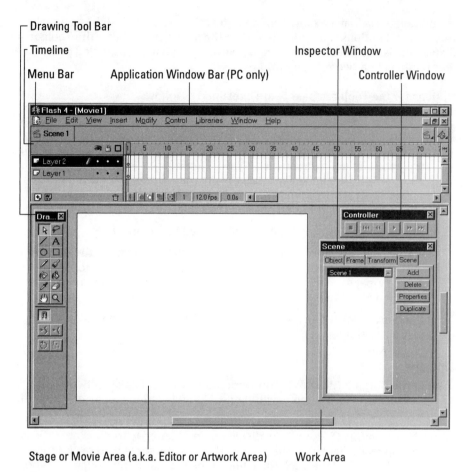

Stage or Movie Area (a.k.a. Editor or Artwork Area)   Work Area

Figure 4-2: Flash on the PC. Note that the controller window and the drawing tool bar are deployed here as floating palettes.

Docking on the PC

The PC version of Flash differs from the Mac version in that the Drawing toolbar and Controller can be docked (or undocked) to the program window. To do this, simply click anywhere on the palette and drag it to the edge of the program window. You can move either the Drawing toolbar or Controller into close proximity of the program window yet prevent docking, by pressing the Ctrl key while dragging.

In addition to the palettes and toolbars, the PC version of Flash has several toolbars and options that aren't found on the Mac. One of these, the Toolbars dialog box, is accessed by choosing Window ➪ Toolbars. This dialog box controls four toolbars and two related options.

Options for the Toolbars palette are explained as follows.

Show

✦ **Standard:** The Standard toolbar is similar to the production toolbars of many programs. It duplicates commonly used tools for easier access, and is generally for those who are unfamiliar with the program. Because it devours precious screen space we urge that it should be disabled. Unfortunately, this is where the Zoom Control is buried on the PC version.

✦ **Drawing:** The Drawing toolbar is discussed in Chapter 1.

✦ **Status:** The Status bar gives text readouts that may explain the use of tools, buttons, and many interface elements. Generally, the text is too limited to be much help. Leave this option disabled; it too devours precious screen space and retards learning.

✦ **Controller:** With buttons similar to a VCR, the Controller is used to test animations.

Options

✦ **Large Buttons (PC only):** This option toggles the display between large and default buttons. It's useful with large, high-resolution monitors and for those with impaired vision.

✦ **Show Tooltips (PC only):** As discussed in Chapter 1, Tooltips are little labels that appear adjacent to the cursor when the cursor is held over a tool, prior to clicking. The labels tell the name of the tools and their related keyboard shortcut. (On the Mac, this option is located in the File ➪ Preferences dialog box.)

Those are the most egregious platform inconsistencies of Flash 4. Although other minor inconsistencies exist, they will be discussed in context with the affected tools and operations as they occur throughout the book.

Contextual menus

Flash contextual menus pop up in response to a right-click (Control+click on the Mac) on a selected item in the Timeline, Library window, or on the Stage. Contextual menus duplicate most functions and commands that are accessible either through the drop-down menus of the menu bar or through the many palettes and dialog boxes that are discussed in this chapter.

The Timeline

On both the Mac and PC, to undock the Timeline and deploy it as a floating palette, click the gray area to the left of the eyeball icon, and then with the mouse button still depressed, drag the palette away from the application window. To prevent the Timeline from docking, press the Control key while dragging. To permanently disable Timeline docking, use File ➪ Preferences and, under Timeline Options, activate the check box for Disable Timeline Docking.

Because animation is the art of making things happen with pictures that change over time, the Timeline might be considered the heart of Flash's animation engine. The Timeline uses Layers and Frames to organize and control a movie's contents over time. Figure 4-3 shows the principal parts of the Timeline.

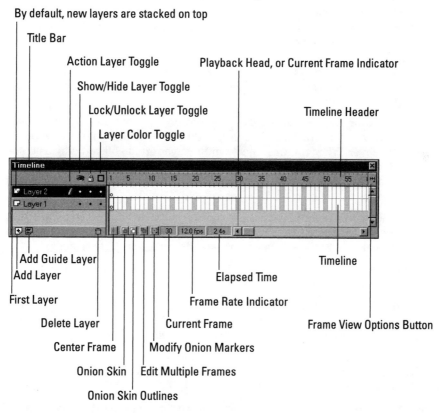

Figure 4-3: New floating Timeline with callouts

As follows, the principal parts of the Timeline are:

✦ **Title Bar:** This does no more than title the palette.

✦ **Active Layer Toggle:** This is more of an icon, really. To make a layer active, either click the layerbar, or select a frame or group of frames. Then the pencil icon appears, indicating that the layer is now active, in addition to the larger clue—the layer bar of the active layer is black, while inactive layer bars are gray. Only one layer can be active at a time.

✦ **Show/Hide Layer Toggle:** Here's a true toggle. Click the dot beneath the eyeball icon to hide the contents of this layer from view on the stage. When the layer is hidden, a red "X" appears over the dot. To return the layer to visibility, click the "X."

Note

Hidden layers will export in the final Flash SWF file and may add considerably to the file size when a Flash movie is published. If you want to prevent a layer from exporting, turn the layer into a guide layer. Of course, you could also delete the layer. Guide layers are discussed in Chapter 8.

✦ **Lock/Unlock Layer Toggle:** This toggle locks or unlocks the layer to either prevent (or enable) further editing. When the layer is locked, a small padlock appears over the dot.

✦ **Layer Color Toggle:** This toggles the colored layer outlines on or off. When on, the dot changes into a small square outline of the same color as the outlines for the layer. When on, the objects in the layer are displayed only as colored outlines, which can be useful for analyzing and finessing animated effects. The Layer Color can be changed with the Outline Color control of the Layer Properties dialog box that is accessed with Modify ➪ Layer.

✦ **Playhead or Current Frame Indicator:** The Playhead indicates the current Frame. Drag it along the Timeline to move from one area of the Timeline to another. Push it beyond the visible area to force-scroll the Timeline.

✦ **Timeline Header:** The Timeline Header is the ruler that measures the time of the timeline: each "tick" is one frame.

✦ **Frame View Options Button:** This button accesses the Frame View Options pop-up menu that affords many options for the manner in which both the Timeline Header and the Frames are displayed.

✦ **Add Layer:** Simply click this button to add a new layer above the currently active layer. By default, layers are given numeric names. Double-click the Layer bar to change the name.

✦ **Add Guide Layer:** Guide layers are used to move elements along a path. This button adds a Motion Guide Layer directly above (and linked to) the currently active layer.

✦ **Delete Layer:** This button deletes the currently active layer, regardless whether it is locked. Of course, the final layer cannot be deleted — there needs to be at least one layer in a Flash movie.

✦ **Center Frame:** Click this button to shift the Timeline so that the current frame is centered in the visible area of the Timeline.

✦ **Onion Skin:** The Onion Skin feature enables you to see several frames of animation simultaneously. (Onion Skinning is further described in the next section of this chapter.)

✦**Onion Skin Outlines:** This enables you to see only the outlines of several frames of animation simultaneously.

✦ **Edit Multiple Frames:** Normally, Onion Skinning only permits you to edit the current frame. Click this button to make each frame between the Onion Skin Markers editable.

✦ **Modify Onion Markers:** Click this button to evoke the Modify Onion Markers pop-up. In addition to manual adjustments, these options are used to control the behavior and range of Onion Skinning.

✦ **Current Frame:** This indicates the number of the current Frame. It's very useful when working with small Frame sizes, which can be specified from the Frame View Options.

✦ **Frame Rate Indicator:** This displays the Frame Rate of the Movie as it plays. It can play no faster than specified in the Movie Properties dialog box, Modify ⇨ Movie. A complex animation may be more than the processor can handle, which will cause playback to drop frames to keep up with the specified frame rate. Note that you should always test your Flash movies as SWF files to accurately see the speed of any playback. Chapter 25 describes how to test Flash movies.

✦ **Elapsed Time:** This indicates the total movie time, measured in seconds, that would elapse from frame 1 to the current frame — provided that the movie is played back at the specified frames per second.

Note By default, new layers are stacked on top of the currently active layer. To rearrange layers, click in the blank area (between the layer name and the layer toggle icons) and drag the layer bar to the desired position in the layer stack.

Tip For enhanced functionality and control, as well as to enable reliable interactivity and ActionScripting, it's a good habit to give your layers meaningful names. Simply double-click the Layer bar and rename.

Onion-skinning

The Onion Skin feature enables you to see several frames of animation simultaneously. When either of the three Onion Skin buttons — Onion Skin, Onion Skin Outlines, or Edit Multiple Frames — is clicked, Onion Skin Markers appear on the timeline, centered on the current frame. These markers indicate the range of frames that will be displayed with Onion Skinning applied. To reposition either of these markers manually, click and drag it to another location on the timeline. As shown in Figure 4-4, in addition to manual adjustments, the Modify Onion Markers pop-up menu offers several other options for managing Onion Markers. For examples of the implementation of the Onion Skinning feature, refer to Chapter 8, the Poser section of Chapter 20, and Chapter 23.

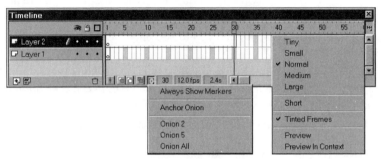

Figure 4-4: Here, the Modify Onion Markers pop-up and Frame View Options pop-up have been combined to show them simultaneously.

Modify Onion Markers

✦ **Always Show Markers:** Check this option to always show the Onion Skin Markers, regardless whether Onion Skinning is on or not.

✦ **Anchor Onion:** Usually, the Onion Skin Markers follow the position of the current frame. Check this option to anchor the Onion Skin Markers at their current position on the Timeline, thus preventing the Onion Skinning effect to move in relation to the position of the current frame pointer.

✦ **Onion 2, 5, All:** These options apply the Onion Skinning effect as follows: (2) to two frames on either side of the current frame, (5) to five frames on either side of the current frame, or (All) to All frames.

Frame View options

✦ **Tiny, Small, Normal, Medium, Large:** These options afford a range of sizes for the width of individual frames. When working on extremely long animations, narrower frames facilitate some operations.

✦ **Short:** This option makes the frames shorter in height, permitting more layer bars to be visible in the same amount of space. When working with many layers, short layers help squelch the tedium of scrolling through layers of layers.

✦ **Tinted Frames:** This option toggles tinted frames on or off. The tints are as follows:

   • **White:** Empty or unused frames (for any layer). This is the default setting and is unaffected whether Tinted Frames is on or off.

- **Gray:** Two kinds of gray frames exist: The "grayed-out" gray frames in the default (empty) timeline are a quick visual reference that indicates every fifth frame. These tinted frames appear regardless of whether Tinted Frames is on or off. The solid "gray" color (which appears when tinted frames is turned "on") indicates that a frame is either filled or otherwise used. Frame usage means that the frame has something in it. That something may be either visible or invisible — as for example, a 0% alpha artwork or hidden symbol.

- **Blue:** Indicates a motion tween sequence.

- **Green:** Indicates a shape tween sequence.

Regardless of whether Tinted Frames is enabled, Flash displays colored tween arrows (and keyframe dots) to indicate the type of tween. A blue arrow indicates motion, while a green arrow indicates shape tweens. (When no other keyframes exist to the right (further along in time), a Motion Tween displays dots while, with a Shape Tween, an arrow still traverses the timeline.)

✦ **Preview:** The preview option displays tiny thumbnails that maximize the element in each frame. Thus, the scale of elements is not consistent from frame to frame. In this animation, a red ball follows an arc through a duration of 15 frames, while a yellow rectangle is moved and scaled about randomly, as its outline disintegrates and disappears.

✦ **Preview in Context:** When previewed in context, the same animation is seen with accurate scale from frame to frame (because elements are not maximized for each frame).

As shown in Figure 4-5, the Timeline offers detailed control of Flash functionality.

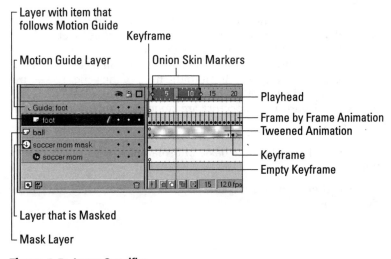

Figure 4-5: Layer Specifics

✦ **Motion Guide Layer:** A Motion Guide Layer is used to guide an animated object along a path, which can be drawn with either the Pencil or the Line Tool.

✦ **Mask Layer:** A Mask Layer is a layer that is used to selectively obscure the layers beneath it.

✦ **Keyframe:** A Keyframe is any Frame where the contents of the Frame differ from the contents of either the previous or subsequent Frames.

✦ **Onion Skin Markers:** As explained in the previous section, Onion Skin Markers define the range of frames that will be affected when Onion Skinning is enabled.

✦ **Playhead:** The Playhead indicates the current frame.

✦ **Frame by Frame Animation:** Frame by Frame Animation is animation composed entirely of Keyframes. In a Frame by Frame Animation, the contents of each individual frame differ from both the previous and subsequent frames. For more information on Frame by Frame Animation, refer to Chapters 8, 20, and 23.

✦ **Tweened Animation:** Tweened Animation is an animation where the movement or change is interpolated, or tweened, over a range of frames that extend between two Keyframes. For more information refer to Chapters 8, 20, and 23.

Scene and Symbol bar

Nested between the menu bar and the top of the Timeline is the Scene and Symbol bar. This bar is shown in context in Figures 4-1 and 4-2. The Scene Name button, at the far left, indicates the name of the current scene. When in Symbol Editing mode, click this button to return to the current scene. To the right is the Edit Scene button, and at the far right is the Edit Symbols button. Click either button to evoke a menu of scenes or symbols that are editable within the current movie.

The Inspectors

Flash has five inspector palettes that consolidate the options and operations specific to particular areas of the application into single, readily accessible palettes. As shown to the left in Figure 4-6, the individual palettes are tabbed and can be ganged together into a gang palette—furthermore, a palette that is not used can be left out of the gang. Click the tab of any inspector to bring it to the front of the gang. The entire gang palette (or each individual palette when deployed separately) can be resized as shown to the right of Figure 4-6. Inspectors are launched from the Window menu, Window ➪ Inspectors.

✦ **Frame:** The Frame Inspector lists basic information about the currently active frame.

✦ **Type:** Tells whether the current frame is a Static, Keyframe, Motion Tween, Shape Tween, and so on.

 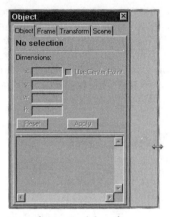

Figure 4-6: Consolidated Inspector palette. Resizing the Consolidated Inspector palette.

✦ **Label:** If the Frame has been labeled, it will appear here.

✦ **Sound:** If this is a sound frame, the file name of the sound appears here.

✦ **Transform:** The Transform Inspector, which is thoroughly discussed in Chapter 6, is used to perform numeric transformations on a selected object.

✦ **Object:** This displays information about the currently selected object. At the top of the Object Inspector, the type of object is displayed. Beneath, X and Y coordinates are displayed for the object's upper-left corner — click "Use Center Point" to display coordinates for the center. W and H are the dimensions of the object. By default, all dimensions are measured in pixels. The unit of measurement can be changed with the Ruler Units Control of the Movie Properties dialog box, at Modify ➪ Movie.

✦ **Scene:** The Scene Inspector lists all scenes in a movie, with the active scene highlighted. To switch scenes, highlight a scene in the list. The Add, Delete, and Duplicate buttons function according to their names. Double-click the scene name or click the Properties button to launch the Scene Properties palette, which is a glorified rename-the-scene control.

✦ **Generator:** The Generator Inspector is not shown here. Generator is a separate but related program, like a database engine that melds to Flash's pictorial and animation engine. Refer to Chapter 16 for an introduction to Generator.

Note

To resize the Inspector on the Mac (pre System 8.5 or if Platinum Appearance is off), grab the palette by the lower-right corner to resize. There's no visual indication that you can do this and the active area is only a 4–8 pixel radius within the double outlines. When using 8.5 or higher there will be the standard corner gripper to drag from.

The individual inspectors can be separated. To separate the inspectors, click the tab for the inspector that you want to remove from the gang, and drag it off the gang palette. To join separate palettes, reverse the process. To organize the tabs of the palettes to suit your work habits, process the order of dragging: Drag the palette that you want on the bottom, with its tab at the far left — the last palette dragged will be on top with its tab at the far right.

From the Menu Bar

Now that we've introduced most of the *major* elements of the Flash interface, we're going to begin at the far left of the menu bar and work through the major points of all the drop-down menus, submenus, and palettes. It's a gruesome, tedious job, but someone has to dive in and make sense of all these interrelated and sometimes seemingly duplicate or parallel operations.

The File menu

The Flash File menu is like the front door of the program. Most of what comes into or out of Flash passes in some fashion through the File menu, as shown in Figure 4-7.

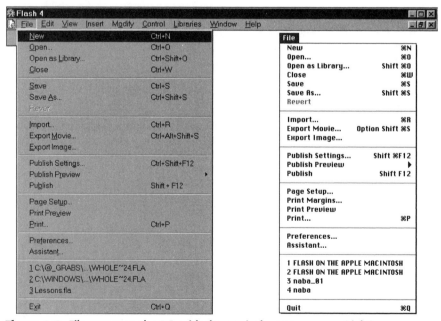

Figure 4-7: File menu on the PC, with the equivalent Mac menu (right)

✦ **New:** By default, Flash opens a new Flash document whenever the program is launched (unless Flash is launched by an extant movie). But once the program is open, File ⇨ New generates all new documents.

✦ **Open:** File ⇨ Open launches the Open dialog box, which is used to browse and locate a Flash compatible file. Compatible formats are:

- Flash Movie — .fla
- FutureSplash Movie — .spa
- Smart Sketch Drawing — .ssk
- Flash Player Movie — .swf

✦ **Open as Library:** Use File ⇨ Open as Library to launch the Open as Library dialog box, and browse for the Flash movie that you want to open as a Library. This makes the components of that movie available for use within another movie. For more about working with the Flash Library, refer to Chapter 9.

✦ **Close:** Close any open movie with File ⇨ Close.

✦ **Save:** Save an open movie with File ⇨ Save.

✦ **Save As:** To save an open movie to another location or with another name, use File ⇨ Save As.

✦ **Revert:** Made a big goof that Edit ⇨ Undo can't undo? Use File ⇨ Revert to revert to the previously saved version of the current movie. Of course, this doesn't spare you much grief unless you *save often*.

✦ **Import:** Many compatible formats can be used directly in Flash. Use File ⇨ Import to launch the Import dialog box for these formats (most, if not all of these formats are discussed later in the book in appropriate sections):

- Enhanced Metafile — .emf
- Windows Metafile — .wmf
- PICT (Mac only) — .pct
- AIFF (Mac only) sounds — .aif
- WAV (PC only) sounds — .wav
- Adobe Illustrator — .eps, .ai
- Flash Player — .swf, .spl
- AutoCAD DXF — .dxf
- Bitmap — .bmp, .dib
- JPEG Image — .jpg
- GIF Image — .gif
- PNG Image — .png

✦ **Export Movie:** Flash can also directly export to a few compatible formats. Use File ➪ Export Movie to write your movie to any of these animation or multimedia formats:

- Flash Player — .swf
- Generator Template — .swt
- FutureSplash Player — .spl
- Windows AVI — .avi
- QuickTime Video (Mac only) — .mov
- QuickTime (supports new Flash media track) — .mov
- Animated GIF — .gif
- WAV Audio — .wav
- EMF Sequence — .emf
- WMF Sequence — .wmf
- EPS 3.0 Sequence — .eps

✦ **Export Image:** Use File ➪ Export Image to output a given Flash frame as a static still image.

- Flash Player — .swf
- Generator Template — .swf
- FutureSplash Player — .spl
- Enhanced Metafile — .emf
- Windows Metafile — .wmf
- EPS 3.0 — .eps
- Adobe Illustrator — .ai
- AutoCAD DXF — .dxf
- Bitmap — .bmp
- JPEG Image — .jpg

Publishing

One of the new features of Flash 4 is the Publish feature, which replaces Aftershock. This powerful, robust aspect of the new Flash 4 is thoroughly covered in Chapter 25. The areas of the File menu which pertain to the Publish feature are:

✦ Publish Settings

✦ Publish Preview

✦ Publish

Printing

Although Flash is considered a Web and animation program, it fully supports printed output. The functionality and specific dialog boxes vary slightly from the Mac to the PC — other variations are subject to which printers and printer drivers are installed on your machine.

The Flash Page Setup dialog box is the most standard aspect of the program and the choices for paper size, margins, center positioning, and orientation are pretty intuitive. However, the Layout area of the PC Page Setup dialog box deserves a little more attention. The options here are:

✦ **Frames:** Use this drop-down menu to choose to print either All Frames of the animation or the ecological default, which is to print the First Frame Only.

✦ **Layout:** There are three options:

- **Actual Size:** This prints the Frame at full size, subject to the Scale setting.

- **Fit on One Page:** This automatically reduces or enlarges the Frame so that it fills the maximum printable area, without distortion.

- **Storyboard:** This option enables you to print several thumbnails per page, in boxes, grid, or blank format. Settings for Frames Across, Frame Margin, and Label Frames make this a great tool for circulating comps and promotional materials. When printing Storyboard Layouts, use File ➪ Print Preview to ensure optimal results.

- **Scale:** At what scale do you want to print your frames? Enter a percentage.

✦ **Print Margins (Mac Only):** Refer to the above discussion of Frames, Layout, and Scale for an explanation of the equivalent options on the Mac. Note, however, the Disable PostScript check box here.

✦ **Print Preview:** Use Print Preview to see an on-screen preview of how the printed output will look, based upon the options you've chosen in the Page Setup and Print Margins (Mac Only) dialog boxes.

✦ **Print:** Just print it!

Note   Problems may occur on PostScript Printers, typically with single large areas of color surrounded by complex borders. If you have such problems, try using the Disable PostScript check box in the Print Margins dialog box (Mac) or in the (PC) Preferences dialog box, which will slow printing. Otherwise, divide the complex area into several simpler areas and also use Modify ➪ Curves ➪ Optimize to reduce the complexity of these areas (which may, however, drastically alter your artwork — so save first!).

Preferences

The Preferences dialog box is one of the main places where you get to tell Flash how you want it to behave. Once you've established your preferences, this is how the program will be configured for every movie that you make. Nearly all options are identical—with the exception of the clipboard settings, which are a reflection of the different way in which the two platforms handle their clipboards.

Bitmaps on Clipboard (PC) Pict Setting for Clipboard (Mac)

✦ **Color Depth (PC):** Choose None if you are only pasting back into Flash. This only copies the Flash vector format, which is faster and conserves system memory. Otherwise, if you want to copy bitmaps to the clipboard (in addition to the default Windows Metafile), choose a bitmap format—which is only useful when pasting into bitmap applications, such as Photoshop.

✦ **Type (Mac):** As with the PC, choose Objects if you are only pasting back into Flash. This only copies the Flash vector format, which is faster and conserves system memory. Otherwise, choose a bitmap format if you want to copy bitmaps (in the PICT format) to the clipboard—which is only useful when pasting into bitmap applications, such as Photoshop.

✦ **Resolution:** Choose the resolution at which you want to capture bitmaps.

✦ **Size Limit (PC):** If your computer has limited memory, choose None. Otherwise, use this entry box to limit the amount of RAM (memory) that will be gobbled up by bitmaps on the clipboard.

✦ **Smooth (PC):** Smooth is antialiasing, which means that the edges of shapes and lines will be dithered to look smooth on screen. Activate smooth to turn antialiasing on.

✦ **Include PostScript (Mac):** Although mostly ignored nowadays the Pict format has the ability to include PostScript objects. This only is available when Objects is chosen. (For a pure bitmap choose Bitmap, 32bit color. Some older Corel clipart collections utilize this format but every piece from these collections has a huge amount of unneeded points. These are straight corner points (no Bézier curves) which means, for example, that a circle in this format is made up of hundreds of points with a straight lines between them—not terribly useful.)

✦ **Gradients on Clipboard (PC):** The Quality drop-down controls the quality of gradient fills that are created when copying to the Windows clipboard. Copying higher quality gradients can be very slow and will also consume system RAM. Choose None if you're only pasting back into Flash, as full gradient quality is preserved regardless.

✦ **Gradients (Mac):** As with the PC, the Quality drop-down controls the quality of gradient fills that are created when copying to the Mac clipboard. Copying higher quality gradients can be very slow and also consumes system RAM. Choose None if you're only pasting back into Flash, as full gradient quality is preserved regardless.

✦ **Undo Levels:** The maximum combined number of undo's and redo's is 200. Undo levels devour system Memory, so work smart and turn your undo's down to 10-25.

✦ **Printing Options (PC):** Disables PostScript output when printing to a PostScript printer. Refer to the previous section on Printing for a full explanation.

✦ **Selection Options:** Shift Select controls how Flash accumulates multiple selections. When Shift Select is ON, Flash behaves normally: Hold down the Shift key to select and acquire additional elements. When OFF, simply click, click, click to continue adding elements to the selection. (Veteran users of Flash will recall that this is how Flash implemented Select when it was Futuresplash and Flash2 as well.)

✦ **Timeline Options (PC):** With Show Tooltips selected, Flash Tooltips — which are identifying text labels — appear when the cursor pauses over tool buttons and other parts of the Flash program interface.

✦ **Timeline Options:** Disable Timeline Docking prevents the Timeline from attaching to the application window once it's been deployed as a floating palette.

The Assistant

The Assistant controls the performance of one of Flash's most celebrated features, the "automated helpers" which aid drawing — these include Line Processing and Shape Recognition. For more about the principles of Line Processing and Shape Recognition, please refer to Chapter 1. In all cases, the Assistant controls the degree of "automatic help" for each of six categories of assistance. For all assistants, the options range from off, to lax, to moderately aggressive, to aggressive as seen in Figure 4-8. Only one assistant has an option that's equivalent to always on. Regardless of the particular assistant here's a universal translation for these somewhat quirky settings:

Off	= OFF
Must be close/Rough/Strict	= Lax
Normal	= Moderately Aggressive
Can be distant/Smooth/Tolerant	= Aggressive
Always snap	= Always ON

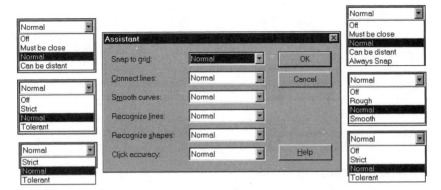

Figure 4-8: Assistant and all drop-down menus

✦ **Snap to grid:** Controls how close an object, symbol, or — while drawing — the end of a line must be to a grid intersection before the object, symbol, or line endpoint snaps to the grid. Snap to grid functions regardless whether the grid has been made visible with View ⇨ Grid — it just snaps to the *invisible* grid.

✦ **Connect lines:** Controls snapping between an extant line and a line that's being drawn. If the line that's being drawn is within the threshold, it will snap to the nearest point of the other line. This setting also controls vertical and horizontal line recognition, which is the aspect of Line Processing that makes nearly vertical or horizontal lines absolutely vertical or horizontal.

✦ **Smooth curves:** When drawing with the Pencil Tool, with the mode set to either Straighten or Smooth, this setting controls how much smoothing will be applied to curved lines.

✦ **Recognize lines:** This setting determines how nearly straight a line segment needs to be in order for Flash to make it perfectly straight.

✦ **Recognize shapes:** In Flash, roughly-drawn circles, ovals, squares, rectangles, and arcs of either 90 or 180 degrees can be recognized as geometric shapes and automatically redrawn with absolute precision. This is called Shape Recognition, and this setting controls the degree of what is "permissible."

✦ **Click accuracy:** This setting controls how close the cursor must be to an item before Flash will recognize the item. A tolerant setting means that you either inadvertently select an item, which is a bother, or that you can be close and easily select an item, which may be cool. We think Normal is the best setting for this.

Finally, at the very bottom of the File menu is the command to close Flash. On the PC, it's File ⇨ Exit, while on the Mac, the equivalent is File ⇨ Quit.

The Edit Menu

The Edit menu (Figure 4-9) is not nearly as complex as the File menu, because it doesn't have a zillion submenus and palettes with infinitesimal options. Still, it's a very important menu because so many of its commands are central to many Flash operations.

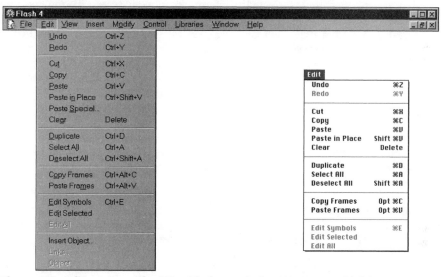

Figure 4-9: Edit menu on the PC, with the equivalent Mac menu (right)

✦ **Undo:** When you make a mistake, before you do anything else — Do the Undo.

✦ **Redo:** The "antiundo," this undoes what you just undid.

✦ **Cut:** This removes any selected item(s) and places it on the clipboard.

✦ **Copy:** This copies any selected item(s) and places it on the clipboard, without removing it.

✦ **Paste:** Disabled if nothing has been copied or cut, this pastes items from the clipboard into the currently active frame on the currently active layer.

✦ **Paste in Place:** This is like Paste, except that it pastes the item precisely in the same place (with regards to X and Y coordinates) from which it was copied.

✦ **Paste Special (PC only):** This is like Paste on steroids, with version control. It pastes or embeds contents from the Clipboard in a specified format; it can also paste and simultaneously generate a link to information in another movie. The Paste Special dialog box has the following fields:

• **Source:** This is readout displays the local path to the source of the item that is on the clipboard.

- **Paste:** This is one of two radio buttons.

- **Paste Link:** This is the other radio button.

- **As:** This field may have several choices, depending both on the nature of the item (including the application that created it) that is on the clipboard, and also on which radio button is activated.

Tip   In the As dialog box, Flash Drawing pastes a portion of a Flash drawing. Object pastes an object together with the information needed to edit it. (You convert the object to an editable Flash element with Modify ➪ Break Apart.) Picture (Metafile) pastes in a form that Flash can edit. Text (ASCII) pastes unformatted text. Text (Native) pastes text with formatting intact.

✦ **Result:** This is another readout. It indicates the result of the selected combination of the Paste/Paste Link and As options.

✦ **Display as Icon:** This check box is enabled when any combination of these options permits the selected item to be pasted as an Icon.

✦ **Change Icon:** This button is evoked when Display as Icon is enabled. Click to open the Change Icon dialog box (complete with browse capability) which facilitates selection of an alternate icon.

Once these settings have been determined, click OK. The enhanced function of this feature almost makes PC's the platform of choice for Flash development. That is, if it weren't for the nagging reality of, "Where *did* you want to go today."

✦ **Clear:** This empties the Clipboard, which is an advisable action after cutting or copying large items, because this will relinquish RAM back to the system.

✦ **Duplicate:** This command duplicates a selected item or items, without burdening the Clipboard. The duplicated item will appear adjacent to the original.

✦ **Select All:** Does what it says.

✦ **Deselect All:** Does what it says.

✦ **Copy Frames:** Copy a selected Frame or Frames with this command.

✦ **Paste Frames:** Pastes the Frame(s).

✦ **Edit Symbols:** Select an instance of a symbol and choose this command to edit in symbol-editing mode.

✦ **Edit Selected:** This is only enabled if a group or symbol is selected on the stage. It will open a group or symbol for editing in a separate "tab" while dimming the rest of the Flash stage—similar to Edit in Place with symbols.

✦ **Edit All:** When editing a group (which is a new feature in Flash 4), Edit All is used to go back to editing the "normal" Flash scene

✦ **Insert Object (PC only):** This and the following commands—Links and Object— are generic Windows options available in most Windows applications. It's part of Microsoft's OLE (Object Linking and Embedding) system, which enables the placement of linked files or content from other applications—when the content is updated in the original application, the placed files are updated. Although this works great in Word and PowerPoint documents, its implementation in Flash is fairly limited. We couldn't get video or sounds to work in a .SWF file when imported with an Insert Object command. Still, creating a WordPad document directly in Flash does work—its text will display in the .SWF file when viewed in the Flash Player.

We recommend that any use of these three commands should be tested thoroughly with the Test Movie/Scene command. Don't simply assume that they will work! Most non-text objects will simply display as red boxes with no interactivity available.

✦ **Links (PC only):** The "Links" command apparently is inoperable; even if a linked file is placed with the Insert Object command (also accessible by right-clicking an empty portion of the Flash stage), this command can not be activated from the Edit menu.

✦ **Object (PC only):** The "Objects" command in the Edit menu can be used whenever a Windows object is selected on the stage—then, chose Edit ⇨ [Document] Object ⇨ Edit, Open, Convert. Note that the text in brackets [...] will vary depending on what type of object is selected.

The View Menu

As shown in Figure 4-10, the View menu is dedicated to controlling how movies— and some tools—are viewed in Flash. A few controls also toggle functionality.

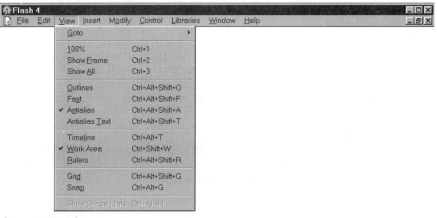

Figure 4-10: View menu

✦ **Goto:** The Goto command leads to a pop-up menu of scenes in the current movie, including four handy shortcuts to the First, Previous, Next, and Last scenes.

✦ **100%:** This is the equivalent of using 100% on the Zoom Control—depending on your monitor and video card, it attempts to show your work at actual size.

✦ **Show Frame:** This command sets the Zoom Level to display the entire frame. It doesn't include objects off stage, regardless whether View ⇨ Work Area is checked. The keyboard shortcut is to double-click the Hand Tool. When in symbol-editing mode (which doesn't display the scene boundaries), this helps to get a sense of scale within the scene frame—though, with the new Edit In Place command, which is the preferred manner for editing symbols, this may be a moot point.

✦ **Show All:** When in View ⇨ Work Area mode, this command sets the Zoom Level to display the entire contents of the current scene—if something is far beyond the scene's boundaries it will include this object in the zoom. When not in View ⇨ Work Area mode, this command zeros in on all active objects—if there's only a tiny object on stage, the viewable area will be filled with that object.

Note

The next four commands: Outlines, Fast, Antialias, and Antialias Text have NO effect on the way in which Flash exports your movie. Quality decisions are made in the Publish Settings, which are covered in Chapter 25. These settings only affect screen quality and screen speed—meaning, "How much longer until this picture appears?"

✦ **Outlines:** Use this command to display all shapes as outlines, and to show all lines as thin lines. This command is useful for reshaping graphic elements, and for getting the general timing and sense of a movie. It also speeds up the display of complex scenes.

✦ **Fast:** This command also speeds up display. It turns off both antialiasing and dithering. Although the default is Off, the recommended setting is On. Unfortunately, this setting is *not* saved as a Preference—it must be set for every movie.

✦ **Antialias:** Not to be confused with the wife of your outlaw cowboy uncle, antialiasing dithers the edges of shapes and lines so that they look smoother on screen. It also slows down the display. It works best with fast, 24-bit video cards. This is really a toggle in opposition with the Fast command: Turn this on and Fast goes off. So, when playback speed is important, turn Antialias off. When image quality is paramount, turn Antialias on.

✦ **Antialias Text:** As with Antialias, this is also a toggle in opposition with the Fast command. It smoothes the edges of text *only* and works best with large font sizes—it can be dreadfully slow when there's a lot of text.

✦ **Timeline:** Use this toggle to show or hide the Timeline.

✦ **Work Area:** This command makes the light-gray area that surrounds the Stage (or Movie Area) visible. This can be useful when your movie has items that are either partially or completely off stage — as, for example, when you have something move into or out of a scene. In order to work with these items (to place or manipulate them) off stage, use View ⇨ Work Area. In order to see the maximum Stage/Work Area, use View ⇨ Work Area, and then View ⇨ Show All.

✦ **Rulers:** This command toggles the Rulers (which display at the top and left edges of the Work Area) on or off — use Modify ⇨ Movie to change units of measurement.

✦ **Grid:** This command toggles the Drawing Grid on or off. To change Grid Spacing use Modify ⇨ Movie and enter a new value in the Grid Spacing Box. Grid spacing also affects Snap sensitivity, because Snap behavior is subject to the Grid.

✦ **Snap:** This command toggles Snap on or off.

✦ **Show Shape Hints:** This toggles Shape Hints to make them visible or invisible. It does not disable shape hinting. Shape Hints are used when tweening shapes.

The Insert Menu

As shown in Figure 4-11, the Insert menu is used to insert Symbols, Layers, Guides, Frames, and Scenes into the current Movie.

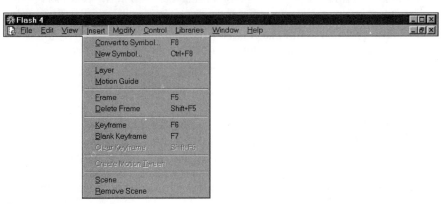

Figure 4-11: Insert menu

✦ **Convert to Symbol:** Use this command to convert a selected item (or items) on stage into a new Symbol and evoke the Symbol Properties dialog box. Refer to Chapter 9 for a full explanation of Symbols.

✦ **New Symbol:** Use this command to create a new symbol and work in Symbol-editing Mode. To use this command, first make sure that nothing is selected by using Edit ⇨ Deselect All.

✦ **Layer:** This command creates a new layer directly above the currently active layer. The new layer becomes the active layer.

✦ **Motion Guide:** Use this command to add a Motion Guide layer (also referred to as a Motion Path). The Motion Guide layer appears above the selected layer.

✦ **Frame:** Use this command to insert a new frame at any selected point on the Timeline. If a frame is selected, then that selected frame (together with all frames to the right on that layer) are shifted to the right to accommodate the new frame — other layers will be left alone. But if no layers (or frames) are selected, then all layers get a new frame at the current frame marker's position and pre-existing frames on all layers shift right.

✦ **Delete Frame:** This command deletes the selected frame.

✦ **Keyframe:** Use this command to convert a selected frame into a Keyframe.

✦ **Blank Keyframe:** This command inserts a new Keyframe at a selected point on the Timeline. If a frame is selected, then that selected frame (together with all frames to the right on that layer) shift to the right to accommodate the new frame — other layers will be left alone. If no layers (or frames) are selected, then all layers get a new frame at the current frame marker's position and pre-existing frames on all layers shift right.

✦ **Clear Keyframe:** This command changes a Keyframe back into a simple Frame, whereupon the contents of the former Keyframe will be replaced with copies of the Keyframe immediately previous in the Timeline.

✦ **Create Motion Tween:** This command is one step in the process of creating a tweened animation.

✦ **Scene:** This command inserts a new, empty Scene immediately following the currently active Scene. By default, new Scenes are numbered — use the Scene Inspector to rename and also to organize Scenes.

✦ **Remove Scene:** This command deletes the currently active Scene.

The Modify Menu

The Modify menu, seen in Figure 4-12, is thick with pop-ups and submenus. Not shown are the pop-ups for the first five items on the menu: Instance, Frame, Layer, Scene, and Movie. The discussion of those items precedes discussion of the menu itself.

✦ **Instance:** The Modify ➪ Instance command evokes the Instance Properties dialog box, which is used to control independent behaviors of Symbol Instances. It has tabs for both Instance Definition and Color Effects.

✦ **Frame:** The Modify ➪ Frame command opens the Frame Properties dialog box. Use the Label Tab of this dialog box to label a frame. Use the Sound, Actions, and Tweening tabs to control those Frame properties. The Frame Properties dialog box is used throughout Flash as an integral part of many operations.

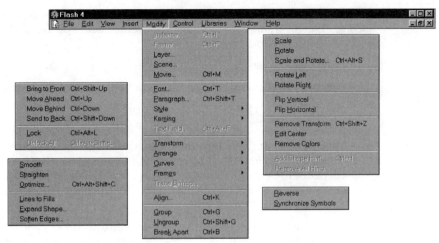

Figure 4-12: Modify menu

✦ **Layer:** The Modify ➪ Layer command leads to the Layer Properties dialog box, which is used to control and edit the properties of the active layer. The Layer Properties dialog box is used routinely in Flash to facilitate Layer operations.

- **Name**—Use this option to change the name of the layer.

- **Show**—With this option checked, the layer is visible. Otherwise, it's hidden.

- **Lock**—This option enables you to lock or unlock the layer.

- **Type**—This option is used to set the type of layer, of which three basic types exist. Normal is the default, used for drawing and animation. Guide layers have two purposes. They can be used either as Motion Guides or as drawing guides. Guide layers aren't exported, so they don't add to the exported file size. Guided layers are linked to a Guide layer. Refer to Chapter 8 for more about Guide Layers. A Mask layer is used in conjunction with a Masked Layer to create special effects. The Masked layer is hidden except beneath filled areas of the Mask it's linked to. For more about Masks, refer to Chapter 8.

- **Outline Color**—Use this to choose the color of the layer's outlines, which will be visible if View layer as outlines is checked. Viewing as outlines speeds the display while editing because all objects are shown as thin outlines.

- **Layer Height**—Use this to increase the height of the layer. This is useful if you use the Preview or Preview in Context timeline settings. It's also useful when viewing the waveforms of sound files.

✦ **Scene:** Modify ➪ Scene opens the Scene Properties dialog box, which has only one function: to rename the current scene.

✦ **Movie:** Modify ➪ Movie leads to the Movie Properties dialog box, which is used to change: Frame Rate, Frame Dimensions, Grid Spacing and Color, Background Color, and also Ruler Units.

- **Frame Rate:** Changes the Frame Rate.

- **Dimensions:** Establishes the Dimensions of the Movie, in pixel units.

- **Match Printer:** This button matches the Movie Dimensions to the currently selected printer's maximum printable dimensions.

- **Match Contents:** This button adjusts the Movie Dimensions to include all active objects, from the upper left-hand corner to the lower right-hand corner of the entire movie (including animation, and the space it may cover during such movements). The expanse includes a narrow zone of white (stage) around it.

- **Grid Spacing/Show Grid:** Use the entry box to set Grid Spacing. The Show Grid Check Box toggles the Drawing Grid on or off. Remember that Grid Spacing affects Snap sensitivity, because Snap behavior is subject to the Grid.

Note

Units: Grid units can be changed by entering the appropriate abbreviation (for example: 25 pt., .5", .5 in, 2 cm, and so on) in the Grid Spacing entry box. Although the specified units will be applied to the grid, they will be translated into the current unit of measurement for the Ruler. Thus, if the Ruler is set to pixels, and the Grid units are changed to 0.5 in, then, upon re-opening the Modify ➪ Movie dialog box, Grid units will be displayed as 36 pix (because pixels are allocated at 72 pix = 1".) Changing Ruler Units also changes Grid Units.

- **Colors:** Click either chip to choose a new Grid or Background Color from the Current Colors pop-up menu.

- **Ruler Units:** Use this drop-down menu to specify Units for the movie. Remember, Ruler Units also changes Grid Units — and impacts Snap behavior.

- **OK:** Applies changes to the current movie only.

- **Save Default:** Much like Preferences, click this button and your settings will become the default for all subsequent movies created with File ➪ New.

✦ **Transform:** Use Modify ➪ Transform to access the Transform pop-up, home to the following commands: Scale, Rotate, Scale and Rotate, Rotate Left, Rotate Right, Flip Vertical, Flip Horizontal, Remove Transform, and Edit Center. These are explained in context in Chapter 6. Of the other commands, Remove Colors is discussed in Chapter 7, while Add Shape Hint and Remove All Hints are explained in Chapter 8.

✦ **Arrange:** Use Modify ➪ Arrange to open the Arrange submenu, which is used to move selected objects, symbols, and groups either forward or backward in the stack of objects that are layered in the currently active Layer. The options — which are pretty intuitive — are as follows:

- **Bring Forward:** This moves the symbol to the absolute front of the stack.

- **Move Ahead:** This moves the symbol one step forward in the stack.

- **Move Behind:** This moves the symbol one step backward in the stack.

- **Send to Back:** This moves the symbol way back to the hinterlands of the stack.

- **Lock:** Use this to lock the symbol in its current position in the stack.

- **Unlock:** Use this to release the symbol from it's locked status in the stack.

✦ **Curves:** The Modify ⇨ Curves pop-up reveals the Curves pop-up menu, home to six commands: Smooth, Straighten, Optimize, Lines to Fills, Expand Shape, and Soften Edges. These commands aren't only for manipulating curves — they're useful for manipulating other things too. See Chapter 6 for detailed explanations in context.

✦ **Frames:** Modify ⇨ Frames yields the Frames pop-up, with two commands:

- **Reverse:** To reverse an animation sequence, first check that there's a keyframe at the beginning and end of the sequence. Next, select the entire sequence — keyframe to keyframe — then, choose Modify ⇨ Frames ⇨ Reverse.

- **Synchronize Symbols:** Sometimes an animation sequence is encapsulated as a symbol and used as a graphic instance in a movie. If the number of frames occupied by this graphic instance doesn't jive with the number of frames in the original sequence, erratic looping occurs. Although this command is supposed to adjust timing to ensure synchronous looping, it rarely works. The optimal solution is to synchronize the animations manually.

✦ **Trace Bitmap:** Use this command to convert an imported bitmap into a vector graphic with editable, discrete areas of color. Please refer to Chapter 7 for a full treatment of the use of various media — including bitmaps — within the Flash vector environment.

✦ **Font, Paragraph, Style, Kerning, and Text Field:** Each of these commands is fully explained in the Text section of Chapter 1, please turn there for more information.

✦ **Align:** The Modify ⇨ Align command elicits the Align dialog box (Figure 4-13), which has intuitive, visual buttons that can be used to align, resize and evenly distribute two or more selected items. These options can be used separately or in combinations. The dialog box has three primary divisions, which function as follows:

- **Vertical:** Vertical Alignment has two option groups, which may be used singly or in any combination. In Align, the options are to align by top edges, centers, or bottom edges. In Space Evenly, the vertical plane items can be evenly distributed according to their adjacent edges, top edges, centers, or bottom edges.

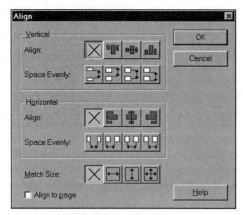

Figure 4-13: Modify ⇨ Align

- **Horizontal:** Horizontal Alignment also has two option groups, which may be used singly or in any combination. In Align, the options are to align by left edges, centers, or right edges. In Space Evenly, the horizontal plane items can be evenly distributed according to their adjacent edges, left edges, centers, or right edges.

- **Match Size:** Items can be resized to match the largest item according to width, height, or both width and height.

✦ **Group:** Use this command to Group two or more selected items. Details and advantages of grouping are discussed in Chapters 6 and 7.

✦ **Ungroup:** This command ungroups items that have been grouped—it's also discussed in Chapters 6 and 7.

✦ **Break Apart:** This command is used to separate groups, blocks of type, instances, bitmaps, and also OLE objects. It can be used to reduce the file size of imported graphics. However, it may not be reversible and also has some unintuitive effects, so refer to the discussion of this command in Chapter 7 before using! Furthermore, because it turns block of type into a graphic, application of this command to type will increase file size—sometimes significantly.

The Control Menu

Despite the alluring title, this is not the menu for Type A personalities. Rather, like the VCR controller, which Type A's always seem to finagle onto their armrest, the Control menu (see Figure 4-14) displays buttons that control the movie playback features within Flash.

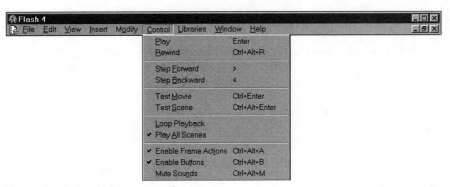

Figure 4-14: Control menu on the PC

✦ **Play:** This command Plays the movie.

✦ **Rewind:** This command returns the movie back to frame one.

✦ **Step Forward:** Use this command to step the movie one frame forward.

✦ **Step Backward:** Use this command to step the movie one frame backwards.

✦ **Test Movie:** Some interactive functions will not work when the movie is played within the Flash-authoring environment. This command utilizes the settings established in the Publish Settings dialog box to export the current movie and instantly play it within a new Flash Player window. The exported movie is *not* a temporary file; it is saved to the same folder as the parent FLA file.

✦ **Test Scene:** This command is similar to the Test Movie command. The only exception is that it tests the current scene only, whereas Test Movie runs the whole shebang.

✦ **Loop Playback:** This command is a toggle that enables looping with all subsequent implementations of the Play, Test Movie, and Test Scene commands.

✦ **Play All Scenes:** The default within the Flash Movie Controller is to play the current scene only. So, like Loop Playback, this is another toggle—it overrides the default single scene playback and enables all scenes to be played with subsequent implementations of the Play, Test Movie, and Test Scene commands.

✦ **Enable Frame Actions:** This is a toggle that controls whether Frame Actions are enabled. Use Enable Frame Actions only during tests and playback within Flash. Otherwise, it may be difficult to edit a movie with Frame Actions enabled.

✦ **Enable Buttons:** Like Enable Frame Actions, this toggle controls whether buttons are enabled. It would be impossible to edit, move, or manipulate buttons if they were continually enabled. So, enable buttons only during tests and playback within Flash.

✦ **Mute Sounds:** This command is a toggle that turns sound on or off.

The Libraries Menu

The Libraries menu is the one menu over which the user has real control. That's because—in addition to the Library items that are placed there in the process of a default installation of Flash—you have the option of placing your own items there too.

The default Libraries menu (see Figure 4-15) contains a selection of buttons and symbols to get you started. These are located in the Libraries folder of the Flash application folder. (And when you're tired of them, you can remove them!) To add your own buttons and symbols, first save them in a Flash file with a descriptive name, and then place that Flash file in the Libraries folder. This is discussed in detail in Chapter 9.

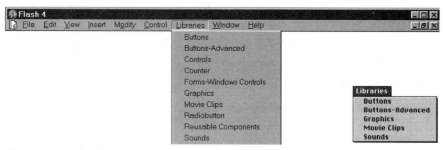

Figure 4-15: Libraries menu on the PC, with the equivalent Mac menu (right)

The Window Menu

The Window menu (see Figure 4-16) is the launch pad for a number of key palettes and windows. It has several commands that are used to control and arrange the display of multiple movies.

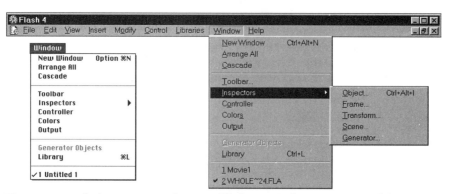

Figure 4-16: Window menu on the PC, with the equivalent Mac menu (left)

✦ **New Window:** This command opens the currently active movie in a new window.

✦ **Arrange All:** This command evenly divides the program window between all open movies and arranges them in horizontal windows from left-to-right.

✦ **Cascade:** This cascades all open windows so that they overlap in a cascade descending from the top left to the bottom right, like fanned out playing cards.

✦ **Toolbar:** This command opens the Toolbars Option palette.

✦ **Inspectors:** This command opens the Inspectors submenu.

✦ **Controller:** This command launches the Controller, which can be used instead of the commands on the Control menu to play a movie within Flash. From right to left, the buttons are: Stop, Rewind, Step Back One Frame, Play, Step Forward One Frame, and Fast Forward.

✦ **Colors:** This evokes the Color window.

✦ **Output:** After export to SWF, this opens the Output window, which shows precise file-size reports on every scene, symbol, text, and so on. It's very helpful for Web work, and is also used for debugging.

✦ **Generator Objects:** This command is disabled, unless you have Generator installed. Generator is a separate program, like database engine that melds to the Flash's pictorial and animation engine.

✦ **Library:** The Library window (left) is not the same as the Libraries menu on the menu bar — yet they are related. Libraries opened from the Libraries menu function like the Library that's accessed with Window ➪ Library. But the Windows ➪ Library is specific to the current movie, while those other Libraries (opened from the Libraries menu) are available whenever Flash is open.

Working with the library

Every Flash movie has its own library, which is used to store and organize symbols, sounds, bitmaps, and other assets such as video files. The Library has many other great features.

If the item is an animation or sound file, the Preview Stop/Play controller pops up to facilitate previewing the item. This is equivalent to the Play option which is found in the Options menu. The Sort Order button toggles the sorting order. For example, A–Z is resorted Z–A. Click the Wide State button to reconfigure the library. The Narrow State button returns the library to a narrow configuration. The New Symbol, New Folder, and Properties buttons are shortcuts for options that also appear in the Options menu, which is displayed to the right of the Library (see Figure 4-17). Both the Properties and New Symbol buttons evoke the Symbol Properties dialog box for the selected item.

The New Folder button simply creates a new folder within the Sort window. Items in the Library can be organized in folders. When a new symbol is created, it is stored at the root of the Library Sort window. To create a new symbol in a folder, select the desired folder first — the new symbol will be placed in the selected folder. Use the Rename option to rename an item. Use the Move to New Folder command to open the New Folder dialog box. Items can be moved between folders by dragging. Click Duplicate to duplicate an item and Delete to delete an item. Click Edit to access the selected symbol in Symbol Editing Mode and you use Select Unused Items to find unused items within the Library. Finally, use the Update option if you've edited items subsequent to importing them into Flash. Items are updated without the bother of re-importing.

Figure 4-17: Library window and Options pop-up menu

Selecting New Symbol, Duplicate, or Properties from the Options menu launches the Symbol Properties dialog box. Use this dialog box to give the symbol a unique name and assign it a behavior. (Note, however, that if the Properties Option is chosen for a sound asset, then the Sound Properties dialog box will appear.

Clicking the Wide State button can also expand the Library. When displayed in this manner, the column headings are all visible in the Sort window. Click any heading to sort the window by Name, Kind, Usage Count, or Date.

The Help Menu

The Flash Help menu directs users to two kinds of help, Offline and Online. Unless you've opted for a custom install or have removed the help files from your Flash installation, the Offline Help resources directly accessible from this menu are: Lessons, Samples, and Flash Help Topics. Online resources, which require an Internet connection, are: Flash Developers Center, and Other Resources. These Flash resources, both Offline and Online are discussed in Chapter 5 — we've also included an extensive list of other resources that you might not otherwise find.

✦   ✦   ✦

Getting Flash Help

Flash ships with Lessons and Samples. If you accepted the default installation, these will be available to you from the Help menu (see Figure 5-1). (Note, however, that you may not have the Lessons or Samples installed if you chose to do a custom install. In this case, you'll probably want to re-install Flash in order to have access to these terrific resources.)

Flash ships with a truly remarkable set of lessons that can be worked through from *within* the program (see Figure 5-2). These are accessed from the menu bar, Menu ➪ Help ➪ Lessons. You'll find over 23 Lessons, and they cover the program thoroughly. They are worthwhile, even for experienced users of Flash. Many lessons are set up so that the information is delivered at the left side of the stage, while the right side is used as a sort of workbook.

Flash also ships with nearly two dozen sample movies that users can deconstruct to get a much deeper understanding of how various effects are accomplished with Flash (see Figure 5-3).

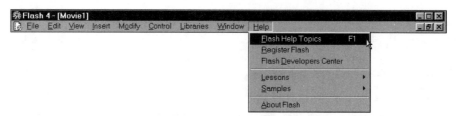

Figure 5-1: The Flash Help menu leads to resources that are both offline and online.

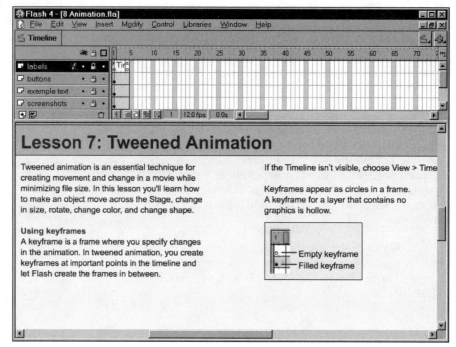

Figure 5-2: The Flash Lessons are among the best tutorials that ship with any program. Here's Lesson 7, the first on Tweened Animation.

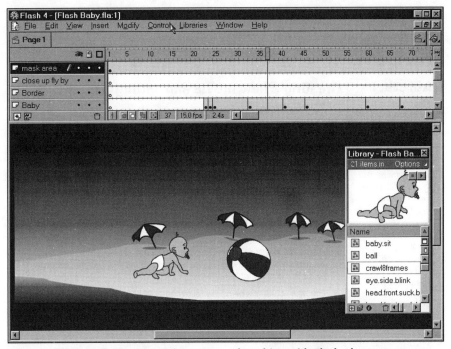

Figure 5-3: Flash Baby, one of the Lessons that ships with Flash, demonstrates a number of mildly complex Flash concepts. Notice the Baby, which appears in both the movie and in the Library. Closer examination of this movie will reveal that the crawling baby is a particular kind of symbol, called a *movie clip*, which is a self-contained movie that is saved in the Library as a *symbol*.

Flash Help Topics

Proceeding from the menu bar, Help ➪ Flash Help Topics will launch your Web browser and open an offline Web page that ships with Flash 4 and is installed as a default with the program. (Note, however, that if you chose to do a custom install, you will not have Flash Help Topics installed. In this case, you'll have to re-install Flash if you want to access this resource.) Flash Help Topics is a thorough series of self-paced tutorials on many aspect of Flash (see Figure 5-4).

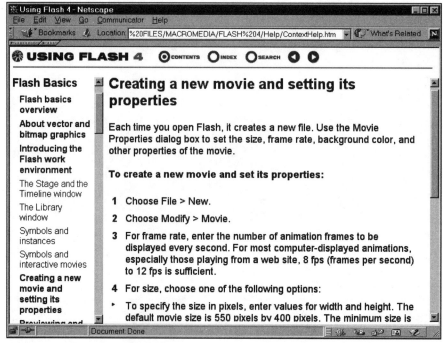

Figure 5-4: The Offline "Help" areas of the Flash Help menu are: *Flash Help Topics, Lessons and Samples.* The Online area is: *Flash Developer's Center.*

Flash Help offers help instruction in the following areas:

✦ Getting Started

✦ Tutorial

✦ Flash Basics

✦ Drawing and Painting

✦ Working with Objects

✦ Using Type

✦ Using Imported Artwork

✦ Using Layers

✦ Using Symbols and Instances

✦ Creating Animation

✦ Creating Interactive Movies

   ✦ Creating Interface Elements

   ✦ Adding Sound

   ✦ Publishing and Exporting

   ✦ Keyboard shortcuts

   ✦ Flash Help

   ✦ Credits

Online

The Flash Help menu also leads to a resource that is viewed through a Web browser and located online called the Flash Developers Center. But many other online resources exist as well, such as FlashPad, FlashLite, or the Quintus Flash Index.

Flash Developers Center

`www.macromedia.com/support/flash/`

This is Macromedia's online resource, the Flash support and developers resource center. It's Macromedia's primary vehicle for the distribution of up-to-date information about Flash and Flash-related topics, so check here regularly for the latest developments. The five main categories have many links and references, as follows:

   ✦ **Learn:** This area is stuffed with information in the following topic categories all of which are subdivided into areas for "Articles," "See Also," and "Technotes."

   • Basics

   • Drawing

   • Animation

   • Symbols

   • Interactivity

   • Sound

   • Final production

   • HTML and scripting

   • Flash Player

   • Top Technotes

✦ **Search:** This area permits a search of the site for specific information.

✦ **Download:** A catalog of trial software, software patches, and technotes. The Flash documentation features downloadable, *printable* manuals of current and prior versions.

✦ **Discuss:** This is the portal to Macromedia's Flash discussion groups. You'll find specific groups to discuss Flash (basic group), Flash Site Design, Open SWF, General Info, and Job Opportunities. You'll also find a button here to submit your feature requests directly to the Flash development team.

✦ **Browse:** As if all that weren't enough, you can find still more resources, tips, lists, and announcements here.

- More resources
- Tip of the day
- Macromedia support programs
- Mailing lists
- Macromedia press
- News and Tips from ZDNet

FlashPad

www.flasher.net/flashpad.html

Recognized as the original Flash developer site (carbon dated at April of 1997), this is our favorite Flash resource site. FlashPad is where we go first when we are researching or have questions to ask. In fact, we hold this site in such high esteem that we asked the site creator, Paul Mendigochea, to be the technical editor for this book. (Paul also helped as a contributor to Part IV of this book — the topic is one in which he is considered one of the leading experts.) FlashPad (see Figure 5-5) is a fast, well-moderated, highly authoritative Flash reference that sports over a dozen separate threaded discussions on the full range of Flash topics, including flasher.newbie, flasher.actionscript, flasher.3d, and flasher.games. If you want to check out the latest in Flash innovation or get your own site debugged, this is the place to start. The interface is built in Flash while the threaded discussions are driven by Flash 4 ActionScript and sophisticated tricks.

Figure 5-5: The FlashPad, at `www.flasher.net`, is the preeminent Flash community Web site featuring related links and information. Shown here is the fs.command forum. Note the menu for other forums, which includes: newbie, design, 3D, sound, sitecheck, coolsites, jobs, swf, and wishlist.

Flash Lite

`www.flashlite.net`

Moderated by Chrissy Rey, this is our favorite site for tutorials. Chrissy contributed several tutorials and loads of enthusiasm for this book. The site is carefully maintained, and newly renovated. In fact, this was the very first site to offer a completely revised library of tutorials to reflect the changes of Flash 4. (That's an impressive indicator of the level of energy that's poured into keeping this site both accurate and up to date!) It's strong on clear, well-developed tutorials for beginners and offers a broad range of Flash-related resources. Highlights are the Newbie Guide and — unique among all the Flash sites — Free Classes. There's also a section with useful tips on distributing Flash content via CD-ROM. Another noteworthy feature of this site is Flashcorps, which is an organization of volunteer Flashers who donate their talents to help fulfill the Web needs of worthwhile charities.

Digging into Other Online Resources

In addition to the lessons and samples available to you from the Help menu of Flash itself, the offline Help Files that can be viewed through your Web browser, and the online Web resources of both Macromedia and FlashPad, many more Web sites are devoted to Flash and Flash developers. These Web sites are not affiliated with Macromedia. They vary widely in design quality and content. Some are apparently motivated by altruism, while others are clearly self-promotional vehicles for the Flash masters who maintain the site. The following is a critical alphabetical listing of such Flash resource sites.

Web sites dedicated to Flash and Flash users

The following Web sites are dedicated to Flash and its users, and should be particularly useful to you in learning more about the product.

Crazy Raven

www.crazyraven.com/

The demonstration movie accessed from this splash page makes a visit to Crazy Raven worthwhile. The preloader alone is fairly amazing! But the tutorials are exceptional, too. Mostly directed at the experienced novice, the topics of these tutorials include pop-up windows, Image maps in Flash, E-mail buttons, and a first-rate button tutorial. Note, however, that high-end Flash is not for the lazy: the preloader tutorial is 44 pages long!

Cruddog

www.cruddog.com/

Cruddog belies its name by sporting a slick, highly kinetic interface with an exemplary dimensional shadow effect. The initial download is a bit long, but it's worth it. There's a link off the home page that leads to a cool 3D demo. Click the front-most yellow bar to find the tutorials, which are both unusual and useful. The basic tutorials are clear and well presented, but our favorite tutorial here is the advanced tip, "Playing the Memory Game" (www.cruddog.com/advtip1/), which shows how to use movie clips for memory storage.

Extreme Flash

www.extremeflash.com/tutorials.htm

Did you ever want to know how to make TV static or how to Blur things with Flash? What about techniques using alpha to make a shadow of text fade or trail away from a word . . . or how to fade text or scale symbols from big to small? The intermediate tutorial sections include all this and more, while advanced tutorials are available on "Tell Target" and preloaders. Although the interface is a bit kludgy, this is a worthwhile site with a broad range of tutorials.

Fay Studio

www.webpagetogo.com/FS/WD/index.html

In addition to a series of six basic tutorials targeted at the beginner, this site has resources on other Web topics as well. You'll find valuable tips on Safe Color in Flash, using bitmaps in Flash, as well as tips on the optimal presentation of your movie.

Flash Academy

www.enetserve.com/tutorials/

This site is closely allied with FlashPad — in fact it reflects the "Etch-A-Sketch" look of FlashPad. But unlike FlashPad, which is *the* authoritative Flash bulletin board, the Flash Academy is a tutorial and general Flash resource site. The tutorials here are mostly for advanced users and vary widely, both in quality and presentation. Still, you can find some flashing gems here.

Flash Central

www.FlashCentral.com/

Second eldest of all the alternative Flash Resource sites, Flash Central features the Flash Tech Resource page, which delivers a staggering list of Flash technical details in outline form. This is also the home of Flash Talk, an online discussion group held each Wednesday night, hosted by John Croteau and Michael Greenberg. (Note, however, that they haven't hosted a chat since Flash2). These guys are highly regarded in the Flash Community for their vast knowledge and technical acumen, not just with Flash but with many other programs as well.

Flash Discussion

www.devdesign.com/flash/

This is a bulletin board, maintained in chronological order, where Flash users can post their work and their questions for feedback, discussion, and answers. As of this writing, the chronology extends just past a year, so this can be a good place to dig around and find . . . well, who knows what you'll find?

Flash FAQ

`sol.inctech.com/flashfaq/`

This site, launched in May of 1999, provides resources to help you resolve problems with Flash. As it matures, it may prove to be a good place to start *before* venturing to the Macromedia Discussion Forum. The FAQ area hosts a question-and-answer-style information resource that is broken into about a dozen categories, ranging from the beginner level to advanced interactivity. Here, you'll find clear, well-presented answers to most of the common questions about Flash. A threaded discussion is also hosted here.

Flash Guide

`www.lunarmedia.com/asmussen/tutorials/index.html`

The Flash Guide covers a gamut of topics that will appeal to both neophytes and experienced users. The beginner tutorials are well presented, and often include the option to access a printable version as well as an example FLA file. The advanced tutorials include Flash Video, Flash 3D, Fullscreen Movies, and Editing Vectors — to mention just a few. Plus, there's an area dedicated to advanced effects, such as creating Filmgrain, Blur, or Drop Shadows. There's also a resource area with links to free fonts, sounds, utilities, and even a freeware video effects program (it's used in the Flash Video tutorial).

Flash Master

`www.flashmaster.nu/`

Here's a sharp, highly designed interface done in what we call the international polychrome mechanoid style — the interface alone is worth investigating. Incidentally, Awall Kejll, the proprietor of FlashMaster, is also the moderator for IDG's Flash Forum in Sweden (`http://eforum.idg.se/`). FlashMaster has too many resources to enumerate them all. The tutorials offer step-by-step instruction for beginners to advanced users. There's also a button dedicated to "Berto's Page." In our opinion, this leads to a better interface and smoother access to the content of BertoFlash (`www.bertoflash.nu`). Berto features great resources on making a Flash clock, integrating Flash with JavaScript, and also use of FS Commands.

Flash Planet

`www.flashplanet.com/`

At the time of this writing, this site was still in early beta, yet it appears to be another promising site. Flash Planet already features tutorials separated into three skill levels that range from "Easy" to "Hard." The site also offers an extensive collection of "Open Source .flas" — Flash files that you can download either to implement in your own site or else (recommended) to study for the development of your own variations. Another interesting feature here is the "question of the week," which is a polling place for Flash related issues.

Flash Resources
www.virtual-fx.net/index.htm

Here's another site with a rather non-descript interface, but loads of useable information. Amanda Farr, an energetic woman in Houston, Texas, moderates the site. The tutorials range from beginner through intermediate to advanced, with an additional area dedicated to effects. Of the effects, we found one most noteworthy. It's a tutorial (www.virtual-fx.net/writeeffect.htm) on the (complex!) technique for creating the illusion of text being handwritten on screen in real time. Another very impressive technique is called the "Dennis Interactive Text Effect." Although both of these techniques were developed for Flash 3, they'll probably be updated to work without a hitch in Flash 4.

Flash Zone
www.flashzone.com

This Flash site, moderated by David J. Emberton , has some authoritative and respected contributors (including moderators from other sites) submitting tutorials and tips. Deep within the archive of downloadable FLA files you'll find a number of Generator examples by Mike Jones — as well as a link to Mike's World, the den of Generator Junkies.

Flasher's Corner
www.insomniac.com/AAL/Flasher.shtml

Although this site is nondescript with humdrum margin-to-margin html text and flat design, it has some good basic tutorials and links to useful resources. Our favorite resource is a link to a Flash ePostCard Machine, which you can purchase for implementation on your own site, using your own Flash animations.

LynxBBS
www.lynxweb.com/bbs/

This threaded bulletin board has considerable turf devoted to Flash. Other threads include many topics that may be relevant to Flash users.

Macromania

www.users.bigpond.com/xtian/

Here's a clean, well-organized interface with well-presented tutorials. This site differs somewhat from the others because, in addition to basic instruction, it offers more advanced tutorials. Advanced topics range from text ("Star Wars" text) and the ever-elusive sketching effects, which is where an image appears to be drawn as the movie progresses.

Mano Artwork

www.manoone.com/

Although this site is done in what we regard as the international polychrome mechanoid style, it is exceptional for the aesthetic sensibility that is evinced within those constraints. The site is designed and maintained by Manuel Clement, a young Frenchman. (He was chosen by the President of France, Jacques Chirac, to serve as one of the judges for the new French Web Site award!) He has a seemingly boundless supply of ideas and tricks for working with Flash and 3D. So, it's not surprising that this site features strong examples and tutorials on topics of 3D and Flash, sound in Flash, and a Magic Button tutorial which explains how to create an animation that only plays on rollover.

Moock Flash

www.moock.org/webdesign/flash/index.html

This is a just a tiny corner of Colin Moock's beautifully designed personal site, featuring excellent tutorials presented with exceptional clarity. The classic design sensibility evinced throughout this site is wondrously refreshing and a lesson on aesthetics as well. Colin has added Flash 4 ActionScript examples and tutorials to his growing resource.

Number A

numbera.cjb.net/

The miscellaneous area of this unique site has a few Flash tutorials and a growing collection of extensions for MM Dreamweaver. "Handtracing," in the 3D section, is probably the most interesting, advanced, and unusual tutorial. We'd like to see more tutorials from this group because of their exemplary design sensibility, as evinced in their capable divergence from the international polychrome mechanoid style.

Open Source

www.fortunecity.com/rivendell/krondor/531/opensource.html

This is a big bulletin board where Flash files are posted both to share and for discussion.

Quintus Flash Index

qfi.flashzone.com

Refreshingly quirky, the whimsical feel and delicate balance of the splash page here feels like a soft collision between Dr. Seuss and the international polychrome mechanoid style (see Figure 5-6). The proclamation of the site mission states, "The Quintus Flash Index makes an attempt to index a huge amount of sites that are created using Macromedia Flash (Shockwave), and preferably in a fresh, nifty, or just plain cool way." In addition, the site hosts threaded discussions on Flash and related topics. The education area is still under development. Future plans include a "cheat-proof" user rating system for the resource links and improved searching. A high five for Quintus!

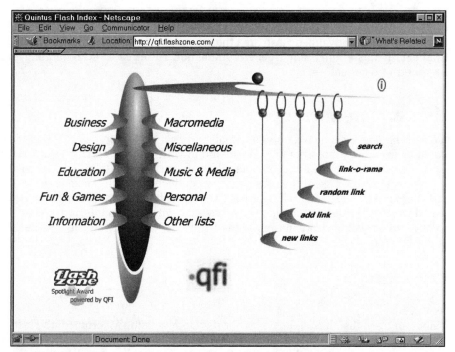

Figure 5-6: QFI, The Quintus Flash Index is refreshingly whimsical, yet hosts and indexes an astounding number of Flash resources.

Stickman Productions

stickman.flashzone.com/tutorials/

These tutorials are highly regarded for their demonstration of a deep knowledge of Flash. It's probably a toss-up as to which of these is the most astounding, but we're pretty sure that if you take a look at "Zoom, Rotate, Pan," you'll understand that some hot licks can be had from this man. We just hope that he'll stick around.

Vectorzone

www.Vectorzone.com/

The Vectorzone is a dazzling, beautiful example of what a Flashed Web site can be. Although it has a tutorial section, it links to tutorials that are sited elsewhere. Thus, its primary value is as an exemplary forum for the delivery of vector-related interviews, news, and notes.

Webmonkey

www.hotwired.com/webmonkey/multimedia/

This area of the Hotwired site is sponsored by Macromedia. Although this is the land of life-saver palettes and over-hyped hype, here you'll find some good introductory Flash tutorials, an advanced Flash area that promises to put you "on the road to Grand Flash Masterdom," and a generic Animation Tutorial for "both budding and seasoned Web animators."

Lists and newsgroups

A *list* or *mailing list* is a collection of e-mail addresses. Members of the list receive postings from other members who correspond with the list. Thus, correspondents converse with the entire list even when they are responding to individual posts. If the mailing list is a digest, then the posts are collected and organized so that list members receive a single mailing, usually once each day. A mailing list can be a useful way for a group of individuals with similar interests to interact and stay up to date with developments in their field of common interest — it can also be an enormous time eater.

Flasher list

www.shocker.com/

This is an open discussion digest list for developers using Macromedia's Flash tools. You simply sign up and the list is e-mailed to you. To sign up, either visit the www.shocker.com site and follow the Flash link. Or, send an e-mail to: list-manager@shocker.com, with "subscribe" in the body of the message.

Much like a list, a *newsgroup* is a group discussion about a subject of common interest, with the primary difference that it is delivered as "News" rather than "E-mail." A newsgroup consists of individual posts submitted to a central Internet site and redistributed through Usenet, which is a worldwide network of news discussion groups. Usenet uses the Network News Transfer Protocol (NNTP), which is usually handled by a Web browser, rather than an e-mail client.

Flash lists

`news://forums.macromedia.com/macromedia.flash`

This is the official Macromedia Flash newsgroup. Enter the address in your browser and a newsgroup window will open up on the latest postings to this resource. Also, check out the following lists:

✦ `news://forums.macromedia.com/macromedia.flash.sitedesign`

✦ `news://forums.macromedia.com/macromedia.open-swf`

✦   ✦   ✦

Creating Flash Graphics

P   A   R   T

◆   ◆   ◆   ◆

Now that you know how to navigate the Flash interface, you're ready to learn how to use Flash tools in combination with each other to quickly create artwork. Chapter 6 will show you how to create shapes and groups, and Chapter 7 will introduce you to the process of importing external media files to your Flash documents. The different types of animation that can be applied to shapes, groups, and images will be discussed in Chapter 8. Finally, you'll learn how to start organizing your Flash movie elements with the Library, using symbols and symbol instances.

Drawing in Flash

Flash has a variety of drawing tools that enable you to create whatever you need for your movies. You should already know how to use these drawing tools from your reading of Chapter 1. This chapter gives you a deeper look at using these tools — and several others — to work with your drawings. We'll manipulate drawings, create special effects, and more.

Simple Shapes and Objects

To learn Flash, it's essential to know how to create simple shapes and objects with the drawing tools, as described in Chapter 1. In fact, drawing simple shapes is quite easy. Individually, these basic drawing tools are quite powerful, but when used in combination with each other they enable you to create an endless array of complex shapes.

Creating shapes

In Flash, it takes little effort to draw most primitive shapes such as circles or rectangles. But what happened to the Triangle tool? And how do you create irregular shapes?

Creating more complex shapes requires adding or removing parts. If you've already been playing around with shapes, one thing that you may have noticed is that, by joining or over-lapping two shapes on the same layer, a brand new shape is created. (If both shapes have the same fill color, you won't be able to pull the pieces apart without using the Undo [Edit ⇨ Undo] command a few times.) This feature is used to create irregular and complex shapes. As shown in Figure 6-1, try adding a circle to a rectangle.

You can also combine shapes of different fill colors for another result. For example, first draw a red circle, and then draw a blue rectangle on top of it. When these shapes are pulled apart, one piece — the blue rectangle — remains intact (the one drawn on last), while the other shape — the red circle — will look like the top shape took a huge bite out of it!

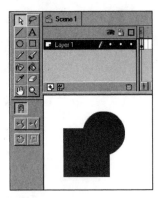

Figure 6-1: Add a circle to a rectangle, and you'll create a brand new shape.

Drawing a triangle

The easiest way to create a triangle is to draw three lines to outline the shape, and then fill it in. But you might be interested in a more precise triangle, as shown in Figure 6-2.

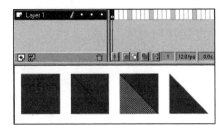

Figure 6-2: This lovely little triangle was created out of a piece of a square.

Here's how to draw a triangle:

1. Select the Rectangle tool. Set your Line Color to transparent, and select a Fill Color. Press the Rounded Rectangle modifier to open the Rectangle Settings dialog box, and make sure that the Corner Radius is set to 0 points.

2. Draw a rectangle that's about twice the size of the triangle that you want to create.

3. Use the Line tool to draw a line from the top-left corner of the rectangle to the bottom-right corner.

4. The line has bisected the rectangle into two triangular filled areas. Use the Arrow tool to select one of the triangular filled areas and drag it away from the rest of the shape. Then select the rest of the shape (the remaining triangle and bisecting line) and delete it. The finished triangle is resting on its side — we discuss how to change that later in this chapter when we move on to "Scale, Rotate, Skew, and Flip."

Drawing a polygon

A polygon is a flat shape with four or more sides. Polygons are more complicated to make than triangles, but they're not difficult. Figure 6-3 shows a five-sided polygon, drawn directly in Flash.

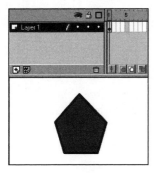

Figure 6-3: This polygon was created with the Line tool, and then filled in with the Paint Bucket.

The simplest way to draw a polygon is to use the Line tool to draw an outline, and then fill it in with the Paint Bucket tool, as shown in Figure 6-3. Another method is to draw several rectangles, rotate and adjust them — using the Scale and Rotate Tools — and then place them on top of each other. Yet another method is to draw a rectangle, and then chop its corners off by drawing intersecting lines, as demonstrated in "Drawing a Triangle." The shape of any polygon can be modified and perfected using the techniques described later in this chapter in "Processing Lines and Shape Recognition."

Creating cutouts

Another effect that you can create by playing around with shapes is a cutout. As shown in Figure 6-4, a circular cutout within a square shape is achieved by drawing the cutout shape on top of the background shape, and then deleting the cutout.

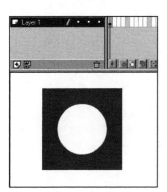

Figure 6-4: This square has a circular cutout.

Here's how to create a cutout:

1. Select the Rectangle tool, choose a fill color, and draw a square.

2. Select the Oval tool, change the fill color, and draw a circle inside the square. If you don't change the fill color for this secondary shape, it will just become part of the square.

3. Use the Arrow tool to select the circle and then delete it. You now have a square with a circular cutout of the center.

You can apply this technique to any number of shapes.

On the CD-ROM

If you'd like to see a SWF example of an advanced implementation of the technique in the following tutorial, open Pill.swf, which is located in the Alien Containment Facility folder located in the ch06 folder of the *Flash 4 Bible* CD-ROM.

Expert Tutorial: Pill Technique
by Larry Larsen

One of the more knowledgeable (and outspoken) participants on the Flash 4 beta team, Larry Larsen is the warden of the Alien Containment Facility (or ACF) that is sited at the fringes of the Flash frontier at www.greenjem.com. *The ACF is a distributor of Flash interfaces, sounds, gradients, tutorials, and tips—which are available online as Flashpacks. In addition to helping us with this tutorial, Larry released a free sample of his aliens for the delectation of the* Flash 4 Bible *readers: Flashpack 1 is on the CD-ROM, in the Alien Containment Facility folder of the ch06 folder.*

Making pill-shaped buttons

Pill-shaped buttons are particularly valuable for text buttons. That's because it can be pretty hard to make circular buttons look good with text on them and because rectangular buttons are just plain boring. It's very easy to create oval buttons in Flash, but Pill-shaped buttons take little bit more work. Thus the procedures used in this tutorial are valuable not only as a solution to the pill problem, but also for their delivery of an advanced way of *thinking* with the Flash drawing tools.

Start by opening a new Flash file with File ➪ New, which should default to a single, active layer. Select the Circle tool, and then click the Fill Color modifier to give it focus. Open the Color window either by clicking the Color Palette button at the top of the Current Fill Colors pop-up, or with Window ➪ Colors. We want to create a gradient fill that can be applied so that the circle will look 3D. To do this, highlight the default black-and-white radial gradient (refer to the following figure), and then click New, as shown.

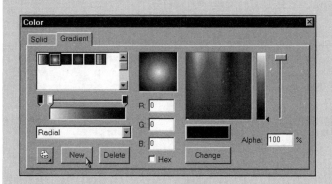

A new black-and-white radial gradient appears in the Current Gradients window. Now, drag two new Color pointers from the "Pointer Well" to about the same positions as shown. (If you have any problems with the color terminology or operations, please refer to Chapter 2, "Flash Color," for a complete explanation before proceeding further.) Next, change the colors of the Color pointers: from left to right, change the first Color pointer to light yellow, the second and fourth to bright orange, and the third to dark red. Finally, click the Change button to apply these pointers and colors to the gradient duplicated from the default black-and-white radial gradient.

Hold down the Shift key a draw a perfect circle, filled with the new gradient color. The circle in the following figure doesn't look very dimensional, does it? The next step will be to reapply the same gradient to this circle in a more convincing way.

Continued

(continued)

Choose the Paint Bucket tool and confirm that the custom gradient is still the Fill Color. (If not, return to the Colors window and select it.) Now, click somewhere in the upper-left corner of the circle. The light yellow highlight of the gradient should appear in the upper left and there should be a dark red shadow in the lower right. Next, use the Arrow tool to select the black outline of the circle and then delete it by pressing the delete key on your keyboard. The resulting orange ball will be used as the basis from which the pill shape is created. Finally, the dimensional orange ball needs to be centered on the Stage. Select the ball with the Arrow tool, and then use File ➪ Cut to cut it. Then, paste the ball back onto the stage using File ➪ Paste. Don't use the Cntrl+Shift+V (Cmnd+Shift+V) keyboard shortcut! This process will center the ball as shown in the following figure.

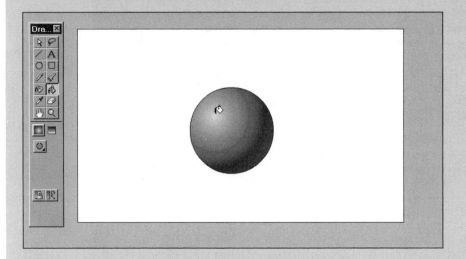

Create a new layer above Layer 1. (When you create this new layer—Layer 2—Flash will make it the current layer, which is what we want.) Then select the orange ball and copy it with Edit ➪ Copy. Next, we need to paste a new copy of the orange ball onto Layer 2, directly over the original. This is easily accomplished with Edit ➪ Paste in Place, which pastes a copy in the same exact position that it was copied from. Now we're going to use a vertical line to bisect the orange ball on Layer 2. To do this, draw a vertical line off to the side of Layer 2 that's taller than the orange ball. Then, select the line with the Arrow Tool and—as with the ball in the previous step—cut it with File ➪ Cut. Paste the line back into Layer 2 using Edit ➪ Paste. This will paste the vertical line in the center of the stage directly over the center of the orange ball, which is also centered on the stage as shown in the following figure.

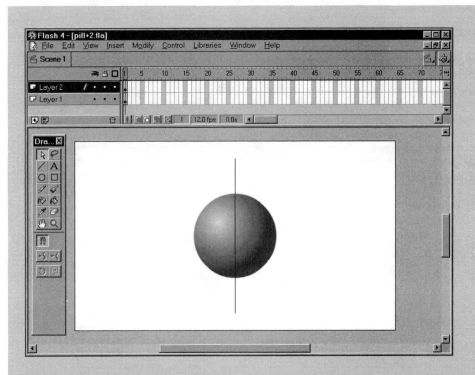

The vertical line that was pasted over the orange ball cut the orange ball in half. Use the Arrow tool to select and delete the line, and then select the right side of the orange ball. (Only the right half of the orange ball should be selected.) Hold down the Shift key (to constrain the movement to the horizontal axis) and move this half over to the right (see the following figure for reference). Repeat this procedure for the left half of the ball.

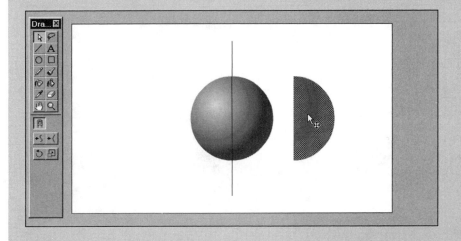

Continued

(continued)

Now, make Layer 1 the current layer. Working off to the side, use the Rectangle tool — with the Fill Color set to "blank swatch" — to draw a very narrow, empty vertical rectangle, taller than the orange ball. Repeat the procedures used with the line to Copy and Paste this rectangle over the center of the orange ball on Layer 1. The lines of the vertical rectangle have cut the orange ball into three pieces as seen in the following figure.

We only need the center piece, so use the Arrow tool to select both the left and right pieces of the orange ball on Layer 1 and delete them, and then delete the rectangle. Select the remaining vertical slice of the orange ball on Layer 1 with the Arrow Tool, and then click the Scale Modifier. Drag the right middle handle out to the right until it snaps to the left edge of the orange ball half on Layer 2 and looks like the following figure.

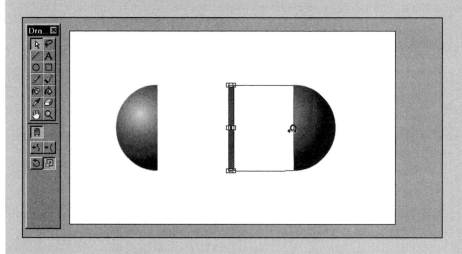

Repeat the procedure on the left side. Drag the left middle handle to the left until it snaps to the left edge of the orange ball half on Layer 2. Finally, Select All, Cut, and then Paste into Layer 1. Then delete Layer 2. This will take all of the pieces and put them on the same layer. Group them together and you have your pill shape, which should look like the following figure. Turn it into a symbol and you won't have to repeat these steps again. (For a discussion of Symbols, refer to Chapter 9.)

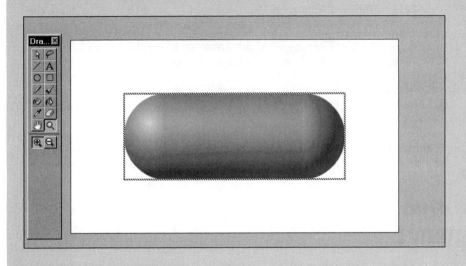

Stacking Order

Flash stacks objects in the order in which they are created, with the most recently created object on top. Thus, in the "Drawing a Triangle" example, when the line was drawn to bisect the rectangle, the line was stacked on top of the rectangle. Similarly, in the "Creating Cutouts" example, the shape that was drawn second (the cutout) was stacked on top of the first shape.

The rules that control the stacking order in Flash are simple: Within a layer, ungrouped, drawn lines and shapes are always at the *bottom* level, with the most recently drawn shape or line at the top of that layer's stack. Groups and symbols stack above lines and shapes in the layer's *overlay* level. To change the stacking order of several drawings, it's often advisable to group them first, as described in "Grouping," later in this chapter. Layers are another factor in the stacking order. No matter how hard you try; you won't be able to stack an object in a lower layer above an object in a higher layer—unless you change the order of the layers.

Changing the stacking order within a layer

Changing the stacking order within a layer is a simple procedure:

1. Select the object that you want to move.

2. Do one of the following:

   • Select Modify ➪ Arrange ➪ Bring to Front or Send to Back to move the object to the top or bottom of the stacking order.

   • Select Modify ➪ Arrange ➪ Move Ahead or Move Behind to move the object ahead or back one position in the stacking order.

Remember the stacking order rules: you won't be able to bring an ungrouped drawing above a group or symbol — if you need that drawing on top, group it then move it.

Tip   To change the stacking order of a layer among several layers, first activate the layer, and then drag the layer bar to the desired position in the Layerstack of the Timeline.

Grouping

Grouping drawings makes them easier to handle. Rather than manipulating a single drawing, group several drawings to work with them as a single object. Grouping also prevents shapes from being altered by other shapes (as discussed earlier in this chapter in "Creating Shapes"). Furthermore, the stacking of groups is more easily controlled than ungrouped drawings, as previously discussed in "Stacking Order."

Creating groups

Here's how to create groups:

1. Select everything that you want to group — any combination of shapes, lines, objects, symbols, and even other groups.

2. Select Modify ➪ Group (Command+G or Ctrl+G).

3. The selected elements are now grouped. To ungroup everything, select the group then use Modify ➪ Ungroup (Command+Shift+G or Ctrl+Shift+G).

Caution   Be careful when ungrouping — your newly ungrouped drawings may alter or eliminate ungrouped drawings below in the same layer (see "Stacking Order").

Editing groups

Editing groups is straightforward:

1. To edit a group, either select the group, and then choose Edit ⇨ Edit Selected, or double-click the group.

2. Everything on stage — except for the parts of the group — will be dimmed, indicating that only the group is editable.

3. To stop editing the group, choose Edit ⇨ Edit All (or double-click an empty part of the stage). Items on stage return to normal color.

Scale, Rotate, Skew, and Flip

Because you've already mastered Chapter 1, you know that the Scale command (or modifier) can be used to resize an object vertically, horizontally, or both. You also know that the Rotate command (or modifier) can be used to rotate an object around its center point. Now you can combine that knowledge with a little Skewing to further manipulate your objects and even develop the effect of perspective.

Refer to Chapter 1 for instructions about using the Scale and Rotate commands in conjunction with the drawing tools.

Flip

The Flip command is used to flip objects on either their vertical or horizontal axis — while leaving the relative position of the object intact. As shown in Figure 6-5, an object is in its original position, and then flipped vertically and then horizontally.

Figure 6-5: The object on the left is the original, while the object in the middle has been flipped vertically, and the object on the right has been flipped horizontally.

Here's what you need to do:

✦ Select the object that you want to flip.

✦ Depending on which axis you want to use to flip the object, choose either Modify ▷ Transform ▷ Flip Vertical or Modify ▷ Transform ▷ Flip Horizontal.

The Inspectors

When drawing in Flash, the Object and Transform Inspectors can be your best friends. Use the Object Inspector to modify the coordinates and dimensions of an object. Or, use the Transform Inspector to scale, rotate, and skew an object.

Cross-Reference Flash has five Inspectors: Object, Frame, Transform, Scene, and Generator. For more information about the first four Inspectors see Chapter 4. The Generator Inspector is introduced in Chapter 16.

The Object Inspector

Use this Inspector to give precise coordinates and dimensions to your objects. Type the numbers in the spaces provided, and your object will be transformed relative to its top-left corner. Or, when working with groups and symbol instances, activate the Use Center Point option to apply changes from the center.

As shown in Figure 6-6, with a shape selected, open the Object Inspector using Window ▷ Inspectors ▷ Object.

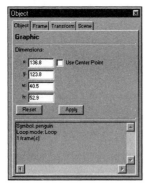

Figure 6-6: The Object Inspector has options to change the location and dimensions of an object.

To use the Object Inspector to change the location of an object, enter new *x* and *y* coordinates, and then press the Apply button. The object moves to the new coordinates, relative to its top-left corner.

Select a shape (or shapes) and group it as previously described in "Grouping." The Use Center Point option on the Object Inspector becomes available. Activate this option, and apply new coordinates to the grouped shape. The shape moves to the new coordinates relative to its center point. Although this option also works on symbol instances, it won't work on ungrouped shapes and lines.

You can also use the Object Inspector to adjust the dimensions of shapes, lines, groups, and symbol instances. The object changes relative to its top-left corner. With groups and symbol instances, the Use Center Point option adjusts the dimensions relative to the center.

The Transform Inspector

This Inspector gives precise control over scaling, rotation, and skewing of an object. Instead of dragging techniques — which are imprecise — numeric values are entered in the appropriate fields and applied directly to the object. When dragging to scale, rotate, or skew an object, the current transformation appears interactively in the Transform Tab — but if the transformations are applied to a shape or line, these numbers disappear when the shape or line is deselected.

Here's the procedure for transformations:

1. With an object selected, open the Transform Inspector with Window ⇨ Inspectors ⇨ Transform, as shown in Figure 6-7.

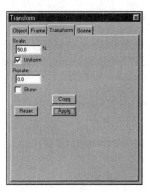

Figure 6-7: Use the Transform Inspector to Scale, Rotate, and Skew objects.

2. Scale the shape — type a new number in the Scale option and press the Apply button. The shape scales to the specified size. To restore the shape to its original shape, press the Reset button. However, once the shape is deselected, it cannot be Reset.

3. Now group the shape and apply new settings. When working with groups and symbol instances, the original settings can be Reset even after the object has been deselected.

4. Apply a rotation to the group by typing a number in the Rotate option, and then click Apply. Objects can be skewed by clicking the Skew option and typing values for the horizontal and vertical angles. Click Apply and the object is skewed to the values entered.

5. Note the Copy button! Press it and Flash makes a copy of the selected object (including shapes and lines), with all Transform settings applied to it. The copy is pasted in the same location as the original.

Stroke and Fill Effects

Flash gives you a number of nifty stroke and fill effects.

Stroke effects

New Feature

Stroke effects—which are controlled by the Line Style modifier of the Line, Oval, Rectangle, and Pencil tools—can be used to give more life to lines. Stroke effects are discussed in detail in "Using the Pencil Tool Line Style Modifier" in Chapter 1.

One really neat way of using this stroke effect is to apply the stroke style (stipple, hatch, and so on) you want to the line, and then turn the line into a fill and apply various effects to the resulting fill. In Flash 3 you couldn't apply gradient or bitmap fills to lines, but now by converting the stroke to fills you *can*, in a roundabout sort of way! Beware that overuse of this technique on complicated styles can significantly increase SWF file size and download time. It may also cause the animation to drag on slower machines.

Cross-Reference

Refer to the section on the Line Style modifier of the Pencil tool in Chapter 1 to learn how to control strokes, and customize their styles.

Gradient fills

Gradient fills are wonderful for giving extra depth and richness to shapes drawn in Flash. These fills are commonly used to give 3D effects to shapes.

Cross-Reference

Colors are discussed in great detail in Chapter 2. Refer to that section to learn more about creating and working with gradient fills.

Spheres

Spheres are very easy to make. To make one, draw a circle on the stage, and then apply a radial gradient fill to it — but don't just stop there! Learn to use the gradient fill to give it some depth by adding highlights and shadows.

Here's how to make a sphere:

1. Select the Oval tool and choose a radial gradient for the fill. (Refer to Chapter 3 for more about working with fills.)

2. Shift-drag across the stage with the Oval tool to make a circle, which should look like the sphere in Figure 6-8.

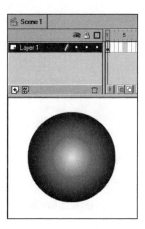

Figure 6-8: A simple sphere

3. To give the sphere a little highlight effect, transform the fill by re-applying it with the bucket tool, so that the lightest part is at the top left of the circle, as shown in Figure 6-9.

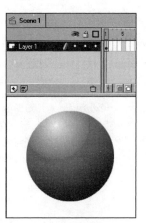

Figure 6-9: Add a highlight effect to the sphere.

4. Now play around with the colors in the fill until you get a nice-looking sphere, as shown in Figure 6-10. Add colors to the radial gradient to tweak the effect of highlight and shadows.

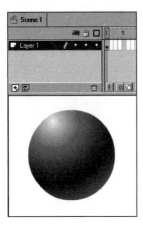

Figure 6-10: Work with the Color dialog box to create a unique radial fill and give highlight and shadow effects to a sphere.

3D-effect fills

The Sphere shown in Figure 6-10, illustrates a very simple 3D effect created with gradient fills. Although it's not really 3D, it does give the illusion of it. Detailed 3D effects can be created using gradient fills.

Refer to Chapter 20 for an in-depth look at creating 3D effects in Flash.

To see the examples for the following tutorial in a real Flash (.FLA) file, open the DNCurves.fla file in the ch06 folder of the *Flash 4 Bible* CD-ROM.

Expert Tutorial: Using Modify ⇨ Curves
by Dorian Nisinson

As the proprietor of Dorian Nisinson Design, Dorian is among the finest Flash Designers. His company Web site, www.bway.net/~dorian/Splash3.htm, *sports a clean, fast splash that really shows what Flash can do. He's one of the major forces behind* www.flashcentral.com *and he was an active, insightful contributor to the Flash 4 beta team. When we asked him to author a tutorial on his favorite facet of the new Flash 4, he chose to focus on some of the permutations of the new Modify ⇨ Curves menu.*

Modify ⇨ Curves ⇨ Lines to Fills

Here are three different situations in which the new Lines to Fills option is indispensable.

Real square corners

How do you get real square corners? First, select the Square tool and draw a square complete with both an outline and a fill. Then, with the Arrow tool, double-click the outline to select all of the line. With only the outline selected, use Modify ⇨ Curves ⇨ Lines to Fills. Now, reselect the converted line with the Arrow tool and click the Straighten modifier. The corners will be nice and sharp, as seen in the following figure.

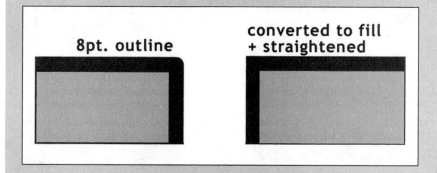

If you create a complex shape and put a line around it, and then use this process, the results will be less predictable. Some corners will gain an extra facet or two.

Real scaleable lines

What about real scaleable lines? In the olden days of Flash 3, an object created with lines would look fine at 100% view, but if an instance was made of that object (which was constructed of lines) and then reduced to 20 %, the thin lines would not scale properly. Instead, they looked huge and ugly. And, because lines (unlike fills) can never be represented by anything smaller than one whole pixel, reducing the line width in the original would not improve the scaled appearance. Now, with the advent of Flash 4, if a symbol will appear at different scales (see the following figure), you can convert those pesky lines into fills — and the fill lines will scale with the artwork!

Continued

(continued)

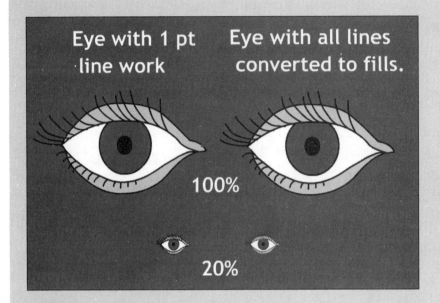

Converting styled lines retains style

That's right, converting a dashed or dotted line maintains line style! For example, select the Pencil tool, choose 8 points for the line width and create a line using the Dotted Line style. This will draw a line with a row of big dots. Now, when you convert those lines to fills, the dots are still there. Yet each dot is a separate item that can be filled and edited much more extensively than lines. So what about lines? As you can see in the example file, now even plain lines can be filled with gradients and even the opacity can be controlled.

Faux 3D with Modify ⇨ Curves ⇨ Soften Edges

Although this new feature of Flash 4 is a natural for dropped shadows or to soften the focus of a shape, here are two Faux 3D uses that may be less obvious.

Making a slightly 3D rectangle

To create the effect shown at the right of the following figure, start with a middle value color for the movie background and draw a rectangle with rounded corners set to 10 and no outline. Fill this rectangle with a linear gradient that goes from blue-green to white and back to blue-green. Now, with the Paint Bucket tool selected, choose the Transform Fills modifier. Click the gradient to select it and then rotate it to approximately 45 degrees. Next, expand or contract the gradient so that the full color ends of the gradient are at opposite corners of the filled shape.

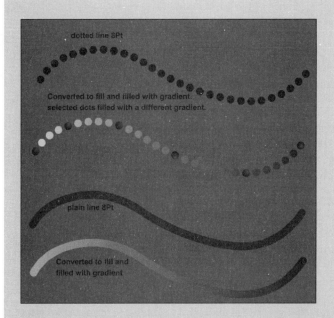

Now, we're ready to make the Faux 3D effect. To do this, select the rectangle with the Arrow tool and use Modify ➪ Curves ➪ Soften Edges with parameters as follows: Distance: 16, Steps: 6 pixels, Expand. Click OK to apply. Then, with the Arrow tool, select the outer ring of this softened shape and copy it. Create a new layer, drag it beneath the first layer and use Edit ➪ Paste in Place to put the outermost ring in the same location as the original rectangle (but on the new layer underneath). Now click the eye icon (in the Layers palette) of the top layer to hide it. With the bottom layer active, fill the center of the pasted shape with a white-to-black opaque gradient. Edit this gradient to a 45-degree angle and squeeze it so that 25% of the filled area is either pure white or pure black. (This can be adjusted later.) When you make the top layer visible again, you'll see the 3D effect.

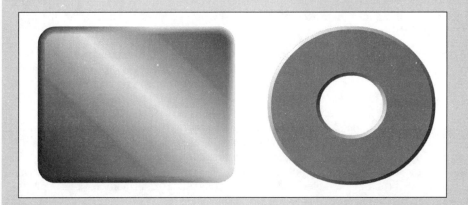

Continued

(continued)

Making a 3D bevel

To create the effect shown at the left of the preceding figure, start with a circle of 150 pixels in diameter filled with an intermediate color. (Remember to hold down the shift key to constrain drawing with the Circle tool to a perfect circle.) Select the circle (with the Arrow tool) and use Modify ➪ Curves ➪ Soften Edges with these parameters: Distance: 140, Steps: 2, Inset. Click OK to apply. Now, select the center of the circle and delete it — a donut shape with a perfectly centered hole remains. Because Soften Edges works by creating a series of rings that is the same color as the original shape, yet of gradually decreasing opacity, it's necessary to fill this donut with a new color that is 100 % opaque. So, select the Paint Bucket tool and fill with a middle value color. Select the donut shape and apply Modify ➪ Curves ➪ Soften Edges with these parameters: Distance: 20, Steps: 2, Expand. Click OK. This results in a donut shape with a ring 10 pixels wide around both the inside and outside edges.

Create a linear gradient that goes from white to a darker shade of the original donut color and fill first the outer and then the inner ring. The rings must be filled individually and with the Lock Fill modifier turned off in order to enable subsequent manipulation of these fills — which completes the 3D effect. Next, with the Paint Bucket tool and Transform Fills modifier, click the outer ring to edit how the gradient is applied. Assuming a light source from the upper left, rotate the gradient approximately 45 degrees until the outer ring is whitest at the upper-left edge and darkest at the lower right. Now, edit the gradient for the inner ring. As a dimensional object, the upper left of the inner ring would be in shadow, while lower right would be illuminated — so, rotate the gradient of the inner ring to the opposite orientation of the outer ring. Now the donut is 3D!

Details about how Soften Edges works

The Options in the Soften Edges palette are:

- ✦ **Distance:** The number of pixels the selected shape will expand or contract.

- ✦ **Number of Steps:** The number of rings around the edges of a shape.

- ✦ **Expand or Inset radio buttons:** Tells Flash 4 whether to enlarge or contract the original shape.

When working with circular shapes, the width of each ring will be equal to the Distance number divided by the Number of Steps. For example, if the Distance is 10 and the Number of Steps is 2, then each ring will be 5 pixels larger or smaller depending on whether Expand or Inset is checked. However, the innermost ring (the ring closest to the original shape) will be the same color as the original shape. This means that that ring will automatically become part of the original shape. Thus, an original circle of 40 pixels in diameter with Expand checked, Distance set to 10 and Number of Steps set to 2 will result in a circle of 45 pixels in diameter with a ring of 5 pixels surrounding it for a total size of 50 pixels in diameter. Using those same original numbers but with Inset rather than Expand, the result will be a circle 35 pixels in diameter and a 5 pixel ring for a total diameter of 40 pixels.

Furthermore, the transparency increases with each successive larger ring. If Distance is 20 and Number of Steps is 6, and then the inner ring will be opaque, while the next smallest ring will have 80 % opacity, the next will have 60 % opacity, the next 40 % opacity. The final, largest ring will have an opacity of 20 %.

Creating Type and Text Effects

Type and text are often necessary to convey information in a Flash movie. You don't have to stick with the standards when adding text, because you have several ways to make text stand out. But remember, don't sacrifice readability for cool effects. The special effects listed in this section are great for text that really needs to stand out, such as headings and button labels. However, the effects aren't advisable for large blocks of text. Although the final decision is up to you, consider the impact that this decision will have on the readability of your movie.

New Feature

Flash 4 now has device font support. The sans serif, serif, and typewriter fonts can be chosen from the Font drop-down. These fonts translate to the default fonts on the end-user's computer. For example, sans serif will usually become Arial, while serif becomes Times, and typewriter becomes Courier. Because these settings utilize the default fonts on the user's machine, these fonts don't need to include their outlines in the SWF—the result is smaller movies that download faster.

Another new feature in Flash 4 is text fields. The content of these text fields can be selected, edited, and changed by the user—depending on how they are set up. Text fields are discussed in detail in Chapter 15.

Cross-Reference

For an overview of the Text tools, refer to Chapter 1. It explains the creation and modification of text in Flash, which is necessary to understand much of this section.

General guidelines to using fonts in Flash

TrueType, Type 1 PostScript, and bitmap fonts can be used in Flash. While Flash exports the system information about the fonts that are used, fonts may still appear incorrectly in the authoring environment if the font is not installed. Such problems can be avoided by using the device fonts available in Flash 4. The device fonts (sans serif, serif, and typewriter) tell the Flash player to use whatever equivalent font is specified on the local computer. Use device fonts for text fields and areas of text that you don't want antialiased. Device fonts also make the final movie size smaller, because Flash doesn't have to export the system information on each font when the movie is exported.

Another way to avoid system conflicts with fonts is by breaking apart all text, which turns it into shapes instead of fonts. Breaking apart text is useful for some of the text effects explained in this section. However, broken-apart text may increase the file size considerably, so use it sparingly. Furthermore, text cannot be edited once it's been broken apart — everything must be written correctly before investing the time required to break the text apart and apply special effects to it.

Note   The font issues just discussed are only pertinent when sharing Flash editor documents (.FLA files) with other people working on the development of a Flash movie. When a Flash movie is exported, any and all font information is embedded within the SWF file — unless it is an editable text field with embedding options turned off. If the font is embedded in the SWF file (which happens by default), the fonts used in the Flash movie will display correctly on any system, regardless of whether the font is actually installed on that system. The primary advantages to using device fonts are that they use very little file space and display consistently across all systems. For more information on optimizing fonts, please read Chapter 25.

Text with drop shadows

Drop shadows are special effects that can be added to text to make it stand out, as shown in Figure 6-11. You have many ways to achieve such effects, and we'll discuss a couple of them here.

Figure 6-11: Drop shadows can really make your text stand out.

Method 1

Here's one way to make a drop shadow:

   1. Type some text then, with it still selected, copy it with Edit ➪ Copy.

2. Paste the copied text onto the stage. Then, select it and change its color to something appropriate for a drop shadow — perhaps dark gray, or something slightly transparent.

3. Now, position the shadow on the stage, and then send it to the back of the stacking order (behind the original text) with Modify ➪ Arrange ➪ Move Behind or Modify ➪ Arrange ➪ Move to Back.

4. Finally, select the original text and position it over the shadow text. Move them around individually until the shadow effect is optimal. To join the shadow and the text, select both and use Modify ➪ Group.

Method 2

Here's another way to make a drop shadow:

1. For a softer shadow, repeat the procedure for Method 1, and then break apart the shadow text using Modify ➪ Break Apart.

2. Soften the shadow's edges by selecting Modify ➪ Curves ➪ Soften Edges. Either leave the settings in the Soften Edges dialog box at their defaults, or play around with them to obtain the ideal, soft shadow.

Tip   Although this soft shadow looks nice, it can add a lot to the file size — particularly if the edges are softened with a lot of steps. This may cause long waits during download and annoyingly slow animations on less capable processors. So use this effect sparingly!

Other text effects

Text effects aren't limited to plain drop shadows. All of the effects and modifications that have been discussed in this chapter can also be applied to text. Skew, rotate, and scale text just like any other object. Use the Soften Edges and Expand Shape commands to create interesting effects. Or, break text apart to apply fills. Finally, to radically reshape text use the methods discussed in "Processing Lines and Shape Recognition."

Glowing text

Give text a glowing look with a method similar to the Drop Shadow effect. First, break apart the "shadow" text. Then apply a light-colored fill to it. Now, soften the edges — just increase the distance in the Soften Edges dialog box — and make sure that the Direction is set to Expand. Then move this modified text squarely behind the original text, as shown in Figure 6-12. Modify this same technique to give an embossed look by simply using a dark fill for the "shadow" text.

Figure 6-12: Give text a glow effect with the Soften Edges command.

Gradient fills in text

Adding gradient fills to text can make it stand out:

1. Select the text — making sure this text is the final copy before you apply this effect to it, because it won't be editable when you're done (if changes need to be made you'll have to redo both the text and the effect).

2. Break apart the text with Modify ➪ Break Apart (Command+B or Ctrl+B). The text appears as selected shapes on the stage. Be careful to keep these shapes selected.

3. Choose the Paint Bucket tool and select a gradient fill from the Current Fill Colors pop-up.

4. Apply the gradient fill to the selected shapes of the broken-apart text. The gradient fills the text as if it were one shape. To add the gradient to each text character individually, deselect the text and apply the fill to each character.

Non-editable text fields

As you'll discover in Chapter 15, most text fields will be editable. However, you may encounter a situation where you need a text field to display information, but you don't want anyone to be able to edit it. For example, you want to display some variable text that users can select, but you don't want them to be able to change the text. The following technique is the solution for just such a situation.

1. Select the Text tool from the Drawing toolbar. Then with the Text Field modifier activated, type your text. If you want the text to be variable, refer to Chapter 15.

2. Once you've finished typing your text, choose the Arrow tool from the Drawing toolbar, and then right-click (or control-click) the text field, and select Properties from the contextual menu.

3. As shown in Figure 6-13, the Text Field Properties dialog box opens. Select the Disable Editing option to prevent editing of this text field. If you also want to disable selection inside the text field, select the Disable Selection option. Press OK to return to the movie.

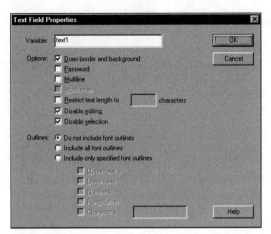

Figure 6-13: The Text Field Properties dialog box has several options available.

4. Test the movie with Control ⇨ Test movie. Try editing the text in this text field.

✦　　✦　　✦

Using Media with Flash Artwork

While you can use the drawing tools in Flash to create a wide variety of graphics, you don't have to limit yourself to just that. Flash has the capability to import artwork from a wide variety of sources. You can import both vector and bitmap graphics, and you can use both types in a variety of ways. In this chapter, we'll discuss the differences between vector and bitmap graphics. We'll also learn how to import external artwork so that it can be used in a Flash movie, and the Flash features used to handle imported bitmap images.

Vector versus Bitmap Images

Flash supports two types of image formats—vector and bitmap. Vector graphics are created with lines and curves and descriptions of their properties. Commands within the vector graphic tell your computer how to display the lines and shapes—what colors to use, how wide to make the lines, and so on. Bitmap (or raster) images are created with pixels. When you create a bitmap image, you are mapping out the place-ment and color of each pixel, and the resulting bitmap is what you see on the screen.

Note   Do not be confused by the name "bitmap." You might already be familiar with the Bitmap format used by Windows. The term "bitmap" can refer to that image for-mat, or it can be applied to raster images in general (GIF, JPEG, PICT, and so on).

The native image type for Flash is vector. Anything that you draw in Flash, using the drawing tools described in Chapter 6, will be vector drawings (with a few notable exceptions, which are discussed in "Using Imported Bitmaps" later in this chapter). Vector graphics have important benefits — they're small in file size and they scale wonderfully. However, they also have drawbacks. Complex vector graphics can have very large file sizes and vectors aren't as useful for continuous tone or photographic quality artwork.

Contrary to popular belief, you can use bitmap images in Flash! Bitmap images are not created natively in Flash — you need to use an external application and then import them into Flash. Unlike vector graphics, bitmap images are not very scalable, as depicted in Figure 7-1. Simple bitmap images are often larger in file size than simple vector graphics, but very complex bitmap images, for example a photograph, are often smaller than comparable vector graphics.

Figure 7-1: Compare the scaled vector graphic on the left to the scaled bitmap image on the right.

Importing External Media

Flash can utilize a wide variety of external media, including vector graphics and bitmap images. You can import this media directly, or you can copy from another application and paste into Flash.

Importing a file into Flash

To import a file into Flash, follow these steps:

1. Make sure that there's a current layer. If no current layer exists, you won't be able to import anything.

2. Select File ➪ Import (Command+R or Ctrl+R).

3. The Import dialog box will open as depicted in Figure 7-2. Browse to the file that you would like to import. Select it and press the Open button. Mac users enjoy greater functionality with this dialog box because the Mac Import dialog box facilitates selection of multiple files from different folders on the hard drive. This is done by selecting and adding the files to the import queue, and then pressing Import.

Figure 7-2: Use the Import dialog box to browse to the file that you would like to import.

Tip

If you attempt to open a file that has a number at the end of its name, and additional files exist with sequential numbers at the ends of their names, Flash prompts you to import the files as a sequence. If that is what you want to do, select Yes when prompted. Otherwise, select No, and only the file that you selected will be opened.

External media recognized by Flash

Flash recognizes a wide variety of file types. Table 7-1 provides an overview of the file types recognized by Flash. You can import media that is not listed in this table, but Flash will attempt to embed it, and it won't actually work in your movie.

Table 7-1				
External Media Recognized by Flash				
File Type	**Extension**	**Description**	**Windows**	**Macintosh**
Adobe Illustrator	.ai, .eps	Adobe Illustrator files are imported into Flash as vector graphics (unless they contain bitmap images). Flash supports import of files saved as Adobe Illustrator 7.0 and earlier.	✓	✓

Continued

Table 7-1 *(continued)*

File Type	Extension	Description	Windows	Macintosh
AIFF Sound	.aiff	Audio Interchange File Format (AIFF) is an audio file format created by Apple Computer. This is the only audio format that can be imported in Mac versions of Flash.		✓
AutoCAD DXF	.dxf	3D DXFs are not recognized by Flash. 2D DXFs don't work so well either. It's advisable to export them from AutoCAD as EPS — that way they'll work just fine.	✓	✓
Bitmap	.bmp, .dib	Bitmap is a Windows format for bitmap images. Don't be confused by the format name — not all bitmap images are Windows Bitmaps.	✓	
Enhanced Metafile	.emf	Enhanced Metafile is a proprietary Windows format that supports vectors and bitmaps internally. This format is generally used to import vector graphics.	✓	
Flash Player	.swf, .spl	Flash Player files are exported Flash movies. The movie is flattened into a single layer and scene, and all animation is converted to frame-by-frame.	✓	✓
GIF Image	.gif	Graphic Interchange Format (GIF) is a bitmap image type that uses "lossless" compression. This type of image is best for images with large areas of solid color.	✓	✓
JPEG Image	.jpg	Joint Photographic Experts Group (JPEG) images are bitmap images that use "lossy" compression. This type of image is excellent for photographic images.	✓	✓

File Type	Extension	Description	Windows	Macintosh
PICT Image	.pct, .pict	A mixed vector and bitmap format. When saved with no compression at 32 bits, it preserves the alpha channel (if any) for compositing.		✓
PNG Image	.png	The Portable Network Graphic format (PNG) is another type of bitmap image. It uses "lossless" compression. This is the best media-type for imported images with alpha settings.	✓	✓
QuickTime Movie	.mov	QuickTime is a multimedia and video format created by Apple Computers. Flash imports it with a link to the original file.	✓	✓
WAV Sound	.wav	WAV is an audio file format created by IBM and Microsoft. This is the only audio format that can be imported in Windows versions of Flash.	✓	
Windows Metafile	.wmf	Windows Metafile is a proprietary Windows format that supports vectors and bitmaps internally. This format is generally used to import vector graphics.	✓	

Using imported vector graphics

Vector graphics from other applications can be easily imported into Flash. These graphics are imported as groups, as illustrated in Figure 7-3, and can be used just like a "normal" group drawn in Flash.

Figure 7-3: Vector graphics are imported as grouped objects.

Refer to Chapter 6 for more information on using grouped objects in Flash.

Using imported bitmaps

Flash is a vector-based application, but that shouldn't stop you from using bitmaps when you *need* to use a bitmap. For example, your movie might require photographic images, which really can't be created as vector drawings. You can import a wide variety of bitmap image types, including JPEG, GIF, BMP, and PICT using the method described previously in "Import a file into Flash." You can also copy a bitmap image from one application and paste it directly into Flash, as illustrated in Figure 7-4.

Figure 7-4: Copy a bitmap from one application (in this case, it's Fireworks) and paste it into Flash.

When you choose to use bitmap images, remember that they won't scale like vector drawings. Furthermore, bitmaps may become distorted when your movie is resized. Compare the two bitmaps in Figure 7-5 — the one on the right depicts a bitmap in an unscaled movie, and the one on the left depicts a bitmap in a scaled movie.

Figure 7-5: Compare these bitmaps — the one on the right is in an unscaled movie with lossless compression, and the one on the left is in a scaled movie with Photo compression. You should notice distortion in the bitmap on the left due to scaling within the movie.

You have a few ways to avoid the kind of image degradation shown in Figure 7-5, or to at least minimize the effects:

✦ Just don't let your movie resize! (See Chapter 25 for setting Scale properties.)

✦ Create your initial bitmap image so that it looks good at the highest screen resolution. Import it at that size and then just scale it down to fit into your movie.

✦ Trace the bitmap to convert it to a vector graphic.

✦ Set the bitmap's compression to Lossless. This setting minimizes but does not eliminate the image degradation upon upscaling.

Importing bitmap images

You have a few ways to bring bitmap images into Flash. You can copy them from an external application, such as Macromedia Fireworks, and paste them directly into Flash. This process is quick and easy, but it doesn't capture any transparency settings, so it may not be the best choice for all of your bitmaps. You can also insert a bitmap as an embedded object if you're a Windows user. The advantage to this method is that you can actually edit the bitmap in a bitmap editor to work with it. Finally, you can import bitmap images, as described in "Importing a File into Flash."

Copy and paste a bitmap image

Follow these steps to copy and paste a bitmap image:

1. Copy the bitmap from the other application.

2. Return to Flash and make sure that you have a current layer in which to paste the bitmap.

3. Paste the bitmap onto the stage by selecting Edit ➪ Paste from the menu (Command+V or Ctrl+V) or pressing the Paste button on the Standard toolbar (PC only). When pasting a selected area from Photoshop, any transparency (alpha channel) is ignored.

Insert a bitmap as an embedded object

Follow these steps to embed a bitmap object:

1. Select Edit ➪ Insert Object. Remember that this only works in Windows!

2. Select the Object Type from the Insert Object dialog box. The available Object Types will depend on the software installed on your computer. Select a familiar Object Type so you know how to work with it.

3. Select Create New if you want to create a new object. You can also Create from File if you have an existing bitmap that you want to use.

4. Click OK and the Flash environment will change somewhat to look like the native environment for the Object Type that you chose.

5. If you chose to create a new object, you can now create your bitmap object in the bounding box provided. When you are done editing, click the stage to return to the "normal" Flash environment.

6. You can Edit, Open, Print, or Convert your object to another type (if possible) by selecting Edit ➪ ObjectType Object from the menu, where ObjectType refers to the original object type.

Tracing bitmaps — converting from bitmap to vector

Tracing bitmaps can be useful when you must convert your bitmap image to a vector graphic.

Trace a bitmap

Here's how to trace a bitmap:

1. Select the bitmap that you want to trace. Note that symbols will not trace. In order for the trace command to become active, the original bitmap must be accessed

2. Use Modify ➪ Trace Bitmap to open the Trace Bitmap dialog box and set the options according to your needs:

   • **Color Threshold** — This option controls the number of colors in your traced bitmap. It limits the number of colors by averaging the colors based on the criteria chosen in Color Threshold and Minimum Area. Color Threshold compares RGB color values of adjacent pixels to the value entered. If the difference is lower than the value entered, then adjacent pixels are considered the same color. By making this computation for each pixel within the bitmap, Flash averages the colors. A lower Color Threshold delivers more colors in the final vector graphic derived from the traced bitmap.

   • **Minimum Area** — This value is the radius, measured in pixels, that Color Threshold uses to describe adjacent pixels when comparing pixels to determine what color to assign to the center pixel.

   • **Curve Fit** — This value determines how smoothly outlines are drawn. Select Very Tight if the curves in the bitmap have many twists and turns. If the curves are smooth, select Very Smooth.

   • **Corner Threshold** — The Corner Threshold is similar to the Curve Fit, but it pertains to the corners in the bitmap image.

Tip If you want your traced bitmap to look more like your original bitmap you should set a low Color Threshold and a low Minimum Area. You should also set the Curve Fit to Pixels and the Corner Threshold to Many Corners. Be aware that using these settings may drastically slow down the tracing process for complex bitmaps, and may result in larger file sizes. When animated, such bitmaps may also retard the frame rate dramatically. Furthermore, if the image is noisy (grainy) it should be smoothed (despeckled) as much as possible prior to tracing to save time and also reduce file size.

3. Click OK. Flash will trace the bitmap. If the bitmap is complex, this may take a while. The traced bitmap will not look exactly like the original bitmap.

Using bitmaps as fills

Working with the Brush and Paint Bucket tools, you can use bitmaps or parts of them, as fills — which is useful for creating patterns. You can also pick solid colors from your bitmap for use as lines or fills.

Turn your bitmap image into the current fill color

You can apply the current fill color to your bitmap image by following these steps:

1. Select the bitmap that you want to use. It has to be either on the stage or in a symbol — you can't just select it in the Library.

2. Select Modify ➪ Break Apart from the menu. The bitmap remains selected, but it's now broken up into separate areas of color. When using a symbol you'll need to select Break Apart twice.

3. Click the bitmap with the Dropper tool — the bitmap will become the current fill and the current tool automatically switches to the Paint Bucket.

4. Switch to the Brush tool to paint your bitmap wherever you need it or just use the Paint Bucket tool to fill shapes with the bitmap pattern. The resulting fill will contain your bitmap.

Setting bitmap properties

Here's how to set a bitmap's properties:

1. Open the movie's library with Window ➪ Library and select the bitmap.

2. Right-click or control-click the bitmap's name and select Properties to open the Bitmap Properties dialog box, which is depicted in Figure 7-6. You can also select Properties from the Library's Options menu or press the Properties button.

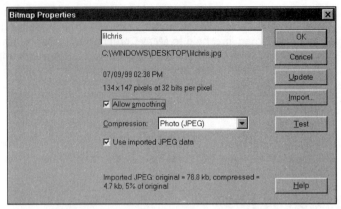

Figure 7-6: The Bitmap Properties dialog box has several
options that can be used to control the look of your bitmaps.

3. Now set the properties of your bitmap as desired:

  • **Preview Window**—This displays the bitmap according to the current
    settings.

  • **Name**—This is the name of the bitmap, as indicated in the Library. To
    rename the bitmap, highlight the name and enter a new one. Beneath the
    name, Flash lists the local path, dimensions, and date information for the
    source of the imported image.

  • **Compression**—The Compression setting enables you to set the
    bitmap's compression to either Photo (JPEG) or Lossless (PNG/GIF).
    Photo is good for very complex bitmap images (photographs for
    example), while Lossless is better for bitmap images with areas of flat
    color. Play around with these settings to see which works best for a
    particular image.

  • **Update**—This feature enables you to re-import a bitmap if it's been
    altered outside of Flash. Flash keeps track of the original location of the
    imported bitmap, and will look for the original file in that location when
    the Update button is pressed.

  • **Import**—This opens the Import Bitmap dialog box. When using this
    button, the new bitmap will replace the current bitmap, while retaining
    the original's name.

  • **Test**—This button updates the file compression information, which
    appears at the bottom of the Bitmap Properties dialog box. Use this
    information to compare the compressed file size to the original file size.

4. Click OK. All copies of this bitmap used in Flash are updated to the new
   settings.

✦   ✦   ✦

Animating with Flash

What's Flash without animation? It's just plain boring!

Animation is the process of creating the effect of movement or change over time. Animation can be the movement of an object from one place to another. It can be a change of color over a period of time. The change can also be a "morph" from one shape to another. Any change of either position or appearance occurring over time is animation.

In Flash, animation is created by changing the contents of successive frames over a period of time. This can include all of the changes just discussed, in any combination. Flash animation can be done frame-by-frame, which is achieved by changing the contents of successive frames. Flash also allows for tweening, which is achieved by defining the contents of the endpoints of an animation, and then enabling Flash to interpolate the contents of the frames in between.

In this chapter, we'll discuss the methods and tools used to create animations in Flash.

Frame-by-Frame Animation

The most basic form of animation is frame-by-frame animation. Because frame-by-frame animation employs unique drawings in each frame it's ideal for complex animations that require subtle changes — for example, facial expression. But frame-by-frame animation has its drawbacks. It can be very tedious and time consuming to draw unique art for each frame of the animation. Plus, all those unique drawings contribute to a larger file size. In Flash, a frame with unique art is called a keyframe. As shown in Figure 8-1, frame-by-frame animation requires a unique drawing in each frame that makes every frame a keyframe.

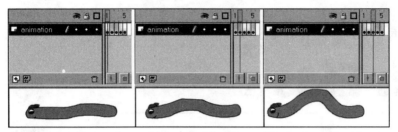

Figure 8-1: This is a frame-by-frame animation with a unique drawing in each frame, which makes every frame a keyframe. Our little inchworm friend takes a few frames to inch his way across the stage.

Adding keyframes

To add a keyframe to the timeline, first, select the frame that you would like to turn into a keyframe. Then do one of the following:

✦ Right-click or control-click the keyframe and select Insert Keyframe.

✦ Select Insert ⇨ Keyframe from the main menu.

✦ Press F6 on the keyboard.

Create a frame-by-frame animation

Here's the process for creating a frame-by-frame animation:

1. Start by selecting the frame where you'd like your frame-by-frame animation to begin.

2. If it's not already a keyframe, make it one by selecting Insert ⇨ Keyframe (F6) from the menu.

3. Either draw or import the first image for your sequence into this keyframe.

4. Then click the next frame and make it another keyframe. Change the contents of this second keyframe.

5. Continue to add keyframes and change the contents of each one until you have a complete animation. Finally, test your animation by returning to the first keyframe and then selecting Control ⇨ Play from the menu.

If you still don't understand the process of creating a frame-by-frame animation, take a look at Frame-by-Frame source file, which is located in the ch08 folder on the CD-ROM.

Tweening

Tweened animation is a huge timesaver because it doesn't require that you draw out your animation frame-by-frame. Instead, you establish endpoints and make drawings for each of those endpoints. Then you let Flash interpolate the changes between them. Tweening is great for a couple of reasons. It minimizes drawing and it also minimizes file size because the contents of every frame in the animation don't have to be saved. In a tween, you only define the contents of the frames at each endpoint, or transition point. This way, Flash only has to save those contents, plus the values for the changes in between. Two kinds of tweens can be created in Flash—Shape and Motion Tweens—each of which has its own unique characteristics.

Shape Tweening

Shape Tweening is useful for "morphing" shapes between your endpoints, as shown in Figure 8-2. Flash can only Shape Tween shapes, so don't even try to Shape Tween a group, symbol, or editable text—it won't work. You can Shape Tween multiple shapes on a layer, but for the sake of organization it usually clearer (and advised!) to put each shape on its own layer. This makes it much easier to return to the animation later and make changes, because it can be nearly impossible to figure out what's going on if a number of tweens share the same layer. Shape Tweening also enables you to Tween colors.

Figure 8-2: Shape Tweening allows for easy morphing of shapes.

Create a Shape Tween

Here are the steps for creating a Shape Tween:

1. Select the frame where you'd like to start the animation. If it's not already a keyframe, make it one.

2. Draw your starting image on the stage. Always remember that Shape Tweening only works with *shapes*—not groups, symbols, or editable text. To Shape Tween such an element, you'll first need to break it apart into shapes (Modify ➪ Break Apart).

3. Add a second keyframe, and draw your ending image on the stage.

4. Open the Frame Properties dialog box by double-clicking on any frame between your two endpoint keyframes. You can also select a frame between the endpoints and select Modify ➪ Frame from the menu (Command+F or Ctrl+F).

5. Select the Tweening tab and choose Shape from the Tweening drop-down menu. You will see several options for modifying the Shape Tween, as shown in Figure 8-3.

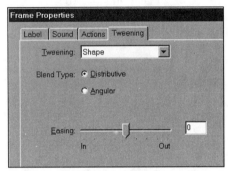

Figure 8-3: The Tweening tab has several options that enable you to modify your Shape Tween.

6. Select a Blend Type. Distributive blending will create smoother interpolated shapes, while Angular blending will create interpolated shapes with corners and straight lines. If your endpoints contain shapes with corners and lines, select Angular blending. Otherwise, select Distributive blending, which is the default.

7. Set the Easing slider if necessary. Easing determines the rate of your animation from start to finish. This is useful if you want to create the effect of acceleration or deceleration. If you want your animation to start out slowly, and then speed up, push the slider toward *In*. For an animation that starts out fast, and then slows down, push the slider toward *Out*. If you want the rate of your animation to stay constant, leave the slider in the middle. You can also type in a number for the Easing value (–100 to 100).

8. Press the OK button once you are satisfied with all of your selections. Test the animation by selecting Control ➪ Play (Enter) from the menu.

On the CD-ROM

Be sure to look at the Shape Tweening source file in the ch07 folder on the CD-ROM.

Shape hints

Shape hints give you more control over complex Shape Tweens. As shown in Figure 8-4, they identify corresponding points on each shape at the endpoints of the Shape Tween. The best way to see why shape hints are so useful is to actually work with them.

Figure 8-4: Shape hints are small, circled letters at the endpoints of a Shape Tween.

Using shape hints in a Shape Tween

You can easily use shape hints in a Shape Tween, as follows:

1. Create your Shape Tween using the method described in "Create a Shape Tween."

2. Select the starting frame of your Motion Tween (you can't add shape hints to the ending frame). Use Modify ➪ Transform ➪ Add Shape Hint, or press Command+H or Ctrl+H to add a shape hint. The shape hint will appear as a red circle with a letter inside of it (the letters start with *a* and go to *z*) as shown previously in Figure 8-4.

3. Move the shape hint to where it's needed — try to visualize points that must correspond from shape to shape over the course of the tween.

4. Now go to the last frame of your tween. You'll see a small green circle with the same letter as your starting shape hint. Place this shape hint at the corresponding point to which the first shape hint will move during the Shape Tween.

5. Play your movie (Control ➪ Play) to see how the shape hint affects the tweening.

6. Continue adding shape hints until you're satisfied with the results. Remember to match shape hints at the start and end frames — *a* goes with *a*, *b* with *b*, and so on.

On the CD-ROM

To get a better idea of just what shape hints do, take a look at the sample for Shape Hints, which is located in the ch08 folder of the *Flash 4 Bible* CD-ROM.

After all that work you might decide that you don't want shape hints in your Shape Tween. To remove all the shape hints use Modify ⇨ Transform ⇨ Remove All Hints. You can also right-click or control-click a single shape hint to open the shape hint pop-up menu. This menu enables you to add a hint (Add Hint), remove a hint (Remove Hint), or Remove All Hints. Using this handy pop-up menu, you can even hide the shape hints by selecting Show Hints (it's a toggle that's on by default). When you want to see the shape hints again, just use this toggle or View ⇨ Show Shape Hints.

Motion tweening

As shown in Figure 8-5, Motion Tweening is useful for animating groups, symbols, and editable text. As the name suggests, Motion Tweening is used to move an element from one place to another, but it can do so much more than that. Motion Tweening enables you to scale, rotate, skew, and move elements. It's also good for changing the color settings and transparency of a symbol over time. Motion Tweening can be applied to only one element on a layer. So, to tween multiple elements, use multiple layers.

Figure 8-5: Motion Tweens are great for showing movement.

It should also be mentioned here that a symbol that's tweened on the layer can be started and stopped as much as you want. Furthermore, the kind of tween can be changed — for example, the symbol can be tweened to rotate in the opposite direction. So, if you use a tween to move a symbol from frame 1 to frame 10 and stop the tween on frame 11; you can have the symbol sit still for 10 frames. Then start a new tween (of same symbol on same layer) on frame 20–30, and so on.

Create a Motion Tween

These are the steps for creating a Motion Tween:

1. Select the frame where you'd like to start your animation. If it's not already a keyframe, make it one by selecting Insert ⇨ Keyframe (F6).

2. Draw or import the image that you would like to tween. You can only Motion Tween groups, symbols, and editable text.

- If you are using an image, group it or turn it into a symbol (see Chapter 9 for more information on creating symbols).

- If you already have the image as a symbol in your movie's library, you can just drag it from the library onto the stage.

- If you are using editable text you don't have to do anything — it's already an object.

3. Select the frame that you would like to end your tween in. Turn this frame into a keyframe by selecting Insert ➪ Keyframe (F6).

4. Position your images in the two endpoints. Remember that you can not only move your tweened elements, but you can also apply other effects such as scaling and rotation. If your endpoint images are symbols, you can also apply color effects to them.

5. Right-click a frame between your two endpoints and select Create Motion Tween. Test out your animation.

6. If you would like to modify the properties of the Motion Tween, double-click any frame between the endpoints to open the Frame Properties dialog box. Select the Tweening tab. You can modify the following properties, as shown in Figure 8-6:

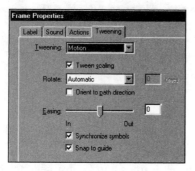

Figure 8-6: The options available for Motion Tweening give you great control over your animations.

- **Tween scaling** — If you are scaling your object (tweening the size) turn this on.

- **Rotate** — You can rotate your objects using this option. Select a rotation type from the drop-down menu and then type the number of rotations in the box. Automatic rotation will rotate your object in the direction that requires the least amount of motion, while Clockwise and Counterclockwise will rotate your object in the indicated direction. In both cases, the rotation will be completed as many times as you specify in the box. If you type 0 in the box, or select None from the drop-down menu, no rotation will occur.

- **Orient to path direction** — When your object follows a path, turning this selection on will force it to orient its center to that path. We will discuss paths in the next section of this chapter.

- **Easing** — Easing determines the rate of your animation from start to finish. This is useful if you want to create the effect of acceleration or deceleration. If you want your animation to start out slowly, and then speed up, push the slider toward In. For an animation that starts out fast, and then slows down, push the slider toward Out. If you want the rate of your animation to stay constant, leave the slider in the middle. You can also type in a number for the Easing value (–100 to 100).

On the CD-ROM

Open the Easing source file on the CD-ROM, which is located in the ch08 folder. Look inside the Frame Properties dialog box, under the Tweening tab. Pay special attention to the Easing option.

- **Synchronize symbols** — This option ensures that your animation loops properly in the main movie. It forces the animation to loop properly even if the sequence is not an even multiple of the number of frames occupied by the symbol in the main movie's timeline. This is only important if your animation is contained within a graphic symbol.

- **Snap to guide** — This option will snap your animated object to a Motion Guide. Motion Guides will be discussed in the next section of this chapter.

New Feature

Flash 4 has a new feature that automatically adds new keyframes between the endpoints of a Motion Tween and can even add new endpoints. This is very useful if you decide to add a third point to your animation (you aren't stuck with only two!). Simply position the current frame marker on the frame where you want the change move the object that it contains to the desired location — your new keyframe appears like magic.

Editing Animation

Once you create your animation, you may find the need to edit it. Flash has features that make such edits quick and easy. You can move frames and keyframes, copy and paste frames and keyframes, insert frames and keyframes, delete frames and keyframes, change the sequence of an animation, and edit the contents of a keyframe. You can also use onion-skinning to view frames at one time, and you can even edit multiple frames at once.

✦ **Moving frames:** Select the frame(s) that need to be moved, and drag them to the new location.

✦ **Copying frames:** Select the frame(s) that you want to copy. Choose Edit ⇨ Copy Frames from the menu.

One of the coolest new features of Flash 4 is the way frames can be copied in the timeline. Now you can select a range of frames that you want to copy and drop them anywhere in the timeline—even if no frames exist in the destination area. Any gaps that might result in the timeline will be automatically filled with static frames. Plus, you can Option (Alt)+drag from one layer to another or even select frames from multiple layers and drag and drop them to multiple layers (provided the destination layers exist prior to the operation).

✦ **Pasting frames:** Select the frame(s) that you want to paste the copied frame(s) into, and select Edit ⇨ Paste Frames from the menu.

✦ **Inserting frames:** Select the point at which you would like to insert a new frame, and select Insert ⇨ Frame (F5) from the menu.

✦ **Inserting keyframes:** Select the point at which you would like to insert a new keyframe, and select Insert ⇨ Keyframe (F6) from the menu.

✦ **Deleting frames:** Select the frame(s) that you want to delete, and select Insert ⇨ Delete Frame (Shift+F5) from the menu. This also works for deleting keyframes, as long as the keyframe isn't part of a tween—to delete that you must first clear the keyframe (shift F6).

✦ **Reversing animation:** Select the animation sequence that you would like to reverse, and select Modify ⇨ Frames ⇨ Reverse from the menu. You must have keyframes at the beginning and end of the selected sequence.

✦ **Editing the contents of a keyframe:** Select the keyframe that you want to edit. Edit the contents of the keyframe.

Onion-skinning

Up to this point, we've worked with only one frame at a time when creating an animation. Flash does have the capability to display more than one frame at a time—it's called onion-skinning. Onion-skinning enables you to view multiple frames at once. The current frame is displayed in full color, while the remaining frames are dimmed out. As shown in Figure 8-7, they appear as if they were each drawn on a sheet of onion skin paper, and then stacked in order. (Note how the frames are dimmed with increasing opacity as they move further from the current time marker. This is an important visual clue that works both in filled and outline modes.) Only the selected frame can be edited, but this feature is useful because it enables you to see how your edits will affect the flow of the entire selected animation. It's also useful for frame-by-frame animation, because you can see each part of the animation without having to switch back and forth.

Figure 8-7: The current frame is shown normally, the surrounding frames are dimmed.

Using onion-skinning

Here's how to skin an onion:

1. Press the Onion Skin button.

2. Move the Start Onion Skin and End Onion Skin markers to contain the frames that you want to view simultaneously.

3. If you'd like to view the Onion Skin as outlines, as shown in Figure 8-8, press the Onion Skin Outlines button.

Figure 8-8: You can view the Onion Skin as outlines, which is useful for complex animations.

4. To edit frames between Onion Skin markers, press the Edit Multiple Frames button.

5. Change the display of the Onion Skin Markers by pressing the Modify Onion Marker button. Choose one of the following from the menu:

   • **Always Show Markers** — This displays the markers whether onion-skinning is on or not.

   • **Anchor Onion Marks** — This option locks the markers at their current positions on the timeline.

   • **Onion 2, Onion 5, and Onion all** — These options display the indicated number (or all) of frames on either side of the current frame.

Guide Layers

Guide layers are useful Flash features that make animation a cinch. Use guide layers to keep the layout of your movie consistent, or to trace images, drawings, or other materials from which you want to develop an object. Guide layers are not exported with the rest of the movie — they're just guides. So use them as you need to.

Using guide layers for layout

Guide layers are great when you need a little help drawing in Flash. You can use them as guides for your layout, aids for drawing a complex graphic, or anything else that you might need. Because they aren't exported with the rest of the movie, you won't see them in the finished product. Guide layers are marked with unique icons next to the layer name.

Adding a guide layer

Add a guide layer as follows:

1. Draw or import your guide art into a layer by itself. This can be anything from a hand-drawn sketch of your layout to a full-blown prototype of your design.

2. Open the Layer Properties dialog box for this layer by double-clicking the icon to the left of the layer's name.

3. Set the Layer Type to Guide (see Figure 8-9), and then click OK.

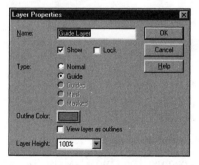

Figure 8-9: Set the Type to Guide in the Layer Properties dialog box.

4. Use Control ⇨ Test Movie to test the movie. Do you see the guide art in the movie? You shouldn't! Remember, because it's a guide layer, it isn't exported with the rest of the movie.

Motion guides

You already know how to move an object from Point A to Point B. What if you don't want to move it in a straight line? This is when tweening along a path comes in handy. Motion Tweening along a path requires a Motion Guide layer that defines the path. This Motion Guide layer is accompanied by one or more guided layers, which follow the path. The guide layer does not export with your movie—it's only visible within the editing environment. Figure 8-10 shows an object and its motion path.

Figure 8-10: Moving objects along a path is simple! Just use a Motion Guide.

Create a Motion Tween along a path

You can create a Motion Tween along a path as follows:

1. Create a Motion Tween as described previously in this chapter.

2. Select the layer containing the tween, and then insert a guide layer by doing one of the following:

   • Click the Add a Guide Layer icon.

   • Right-click or Control-click the layer and select Add a Motion Guide from the pop-up menu.

   • Use Insert ⇨ Motion Guide from the main menu.

3. Draw a path in the guide layer. You can use the Line, Oval, Rectangle, Pencil, or Brush tools to do this.

4. Snap the center of the objects in the endpoint keyframes to the path. If you selected Snap to guide in the Tweening tab of the Frame Properties dialog box, it should snap automatically to the object in the starting keyframe.

5. If you want the object to orient itself to the path it's following, select a frame between your Motion Tween's endpoints, open the Frame Properties dialog box, choose the Tweening tab, and make sure that the Orient to Path Direction option is selected. This will force the object to move so that its center remains parallel to the path. See Figure 8-11 for an example.

Figure 8-11: An example of the Orient to Path Direction option.

Be sure to look at the Motion Guide source file, located in the ch08 folder of the *Flash 4 Bible* CD-ROM. It should help you understand this process a little better.

✦   ✦   ✦

The Flash Library: Symbols and Instances

I n this chapter, you will learn how to create and edit symbols. You'll also learn how to use symbols, both within the movie and within other symbols, and how to modify each instance of a symbol.

Symbol Types

A *symbol* is a reusable element that resides in either the Flash libraries, which are accessed directly from the Libraries menu, or in the current movie's library, which is accessed with Window ⇨ Library. Each time you place a symbol on the stage or inside of another symbol, you're working with an *instance* of that symbol. Unlike using individual graphic elements, you can use many instances of a given symbol, with little or no addition to the file size.

Using symbols helps reduce the file size of your finished movie because Flash only needs to save the symbol once. Each time that symbol is used in the movie, Flash refers to this original profile. Then, to support the variations of an instance, Flash only needs to save information about the differences — such as size, proportions, and color effects. If a separate graphic were used for each change, Flash would have to store a complete profile of all the information about that graphic — not only the size and color, but also what the graphic looks like.

CHAPTER

9

◆　◆　◆　◆

In This Chapter

Symbol types

Graphic symbols

Movie clips

Button symbols

Adding symbols to movies

Editing symbols

Modifying instance properties

◆　◆　◆　◆

Furthermore, symbols can save you a lot of time and trouble, particularly when it comes to editing your movie. That's because changes made to a symbol are reflected in each instance of that symbol throughout the movie. Let's say your logo changes halfway through production. Without symbols, it might take hours to find and change every individual copy of the logo. But if you've used symbol instances, you need only edit the original symbol — the instances will be updated throughout the movie, automatically.

Three types of symbols exist. Each type is unique, and suited for a particular purpose. Figure 9-1 illustrates the icons associated with each type of symbol.

Figure 9-1: Each symbol type has an icon associated with it.

✦ **Graphic symbols** are great for static images and simple animations controlled by the main movie's timeline. However, Flash ignores sounds or actions inside a graphic symbol.

✦ **Movie clips** are actually like movies within a movie. They're good for animations that run independently of the main movie's timeline. They can contain actions, other symbols, and sounds. Movie clips can also be placed inside of other symbols, and are particularly useful for creating animated buttons.

✦ **Button symbols** are useful for creating interactive buttons. Buttons have various states (Up, Over, Down, and Hit), each of which can be defined with graphics, symbols, and sounds. Once you create a button, you can assign actions to its instances within both the main movie and movie clips.

Graphic symbols

Graphic symbols are the simplest kind of Flash symbol. Use them for static images, as well as animations. Note, however, that animations within graphic symbols are tied to the main timeline of the movie — when you stop the movie, the animated graphic symbol stops too. Furthermore, actions and sounds don't work within graphic symbols.

Create a graphic symbol with selected elements

Here's how to create a graphic symbol with selected elements:

1. Select the element or elements that you want to include in the symbol.

2. Use Insert ➪ Convert to Symbol (F8) to access the Symbol Properties dialog box.

3. Type a name and select a Behavior for the symbol, as seen in Figure 9-2. The Behavior setting specifies the default behavior of this symbol as a Graphic, a Button, or a Movie Clip. Note that a different behavior can be applied to each instance of a symbol. For this symbol, set the Behavior to Graphic, and then click OK. You've got a symbol!

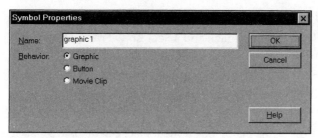

Figure 9-2: Type in a name in the Symbol Properties dialog box, and then select the behavior type.

Create an empty symbol

The following steps demonstrate how to create an empty symbol:

1. Use Insert ➪ New Symbol (Ctrl+F8) to initiate a new, empty symbol. This, too, opens the Symbol Properties dialog box.

2. Enter a name for your symbol and select a Behavior — Graphic, Button, or Movie Clip.

3. Press OK. You'll be taken to the Symbol Editor, where you can create content for your symbol just as you might normally do in the Movie Editor.

4. When you've finished the symbol and are ready to return to the Stage, use Edit ➪ Edit Movie (Command+E or Ctrl+E) to exit the Symbol Editor.

Movie clips

Movie clips are mini-movies inside the main movie. You can add animation, actions, sounds, other symbols, and even other movie clips to movie clips. Movie clips have their own timelines, which run independently of the main timeline. This can be useful for animations that continue running after the main movie has stopped. Unlike animated Graphic Symbols, Movie Clips only need a single keyframe (the initial one) in the timeline of the main movie to play.

Creating a movie clip using existing animation

The simplest way to create a movie clip is to use existing animation from the main movie.

1. Select every frame of every layer of the existing animation that you want to turn into a movie clip.

2. Copy the animation by doing one of the following:

   - Right-click or control-click and select Copy Frames from the pop-up menu.

   - Select Edit ⇨ Copy Frames (Option+Command+C or Ctrl+Alt+C) from the main menu.

3. Select Insert ⇨ New Symbol (Command+F8 or Ctrl+F8) from the main menu.

4. The Symbol Properties dialog box appears as seen in Figure 9-3. Give the symbol a name and select Movie Clip as the Behavior. Click OK.

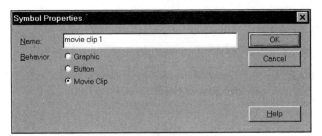

Figure 9-3: The Symbol Properties dialog box also appears when you create a new movie clip. Set the Behavior to Movie Clip and name the symbol.

5. Now select the first frame of the Timeline in the new symbol that was just created, and paste the frames you copied by doing one of the following:

   - Right-click (Ctrl+click) and select Paste Frames from the pop-up menu.

   - Select Edit ⇨ Paste Frames from the main menu.

6. Use Edit ⇨ Edit Movie (Command+E or Ctrl+E) to return to the main movie.

7. Select the frames from the main movie's Timeline (if they aren't still selected from the first step), and delete them with Insert ⇨ Delete Frame (Shift+F5).

Button symbols

Button Symbols have four "states," based on the mouse states. Each button state can present a different image. Buttons can also have actions assigned to them for each of the four mouse states. The images are set inside of the button symbol, while the actions are set in each of the button's instances. Actions cannot be assigned directly to the button symbol itself — only to an instance (or instances) of the symbol.

 Refer to Chapter 13 for more about adding actions to button instances.

The timeline for a Button Symbol, as illustrated in Figure 9-4, is different from other symbols. It consists of four frames, each one labeled for a mouse state: Up, Over, Down, and Hit. These are the only frames that can be used when creating a button; but you can use as many layers as you like. Go ahead get crazy.

Figure 9-4: The Button Symbol timeline consists of four keyframes labeled Up, Over, Down, and Hit.

Creating a simple button

Creating a button is a simple procedure:

1. Select Insert ➪ New Symbol to create a new (empty) symbol and launch the Symbol Properties dialog box. Name the button and set the Behavior to Button. Click OK.

2. Now the Symbol Editing window opens to display each of the four named states as a separate frame: Up, Over, Down, and Hit. The initial state will automatically have a keyframe. Draw a graphic for this initial state of the button — the Up state. Note that a graphic symbol, imported graphic or bitmap may also be used, or pasted into, the keyframe for the Up state.

3. Next, insert a keyframe (Insert ➪ Keyframe) in the Over state. This is the frame that appears when the mouse passes over the button. If you'd like your button to do something interesting on mouse over, this is where you make it happen. A graphic symbol, imported graphic or bitmap (or even a movie clip) may also be used, or pasted into, this keyframe for the Over state — as well as for the next two, final states.

4. Insert a keyframe in the Down state. This is the frame that appears when the button is pressed. If you don't want the button to change when it's hit, just insert a frame here instead of a keyframe.

5. Finally, insert a keyframe in the Hit state. This frame defines the effective hit area of the button. If you're only using text for your button, this is particularly important, because without a Hit state the effective hit area is limited to the text itself — which makes it very hard to hit the button. So, in this frame, draw a shape to define the hit area. Because this state is never actually seen by the user it doesn't matter what it looks like. But it's good practice to add a Hit state to every button you make — this way you won't forget to add one when it's necessary.

Adding an animated state to a button

You can add an animated state to a button as follows:

1. Follow the preceding steps for "Creating a simple button" to make a new button.

2. Next, follow the procedures in "Creating a movie clip" to create a movie clip for the animated state.

3. Now, open the Library with Window ➪ Library (Command+L or Ctrl+L). Next, find and select the button you just made, and then open it in symbol editing mode by right-clicking it and then selecting Edit from the contextual menu.

4. Select the frame to which you want to add an animated state. This can be the Up, Over, or Down state. (Because the Hit state is never seen in the movie, there's no reason to animate it.)

5. If the frame doesn't have a keyframe, add one with Insert ➪ Keyframe (F6).

6. Now, return to the Library with Window ➪ Library (Command+L or Ctrl+L), and select the movie clip that you created for the animated state. Then, with the appropriate keyframe active for the desired state, drag the movie clip into place, as shown in Figure 05.

7. Finally, test your work by selecting Control ➪ Test Movie (Command+Enter or Ctrl+Enter).

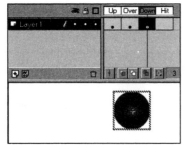

Figure 9-5: This figure illustrates a movie clip added to the Down state of a Button symbol.

Refer to Chapters 10 and 11 for more information about importing external sounds, such as AIF or WAV files. Adding sounds to button symbols (and various button states) is discussed in Chapter 11.

Adding Symbols to Movies

Now that you've created some symbols, you can use them in movies and modify each instance. Use the Library to put them in a movie. But remember that in addition to putting symbols on the stage of the main movie, you can also add them to other symbols as well.

Adding symbols to the stage

Here's how to put symbols on the stage:

1. First, use Window ⇨ Library (Command+L or Ctrl+L) to open your Library. A sample Library is depicted in Figure 9-6.

Figure 9-6: The Library contains all of a movie's symbols.

Don't choose Library from the main menu. Those libraries come with Flash and — unless you've put them there — won't contain your symbols.

2. Use the Library to find and select the symbol that you want to add to the movie.

3. Drag the symbol onto the Stage by dragging either the graphic of the symbol from the Preview Window or the symbol's name as it appears in the Sort Window.

Editing Symbols

Every instance of a symbol is a copy of the original and each edit applied to that original is applied to every instance. You have several ways to edit a symbol.

Editing a symbol in the symbol-editing mode

You can edit a symbol as follows:

1. Select an instance of the symbol that you want to edit.

2. Do one of the following:

    • Use Edit ➪ Edit Symbol (Command+E or Ctrl+E) from the main menu.

    • Right-click (Ctrl+click) the instance and choose Edit from the Contextual pop-up menu.

    • Double-click the instance to open the Instance Properties dialog box. Select the Definition tab and press the Edit Symbol button as seen in Figure 9-7.

 Figure 9-7: Press the Edit Symbol button in the Instance Properties dialog box to open the symbol-editing mode.

Editing a symbol in a new window

This method is useful if you want to quickly open a new window to work in. When editing in a new window, the movie remains open and available. You can switch between these windows by choosing from the Window menu. Or, you can divide the workspace between both windows by choosing Window ➪ Arrange All.

✦ First select an instance of the symbol that you want to edit.

✦ Then right-click (Ctrl+click) the instance and select Edit In New Window from the contextual pop-up menu.

Editing a symbol in place

New to Flash 4, Edit in Place Mode is very useful. The advantage is that, rather than opening the symbol-editing mode, you simply edit your symbol as part of the main movie. Everything else on the stage is visible, but dimmed out. To do this:

✦ Select an instance of the symbol that you want to edit.

✦ Right-click (Ctrl+click) the instance, select Edit In Place from the contextual pop-up menu.

Editing symbols from the library

You might not have an instance of your symbol available to select for editing, but you can still edit it. Just edit it from the library.

✦ Open your movie's library with Window ⇨ Library (Command+L or Ctrl+L) from the main menu.

✦ Select the symbol that you want to edit and do one of the following:

  • Double-click the symbol.

  • Right-click (Ctrl+click) and select Edit from the Contextual pop-up menu.

Returning to the movie after editing a symbol

Once you've edited your symbol, you'll want to go back to the movie to make sure that your changes work properly. Just do one of the following:

✦ Select Edit ⇨ Edit Movie (Command+M or Ctrl+M) from the main menu.

✦ Select the scene name in the left corner of the timeline as depicted in Figure 9-8.

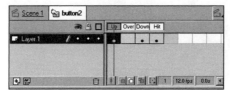

Figure 9-8: Select the scene name to return to editing the movie.

Modifying Instance Properties

Every instance of a symbol has a number of properties that can be modified. These are properties that only apply to the specific instance — not to the original symbol. Properties such as the brightness, tint, alpha (transparency), and behavior can all be modified. An instance can also be scaled, rotated, and skewed. As previously discussed, any changes made to the original symbol will be reflected in each instance — this still holds true even if the instance's properties are modified.

Modifying color effects

Each instance of a symbol can have a variety of color effects applied to it. The basic effects are changes of brightness, tint, and alpha (transparency). Tint and alpha changes can also be combined for special effects. To apply color effects:

1. Select the instance that you want to modify.

2. Open the Instance Properties dialog box by doing one of the following:

   • Double-click the instance.

   • Right-click or control-click the instance, and then select Properties from the pop-up menu.

   • Select Modify ⇨ Instance (Command+I or Ctrl+I) from the menu.

3. Select the Color Effect tab and select one of these options from the drop-down menu. Figure 9-9 depicts the Color Effect tab with the Tint option selected.

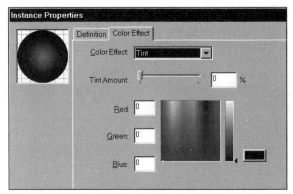

Figure 9-9: The Color Effects tab of the Instance Properties dialog box has several options to choose from.

   • **Brightness**—This option adjusts the relative brightness or darkness of the instance. It ranges from 100% (black) to 100% (white). Use the slider to change the value or just type a numeric value into the box.

   • **Tint**—The tint option enables you to add color to an instance. Either select a hue with the color picker, or enter the RGB values directly. Then, select the percentage of saturation (Tint Amount) by using the slider or by entering the percentage in the box. This number ranges from 0% (no saturation) to 100% (completely saturated).

- **Alpha** — Alpha enables you to modify the transparency of an instance. Select a percentage by using the slider or by entering a number directly. The Alpha percentage ranges from 0% (completely transparent) to 100% (no transparency).

- **Special** — This option enables you to adjust the tint and alpha settings of an instance. The controls on the left reduce the tint and alpha values by a specified percentage, while the controls on the right enable either reduce or increase the tint and alpha values by a constant value. The current values are multiplied by the numbers on the left, and then added to the values on the right.

Changing the behavior of an instance

You don't need to limit yourself to the native behavior of a symbol. There may be times when you need to turn an animated graphic symbol into a movie clip. You don't have to go through the extra effort of creating a new symbol — just change the behavior of the instance as needed. To change the behavior of an instance:

1. Select the instance that you want to modify.

2. Open the Instance Properties dialog box, as described in "Modifying Color Effects."

3. Click the Definition tab and, in the Behavior area, select the desired behavior. You can select Graphic, Button, or Movie clip. The Definition tab is illustrated in Figure 9-10.

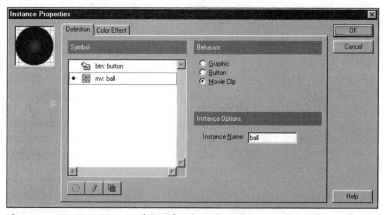

Figure 9-10: You can set the Behavior of an instance from the Definition tab of the Instance Properties dialog box.

Each type of symbol has options that can be modified in the Definitions tab:

- **Graphic Behavior** gives you the Loop, Play Once, Single Frame, and First Frame options. The options are pretty self-explanatory—Loop makes the Graphic Symbol loop, Play Once will make it play through its animation once, and Single Frame will make the Graphic Symbol static. The First Frame setting enables you to designate the first frame of the Graphic Symbol.

- **Button Behavior** gives you the Track as Button and Track as Menu options. Selecting Track as Menu Item is useful when you create pop-up menus, while Track as Button is useful when you are using single buttons.

- **Movie Clip Behavior** gives you the Instance Name option. The Instance Name is used with actions such as Tell Target.

Switching symbols

There may be times when you need to replace an instance of one symbol with another symbol. You don't have to go through and recreate your entire animation to do this—just use the Switch Symbol feature. This feature only switches the symbol contained in the instance. All other modifications applied to the instance will remain the same. Here's how to switch symbols:

1. Select the instance that you want to switch.

2. Open the Instance Properties dialog box as described in "Modifying Color Effects."

3. Click the Definition tab and, from the list in the Symbol area, select the symbol that you want to switch to.

4. Press the Switch Symbol button.

✦   ✦   ✦

Sound Planning

One of the most neglected (or perhaps understated) aspects of multimedia development is sound. Because the majority of people who use Flash (or create multimedia) come from graphic arts backgrounds, it's no surprise that sound is often applied as the last "effect" to a visually stunning presentation — there may be little or no consideration for the soundtrack in early stages of development. Moreover, it's the one element that is usually taken from a stock source, rather than being original work by the Flash designer. (Exceptions exist, of course, as many Flash designers have demonstrated time and time again.)

With this in mind, we sought to provide you with a basic overview of digital sound and sound quality in Chapter 10, so that you would know how to judge the quality of different bit depths and sampling rates. Chapters 11 and 12 will also guide you through the use of audio within a Flash movie, and suggest tips for getting the most bang per byte in the final .SWF file.

Understanding Sound for Flash

This chapter provides an introduction to the basics of digital audio for Flash. When done properly, the integration of sound into your Flash project can add dimension, ease of use, and impact to your final product. Careful planning and attention to technical detail can help you use sound to your advantage, and create a seamless sensory experience for your audience.

Basics of Sampling and Quality

When using sound in your Flash project, it is important to get a handle on the basics of digital audio. What follows is a crash course that will introduce you to sampling, bit resolution, and file size.

What is sound?

Essentially, sound is the aural sensation produced by vibrations in the air. The frequency produced by these vibrations (waves) determines the pitch of the sound (for example, how low or high it is.)

The frequency of sound is measured in Hertz. Ideally, humans have the ability to hear frequencies that are in the 20 to 20,000 Hz range. It is important to not confuse sound frequency with sample rate. In the late 1940s, Harry Nyquist and Claude Shannon developed a sampling theorem that describes how a sampling rate needs be twice the value of the highest frequency of a signal. We will see how this theorem applies to sound in the next section.

Things you should know about sound for Flash

When incorporating sound into Flash, you should keep a number of factors in mind when it comes to quality and file size. Foremost among these are *sample rate* and *bit resolution*.

Sample rate

A sample rate describes the number of times an audio signal is sampled when it is recorded digitally. This rate is measured in hertz (Hz) or kilohertz (kHz). The higher the sample rate, the better the audio range. For example, a sound that is sampled at 44.1 kHz will analyze the sound 44,100 times per second, and record the differences between each analysis. Higher sample rates generally result in a richer, more complete sound. As we indicated in the last section, Nyquist and Shannon's sampling theorem tells us that, in order for the audible range of 20 to 20,000 Hz to be sampled correctly, the audio source needs to be sampled at a frequency no lower than 40,000 Hz, or 40 kHz. This is why CD audio is sampled at 44.1 kHz—it very closely resembles the source sound. The less a sound is sampled, the less the reproduction will resemble the original sound.

Note   A sound sample refers to one "analysis" of a recorded sound, whereas as sound file refers to the entire collection of samples recorded.

When you decrease the sample rate of a sound file, the file size will drop proportionately. For example, a 300Kb, 44.1kHz sound file would be 150Kb when saved as a 22.05kHz file. Table 10-1 delineates sample audio rates and their qualities.

	Table 10-1	
	Audio Sample Rates and Quality	
Sample Rate	**Quality Level**	**Possible Uses**
48 kHz	Studio Quality	Sound or music recorded to a digital medium such as miniDV, DAT, DVCam, and so on
44.1 kHz	CD Quality	High Fidelity sound and music
32 kHz	Near-CD Quality	Prosumer digital camcorders
22.05 kHz	FM Radio Quality	Short, high quality music clips
11 kHz	Acceptable for music	Longer music clips, high quality voice, SFX
5 kHz	Acceptable for speech	"Flat" speech, simple button sounds

Bit resolution

Another key factor that influences audio quality is *bit resolution*. Bit resolution (or bit depth) refers to the number of bits used to describe each audio sample. It is also exponential, meaning that an 8-bit sound sample will have a range of 2^8, or 256, levels, and a 16-bit sound sample will have a range of 2^{16}, or 65,536, levels. A 16-bit sound will therefore have far more information to describe the sound than an 8-bit sound of equal length. The extra information in a 16-bit sound will keep the background hiss to a minimum, and will be clearer and less washed out than the same sound at 8 bits.

It is possible to convert a sound from a higher bit resolution to a lower one, the same way it is to "desample" a sound with a high sample rate to a lower one. This can be done with hardware conversion, or (more likely for use with Flash) through a software application. For more information on desampling and conversion in applications other than Flash, see Chapter 19.

Tip

If you're having difficulty understanding the significance of bit depths and are familiar with scanning photographic images, think of the difference between an 8-bit grayscale image and a 24-bit color image. While the 8-bit grayscale image (like a black and white photograph) is much smaller than the 24-bit color image (like a color photograph), the 8-bit black and white image doesn't contain as much information—only 256 levels of gray. On the other hand, the 24-bit color image contains 256 levels in each of the R, G, and B channels, yielding a possible 16.7 million color range. Sound samples intended for human ears do not need anything close to a 16.7 million range of values. 16-bit sound samples provide a dynamic range of over 64,000 values, which is more than the human ear can detect.

One thing to keep in mind is that a 16-bit sound file would be twice the size of the same file saved at 8-bit quality. This is due to the increased amount of information needed to describe the higher quality file. Table 10-2 describes a few audio bit resolutions and their qualities.

Table 10-2
Audio Bit Resolution and Quality

Bit Depth	Quality Level	Possible Uses
16-bit	CD Quality	High Fidelity sound and music
12-bit	Near-CD Quality	Prosumer digital camcorder audio
8-bit	FM Radio Quality	Short, high quality music clips
4-bit	Acceptable for music	Longer music clips, high quality voice, sound effects

To compare the differences between sounds at different sample rates and bit depths, refer to Figures 10-1 and 10-2. Both figures represent the same original source sound file, but at varying sample rates and bit depths. Notice how the waveform of the 16-bit 44.1 kHz sound has many more "points" or samples of information than the 8-bit 11.025 kHz sound. By having more samples, the difference between each sample isn't as large as the 8-bit 11.025 kHz sound. As a result, more samples provide much cleaner sound.

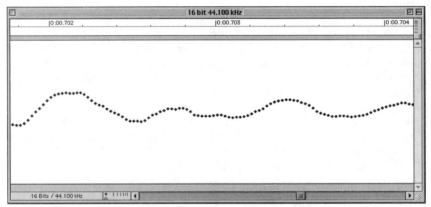

Figure 10-1: A sound sampled at 44.100 kHz with a 16-bit resolution

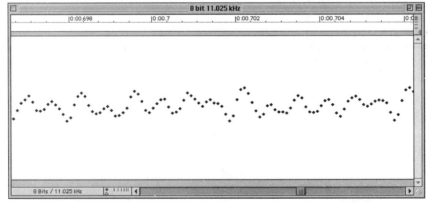

Figure 10-2: The same sound shown in Figure 10-1, but downsampled to 11.025 kHz with a 8-bit resolution

Channels

All audio files are either stereo (left and right) or mono (single channel). Stereo files will be twice the size by virtue of having twice the amount of information. In most audio-editing applications, you should be able to save, or export a stereo sound to a one-channel mono sound, by mixing the two channels together. It is also possible to save the right or left channel of a stereo sound separately as a .WAV or .AIF file.

In multitrack editing applications, such as Deck II, ProTools and AudioLogic, it is possible to have more than 8 tracks of audio, depending on your system configuration. These multitrack audio project files then need to be "bounced" or mixed down to a stereo or mono file in order to be saved as WAV or AIF files. For a more detailed description of this process, please see Chapter 19.

File size

You should be concerned about your audio clip's file size for a number of reasons. First, sound files can take up a relatively large amount of drive space. Second, moving them around, and importing them into Flash can be cumbersome and slow. Third, download times for large, elaborate sound clips (even when exported from Flash as heavily compressed audio) can be excruciating if you don't have a fire hose of an Internet connection.

When working with external audio applications, (which are discussed in detail in Chapter 19) it is important to create the shortest audio clips possible. That means trimming off any excess sound you don't need, especially any blank lead-in or lead-out ("handles") at the beginning or the end of a clip.

If you are planning to have a music soundtrack in your Flash project, it is a good idea to use a small audio clip that can be looped. Looping audio clips is discussed in Chapter 11.

Here is a simple formula to determine the file size, in bytes, of a given audio clip:

Seconds of audio × sample rate* × # of channels × (bit depth ÷ 8**) = file size

---

* Expressed in hertz, not kilohertz.

** There are eight bits per byte.

Thus, a 20 second stereo audio loop at 8 bits, 11kHz would be calculated like this:

20 sec ×11,025 Hz × 2 channels × (8 bits ÷ 8 bits/byte) = 441,000 bytes = 430KB

Note When using sound in Flash, it is a good idea to start with the highest quality audio source files possible (16 bit, 44.1kHz is ideal) and then let Flash compress it when exporting. See detailed information on sound export settings for SWF movies in Chapter 12.

Sound File Import Formats

Flash 4 can import a few different file formats into Flash. The format you choose will depend primarily on what platform you are using to develop your content. Note that regardless of whether a sound file has been imported on a Mac or PC, the resulting FLA file can be edited by either platform.

✦ **.WAV (Windows Wave):** WAV files are the standard for digital audio on Windows PC's. Flash can import WAV files created in other programs, like Rebirth, SoundForge, and so on. Wave files can be either stereo or mono, and support varying bit and frequency rates. Flash 4 for Macintosh cannot import this file format. However it will recognize FLA files that contain WAV clips created on a Windows PC.

✦ **.AIFF or .AIF (Audio Interchange File format):** The AIF format is commonly used for digital audio on the Mac. Flash can import AIFF sounds created in other programs, like PEAK, DECK II or Rebirth. Like WAV, AIFF supports stereo and mono, variable bit and frequency rates. Flash 4 for PC cannot import AIFF sounds. However, it will recognize FLA files that contain AIFF clips that were created on a Macintosh.

✦ **QuickTime:** It is important to note that QuickTime Audio files (.QTA or .MOV files) cannot be imported into Flash directly. You can, however, save QuickTime audio files as WAV's or AIFF's, and then import them in Flash. In order to do this, you will need to have QuickTime Pro 3.0 or greater installed. This software is available from Apple at `www.apple.com/quicktime`.

Note   If you depend on the embedded sound in the FLA file as your master audio file, you will lose the ability to update sound files from the original *when the Flash file is edited on a different platform*. This can be worked around by saving all changes to the original audio file (the true master) in both WAV and AIF from your sound editing program and re-importing them accordingly when working in a mixed platform environment.

Sound Export Formats Used by Flash

When exporting FLA project files to SWF movies (see Chapter 25), you will need to decide what export format to use for audio. The default in Flash 4 is to export all audio as MP3, but you can individually specify a compression scheme for each sound by using the Flash Library. The benefits and drawbacks of each format appear in the following list. For more information on export settings for sound, please see Chapter 12.

✦ **ADPCM (Adaptive Differential Pulse-Code Modulation):** ADPCM is an audio compression scheme that converts sound into binary information. It is primarily used for voice technologies, such as fiber optic telephone lines, because the audio signal is compressed, enabling it to carry textual information as well. ADPCM works well, because it records only the difference between samples, and adjusts the encoding accordingly, keeping file size low.

Note

ADPCM is the default setting for older versions of Flash, such as Flash 2 and 3. It isn't as efficient as MP3 encoding, but is the only choice for those who want to maintain compatibility with older Flash Players.

✦ **MP3 (MPEG-1 Audio Layer 3):** MP3 is the emerging standard for digital audio distributed on the Internet. Despite (and perhaps because of) controversy surrounding the availability of "pirated" music in MP3 format on the internet, MP3 has achieved critical mass and become a common acronym in netspeak. MP3 is a very effective codec because it can cut file size down significantly without any clearly noticeable difference in audio quality. To do this, it uses perceptual encoding techniques, which reduce the amount of overlapping and redundant information that describe sound. While MP3 encoding provides excellent audio quality with minimal file-size cost, it is much more processor-intensive than most audio compressors. This means that slower computers may have more difficulty playing high-bit-rate MP3 audio while performing other tasks, like processing complex animations and tweens. If in doubt, test your Flash movie with MP3 audio on slower computers.

Tip

Flash 4 can export SWF files with MP3 encoding as its means of audio compression. It may be interesting to note that Shockwave Audio, the default audio compression scheme for Director-based Shockwave movies, is actually MP3 in disguise. MP3 is not supported by earlier versions of the Flash Player, such as Version 3.

✦ **RAW (Raw PCM):** Flash can export sound to SWF files in a RAW format. Flash will not recompress any audio if you use this setting. Uncompressed sound tends to be very large in file size, and would most likely be useless for Internet-based distribution. The only advantage we can think of for exporting sounds as RAW would be its backward compatibility with earlier versions of Flash. Even for those people who wish to develop Flash content for QuickTime, it would be more effective to add uncompressed sound to a Flash-originated animation in a program like Premiere or Final Cut. Tables 10-3 and 10-4 list Flash 4 audio import and export formats.

Table 10-3
Audio Import Formats in Flash 4

Import Formats	Compatibility			Comments
	Mac	PC	Flash 3	
AIF	Yes	No	Yes	Default sound format for Macintosh
WAV	No	Yes	Yes	Default sound format for PC

Table 10-4
Audio Export Formats in Flash 4

Export Format	Compatibility			Comments
	Mac	PC	Flash 3	
ADPCM	Yes	Yes	Yes	Good encoding scheme, Flash Player 3 and earlier compatibility.
MP3	Yes	Yes	No	Best encoding scheme, not compatible with earlier versions of Flash Player
RAW	Yes	Yes	Yes	No compression, lossless, large file sizes

✦   ✦   ✦

Controlling Sounds in Flash

✦ ✦ ✦ ✦

In This Chapter

How to add sounds
to buttons

Understanding
sync settings

Controlling in
and out points

How to add basic
effects to Flash
sounds

✦ ✦ ✦ ✦

This chapter focuses on importing and integrating sound
files into your Flash project. Sound can be used in Flash
to enhance interactive design elements, such as buttons, to
play a background soundtrack, or for more experimental
narrative uses.

Importing Sounds into Flash

As discussed in Chapter 10, Flash can import AIFF (Mac) or
WAV (PC) audio files. Unlike other imported files, Flash does
not automatically insert the imported file into a layer's frames
in the timeline. You don't have to have any specific layer or
frame selected before you import, but you do need to have at
least one unlocked layer in your Flash movie. You can assign
an imported sound to a keyframe after you have imported it
into Flash.

To import an audio clip into the Flash authoring environment:

1. Choose File ➪ Import

2. Select the AIFF or WAV clip you want.

3. Click Open.

The sound clip you selected is now imported into your Flash
editor document (.FLA file). You can find the imported sound(s)
in the Flash Library (Command+L or Ctrl+L). When you highlight
the sound clip in the Library, you can see the audio file's
waveform (see Figure 11-1). You can listen to your sound by
pressing the Play button above the waveform.

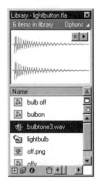

Figure 11-1: This is a sound in the Flash Library.

Cross-Reference   In Chapter 12, we discuss how to specify unique compression settings for each sound in the Flash Library.

Assigning a Sound to a Button

Sound effects can be easily added to button states to enhance interactivity. Sounds can be added to the Over and Down states of a button, meaning that you can use a different sound for a mouseover and a mouse click, respectively. For general information about creating buttons, see Chapter 9.

To add sounds to a Flash button:

1. In the Library, choose the button that you want to play the sound and double-click it, or choose Edit from the Library window menu.

2. Add a new layer to the button's timeline, and insert keyframes in the Over and Down columns. Refer to Figure 11-2 for an example.

3. Select the frame of the button state that you want to use the sound, and choose Modify ➪ Frame (or double-click the frame).

4. Click the Sound tab of the Frame Properties dialog box (see Figure 11-3).

5. In the Sound drop-down menu, choose the sound clip you want to use. Note that this menu always lists all the sounds that are currently available in the movie's Library.

6. Now choose how you want to the sound to play in the Sync drop-down menu. For now, use the Event option. The Sync menu is discussed in the next section.

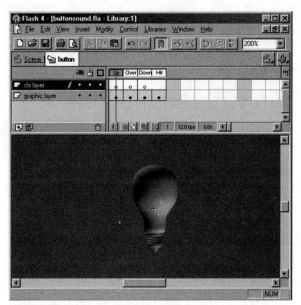

Figure 11-2: Your button's timeline should resemble this.

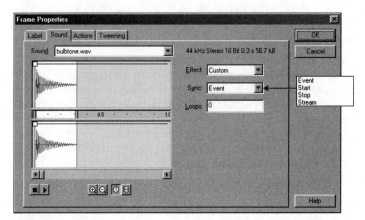

Figure 11-3: The Sound tab of the Frame Properties dialog box

You have now added sound to your button state. To try it out, go back to the movie editor (Command+E or Ctrl+E) and choose Control ➪ Enable Buttons, or Control ➪ Test Scene. You can add another sound to either the other button state (either Over or Down, depending upon which state you used in Step 3).

You can refer to the buttonsound.fla tutorial Flash movie located in the ch11 folder of the *Flash 4 Bible* CD-ROM. This movie has a pre-made button with sounds attached. It was made with the same technique described in this section.

Synchronizing Audio with Animations

To *synchronize*, or *sync* in film editor's lingo, means to precisely match picture to sound. It is derived from the Greek word for time, *chronos*. In Flash, you can sync, or synchronize audio to the timeline. Synchronizing sound in Flash involves synchronizing the audio to animation on the timeline. Several different sync options exist in Flash, each with a specific use in mind. These are discussed later.

Types of sound synchronization in Flash

You can use sync to create complex multimedia animations, button-triggered sounds, and even synced cartoons. The sync options you choose depend upon what you want your sound to do:

✦ **Event:** Event sounds begin on the keyframe they are added to, and play independently of the timeline. If the event sound is longer than your movie, it continues to play even if the movie stops. Event sounds are useful for background soundtracks and other sounds that don't need to be synced. Event is the default setting in Flash.

✦ **Stream:** Stream sounds are like a traditional track in a video-editing application. A Stream sound essentially locks to the timeline, and Flash animation attempts to keep the animation in pace with the sound. Although this works in theory, when animations get too complex or run on slower machines, Flash tends to skip, or "drop" the frames in order to keep up with the Stream sound. The sound stops either once the animation comes to an end (for example, at the end of the timeline) or, more specifically, when the playback head reaches the last frame that includes the waveform of the streamed sound.

✦ **Start/Stop:** Selecting Start is similar to an Event sound. Choosing Start begins the sound again if it is already playing. This option can be useful when you have a longer sound that plays on a button instance. For example, you might have three identical buttons that play the same two-second audio clip on the "over" state. The sound begins when the first button is moused over. If the second or third button is moused over, the sound plays again. Selecting Stop is similar, but when activated, the selected sound stops playing.

Incorporating Sound in the Timeline

In order to incorporate sound in the Flash timeline, you should first import the sound (described previously) and create a new layer for it. You may have as many sound layers as you like in your project, and Flash mixes them all equally. However, keep in mind that not only do more sound layers increase a movie's file size, it also strains the processing power of the computer it's being run on.

One thing to keep in mind is that the Frame Rate you specify in the Movie Properties dialog box affects the number of frames your sound takes up on the timeline. For example, a 30-second sound clip takes up 360 frames on the timeline, if you are using Flash's default setting of 12 frames per seconds (fps). The same 30-second clip at 18 fps takes up 540 frames.

You can use the sample sound ninjabeat.wav (PC) or ninjabeat.aif (Mac) for this exercise. You can find these sounds in the ch11 folder of the *Flash 4 Bible* CD-ROM.

Adding sound files to the timeline is similar to assigning sound to a button. To add sounds to a movie's timeline, follow these steps:

1. Create a keyframe in your sound layer where you want the sound to begin.

2. Select the keyframe and choose Modify ➪ Frame (or double-click the frame).

3. Click the Sound tab in the Frame Properties dialog box.

4. Choose the sound file you want to add using the Sound drop-down menu at the top of the window.

5. Now choose how you want to the sound to sync in the Sync menu (see earlier section for more details).

6. Specify how many times you want the sound to loop. If you want it to loop indefinitely, enter a high number, such as **50**. Note that no matter how many times you tell a Stream sound to loop, it still stops at the end of the its duration in the timeline. You can add as many frames as you wish to a stream sound's layer to extend its looping capacity.

7. Perform any last minute editing or finessing of the sound file (see the "Editing Audio in Flash" section later in this chapter).

8. Click OK.

Your sound is now part of the timeline. You can see it in waveform on the layer to which it was added. You can test your sound by pressing Enter on your keyboard, which plays the timeline. To more accurately test the sound, choose Control ➪ Test Scene to see it as a SWF file.

Tip If you are syncing anything to the timeline using the Stream feature, you should test your SWF movie on various platforms and machines with different processor speeds. What looks and sounds good on your brand new Power Macintosh G3 450 could be a mess on a lowly Pentium 133.

If, at any keyframe on the timeline, you wish to stop all sounds that are playing, do the following:

1. Select the keyframe where you want all the sounds to stop.

2. Choose Modify ➪ Frame to access the Frame Properties dialog box, and click the Actions tab.

3. From the + pop-up menu, select the Stop All Sounds action (see Figure 11-4).

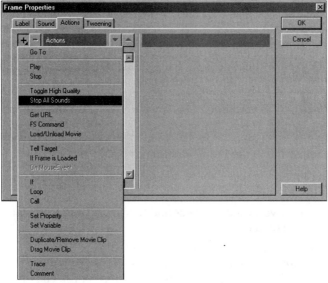

Figure 11-4: All the sounds playing in the timeline stop when the Stop All Sounds keyframe is reached.

4. Click OK.

Editing Audio in Flash

Although not intended as a full-featured sound editor, Flash can be used in a pinch for basic sound editing. If you plan on using sound extensively in Flash, we strongly recommend you purchase a professional sound editing application. The amount of money you spend on a good editor certainly pays off with fewer headaches and more control over your final product. We discuss external sound applications used in concert with Flash in Chapter 19.

Sound editing controls in Flash

Flash has some useful (albeit basic) sound editing controls in the Sound tab of the Frame Properties dialog box. You can change the In and Out points of a sound, and use the envelope handles to create Fade-in and Fade-out effects.

A sound's In point is where the sound starts playing, and a sound's Out point is where the sound finishes. To change a sound's In and Out points:

1. Select the keyframe of the sound you want to edit.

2. Choose Modify ➪ Frame, and click the Sound tab of the Frame Properties dialog box.

3. Drag the Time In and Time Out control bars (see Figure 11-5) to mark the section of audio you want to use.

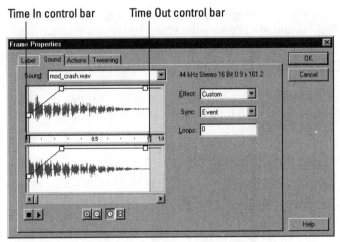

Time In control bar   Time Out control bar

Figure 11-5: Drag the Time In and Out control bars on the sound's timeline to restrict which section is played.

4. Click the Play button to hear the sound as marked, and click OK after you have finessed the points.

Creating effects in the Sound tab

You can use Flash's preset fades and other effects by using the Effect menu in the Sound tab of the Frame Properties dialog box, but it is often better to create these effects in a dedicated sound-editing application. Flash's preset effects are described in detail here:

✦ **None:** No effect is applied to the sound channels.

✦ **Left Channel/Right Channel:** Play only the right or left channel of a stereo clip.

✦ **Fade Left to Right/Fade Right to Left:** Creates an effect that lowers the levels in one channel while raising them in the other, creating a "panning" effect. This effect takes place over the entire length of the audio clip.

✦ **Fade In/Fade Out:** Fade In gradually raises the level of the beginning of an audio clip. Fade Out gradually lowers the level at the end of an audio clip. The default Fade In/Out length is approximately 25% of the length of the clip. Note that even if you change the size of your selection with the control bars, inexplicably, the Fade In/Out length remains the same. Thus, a 35-second sound clip with an original default Fade In time of 9 seconds *still* has a 9-second Fade In time even when the selection's length is reduced to, say, 12 seconds. Creating a Custom Fade can solve this problem (see the next section for more information).

✦ **Custom:** Any time you manually alter the levels or audio handles on this screen, Flash automatically sets the Effect menu to Custom.

Creating a Custom Fade In or Out

For more control, use the Envelope Handles to create custom fades or lower the audio levels, or amplitude, of a given section of audio. Besides fading in or out, lowering the levels can be used for low-volume sounds that play subtly in the background.

1. Select the keyframe of the sound you want to edit.

2. Choose Modify ➪ Frame, and click the Sound tab.

3. Click the envelope lines to create envelope handles (see Figure 11-6).

Once these handles have been created, you can drag them around to create your desired volume/fading effects. The lines themselves show the volume level of the sound. Thus, when you drag an envelope handle down, the line slopes down, indicating a decrease in the volume level. Keep in mind that you can have only eight envelope handles per channel. (For example, eight for left, and eight for right.)

Envelope handles
(Left Channel)

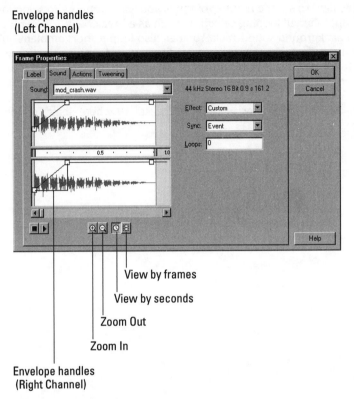

View by frames

View by seconds

Zoom Out

Zoom In

Envelope handles
(Right Channel)

Figure 11-6: The sound-editing tools and options of the
Sound tab

Other controls in the Sound tab

Aside from what was mentioned previously, other useful tools in the Sound tab
warrant mention. Refer to Figure 11-5 for their locations in the Sound tab.

✦ **Zoom In/Zoom Out:** Use these sophisticated tools to, you guessed it, enlarge
   the view of the waveform (Zoom In) or shrink the view of the waveform (Zoom
   Out). This is particularly helpful when you are altering the In or Out points or
   envelope handles.

✦ **Seconds/Frames:** AIFF and WAV audio files represent time in seconds.
   However, you can toggle between viewing time in seconds or Flash frames by
   clicking these buttons. Viewing time in frames is advantageous for syncing
   sound with the Stream option.

✦ **Loop:** Use this field to set the number of times you want your audio selection to repeat (or loop). A small looping selection, such as a break beat or jazz riff can be used for a background soundtrack. You can also loop a short ambient noise for an interesting effect. You can test the quality of your looping selection with the Play button. If your loop isn't perfect, you may need to trim off blank or repeating sections with the control bars.

Cross-
Reference

We show you how to create precise loops in Chapter 19 where Sonic Foundry's Acid Pro software is discussed.

✦   ✦   ✦

Optimizing Flash Sound for Export

CHAPTER

12

After you have added sound to buttons and timelines in a Flash movie, you need to know how to modify the audio's export settings for optimal sound quality and file size. This chapter discusses the intricacies of controlling audio output within the Publish Settings dialog box and the Flash Library.

Sound Optimization Overview

As discussed in Chapter 10, when exporting your Flash sound, you have a number of things to consider. For Web-based delivery, your primary concern should probably be trying to find a middle ground between file size and audio quality. On the other hand, perhaps you are creating a Flash Web site for a record company. In this case, sound quality would be slightly more important than file size. Your audience and your method of delivery should determine the export settings you choose.

You have two ways of optimizing your sound for export. The quickest, simplest way is to use the Publish Settings. If your Flash project uses a combination of audio types, such as button sounds, background music, speech, and so on, it is better to fine-tune your audio settings in the Library. This gives you better control over output.

 Cross-Reference This chapter discusses the Publish feature of Flash 4, which is explained more thoroughly in Chapter 25.

Publish Settings for Audio

You can use the Publish Settings to easily control audio output quality for Flash movies by choosing File ⇨ Publish Settings and selecting the Flash tab (see Figure 12-1). See Chapter 25 for detailed information about Publish Settings.

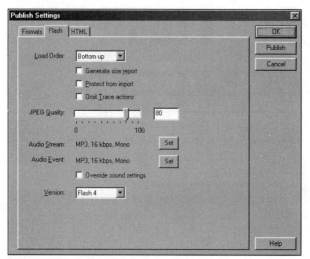

Figure 12-1: The Flash tab of Publish Settings has options that control audio quality.

New Feature

In previous versions of Flash, audio export settings were specified in the Export Movie dialog box. Flash 4 adds a new Publish feature to more easily export your Flash editor documents (.FLA files) as Shockwave Flash movies (.SWF files).

You can specify the following Publish Settings:

✦ **Audio Stream:** Controls the export quality of Stream sounds (see Chapter 11 for more information on Stream sounds in Flash.) To customize, click Set. This gives you a number of options, described later.

✦ **Audio Event:** Controls the export quality of Event sounds. (See Chapter 11 for more information on Event sounds in Flash.) To customize, click Set. This gives you a number of options, described later.

✦ **Override Sound Settings:** If this box is checked, Flash uses the Publish Settings, rather than individual audio settings fine-tuned in the Library. For more information, see the "Fine-Tuning Audio Settings in the Library" section later in this chapter.

The Set options

Audio Stream and Audio Event have individual compression settings, specified by their respective Set button options. If you click either Set button on the Flash Tab, you can see more settings related to audio quality in the Sound Settings dialog box (see Figure 12-2). The settings listed differ depending on what you choose in the compression menu.

Figure 12-2: The Sound Settings dialog boxes

The Sound Settings options are based on the audio-encoding scheme selected in the Compression drop-down menu:

✦ **Disable.** This option turns off all sound for either Audio Stream or Audio Event. If this option is selected, no sound is exported to the SWF movie.

✦ **ADPCM.** If ADPCM is selected in the Compression menu, you can set the following options:

   • **Convert Stereo to Mono:** Mixes the right and left channel of audio into one (mono) channel.

   • **Sample Rate:** Choose sampling rates of 5, 11, 22, or 44 kHz. Note that increasing the sample rate of an audio file to something higher than the imported file's simply increases file size, not quality. For example, if you imported primarily 22kHz sounds into the Flash movie, selecting 44 kHz will not offer any sound quality improvement. For more information on Sample Rates, see Chapter 10.

   • **ADPCM Bits:** Set the number of bits that ADPCM uses for encoding. You can choose a rate between 2 and 5. The higher the ADPCM bit number, the better the audio quality. Flash's default setting is 4 bits.

✦ **MP3.** If you select MP3 in the Compression menu, you can set the following options:

- **Convert Stereo to Mono:** See the description for the equivalent ADPCM setting.

- **Bit Rate:** MP3 measures compression in kilobits per second (Kbps). The higher the bit rate, the better the audio quality. Because of the efficiency of the MP3 audio compression scheme, you can set the bit rate relatively high, and the file size still remains relatively small. See Table 12-1 for more information.

- **Quality:** Choose Fast, Medium, or Best quality. Fast optimizes the audio file for faster delivery on the Internet, although some quality is lost. Use Best for files distributed through other media, such as Intranets or CD-ROMs.

✦ **Raw:** If Raw (a.k.a. *Raw PCM audio*) is selected in the Compression menu, you can specify the following options:

- **Convert Stereo to Mono:** See the equivalent setting in ADPCM.

- **Sample Rate:** This option specifies the sampling rate for the Audio Stream or Audio Events sounds. For more information on sample rate, please see Chapter 10.

Table 12-1
MP3 Bit Rate Quality

Bit Rate	Sound Quality	Good For
8 Kbps	Very bad	Nothing. Don't use this unless you want horrible, unrecognizable sound.
16 Kbps	Barely acceptable	Very large audio files where quality isn't important, simple button sounds.
20, 24, 32 Kbps	Acceptable	Speech or voice.
48, 56 Kbps	Acceptable	Large music files, complex button sounds.
64 Kbps	Good	Large music files that need good audio quality.
112–128 Kbps	Excellent	Near-CD quality.
160 Kbps	Best	Near-CD quality.

As a general rule, if you are using the Publish Settings to select your audio export options, we would recommend choosing MP3 at 64 Kbps, for moderate-to-good sound quality. At this setting, the resulting file size-to-quality ratio is relatively good, and suitable for most Flash projects.

Caution You may notice that when Flash exports certain audio files and plays the final movie in the Flash Player, a distinct "crackle" can be heard, especially at higher bit rates. When you check the original audio file in an external audio application, you won't hear the crackle. This could be due to an unresolved bug in the Flash Player, or a conflict with the Player and an outdated sound card driver in Windows 95/98/NT. Strangely, these audio problems are not always reproducible with the same file when used across different systems. Although there's no sure-fire way to eliminate this problem, you could try using your preferred audio application to save the problematic sound file again at a different bit-depth or sample rate. We have been informed by a couple of audio experts that exported Flash movies clip audio tracks that peak at 98 to 100 percent. As such, any and all audio imported into Flash should be normalized to no more than 95 percent. Normalization is discussed in Chapter 19.

One thing to consider, however, is that MP3 is not supported by Flash 3 (or earlier) players. Many Web users out there haven't upgraded their Flash Player plug-in to version 4. Although people should eventually upgrade, it would be wise to implement a transitional solution. For example, you could provide both a Flash 3 movie with ADPCM encoded audio and a Flash 4 movie with MP3 encoded audio on your Web site. Include information about Flash 4's ability to cut down download times and increase audio quality as an incentive for visitors to upgrade, and provide a link to Macromedia to download the new plug-in. Another, more "invisible" solution would be to add a "plug-in detection" script that would automatically serve users the movie that corresponds to the version of the Flash Player they have installed.

Cross-Reference To add plug-in detection to your Flash movies, use one of the HTML templates installed with Flash 4. HTML templates are discussed in the "Using the HTML Settings" section of Chapter 25.

Fine-Tuning Sound Settings in the Library

For more control over Flash compression of sound, you can customize some or all of the settings for your audio clips individually in the Flash Library. The Publish Settings menu exports all of your "noncustomized" Stream sounds or Event sounds at the same rate. However, if you have many sounds and need to export them at different rates, it is best to fine-tune them in the Library.

You can also use a combination of the two methods. For instance, you have 3 different Event sounds in your Flash project. Two of these are simple button sounds you want to set as MP3 at 48 Kbps. The third is a background jazz loop that needs to be near CD quality. In this case, you would set the better quality music loop in the Library to 112 Kbps. In the Publish Settings menu, you could have the other two Event sounds default to MP3 at 48 Kbps.

Settings for audio in the Library

Audio settings in the Library are similar to those discussed previously for the Publish Settings. To access these settings, select the sound in the Library and double-click it, or press the Properties button (see Figure 12-3).

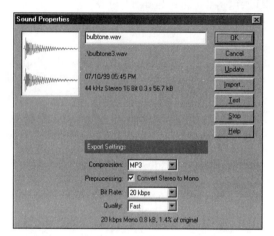

Figure 12-3: The Sound Properties dialog box enables you to control compression settings for each sound in the Library.

In the Sound Properties dialog box, you can see a window with the waveform of the audio you selected. The top half of the dialog box displays the sound file's information: location, date, sample rate, channels, bit depth, duration, and file size. The lower half of the dialog box has a section titled "Export Settings." There, you can find a drop-down menu to choose the Compression scheme. The options listed in this menu are exactly the same as the options in the Sound Settings dialog box discussed earlier in this chapter. Unlike the Publish Setting's options, though, the Export Settings in the Sound Properties dialog box can display the estimated final file size (after compression) of the clip, and show you what percentage it was reduced by.

The buttons on the right-hand side of the Sound Properties dialog box offer other options as well:

✦ **Update.** Flash checks to see if the original WAV or AIFF file on your drive has been modified, and updates it accordingly.

✦ **Import.** Enables you to import another audio file into the Flash environment. For more information on importing audio files, see Chapter 11.

✦ **Test.** This is an excellent feature that enables you to preview the export quality of you selected from the Compression menu.

✦ **Stop.** Pressing this button silences the sound preview.

✦ **Help.** Launches the Web browser-driven help interface.

One benefit of fine-tuning your audio in the Library is the Test function of the Sound Properties dialog box. Using the Test feature is an excellent way of previewing what your audio file will sound like with different compression schemes and bit rates. Also, you can see the effect of each setting on the final compressed file size of the sound.

Publish Settings for QuickTime

A hot new feature in Flash 4 is the ability to export your Flash movies as QuickTime Flash movies. This section will briefly cover the audio options available within the QuickTime (QT) architecture. These options only pertain to a Flash sound that is converted to a QuickTime sound track. This new QuickTime sound track is not merged with pre-existing QT sound tracks. In general, you can keep Flash sound embedded with its original Flash media track by disabling QuickTime sound compression. However, if you want Flash sounds, such as background music sound to use compression schemes currently unavailable in Flash 4, then you can opt to convert the Flash sound to a QuickTime-supported audio codec such as QDesign Music.

Cross-Reference   For more information on QuickTime support in Flash, see Chapter 21.

To access the QuickTime audio export options:

1. Choose File ⇨ Publish Settings.
2. Check the QuickTime option in the Formats tab.
3. Now click the QuickTime tab that appears.
4. Check the Use QuickTime Compression option in the Streaming Sound setting.
5. Now click the Settings button. See Figure 12-4 for an example.

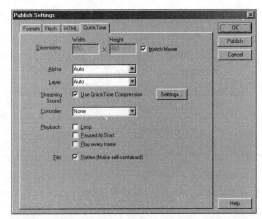

Figure 12-4: The QuickTime tab of Publish Settings enables you to convert Flash sounds into QuickTime audio tracks with the Streaming Sound setting.

You can now see a new window that enables you to select your audio compression settings.

The QuickTime audio encoding options available differ according to the configuration of your machine. What you decide to use should depend on the end use of your QuickTime movie, which could be Internet distribution, to put on CD-ROM, or something else. Table 12-2 explains some of the popular encoding methods available for QuickTime.

Table 12-2
QuickTime Sound Compressors

Popular Codecs	Best For	Description
Qdesign Music Codec	Internet	Very good compression ratio, great for music. Progressively downloads.
Qdesign ver. 2	Internet	Excellent compression ratio, great for music, streaming audio.
Qualcomm PureVoice	Internet	Excellent compression ratio. Very good for voice.
IMA	CD-ROM	Good quality, only encodes 16-bit audio. Not great for music with very low frequencies (such as booming bass) or for Web use.

Other Formats	Description
24-bit Integer, 32-bit Integer	Increases bit rate to 24-bit and 32-bit, respectively.
32-bit Floating Point, 64-bit Floating Point	Increases bit rate to 32-bit and 64-bit, respectively. Note that current computer systems generally are only capable of playing back 16-bit sound.
Alaw 2:1	European standard compression scheme. Low quality, not recommended.
MACE 3:1, MACE 6:1	Old Macintosh standards. Low quality, high file size. Forget about using these codecs.
uLaw 2:1	Old Internet standard for Japan and North America. Low quality, high file size.

✦   ✦   ✦

Flash Interactivity: Making Things *Happen*

So far you've been learning how to make *things* — drawing shapes, creating symbols, working with frames, and adding sound. In the next three chapters, you're going to learn how to make things *happen*. If you can't wait to make buttons work, sounds play and stop, Web pages load, or animations really go, you've come to the right place. Start with Chapter 13, which introduces you to the concepts that you should know when adding interactivity to your movies. Chapter 13 also examines the fundamental Flash Actions (*Go to*, *Play*, *Stop*, and *Get URL*) and Event Handlers (button clicks and general mouse/button interaction, keypresses, and keyframes). Once you're ready to get your hands a bit more dirty, move on to Chapter 14, where we see how to use some more-involved Flash Actions, and show some practical examples of how to make them work. Then, to bring the interactivity in your movie to a higher level, visit Chapter 15, where we explore the brand-new world of ActionScript programming in Flash 4.

Understanding Basic Interactivity: Actions and Event Handlers

Interactivity in a Flash movie can broadly be thought of as the elements that react and respond to a user's activity or input. A user has many ways to give input to a Flash movie, and Flash has even more ways to react. But how does interactivity actually work? It all starts with Actions and Event Handlers.

Actions and Event Handlers

Even the most complex interactivity in Flash is fundamentally composed of two basic parts: 1) the behavior (what *happens*), and 2) the cause of the behavior (what makes it happen). Here's a simple example: Suppose you have a looping soundtrack in a movie and a button that, when clicked, turns the soundtrack off. The *behavior* is the sound turning off, and the *cause* of the behavior is the mouse clicking the button. In Flash, behaviors are referred to as *Actions*. The first step in learning how to make interactive movies is becoming familiar with the list of possible Actions. But Actions can't act without being told to act *by* something. That something is often the mouse coming in contact with a button, but it can also be a keystroke, or simply a command issued from a keyframe. We refer to any occurrence that can cause an Action to happen (such as the button click in the preceding example) as an *Event*. The

mechanism we use to tell Flash what Action
to perform when an Event occurs is known as an *Event Handler*.

This cause-and-effect relationship seems obvious, but it is an extremely important concept. For the purposes of creating basic interactivity, the difference between an Action and the cause of an Action is merely a practical detail. But with Flash 4's new programmatic Actions and the scripting capabilities they provide, understanding the relationship between Actions and the things that cause them can be the key to adding more sophisticated behavior to your movies with traditional-style programming techniques.

Don't worry, we're taking it one step at a time. First, let's take a look at some basic Actions (one of which is the Stop All Sounds Action referred to in the preceding example), and then let's see how to call those actions in various ways with three kinds of Event Handlers: button manipulation, keyframes, and keystrokes.

What Actions can do

Right, enough theory. Let's take a look at some Actions. Access the Instance Properties dialog box (Figure 13-1) by selecting a button on stage and choosing Modify ⇨ Instance (Command+I or Ctrl+I):

Figure 13-1: The Actions tab of the Instance Properties dialog box

Figure 13-1 shows all of the Flash Actions. Not too daunting a list, right? But a lot of possibilities are buried in there. If you used Flash 2 or 3, you should recognize many of the Actions, but you should also notice that some are new in Flash 4.

The actions are organized into semi-logical divisions according to the functions they can perform. The first two divisions, comprised of Go to, Play, and Stop, control the playback of the movie. The third division, which includes Toggle High Quality and Stop All Sounds, provides global tools for handling sounds and visual quality. The fourth division—Get URL, FS Command, and Load/Unload Movie—let movies load external files and communicate with the browser, a Web server, or the standalone player. The fifth division is effectively made up of Tell Target and If Frame Is Loaded. These two Actions afford, respectively, communication between Movie Clips and control over the display of movies as they are downloading.

Note   We omit OnMouseEvent from division five because it's not actually an Action—it's a list of Event Handlers for buttons. Now you see why we called the Action grouping semi-logical.

The remaining Action divisions primarily offer ActionScript programming capabilities.

Your First Six Actions

So, now that you have a general picture of what Actions do, let's look at the first six in detail (the remaining Actions are covered in Chapters 14 and 15). At this point, we're only describing the function of each Action, not how to add an Action to your movie. Information on adding an Action is covered in the next section, "Making Actions Happen with Event Handlers."

As they appear in the Flash interface, the Actions are coincidentally sorted from top to bottom roughly according to their complexity. Let's take it from the top.

Go to

The Go to Action changes the current frame of the movie to the target frame specified in the Go to settings. The Go to Action has two variations:

✦ **Go to and Stop:** Changes the current frame to the frame specified and then halts playback. Go to and Stop is often used to produce toolbar-style interfaces where the user clicks buttons to view different areas of content in a movie.

✦ **Go to and Play:** Changes the current frame to the frame specified, and then executes a Play Action. Like Go to and Stop, Go to and Play can be used to create toolbar interfaces, but would provide the capability to show animated intro sequences as preludes to individual content areas. Go to and Play also gets frequent use in choose-your-own-adventure style animations, where the user guides an animated character through different paths in a narrative. Note that Go to and Stop is the default type of Go to Action. To create a Go to and Play Action, you must first add a Go to Action, and then check the Go to and Play option of the Control setting.

Setting the target frame of Go to Actions

You have five methods of specifying the frame to which the movie should go when it receives a Go to Action. You set the method by selecting the appropriate Frame setting. Once you've chosen the method you're using to refer to your target frame, enter or select the frame's name or number under that setting's options (see Figure 13-2).

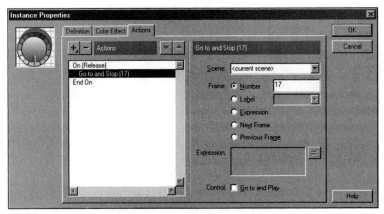

Figure 13-2: Setting the Go to Frame Number Action

The methods are as follows:

✦ **Number:** Specify the target frame as a number. Frame 1 is the beginning of the movie or scene. Number spans scenes, so if you have a movie with two scenes, each containing 25 frames, and you add a Go to Action with Frame Number set to 50, your Action advances the movie to the 25th frame of the second scene.

Using frame numbers to specify the targets of Go to Actions can lead to serious scalability problems in Flash movies. Adding frames at the beginning or in the middle of a movie's timeline causes the following frames to be renumbered. When those frames are renumbered, all Go to Frame Number Actions must be revised to point to the correct new number of their target frames.

In the vast majority of cases, Go to Actions that use Label to specify target frames are preferable to Go to Actions that use Number to specify target frames. Unlike numbered frame targets, Go to Actions with labeled frame targets continue to function properly even if the targeted frame changes position on the timeline.

✦ **Label:** Individual keyframes can be given names via the Label tab in the Frame Properties box. Once a frame is labeled, a Go to Action can target it by name. To specify a Label as the target of a Go to Action, select the Label option of the Frame setting. Then either type the name of the frame into the Label text field, or select it from the automatically generated list of frame Labels in the Label drop-down menu as seen in Figure 13-3.

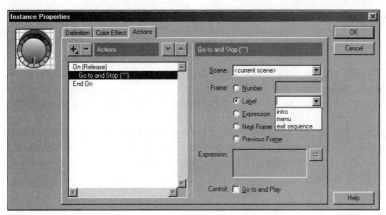

Figure 13-3: Setting the Go to Frame Label Action

Note The automatically generated list of Labels that appears in the Label drop-down can include Labels from other scenes, but cannot include Labels inside Movie Clips. To target a Label in a Movie Clip, you have to embed the Go to Action in a Tell Target Action and type the Label in manually. For more info, see Chapter 14.

✦ **Expression:** Specify the target frame as an interpreted ActionScript code segment. Used to dynamically assign targets of Go to Actions.

✦ **Next Frame:** Specify the target frame as the frame after the current frame. Next Frame can be used in conjunction with previous frame to quickly set up a slide-show-style walkthrough of content, where each of a series of contiguous keyframes contains the content of one "slide."

✦ **Previous Frame:** Specify the target frame as the frame before the current frame.

✦ **Scene:** You can specify frames in other scenes as the target of a Go to Action with the Scene drop-down. In the Scene drop-down, you can find a list of all the scenes in your movie, as well as built-in references to <current scene>, <next scene>, and <previous scene>. The Scene drop-down can be used together with the Number, Label, and Expression settings to target a frame in any Scene in a movie.

Play

This simple action is one of the true foundations of Flash. Play sets a movie or a movie Clip in motion. When a Play Action is executed, Flash starts the sequential display of each frame's contents along the current timeline. The rate at which the frames are displayed is measured as Frames Per Second, or FPS. The FPS rate can be set from 0.01 to 120 (meaning that the Play Action can cause the display of as little as 1 frame every hundred seconds to as many as 120 frames in a single second, subject to the limitations of the computer's processing speed). The default FPS is 12. Once Play has started, frames continue to be displayed one after the other, until another Action interrupts the flow or the end of the movie or Movie Clip's timeline is reached. If the end of a movie's timeline is reached, the movie either loops (begins playing again at frame 1, scene 1), or stops on the last frame. (Whether a movie loops or not depends on the Publish settings described in Chapter 22.) If the end of a Movie Clip's timeline is reached, playback loops back to the beginning of the clip, and clip continues playing (to prevent looping, add a Stop Action to the last frame of your Movie Clip).

Note   A single Play Action affects only a single timeline, whether that timeline is the main movie timeline or the timeline of a placed Movie Clip. For example, a Play Action executed inside a Movie Clip does not cause the main movie timeline to begin playing.

Stop

Stop, you guessed it, halts the progression of a movie or movie clip that is in a play state. Stop is often used with buttons for user-controlled playback of a movie, or on frames to end an animated sequence.

Tip   Movie Clip instances placed on timelines begin playing automatically. It's important to remember to add a Stop Action on the first frame of a Movie Clip if you don't want it to play right away.

Toggle High Quality

Here's a straightforward Action that changes Flash's visual-rendering-quality setting to High if it is currently set at Low and to Low if it is currently set at High. In High Quality mode, the edges of lines and text appear smooth because they are antialiased (or blurred slightly between shifts in color). In Low Quality mode, the edges of lines and text appear choppy because they are not antialiased. Low Quality is occasionally set on movies that are played back on slower computers because it causes animation to play back more quickly. See the difference in Figure 13-4.

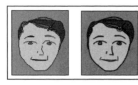

Figure 13-4: High Quality versus Low Quality

Tip   The Toggle High Quality Action is most frequently used to set the Quality of standalone Flash movies. (On the Web, the quality of a movie can be set with HTML attributes.) If the Quality is not explicitly set to High, it defaults to an automatic mode where the Quality shifts between High and Low depending on how demanding each frame of the movie is on the computer. The effect is rather jarring, so most designers avoid it by simply choosing the often slower, but more attractive High Quality.

Stop all sounds

A simple but powerful Action that mutes any sounds playing in the movie at the time the Action is executed. Note that Stop All Sounds does not disable sounds permanently, it simply cancels any sounds that happen to be currently playing. It is sometimes used as a quick and dirty method of making buttons that shut off background looping soundtracks. Stop All Sounds is not appropriate for controlling whether multiple sounds are played or muted. For information on more accurate control over sounds, please see Part III.

Get URL

Want to link to a Web page from a Flash movie? No problem. That's what Get URL is for. Get URL is simply Flash's method of making a conventional hypertext link (it's nearly exactly the equivalent of an Anchor tag in HTML, except that it also allows for form submission). Get URL can be used to link to a standard Web page, an ftp site, another Flash movie, an executable, a CGI script, or anything that exists on the Internet or on an accessible local file system. Get URL has three settings that are familiar to Web builders (the first setting, URL, is required for this Action to work):

✦ **URL:** This is the network address of the page, file, script, or resource to which you are linking. Any value is permitted (including ActionScript expressions), but of course, the linked item can only be displayed if the reference to it is correct. URL is directly analogous to the HREF attribute of an HTML Anchor tag. Examples:

```
http://www.yoursite.com/
ftp://ftp.yoursite.com/pub/documents.zip
```

New Feature

Get URL can now link to documents on the Web from the standalone Flash player. Execution of a Get URL action in the standalone player causes an external Web browser to launch and load the requested URL (see Figure 13-5).

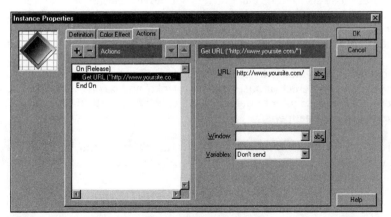

Figure 13-5: Setting the URL of a Get URL Action

✦ **Window:** This is the name of the frame or window in which you wish to load the resource specified in the URL setting. Window is directly analogous to the TARGET attribute of an HTML Anchor tag. In addition to enabling the entry of custom frame and window names, Window provides four presets in a drop-down menu:

- **_self:** Loads the URL into the same frame or window as the current movie.

- **_blank:** Creates a new browser window and loads the URL into it.

- **_parent:** Removes the current frameset and loads the URL in its place. Use this option if you have multiple nested framesets, and you want your linked URL to replace only the frameset in which your movie resides.

- **_top:** Loads the URL into the current browser and removes all framesets in the process. Use this option if your movie is in a frame, but you want your linked URL to be loaded normally into the browser, outside the confines of any frames.

✦ **Variables:** This option enables Get URL to function like an HTML form submission. For normal links, the Variables setting should be left at its default value, Don't Send. But in order to submit values to a server-side script, one of the submission methods (Send Using GET or Send Using POST) must be selected. For a complete tutorial on using Get URL to submit data to a server, see "Submitting Values to CGI Scripts" in Chapter 15.

Note   Get URL does not function in the Test Movie environment. To see your Get URL links work, you have to view your movie in a browser or in the standalone Flash player (Flash 4 only).

Making Actions Happen with Event Handlers

The first six Actions — Go to, Play, Stop, Toggle High Quality, Stop All Sounds, and Get URL — provide all the behaviors you need to make an interesting interactive Flash movie. But those six Actions can't make your movies interactive on their own. They need to be told when to happen. To tell Flash when an Action should occur, you need Event Handlers. Event Handlers specify the condition(s) under which an Action can be made to happen. For instance, you might want to mouse-click a button to initiate a Play Action, or you might want a movie to stop when a certain frame in the timeline is reached. Creating interactivity in your movies is simply a matter of deciding what event you want to detect (mouse click, keystroke, and so on), and then adding the appropriate Event Handler to detect it, and specifying the Action(s) that should be performed when it happens.

Before we describe each individual Event Handler in detail, let's see an example of exactly how an Event Handler merges with an Action to form a functioning interactive button.

Combining an Action with an Event Handler to make a functioning button

Imagine you have a short, endlessly looping movie in which a square spins. Now imagine that you want to add a button to your movie that, when clicked, stops the square from spinning by stopping the playback of the looping movie. Here's what you need to do:

1. Make a new Layer.

2. Place a button on the new Layer. (You could use Flash 4's sample VCR stop button found in Libraries ⇨ Buttons.)

3. Bring up the Instance Properties dialog box for the button by selecting it on stage and choosing Modify ⇨ Instance (Command+I or Ctrl+I).

Tip   Selecting buttons and editing button properties can be sometimes be tricky if buttons are enabled in the Flash authoring environment. For easier button manipulation, disable buttons by unchecking Enable Buttons under the Control menu. Once disabled, you can double-click a button to view its properties.

4. Select the Actions tab.

5. Click the button with the plus sign (+) on it in the top-left corner of the Actions tab. A list of all the actions appears.

6. Select OnMouseEvent. A list of settings for OnMouseEvent appears on the right side of the Actions tab. This list contains all the Event Handlers for buttons.

7. Select the Release option of the Event setting. The Release Event Handler is one of two kinds of mouse-click Handlers (the other is Press; both are described later). Once you have checked Release, you should notice that the Actions listbox has been updated to show the Event Handler you've selected. You've now told Flash that you want something to happen when the mouse clicks the button. All that's left is to tell it what should happen. In other words, you need to add an Action as seen in Figure 13-6.

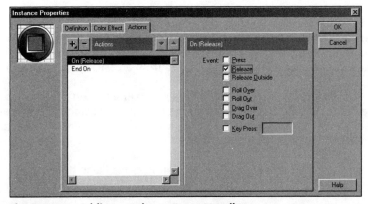

Figure 13-6: Adding a Release Event Handler

8. With the words On (Release) highlighted in the Actions listbox, click the plus (+) button in the top-left corner of the Actions tab.

9. Select Stop. A Stop Action can be placed between the words On (Release) and End On. The Actions listbox should now read as follows:

```
On (Release)
        Stop
End On
```

The Stop Action (represented by the word Stop) is contained by the words On and End On, which mark the beginning and end of the list of Actions that are executed when the Release Event occurs (there could be any number of Actions).

10. Click OK.

Tip

In this example we selected the Event Handler before adding our Action. This helped illustrate the individual role that each of those components plays. During real production, however, you may simply add any Action without first specifying an Event Handler—Flash automatically adds a Release Event Handler to Actions that are added to buttons.

We now have a button in our imaginary movie that stops the movie's playback when it is clicked. To make any interactivity in your movies, you simply have to apply the basic principles we used to make the stop button: decide which Action (or Actions) you want to happen, and then indicate when you want that Action to happen with an Event Handler. In the first part of this chapter, we explored six Actions. Let's look now at the list of Event Handlers you can use to make those Actions happen.

The Flash Event Handlers

Three kinds of Event Handlers exist in Flash. Those that detect mouse activity on buttons (Button Manipulation), those that recognize when a key is pressed on the keyboard (keystrokes), and those that respond to the progression of the timeline (keyframes).

Button manipulation

Event Handlers that occur based on the user's interaction with a button rely entirely on the location and movement of the mouse pointer. If the mouse pointer comes in contact with a button's Hit area, it changes from an arrow to a hand symbol (See Chapter 7 for information on Hit areas). At that time the mouse is described as "over" the button. If the mouse pointer is not over a button, it is said to be *out* or *outside* of the button. General movement of the mouse *without* the mouse button depressed is referred to as *rolling*. General movement of the mouse *with* the mouse button depressed is referred to as *dragging*.

The following are the mouse-based Event Handlers for Flash buttons.

Event Handlers and Actions on buttons must be placed only on button instances on the stage, not on the four frames in the timeline of the original button symbol. Though the Actions tab is available in the Frame Properties dialog box of button frames, Actions placed on those frames are ignored.

Press

A single mouse click can actually be divided into two separate components: the down-stroke (the *press*) and the up-stroke (the *release*). A Press Event occurs when the mouse pointer is over the Hit area of a button *and* the down-stroke of a mouse click is detected. Press is best used for control-panel style buttons, especially toggle switches. Press is not recommended for important user moves (such as irreversible decisions or primary navigation) because it does not give the user any opportunity to abort their move.

Release

A Release Event occurs when the mouse pointer is over the Hit area of a button *and* both the down-stroke and the up-stroke of a mouse click are detected. Release is the standard button click Event Handler.

Release Outside

A Release Outside Event occurs in response to the following series of mouse movements: the mouse pointer moves over a button's Hit area; the mouse button is pressed; the mouse pointer is moved off the button's Hit area; the mouse button is released. Release Outside can be used to react to an aborted button click.

Roll Over

A Roll Over Event occurs when the mouse pointer moves onto the Hit area of a button without the mouse button depressed.

The Roll Over Event Handler should not be used to make visual changes to a button (such as making it appear "active" with a glow or size increase). Flash has a built-in method of handling strictly visual changes on buttons that is described in Chapter 7. The Roll Over Event Handler should only be used to initiate Actions. For a practical example of when to use the Roll Over Event Handler, please see Chapter 14.

Roll Out

A Roll Out Event occurs when the mouse pointer moves off of the Hit area of a button without the mouse button depressed.

Drag Over

A Drag Over Event occurs in response to the following series of mouse movements: The mouse button is pressed while the mouse pointer is over the Hit area of a button; the mouse pointer moves off the Hit area (mouse button still depressed); and the mouse pointer moves back over the Hit area (mouse button still depressed). Drag Over is rather obscure, but could be used for special cases of interactivity such as revealing an Easter egg in a game.

Drag Out

A Drag Out Event occurs in response to the following series of mouse movements: the mouse button is pressed while the mouse pointer is over the Hit area of a button; the mouse pointer moves off the Hit area (mouse button still depressed).

Keystrokes

The keystroke Event Handler lets you execute an Action when the user presses a key on their keyboard. The implementation method for keystroke Event Handlers is potentially confusing: To add a keystroke Event Handler, you must first place a button onstage at the frame where you want the keyboard to be active. You then attach the keystroke Event Handler to the button.

Tip   If you are only using the button as a container for your keystroke Event Handler and you do not want the button to appear on stage, you should make sure that (in Symbol editing mode) all the frames of the button are blank.

The keystroke Event Handler, which is new to Flash 4, opens up many new possibilities for Flash. Movies can now have keyboard-based navigation, buttons can have keyboard shortcuts for convenience and accessibility, and games can have keyboard-controlled objects (such as ships and animated characters). But watch out for some potential "gotchas" to keyboard usage. If you're planning on ambitious keyboard-based projects, you may want to check this list of potential issues first:

✦ The Esc key does not work as a keystroke.

✦ Multiple key combinations are not supported. This rules out diagonals as two-key combinations in the classic four-key game control setup. It also means shortcuts such as Ctrl+S are not available. Uppercase is functional, however.

✦ If presented in a browser, the Flash movie must have "focus" before keystrokes can be recognized. To "focus" the movie, the user must click anywhere in the space it occupies. Keyboard-based movies should include instructions that prompt the user to perform this initial mouse click.

Note   Keystrokes cannot function until the user has clicked at least once somewhere in the Flash movie.

✦ Because the Enter, less than (<), and greater than (>) keys are used as authoring shortcuts in the Test Movie environment, you may want to avoid using them as control keys in your movies. If you need to use those keys in your movies, make sure to test in a browser.

✦ Keystroke events are case sensitive. For example, an UPPERCASE letter "S" and a lowercase letter "s" could trigger two different Actions. No case-insensitive keystroke Event Handler exists (one that would enable both cases of a letter to trigger the same Action). Achieving case-insensitivity would require duplication of Event Handler and Action statements.

Keyframes

The keyframe Event Handler depends not on the user, but on the playback of the movie itself. Any action can be attached to any keyframe on the timeline. An Action attached to a keyframe is executed when the playhead enters the keyframe, whether it enters naturally during the linear playback of the movie or as the result of a Go to Action. So, for instance, you may place a Stop Action on a keyframe to pause the movie at the end of an animation sequence.

In some multimedia applications, keyframe Event Handlers could differentiate between the playhead *entering* a keyframe and *exiting* a keyframe. Flash has only one kind of keyframe Event Handler (essentially, On Enter). Hence, as an author, you do not need to add keyframe Event Handlers explicitly — they are a presumed component of any Action placed on a keyframe.

Tip

Complex movies can have dozens, or even hundreds of Actions attached to keyframes. In order to prevent conflicts between uses of keyframes for animation and uses of keyframes as Action containers, it is highly advisable to create an entire Layer solely for Action keyframes. Name the Layer **Actions** and keep it on top of all your Layers for easy access. Remember not to place any objects, text, or artwork on your Actions Layer.

✦　　✦　　✦

Gaining Advanced Control Over Your Movies

One of the most powerful additions to Flash 3 was the Movie Clip symbol. Movie Clips enabled Flash developers to create complex behaviors by nesting self-contained sequences of animation or interactivity inside each other. These sequences could then be placed as discreet, self-playing modules on the main timeline. The key to the power of Movie Clips was their ability to communicate with and control each other via the Tell Target Action.

Controlling Movie Clips with Tell Target

In Flash 4, the role of Movie Clips has been expanded: They are now also used with ActionScript. Now more than ever, Movie Clips are the foundation of advanced interactivity in Flash.

Movie Clips reviewed

Previous to this chapter, Flash movies have been dealt with as a single sequence of frames arranged along a single timeline. Whether the playback along that timeline was linear (traditional animation) or nonlinear (where the playhead jumps arbitrarily to any frame), so far our example movies have normally comprised only the frames of a single timeline. Ostensibly, a single timeline may seem to provide everything you'd need to create any Flash behavior, but as you get more inventive or ambitious, you'll soon find yourself conceiving ideas for animated and interactive segments that will be thwarted by the limits of a single timeline.

Suppose you want to create a looping animation of a character's face. You decide the character's eyes should blink every two seconds, and the character's mouth should yawn every 15 seconds. On a single timeline, you'd have to have a loop of 180 frames for the mouth (assuming a frame rate of 12 frames per second), and repeating keyframes for the closed eye artwork every 24 frames. Though creating your face in that manner would be a bit cumbersome, it wouldn't be impossible — until your character's face had to move around the screen as an integrated whole. Making the mouth and eyes loop while the whole face moved around complex paths for extended periods of time would quickly become impractical, especially if the face were only one part of a larger environment.

Now imagine that you could make your character's face by creating two whole separate movies, one for the eyes and one for the mouth. Could you then place those movies as self-contained animating objects on the timeline of your main movie, just like a graphic or a button. Well, you can — that's what Movie Clips are all about. Movie Clips are independent sequences of frames (timelines) that can be defined outside the context of the main movie timeline and then placed onto it as objects on a single frame. You create Movie Clips the same way you create a Graphic symbol (in the Edit Symbol environment), but, unlike a Graphic symbol, a Movie Clip (as the name implies) acts in most cases just like a full-fledged SWF file, meaning, for instance, that Frame Actions in Movie Clip timelines are functional. Once you have created a Movie Clip as a symbol, you drop instances of it onto the main movie stage or onto any other Movie Clip stage.

During playback, a Movie Clip instance placed on a timeline begins to play as soon as the frame on which it occurs is reached, whether or not the main movie is playing. A Movie Clip plays back autonomously, meaning that as long as it is present on stage it is not governed by the playing or stopping of the main timeline. Movie Clips can play when the main timeline is stopped, or stay halted when the main timeline plays. And like a graphic or a button symbol, Movie Clips can be manipulated on the stage — you can size them, skew them, rotate them, place effects like Alpha blending on them, or Tween them, all while the animation within them continues to play. In our character face example, the animated eyes and mouth could be looping Movie Clips, and then those movie clips could be grouped and Tweened around the stage on the main timeline to make the whole face move. The same principle could be used to move a Movie Clip of a butterfly with flapping wings along a motion path.

Tell Target explained

If you already studied Movie Clips in Chapter 7, you probably know that they provide the solution to our animated face problem. But you might not have guessed that Movie Clips can add also add logic to animation and Flash interfaces. Let's take our animated face example a little further: When people yawn, they generally close their eyes for as long as they are yawning. Our hypothetical character's face may look strange if it is blinking and yawning at the same time. Suppose we wanted to make our character's eyes stay closed during every yawn. We'd have to have some way for the mouth Movie Clip to control the eyes Movie Clip so we could tell the eyes to go to a "shut" frame when the mouth opens, and then tell them to return to their blink loop again when the mouth closes. Well, we do have a way to control the eyes Movie Clip from the mouth Movie Clip. It's called Tell Target. Tell Target lets Actions on any timeline (including Movie Clip timelines and the main movie timeline) control what happens on any other timeline. How? Tell Target simply provides a mechanism for extending Actions, enabling them to specify the timeline upon which they should be executed.

We're going to let Colin Moock explain the nuts and bolts of it by showing how he uses Tell Target and Movie Clips with GWEN!, the star of his online animated series by the same name. (If you want to see more of GWEN! after you've finished the tutorial, you can visit www.moock.org/gwen/).

To do this tutorial, you'll need the gwen.fla file in the ch14 folder on the *Flash 4 Bible* CD-ROM. If you want to see the finished product, open gwen-finished.fla located in the same folder.

Expert Tutorial:
Making GWEN!'s Eyes Shut When She Yawns
by Colin Moock

GWEN! was born as a Flash 2 animation. In Episode One, she didn't blink much, or yawn at all. By the time Episode Two was nearly finished, Flash 3 had hit the streets, and oh, the joy to GWEN! when she discovered Movie Clips and Tell Target. Now, after much convincing, GWEN! has agreed to be dismantled a little so you can see how her eyes and mouth work. We're going to show you how to put her back together in this tutorial. Don't worry, GWEN!, this won't hurt a bit.

Begin by opening gwen.fla (it's in the ch14 folder on the *Flash 4 Bible* CD-ROM). Open the library for gwen.fla by choosing Window ➪ Library. In the library you'll see five objects and one folder: gwen's face, gwen's eyes, gwen's eyes shut, gwen's mouth, gwen's mouth open and the folder face artwork. Drag a copy of the gwen's face graphic symbol from the library onto the stage.

Continued

(continued)

Next we're going to make a Movie Clip with GWEN!'s eyes blinking. Make a new Movie Clip by choosing Insert ⇨ New Symbol. In the Symbol Properties dialog box, enter the name **eyes** and make sure to select the Movie Clip option of the Behavior setting. Click OK.

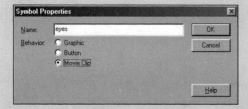

When you create a new Movie Clip symbol, you are automatically taken into the Symbol Editing mode where you work on your Movie Clip. Rename Layer 1 to **Eyes Blinking**. Click Frame 24 of the Eyes Blinking layer, and then select Insert ⇨ Frame. While still on Frame 24, select Insert ⇨ Blank Keyframe.

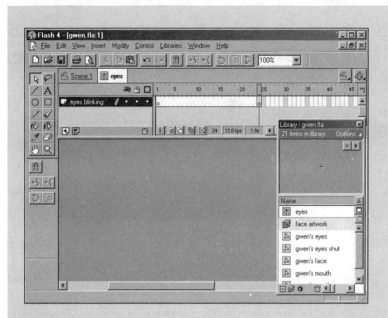

Click Frame 1 and drag the symbol gwen's eyes onto the stage. Make sure gwen's eyes is still selected, and then choose Modify ➪ Align. Center the symbol on the stage by clicking the third button of the Vertical and Horizontal Align settings, then checking the Align to Page check box, and clicking OK.

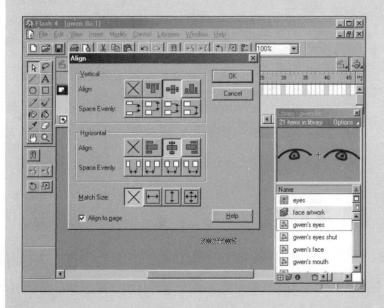

Continued

(continued)

Click Frame 24 and drag the symbol gwen's eyes shut onto the stage. Center the symbol on stage as you did in the previous step.

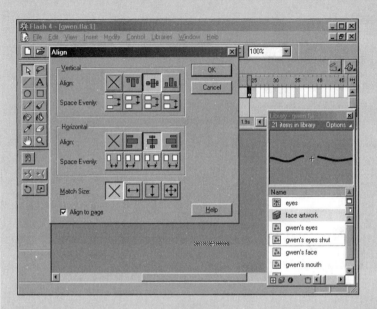

Next we need to label our "eyes shut" frame so we can move to it whenever GWEN!'s mouth opens. Add a new layer by choosing Insert ⇨ Layer. Name the new layer **Labels**. Labels should always be kept on their own layer. Click Frame 24 of the Labels layer, and then select Insert ⇨ Blank Keyframe. Choose Modify ⇨ Frame (or double-click the Frame), and then select the Label tab of the Frame Properties dialog box. In the Name text field, type **shut**. Make sure the Behavior setting is set to Label (it is by default), and then click OK.

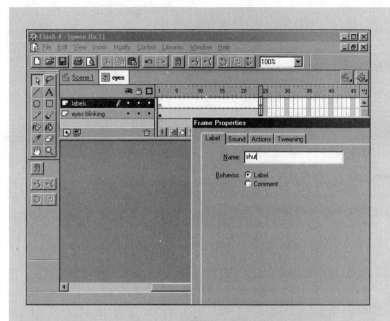

We're done with the eyes, so let's make the mouth. Make a new Movie Clip by choosing Insert ➪ New Symbol. In the Symbol Properties dialog box, enter the name **mouth** and select the Movie Clip option of the Behavior setting. Click OK.

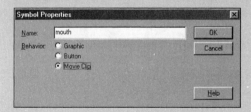

As with the eyes, you are automatically taken into Symbol Edit mode for your new Movie Clip. Rename Layer 1 to **Mouth Yawning**. Click Frame 180 of the Mouth Yawning layer, and then select Insert ➪ Frame. Click Frame 160 and select Insert ➪ Blank Keyframe.

Continued

(continued)

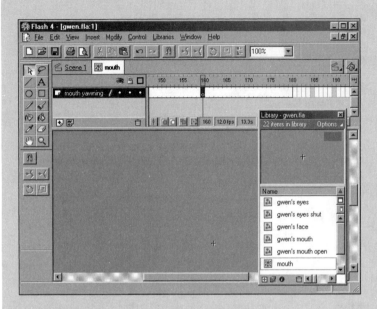

Click Frame 1 and drag the symbol gwen's mouth onto the stage. Make sure gwen's mouth is still selected, and then choose Modify ⇨ Align. Center the symbol on the stage by clicking the third button of the Vertical and Horizontal Align settings, checking the Align to Page check box, and then clicking OK.

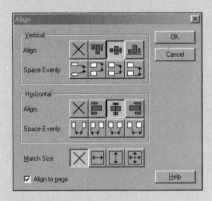

Click Frame 160 and drag the symbol gwen's mouth open onto the stage. Center the symbol on stage as you did in the previous step.

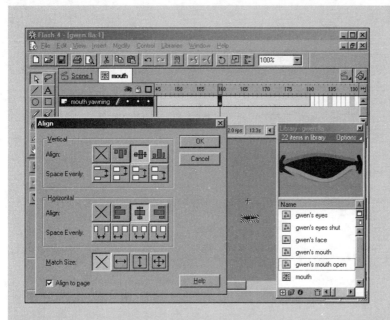

It's time to place our eyes and mouth onto GWEN!'s face. Return to the main stage by choosing Edit ⇨ Edit Movie (Ctrl+E or Command+E). Drag the newly created Movie Clip symbols, eyes and mouth, out of the library onto GWEN!'s face.

Continued

(continued)

At this point, you've got a fairly functional animated girl. If you test your movie now, you'll see that GWEN!'s eyes blink, and her mouth opens for her yawn, but we still have to add the advanced interactivity that lets the mouth tell the eyes when to shut and reopen. To do that, we first have to name the instance of the eyes Movie Clip you created and dragged onto the stage so the mouth Movie Clip instance can identify it. Then we have to add the Tell Target Actions which control the eyes. Hang on GWEN!, we're almost there!

Select the eyes Movie Clip on stage, and then choose Modify ⇨ Instance. The Instance Properties dialog box appears with the Definition tab selected. Under Instance Options, you'll see a text field next to Instance Name. That text field is where we give our embedded Movie Clip instance a unique identification. Instance names are something like serial numbers: they enable Actions in the movie to address a specific copy of a Movie Clip. Type **her-eyes** in the Instance Name text field (without the quotes), and then click OK.

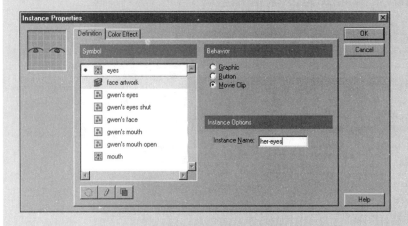

Remember that, like any symbol, a Movie Clip that is placed on stage is only a replica of the symbol in the Library. That's why you name the symbol Instance on stage, rather than simply referring to the symbol by name in the Library. You could place multiple copies of GWEN!'s eyes on the stage and give them all different names so that each could be individually controlled and manipulated without any effect on the others. With eyes, the results can be a little trippy . . . take a look at Episode Two of GWEN! at www.moock.org/gwen/.

Now that the eyes Movie Clip Instance is named her-eyes, we can return to the mouth to add the Tell Targets that control the her-eyes instance. Deselect all selections by clicking a blank area of the stage, and then select only the mouth symbol. Choose Edit ⇨ Edit Selected to resume work on the mouth Movie Clip. Add a new layer by choosing Insert ⇨ Layer. Name the new layer **Actions**. Actions should always be kept on their own layer.

Click Frame 160 of the Actions layer, and then select Insert ⇨ Blank Keyframe. Choose Modify ⇨ Frame (or double-click the Frame), and then select the Actions tab of the Frame Properties dialog box. Click the plus (+) button and select Tell Target. In the Target text field type **/her-eyes**. Now every Action we add between the Begin Tell Target and the End Tell Target lines in the Actions listbox is applied to the Movie Clip instance named her-eyes on the main movie timeline. We're now ready to add the Action that controls the playback of the eyes Movie Clip.

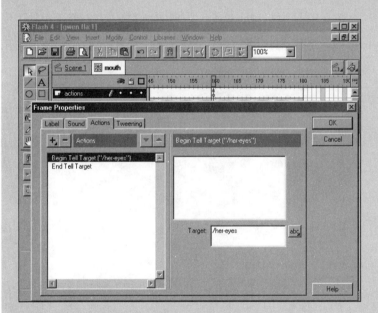

Note on identifying instances with Tell Target

From inside a Tell Target Action, references to Movie Clip instance names work just like references to a directory structure. To refer to a Movie Clip instance named clip1 on the current timeline, you would simply enter **clip1** as the Target. But to refer to clip1 if it was placed inside another Movie Clip instance on the current timeline that was named logo-spin, you'd enter **logo-spin/clip1** as the Target. And to refer to clip1 if it resided one timeline above the current timeline (for example, on the main timeline if the current timeline is a Movie Clip), you'd enter **../clip1**. To target the main movie timeline you enter **/** as the Target.

Continued

(continued)

All Movie Clip instance names may also be referred to relative to the main movie timeline. To target Movie Clip instances in relation to the root or main movie timeline, compose your Target in the following way: start with a /, meaning the main movie timeline, and then add the name of the Movie Clip instance you want to target, for example, /clip1. If your target is embedded inside clip1, enter another / and then its name (for example, /clip1/clip2); repeat until you reach your Movie Clip. It may be helpful to think of the main movie timeline as the root of a tree and embedded Movie Clip timelines as the branches. To reach any end branch, you have to describe the complete route you would take to get there if you started at the root of the tree.

With the words Begin Tell Target ("/her-eyes") highlighted in the Actions listbox, click the plus (+) button and select Go to. Select the Label option of the Frame setting, and type **shut** in the Label text field. This makes the eyes Movie Clip instance playhead move to the shut frame and stay there until told otherwise.

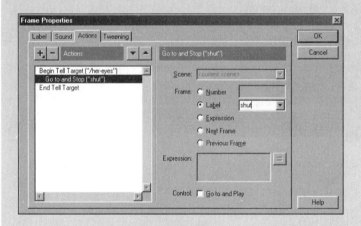

The Actions listbox should now read as follows:

```
Begin Tell Target ("/her-eyes")
    Go to and Stop ("shut")
End Tell Target
```

Click OK.

Click Frame 180 of the Actions layer, and then select Insert ➪ Blank Keyframe. Choose Modify ➪ Frame (or double-click the Frame), and then select the Actions tab of the Frame Properties dialog box. Click the plus (+) button and select Tell Target. In the Target text field type **/her-eyes**. With the words Begin Tell Target ("/her-eyes") highlighted in the Actions listbox, click the plus (+) button and select Play. This will make the eyes resume their two-second blink loop. Click OK.

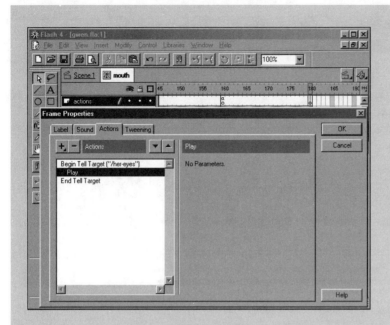

That's it. You should now be able see GWEN!'s eyes close when she yawns by testing your movie with File ➪ Publish Preview ➪ Flash (Ctrl+Enter or Command+Enter). If things aren't working perfectly, compare your work closely with the finished version of GWEN!, called gwen-finished.fla, in the ch14 folder of the *Flash 4 Bible* CD-ROM.

A final hint: Tell Targets can be a little finicky — always be sure to check your target names and instance names to be sure they match, are in the correct location, and are referred to correctly. You may have to make a few mistakes at first, but it's not long before you'll know where to look to find the cause of the most common problems. Oh, and if you want to play with GWEN! some more, visit her at www.moock.org/gwen/. She's kind of snooty, but you never know . . . she might pay more attention to you now that you've seen how she works. Don't forget to pinch her cheeks.

Using Tell Target and Movie Clips with interfaces

GWEN! shows you an example of using Tell Target to create enhanced animation. ut the same technique can also be used to produce interfaces. Interface-based Tell Targets are often implemented on buttons. Just as you used Tell Targets with Actions on keyframes in Colin's tutorial, so can you also use Tell Targets with Actions on buttons. While working at ICE during the spring of 1999, Colin produced much of the interactive component of McClelland & Stewart's *The Canadian Encyclopedia 1999* CD-ROM in Flash. Most of the interactive pieces used Movie Clips and Tell Targets extensively. A simple but good example of using Tell Targets to enhance an interface comes from the Painting Retrospective in the encyclopedia as seen in Figure 14-1.

Figure 14-1: The Painting Retrospective, from McClelland & Stewart's *The Canadian Encyclopedia 1999*

Figure 14-1 depicts the Painting Retrospective in action. Painting thumbnails are shown on a carousel which the user moves around by clicking the right and left arrows. Below the carousel is a status window that displays the painting title, date, and artist when the user rolls their mouse over a painting. The status window is a Movie Clip that has one frame for each of the painting descriptions. The painting thumbnails in the carousel are all buttons. When the user points to a painting, the button's Roll Over Event Handler initiates a Tell Target Action that makes the status window Movie Clip Go to the frame that contains the appropriate painting description. Even when the paintings are moved along the carousel, the status window stays put because it's a separate Movie Clip, not a part of the thumbnail buttons.

How Movie Clips can add logic to a movie

A not so obvious yet significant aspect to Movie Clips is that they do not need to have any content in them. They can be used solely as empty devices that instigate interactive behavior. A Movie Clip can be just a string of empty frames with only

Labels and Actions. Tell Targets from other timelines can move the playhead of empty Movie Clips in order to achieve basic levels of memory and logic in a Flash movie. We refer to these empty Movie Clips as *Logical Movie Clips*. One example of how you can create interactivity with a Logical Movie Clip is keeping score in a simple game.

Suppose you have a movie consisting of three true-or-false questions with a true button and a false button for each question. The user answers each question by clicking one or the other button. You also have a Logical Movie Clip with four keyframes. The first frame has a stop action on it. The last frame has a Tell Target Action on it that tells the main movie timeline to go to a keyframe that has a congratulations message. Finally, all the "correct" answer buttons have Tell Target Actions that tell the Logical Movie Clip to Go to Next Frame. Here's what happens when the user plays and gets all the questions right: question one, the user clicks the correct button, and the Logical Movie Clip moves to frame 2; question two, the user clicks the correct button, and the Logical Movie Clip moves to frame 3 and so on. When the user gets to frame 4, the last frame of the Logical Movie Clip, it tells the main movie timeline to go to the congratulations frame, which says "Congratulations, you got a perfect score!" So what happens if the user gets a question wrong? Well, when the user gets any of the questions wrong, the Logical Movie Clip does not advance, so by the end of the game, the playhead will never reach frame 4, and the Tell Target Action which causes the congratulations message to be displayed will not executed.

Tricks such as the score keeper were common tools for Flash 3 developers. Using Logical Movie Clips, inventive developers produced impressive results: even a primitive version of Pac Man exists as a Flash 3 movie (see `www.spookyandthebandit.com/` for the game and to download the free .FLA file). However, now that Flash 4 supports variables and scriptable Movie Clip properties, those kinds of Movie Clip uses are less important. But conceptually, it's useful to understand that Movie Clips can serve as more than just devices for embedded animation. They can also serve as containers for meta-information stored in movies.

Drag'n'Drop in Flash

A new feature in Flash 4 is drag'n'drop, which enables the user to pick up objects with the mouse pointer and move them around the movie stage. Drag'n'drop in Flash is based entirely on Movie Clips. The only objects that can be moved with the mouse are Movie Clip instances. So if you want a drawing of a triangle to be moveable by the user, you have to first put that triangle into a Movie Clip, and then place a named instance of that clip onto the stage. Flash's drag'n'drop support is fairly broad, but more-complicated drag'n'drop behaviors require a little ActionScript knowledge. We'll cover building drag'n'drop Movie Clips in two parts: "Drag'n'Drop Basics" and "Advanced Drag'n'Drop."

Drag'n'drop basics

In mouse-based computer interfaces, the most common form of drag'n'drop goes like this: A user points to an object with the mouse pointer, clicks the object to begin moving it, and then releases the mouse button to stop moving it. Because drag'n'drop in Flash only works with Movie Clips and because buttons are the only objects that can respond to mouse clicks, this common form of drag'n'drop in Flash is produced by embedding a button in a Movie Clip and then attaching a Drag Movie Clip Action to that button. Here's how:

1. Start a new movie. Create a new Movie Clip named **drag object**.

2. Create a simple button and place it on Frame 1, Layer 1 of the drag object Movie Clip.

3. Return to the main stage by choosing Edit ➪ Edit Movie (Ctrl+E or Command+E). Place a copy of the drag object Movie Clip on stage and, with it still selected, choose Modify ➪ Instance. On the Definition tab under Instance Options, type **drag-me** in the Instance Name text field (without the quotes), and then click OK. This names our Movie Clip Instance so it can be referred to in the Drag Movie Clip Action.

4. Return to the drag object Movie Clip stage by choosing Edit ➪ Edit Movie (Ctrl+E or Command+E). Bring up the Instance Properties dialog box for the button you placed on the stage by selecting it and choosing Modify ➪ Instance (Command+I or Ctrl+I).

5. Click the plus (+) button in the top-left corner of the Actions tab and select Drag Movie Clip. Make sure the Start Drag Operation radio button is selected, and then type **/drag-me** in the Target text field. The Target option specifies which Movie Clip should begin dragging when the Drag Movie Clip Action is executed. Note that though our Drag Movie Clip action will be applied to the same Movie Clip that houses our button, a Drag Movie Clip Action can refer to any Movie Clip from any button, or even from any keyframe.

6. Now remember that we want to make our Movie Clip start moving as soon as the user depresses the mouse button. So change the button's Event Handler from On (Release) to On (Press) by selecting the On (Release) line in the Actions listbox, and then unchecking the Release option of the Event setting and checking Press.

7. So far our button, when clicked, will cause the drag-me Movie Clip Instance to start following the mouse pointer. Now we have to tell the Movie Clip to stop following the pointer when the mouse button is released. With the words End On highlighted in the Actions listbox, click the plus (+) button and select Drag Movie Clip. Then select the Stop Drag Operation radial button. The default Event Handler added is On (Release), which is what we want, so that's all we have to do. The Stop Drag Operation Action stops any current dragging Movie Clip from following the mouse pointer. Because only one Movie Clip can be dragged at a time, it's not necessary to specify a Target as we did with Start Drag Operation. Click OK to finish.

Caution It is possible to use a button that is not contained in the draggable Movie Clip to stop the dragging Action. If you use a button like that, remember that when your only Event Handler is On (Release) your Action will not be executed if the mouse button is released when it is no longer over the button (which is likely to happen when the user is dragging things around). You should also add an On (Release Outside) event handler to capture all Release events.

8. Test your movie with File ⇨ Publish Preview ⇨ Flash (Ctrl+Enter or Command+Enter).

So it worked? Great, now we can tell you about the other basic settings for Drag Movie Clip.

Constrain to rectangle

Check this setting in order to specify the limits of the rectangular region within which a draggable Movie Clip instance can be dragged. Once you've checked Constrain to Rectangle, enter the pixel locations of the four corners of the rectangle. The pixel coordinates are set relative to the top-left corner of the stage upon which the draggable Movie Clip instance resides. For example Start Drag ("/drag-me," L=0, T=0, R=300, B=300) would constrain the draggable Movie Clip instance named drag-me to a 300 pixel square region in the top-left corner of the main stage.

 Note If the draggable Movie Clip instance is located outside of the defined drag region when the Drag Movie Clip Action occurs, then the instance is automatically moved into the closest portion of the drag region.

Lock mouse to center

This setting makes the dragged Movie Clip instance center itself under the mouse pointer for the duration of the drag. If the dragged Movie Clip instance is not already under the mouse pointer when the Drag Movie Clip Action occurs, the instance will automatically be moved under the pointer, providing that the pointer is not outside the region defined by Constrain to Rectangle.

Advanced drag'n'drop

In "Drag'n'Drop Basics" we showed how to make Movie Clip instances that can moved around by the user. But what if we wanted to force the user to move an object into a certain location before we let them drop it? For instance, consider a child's shape matching game where a small circle, square, and triangle should be dragged onto corresponding larger shapes. If the child drops the small circle onto the large square or large triangle, the circle returns to its original location. If, on the other hand, the child drops the small circle onto the large circle, the small circle should stay where it is dropped, and the child should receive a "Correct!" message. That kind of game is quite possible in Flash but it requires some understanding of Get Property and Set Property.

Here's how it works — we'll take the circle as an example. First, create a draggable instance of the little circle Movie Clip just as you did earlier in the "Drag'n'Drop Basics" section (put a button in a Movie Clip, put a named instance of that clip on stage, and then attach the start and stop Drag Movie Clip Actions to the button). Then, you create a large circle graphic Symbol, put it into a Movie Clip, and place an instance of that Movie Clip onto the main stage. Name the large circle Movie Clip **circle-big**. Here's where the new Flash 4 Movie Clip Properties come in: When the user drops any Movie Clip instance, the instance's _droptarget Property is updated. The _droptarget Property specifies the name of the Movie Clip instance upon which the dragged Movie Clip instance was last dropped. So if the user dropped the little circle Movie Clip instance onto the large circle instance, the _droptarget Property for the little circle instance would be set to /circle-big. Knowing that, we can add an If . . . Else condition to check whether or not the little circle was dropped onto the big circle. If it was, we simply let the little circle stay dropped, and then we display a "Correct" message using Tell Target to update a status-message Movie Clip. If it wasn't, we return the little circle to its place of origin by setting the x and y coordinates of the little circle instance with Set Property. Here's what the code on the little circle button would look like (note that the Stop Drag Action must occur before we check the _droptarget Property):

```
On (Press)
      Start Drag ("/circle")
End On
On (Release)
      Stop Drag
      If (GetProperty ("/circle", _droptarget ) eq ¬
"/circle-big")
            Begin Tell Target ("/status")
                  Go to and Play ("correct")
            End Tell Target
      Else
            Set Property ("/circle", X Position) = "112"
            Set Property ("/circle", Y Position) = "316"
      End If
End On
```

On the CD-ROM

For further study, we've included this basic child's drag'n'drop game as a sample movie called dragndrop.fla on the *Flash 4 Bible* CD-ROM in the ch14 folder.

Managing Smooth Movie Download and Display

Because most Flash movies are downloaded and viewed over the Web, Flash has a number of advanced Actions that are dedicated solely to controlling the download and display of movies. If Frame is Loaded lets developers prevent a movie from playing before a specified portion of it has finished loading, and Load/Unload Movie lets movies be broken into small pieces that are downloaded only if required based on the user's navigational choices.

Ensuring proper movie playback

When Flash movies are played back over the Internet, they *stream*, meaning that the plug-in shows as much of the movie as it can during download, even if the whole file has not been transferred to the user's system. The benefit of this feature is that users start seeing content without having to wait for the entire movie to finish downloading. But streaming has potential drawbacks. First, during streamed playback, the movie may unexpectedly halt at arbitrary points on the timeline because a required portion of the movie has not yet downloaded. Second, Actions are ignored when they refer to segments of the movie that have not downloaded. These drawbacks can lead to unpredictable and often undesired playback results.

Thankfully, there's a solution. You can regulate the playback of the movie by using the If Frame is Loaded Action to prevent the movie from playing until a specified portion of it has downloaded. This technique is often referred to as *preloading*. A common preload sequence, or *preloader* involves displaying only a short message, such as "Loading . . . Please Wait," while the movie loads. Once the appropriate amount of the movie has been retrieved, the movie is allowed to play. Flash provides both a basic and an advanced method of producing a preloader.

Building a basic preloader

In this example, we'll explain how to create a preloader for a 100-frame movie, where the movie doesn't begin playing until all 100 frames have been downloaded:

1. Create a new movie with 100 frames. Rename Layer 1 to **Actions**.

2. Create a new layer and name it **Labels**. On the Labels layer, create a blank keyframe on frames 2, 5, and 100. Label those frames **preload-loop**, **begin-movie**, and **miminum-loadpoint**, respectively.

3. Create a new layer and name it **Content**. Create blank keyframes at frame 5 and frame 100. On each of those keyframes, place a large symbol such as a complex vector shape or a bitmap (you need some content in order to see the load sequence working in Test Movie mode). On frame 1 of the Content layer, use the Text tool to type the words **Loading . . . Please Wait**. See Figure 14-2.

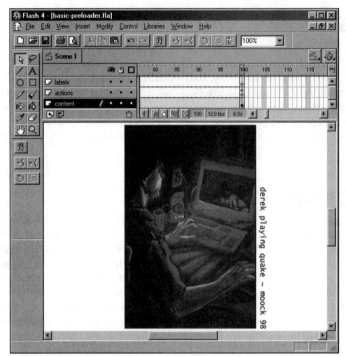

Figure 14-2: Add content that will be preloaded.

4. On the Actions layer, create a blank keyframe at frames 3, 4, and 100.

5. Edit the Frame Properties of Frame 3 by double-clicking it in the timeline, and then click the plus (+) button in the top-left corner of the Actions tab and select If Frame is Loaded. Choose the Label option of the Frame setting, and select minimum-loadpoint from the Label drop-down menu.

6. With the words "If Frame is Loaded" highlighted in the Actions listbox, click the plus (+) button and select Go to. Choose the Label option of the Frame setting, and then select begin-movie from the Label drop-down menu. Then check the Go to and Play option of the Control setting. This Go to Action, which starts playback of the real movie, will only be executed if the frame labeled minimum-loadpoint has been downloaded.

7. The If Frame is Loaded Action is a one-time check. If the frame specified in the If Frame is Loaded Action has already downloaded, then the Action(s) contained within the If Frame is Loaded statement are executed. If, on the other hand, the frame specified has not yet been downloaded, then the Action(s) contained are not executed, and the movie simply continues playing. In most cases, however, you won't want the movie to carry on playing until your desired frame has been downloaded, so you have to force the movie to perform the If Frame is Loaded

check over and over until the specified frame is loaded. To do that, edit the Frame Properties of Frame 4 on the Actions layer by double-clicking it in the timeline. Select the Actions tab and add a Go to Action. Choose the Label option of the Frame setting, and then select PreloadLoop from the Label drop-down menu. Then check the Go to and Play option of the Control setting.

8. Finally, add a Stop Action on frame 100 of the Actions layer. Now you're ready to test your movie and see the preloader work its magic. Choose Control ➪ Test Movie (Command+Enter or Ctrl+Enter). Once in Test Movie mode, you'll have to configure the environment a bit to watch the simulated download. Enable the Bandwidth Profiler by checking View ➪ Bandwidth Profiler. Click Frame 1 in the Profiler timeline. Select View ➪ Frame by Frame Graph. Choose Control ➪ 28.8 (2.3KB/s) (this simulates a 28.8-baud modem). To watch your movie playback as it would over the Web, choose Control ➪ Show Streaming. You'll see the playhead in the timeline looping around your If Frame is Loaded Action while it waits for the movie to download. The green bar in the timeline indicates how much of the movie has downloaded.

On the CD-ROM For further study, we've included this basic preloader movie as a sample movie called basic-preloader.fla on the *Flash 4 Bible* CD-ROM in the ch14 folder.

A couple of notes on preloaders: First, preloaders do not work inside Movie Clips. You cannot preload individual portions of a Movie Clip. If a Movie Clip instance is placed on a frame, the frame is not considered loaded until the entire instance has finished loading. Second, you don't need to preload the entire movie when using preloaders. In our previous example, you could move the minimum-loadpoint keyframe to any point in the movie after frame 5. By using the streaming emulator in Test Movie mode, you can determine approximately how much of your movie should be loaded before you allow it to play. Also, by using more than one preloader you can show the first part of a movie and then re-enter a loading state before showing any subsequent parts.

Building a more sophisticated preloader

In Flash 3, the only tool developers had to create preloaders was the If Frame is Loaded Action. Using multiple preloaders, developers attempted to simulate a percentage-loaded feature that told the user how much of the movie had been downloaded. Though they demonstrated the ingenuity of the developers, these percentage-loaded indicators were mostly inaccurate. But with the introduction of ActionScript in Flash 4, developers now have a way to precisely determine the percentage of frames that have been downloaded to the user's system. You'll need to be familiar with ActionScript to create your own advanced preloaders, but if you're not, you can still use the template sample file, advanced-preloader.fla, in the ch14 folder included on the *Flash 4 Bible* CD-ROM.

Here's an example of how to build one kind of advanced preloader: Create a keyframe where you wish to halt playback until the desired amount of the movie is loaded. Then create a keyframe somewhere before that keyframe and label it **preload-loop**. Then create a keyframe where the movie really starts and label it **begin-movie**. On the keyframe where you want playback to halt, add the following ActionScript:

```
Set Variable: "loadedFrames" = GetProperty ("/",_framesloaded)
Set Variable: "totalFrames" = GetProperty ( "/",_totalframes)
If (loadedFrames < totalFrames)
        Set Variable: "percentageOutput" = int((loadedFrames / ¬
totalFrames) * 100)
        Go to and Play ("preload-loop")
Else
        Go to and Play ("begin-movie")
End If
```

Then, on the main stage at the same point as the preload-loop keyframe, create a Text Field Variable called percentageOutput.

When the playhead reaches the frame on which the preceding ActionScript is placed, Flash executes the script. If, at that time, it finds that the number of frames downloaded is fewer than the number of total frames in the movie, it sends the playhead back to the preload-loop keyframe. Then it updates the percentageOutput variable to show, as a percentage, how many frames have loaded relative to the total number of frames in the movie. If, on the other hand, the number of frames loaded is not less than the total number of frames in the movie (in other words, if all the frames have loaded), then the playhead is moved to the begin-movie keyframe, and the movie proper starts playing.

An interesting variation on this advanced style of preloading is a graphical preload bar. A preload bar would simply be a small Movie Clip that contains a rectangle shape. Once placed on stage, the width of the bar would be set using Set Property to adjust the X Scale (width percentage) Property of the rectangle Movie Clip instance.

Note   Both the text based and graphical advanced preloaders are not accurate measurements of downloaded file size. They measure only the number of frames that have been downloaded. So, if the content of your movie is distributed evenly over the frames of the timeline, the frames-based percentage values will closely match the real file size transfer percentage. If, however, your heaviest content occurs only on sporadic frames, the frames-based percentage values may appear imprecise to the user.

Load/Unload Movie

Long sequences of animation in Flash naturally require the preloading capabilities of the If Frame is Loaded Action to guarantee smooth playback. But traditional information-based Web sites done in Flash require a different kind of download management. Suppose you're building a Web site with three sections: products, staff, and company history. Each section is roughly 100KB in size. In a normal Flash movie, you'd place those sections in a sequential order on the main movie timeline. The last section you place on the timeline would, of course, be the last section to download. Might sound fine so far, but here's the problem: what if the section that appears last on the timeline happens to be the first and only section the user wants to see? They'd have to wait for the other two sections to download before they could view the one they want — but they don't even want to see the other two sections, so really they're waiting for nothing. The solution to this problem is the Load/Unload Movie Action.

Load/Unload Movie provides a means of inserting one or more external SWF files into a Flash movie (whether that movie resides in a browser or on its own in the standalone player). Load/Unload Movie can be used to replace the current movie with a different movie or to display multiple movies simultaneously. It can also be used, as in our company Web site example, to enable a parent movie to retrieve and display content kept in independent SWF files on a need-to-retrieve basis (similar to the way a frame in an HTML frameset can call external pages into different frames).

Where are the multiple movies stored?

You may already be wondering how these newly loaded movies are managed relative to the original movie. Flash uses the metaphor of *levels* to describe where the movies are kept. Levels are something like drawers in a cabinet; they are stacked on top of each other, and can contain things; you can place things in any drawer you like, but once a drawer is full you have to take its contents out before you can put anything else in. Initially, the bottom level, referred to as Level 0, contains the original movie. All movies subsequently loaded into the Flash Player must be placed explicitly onto a target Level. If a movie is loaded onto Level 1 or higher, it appears visually on top of the original movie in the Player. If a movie is loaded onto Level 0, it replaces the original movie, removing all movies stored on Levels above it in the process. When a loaded movie replaces the original movie, it does not change the frame rate, movie dimensions, or movie background color of the original Flash stage. Those properties are permanently determined by the original movie and cannot be changed (though you can effectively change the background color of the stage when you load a new movie by creating a rectangle shape of your desired color on the lowest layer of the movie you are loading).

How to load an external SWF file into a movie

A new movie is imported onto the main movie stage when a Load Movie Action is executed. Here's how to make a button click load an external movie named movie2.swf:

1. Place a button on the stage of your main movie. Bring up the Instance Properties dialog box for the button by selecting it and choosing Modify ⇨ Instance (Command+I or Ctrl+I).

2. Click the plus (+) button in the top-left corner of the Actions tab and select Load/Unload Movie. Select the Load Movie into Location radial button of the Action setting, and then type **movie2.swf** into the URL text field. The URL text field contains the network path to the movie file you want to load. That path must be specified relative to the location of the page that contains your main movie, not relative to the location of the movie itself. In order for Load Movie to work in Test Movie mode, all movies (including the original and the loaded movies) must reside in the same directory.

3. Select the Level option of the Location setting, and enter **1** into the Location text field. This instructs Flash to load movie2.swf onto Level 1. If there had already been a movie loaded into Level 1, it would automatically have been replaced by movie2.swf.

4. Click OK.

Note   When a movie is loaded above any other movie (including the main movie), the buttons in the movies on lower levels will continue to be active, even though they may not be visible. To prevent this undesired behavior, you need to send movies on lower levels to an idle or blank frame where no buttons are present. Do that by adding a Go to Action before your Load Movie Action that sends the current movie to the idle frame. This technique is known as "parking" the movie. If you have to park multiple movies, you'll need to know how to communicate between movies on different levels.

How Flash handles loaded movies of differing sizes

A movie loaded onto Level 1 or above that is smaller than the Level 0 movie is positioned in the top-left corner of the stage. In this situation, objects on the Level 1 movie's stage are displayed even when they go beyond the bottom and right dimensions of the Level 1 movie. To prevent objects from being displayed off stage you would have to create a curtain layer above all the other layers in the Level 1 movie that covers up the work area (the space outside the movie's stage).

Movies loaded onto Level 0 that are smaller than the original Level 0 movie are automatically centered and scaled up to fit the size of the original movie (the manner in which they are scaled depends on the Scale setting in the Publish settings).

Movies loaded onto Level 0 that are larger than the original Level 0 movie are cropped at the right and bottom boundaries defined by the original movie dimensions.

Placing, scaling, and rotating externally loaded SWF files

Especially when your movies are different sizes, it's not very convenient to have newly loaded movies dropped ingloriously in the top-left corner of the stage. To give you more flexibility with the placement, rotation, and scale of your loaded movies, Flash 4 now provides the capability to load a movie into a Movie Clip instance. So far, this may not make a whole lot of sense. Loading a movie into a Movie Clip instance seems like a strange feature at first, until you find out what it can do—then it seems indispensable. The easiest way to understand what happens when you load a movie into a Movie Clip is to think of the Load Movie Action as a Convert Loaded Movie to Movie Clip Action.

When a Movie is loaded into a Movie Clip instance, it replaces the instance's timeline, and takes on its name, scale percentage, rotation, and placement. To load a movie into a Movie Clip instance, add a Load Movie Action as usual, but check the Target option of the Location setting. Then enter the name of the Movie Clip instance into which you want to load your external SWF file (the instance must be resident on stage at the time the Load Movie Action occurs). Your SWF file's top-left corner will be placed at the center point of the Movie Clip it is loaded into. The movie can then be controlled via Tell Target as though it were the Movie Clip instance.

On the CD-ROM For further study, we've included a Load/Unload Movie example as a group of files on the *Flash 4 Bible* CD-ROM in the ch14 folder under load movie. Open movie1.html in a browser to view the files in action.

Communicating between multiple movies on different levels

Once you've got a movie or two loaded onto different levels, you may want each timeline to control the other, just as Movie Clips can control each other. Lucky for you, you already know how to do this (you did read the first half of this chapter, right?). To communicate between different Levels you simply embed Actions in a Tell Target. The method for creating a Tell Target that controls a timeline on a different Level is identical to the method for creating a Tell Target that controls the timeline of a Movie Clip instance, except for one small change. You have to indicate the name of the Level you want target rather than the name of the Movie Clip. Level names are constructed like this: first, there's an underscore (_), then there's the word "level," and then there's the number of the Level you want your Action to occur on. Here are some examples:

```
Begin Tell Target ("_level1")
  Go to and Stop (50)
End Tell Target
```

This tells the movie loaded onto Level 1 to Go to frame 50.

```
Begin Tell Target ("_level0")
  Go to and Stop (50)
End Tell Target
```

This tells the main movie timeline to Go to frame 50.

You can also target Movie Clips that reside on the timelines of movies on other levels. Here's an example:

```
Begin Tell Target ("_level3/products")
  Play
End Tell Target
```

This sends a Play Action to the Movie Clip named products on the timeline of the movie loaded onto Level 3.

Unloading movies

Even though movies loaded onto levels that already contain a movie will automatically be removed before the new movie is displayed, the transition can be choppy. To ensure a smooth transition between movies, or to lighten the memory required by the Flash player, you can explicitly unload movies on any level using the Unload Movie From Location option of the Load Movie Action setting.

✦   ✦   ✦

Programming Flash with ActionScript

CHAPTER

15

◆ ◆ ◆ ◆

In This Chapter

Learn how to write
ActionScript

Use text documents
to store variables
and values

Create Flash forms
that interact with
CGI scripts

Controlling movie
and movie clip
properties

◆ ◆ ◆ ◆

For many serious Web developers, Flash 4's new programming capabilities are the single most important new
feature of the product. Elements inside Flash movies can now
be dynamic, have machine-calculated properties, and respond
to user input. Movies can now communicate with server-side
apps and scripts by sending and receiving processed and raw
data. What does this mean for your movies? It means you now
have the tools you need to produce truly advanced movies
(things like Flash asteroids, a multi-player role-playing adven-
ture game, or a navigational interface with a memory of the
user's moves are now possible). It also means that Flash can
now be used to produce many complex Web-apps (such as
database-driven e-commerce product catalogs) without the
need for Macromedia Generator. This chapter shows you the
new programming tools (collectively known as ActionScript)
and explains how to use them in your movies.

The Basic Context for Programming in Flash

The programming environment in Flash is not, in the strict
sense of the word, a programming "language." It is an assort-
ment of scripting commands, conventional Flash Actions, and
alterable movie properties that can be combined to achieve
programmatic behavior in a Flash movie. Together these
various elements are referred to as ActionScript. Writing
ActionScript consists primarily of attaching scripting Actions
to keyframes and buttons, and selecting parameters for those
commands from drop-down menus (or entering parameters by

hand into text fields). Though this method of programming can feel unnatural to traditional programmers, the resulting ActionScript looks and reads very much like conventional languages. Syntactically, ActionScript bears some similarity to PERL. And like those languages, ActionScript is composed of many familiar building blocks: variables, operators, conditionals, loops, expressions, built-in properties, subroutines, and native functions.

The Parts of Its Sum: ActionScript's Components

Many of the basic ActionScript commands can be found easily in the Flash interface under the plus (+) button on the Actions tab of a Frame or Instance Properties dialog box. Others, however, are hidden in the expression editor or not represented at all in the Flash interface. While it is beyond the scope of this book to fully explain fundamental programming principles, we can give a sense of the whole of Action-Script by providing you with an organized reference to each of its parts. For information on structuring ActionScript programs, see Colin Moock's Expert Tutorial later in this chapter.

"Writing" code

Every line of code in ActionScript is born from a mouse click. Whether you're declaring or updating a variable, checking a condition with an if/else statement, looping a series of statements, or setting a property on a Movie Clip, you start by adding an Action with the plus (+) button on the Actions tab of a Frame or Instance Properties dialog box. Once you've added your desired operation or command, you specify its parameters in the options for that statement on the right side of the Actions tab. For example, in code, assigning a variable "counter" a value of "1" would look like this:

```
Set Variable: "counter" = "1"
```

But in the Flash interface, it would appear as shown in Figure 15-1.

Note   Nearly every ActionScript statement option can be set as either a literal string value or as an expression (an interpreted code fragment). The abc button on the right of each option determines the setting: abc indicates a string, two lines (=) indicates an expression. This setting can easily be overlooked, but the difference in behavior is extremely important. Improper string/expression setting is often the cause of ActionScript errors. For a list of common examples, see the "Expressions" section later in this chapter.

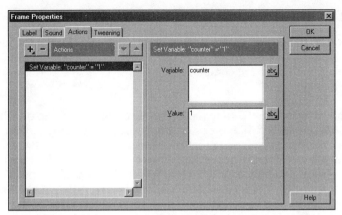

Figure 15-1: "Writing" code with Flash's menu-based Actions editor

To add a line of code below any existing statement, highlight the existing statement in the Actions listbox, and then add your Action. If you accidentally add your code in the wrong place, or if you want to move code around, simply select the lines you want to move and drag them with the mouse. You can also cut, copy, and paste code within the Actions listbox or from one listbox to another using Command+X or Ctrl+X, Command+C and Ctrl+C, and Command+V or Ctrl+V, respectively.

Variables

Variables are named storage places for changeable pieces of data (numbers and letters). To create ("declare") or alter a variable in ActionScript add a Set Variable Action and type the variable's name and value in the text fields under the Action options. Both the variable name and the variable value can be strings or expressions. To assign the literal string value wendy to the variable named first_name, use Set Variable: "first_name" = "wendy" with both the name and value set to strings. To assign a computed value to a variable, such as x = x + 1, you must be sure the value option is set to expression (change the abc button to the two horizontal lines, =). You can also dynamically create variable names by specifying the name of the variable as an expression. The following loop would create five variables named product_1 through product_5, and assign each of them the same value, "empty":

```
Set Variable: "count" = "1"
Loop While (count <= 5)
    Set Variable: "product_" &count = "empty"
    Set Variable: "count" = count + 1
End Loop
```

Use dynamic variable name assignment and retrieval to emulate arrays.

Variables in ActionScript are not "typed," meaning that their value is not explicitly set to be either a number or a letter. When working with variables, you must therefore be sure to use the appropriate string or numeric operators. For instance, the numeric comparisons `if (version = 1.0)` and `if (version = 1)` would both return the same result, but the string comparisons `if (version eq "1.0")` and `if (version eq "1")` would not.

Variables in Flash are attached to the timeline of the movie or Movie Clip on which they are created. If you create a variable x on the main movie timeline, that variable is available for other scripting Actions on that timeline. But from other Movie Clip timelines, the variable is not directly accessible. To access the value of a variable on another timeline (such as a Movie Clip), enter the Tell Target path to the clip in which the variable resides, then enter a colon (:), and then enter the variable name. For instance, this statement sets the variable x to be equal to the value of the variable y in Movie Clip named "ball": `Set Variable: "x" = /ball:y`. Whereas this statement sets the variable "y" to be equal to the value of the variable x on the main movie timeline: `Set Variable: "y" = /:x`.

Tip   Variables in ActionScript are not case sensitive and cannot start with a number.

Loading variables from an external text file

In addition to setting variables inside Flash, you can load variables into Flash from an external text file using the Load/Unload Movie Action. Simply add the Action, and then select the Load Variables into Location option of the Action setting. In the URL text-field, enter the path and name of the file from which you want to load your variables, and then choose either the level or target Movie Clip into which you want the variables loaded. The text file that contains the variables must be structured like the text of a standard MIME format known as application/x-www-urlformencoded. In this format, spaces are represented by the plus sign (+), and multiple variables are separated by ampersands (&). For example, to load the variables var1 and var2 you would use something like this:
`var1=hello&var2=there+world`.

On the CD-ROM   You'll find a working example of a movie containing a simple load-variables statement in the ch15/loadvars folder on the *Flash 4 Bible* CD-ROM.

Using Load/Unload Movie, you can also load variables from, and send variables to, a CGI script.

Operators

Operators are used to compare and combine variable values and to phrase logical statements in expressions. Flash has three kinds of operators: numeric, string, and logical. These are explained in Table 15-1.

Table 15-1
ActionScript Operators

Operator	Explanation
Numeric Operators	
+	Add
-	Subtract
*	Multiply
/	Divide
=	Equals. Used both for assignment and for comparison. ActionScript does not use separate operators for those different operations (no == exists).
<>	Does not equal. (Often represented as ! = in other languages.)
<	Less than.
>	Greater than.
<=	Less than or equal to.
>=	Greater than or equal to.
( )	Group operations together, as in x = (x + y) * 3
String Operators	
" "	Indicate that the enclosed value should be interpreted as a string, not an expression.
eq	Is equal to, or the same as. Example: if (name eq "derek").
ne	Is not equal to. Example: if (name ne "null").
lt	Alphabetically before. So ("a" lt "b") is true. If the strings compared have multiple characters, the first character determines the alphabetical position. So "apple" comes before "beet." The lt, gt, le, and ge operators are based on ASCII values.
gt	Alphabetically after.
le	Alphabetically before or the same as.
ge	Alphabetically after or the same as.
&	Join two strings together, or add a string to a variable. Example: "he" & "llo" returns "hello".

Continued

Table 15-1 *(continued)*	
Operator	**Explanation**
Logical Operators	
and	Require that two or more conditions be met in a single comparison. Often represented in other languages as &&. **Example:** While (counter < 10 AND quit eq "false").
or	Require that one of two or more conditions be met in a single comparison. Often represented in other languages as ||.
not	Require the opposite of a condition to be met. **Example:** if (not (status eq "member").

Note   For quick reference within the application, the Flash operators are listed at the bottom left of the Expression editor.

Conditionals

A conditional is a container for a statement or series of statements that are only executed if a specified circumstance is true. A basic conditional consists of three components: the prerequisite (the condition that must be met), the statements which are executed if the prerequisite is met, and the termination of that list of statements. Table 15-2 lists the components of a conditional statement.

Table 15-2 **Conditional Statement Components**	
Prerequisite	**If (x = 1)**
Statements to be executed	Set Variable: "name" = "margaret"
Termination of Conditional	End If

If the prerequisite set by an If statement is not met, one or more subsequent conditions may be tested via the Else If statement. If none of the prerequisites set by a series of If/Else If statements are met, an Else statement can be added to specify a statement or group of statements to be executed as a last resort. Here is an example of an If/Else If/Else construction:

```
If (x = 1)
   Set Variable: "name" = "margaret"
```

```
Else If (x = 2)
   Set Variable: "name" = "michael"
Else
   Set Variable: "name" = "none"
End If
```

To add an `If` statement in ActionScript, choose the If Action from the plus (+) button in the Actions tab. In the Condition text field, enter the expression that identifies what circumstance must exist for the statements in your conditional to be executed. Remember that, in your expression, literal strings must be quoted, and the `eq` operator must be used for string comparisons. To add an `Else` clause, select the first line of the `If` statement, and then click the Add Else/Else If clause button. An `Else` statement replaces the original `End If` statement, and a new `End If` statement will be added. To add an `Else If` clause Select the new `Else` statement, and then select the Else If option of the Action setting. The `else` will become an `else if`, and you can enter your new condition in the Condition text field.

Loops

A `Loop` is a container for a statement or series of statements that are repeated as long as a specified condition is exists. A basic `Loop` is made up of four parts: the condition, the list of statements to be repeated, a counter update, and the termination of the list of repeated statements. Loop components are listed in the following table.

Condition	Loop While (count <= 10)
Statements to be repeated	Set Property ("/clip_" &count, X Scale) = 100 / count
Counter update	Set Variable: "count" = count + 1
Termination of Loop	End Loop

To create a `Loop`, add the Loop Action using the plus (+) button on the Actions tab. In the Condition text field, enter an expression that describes the conditions under which the `Loop` should continue repeating. Before the end of the `Loop`, be sure to update whatever the `Loop` relies on in order to continue, usually a counter. If you forget to update a counter, you are now stuck forever in the `Loop`, and Flash imperiously stops the script from continuing.

Infinite or even high-repetition `Loops` are not supported in Flash. Theoretically, the most number of times any series of Actions can be executed in Flash is 200,000. Flash's stated `Loop` limit is 20,000, but in our testing, the highest count we could achieve was 12,500. Whatever the specific number, this limitation means that Loops in Flash are not appropriate for running background processes that listen for conditions to become true elsewhere in the movie. While a Loop is in progress, the screen is not updated and no mouse events are captured, so most Flash Actions are effectively not executable from within a Loop. The Loop Action is best suited to abstract operations like string handling (for example: to check each letter of a word to see if it contains an @ symbol) and dynamic variable assignment. Loops to execute repetitive Actions, which affect tangible objects in the movie, should be created as repeating frames in Movie Clips. To create a permanently running process, make a Movie Clip with two keyframes. On the first frame, call the sub-routine or add the statements you want to execute, on the second frame use a Go to Action to return to the first frame.

Expressions

Flash uses the term *expression* to refer to two separate kinds of code fragments in ActionScript. An expression is either 1) a phrase of code used to compare values in a Conditional or a Loop (these are known as *conditional expressions*), or 2) a snippet of code that is interpreted at run-time (these are known as *numeric expressions* and *string expressions*).

Numeric and string expressions are essentially just segments of ActionScript code that are dynamically converted to their calculated values when a movie runs. For instance, suppose you have a variable, y, set to a value of 3. In the statement $x = y + 1$, the $y + 1$ on the right side of the equal sign is an expression. Hence, when the movie runs, the statement $x = y + 1$ actually becomes $x = 4$, because the value of y (which is 3) is retrieved (or "interpreted") and the calculation $3 + 1$ is performed. Numeric and string expressions are an extremely potent part of ActionScript because they permit nearly any of the options for Actions to be set based on mathe-matical calculations and external variables rather than requiring fixed information. Consider these two examples: 1) the Frame option of a Go to Action could be set as an expression that returns a random number in a certain range, sending the movie to a random frame and 2) the URL option in a Get URL Action could be made up of a variable that indicates a server name and a literal string which is the file path. To change all the URLs in your movie from a staging server to a live server you'd just have to change the value of the server variable. Anywhere that you see the word "expression" in any Action options or you see the little abc button, you can use an interpreted ActionScript expression to specify the value of the option. Just enter the code, and then click the abc button and select the expression setting, the two lines (=).

Within the context of ActionScript code itself, that little abc button plays an extremely important role: If you write an expression in a text field but do not change the button to the expression setting, the code cannot be executed. Instead, the actual string of text that makes up the code segment is used as the value of the parameter in question. Even if you just want to assign one variable value to another variable, you *must* set the button to expression so that the second variable is interpreted. Here's an example: suppose you have two variables: x = 5, and y = 10. If you use `Set Variable` to make x = y but forget to set the abc button to expression, you're actually literally setting x equal to the letter y, not to the number 10. In your code, you can see the difference: expressions are not quoted, and strings are quoted (for example: x = "y" sets x to the string "y," but x = y sets x to the value of the variable y). Be especially careful to set the abc button correctly when assigning dynamic variable values and when using the Trace Action to return variable values.

To use a string inside an expression, simply add quotation marks around it. Anything surrounded by quotation marks is taken as a literal string. For example, the conditional: `if (status eq ready)` wrongly checks to see if the value of the variable `status` is the same as the value of the nonexistent variable `ready`. The correct conditional would check to see if the value of status is the same as the string "ready" by quoting it, as in: `if (status eq "ready")`.

Properties

Properties are characteristics (such as width and height) of movies and Movie Clips that can be retrieved and set with GetProperty and Set Property. Table 15-3 explains each property and lists its name as it is differently used by Get and Set Property (those without an entry in the Set Property column are read-only and can not be set with ActionScript).

Table 15-3
Flash Movie and Movie Clip Properties

GetProperty Name	Set Property Name	Property Of	Definition
_x	X Position	MC	The horizontal distance between a Movie Clip's center point and the top-left corner of the stage upon which it resides. Increases as the clip moves to the right. Measured in pixels.
_y	Y Position	MC	The vertical distance between a Movie Clip's center point and the top-left corner of the stage upon which it resides. Increases as the clip moves downward. Measured in pixels.

Continued

Table 15-3 *(continued)*

GetProperty Name	Set Property Name	Property Of	Definition
_width		MC, Movie	Returns the width, in pixels, of a movie clip or the main movie stage. Determined not by the width of the canvas but by the width of the space occupied by objects on the stage (meaning it can be less or greater than the canvas width set in Movie Properties).
_height		MC, Movie	Returns the height, in pixels, of a movie clip or the main movie stage. Determined not by the height of the canvas but by the height of the space occupied by objects on the stage.
_rotation	Rotation	MC	The amount, in degrees, a Movie Clip is rotated off plumb. Returns values set both by the rotation tool and with Set Property. **Warning:** Setting the rotation property of a Movie Clip instance also scales that instance down slightly. Routines that spin an object should be written to compensate for this bug.
_target		MC	Returns the exact string you'd use to refer to the Movie Clip instance with a Tell Target Action.
_name	Name	MC	Returns or reassigns the Movie Clip instance's name (as listed under Instance Properties).
_url		MC, Movie	Returns the complete path to the .SWF file in which the Action is executed, including the name of the .SWF itself. Could be used to prevent a movie from being viewed if not on a particular server.
_xscale	X Scale	MC, Movie	The width of a Movie Clip instance (or movie) as a percentage of the parent's actual size.

GetProperty Name	Set Property Name	Property Of	Definition
_yscale	Y Scale	MC, Movie	The height of a Movie Clip instance (or movie) as a percentage of the parent's actual size.
_currentframe		MC, Movie	Returns the number of the current frame (for example, the frame on which the playhead currently resides) of the movie or a Movie Clip instance.
_totalframes		MC, Movie	Returns the number of total frames in a movie or Movie Clip instance's timeline.
_framesloaded		Movie	Returns the number of frames that have downloaded over the network.
_alpha	Alpha		The amount of transparency of a Movie Clip or movie. Measured as a percentage: 100% is completely opaque, 0% is completely transparent.
_visible	Visibility	MC, Movie	A Boolean value which indicates whether a Movie Clip instance is shown or hidden. Set to 1 to show, 0 to hide. Buttons in "hidden" movies are not active.
_droptarget		MC	Returns the name of the last Movie Clip upon which a draggable Movie Clip was dropped. For usage, see "Drag'n'Drop in Flash" in Chapter 14.
_highquality	High quality	Movie	The visual quality setting of the movie. 1=Low, 2=High, 3=Best. For details, see "Toggle High Quality" in Chapter 13.
_focusrect	Show focus rectangle	Movie	A Boolean value that indicates whether a yellow rectangle is shown around buttons when accessed via the TAB key. Default is to show. When set to 0, the Up state of the button is shown instead of the yellow rectangle.

Continued

GetProperty Name	Set Property Name	Property Of	Definition
_soundbuftime	Sound buffer time	Movie	The number of seconds a sound should pre-load before it begins playing. Default is 5 seconds.
.scroll		Text Field Variable	The topmost displayed line in the viewable region of a text-field variable. May be set with Set Variable; for example: `Set Variable: "var1.scroll" = "3"`.
.maxscroll		Text Field Variable	Returns the number of the lowest line that may be displayed as the top line in the viewable region of a text-field variable. Retrievable by simply stating the variable name and appending the .maxscroll command, as in `var1.maxscroll`.

Table 15-3 *(continued)*

Using GetProperty

GetProperty is not available as an Action, but must be typed in as an expression anywhere an expression is permitted. It takes the following syntax: `GetProperty ( target, _propertyname )`. The target is the full path to the name of the Movie Clip instance or Level that is being inspected. Target must be surrounded by quotation marks — for example, `GetProperty ( "/testmovie", _x )`. For more information on constructing target paths, see "Controlling Movie Clips with Tell Target" in Chapter 14.

Using Set Property

To set a property of a Movie Clip or movie, add a Set Property Action using the plus (+) button on the Actions tab. Choose the property you wish to set using the Set drop-down menu. Then specify the target movie or Movie Clip instance in the Target text-field (the target, which can be an expression, is the same as it would be for a Tell Target Action). Finally, enter the value of the property in the Value text-field. If the assigned value is an expression (for example, if it contains calculations or variables), remember to set the abc button to expression (see "Expressions" earlier in this chapter). GetProperty can be used in combination with Set Property to alter a movie or Movie Clip instance relative to its original state. For instance, the following code would double the current width of the Movie Clip instance named testmc:

```
Set Property ("/testmc", X Scale) = GetProperty ("/testmc",_x) * 2
```

Built-in functions

ActionScript contains a number of native programming commands known as *functions*. To execute a function, type its name (or select it in the Expression Editor), and supply the correct parameters. Table 15-4 outlines the ActionScript functions.

Table 15-4
ActionScript Functions

Function Name	Syntax	Example	Definition
Eval	eval(variable or expression)	`eval("product" & count)`	Performs the operations in parentheses, and then returns the resulting value as a variable name.
True	True	`Set Property ("/ball", Visibility) = True`	Long-hand version of Boolean "on" state. Equivalent to "1."
False	False	`Set Property ("/ball", Visibility) = False`	Long-hand version of Boolean "off" state. Equivalent to "0."
Newline	Newline	`Set Variable: "name" = "Andy" & Newline & "Harris"`	Adds a line break to a string value.
GetTimer	GetTimer	`Set Variable: "time" = Int (GetTimer / 1000)`	Returns, in milliseconds, the time elapsed since the movie started.
Int	Int(number)	`Set Variable: "foo" = Int (5/2)`	Returns just the integer of a variable, number, or expression. (for example, the Int of both 2.3 and 2.9 is 2)
Random	Random (number)	`Set Variable: "dice" = Int (Random (6)) + 1`	Returns a random number from 0 to the number −1. Number may be a variable, number, or expression.

Continued

Table 15-4 *(continued)*

Function Name	Syntax	Example	Definition

Substring	Substring (string, index, count)	`Set Variable:`
		`"second_char"`
		`= Substring`
		`(name, 2, 1)`
			Returns a portion of a string or variable value. The returned portion has a length of "count," starting at the character number "index."

Length	Length (string)	`Set Variable:`
		`"num_chars"`
		`= Length (name)`
			Returns the number of characters in a string.

Chr	Chr (asciiCode)	`Set Variable:`
		`"character"`
		`= Chr (65)`
			Returns the character representation of the given ascii value.

Ord	Ord (character)	`Set Variable:`
		`"ascii_num"`
		`= Ord ("A")`
			Returns the ascii value of the first letter in the supplied string or variable value.

MBSubstring	MBSubstring (string, index, count)	`Set Variable:`
		`"second_char"`
		`= MBSubstring`
		`(name, 2, 1)`
			Same as Substring, but for multibyte characters.

MBLength	MBLength (string)	`Set Variable:`
		`"num_chars"`
		`= Length (name)`
			Same as Length, but for multibyte characters.

MBChr	MBChr (asciiCode)	`Set Variable:`
		`"character"`
		`= Chr (65)`
			Same as Chr, but for multibyte characters.

MBOrd	MBOrd (character)	`Set Variable:`
		`"ascii_num"`
		`= Ord ("A")`
			Same as Ord, but for multibyte characters.

Retrieving text input and returning text output

Flash 4 enables users to type text into text fields. The contents of a text field can be retrieved or set with ActionScript just like the value of any variable. Text field variables can, therefore, be used both to accept user input and to return ActionScript output.

Creating a text field variable to accept user input

To create a text field variable that can be altered by the user, follow these steps:

1. Select the text tool and click anywhere on the stage. A text field is created.

2. Make sure the Editable Text Field (or ab|) button located at the bottom of the tool bar is depressed. This indicates that your text field is a text field variable.

3. Choose the size, font, and font size for your text field. Then, with your text field selected, choose Modify ➪ Text Field. In the Text Field Properties dialog box, enter the name of your variable (the default is TextField1). Check your desired options, and then be sure that Disable Editing is not checked, and click OK.

You now have a text field variable that can be altered by a user. You can retrieve the variable's value at any time in the same way you get the value of any other normal variable (see the preceding "Variables" section). If desired, you can limit the number of characters the user can type into the text field by checking the Restrict Text Length To option and specifying the number of characters.

Sending output to a text field variable

You can set the value of any text field variable using Set Variable in exactly the same way you set the value of normal variables. Any new value you give to a text field variable is displayed in that text field during playback of the movie. Normally you don't want these output windows to be editable or selectable by the user, so make sure to check the Disable Editing and Disable Selection check boxes in the Text Field Properties dialog box. Also, if your output content is more than can be displayed within the viewable region of the text field, you'll likely want to check the Multiline and Word Wrap options of the Text Field Properties so your content isn't truncated.

On the CD-ROM   The source files (flashmail.fla, flashmail.swf) and the script for this tutorial are located in the ch15 folder of the *Flash 4 Bible* CD-ROM.

Expert Tutorial: Sending a Form to an E-mail CGI Script
by Paul Mendigochea

One of the first true Flashmasters, Paul Mendigochea has been working with the program since the release of FutureSplash. He's renowned as the architect of the award-winning Flashpad Web site (`www.Flasher.net/Flashpad.html`), which was the first community forum for Flashers. Flashpad is built entirely in Flash 4, with exemplary use of the new ActionScript and CGI script interlinkage. According to Paul, "Flash 4's robust forms and client/server features make Flash 4 a viable alternative to HTML-based Web sites." Paul predicts that these new features will propel "The great Internet facelift era," meaning that clunky HTML interfaces will soon be replaced with easy-to-use Flash front ends. In an effort to kick-start this era, Paul also maintains the Flash CGI Web site (`www.flashcgi.com`), which delivers support to developers who build Flash-based client/server applications — to learn more about FlashMail, simply go there.

Flash Forms and CGI Scripts

One of the hidden yet powerful features of Flash 4 is its ability to communicate with a Web server using Flash Forms. Flash Forms are simply user data entry forms that are created in Flash, using editable text fields. When a user types information in these text fields, the information is stored as *variables*. The *values* of these *variables* are then sent to a specified Web server using standard GET or POST communication. These same *variables* are available to the Web server and can be processed there by a CGI (Common Gateway Interface) program or script. CGI programs can be written to e-mail this information, manipulate it, store it in a database, or perform many other applications. The same CGI script can also return *values* to Flash — these can then be displayed or used by the originating Flash movie.

Because Flash conforms to standard GET and POST communications, it's very simple to replace an existing HTML form with a Flash form. In this tutorial, we'll cover how to get your Flash movies to talk to a server (send *values*) and listen for a response (receive *values*). We'll build a simple Flash feedback form that enables users to send their comments to the Webmaster. Don't worry about CGI programming, we'll use the free FlashMail fuelpack from Flashcgi.com. With just one command, we can configure the fuelpack to have our Flashform e-mail the text and *values* people enter.

As an example, we'll go behind the scenes at Flashpad to see how the feedback form works. It's a basic feedback form used to solicit feedback about a Web site and give visitors an opportunity to submit comments, report bugs, or make suggestions for improvement. As each form is submitted, it's e-mailed directly to the site administrator — a great way to keep in touch with the audience.

Open Flashmail.fla, go to scene *"sample_form,"* and select the keyframe *"form."* It has three text fields in which visitors can enter their name, e-mail, and comments. When a visitor enters information into these form fields, the information becomes the values of individual *variables* that's posted to the server. This form can be modified by adding other text fields, each with a declared *variable* name. Whatever is entered will be sent to the CGI program. How is that done? To find out, double-click the send button, which opens the Instance Properties dialog box. Click the Actions tab and take a look at the ActionScript code assigned to the "On (Release)" event:

```
On (Release)
     Set Variable: "mailto" = "your@email.com"
     Set Variable: "fcgi_datetime" = ""
     Load Variables ¬
("http://www.Flashcgi.com/sandbox/Flashmail.php3", "",
vars=POST)
     Go to and Play ("server check")

End On
```

This code consists of four lines. The first line, *Set Variable*, assigns the *mailto* variable to the e-mail address where the mail will be sent. (You can change that variable to your own e-mail.) The next *Set Variable* declares an empty variable called "fcgi_datetime" in order to get the date and time returned by the CGI script. The third line, *Load Variables*, is used to send the variables to the server. It sends all variables in the current timeline to the specified URL. Either of two possible methods — GET or POST — may be used to transmit the variables to the Web server. So what's the difference between the GET and POST method? Both methods use HTTP (hypertext transfer protocol) to encode the *variable name/variable value* in the header of the request. Each *variable name/variable value* pair is separated by an ampersand (&) and the values are *URL encoded*. The fourth line sends the Flash Timeline to the frame label "server check," which will be discussed in just a moment.

The GET method sends *values* as part of the URL string. Meaning that *values* from the form are simply attached to the end of the URL string. (For example, in most search engine search results, the results have a link with a rather obscure URL, such as www.info-sources.com/cgi-bin/showan?an=02423106.) This method is limited because the string can only be 1024 characters long. In addition, the GET method isn't secure because it exposes all of the variable names, which makes it easier to study how the movie and script works. Therefore, it's better to send by POST. With POST, more variables can be sent, and — although the HTTP transmission can be snooped (unless it's a secure connection) — the transmission is not as plainly visible as with GET.

Back to the feedback form: we set the Load Variables action to *"send using POST"* and the target to "" (blank), which causes it to return all variables to the current timeline. For the URL, type the path to the installed FlashMail script — this sends all variables in the timeline (name, e-mail, comments, and mailtos) to FlashMail.cgi. Upon receipt, the CGI will process the variables and automatically create an e-mail message that's mailed to the e-mail address (*value*) assigned to the *mailto variable*.

So what happens after someone clicks the *Send* button? Flash submits the *variables* for each entry field *without* any feedback to the sender. So, it's up to you to design a feedback mechanism so the user will know what's occurred. A simple way is to provide a message thanking the user for their feedback. Just for kicks, this message can also display the date and time the form was submitted.

Continued

(continued)

But to do this we need to a way to test if a server has sent back any *values. Variables* are sent back in the same format in which they are sent: as a string of *variable name/variable value* pairs, each separated by an "&" with the value portion URL encoded. As soon as Flash receives this string, it sets (employs) all *variables* on the timeline that received them. The key to knowing when the server has finished its work is to test for a *variable* that the server has sent back. This *variable* is called the "server response code." This can be as simple as *&result=okay*. With a looping movie clip, we can use an if/then condition to test if result eq "okay." That is, if the *variable "result"* has been set and is equal to *"okay,"* then the if/then condition becomes true. If it is, then we use the *Goto and play* ActionScript to get out of the loop and make the movie proceed to the keyframe with the thank you message. Otherwise, the movie clip keeps looping until it receives the *value* back from the server. You can find this ActionScript code in the first keyframe of the "check server loop":

```
If (result eq "okay")
      Go to and Play ("thankyou")
Else
      Play
End If
```

If all parts of the movie are functioning properly, the server sends the visitor's e-mail to the specified *mailto* address and returns the date and time of submission to the visitor's browser. The FlashMail CGI sends this back as a *variable* called *"fcgi_datetime."* To display this *variable* a text field named *"fcgi_datetime"* must be created on the *"thank you"* frame. When the player hits this frame, it displays the submission date and time—as sent by the CGI program—inside this *"fcgi_datetime"* text field.

That's all there is too it. The neat thing about the FlashMail script is that it can handle any number of *variables*. Although this sample feedback form only deals with three *variables*, with strong form design by using consistent variable names a survey, product questionnaire, order form, or other data sheet can be created using these same procedures and the Flashcgi script.

Duplicating and removing movie clip instances

A form of object creation and destruction can be achieved in ActionScript via the Duplicate/Remove Movie Clip Action. Once you have placed an instance of a Movie Clip on stage, you can make a copy of that instance by adding a Duplicate/Remove Movie Clip Action. Under the Action setting, choose Duplicate Movie Clip. In the Target text-field, specify the name of the instance you want to duplicate. In the New Name text field, enter the new instance's name (which lets you control the instance later with Tell Target, Set Property, and so on). Finally, in the Depth text field, enter the layer upon which you want to place the new instance, relative to the original instance. Depth starts at 0 (lowest). Only one duplicated instance can exist at a time on a depth level (placing an instance on an occupied depth level removes any existing instances). No duplicated instance can be placed underneath its parent instance. Note that a duplicated instance is placed exactly on top of its parent. To see the new instance, set the _x and _y properties to move it off its parent.

Note To remove a duplicated instance, choose the Remove Duplicate Movie Clip option of the Action setting of the Duplicate/Remove Movie Clip command, and then specify the instance you want to remove by entering its full Tell Target path and name in the Target text field.

Creating and calling subroutines

Whether they're called functions or subroutines, most programming languages provide a mechanism for programmers to create self-contained code modules that can be executed from anywhere in a program. ActionScript supports subroutines through the use of frames and labels. To create a subroutine in Flash, first attach an Action or series of Actions to a keyframe. Next, give that keyframe a label. That's it, you've got a subroutine. To call your subroutine from any other keyframe or button, simply add a Call Action, and then enter the name of the subroutine into the Frame text field using the following syntax: Start with the Tell Target path to the timeline on which the subroutine keyframe resides, enter a colon (:), and then enter the subroutine name (for example: `Call ("/bouncingball:getRandom")`). When you call a subroutine, all the Actions on the specified keyframe are executed. The subroutine must be present on the movie timeline (either as an active keyframe or an embedded Movie Clip instance) for it to work.

Note Subroutines in Flash do not accept passed parameters, nor do they return any values. To simulate passing and receiving variable values, set the necessary variable values in the Action list that calls the subroutine before it is called, and then have the subroutine set other variables that can be retrieved afterward by any other Actions.

Debugging your code

Flash offers three built-in methods of tracking down errors in your code:

✦ **List Objects.** While in Test Movie mode, use Control ⇨ List Objects to obtain a list of every element currently present on the movie stage, including Movie Clip instances, buttons, graphics, shapes, and text. List Objects displays the full names and paths of any Movie Clip instance or loaded movies. Useful for checking target names.

✦ **List Variables.** While in Test Movie mode, use Control ⇨ List Variables to obtain a list of all variables currently initialized, and to find out their locations and values. Very useful for checking whether a variable is resident at specific points on the movie timeline and for checking the name of the timeline upon which the variable resides.

✦ **Trace.** Add a Trace Action to send a string or the value of an interpreted expression to the Output Window during Test Movie mode. The value is sent when the Trace Action occurs. Make certain that the abc button is set to expression if you want to send the value of a variable or a computed value. As a debugging tool, Trace is analogous to alert() in JavaScript.

You can also create a temporary text-field variable for the purposes of displaying code output during development. Put temporary text-fields on their own layer and make that layer a guide when exporting the production version of your movie.

Expert Tutorial: A Model for Making ActionScript Programs
by Colin Moock

The smallish world of Flash has suddenly become a galaxy with the introduction of ActionScript. No longer must developers struggle with poorly supported FS Commands to achieve good internal programmatic behavior in Flash. But with this new power comes a new challenge: how can we create sophisticated programs in spite of ActionScript's potential for organizational chaos? Variables on buttons, properties set by frames, calculations performed in unlabeled Movie Clip instances; how can a developer keep track of all the pieces when each one could be anywhere? The answer may be to emulate existing methodology found in established languages. For Web developers, the object-oriented framework of JavaScript may provide just the model needed to maintain ActionScript sanity.

Here are some JavaScript-based ActionScript guidelines that can ease the code management burden of ActionScript development:

1. Wherever possible, group the functionality of your ActionScripts into self contained subroutines.

2. Keep all your subroutines in one place. Make a Movie Clip called "subroutines" and place an instance of it on the main movie timeline on its own layer, also called "subroutines." (Make sure there's a Stop Action on the first frame of your subroutines Movie Clip so your subs don't all fire off autonomously when your movie runs.)

3. Consider keeping all your variables in one place. Make a Movie Clip named "variables" and place an instance of it on the main movie timeline on its own layer, also called "variables." It may require a little extra typing, but then no matter where you're setting or retrieving a variable, you always know where to find it. You may want to simulate local variables by storing them outside the general variable Movie Clip.

4. Don't place ActionScript code on buttons. Instead, use button Actions only to call subroutines in your subroutines Movie Clip, just like you use Event Handlers in JavaScript to call functions.

5. Don't be afraid to call subroutines from inside subroutines. Rather than placing multiple subroutine calls on a button, create a single subroutine that calls the other subroutines (for example, an initMovie container subroutine). The less you hard-code onto a button, the easier it is to port your behavior from one button to another or onto a keyframe, and the easier it is to follow your code conceptually if you return to it after putting it down for a while or if you pass it on to another developer.

6. You can't "comment out" code in ActionScript with the Comment Action, but you can do this: Make a dummy keyframe in your subroutines Movie Clip called "temp." When you want to disable some code in a subroutine, cut and paste it to the temp keyframe and then copy it back if you need it again.

These are just some basic tenets to start with, but in general it may be useful to think of how you would do a task in another language before you try to do it in ActionScript. As I discover more useful principles, I'll post them at www.moock.org. Until then, you can study this sample movie that demonstrates the methodology:

On the
CD-ROM

Colin's approach to ActionScripting can be seen in his demonstration movie starfield.fla in the ch15 folder on the *Flash 4 Bible* CD-ROM.

✦   ✦   ✦

Revving Up Flash Generator

◆   ◆   ◆   ◆

In This Chapter

The difference between Generator Server and Studio

An overview of Generator objects

Creating a Generator template

◆   ◆   ◆   ◆

Despite the new capabilities that ActionScript has brought to Flash 4, the program still can't do some things — at least, not without a little help. That's where Macromedia Generator 2 comes to the rescue. For example, if you want to dynamically insert or update graphics into Flash movies, then you need Generator. Generator can do a whole lot more, so without further ado, let's get started.

How this Chapter was Written

Generator is a specialized branch of Flash. In fact, it's not really a part of Flash — rather, it's an add-on. And, despite its importance, there aren't many bona fide Generator experts. In order to ensure that this chapter would deliver some solid material, we invited Mike Jones to submit a guest tutorial. Yet when he delivered his material, we discovered that he'd essentially written the whole chapter. So we opted to honor our good fortune and go with this chapter pretty much as Mike submitted it.

Mike Jones is one of the original team members of Spooky and the Bandit, which is a Flash design and development team (`www.spookyandthebandit.com`). Several years ago, when Spooky was invited to beta test the original Generator, he "jumped right in." As Mike recalls, he was "Excited about the whole process . . . after all, Flash is my one great passion. So to be able to create Flash content that could be updated dynamically really struck a chord." Then Mike's involvement with Generator was given a boost when he was asked to write a few articles on Generator directed at new users who weren't too sure what Generator was. The articles were so popular that he decided to create an online resource for people who want to use Generator but are unsure where to start. That's how FlashGen.Com — the premiere online resource for Generator information, tutorials, and tips — was born. As shown in Figure 16-1, FlashGen.Com is located at `www.flashgen.com`.

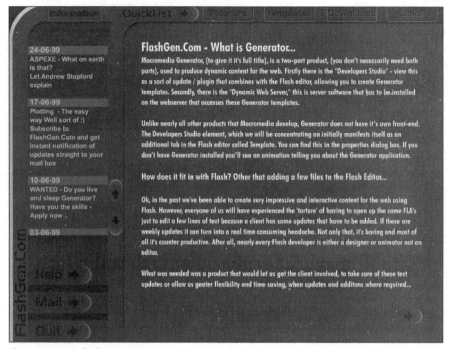

Figure 16-1: FlashGen.Com

What is Generator?

Macromedia Generator 2 is both a tool and a server application used to develop and deploy automated and/or personalized Web-based graphics. The Web graphics can be SWFs, GIFs, JPEGs, PNGs, image maps, or animated GIFs. All of these can be produced by Generator to deliver personalized content for individual users. They can also be produced by Generator for inclusion within scheduled, updated interactive Web applications such as banner ads, stock market tickers, scrolling lists, 3D pie charts, maps, calendars, and headliners.

Caution   This entire chapter is based on Generator version 2. Generator 1.0 is not compatible with Flash 4. Do not try to reinstall Generator 1.0 to use with Flash 4. You need Generator 2 to create templates in Flash 4.

Macromedia's concept was to separate the design-based elements from the actual content, which gives the developers greater flexibility and control when updating or altering graphics on the Web. The basic idea is that Generator performs, as Macromedia describes it, ". . . a similar function as a mail merge." Generator takes a given set of data elements, and applies them to a given list of variables. This saves developers time and money in the management of content, and leaves the designers to do what they do best — Design!

To do this they created a "hybridized" application. To create Generator content you need to own and install the Generator Developer's Studio for Flash. To dynamically serve these Generator "templates" from your site you also need to own and install the Generator Dynamic Graphics Server application on your Web server. The Generator Dynamic Server is only available for either Windows or Solaris. These two products are separate applications, you don't need to have both to serve Generator pages.

Thus, developing for Generator is a two-part process: First, Generator Developer's Studio is used to design and incorporate graphical Web templates. Then, when implemented, the Generator Dynamic Graphics Server takes these templates and combines them with data provided from an external source thus creating "live" Web graphics, (.SWF, .GIF, .GIF89, .JPEG, or .PNG).

Before moving on to the Generator Developer's Studio, let's take a brief look at the Generator Dynamic Graphics Server application.

Generator Dynamic Graphics Server

As mentioned previously, if you want to serve Generator content you have to purchase and install the Generator Dynamic Graphics Server application on either your Windows or Solaris server. This is truly the Generator: It sits on your Web server, takes the templates that you have produced with the Developer's Studio, (DS), applies the specified datasources to these files, and then delivers them to the user.

Generator is not only capable of producing interactive content solely based in Flash; the Generator Dynamic Graphic Server application, (GS), can also convert this Flash content (or any SWT) into a GIF, JPEG or PNG. Generator can also remove all textual elements from a SWT and it's datasource and save these elements to a standard text document. (Note, however, that Generator doesn't format the text.) In addition, Generator can generate image maps — both client and server side. All of these items can be produced in either a "per-user" (Online), or a scheduled (Offline), capacity.

Online/Offline?

So what exactly is Online/Offline, and how do they differ? Basically the Online functions of Generator are employed when you need to update dynamic content on a per-user basis. Examples of this might be stock market tickers, weather maps, booking information, and that sort of thing. An Online process is evoked every time a SWT is called from the server by a user, or when a script is run that returns updated information that is constantly changing minute by minute.

Note Online deployment of content along the lines of navigation links, nondated textual information, and any files that are not updated too regularly, is a waste of the Generator resource. Plus, it can put unnecessary strain on your Web server. These types of information are more suited to Offline functions.

Offline functionality schedules Generator to create files locally and place them wherever required, such as on a remote server. This means that you can set up command lines using standard DOS naming conventions and evoke the Generator executable, pointing it at the SWTs you wish to use. You can schedule these commands to be run only when necessary or once a week. These command lines are placed directly on the Web server.

Caution Online functionality can only be provided by the Generator Dynamic Graphics Server software. Because this server software is only available for Solaris and Windows operating systems (primary NT Server with IIS 3.0 or 4.0 or Windows 95/98 Personal Web Server), Macintosh or non-Solaris/Windows users have to be content using the Developer's Studio to design templates—not serve them. Macromedia produces server software for Solaris and Windows as most Web servers are UNIX or NT-based

Generator Developer's Studio

Now that you've been introduced to the concepts behind serving Generator templates, all you need to know is how to make them.

Generator Developer's Studio, in conjunction with Flash, is used to make Generator templates. Currently, the Generator Developer's Studio is only available for Flash 3 and 4—although some content can be created for Flash 2, it has limited functionality.

Unlike other products that Macromedia develops, Generator doesn't have its own front-end application or GUI (graphical user interface). You can access Generator elements from a variety of places within the Flash 4 authoring environment. The main Generator element appears as an additional file type in the Formats tab of the File ➪ Publish Settings dialog box. When you enable the Generator Template (.SWT) check box in the Formats tab, you'll be able to access another Publish Settings tab called Generator. This is shown in Figure 16-2.

There's also an Inspector in Flash for Generator which is accessed with Windows ➪ Inspectors ➪ Generator, but unless you have the Developer's Studio installed, this only displays an animation. This is shown in Figure 16-3.

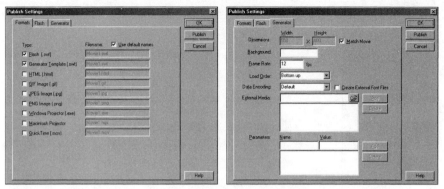

Figure 16-2: The Generator tab appears within the Publish Settings. If you do not have Generator installed, then the Generator Template file format is disabled in the Formats tab.

Figure 16-3: The Generator Inspector only functions when the Generator Developer's Studio is installed. If Generator isn't installed, you see an advertisement promoting Generator. If you have Generator installed, the Inspector is blank until you start working with Generator variables and content.

We're ready to start using Flash to create Generator templates, which are referred to as SWT files. But, before looking at an example of how Generator content is created, let's look at the objects that are available once the Developer's Studio is installed. You can access a tool window for Generator objects by using the Windows ➪ Generator Objects command (see Figure 16-4).

Figure 16-4: The Generator Objects window is used to place dynamic content placeholders in Flash movies.

✦ **Basic Charts:** This template facilitates the creation of charts, which come in various "flavors": Bar, Stacked Bar, Line, Stacked Line, Area, Stacked Area, Scatter & Scatter Line.

✦ **Insert Flash Movie:** This option enables the insertion of a Flash movie from another source directly into the SWT. In the output, Generator merges the two files into one. The source files can be external to the SWT, either locally or remotely.

✦ **Insert GIF:** As mentioned previously, GIF files can also be acquired from their native format and inserted directly into the SWT.

✦ **Insert JPEG:** As Insert GIF.

✦ **Insert PNG:** As Insert GIF.

✦ **Insert Sound:** This option enables sounds to be merged into an SWT.

✦ **Insert Symbol:** This option enables a symbol to be taken from the library of the SWT and inserted directly into the SWT file. Symbols don't have to be taken from the same SWT, they can be held in separate SWTs.

✦ **List:** Enables the display of information in either a Vertical or Horizontal field.

✦ **Pie Chart:** Enables data to be feed into a Pie chart format, which can even be 3D (and exploded) to show breakdown of data.

✦ **Plot:** Plot enables the placement of an element from the library onto the canvas at specified coordinates. Scaling and rotation can also be applied via this template.

✦ **Scrolling List:** A scrolling version of the List template. This is like the List template except that it uses one symbol to replicate information, which can be displayed either as a vertical or horizontal scrolling template.

✦ **Stock Chart:** This option facilitates the display of data pertaining to stock market quotes. This template is able to display figures in various data sets as either: High-Low-Close, Open-High-Low, or Candlesticks.

✦ **Table:** The table template enables the display of textual information such as calendars and scheduling information

✦ **Ticker:** Based on the Scrolling List, this template is especially useful for a banner header or quote ticker. The data can be displayed either vertically or horizontally.

How do I start to use Generator?

So you've installed the Generator Developer's Studio and you're ready to make a template. The first thing that you'll need to decide is what your datasource is. This can be either a humble text file, or a middleware solution—such as Perl, ColdFusion, Active Server Pages (ASP), or it can even be a direct link to a database. For this simple example we'll be using a text document.

1. Create a directory on your local machine. The exact location is up to you. Call it `GenDev` and in this folder make two more folders, one called `data` and the other called `swt`.

2. Create an empty text file. Save that text file in the `data` folder and name it `info.txt`.

3. Open the text file in an ASCII editor, either Notepad (PC) or SimpleText (Mac), another good editor is UltraEdit (PC), but the choice is yours.

4. At the top of the text document write the following words—make sure you observe the syntax carefully:

   `name, value`

5. Save the text file and close it.

6. Open your `GenDev` folder and make another folder inside of it called `fla`. This is where we'll put our source files.

7. Open Flash, if you haven't already, and save a new empty Flash editor document (.FLA file) as lesson1.fla in the `fla` directory.

This is the procedure—you're advised to get into this routine. It's far trickier to track down rogue bugs in Generator than in Flash. So getting into this type of routine minimizes errors.

Now's a good time to explain the logic behind the folder structure that we've just created. Using relative paths for your data source makes it very easy to migrate the final files to your Web server for final deployment. Also, the current folder configuration affords the extra advantage that the final SWT files can easily find other source files. The exported SWF files that are created with Flash's Test Movie and Scene commands are also saved to the FLA source folder, where the final SWTs can find them.

To set your data source, look to the top right of the Flash application, above the Timeline header of the main movie, where—as shown in Figure 16-5—you'll see the Generator logo. It's there to signify that this installation of Flash is Generator enabled. It also opens the Generator Set Environment dialog box. To insert Environment parameters, click this logo and a dialog box opens.

Click to insert a Generator
environment variable

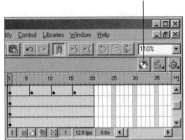

Figure 16-5: Click the Generator Logo Button (to the left of the Scenes pop-up menu) to open the Generator Set Environment dialog box.

New Feature

Formerly, in Generator 1, the environment parameters were set in the Timeline. But with the release of Generator 2, this has been altered as discussed previously. Other changes in Generator 2 are that specific selections for Set Environment and Set SQL Environment no longer exist. Both of these have been combined in the new Set Environment dialog box. Once you have made your settings in this box you can check them at any point by clicking the Generator logo.

As shown in Figure 16-6, two icons appear at the top-right corner of the Set Environment dialog box: Column Name/Value Data Layout and Name/Value Data Layout. Basically, these variable containers enable you to input names and values in the same manner as we are going to in our text file. You can browse to a data source via the small folder icon in the top left. Remember though, keep the paths *relative*.

Column Name/Value data layout

Click to browse to a file   Name/Value data layout

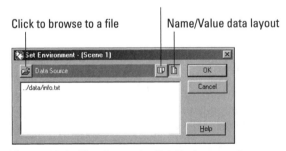

Figure 16-6: The Generator Set Environment dialog box

Now that you're more familiar with the turf, let's enter the data source we have just saved in text form. If you aren't there already, switch back to Flash and click the Generator logo. When the dialog box opens, type this directly into the text field:

```
../data/info.txt
```

Click OK and save the file. That's the path to the data source set in the text file, named `info.txt`. Remember, if you used the browser icon you need to crop off the front part of the absolute path and enter a relative one instead. As follows:

```
C:\gendev\data\info.txt
```

would need to be cropped to match the preceding string.

Tip If you don't already work this way, it's advised that you separate the recurring elements of your files — Actions, labels, and sounds, (to name a few) into different layers. This makes it easy to locate and alter these parts — instead of wading through a frame that has Actions, labels, sounds, and so on, all tossed into the same layer's frames.

Now you're ready to make your mark on the Flash stage. Select the Text tool and change the font to Arial/Helvetica (depending on your platform). Make the color Black and the size about 20pts. Then click the stage to activate the text-input box, and type the following: **{btext}{ntext}**. Refer to Figure 16-7 for how they'll look in the editor.

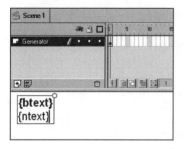

Figure 16-7: Making Generator Text in the Flash Editor

Tip Note that {btext} is bold in the editor. If you want particular formatting for elements of text, you'll need to add these to the variable, as they can't be added via the data source.

As you can see, the text layout properties are still active. If we just left it like this, we'd get strange letter layout when our text is added upon generation. That's due to the fact that there's only space for seven characters. To resolve this, set the size of the text box by "grabbing" the circle in the top right corner and drag while the mouse button is still pressed, as shown in Figure 16-8.

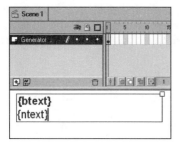

Figure 16-8: Resetting the size of the text box

Now save the file — make sure that it's saved in the `fla` folder of the `GenDev` folder. As we continue adding more and more information to this file, you'll need to keep backing it up. Therefore, it's recommended that you make an incremental save to the file *before* you make any major changes to it. If these new changes are successful, then you should save the file as the next file in order, as follows: gen_01.fla, gen_02.fla, and so on.

Switch to your text editor and open the text file called `info.txt`. This file should only contain the two words that we entered at the very beginning. As a recap these should be:

```
name, value
```

Under this entry, we'll insert a carriage return and — on the next line down — we'll add our first variable, {btext}, and then on the next line we'll add our second variable, {ntext}:

```
name, value
btext,
ntext,
```

Note that a comma follows each of the variables and that the brackets (that surrounded the equivalent variable in the Flash editor) have been removed. The comma is what is known as the delimiter — that means that anything appearing after the comma is treated by Generator as a variable value.

Knowing this, you might imagine that problems arise when you need to include a whole sentence or a string of characters that may or may not be separated by a comma. We solve this by putting the value of the variable in double quotes. The downside of this solution is that you can't put double quotes inside a value — because it would have the same effect as placing a comma outside double quotes, which would cause the text to end abruptly. You can, however, use single quotes inside double quotes with no adverse effects. Then, if you need to use double quotes, use a \ as a delimiter. Therefore, to recap, in order to double quote within a set of quotes, write the sentence thus:

```
This section of \"text\" is in quotes.
```

Tip

If only part of the text is being generated from your template, Generator is not at fault. A syntax error is more likely in your text source than in the generation process itself. If no text is generated, check all elements before looking at Generator as the source of the problem. Remember a lot of user elements can cause a template to fail — especially the old "forgot to set my file as a Generator template" one. That's not saying Generator is foolproof though!

Now let's add values for both variables. The first variable, btext, has the value:

```
Generator
```

Our second variable, ntext, has the variable:

```
Welcome to a new era
```

So now our final text document should look something like this:

```
Name, value
    btext, Generator
    ntext, Welcome to a new era
```

Finally, save the file and close your text editor. That's all the text manipulation we need to do. Now, if you closed Flash while working on the text you'll need to open it again. So . . . back into Flash for our last time.

Note

A side note here is very relevant. If your development machine does not have a Web server on it, *or*, if you're using a Mac, you'll only be able to use the built-in editor functions for creating Generator content. However, if you do have a Web server on your machine you can use that to deliver dynamic content straight to your browser. However, you'll have a gray/black Macromedia watermark on all Generator files produced by the server. To get rid of them you'll have to buy the Dynamic Web Server for Generator.

Now, we test our file to see if it works. Open lesson1.fla and double-check your Environment dialog box one more time to make sure it's pointing to your text document. Click Publish Settings in the File menu and make sure that Generator is checked in the Formats tab. This box is the equivalent to the Settings dialog box that you encountered in Generator. Ignore the rest of the Generator settings for this exercise. Click OK. Now, *save* the file!

Done that? Good, let's try it. Choose File ➪ Publish Preview (F12) or use the Control ➪ Test Movie command. Behold . . . it worked. Well done! You've taken your first step on the dynamic road of Generator. Note that if you opt to use the Publish (or Publish Preview) command, the file won't open in the editor — it does, however, export a self-contained, playable, SWF file as well as the SWT.

✦   ✦   ✦

Using Flash with Other Programs

In Parts I through IV, you learned that Flash can tackle some of the most complex graphic, animation, sound and interactive projects. But, as we all know, no one program can do it all—every computer application (or *app*) fits into a workflow with other apps. Unlike most computer books, this Bible seeks to find a place for Flash amongst all those other applications that you use in your multimedia work.

Part V will show you how to use Flash with everything from Adobe Photoshop to Kinetix 3D Studio MAX to QuickTime 4 to Macromedia Director. This section has been broken into chapters of application "families." At this point, you can skip around to different chapters to study a certain aspect of Flash content creation more closely. If you want to get back to working solely with the Flash authoring environment, jump to Part VI, where we will discuss how to publish Flash movies for use on the Web, or in stand-alone projectors and players.

Working with Raster Graphics

Flash 4 is an amazingly versatile application that can import and export just about any raster (a.k.a. *bitmap*) image format. This chapter shows you how to use Flash artwork in raster-based applications such as Adobe Photoshop. You'll also learn how to create alpha masking channels in Photoshop, three-state buttons in Macromedia Fireworks, and animation sequences from Live Picture.

Preparing Bitmaps for Flash Movies

By this point in the book, you already know how to work within the Flash authoring environment. You also know how to import external media into your Flash movies. What you may not know is how to ready your raster graphics before you use the Import command in Flash.

Cross-Reference Please read Chapter 7 for details on importing all types of external media, including raster images, into Flash movies.

A word of caution regarding bitmap use

Flash 4 supports bitmap graphics extraordinarily well, considering that it is a vector-based program. Because the main use of Flash movies is Web presentations, however, you always need to keep file size in mind — at least until faster Internet connections are more widely available and in use. Unfortunately, raster images usually use a lot more of the computer's memory than vector graphic equivalents to display on the screen. Because of that, try to follow these general guidelines when you are creating Flash movies:

✦ Limit the number of bitmaps used in any one frame of a Flash movie. Remember that regardless of how many times the bitmap is placed on the stage, the actual bitmap (or its compressed version in the .SWF file) is downloaded during the first occurrence of the bitmap (or its symbol instance). Try spreading out bitmap usage, or hide a symbol instance of the bitmap in an earlier frame before it is actually needed.

✦ Apply compression settings to each individual bitmap in the Flash Library to determine the quality you need before you use the general JPEG settings in the Export Movie or Publish Settings dialog box.

JPEG export settings for Shockwave Flash movies (.SWF files) are discussed in greater detail in Chapter 25.

✦ If you need to include several high-quality bitmap images in your Flash movie, consider the use of an ActionScript preloader (see Chapter 14), or try breaking up the Flash movie into several linked Shockwave Flash movies. These linked movies would use the Load Movie action to appear in the main (or parent) Flash movie (see Chapter 14 as well).

Raster images: Resolution and dimensions

Resolution refers to the amount of information per a given unit of measurement. Greater resolutions mean better quality (or better resemblance to the original). With respect to raster images, resolution is usually measured in pixels per inch (when viewed on a monitor) or dots per inch (when output on film or paper).

What is Resolution?

The resolution of an original image changes if the dimensions of the original image are changed, and the pixel dimensions are fixed. This means that, if you have a 2" × 2" original photograph scanned at 300 pixels per inch (ppi), then changing the dimensions to 4" × 4" results in a resolution of 150 ppi. Of course, you can interpolate a 4" × 4" image at 300 ppi from the original image, but you're not really gaining any true resolution in such a jump. When enlarging an image in such a manner, you're simply telling the graphics application to double every pixel already present, which ends up softening the image considerably. This effect only applies to creating an image that is larger than its original. Reducing the scale of an image has few undesirable side effects. A smaller version of the original can, however, reduce or destroy fine details.

A better way of referencing raster images is by using the absolute pixel width and height of an image. After all, all raster images consist of pixels, and resolution simply describes how those pixels should be packed. For example, a 4000 × 5000 pixel image can be printed or displayed at any size with variable resolution. For example, this image could be 4" × 5" at 1000 ppi, or it could be 8" × 10" at 500 ppi. Remember that resolution simply describes how much information is shown per unit. When you reduce the pixel width and height of an image, the resolution becomes lower as well. Once any pixels are thrown out or discarded, they're gone for good.

When you want to bring raster images into Flash movies, you should know what portion of the Flash Stage the image occupies. By default, Flash movies are 550 × 400 pixels. So, if you want to use a bitmap as a background image, it doesn't need to be any larger than 550 × 440. Assuming you are starting with a high-resolution still image, you should downscale the image to the largest size at which it appears in the Flash movie before you import into the Flash authoring environment. Use an image-editing program such as Adobe Photoshop (discussed later in this chapter) to resize the pixel width and height of your image. Also, if you mask bitmaps with a Mask Layer in the Flash Timeline, the entire bitmap is still exported. You should crop any images that you intend to mask in Flash. For example, if all you need to show in an image is someone's face, then crop the image so that it only includes the face and a bare minimum of extraneous detail surrounding the face.

Caution
You need to consider how you are setting up the scale attribute of Flash movies on the Web, or whether the bitmap is to be zoomed in a motion tween. If a Flash movie scales beyond its original pixel width and height, then any placed bitmap images may appear at a lower resolution. Scaling Flash movies is discussed in Chapters 25 and 26.

Be aware that Flash doesn't automatically resize (or resample) an image to its actual placed size when a Shockwave Flash movie (.SWF file) is created. We tested the same image with two different pixel dimensions in two different Flash movies (that is, one version per movie). The first version of the image had a 575 × 634 pixel dimension, while the second version had a 287 × 317 pixel dimension — exactly half the size of the first. In one Flash movie (we'll call it Movie A), the first version was imported and resized to the size of the second, using the Transform Inspector. In another Flash movie (Movie B), the second version was imported and placed as is, occupying the same amount of the Flash stage as the first movie. Even though both Flash movies contained a bitmap at the same apparent size on the Flash Stage, the resulting SWF files, which used the same level of JPEG compression on export, had drastically different file sizes. Movie A was 44.1KB, while Movie B was 14.8KB! Movie A is nearly three times larger than Movie B. However, it should be noted that you can see the difference in resolution whenever a view larger than 100 percent was used within the Flash Player.

Tip
If you are unsure of the final size you need for a bitmap in Flash, then import a low-resolution version of the image into Flash. Don't erase or overwrite your high-resolution version in the process! Immediately make a symbol with a graphic behavior and place the low-resolution bitmap into that symbol. Whenever you need to use the bitmap, place its symbol on the Flash Stage. If you determine that a better quality bitmap is required during final production and testing, import a higher resolution image then. Double-click the original low-resolution bitmap in the Flash Library to access the bitmap's properties. In the Bitmap Properties dialog box, click the Import button and select a new version of the bitmap. Upon reimport, all symbols and symbol instances update automatically.

Raster images: Bit depth

The other factor that influences image quality and file size is bit depth. Bit depth refers to the breadth of information stored in every pixel of a given image. The most common bit depths for images are 8-bit and 24-bit, although many others exist. An 8-bit image can contain up to 256 colors, while a 24-bit image can contain values within a 16.7 million–color range. Some images, depending on their format, can also use an 8-bit alpha channel, which is a multi-level transparency layer. As you would expect, each addition to an image's bit-depth comes at a great file size increase. A 24-bit image contains three times as much information per pixel as an 8-bit image does. Mathematically, you can calculate the file size (in bytes) of a given image with the following formula (all measurements in pixels):

width × height × (bit depth ÷ 8*) = file size
* There are 8 bits per byte.

Flash favors 24-bit image display, given the fact that it uses JPEG compression for all exported bitmaps in Shockwave Flash movies. As a rule of thumb, you should keep your images at 24 bit to use in Flash movies. You can, however, import 8-bit images in formats such as GIF, BMP, and PICT. For people viewing your Flash artwork with 8-bit video adapters, you have a greater degree of viewing predictability with 8-bit images that use Web-safe color palettes.

Tip   Use care with managing the properties of 8-bit raster image types in the Flash Library. The Smoothing option renders custom pre-dithered hybrid Web colors quite differently from the way the originals did.

Raster images: File formats

Images can be saved in any number of file formats, and Flash can import images in just about every major format available. Actually, Flash's export formats for raster images are exactly the same as its import formats. Refer to Table 17-1 later in this chapter for a description of these image formats.

Because Flash 4 offers full support for the PNG image format (including lossless compression and multi-level transparency), you should use the PNG format for images that you import into Flash. The PNG format has two types, PNG-8 and PNG-24. While both provide greater flexibility with compression, only PNG-24 images can use an alpha channel and 24-bit color depth. The PNG format is discussed later in the Photoshop section of this chapter.

Ideally, Flash would be able to import TIF-formatted images, as this is a widely used professional image format. As it stands, you'll have to convert any unsupported image types such as TIF or PSD to Flash-friendly import types in your preferred image-editing applications. Again, if you are going through this conversion process with your images, use the PNG format, because the image quality and resolution are unaffected. Note that Flash's PNG support is browser-independent, meaning that Flash can use the PNG format regardless of the Flash Player's hosting environment.

Caution

While Flash does retain JPEG compression levels on any imported JPEG images, it reapplies JPEG compression (unless otherwise specified in the Library) to the already-compressed image, resulting in further artifacting of the image. If you do use the JPEG image format for imported bitmaps, make sure you test the results of further JPEG compression and/or choose the Lossless compression setting in its Bitmap Properties dialog box, accessible from the Flash Library. Refer to Chapter 7 for more information on using raster artwork in Flash movies.

Using Photoshop to Create Images with Alpha Channels

Adobe Photoshop 5.5 is perhaps one of the most revolutionary upgrades to this premiere image-editing program. When you're preparing bitmaps for use in Flash, look no further. Photoshop 5.5 adds some extremely useful and powerful Web features that make saving high quality JPEGs and PNGs a snap. We mentioned earlier that the PNG-24 format is a great format to use with Flash, because this file format supports lossless compression and can use an alpha channel (a.k.a. *transparency mask*). In this section, we'll show you how to export a Photoshop image (.PSD file) as a PNG-24 image to use in Flash.

Photoshop has superior selection and masking tools for the most complex images. While some third party plug-ins can make the task a lot simpler, a little know-how with Photoshop tools can also go a long way toward simplifying your task. In the following tutorial, we take an image of some houses along the beach and mask the background sky. This lesson assumes you have a working knowledge of Photoshop layers and layer masks.

On the CD-ROM

Use the sample image beachhouses.psd in the ch17 folder of the *Flash 4 Bible* CD-ROM for this section. The completed PSD and PNG versions of the masked image titled beachhouses_masked.psd and beachhouses_masked.png are also on the CD-ROM.

1. Open the beachhouses.psd file from the CD-ROM. If you receive a message about a color profile mismatch, choose Don't Convert. For more information about color profiles and Flash, see the Color Management in Photoshop 5.5 sidebar in this section.

2. To more easily separate the color tones of the sky from the foreground, add a grouped Levels adjustment layer to Layer 0 (the layer with the actual image). Do *not* use the regular Levels command, which permanently applies its effect to the image. We only need a temporary Levels effect to increase the contrast. See Figure 17-1.

Figure 17-1: The image with a Levels adjustment layer

On the CD-ROM You can achieve the right levels values in the Levels dialog box by loading the separation.alv file into the dialog box, using the Load button. This file is in the ch17 folder of the *Flash 4 Bible* CD-ROM.

3. Select the Magic Wand tool in the Photoshop tool palette. In the Magic Wand Options tab of the Option window, enter **15** in the Tolerance field, and make sure Anti-Aliased and Contiguous are checked. Click the uppermost area of the now-darkened sky to select it. Shift-click additional areas until the entire sky is selected. See Figure 17-2.

Figure 17-2: Shift-click with the Magic Wand tool to add to your initial selection. If you grab anything in the foreground, either undo or start over (Select ➪ None). Pay particular attention to the edges of the rooftops.

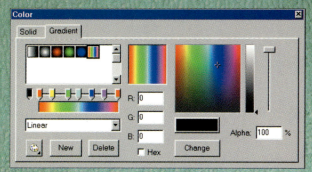

Color Plate 1. Chapter 2 shows you how to set colors in the Gradient tab of the Colors window.

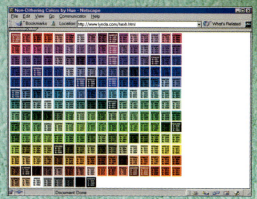

Color Plate 2 and 3. Lynda Weinman's color chart and Color Mix's Web color utilities can help you decipher the Web-safe color cube.

Color Plate 3.

Color Plate 4. This is the Flash log-in screen for Paul Mendigochea's FlashPad (www.flasher.net). In Chapter 15, Paul shows you how to create a Flash form that sends visitor comments to your e-mail address.

Color Plate 5. In Chapter 17, you learn how to create alpha-channel PNG images in Photoshop and Fireworks and use them in Flash.

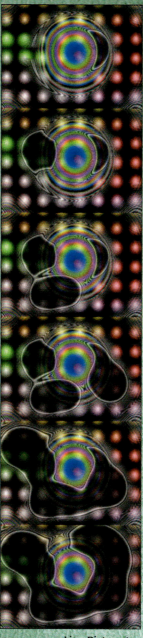

Color Plate 6. On the Mac, you can use Live Picture to create PICT sequences and use them for animation in Flash. Refer to Anders F. Rönnblom's tutorial in Chapter 17 for details.

Color Plates 7 through 10. In Chapter 18, Todd Purgason of JUXT Interactive shows you how to use Macromedia Freehand to plan and present your Flash movies for client Web sites.

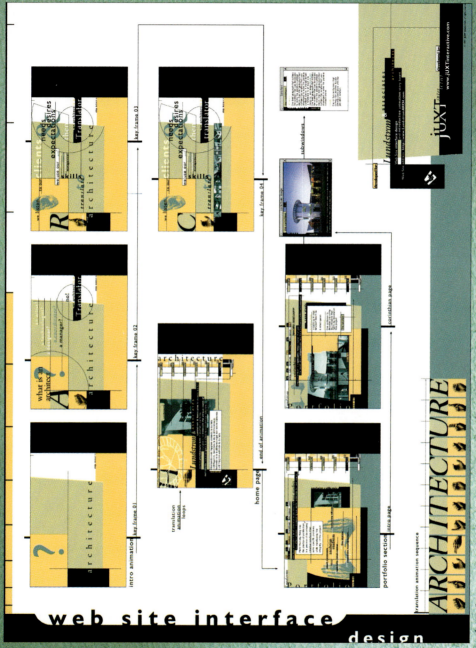

Color Plate 8.

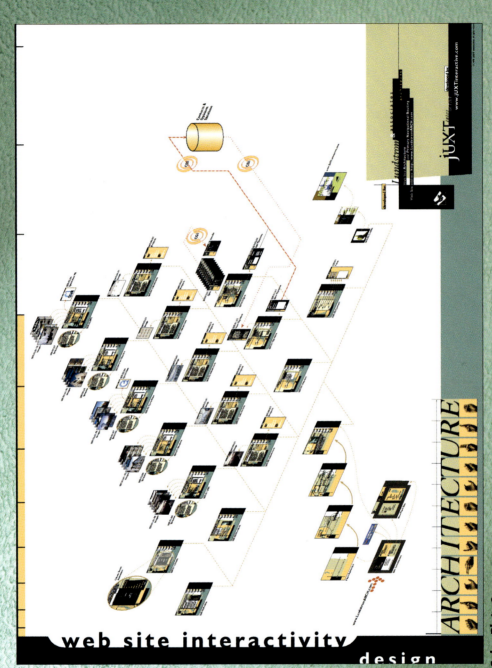

Color Plate 9.

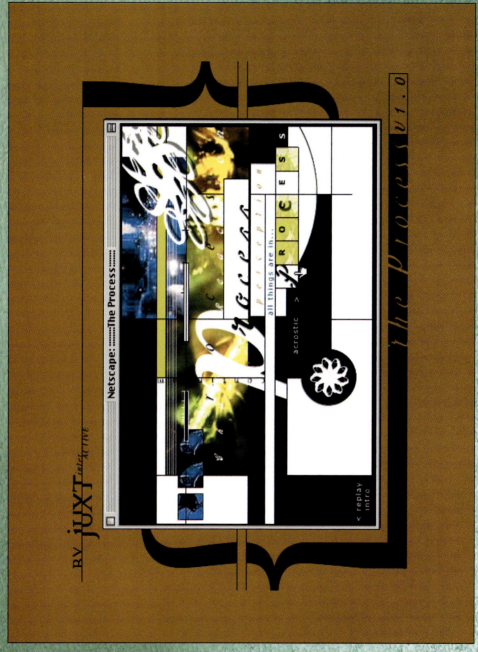

Color Plate 10.

Color Plate 11. Learn how to trace bitmaps imported into Flash in Chapter 18.

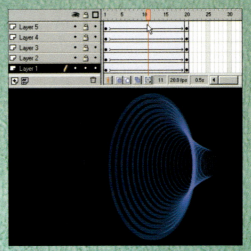

Color Plate 12. In Chapter 20, award-winning 3D Flash designer Manuel Clement shows you how to create an animating vortex effect.

Color Plate 13. You can combine interactive Flash movies with QuickTime and QTVR movies. Find the details in Chapter 21.

4. With Layer 0 highlighted in the Layers window, Option-click (Mac) or Alt-click (PC) the Add layer mask icon at the bottom of the Layers window. This uses the selection of the sky as a mask. See Figure 17-3.

Figure 17-3: Option- or Alt-clicking the Add layer mask icon uses the active selection as the black area of a layer mask. If the Add layer mask icon was clicked without holding Option or Alt, then the foreground elements would have been masked instead.

5. Now that we have masked out the sky, we don't need the Levels effect anymore. Turn off the Levels adjustment layer, or delete it.

6. Before we save this image as a PNG-24 file, we should crop all unnecessary information from the image. In this example, the masked sky should be almost entirely eliminated. See Figure 17-4.

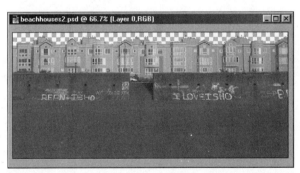

Figure 17-4: The image of the beach houses should now look like this. It's always a good idea to crop unnecessary information (especially if it's hidden by a mask) from the image before importing it into Flash.

7. In the previous section on resolution and dimensions, the effects of larger-than-necessary bitmaps were discussed. Because the image width is currently larger than the default Flash movie width, we'll also use the Image ➪ Image Size command to change the width from 755 to 550.

Caution   Make sure you double-check the layer mask by viewing it separately in the Channels window. If any faint gray lines appear along the top edges of the mask, paint over them with a black brush. If any gray appears in the black area of the mask, then it shows up in the Flash movie.

Caution   Be careful when using the Image Size command. For this example, the Constrain Proportions and Resample Image: Bicubic options should be checked.

8. We're ready to save the image as a PNG-24 file, using the new Photoshop 5.5 Save for Web command (Option+Shift+Command+S or Ctrl+Shift+Alt+S), located in the File menu. Once you have chosen this command, the image appears in LivePreview mode within the Save for Web dialog box (see Figure 17-5). Click the 2-Up tab to view the original image with the optimized version. In the Settings section, choose the PNG-24 preset. Make sure the Transparency option is checked — this exports the layer mask as an alpha channel in the PNG file. Do not use the Interlaced or Matte options for Flash import. Click OK and Photoshop asks you to specify a location and filename for the PNG-24 image. Note that the PNG image format is already selected in the Save as Type drop-down menu. It is not necessary to check the Save HTML File option for Flash use.

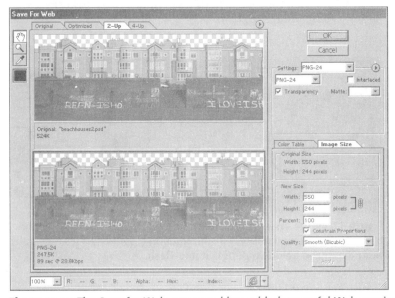

Figure 17-5: The Save for Web command has added powerful Web previewing features to Photoshop 5.5. You may need to resize this dialog box in order to display horizontal images on top of each other, as shown in this figure.

Tip

The Save for Web dialog box has many other cool features. While the 4-Up effect is not necessary for PNG-24 files (there are no compression options to worry about), you can preview your original with three different JPEG or GIF versions, each at a different compression setting. You can use the Preview Menu to see the effect of 8-bit browser dither (by checking the Browser Dither option), and you can use color profiles using Photoshop Compensation or Uncompensated Color. For PNG-24 files, always use the Uncompensated Color preview, because it is the most accurate for Flash use. See the sidebar titled Color Management in Photoshop 5.5 for more information on color compensation. Note that you can also resize the optimized image in the Image Size tab, instead of performing this action in step 7.

9. We're ready to import the PNG file into Flash, which recognizes the alpha channel in the PNG-24 version of our image. Open a movie in Flash 4 (or create a new one), and choose File ➪ Import (Command+R or Ctrl+R). Select the PNG image and Flash places the image on the current frame of the active layer. Remember that all bitmaps are stored in the Flash Library. If you delete the instance of the bitmap on the Stage, you can always replace it with the bitmap in the Library. That's it! You've successfully imported an image with an alpha channel into Flash (see Figure 17-6).

Figure 17-6: Using a bitmap with an alpha channel enables you to seamlessly place other elements behind the bitmap in a Flash movie.

 On the CD-ROM

Check out the sample Flash movie, alphabitmap.fla, in the ch17 folder of the *Flash 4 Bible* CD-ROM. You can also see a color version of the final Flash scene in the color section of this book.

Color Management in Photoshop 5.5

Many strategies exist for color calibration on desktop computer systems. Macintosh computers have had a leg up in this area of graphics creation and output ever since the development of ColorSync. Apple's ColorSync software provides one of the most complete system-level color management solutions for desktop publishing. Unfortunately, while Windows 98 does include ICC profile support, it's not nearly as comprehensive as Apple's ColorSync. Since Photoshop's 5.0 release, ICC color profiles can be specified and attached to images. In a nutshell, ICC profiles describe the color capabilities of a given input or output device, such as a computer monitor, printer, or scanner. When an ICC profile is attached to an image, it tells the application that is using the image how the colors in the image should be interpreted. If every program in your workflow supports ICC profiles, then technically, this provides a high-level of predictable display and output of all graphics.

However, while Photoshop and most page-layout programs recognize ICC profiles, the majority of applications do not. Current Web browsers do not support embedded image profiles, although Apple has proposed many ICC tags to make color management a reality for the Web (see `www.apple.com/colorsync/benefits/web`). More importantly, Flash 4 does not support ICC profiles. Neither does the current implementation of the PNG-24 format. JPEG images are the only current Web-image format that supports embedded profiles. Moreover, ICC profiles typically add about 500 to 800 bytes to an image's file size.

Herein lies the problem for serious graphic designers who routinely work under tight color management. If you specify a RGB space within the RGB Setup preferences (File ⇨ Color Settings ⇨ RGB Setup) *other than* Monitor RGB or Simplified monitor RGB *and* have Display Using Monitor Compensation checked, then what you see in Photoshop is not what you see in Flash when you import the image. This is why Photoshop 5.5's new Save for Web feature and its Preview Menu are so invaluable: They enable you to see how the JPEG, GIF, or PNG looks without Photoshop Compensation. If you work primarily with Web or screen graphics, then you should probably change your RGB working space to Monitor RGB or Simplified monitor RGB in Photoshop, or turn off Display Using Monitor Compensation if you continue to use other RGB spaces. Either method enables you to work with your images so that the Photoshop Compensation and Uncompensated Color settings render the image exactly the same within the Save for Web preview panes.

Now that you understand what an alpha channel is and how it works, let's move on to the next section where you'll learn how to use PNG images as semi-transparent states for Flash buttons.

On the CD-ROM   For your viewing pleasure (or cheating comfort), we have included the finished Flash movie, called Flash_Fireworks_Tutorial.fla. You can find it on the *Flash 4 Bible* CD-ROM, in the ch17 folder.

Expert Tutorial:
Using Fireworks 2.0 to Create Flash Buttons
by Christian Honselaar

Chris Honselaar is an educational developer committed to building future-conscious Internet content and enhancing conceptual communications over new media. To implement his ideas, Christian and his partner, Fabian Gort, established a Web design company, HTMWell, which is dedicated to human interaction. As such, HTMWell intends to redefine PR for the net. Reflecting its multifaceted attitude, HTMWell employs seasoned graphic designers and commercial consultants and utilizes the forefront of Web technology to build Internet solutions that stands the test of time. You can chat, or chew their eye candy at www.HTMWell.com.

Nobody can accuse Flash of having all its eggs in one basket. Vector design and animation alone would have made it one of the finest Web design tools available. But you probably have hundreds of bitmap images on your hard-drive, and some great paint tools. You don't want to throw those away, and neither does Flash. In a successful attempt to create a Web tool that really has it all, Macromedia integrated bitmap support in all shapes and sizes: You can import, vectorize, tile, shake, *and* stir bitmaps, in perfect harmony with their vector friends! As if that's not enough, Flash then went and implemented what Explorer and Netscape should have done a zillion years ago: Full PNG support now enables you to have ultimate transparency control, along with funky compression! By far the easiest software to use to create impressive bitmap/transparency effects is Macromedia Fireworks.

While you can simulate a see-through effect in any static JPEG picture or have a simple on-or-off transparency in a GIF bitmap, the advantages of having a separate transparency channel are often immediately apparent. The true potential of the PNG format is unleashed when transparent pictures move over other images, or when the transparency itself changes. This dynamic transparency effect is possible only with PNG images.

The following workshop shows you in crystal-clear steps how to make a translucent button in Fireworks and make it work in your Flash project! Please note that we assume you use Fireworks 2. Don't worry if you are still using Fireworks 1.0 — it has all the features we need right now.

1. Open Fireworks. Choose File ➪ New (Command+N or Ctrl+N). The Canvas Size should be 150x100 pixels, and the Canvas Color setting should be Transparent.

2. Select the Rectangle tool. For a more fashionable look, soften the corners by increasing the Corner size to 50 in the Tool Options window (Option+Command+O or Ctrl+Alt+O). Now draw a rectangle covering a large part of the canvas.

3. Choose a solid fill color using the Fill window. Switch to the Stroke window and choose the Unnatural option in the Stroke Category drop-down menu. Then, in the Stroke Name drop-down menu, choose Outline.

Continued

(continued)

4. A button would probably be incomplete without some text, so let's add a little. Choose the Text tool and click in our rectangle. With the Arial (or Helvetica) font at 20 to 30 points, write some suitable text, such as Hot Stuff, and click OK. With the text selected, choose the Emboss option in the drop-down menu of the Effects window. Compare your canvas to the following figure.

Fireworks canvas showing initial button state

5. Our current canvas is the Up state of the button. Now we need to add two more frames to the image to add the Over and Down states of the button. Open the Frame window (Option+Command+K or Ctrl+Alt+K) and access its pop-up options menu by clicking the arrow icon, located in the top right corner of the Frame Window. Choose Duplicate Frame. In the following dialog box, set the number of frames to be added to **2** and in the Insert new frames setting choose After current frame. The new frames contain the Over and Down states of our button. Creating your buttons in this manner also eases the workload for converting to a JavaScript rollover button (for example, as an alternative to Flash content): Fireworks automatically creates buttons using these frames.

6. Click frame 2 in the Frame window to show our button's Over state. Select the main rectangle and apply the Emboss effect. Instant transparency! Embossing automatically creates a gradient in the Alpha channel, which is saved along with a PNG bitmap image. Now set the Emboss options for the rectangle, as shown in the following figure.

Fireworks Emboss effect options

7. The text is already transparent, as you notice. To make the text easier on the eye, however, you can change its Emboss options in the Effect window as well. Try reducing its Softness setting and/or increasing its Contrast setting in the Emboss options. Use the Emboss effect options wisely when handling text and detailed images. Decrease the Softness, increase Contrast, and toy with the Width to preserve legibility!

8. Select frame 3, the Down state of the button. What is that? It doesn't look down to you? Simulating an object that is inset can be done by changing the lighting. Shift-click both the rectangle and the text. Now reverse the Angle setting in the Emboss options by changing the value from 135 to 315 degrees.

9. When you are satisfied with the button, it's time to export it to Flash. Click the Export icon in Fireworks' toolbar (Windows version only), or choose the File ⇨ Export (Shift+Command+R or Shift+Ctrl+R). For the Format, choose PNG. Change the Bit Depth setting to Millions +Alpha (32 bit). Click Set Defaults at the bottom of the dialog box. Now that Fireworks knows how to treat our pictures, choose File ⇨ Export Special ⇨ Export as Files. This command enables us to automatically save sequential frames, layers, and slice objects as separate files. In the Files From drop-down menu, choose Frames. Now pick your destination folder and type **GhostButton.png** as the file name. Fireworks will append _F and two numbers (indicating the frame) to this name. Click Save.

10. Open Flash 4. Make sure the stage is set to the default size of 550×400 and a black background color.. Choose File ⇨ Open as Library (Shift+Command+O or Ctrl+Shift+O). Open the finished tutorial example, Flash_Fireworks_Tutorial.fla located on the *Flash 4 Bible* CD-ROM. The Flash Library window then pops up. Drag the Symbol called Spotlight to the stage.

11. Now our Fireworks button makes its entrance. Choose Insert ⇨ New Symbol (Command+F8 or Ctrl+F8). Name it GhostButton and pick the Button behavior. Click OK. Choose File ⇨ Import (Command+R or Ctrl+R) and locate the files you created in Fireworks. Open GhostButton_F01.png. Flash detects the fact that this is a sequence of images and asks permission to import them all. Click Yes. Presto, a button is born (as the following figure shows)! Choose Edit ⇨ Edit Movie (Command+E or Ctrl+E) to return to the movie editing workspace. Make sure the Flash Library is shown (Command+L or Ctrl+L) and drag our fresh button to the stage, in the middle of the spotlight.

That's it! You can now test your movie by choosing Control ⇨ Test Movie (Command+Enter or Ctrl+Enter). You can also test the button states within the Flash authoring environment by choosing Control ⇨ Enable Buttons (Option+Command+B or Ctrl+Alt+B).

The rotating spotlight effect may demonstrate Flash's impressive transparency handling, but it also demonstrates a quick way to get a headache! Using it too much in a Web site may result in:

✦ Web surfers suing you because of an epileptic fit!

✦ Timothy Leary materializing in your bedroom and abducting your visual cortex!

Continued

(continued)

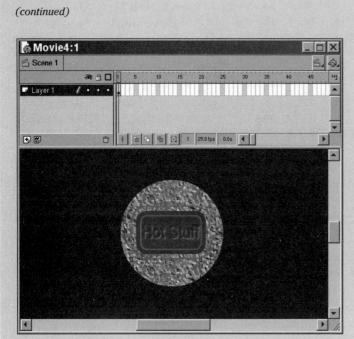

Completed button Movie in Flash

The point here is, don't choke your pages with psychedelic effects, unless you really feel like it. They can attract people to your site, but misuse can scare them away even more easily. Because intricate transparency has until now been barred by lack of implementation in all browsers, it is a promising field indeed. We leave it up to your imagination to take on the next frontier in Web design!

Using Live Picture to Create Animations

What's Live Picture?

Live Picture is neither a raster graphics program nor a vector graphics program. Rather, it's a unique resolution-independent technology based on proprietary code and file scheme. It's the flagship product of Live Picture Inc. (www.livepicture. com), the company that developed the Flashpix format.

Working with Live Picture enables a designer to work in real-time and either generate or manipulate huge files with remarkably little RAM. As a compositing tool, Live Picture is incredibly powerful. Live Picture's resolution independence means that you can lay out a huge billboard with the same screen conditions (resolution and file sizes) that you would use if you were designing a tiny stamp. Conversely, it also means that, if your client returns six months later because she wants her Web graphic printed in a high-quality annual report, or because she wants to use it as a big glossy four-color poster, you won't have to rework a 72 dpi Web image into 300 dpi hi-res files. Unfortunately, for those of you who use the PC, Live Picture is only available for the Mac and no plans exist for a PC version.

We chose to include a discussion of this program as an adjunct to Flash because it's useful for the creation of a series of still images that is animated in Flash. Because it employs raster images for input and builds raster images as output, we've grouped it here with other raster graphics programs. We felt that it would be especially interesting for designers who find that they must deliver imagery for delivery to multiple formats. So, if you find that your work runs the gamut from high resolution billboards to glossy magazine art, as well as the Web — then Live Picture can dramatically increase your design options and also save you a lot of time.

The following guest tutorial, based on materials supplied by Anders F. Rönnblom, is intended to give you a glimpse of the possibilities inherent in the linkage between Flash and Live Picture.

Expert Tutorial: Setting up for Stills from Live Picture by Anders F. Rönnblom

Anders F. Rönnblom is the publisher of Mac Art and Design, *Sweden, (macartdesign@ matchbox.se).* Mac Art and Design *is, arguably, the world's most beautiful digital art magazine. It's a remarkably visual magazine with deep, rich layouts and spreads that run across multiple pages. Unlike any other magazine that we know of,* Mac Art and Design *is laid out entirely in Live Picture. We asked Anders to share his experience in using Live Picture with Flash because we knew that his perspective would, as with the other guest tutorials in this book, broaden the scope of the* Flash 4 Bible.

Let's start a huge project. A client comes to you wanting some illustrative elements and small animations for his Web site, some exclusive folders, stickers, a large trade show display . . . oh, and he's also got some ideas for a promotional video that would substantially depend on your initial designs. Then he mumbles something about an upcoming annual report and starts asking about expressive fine art pieces. He wants you to come up with it — all of it. A huge project such as this is bound to scare anyone off. But, if you're used to working with Live Picture, you'll keep your cool and see a very exciting challenge.

For this tutorial, you won't be working with photographic images. Because the design calls for a richly textured background, we'll design the graphic elements directly in Live Picture, with its 48-bit color space, utilizing its amazing Texture World. You can design very sophisticated and complicated textures for very large image files, and use the resolution-independent brushes to smoothly brush in layer upon layer with these textures. This would be nearly impossible with a pixel-based program.

Continued

(continued)

I'll start with some basic steps to set up the project, show you how to build rich and exciting textures, and then, finally, I'll explain how to export a series of these textures to create a simple Flash animation.

To begin, open Live Picture and select File ➪ Document Setup. In this dialog box, we define the dimensions of the largest piece that is rendered as a raster-based TIF image. The client requested a trade show display at 5 by 3 meters, so type in **500** centimeters for Width, **300** centimeters for Height, and a resolution of **300** dpi. Click New. This results in a new, untitled file, containing a large empty rectangle with title box at the upper right, informing you that this is View 1 as seen in the following figure.

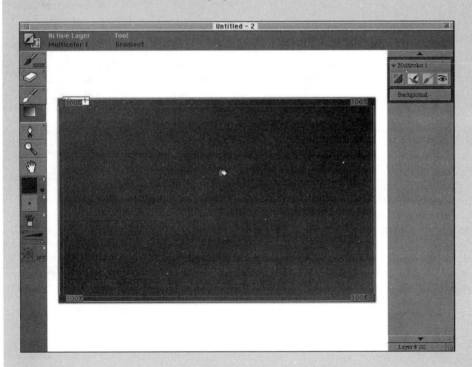

Now, create a new Multicolor layer with Create ➪ Multicolor. (Note: this project was created on a system with dual monitors, thus the menu bar isn't visible in the examples.) A new layer appears in the Layer Stack to the right. Find the Fill Rectangle Tool, which is the fourth from the top in the Tool Stack on the left, and choose Gradient ➪ 4 Point. This tool is used to create a multicolored gradient with different colors and opacity settings at each corner of the rectangle. Now drag out a rectangle to cover View 1. The rectangle is empty, with a color tab on each corner. Double-click each tab to invoke the Color Picker. Select a bright red color for two opposite corners, and black for the remaining corners. Now click inside the rectangle to fill it with the color gradient.

Find the Brush Effects Button, which is third from the bottom in the Tool Stack (and looks like a little can filled with brushes), and choose the TextureWorld option. In the TextureWorld dialog box (shown in the following figure), select a symmetrical dot-like pattern. Use the sliders located on the right to adjust the size and the amount of the effect, and then click OK.

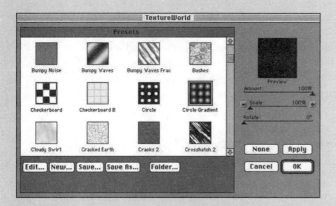

Next, to make three copies of this layer, hold down the option key, click the layer, and drag the layer up in the Layer Stack. Make the middle layer active by double-clicking it in the Layer Stack, and then repeat the procedure for setting up a 4-Point Gradient. This time, use yellow and blue. Next, activate the third, or bottom, layer and create a 4-Point Gradient there with orange and green (shown in the next figure).

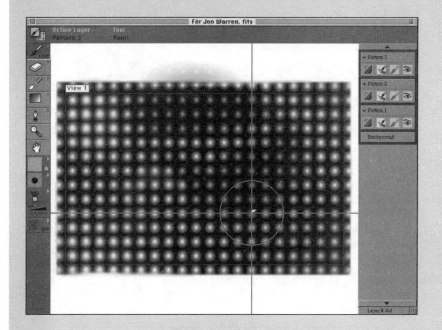

Continued

(continued)

With this simple three-layer set-up, you can now use any combination of Brush, Eraser, and Rectangle tools to easily adjust the colors and the opacity of the layers. See how the colors from the three layers show through each other! You now have an impressive 5- by 3-meter textured background, created in 48-bit color at 300 dpi, and ready to be ripped to film for high-quality printing. (Remember to save the file. The Live Picture format is saved to a FITS file. This is our working file — it includes all the mathematics and directions for rendering the different pieces of this project.) Now all of the pieces for this sprawling project are derived from the design of this single FITS file.

For the next step, you'll create some exciting gradient effects by generating a new layer from Create ⇨ Artwork. An Effects Menu appears at the top middle of the screen (this contains the options for the new Artwork layer that you've just created). Choose the Prismatic Effect. Then choose a silver color and draw out a 4-Point Gradient. Set the opacity at 100 percent in two opposite corners, and at 25 percent in the other two. Click inside the rectangle to fill the rectangle with these settings. The Prism forms its center where you click, so click again if you want to change the center. Wow! Remember, this is a fully editable, resolution-independent graphic element, in 48-bit color, covering a 5 by 3 meter canvas, separated on its own layer.

Choose a large Eraser brush (second from the top in the tool stack) and make a circular hole in the middle of our canvas. Brush smoothly in a circular motion and note how the gradient pattern changes its form. Change brush sizes and opacity, try different pressure settings, and create more circular patterns as shown in the following figure.

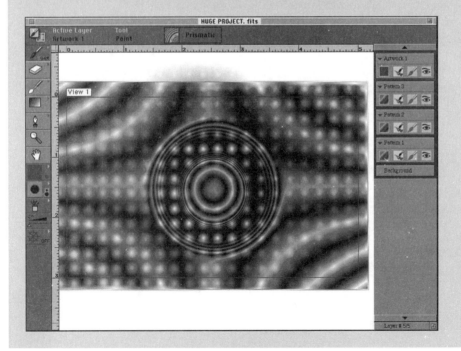

Change the color to a darker gray. The change is instant—pure magic! This project can be developed in more ways. Duplicate the Artwork layer by option-clicking and dragging the layer up in the Layer Stack. Flip the layer and you have a symmetrical design. Modify the circular gradient patterns with the eraser brush constrained to horizontal movement. Now, go back to the top Artwork layer, and change the effect there to Disco Light.

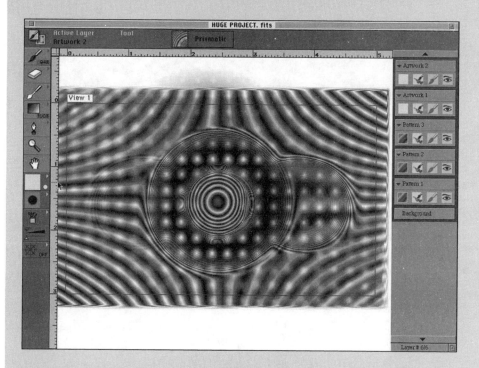

Double-click Artwork layer 2 and see the mix of the two gradient effects as shown in the preceding figure. Although you could continue to manipulate and discover many more exciting textures, stop here with this background. It is used as the source to generate a variety of related materials: brochures, stickers, and other printed material, but also the backgrounds and animation for a Web site.

Now, to prepare for animation, you have many ways to go, of which two are most obvious. One alternative is to build (or render) all of the layers into a single composite file that can be reinserted (Create ➪ Image Insertion) by opening a new image with 72-dpi screen resolution and/or smaller scale. Instead, use this composite at 300 dpi, zoom into an area of interest in the middle of the design, and set up a new View (View ➪ Add/Edit). By default, this generates View 2.

You can specify any number of Views (see the following figure), all of which can be rendered out by using the View ➪ Shoot command. Select View ➪ Shoot to shoot a 72-dpi PICT file of any View that you have specified.

Continued

(continued)

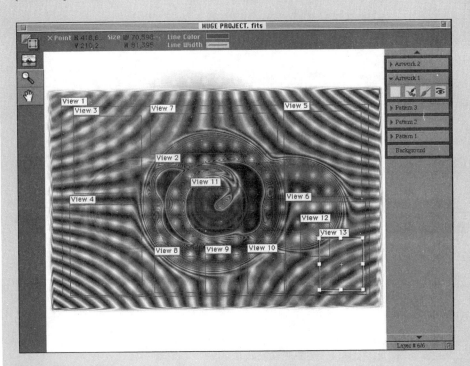

Or, using many layers, and big image files, you can change and distort your image slightly and shoot a PICT file for every little modification. This method is unsurpassed when you want to generate a uniquely creative sequence of images. You'd probably need around 60-100 frames for a high-quality two-second video sequence, but only about 5-10 for successful Web animation. (To see this image in full color, refer to the color insert at the center of the book.)

Depending on the nature of the project and the relative care with which you've taken your shots, the final numbered PICT files might be brought into a post production program, such as After Effects or Premiere for additional compositing effects before exporting them to Flash. Or, you might set it up so that you can go directly to Flash.

(By the way, when saved, the file size for the final Live Picture FITS for this tutorial, based on a 5 by 3-meter artwork, was a modest 1.5MB.)

Cross-Reference For more information on importing a PICT sequence into Flash, see the Poser section of Chapter 20, or the "Importing a Sequence into Flash" section of Chapter 21.

Exporting Raster Images from Flash

If you've been wondering how to use your artwork in Flash with other raster-based applications, then this section is for you. Many people prefer to use Flash as their primary drawing and illustration tool, thanks to Flash's unique approach to vector artwork that doesn't involve confusing Bézier handles and anchor points.

Combined with a pressure-sensitive graphics tablet, Flash can indeed become a powerful illustration program.

Why would you want to export raster-based images from a vector-based application? The answer is quite simple: Some applications work better with raster (or bitmap) images than they do with vector images. As you'll see in Chapter 22, video-editing applications usually prefer working with bitmaps over working with vectors. If the application in which you want to use Flash artwork supports vector file formats such as EPS or AI, then you most likely want to use those instead of bitmap-based formats such as BMP or PCT.

Cross-Reference   We'll discuss using external vector applications in Chapter 18. If you want the best quality artwork from Flash, jump over to that chapter.

If you are unsure of the format to use in your graphics program, refer to Table 17-1. Afterward, we'll show you how to export a frame's artwork as a static raster image.

Table 17-1
Raster Image Formats for Flash Export

Flash Export Format	*File Extension*	*Comments*
BMP (PC only) Windows Bitmap	BMP	Can be used with all PC and some Mac applications. Variable bit depths and compression settings with support of alpha channels. Supports lossless compression. Ideal for high quality graphics work.
GIF Graphics Interchange File	GIF	Limited to a 256-color (or less) palette. Not recommended as a high-quality Flash export format, even for Web use.
JPEG Joint Photographic Experts Group	JPG	Supports 24-bit RGB color. No alpha channel support. Recommended for most high-quality graphics work. Note that this format does throw out color information due to its lossy compression method.
PICT (Mac only) Picture	PCT	Can be used with many PC and all Mac applications. Variable bit depths and compression settings with support of alpha channels. Supports lossless compression. Can contain vector and raster graphics. Ideal for high quality graphics work.
PNG Portable Network Graphic	PNG	Supports variable bit depth (PNG-8 and PNG-24) and compression settings with alpha channels. Lossless compression schemes make it an ideal candidate for any high-quality graphics work.

To export a raster image format from Flash 4:

1. Move the Current Frame Indicator in the Flash Timeline to the frame that contains the artwork you wish to export.

2. Choose the File ⇨ Export Image command.

3. Select a destination folder and enter a file name. Select your preferred raster image format in the Save as Type drop-down menu.

4. Depending on the file format you selected, you are presented with an export dialog box with options specific to that file format. Next, we take a look at the general options and at some file-specific settings.

General export options in raster formats

Every raster image format in Flash's Export dialog box has the same initial options. All of these options (as seen in Figure 17-7) pertain to the image size, resolution, and bit depth. You can also trim any unused stage area from the final exported image.

A. Dimensions. The Width and Height options control the image's width and height, respectively, in pixels. Note that the aspect ratio of these values is always locked. You cannot control the Width value independently of the Height value.

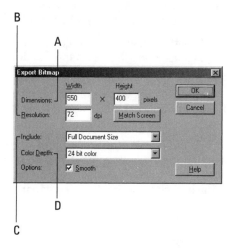

Figure 17-7: The general options of the Export dialog box for raster image formats

B. **Resolution.** Measured in dpi (dots per inch), this setting controls the quality of the image, in terms of how much information is present in the image. By default, this setting is 72 dpi. If you want to use Flash artwork in print or high-resolution graphics work, enter a higher value such as 300 or 600. If you change this setting accidentally, pressing the Match Screen button reverts the value to 72 dpi, the resolution of most computer monitors. Note that changing the value for this setting also changes the Width and Height values in the Dimensions setting.

C. **Include.** This drop-down menu determines what Flash content is included in the exported image.

- **Minimum Image Area.** When this option is selected, the image size (a.k.a. *dimensions*) is reduced to the boundary of Flash artwork currently on the Stage. This means that, if you only have a circle in the middle of the Stage, then the dimensions of the exported image match those of the circle—the rest of the Flash Stage or background is be included.

- **Full Document Size.** When this option is selected, the exported image looks exactly like the Flash stage. The entire frame dimensions and contents are exported.

D. **Color Depth (or Colors).** This drop-down setting controls the color range of the raster image. The higher the bit depth, the wider the color range. Depending on the file format, not all options are identical. We define the most frequently occurring options here. Note that this option is not available for the JPEG format, as that format must always be 24-bit.

- **8-bit grayscale.** This option limits the image to 256 levels, or values, of gray. It is equivalent to a typical scan of a black and white photograph.

- **8-bit color.** This option reduces the image to 256 colors. You may notice unsightly dithering in the image as a result. See Chapter 25 for more information regarding dither.

- **24-bit color.** This option enables the image to use any of the 16.7 million colors available in true RGB color space. Use this option for the best color quality.

- **32-bit color w/ alpha.** This image enables the same range of colors as 24-bit color, but also adds an alpha channel using the Flash movie's background color as a guide. If your raster image program can read alpha channels, then the Flash background color is transparent.

Other raster file format options

Each file format may have additional export options. In this section, we'll look at the additional options available for BMP (PC only), PCT or PICT (Mac only), and GIF. These options have not changed from the previous release of Flash. In fact, you may have more control with export file formats using the Export Image command instead of the Publish Settings/Publish commands.

The JPEG, GIF, and PNG format options are discussed in Chapter 25. Because a problem exists with publishing adaptive GIFs in the Macintosh version of Flash, however, we explore the GIF export options here.

BMP (PC only) options

The Windows Bitmap (.BMP) file format has numerous options. In addition to the general export settings, the .BMP export dialog box has an Options setting containing a check box for Smooth. When this option is checked, Flash antialiases all Flash artwork, making the edges nice and smooth. If this option is unchecked, then Flash artwork is rendered in an aliased fashion, in which edges appear jagged and rough.

In most external graphics applications, the 32-bit w/ alpha option in the Colors drop-down menu is not supported. You should use the 24-bit option if you experience difficulties using 32-bit BMP files. If you need to export an image with alpha channel support, use the PNG format in the Windows version of Flash 4.

PICT (Mac only) options

The PICT (short for Picture) format is a standard Macintosh graphic file format. Any Macintosh application that uses graphics can use it, and, with QuickTime, you can use PICT (or .PCT) files on Windows computers. PICT files can contain both vector and raster (bitmap) information. Usually, only raster-based PICT files are truly cross-platform. See Figure 17-8.

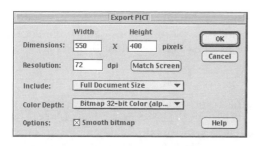

Figure 17-8: The PICT format has a unique Objects option in addition to traditional raster-based options.

✦ **Color Depth.** This drop-down menu is the same as the Colors setting for other raster-image file formats. It has a few peculiarities that are defined next.

- **Objects.** Due to the transgender nature of PICT files, you can specify Objects to export Flash artwork as vector-based images. Note that selecting this option enables you to select Use PostScript in the Options setting. Use PostScript that contains PICT output with caution, as it can produce undesirable results. If you need PostScript output, it is better to use Illustrator or EPS as the format.

- **Bitmap 1-bit B/W.** This option converts all colors to either black or white, with no in-between values of gray. It is equivalent to the Bitmap image mode in Photoshop, and gives a fax document look to your Flash artwork.

- **Bitmap 8-bit Gray.** This option converts your Flash artwork colors to 256 values of gray.

- **Bitmap 8-bit Color.** This option creates an adaptive palette of 256 colors for the exported image.

- **Bitmap 24-bit Color.** This option produces the highest-quality raster-based PICT files, enabling any color in the RGB color space to be represented. By default, you should use this option for graphics work in other applications.

- **Bitmap 32-bit Color (alpha channel).** This option has the same color depth as 24-bit color, with the addition of an alpha channel (or transparent mask). An unoccupied area of the Flash Stage is used to determine the transparent areas of the alpha channel.

✦ **Options.** The PICT export dialog box displays one option. The option displayed varies depending on the Color Depth setting.

- **Smooth bitmap.** If you chose any of the Bitmap color options in Color Depth, then you have the option of antialiasing (or smoothing) Flash artwork. Smoothing produces cleaner edges on Flash vector-based artwork.

- **Include PostScript.** If you choose Objects from the Color Depth menu, then you can enable the Include PostScript option. This option optimizes the file's settings for output to a PostScript-compatible printer.

GIF options

The majority of the options listed in the Colors section of the GIF export dialog box are discussed in Chapter 25's section "Using the GIF Settings." The Colors drop-down menu is slightly different, however. Also, as mentioned in a previous note, the Publish settings in the Macintosh version of Flash 4 do not create adaptive GIF images (even if you have selected the option to do so). You can, however, create suitable GIF images in both Windows and Macintosh versions of Flash 4 using the Export Image command. See Figure 17-9.

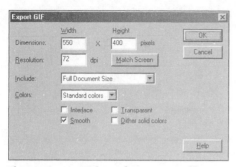

Figure 17-9: Options that are specific to the GIF format

You can see the effect of each of these color options by looking at a series of GIF images created from a test Flash movie, gifcolors.fla, located in the ch17 folder of the *Flash 4 Bible* CD-ROM. Each GIF color depth setting was applied to this movie, and saved as a separate GIF image.

✦ **Colors.** As stated in the discussion regarding general options, this setting controls the range of colors contained in the exported image. GIF images can use a variety of bit depths with the overall 8-bit color depth setting. The fewer colors, the smaller the resulting GIF file.

• **Black & White.** This option is equivalent to a 2-bit color depth, and converts all Flash colors to one of three colors (Web hex in parentheses): black (#000000), middle gray (#808080), or white (#FFFFFF).

• **4, 8, 16, 32, 64, 128 or 256 colors.** These options create the respective color ranges within the GIF format. Note that Flash determines what colors are used for each setting, similar to the adaptive palette type in Photoshop.

• **Standard Colors.** This option creates GIF images that use the 216 Web-safe palette.

✦   ✦   ✦

Working with Vector Graphics

While Flash 4 has effective drawing tools, don't be mistaken: It is not a replacement for a full-featured illustration program like Macromedia FreeHand or Adobe Illustrator. Creating complex artwork can be accomplished much more easily in these programs — and integrating the final artwork with Flash is a cinch.

Preparing Vector Graphics for Flash Movies

Earlier in this book, we discussed the use of external media in Flash movies. However, not all vector graphics are created the same. Some vector graphics may be simple objects and fills, while others may include complex blending or paths that will add significant weight to a Flash movie. Even though most vector graphics are by nature much smaller than raster graphics equivalents, don't assume that they're optimized for Flash use.

Cross-Reference   Please read Chapter 7 for details on importing all types of external media, including vector artwork, into Flash movies.

Guidelines for using external vector graphics in Flash

Because Flash is primarily a vector-based application, using vector graphics from other applications is rather straightforward. However, because most vector graphics applications are geared for print production (for example, publishing documents intended for press), you need to keep some principles in mind when creating graphics for Flash in external graphics applications:

✦ Limit or reduce the number of points describing complex paths. This chapter takes a look at using FreeHand's Simplify command and Illustrator's Pathfinder window to accomplish this task.

✦ Limit the number of embedded typefaces (or fonts). Multiple fonts add to the final SWF movie's file size. This chapter shows you how to convert fonts to outlines in both FreeHand and Illustrator.

✦ To insure color consistency between applications, use only RGB colors (and color pickers) for artwork. Flash can only use RGB color values, and converts any CMYK colors to RGB colors. Color conversions usually produce unwanted color shifts. This chapter shows you how to set up FreeHand and Illustrator to avoid this.

✦ Gradients created in other drawing applications are not converted to Flash gradients when the file is imported. Unless you're using Macromedia Free-Hand, you need to replace externally created gradients with Flash gradients or accept the file size addition to the Flash movie. This chapter teaches you how to redraw gradients in Flash.

✦ Some vector formats can use layers, and Flash recognizes these layers if the graphic file format is correctly specified. Layers keep graphic elements separate from one another.

Reducing path complexity

All vector graphics are made up of paths, in one shape or another. A path can be as simple as a straight line with two points, a curved line with two points, or 500 or more points along an irregular shape or fill. This is why vector graphics are well suited for noncontinuous tone images, like logos, architectural drawings, clip art, and so forth. Fonts are also made up of paths. As we've seen with Flash-drawn graphics, you can scale them at any size without any loss of resolution. You learned in the last chapter that raster (bitmap) artwork can not scale larger than the original size without loss of resolution.

Note

Vector graphics are eventually "rasterized," so to speak. The vector formatting for drawn shapes and text is more of a simplified storage structure that contains a mathematical description (that is, smaller than a bit-for-bit description) of an object or set of objects. When the vector graphic is displayed, especially with antialiasing, the video card needs to render the edges in pixels. Likewise, the PostScript RIP (Raster Image Processor) of a laser printer needs to convert the vector information or an EPS (Encapsulated PostScript) file into printer "dots."

When you are using imported vector graphics in Flash movies, you should minimize the number of points describing curved lines or intricate outlined graphics (for example, "traced" raster images). One of the biggest problems with creating cool graphics in vector-based applications like Illustrator, FreeHand, and 3D Studio Max is the number of points used to describe lines. When these graphics are imported into Flash, animations will be slower and harder to redraw (or refresh) on the computer screen. Also, the file size of the Flash movie will grow considerably.

Simplify paths in FreeHand

Complex artwork can be "simplified" in FreeHand. Simplifying will reduce the number of points to describe a path (or a set of paths). To simplify any artwork, select the paths that describe the object and choose Modify ➪ Alter Path ➪ Simplify (see Figure 18-1).

Figure 18-1: The Simplify dialog box in FreeHand 8 can reduce the complexity of vector artwork.

The slider and/or text field of the Simplify dialog box controls how much information is discarded from the original artwork. While it might seem tempting to use the highest setting (10), you may end up drastically changing the look of the original artwork. See Figure 18-2 for an example.

a) Original artwork   b) Simplify "5"   c) Simplify "8"

Figure 18-2: Compare the effects of the Simplify command at different settings.

While the visual difference between the Simplify settings may not be readily apparent, the resulting SWF file sizes are noticeably different. The original artwork's SWF file (when copied, pasted, and exported from Flash 4) was 49KB. The simplified "5" version of the original produced a 32KB SWF file, and the simplified "8" version resulted in a 30KB SWF file.

On the CD-ROM

To see the differences for yourself, check out seashell_normal.swf, seashell_5.swf, and seashell_8.swf in the ch18 folder of the *Flash 4 Bible* CD-ROM.

Granted, those are still pretty large SWF movies, but it does illustrate the file-size savings that the Simplify command can accomplish.

Optimize curves command in Flash

You can also reduce the complexity of paths within Flash 4, by using the Modify ➪ Curves ➪ Optimize command. This has the same effect as the Simplify command in

FreeHand, with a couple of extra options. Be sure to use the Modify ➪ Break Apart command before you use the Optimize command — you can't optimize groups or symbols. In Figure 18-3, you can see the effect of maximum smoothing on the seashell 5 graphic from the previous section.

Figure 18-3: Flash 4's Optimize Curves dialog box enables you to specify multiple passes, which means that Flash will optimize the graphic at a given setting as much as it possibly can.

On the
CD-ROM

You can test the Optimize Curves effect on the seashells_5.fla file, located in the ch18 folder of the *Flash 4 Bible* CD-ROM.

Using the Pathfinder window in Illustrator 8

You can use the Pathfinder window in Illustrator 8 to join overlapping paths. Not only does this reduce the complexity of the path but it makes the graphic easier to handle as a group.

Select the overlapping paths by Shift-clicking each object. In the Pathfinder window, select an operation that is suitable for the overlapping elements. In Figure 18-4, the Unite command is used to combine the individual components of the crosshair into one unified path.

Tracing complex vector artwork in Flash

Many graphics programs like Kinetix, 3D Studio Max, and Adobe Dimensions can create some astonishing vector-based graphics. However, when you import EPS versions of those graphics into Flash, they either fall apart (display horribly) or add unrealistic byte chunks to your Flash movie. Does this mean you can't use these intricate graphics in Flash movies?

You can try to do a number of things with intricate vector artwork, including using the methods described previously. Depending on the needs of the artwork, you may be able to output small raster equivalents that won't consume nearly as much space as highly detailed vector graphics. Or, you can try redrawing the artwork in Flash. Sound crazy and time-consuming? Well, it's a bit of both, but many Flash designers will spend hours on end getting incredibly small file sizes from "hand-tracing" vector designs in Flash.

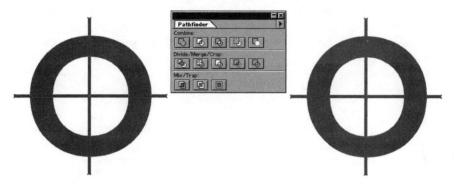

Figure 18-4: Combine paths into single path with the Pathfinder window.

For example, if you made a highly detailed technical drawing of a light bulb, and wanted to bring into Flash, you could import the original EPS version of the drawing into Flash, place it on a locked layer, and use Flash drawing tools to recreate the object (see Figure 18-5).

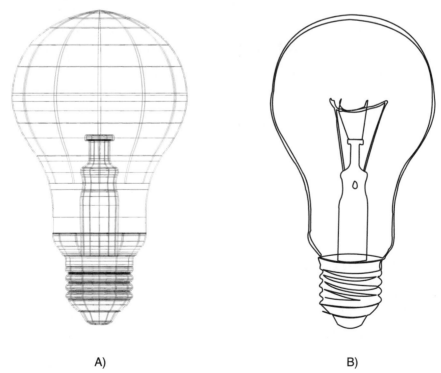

A)   B)

Figure 18-5: Compare the original artwork of the light bulb (A) to the simplified version drawn in Flash (B).

Converting text to outlines

Another aspect of vector graphics that you need to keep in mind — especially when working with other designers — is font linking and embedding. With most vector file formats like Illustrator, FreeHand, or EPS (Encapsulated PostScript), you can link to fonts that are located on your system. But, if you give those files to someone else who doesn't have those fonts installed, then he/she won't be able to see or use those fonts. Some formats enable you to embed fonts into the document file, which circumvents this problem. However, whether the fonts are linked or embedded, you may be unnecessarily bloating the size of the vector graphic.

You can convert any text into outlines (a.k.a. *paths*) in any drawing or illustration program (see Figure 18-6). In FreeHand 8, select the text as a text block (not with the Text tool) and choose Text ⇨ Convert to Paths. In Illustrator 8, select the text as an object and choose Type ⇨ Create Outlines.

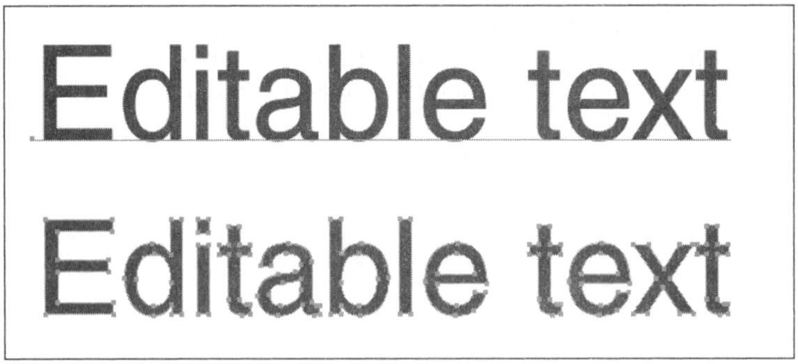

Editable text
Editable text

Figure 18-6: Make sure you have finalized any text editing before you convert the text to outlines. The text at the top can be edited, whereas the text at the bottom (the same text converted to outlines) cannot be.

If you have a lot of body text in the graphic, you may want to copy the text directly into a Flash text box and use a _sans, _serif, or _typewriter device font. These fonts do not require any excess file information (such as embedded fonts) when used in a Flash movie.

Controlling color output

Flash 4 can only use a RGB color space, meaning that it renders colors in an additive fashion — full red, green, and blue light added together will produce white light. Whenever possible, use RGB color pickers in your preferred drawing application. If you use CMYK (subtraction colors), then you will notice color shifts when the artwork is imported into Flash 4. If you're using Adobe Illustrator 8, then make sure you specify colors with the RGB color picker — this will insure that both copy-and-pasted objects and exported files will appear as you see them in the Illustrator workspace. If you're using Macromedia FreeHand 8.0.1, then you have a wider range of clipboard options.

Setting up preferences in FreeHand

Macromedia FreeHand 8.0.1 has controllable clipboard options, accessible via File ⇨ Preferences. In the PC version of FreeHand, click the Import/Export tab of the Preferences dialog box. In the Mac version of FreeHand, click the Export category of the Preferences dialog box. There, you'll find a Convert Colors To drop-down menu. If you are using a mix of CMYK and RGB color in a FreeHand document, then choose "CMYK and RGB." However, this may render CMYK artwork differently in Flash 4. If you want WYSIWYG (What You See Is What You Get) color between FreeHand and Flash, you may opt to use the solitary RGB option. This option converts all artwork to RGB color space, regardless of the original color picker used to fill the object(s).

Saving in the proper file format

Some vector file formats cannot save artwork color values in RGB space. If you are using Adobe Illustrator 8, make sure you specify Illustrator 7 in the Illustrator document options when saving. If you choose the Illustrator 6 or lower format, then RGB values will not be saved and color shifts will result. If you are exporting EPS files from FreeHand 8, use the Setup (PC) or Options (Mac) button in the Export Document dialog box to access the same color options available in the FreeHand Preferences, discussed previously. Because FreeHand 8.0.1 supports direct export to SWF files, you should use this option to insure complete color compatibility with Flash 4.

Replacing blends with Flash gradients

A favorite trick among 3D Flash designers, replacing externally-rendered "blends" with Flash gradients, drastically cuts down on Flash movie (.SWF) file sizes. Unless you're using FreeHand 8.0.1, gradients or blends created in drawing, illustration, or 3D programs will not be converted to Flash gradients when the graphic(s) are imported into Flash.

On the CD-ROM Use the 3Dgraphic.eps file, located in the ch18 folder of the *Flash 4 Bible* CD-ROM, if you need a sample image for the following steps.

Because the vast majority of applications do not render Flash-style gradients, it's up to you to decide to accept the file size "weight gains" of shaded blends or to recreate the blends with Flash gradients after the artwork has been imported into the Flash authoring environment. Here's the general process for replacing externally created blends in Flash:

1. Once the artwork has been rendered as an EPS or AI file, open Flash 4. Create a new graphic symbol and open this symbol in the Symbol Editing stage. Import the EPS graphic into the first frame of the symbol.

2. Break apart (Command+B or Ctrl+B) or ungroup the imported vector artwork to the point where you isolate the blend separately from the rest of the graphic. If you break apart the imported vector graphic, then it should be reduced to "symbol" parts and groups in one step as seen in Figure 18-7. Note that Flash will convert EPS blends to symbols (accessible from the Flash Library). These symbols will contain two layers: a mask layer and a blend layer.

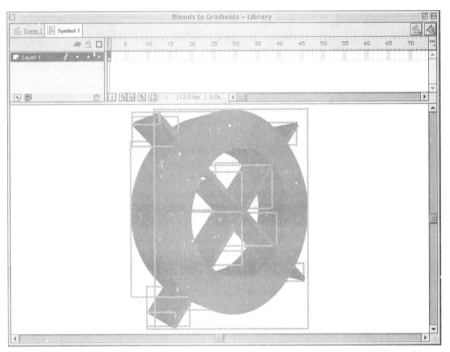

Figure 18-7: When the Break Apart command is applied to the imported graphic, you can access the individual groups within the graphic.

3. Select each symbol that contains a blend, and use the Edit in Place feature to erase the "blend" graphics. Keep the original mask layer intact, but replace the blend layer contents with a Flash gradient. Refer to Figures 18-8 and 18-9 for more details.

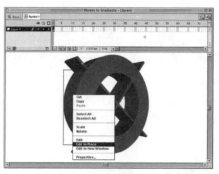 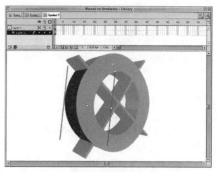

Figure 18-8: Ctrl-click (Mac) or right-click a selected symbol, and choose Edit in Place. Replace the blend in the lower layer of the symbol with a Flash gradient. You may need to make a three- or four-color gradient, and use the Transform Fill modifier of the Paint Bucket tool to modify the direction and size of the gradient.

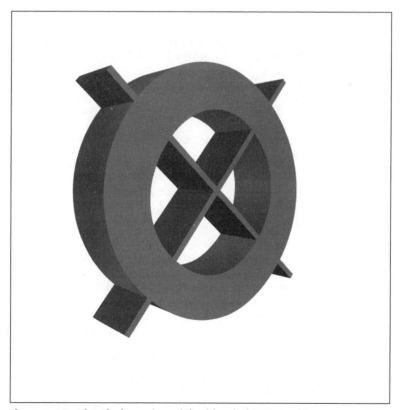

Figure 18-9: The Flash version of the blended EPS graphic

When you are done replacing each blend's symbol with a Flash gradient, you'll have a better-looking (and slightly smaller) Flash movie. If you are working with multiple imported vector graphics that have blends, you'll end up with much smaller Shockwave Flash movies — which means Web visitors will spend less time waiting to see your movies.

Tip

Remember that gradients created in Macromedia FreeHand 8.0.1 can be directly exported to SWF files as Flash gradients. FreeHand's transparent colors will also convert to Flash alpha colors.

Using layered EPS or Illustrator files

A handy feature of many popular illustration programs is support for layers. Just like layers in a Flash editor document (.FLA file) or a Photoshop image (.PSD file), layers in illustration programs enable you to keep individual groups of graphics separate from one another. A simple "trick" with animating vector graphic files is to animate or tween each layer separately in the Flash authoring environment.

A quick example of an easy Illustrator-to-Flash layered movie is a business card. If you have laid out any promotion materials in Illustrator or FreeHand and have kept the elements separated by layers, then you can create an interactive business card.

On the CD-ROM

You can use the sample business card, businesscard.eps, in the ch18 folder of the *Flash 4 Bible* CD-ROM for this exercise.

1. Create a layered graphic in Illustrator or FreeHand. Before a new element is created, make a new layer for it.

2. If you used extensive text controls (such as kerning, leading, tracking, and so on), then convert the text to outlines (or paths).

3. Save the layout as an EPS file. If you have used RGB colors in the document and want them to appear the same in Flash 4, make sure you save it as an Illustrator 7 file — artwork saved as an Illustrator 8 file may not import correctly into Flash. In FreeHand, you may have difficulty with the exported EPS file format. We recommend that you export your FreeHand documents as Illustrator 7 documents for better layer compatibility with Flash.

Caution

CMYK colors will shift when imported into the RGB color space of Flash. Moreover, some masking and cropping information (for bleeds) may not be interpreted by Flash.

4. Import the EPS or AI file into Flash 4. You may want to create a new scene or symbol to contain the imported graphic(s). Otherwise, the layers from the EPS or AI file will be stacked on top of or below your current layers. See Figure 18-10 for reference.

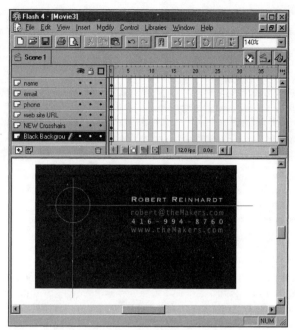

Figure 18-10: When a layered EPS or AI is imported into the Flash, the layers will be converted to Flash layers.

5. Even though Flash recognizes the layers in the EPS or AI file, it will not group elements on each layer. So, select any one layer and lock the others. Select everything on the active unlocked layer (Command+A or Ctrl+A) and group it (Command+G or Ctrl+G). Alternatively, you can convert the selection into a symbol for easier manipulation later. You will need to make button symbols for any element that you want to use interactively (such as clicking the name to e-mail the person, and so on). Repeat this step for every layer.

6. Now add any Flash tweens or actions to the groups or symbols in each layer. At this point, continue creating a full Flash movie with other components, or export a Shockwave Flash movie.

As you can see, in just six straightforward steps, you can create an interactive business card that can be put on a floppy disk or in an e-mail. Whenever you're developing complicated layered work in an illustration application like Illustrator or FreeHand, you can take advantage of those layers in Flash. However, if you want to see how to use FreeHand as a complete concept planner for Flash movies, don't stop here — read the next section.

On the CD-ROM Check out the completed interactive business card, businesscard.fla or business-card.swf, located in the ch18 folder of the *Flash 4 Bible* CD-ROM.

Expert Tutorial: Focus on FreeHand:More Than Just an Extended Flash Toolbar *by Todd Purgason*

Todd Purgason is the Creative Director for Juxt Interactive, a southern California-based Web design shop specializing in Internet strategy and Flash-based interactive Web sites. Todd has led Juxt in creating innovative work that has been highlighted in several Web and print publications including HOW Magazine, Communication Arts, High Five, eMarketer, Netscape *and others. They have been honored with five Macromedia "Shocked Site of the Day" awards and are featured in both the Flash and FreeHand Galleries on Macromedia's Web site.*

Flash 4 is a very powerful tool for developing intelligent and sophisticated Web sites and interactive environments. But as most of us in the digital design arena know, no single tool does it all. We have all mastered many applications that enable us to design and produce the images and interfaces that are imagined in our mind's eye. The old cliché, "the right tool for the job," holds just as true in the digital arena as it does in your grandpappy's garage. By adding FreeHand to your Flash toolbox, you go from having four drawers of specialized tools to having eight drawers of specialized tools. FreeHand is an extremely powerful illustration and typography tool that brings more than ten years of research, design and refinement to all your Flash projects. By tapping the strengths of FreeHand, your Flash 4 applications can be that much more effective.

What advantages can FreeHand give to Flash 4 projects?

For starters, familiarity: Flash 4 is a new tool with a new paradigm for creating vector graphic artwork. It works with vectors but often feels like a raster-based authoring application. Many of us are very used to objects with lines, curves, points, and fills that are the basic foundations of applications like FreeHand and Illustrator. We have become quite proficient in this working model and setting these skills aside would be a terrible waste. FreeHand brings much more than familiarity to the table. It has very powerful tools for illustration and—my personal favorite—typography.

One of the huge benefits of using FreeHand in the Flash design process is conceptualizing a design. Using FreeHand's multi-page format, you can layout moments in time or keyframes to visualize and study the interface and motion graphics you will be executing in Flash. This is one of the big advantages of using FreeHand as opposed to Illustrator for your conceptualizing needs—Illustrator is limited to one page documents. In addition, Macromedia has spent a great deal of time and effort on things like the animate to layer tool and SWF export in FreeHand. These features enable FreeHand to live symbiotically in the same design space as Flash.

In my opinion the greatest asset FreeHand brings to the Flash table is PRINT. Ooooo . . . that nasty word: the old medium of print. Don't we live in the paperless society yet? Guess again. While developing your design in FreeHand you are actually doing production and comping at the same time. After you have visualized an animation over several pages in FreeHand, it is a very simple task to bring those pages together onto a large format presentation board that you can output to a printer. These presentations blow the clients away!

Once you get approval, it is on to Flash. You breathe life into the design you have been carefully planning in FreeHand. And if your clients are like mine, they'll come back and want you to do print promotions, ads and even identity materials based off the site. You already have all the print assets developed in your page comps. What a bonus! I just hate getting more billable work, don't you?

Developing a process model

As the complexities of this process would require several chapters, what I will do now is walk you through the key steps using visuals from a recent project of my own. The piece I will be using is appropriately titled "The Process," an in-house marketing project. It is basically a reflection of our creative philosophy at Juxt Interactive. You can see this project at `www.juxtinteractive.com/theprocess`. Refer to the color section of this book for an image of this Web site.

Design

Just about every Flash project I have seen is carried out over one or several layouts that I call *scenes*. The term *scenes* is appropriate because oftentimes they are just that — scenes in the Flash movie. After I have developed a concept in my head and scribbled sketches on paper, I go to FreeHand and start sketching out scenes. The following figure is an example of such scenes.

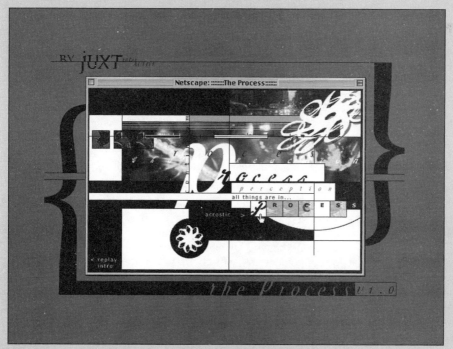

The Process scene, as seen in a Web browser with the Flash Player plug-in

Continued

(continued)

Next, I start building moments in time, or keyframes, which bring elements (characters) into the scene to be laid out and experimented with. I typically start by developing a moment in time that is very heavy visually—typically the end of the first major scene. Once I am happy with the scene and the way the elements or characters are working together, I duplicate the page in FreeHand. Using the duplicated page(s), I then experiment with the relationships of the all the characters. During this step, I keep in mind what motions will be employed to get me to and from this moment. I continue to develop a number of keyframes that explain to me what I intend to do. Kyle Cooper of Imaginary Forces, the renowned film title designer, has been a great inspiration to me and many others. He once said, "I think that, in the end, I should be able to pull any frame out of my title sequences and it should be able to stand on its own as an effective illustration." By studying my design as snapshots in time in FreeHand I am able to ensure that the motion is not destroying the concept, but rather enhancing its effectiveness.

Realness of presentation

Now, I have many pages that help me understand just how to pull this project off. I take those keyframe pages and lay them out onto a large format sheet that will be printed on our large format HP Design Jet at roughly 30" × 40". Many people ask me why I continue to print in this day and age. I will tell you why: communication. Half of the job of design is selling the design you create, especially if you are asking the client to take risks pushing the envelope that they are accustomed to. A digital presentation has many advantages, but so does a good old tangible printed piece.

We have developed a presentation process at Juxt that I affectionately call the 2×4 approach. It is based on the old idiom, "How do you get the attention of a donkey? Hit him over the head with a 2×4." Don't get me wrong—I'm not insulting any clients out there. The point is to make an impact. When we go into a presentation, it is our intention to exceed the client's expectations and to make the client very happy. With a presentation board, I can show many keyframes or screens simultaneously as I walk the client through the animation, explaining the process of the motion or the interaction of the interface without having to commit the resources to create an actual working prototype at this early stage.

But the advantages are far greater than saving time. The clients can absorb the design when it is all laid out for them. They can see how their brand is working across the piece. They can grasp the wholeness of it. And the print piece is very tangible. They can take ownership of it emotionally. The digital medium is so abstract where print is so real. But most importantly, it communicates to the client that you are good at what you do. They will have more faith in the decisions that you are going to make for them during the process of creating the project. Refer to the following figure.

Instant changeability

So you have presented the project and your client is blown away but his partner walks in and says, "Ewwwwwwwwww . . . I just hate that green." You try to objectively explain its purpose and importance to the piece, but he won't budge. If you had completed a prototype in Flash, you would have to go back and spend many tedious hours changing that green to tan. But because you laid it out in FreeHand, you can change that green to tan across the entire piece in all of about 5 seconds. You simply select the new tan color in FreeHand's Web-safe color palette, drag and drop it on top of the banished green in the color list, and voila, every instance of the green is now tan. No matter if it is on lines, files, patterns, text, or even colored bitmaps, it is now tan.

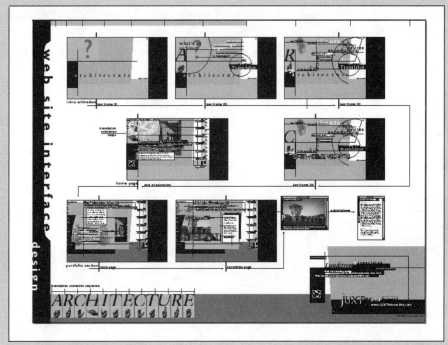

The Process board, to use as a printed presentation for clients. Refer to the color section of this book for another process board example.

Before you have time to gloat, the client's lackey graphics guy tells you that you were given the old corporate design standards manual. Instead of Franklin Gothic (the font you used on 75% of the typography), you are supposed to be using Meta Plus. Well, because you still have all your pages in FreeHand, you can simply use the graphic search-and-replace feature to instantly change every bit of Franklin Gothic to Meta Plus. After a few minutes of double-checking kerning effects, you are back to where you started. Now go ahead and feel proud of yourself. Your client will love the fact that these changes won't cost the company a dime.

Moving artwork from FreeHand to Flash

You have two ways to get your artwork from FreeHand to Flash: the SWF Export feature and the good old copy-and-paste method.

Continued

(continued)

Using the SWF export for static Flash movies

The SWF Export feature is generally the best method for outputting FreeHand files as Flash movies, as it creates the most optimized result and does much of the tedious work for you. For instance, if you have a tinted black and white TIFF image pasted inside a circle shape in a FreeHand drawing, you can export an optimized SWF movie. When you import that SWF file into Flash, your image will have automatically converted to a Flash bitmap image with a mask of the circle shape.

You can access the SWF Export feature by choosing File⇨Export (Shift+Command+R or Shift+Ctrl+R), and selecting Flash (.swf) (PC) or Flash SWF (Mac) in the Save as Type (PC) or Format (Mac) drop-down menu. Click the Options button (Mac) or the Setup button (PC) to access the conversion properties used for the Flash SWF file (see the following figure).

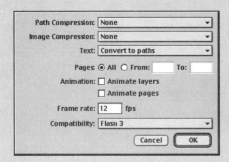

In the Export Document dialog box, you can access the SWF file settings by clicking the Options button (Mac) or Setup button (PC). Note that you can only choose Flash 3 as the SWF version format, which is perfectly fine for Flash 4 artwork. The Flash 4 SWF format has not changed any artwork specifications that were used in Flash 3.

In this section, we'll output a set of FreeHand objects as the basis of a Flash scene. Before you export a FreeHand document as a Flash file, you need to prepare the FreeHand artwork for optimal export. In the FreeHand file, select all the objects on a "moment in time" page that has the scene completely built and some of the elements or characters on the stage. Copy that page and paste it into a new FreeHand document, aligning the upper left-hand extents of objects with the upper left-hand extents of the page. If you have some complex typography elements with special kerning as well as body text, you will want to select the illustration text elements and convert them to paths using the Text⇨Convert to Paths command.

You will lose kerning of text if you export with the Maintainblocks option enabled. Always convert type elements that use special kerning or FreeHand-specific text effects. If you do *not* have body text, I recommend setting the text option of the SWF Export dialog box to

Convert to Paths. This will convert the characters to paths and create symbols of each character in the process.

Now access the Flash file properties in the Export Document dialog box. Because you are exporting a particular moment in time, turn off the Animate Pages and Animate Layers options in the Animation setting. Because this export is a transition from FreeHand to Flash and *not* a final file, you will want to eliminate any file degradation by setting the Path Compression and Image Compression drop-down menus to None. Export the file import it into Flash 4.

Once in Flash, you will want to go through a process of organizing your file and optimizing the imported artwork. The objects exported from FreeHand will come into Flash as a group. Some objects are often in nested groups. You will want to go through the process of moving key elements to separate Flash layers. As you do this, ungroup the objects and create logically named Flash symbols out of them. Once the scene is organized with objects grouped (as symbols) and arranged on their own layers, you are ready to animate.

Using copy and paste

You can also copy elements from a FreeHand document and paste them into Flash movies, using the Edit ➪ Copy and Edit ➪ Paste commands in each application, respectively. The copy-and-paste method can complement the SWF Export method — you can move through the process of building your animation by copying and pasting small pieces while SWF exporting large pieces as you see fit. For certain typography elements, I find it just as easy to recreate them in Flash using my FreeHand layout as a visual reference.

Using the SWF export for animating Flash movies

One other avenue for small simple animations is to use an "animate to layer" process in FreeHand to build a frame-by-frame animation in Flash. Go ahead and try this out for yourself, following these steps:

1. Create a circle and a square in FreeHand. Keep some distance between the two objects.

2. Select both objects and blend them together using the Modify ➪ Combine ➪ Blend command (Shift+Command+B or Shift+Ctrl+B), or Xtras ➪ Create ➪ Blend. Open the Object Inspector window. With the blend selected, change the Number of Steps value to 30 steps.

4. Select Xtras ➪ Animate ➪ Release to Layers. This will release each blend step to a unique layer.

5. Choose File ➪ Export, and access the Flash SWF options. Check the Animate Layers option, and set the Frame Rate to 15 fps. Click OK and export the SWF file.

6. Open Flash and import the SWF file. You will see 30 keyframes in the Flash Timeline, each containing a step in the blend.

Continued

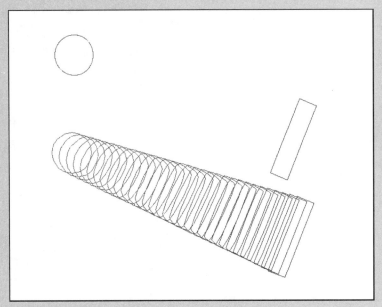

This FreeHand document shows the outlines of the two individual shapes, as well as the outlines of the 30-step blend between them.

While the Release to Layers function can be a quick way to produce shape morphing animations, it's not necessarily the best method. This feature was extremely useful prior to Flash 3, because shape morphing with hints was not supported within the Flash authoring environment.

General guidelines when using FreeHand with Flash

Once you get used to the process of exporting artwork to Flash, you'll find that it's relatively simple. However, you need to keep some "rules" in mind while working:

✦ If you are using Flash 3 or 4, you must set the Import/Export tab (or the Export category in the Mac version) of the FreeHand Preferences dialog box to use RGB color conversion (in the Convert Colors To drop-down menu). If you fail to do so, unexpected color shifts appear in your FreeHand and Flash artwork.

✦ When exporting .SWF files from FreeHand, do not include large amounts of body text. Recreate the body text (for example, copy and paste the text into a text box) in Flash.

✦ Remember that elements from FreeHand will be put into groups, often stacked or nested within other groups. If you can't edit an element, ungroup it or break it apart.

♦ Organize your FreeHand artwork into logical Flash layers. Develop a consistent system that you and others on your team can recognize and implement.

♦ You must be using FreeHand 8.01 or greater to export Flash 3 SWF files. There is no change in the artwork format used by Flash 4.

Using FreeHand to start your Flash project gives you huge advantages that don't detract from Flash as a tool. Rather, FreeHand can only enhance your understanding of animation and interactive concepts. With FreeHand, you have a fast, powerful tool to study your design and develop it without countless wasted hours of tweening that may or may not make the final cut. You will have fantastic print deliverables to sell your design approach. For me, this is the icing on the cake—I have print-ready materials if the client needs anything from the FreeHand concepts. That means I don't have to create my artwork or designs twice—I have more time to dedicate elsewhere in the design process.

Converting Rasters to Vectors

Have you ever wanted to take a scan of a "real" pen and ink drawing you made and turn it into a vector graphic? It's not incredibly hard to do, and the results are usually pretty close to the original (see Figure 18-11). You can also turn continuous tone or photographic images into vector art, but the converted version will not likely bear much resemblance to the original. However, this can be useful for aesthetic effects.

Figure 18-11: Compare the raster version (on the left) of the sketch to its traced vector version (on the right).

You can trace raster artwork with a handful of applications, including Flash 4. In the following sections, we'll compare the tracing abilities of Flash, FreeHand, and Adobe Streamline. With all of these tracing applications, keep in mind the following points:

✦ Higher resolution images will always yield better "traced" vector artwork. With more pixels to define edges, the application can better detect shapes.

✦ Sharper images (such as clearly focused images) and higher contrast images will produce better-traced artwork. Oftentimes, applying Photoshop art filters to an image can reduce the complexity of a photographic image, making it easier to trace.

✦ One-color images or scans, like those of hand-drawn sketches with pencil or ink, will produce the best-traced artwork.

Caution

Ironically, the results of some traced raster images can produce even larger vector images. Remember that vectors were designed for solid colors, blends, lines, and points. Every file format has its purpose, and sometimes raster images are smaller than their traced counterparts. With a little practice, you'll be able to judge what kind of images will produce small "traced" versions.

Flash's Trace Bitmap command

After you have imported a bitmap into Flash, you can use the Modify ➪ Trace Bitmap command to convert the image into Flash lines and fills. This method is by far the simplest and quickest method of tracing artwork to use in Flash movies. The benefits are that you can perform it directly in Flash 4 without the aid of external applications, you have moderate control of the conversion settings, and, most importantly, the artwork is converted directly into Flash lines and fills (see Figure 18-12 for an example).

If the results of the Trace Bitmap command are less than desirable, then use as many undo steps as necessary to get back to your original bitmap image.

Cross-
Reference

See Chapter 7 for more information on the Trace Bitmap settings.

FreeHand's Autotrace tool

Macromedia FreeHand also has tracing abilities, and arguably, they are more expansive than Flash's Trace Bitmap command. You can access the Autotrace tool in the FreeHand toolbox (see Figure 18-13). By double-clicking it, you can adjust the sensitivity of the Autotrace tool for imported bitmapped artwork. When you're ready to trace the bitmap, simply double-click the bitmap image with the Autotrace tool selected in the toolbox.

Figure 18-12: The Trace Bitmap command can be used to convert bitmap images into vector Flash artwork. Higher Minimum Area and Color Threshold values will reduce the complexity of the resulting Flash artwork, which means smaller Shockwave Flash movies. Refer to these same figures in the color section of the book.

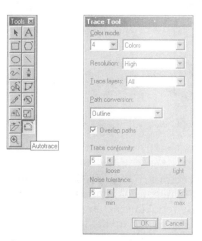

Figure 18-13: FreeHand's Autotrace tool has an array of options for precise tracing.

Because the nature of bitmapped artwork varies by subject matter, we recommend that you use a "trial and error" method for using the FreeHand Autotrace tool. If the results are not satisfactory, then simply undo the trace command. Or, refer to Deke McClelland's coverage of the Autotrace tool in the *FreeHand 8 Bible* (from IDG Books Worldwide).

Note   FreeHand retains the original bitmapped artwork behind the traced vector artwork. If you no longer need the bitmapped version, delete the bitmap image after you have moved the traced objects to a new location. Group the traced objects for greater ease in moving them.

Tracing with Adobe Streamline

While you can trace images in Adobe Illustrator, Adobe has a standalone product completely designed for the purpose of tracing raster artwork—Streamline 4.0. With Streamline, you have the most conversion options, and, more importantly, you can optimize the results with smoothing commands. See Figure 18-14 for an example of Streamline 4.0.

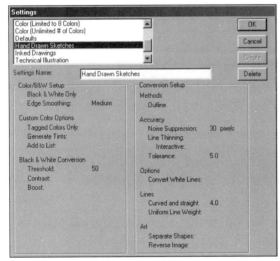

Figure 18-14: Streamline 4.0 hosts a wide range of presets in the Settings dialog box.

After you have converted a bitmap image to vector artwork, you have the option of "smoothing" the results. Smoothing means eliminating redundant or excess points to create simpler shapes and curves. By reducing the complexity of points in vector artwork, you can reduce the overall file size dramatically.

In the Edit menu, you can access two types of smoothing: Smooth Paths and Smooth Direction Points. Smooth Paths will eliminate anchor points within selected paths, and Smooth Direction Points will change hard-edged corners into rounded edges. Each command has a Minimum, Normal, and Maximum setting. For more information on the exactness of these settings, refer to the online Streamline help.

Caution   Be extremely careful of "over smoothing." While we all would like smaller file sizes, don't lose sight of the effect of smoothing on image quality.

Exporting Vector Graphics from Flash

In the previous chapter, you learned how to export raster image formats from Flash. If you've created artwork in Flash that you want to share with other drawing applications, then you can export any frame (or series of frames) from Flash — in any of the popular vector file formats.

Why would you want to export vector-based images from Flash? If you're a design or graphics professional, then you probably need to reuse your artwork in a number of different media for print, multimedia, or broadcast delivery. As such, you don't like wasting valuable time recreating the same artwork twice. Most Flash artwork exports flawlessly to the file formats listed in Table 18-1.

Cross-Reference   If you want to export a series of vector images from a Flash movie to use with video or other multi-frame applications, check out Chapter 22.

If you are unsure of the format to use in your graphics program, then refer to Table 18-1. Afterward, we'll show you how to export a Flash frame's artwork as a static vector image.

Table 18-1
Vector Image Formats for Flash Export

Flash Export Format	File Extension	Comments
EPS 3.0 Encapsulated PostScript	EPS	Universal vector format recognized by most applications. However, any gradients created in Flash will not export well with this format.
Illustrator Adobe Illustrator	AI	Proprietary file format mainly used by Adobe applications. However, any gradients created in Flash will not export well with this format.

Continued

Table 18-1 (continued)		
Flash Export Format	File Extension	Comments
DXF Drawing eXchange Format	DXF	AutoCAD 2D/3D file format.
PICT (Mac only) Picture	PCT	Strange as it may seem, the transgender Macintosh PICT format can contain vector and raster information.
WMF/EMF (PC only) Windows Meta File/ Extended Meta File	WMF EMF	Only some Windows applications support these formats. These formats are not widely used on either Mac or PC systems.

To export artwork as a vector file format from Flash 4:

1. Move the Current Frame Indicator in the Flash Timeline to the frame that contains the artwork you wish to export.

2. Choose the File ➪ Export Image command.

3. Select a destination folder and enter a file name. Select your preferred raster image format in the Save as Type drop-down menu.

4. Click Save, and use the new vector file in your drawing or illustration program.

Note

Unlike exported raster image formats from Flash, the exported vector file formats do not have any additional settings for image quality, contents or size. This is due primarily to the fact that these settings are not necessary for vector file formats. By their nature, vector graphics can be scaled at any size.

A word of caution using vector formats from Flash

Generally speaking, the quality of exported vector files from Flash is less than desirable. While it would seem that Flash's vector exports would be better than its raster exports, this simply isn't the case. Because RGB color space (as the "end" product) is relatively new to the world of print-based production, most vector file formats need to encode color information as CMYK. This presents a couple of problems, as we'll see in the following headings.

Color consistency

Flash works within a RGB color model, meaning that all color is defined by three numbers, one assigned to each color channel of the image (for example, red, green, and blue). Most standard vector file formats do not encode the color information in this manner. Rather, they use CMYK (cyan, magenta, yellow, and black) colors that have a much more restricted color gamut (range) than RGB.

As such, most, if not all, of your Flash artwork will display quite differently when exported as a vector file format like EPS or AI. Is this yet another reason to start projects intended for multiple media in Macromedia FreeHand? Yes and no. While starting projects in FreeHand lends itself to greater flexibility for the re-use or repur-posing of artwork, you have an alternative to exporting vector files from Flash: good old copy-and-paste. If you select Flash artwork, choose Edit ➪ Copy, switch to your illustration program and choose Edit ➪ Paste, the newly pasted artwork should match your original Flash artwork.

Why is this so? Most likely, this phenomenon is due to the fact that Flash's export file formats (or the versions of these formats) don't seem to support RGB colors. However, the clipboard can support a multitude of data types, and Adobe Illustrator and FreeHand can recognize RGB colors. Therefore, the copy-and-pasted colors show up as RGB colors in these programs.

Note
Interestingly, if you choose Adobe Illustrator (.ai) as the export file format from Flash, you can only choose up to and including Illustrator 6 formats. RGB color support was only introduced with the Adobe Illustrator 7. It is also likely that the EPS 3.0 format is an older version of the format that does not support RGB colors.

Flash gradients

Another troublesome spot for exported vector files from Flash is the re-rendering of Flash gradients as CMYK "blends." Depending on the vibrancy of the original gradient in Flash, the exported vector equivalents might end up very muddy or brownish—especially in the middle range of the gradient. Again, you can avoid this color-shifting by copying and pasting the Flash gradients directly between applications. Note that this still converts Flash gradients to blends, but it will retain the RGB color values of the original Flash gradient.

Tip
If you need absolutely perfect exported material from Flash, you might consider exporting high-resolution bitmap (a.k.a. *raster*) files instead.

✦   ✦   ✦

Working with Audio Applications

Although Flash has rudimentary sound editing controls, those who are serious about integrating sound and music in their projects should consider purchasing other audio applications. Using professional-quality sound editors such as Peak (for Macintosh) or Sound Forge (for PC) can facilitate the manipulation and optimization of high-quality audio in your Flash projects.

Preparing Audio for Use in Flash

Because of the limited number of options for editing audio in Flash, we recommend you optimize and experiment with your sound clips in an external application before importing them into the Library.

When creating or editing audio for use in Flash, we *cannot stress enough* the importance of starting out with the highest sample and bit conversion rates possible. Remember, sound quality in general is simple to degrade, but can be difficult or impossible to restore, so it's not a good idea to skimp from the beginning. Ideally, your original files will be 16-bit 44.1 kHz. From this point on, we are assuming that your audio clips are of reasonable quality and were captured or created from a good 16-bit source, such as an audio CD or a sound effects application like Propellerhead's Rebirth (discussed later in this chapter).

Sound editing and creation software

Just about every multimedia or video software package includes a sound-editing application. For the most part, you'll find limited edition (a.k.a. *LE*) versions of popular sound applications bundled with Macromedia Director or video application suites like Digital Origin's EditDV. For a price, you can upgrade these LE versions to full versions, or purchase them separately if you don't need or want a multimedia production software package. While none of the following applications are available on both Macintosh and Windows platforms, their functionality is virtually identical.

Note   You can perform the same basic functions (described in this chapter) in either the LE or fully featured versions of the sound-editing application. LE versions usually have less effects-oriented controls like sound filters and enhanced noise reduction.

Sonic Foundry's Sound Forge (PC only)

Sound Forge is a powerful, yet easy to use waveform sound editor for the PC environment. One of the great features of Sound Forge is nondestructive editing. Sound Forge can also be integrated with Sonic Foundry's Acid software.

Sound Forge supports both of the Flash-compatible audio import formats, AIFF and WAV. You can open up an existing sound file, edit it, and save it as WAV or AIFF at several different sampling and bit rates.

You can download a trial version of Sound Forge at www.soundforge.com/download.

Sonic Foundry's ACID Pro (PC only)

ACID is a powerful, loop-based sound-editing program that is ideal for use with Flash (see Figure 19-1). With ACID, you can very easily take loops created in other programs, and arrange them on multiple tracks. One of ACID's great features is the ability to change the speed of the loop without changing the key. ACID Pro also comes with over 100 ready-to-use loops, so you can arrange an audio track in a pinch.

You can download a trial version of ACID at www.sonicfoundry.com/download.

Tip   Point your browser at the Chapter 19 section of the *Flash 4 Bible*'s Web site, www.theflashbible.com/ch19, for more tips and tricks on Sonic Foundry's Acid Pro.

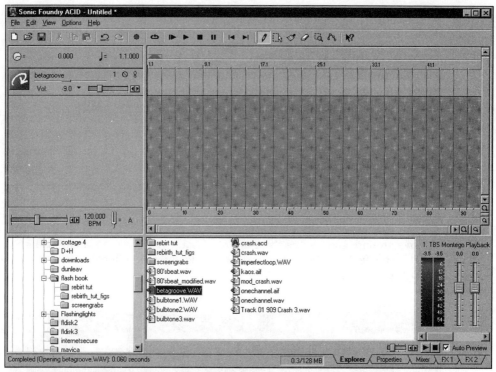

Figure 19-1: In ACID, you can very easily preview an audio clip, add it as a track, and move it around a timeline.

Macromedia SoundEdit 16 (Mac only)

SoundEdit has had a relatively long history with Macintosh users as a sound-editing workhorse, especially for use with multimedia. Although still widely used, SoundEdit 16 is no longer being produced by Macromedia, and Mac users are slowly migrating to the more robust, full featured Peak.

Bias Peak (Mac only)

Peak, produced by BIAS, is the successor to SoundEdit 16, and is rapidly becoming one of the most widely used audio-editing applications for multimedia on the Macintosh. It is available in both Full and LE versions. It is simple to use and supports a wide variety of plug-ins (including Premiere) and audio formats. It also has advanced loop-finding capabilities.

You can download a demo version of Peak at www.bias-inc.com.

Bias Deck (Mac only)

Deck is a powerful multitrack editor for the Macintosh platform. In addition to being able to play back up to 64 tracks at once, Deck can also function as a multitrack recorder, enabling you to create your own music or sound effects. It is a fair bit less expensive than other similar software packages, and can be closely integrated with Bias Peak.

You can download a demo version of Deck at `www.bias-inc.com`.

Setting in and out points

One of the first things you will want to do with your audio file before you bring it into the Flash environment is set its In and Out points. These points, respectively, control where the sound will start and end. By precisely placing In and Out points, you can minimize the sound's file size (see Figure 19-2), making it less cumbersome to move around, and reduce the amount of time you'll have to spend using Flash's less-than-full-featured interface. You can set In and Out points in most, if not all, audio applications.

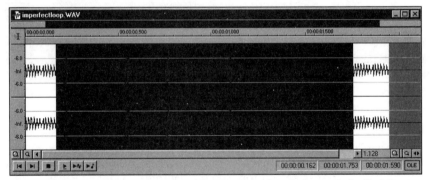

Figure 19-2: You can greatly reduce the file size of a Flash movie by limiting an audio track to its essential portion.

In Sound Forge, Peak, and Sound Edit 16, follow these steps to set the In and Out points of a sound:

1. Highlight the area you want to keep.

2. Test your selection by pressing the Play Loop or Play Normal button. (Sound Forge).

To create a new audio file with your selection:

1. Select File ➪ Copy (Command+C or Ctrl+C).

2. Select File ➪ New (Command+N or Ctrl+N).

3. A new window will open. Select Edit ➪ Paste (Command+V or Ctrl+V).

4. Your selection will now be a new audio file.

Normalizing audio levels

You can use the Normalize function to optimize your sound levels, and prevent your audio file from "clipping." (Digital clipping occurs when an audio clip is recorded at too high a level. The clipping sound is distorted, resulting in an undesirable crackling or buzzing sound.) Normalize can also be used to boost levels when your audio file was recorded too low. Normalization may also reduce the risk of having to deal with the Flash sound export bug described in Chapter 12. Normalize is an option in most audio applications.

Tip   If you are gathering sound samples from a number of different audio sources (such as audio CD, direct recordings with a computer microphone, DAT recordings, DV camcorder audio, and so on), it's best to normalize all of them to a consistent audio level.

To normalize in Sound Forge:

1. Select part or all of the clip to be normalized.

2. Choose Process ➪ Normalize

3. The Normalize Window appears (see Figure 19-3). You can click Preview to see what the default settings do.

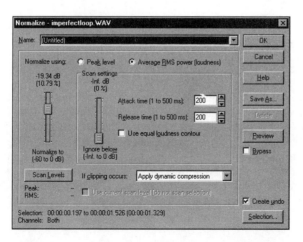

Figure 19-3: Sound Forge's Normalize window enables you to preview the settings before you apply them to the audio clip.

Watch the Play Meter on the right-hand side of the screen, if the levels seem high, (constantly in the red,) lower the levels with the slider bar on the left-hand side of the Normalize Window. On the contrary, if your levels are too low, gradually raise the slider bar. Click OK, and your file is now Normalized. Note that many other options exist in the Normalize Window. If you like, you can experiment with these settings to get the result you are looking for.

To normalize in Peak and SoundEdit:

1. Select part or all of the clip to be normalized.

2. In Peak, choose DSP ⇨ Normalize. In SoundEdit, choose Effects ⇨ Normalize.

In Peak's Normalize dialog box, you can move the slider bar back and forth to choose the Normalization percentage. The number you choose will normalize to a percentage of the maximum level. After you click OK, you can listen to the Normalized selection by pressing Option+spacebar. Watch the levels for any clipping.

Caution   If you are recording your own sounds with a microphone attached to your computer's sound card, make sure you have adjusted the mic's volume level (or gain) in the sound-recording application. If the levels are too high during recording, you won't be able to normalize the sound — the resulting sound will be very distorted and "clip" on playback.

Fade in and fade out

As discussed in Chapter 11, Fading In means increasing the volume of a sound over time, and Fading Out is decreasing it. Most audio-editing applications have more sophisticated Fading effects than Flash.

To fade audio in Sound Forge:

1. Select the part of the audio you wish to Fade In or Out.

2. Choose Process ⇨ Fade ⇨ Graphic.

3. The Graphic Fade Window appears (see Figure 19-4).

You should now see your selected sound as a waveform (that is, a graphic representation of sound waves). The interface for customizing your fade is vaguely similar to the one used in Flash. You create Envelope Handles by clicking points on the Envelope Line at the top of the waveform. Drag these Handles around to create your desired volume/fading effects. The lines themselves show the volume level of the sound. Thus, when you drag an envelope handle down, the line slopes down, indicating a decrease in the volume level. Click Preview to hear your custom fade. Click OK when you are satisfied.

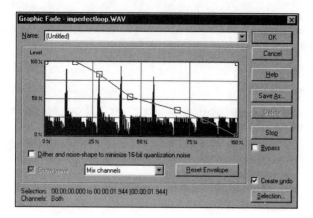

Figure 19-4: Sound Forge enables you to save custom fade effects to apply to other sounds.

Using Peak to fade audio:

1. Select the section of audio you want to fade in or out.

2. Choose Preferences ⇨ Fade In Envelope or Fade Out Envelope.

3. The Fade In Envelope or Fade Out Envelope Window will appear.

4. You can use the default fade shape, or create your own by using a similar technique to the one described previously, in the Sound Forge instructions.

5. Choose DSP ⇨ Fade Out. Peak will apply the fade to your selection.

6. To hear your Fade, press Option+spacebar.

Fading with SoundEdit:

1. Select the section of audio you want to fade in or out.

2. Choose Effects ⇨ Fade In or Effects ⇨ Fade Out.

3. Create your fade using a similar technique to the one described in the Sound Forge instructions. SoundEdit also has Slow, Medium, or Fast fade presets. Click OK when finished.

Creating a reverb effect

Adding Reverb to a sound file can create an interesting effect. Reverb creates the auditory illusion of acoustic space. For example, you could simulate the sound of water dripping in a cave.

To add a reverb to an audio sample in Sound Forge:

1. Select the section of sound you want to add reverb to.

2. Choose Effects ⇨ Reverb.

3. The Reverb Window appears.

4. Select a Reverberation Mode from the drop-down menu. Per our previous example, choose Cavernous Space.

5. Press the Preview Button to hear how it sounds. Play with some of the sliders and other options until you achieve the desired effect. When done, click OK.

Peak does not come with a Reverb effect. However, a variety of third-party effects plug-ins are available on the market that are compatible with Peak.

SoundEdit 16 has a similar effect to Reverb called Echo. To add Echo to a selection, choose Effects ⇨ Echo.

Other effects

Many other effects and processes are available in these audio-editing applications, and to list them all would be beyond the scope of this book. A great feature of many of these software packages is nondestructive editing. You can make as many changes to your audio clips as you like without destroying the original source files. Set aside some time to experiment, and let your creativity take over.

Expert Tutorial: Using Propellerhead's Rebirth to Create Loops for Flash *by Justin Jamieson*

Justin Jamieson (justin@mediumLarge.com) started using his first computer when he was eight years old. Years later, after studying design and cinematography, he combined his training with his computing knowledge to co-found mediumLarge (www.mediumLarge. com), a new media design firm in Toronto. In 1997, while developing a Web site for a local Toronto rap group, Justin began his research into the use of sound on the Internet and there's been no turning back. He recently began an online record company for unsigned Canadian acts that will distribute CDs and MP3s to listeners around the world.

Rebirth is an innovative sound creation tool that accurately replicates vintage analog synthesizers and drum machines. Simply put, it enables you to easily create electronic music without investing tons of money in hardware.

With Rebirth, you can create looping music for Sync or Event sounds in Flash. You can also create some pretty weird effects by tweaking the various knobs and adding distortion. Prepare yourself to spend long hours and sleepless nights experimenting with this program. That's not to say that it's extremely difficult — it's not. Rebirth is actually quite easy to get the hang of, but you'll soon be keeping the neighbors awake at night with heavy bass and spacey frequencies.

Rebirth emulates two synthesizers, Roland 303's, and two drum machines, a Roland 808 and a 909. Countless Mods (modifications) are available on the Internet, with different graphics and sample sets. Some of these sample sets specialize in certain types of electronic music, such as drum and bass, dub, industrial, and so on. For the purposes of this tutorial, however, we will use the default Mod, which has controls that are fairly easy to get used to (and that sought-after '80s Electro sound.)

Getting started with Rebirth

First, try and get used to some of Rebirth's controls. See the following figure for the main Rebirth window. A fair number of them exist, and the Rebirth manual describes them very well. You should have a basic knowledge of Rebirth for the purposes of this tutorial.

The main Rebirth Window

Although you can use the demo version of this software for the purposes of this tutorial, it lacks the capability to save any final audio files and shuts down after 15 minutes.

Creating your first simple beat in Rebirth

In pattern mode, press Play and look at the 909 at the bottom of the screen. You'll notice red lights moving from left to right over the 16 step buttons. This represents one musical measure. To modify the beat that is playing, you can clear some or all of the buttons and add your own. You can also select pre-made beats by pressing the pattern buttons on the left-hand side of the screen.

Continued

(continued)

Note: To clear an entire pattern, move the red Focus Bar down to the bottom of the screen using the down arrow key, and then choose Edit ⇨ Clear.

To begin creating your own beat, or to modify an existing one, you will want to "solo" the 909, so the other sections don't get in the way. To do this, click the Mix buttons to turn off the green lights in all but the 909 section. You should now only hear the 909. You can also select how many beats per minute by altering the number on the BPM selector at the top left-hand side of the screen.

More advanced musicians may want to change the time signature by altering the number in the value display on the left-hand side of the 909 (reference the following figure). When you change the number, you are altering the total of 16th notes within a bar. Thus, if you change it to 14, there will be 14 16th notes between the beginning and end of a bar.

The 909 is "soloed" in the main Rebirth window.

To select different drum sounds to play, you can either use the rotary dial on the right-hand side, or you can click the sound names above the 16 step buttons. Each step button also has two instance levels — the first time you click a step button, a faint red light appears, indicating a lighter drum hit. The second time you click the same step button, the heavier red light appears, indicating a heavier hit. The third time you click the same button, you clear it. No sound will be produced.

The 909 also has a Flam feature, which simulates the sound of a percussionist hitting a drum with both sticks at slightly different intervals (see the following figure). To uses this feature, click the Flam button on the 909, and choose the step button that you want to hear the Flam on. The dial above the Flam button adjusts the "width" of the Flam — the actual time interval between the two simulated "stick hits."

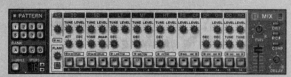

Various instance levels of the 909. The faint light indicates a "light hit." The heavier one indicates a "heavy hit." The green light indicates a "Flam," which is similar to the sound of a drummer hitting a drum with both sticks at slightly different intervals.

The process of creating your own beat involves clearing all or some of an existing drum pattern by manually clicking the step buttons for the various drum sounds, and clicking in new ones. Once you have found a suitable bar of beats, at a suitable speed, you are now ready to add some 303 synth.

Adding sound from the 303

The two top sections are digital replications of the vintage Roland TB 303 analog synthesizer. These are a little bit more difficult to program than the 808's, and those new to Rebirth may find it a little frustrating. A good way to begin is to customize an existing pattern.

Use the up arrow keys to move the focus bar to the 303 you want to use. Solo it, the same way you soloed the 808, previously. Press play, and begin the process of choosing a pattern.

You can choose the pattern either by using the Pattern Selector on the left-hand side of the 303 (see the following figure), or by pressing Ctrl+R, to randomly "surf" the patterns. Once you find a suitable pattern, you can begin to modify it using the Synth Sound Controls.

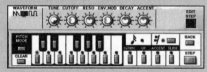

The various synth sound controls on the 303. Experiment with these knobs and buttons to achieve interesting results.

The Synth Sound Controls can create interesting results. For a detailed description of what each control does, consult the Rebirth manual. Keep in mind that experimentation is key. Set aside some time to create the perfect synth lick by playing with these controls.

Using the 808

The 808 drum section, above the 909, is fairly similar to the 909, but with a few distinct differences. For one, the drum sounds are different. Also, the controls aren't quite the same. When you are creating or editing beats in the 808, you only have one instance level on the key buttons. The 808 instead uses the Accent feature (AC.) to create heavier beats. The AC is located over the first key button, and when chosen you can add accents just like you would add a sound or beat. When you add an accent to a key button, all other sounds that occur on the same key button are emphasized.

Continued

(continued)

Other controls in Rebirth

Other effects and controls in Rebirth can help you find the sound you are looking for. Here are some of the basic ones:

✦ **Distortion (Dist):** Distortion is an effect similar to cranking up a guitar amp to full volume. It creates a harsher, louder sound. Distortion can be used by clicking the Dist button on the right side of any of the four sections. Note that although distortion can be applied to any or all of the sections at the same time, only one master control exists for all sections. It is located on the right side of the Rebirth window.

✦ **Pattern Controlled Filter (PCF):** The PCF is a versatile filter that can be applied to one section at a time, and has a master control on the right-hand side of the Rebirth window. The PCF radically modifies the sound essentially by reshaping it. To experiment with the PCF controls, move the four slider bars up and down.

✦ **Compressor (Comp):** The Compressor evens up the audio signal, making it sound tighter. You can use the Compressor for either one individual section, or for the Master Output.

✦ **Delay:** The Delay creates an echo effect for a given sound. You'll find delay knobs on the right side of each section, and one master control on the right-hand side of the Rebirth window.

✦ **Level Controls:** You can control the Levels going out to mix by using the mix slides to the right of each section. Keep in mind that as discussed in earlier sound chapters, Levels are an important thing to consider before you import your final sound or music loop into Flash. A Master Output slide also exists that controls the Levels going out. Make sure that the meter isn't spending too much time in the red, or clipping will occur.

Preparation, mixing, and exporting Rebirth loops

At this point you should have a loop created that you want to export to AIFF or WAV format. Before you do, you should take a few steps to ensure good-quality output.

✦ **Final Mixing:** Make sure that all the sections you want to mix are no longer soloed. To do this, make sure that all of your sections are set to go to the mix (green light on.) Set the Levels on your sections individually to your liking, by adjusting the Level Controls, as described previously. Bring them down if they are too "hot" (too much in the red), and set the Master Output Levels in a similar way.

✦ **Switch to Song Mode:** In order to export your Rebirth Loop to AIFF or WAV, you will need to switch to Song Mode. To do this, click Song Mode at the top of the screen. In Song Mode, choose Edit ➪ Initialize Song From Pattern Mode. Press Play to test your loop.

✦ **Exporting:** In order to export your loop, choose File ➪ Export Loop as Audio File. You will be given the option to save your loop as a WAV or AIFF file. The quality is automatically set to 44.1 kHz, 16-bit.

You should now have a one bar loop in AIFF or WAV format. You can test it in another audio application, such as Peak or Sound Forge and make any necessary changes, or add additional effects, or import it directly into Flash.

Advanced methods to create multiple bar loops in Rebirth

Once you get the basics down, you will no doubt want to get more complex. Creating a one-bar loop in Rebirth is just the beginning—you can use Rebirth's recording and Loop features to make complex songs. Rebirth can also be integrated with other audio applications, such as Cubase VST. For more information on how to create a more complex sound in Rebirth, see the very comprehensive Rebirth manual.

With the greatly improved MP3 compression available with Flash 4, an incentive now exists to create complex, high-quality electronic music with an application such as Rebirth, without having to worry as much about file size. And the rewards for creating your own samples, loops, and songs are tremendous.

Note

Rebirth is available for Macintosh and Windows platforms. You can download a demo version of Rebirth from the Propellerhead Web site at `www.propellerheads.se/demo`. You can also find information about Rebirth at `www.steinberg.net/products/rebirthmac.html` or `www.steinberg.net/products/rebirthpc.html`.

✦　　✦　　✦

Working with 3D Graphics

Although Flash has no true 3D art tools, with a little time and effort, you can mimic three dimensionality. If you have other 3D applications, you'll learn how to export optimized EPS or bitmap sequences to use as movie clips in a Flash movie. As interest in 3D Flash artwork is growing, developers are star-ting to include direct SWF output capabilities with their applications.

Introduction to 3D Modeling

Because computer monitors have only two dimensions, width and height, working with three-dimensional objects can be a bit unnerving for a novice to 3D computer modeling. That's because 3D artwork occurs in what is called 3D space, which is a simulation of real space. Three-dimensional space has three axes: X (width), Y (height), and Z (depth). While conceptualizing three dimensions may not be difficult, controlling views of objects and cameras, or rotating objects with a mouse and keyboard can prove to be an arduous task. Likewise, most 3D graphics are displayed on flat computer screens. So, what makes a graphic appear to have depth in a 2D space? See Figure 20-1 for an example.

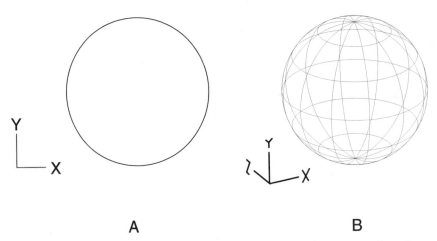

A   B

Figure 20-1: The left diagram illustrates a two-dimensional representation of space, whereas the right diagram depicts a three-dimensional one.

Art history teaches us that several factors can give the illusion of depth on a flat surface. All of these factors are central to the arrangement of subject matter within a frame, also known as the composition. Most artwork achieves the appearance of depth through the use of perspective, wherein the proportion of the composition's foreground and background spaces lend a perceived depth. With linear perspective, parallel lines are drawn as converging lines, usually to a single vanishing point on a horizon line (see Figure 20-2). The diminution of scale is integral to the concept of linear perspective. Objects closer to the viewer appear larger, while objects farther from the viewer appear smaller. Similarly, atmospheric perspective adds to a composition's sense of depth by reducing the visibility of objects as they approach the horizon.

In most 3D computer applications, you can also choose a viewpoint known as orthographic perspective, in which objects and scenes are shown from a strict mathematical viewpoint—without any sense of depth (see Figure 20-3). Technically, because orthographic views do not use perspective, this viewpoint should be referred to as orthographic projection. That's because an orthographic view renders an object or scene with mathematical accuracy instead of perspective accuracy. Some applications may also have an *isometric* view. As far as 3D computer drawing programs are concerned, *isometric* and *orthographic* views are the same.

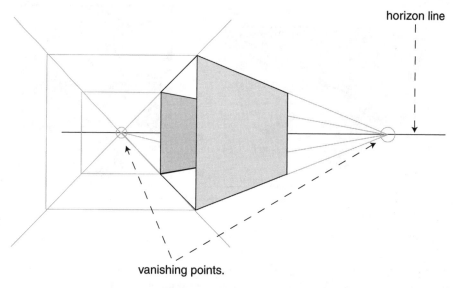

Figure 20-2: The line drawing illustrates the concept of linear perspective. The image created in MetaCreations Bryce 3D shows linear and atmospheric perspective.

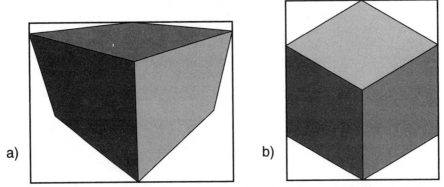

a)   b)

Figure 20-3: Linear perspective of a cube on the left; orthographic projection of a cube on the right

With the advent of photography, depth-of-field effects have also become factors that can be used to contribute to a sense of perceived depth within a two-dimensional plane. *Depth –of field* refers to the range of clear focus in either the foreground or the background of a composition. A low depth of field means that objects appear in focus only within a short distance range from the viewer (see Figure 20-4). For exam-ple, if a camera lens is focused on a person with mountains in the distance, then the person is in focus, while the mountains are not. A high depth of field means that objects can be farther apart from one another while maintaining the same focus clarity. Using the same previous example, a high depth of field would enable both the near person and the distant mountains to appear in focus.

Figure 20-4: Low depth of field on the left; high depth of field on the right

Most 3D creation programs not only strive to render scenes with accurate perspective, but also strive for a sense of near-photographic realism. Given the nature of Flash's vector-based framework, most highly textured 3D artwork won't mesh well with small vector file sizes. Nevertheless, simpler 3D objects and anima-tions can be imported into Flash while maintaining reasonable file sizes (less than 60KB). The 3D programs use the following processes or enhancements to add realism and depth to artwork:

✦ **Extruding.** This is the process of importing a 2D vector graphics file (such as Illustrator EPS) into a 3D modeling program, and giving depth to an otherwise flat object — usually by extending points or lines along the Z axis (see Figure 20-5).

Figure 20-5: A flat 2D graphic on the left; an extruded 2D graphic on the right

✦ **Lighting.** The most important factor in creating the illusion of spatial depth is adding and positioning light sources. A well-lit 3D model emphasizes planar depth; poorly lit 3D objects look flat (see Figure 20-6).

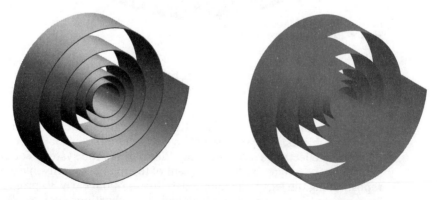

Figure 20-6: A well-lit 3D object on the left; a poorly lit object on the right

✦ **Texture Mapping.** Textures (images of patterns or surface materials) can be stretched across an object's surface(s) or facets (see Figure 20-7). Through the use of color contrast, pattern, and opacity, texture mapping gives an object unique, realistic attributes.

Figure 20-7: A texture-mapped object

✦ **Wireframe.** A wireframe is the most basic model structure of a 3D object. It renders objects using lines to represent the edges of polygons and surfaces (see Figure 20-8).

✦ **Inverse Kinematics.** Kinematics is the study of the motion of objects or of a system of objects. Inverse kinematics (IK) refers to how motion in one area of the system effects the movement of other parts in the system. For example, in respect to the human body, movement of the hip necessarily involves repositioning the legs to accommodate that motion. Early 3D programs didn't incorporate IK very well. Most high-end 3D applications such as 3D Studio Max have advanced control of IK effects, while most prosumer 3D applications, such as MetaCreations Poser, have some level of IK support. Although IK support doesn't necessarily affect the three-dimensional feel of an object, it adds automated realism to animated figures and complex objects.

Figure 20-8: A PostScript view of an extruded letter R in Adobe Dimensions; a wireframe view of the same model

A variety of common cross-platform 3D file formats exist: 3DMF, DXF, and VRML. However, Flash 4 only recognizes two-dimensional DXF files, such as those created by CAD programs. Consequently, for most 3D artwork imported into Flash, we recommend that you export either EPS/AI files (on the vector side) or PICT/BMP files (on the raster side) from the parent 3D application.

Tip   At the time of this writing, only two plug-ins for Kinetix 3D Studio Max provide for direct export of 3D objects or animations to the Flash SWF format — Digimation's Illustrate! 4 and Vecta3D by Ideaworks. Because Macromedia has opened the Flash SWF source code to the public, we expect to see more applications that can either save as or export to the SWF file format.

A variety of 3D applications are on the market, and they vary greatly in price and quality. Although a program such as Kinetix 3D Studio Max offers the broadest range of advanced controls, you might not need (or want) to take the time to learn it. Simpler programs such as Adobe Dimensions or MetaCreations Poser sacrifice the finer controls but offer the ease of use that Web designers expect from other graphics applications. Without further introduction, let's get started with some simple yet effective 3D work, created in Flash with the help of Freehand or Illustrator.

Simulating 3D with Flash

In this section, Manuel Clement, foremost master of Flash 3D graphics, shows you how to create a 3D vortex.

On the CD-ROM   If you'd like to see the fully constructed Flash (.FLA) file for this tutorial, see Vortex.fla in the ch20 folder on the *Flash 4 Bible* CD-ROM.

Expert Tutorial: Vortex: The Illusion of 3D with Flash by Manuel Clement

Manuel Clement is a young Frenchman who is known in the Flash community for his sharp handling of 3D effects with Flash. He has published a series of articles and tutorials in the 3D area of www.flashzone.com and, until February 1999, was the 3D pad moderator at www.flasher.net. His personal site, "Mano Artwork Project" (www.manoone.com), was awarded Macromedia Shocked Site Of the Day on February 3, 1999. He was recently invited by the president of France, Jacques Chirac to serve as a judge for a French National Web Site award. Manuel says this of his recent work; "I am influenced by the artist Victor Vasarely, who is distinguished in contemporary art for the exceptional results which he brought [to] geometrical abstract painting, under the name of cinetism." (Vasarely's work can be viewed online at www.netprovence.com/fondationvasarely/) "This vortex," Manuel continues, "reminds me of his paintings. . . . I created it for The Hypersite Network at www.hypersite.net — where I placed several animated transitions that were developed with this same technique."

Illusion: The vortex

A common drawback to 3D animation delivered over the Web is that the results can vary widely due to variables of systems and connections. Yet this animation has been tested over many connections on systems ranging from 200Mhz to 450Mhz and is drawn smoothly even on slower systems.

The vortex is a 3D effect created without an external modeler, using only the Flash drawing tools, timeline, and layers. Once you've followed this tutorial, you'll be able to create similar effects using the same technique, which is to simulate 3D with one object of the library, a semi-visible ring, by decreasing the size of the symbol on successive layers. As you'll see, the possibilities are endless.

To begin, create a new movie and modify it so that it has a black background with Modify ⇨ Movie ⇨ Background. (Save this, and don't forget to save your work using Ctrl+S [Command+S] each time you make one more step.) Next, select the Oval tool and set Fill Color to neutral, Line Color to white, and Line Thickness to H (thinnest setting). Now, draw a large circle at the default keyframe 1.

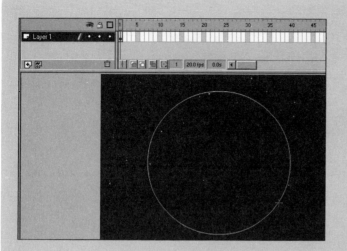

Select the circle. Copy it using Ctrl+C (Command+C) and then Paste it using Ctrl+V (Command+V) into the same (first) keyframe, as seen here.

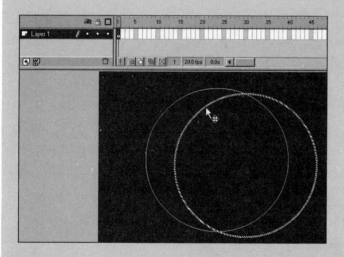

With the circle still selected, use the Arrow tool with the Scale Modifier to first reduce the size of the new circle, and then drag it to the middle of the original circle as seen in the following figure.

Continued

(continued)

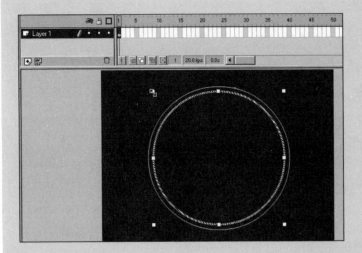

Choose the Paint Bucket tool and create a new color with a 30-percent Alpha. For more information on creating a new color, refer to Chapter 2. For this example, a blue with a 30-percent Alpha was used. The Alpha setting is important for the optical illusion that we are creating. (Be sure to press the New button to add your new color to the Current Colors pop-up menu.) Now fill the space between the two circles. We now have a filled shape with two outline circles. Delete these outline circles by selecting each circle with the Arrow tool and then pressing the Delete key. You should now have a transparent ring that looks like this figure:

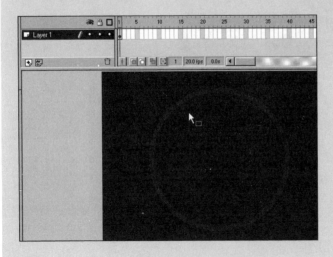

Select the ring and convert it to a movie clip (Insert ⇨ Convert to Symbol). In the ensuing Symbol Properties dialog box, type the Name of the symbol and select Movie Clip as the Behavior.

Now, with the Arrow tool and the Scale Modifier, select the ring and reduce its size — we're going to need a lot of space to create the vortex (see the following figure). If you haven't saved your project yet, do so now.

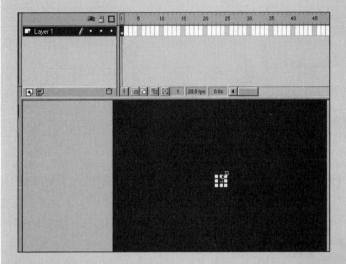

Select the keyframe and copy it by right-clicking the keyframe and selecting Copy Frames from the ensuing pop-up menu. Create a new layer with Insert ⇨ Layer (or by clicking the Add Layer button on the timeline). Now Select the first keyframe of the new layer and paste the previously copied keyframe with a right-click into the keyframe followed by selecting Paste Frames from the ensuing pop up menu. At this point, there should be two layers with identical keyframes, as shown. Lock the previous layer to prevent future mistakes.

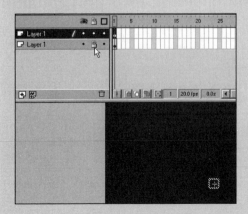

Continued

(continued)

In order to see exactly what you are doing, go to the Zoom control and select Show All (alternately, use View ⇨ Show All). With the original layer locked and the new layer active, use the Scale Modifier of the Arrow tool to select the ring and enlarge it slightly. This becomes the basic procedure: each time we create a new layer with its new ring, we make that layer larger than the previous one.

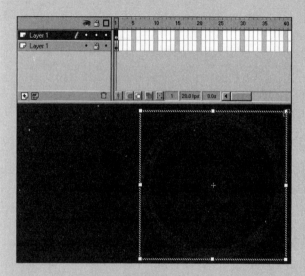

Mimic the previous procedures to copy the latest keyframe, create a new layer, and then paste the frame on the newest layer's first keyframe. Again, lock the previous layer to prevent future mistakes. Finally, enlarge the newest ring and save.

Repeat the previous steps a few more times, until you have about 21 rings (on 21 layers). Note that, although the process remains the same, the effect varies depending on the number of rings: the more rings you add, the bigger the vortex.

Now we're going to animate the vortex. Select frame 20 of *all* the layers: to do this, start at the bottom of the timeline, click frame 20, and hold the Shift key while selecting all remaining layers. Now, with all the frames that you've selected still selected, make frame 20 of each layer into a keyframe by pressing F6.

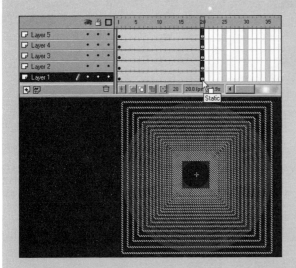

As shown in the previous image, all of the rings should still be selected and you should be at keyframe 20. If not, shift click to select keyframe 20 of all layers and select all of the rings simultaneously with Edit ⇨ Select All. Now, use the Scale Modifier of the Arrow tool to reduce the width of the rings on the X-axis, as shown next. Then, lock the top layer.

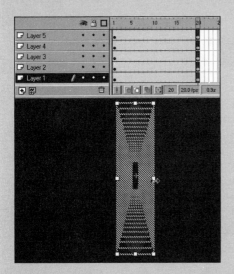

Continued

(continued)

If they are not selected, reselect all of the rings again and then press the right arrow key 10 times. This moves all the selected rings (except for those rings on layers that are locked) toward the right along their X-axes. Finally, lock the topmost layer of the unlocked layers.

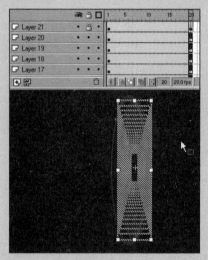

Once again, reselect all of the rings (if they are not selected) and press the right arrow key 10 times. This moves the selected rings (on all unlocked layers) farther to the right along the X-axis. (You can see the shape of the vortex starting to appear.) Lock the topmost, unlocked layer.

Repeat the previous procedure until all layers are locked and the vortex is drawn. Your vortex should look just like the one shown here.

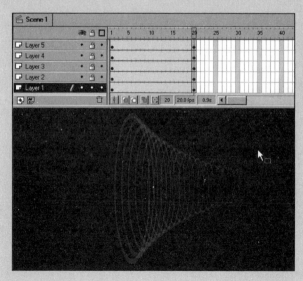

Now select the first keyframe of all layers by starting at the bottom layer and shift-clicking on the first keyframe of each layer until you've selected the first keyframe of each layer. With all first keyframes still selected, access the Frame Properties dialog box with Modify ⇨ Frames. Set the Tweening to motion with the same settings as shown.

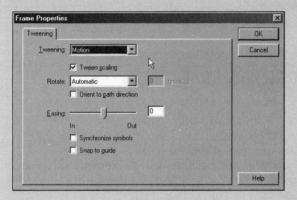

An arrow appears between keyframes, passing through the frames of each layer to indicate a motion tweening transition between frame 1 and frame 20. Save, and then press Enter to see the vortex animate!

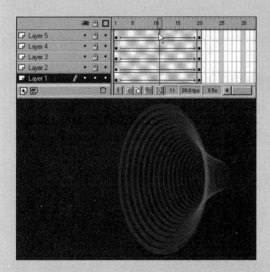

The file size of this seemingly complex animation is only 6KB. That's because it's built from a single, simple ring symbol. With more rings or keyframes, your file size might be a little larger, but not much. Although this vortex animation is only a transition between two keyframes, once you understand the principle, you can create your own varied effects. You

Continued

(continued)

may get some interesting results by editing the ring movie clip in the gallery and changing its shape or color, or maybe even by animating the clip itself. The vortex differs with each change made to the ring symbol.

Using Adobe Dimensions to Create 3D Objects

Many Flashers create 3D designs and animations for Flash movies with Adobe Dimensions 3.0. That's because Dimensions offers one of the most intuitive interfaces for elementary 3D design. If you've never used a 3D program before, then Adobe Dimensions is a great place to start. The interface has familiar tools found in other 2D drawing programs. These include pen, text, and object tools. Although Dimensions' support of animation isn't as advanced as that of other applications (such as 3D Studio Max or even Extreme 3D 2) you can use it to create great-looking 3D animations to use in Flash — and also maintain small file sizes! This section shows you how to turn an existing 2D design into a simple — yet effective — 3D sequence that can be imported into Flash. (If you aren't acqua-inted with the basic interface of Dimensions, please read Chapter 1 of the *Adobe Dimensions 3.0 User Guide,* which comes with the software, before proceeding with this section.)

How to extrude vector artwork

In Dimensions 3.0, you can create 3D artwork from scratch, using the various drawing tools in the toolbox. You can also use Dimensions to generate dimensional artwork from any vector file, such as EPS or AI files. In this section, we describe how to extrude an imported Illustrator file.

✦ Make sure you have installed Dimensions 3.0 on your Windows or Macintosh computer. Open the application.

✦ In the Render Mode drop-down menu of the Untitled-1 document window, choose PostScript.

✦ Open the Extrude window by choosing Operations ➪ Extrude or Command ➪ Ctrl+E. This command or shortcut can hide the Extrude window as well.

✦ In the lower left-hand corner of the Extrude window, click the New Base button.

✦ With the Extrude base window active, import an EPS file that you want to turn into animated 3D artwork for Flash. To do this, choose File ➪ Import (Command+Option+I or Ctrl+Alt+I), and select a vector file. (You can use the crosshairs.eps file in the ch18 folder on the *Flash 4 Bible* CD-ROM.)

Tip

You can export an EPS or Illustrator file from Flash to use in Dimensions. For more information on exporting vector file formats from Flash, see Chapter 18.

In the Extrude window, enter a value in the Depth text field. By default, all values in Dimensions are points. After you enter a value, click the Apply button in the lower right-hand corner of the Extrude window (see Figure 20-9). A value of 75 points was used for the crosshairs sample file.

Figure 20-9: Using the Extrude window, you can convert a 2D vector file to a 3D object.

With the object selected in the document window, open the Camera window (Window ⇨ Show Camera), which controls the view angle of the 3D window. Enter **75** for the Lens value, and **0** for Lon, Lat, and Roll.

Open the Move window (Operations ⇨ Transform ⇨ Move). Choose Absolute for the Coordinates property, and enter **0** for X, Y, and Z values. Click Apply. If you're using the crosshair sample file, your object should resemble Figure 20-10.

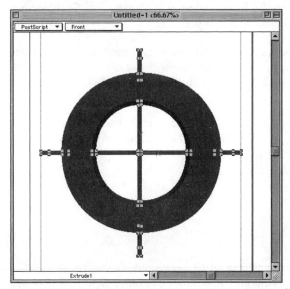

Figure 20-10: After applying a new Camera view and object coordinates, the crosshairs object has a much more dynamic look.

The next step is to generate a series of still images from Dimensions to use in Flash. (The process is similar to using the Auto-Distort command in the Paint window of Macromedia Director.) To do this, we use Dimensions to record the position and scale of the object as it is rotated and moved in the 3D window. A start point and an end point are specified. Then Dimensions creates the in-between keyframes similar to tweening in Flash.

With the 3D object selected and in a starting position, choose Operations ➪ Generate Sequence. The alert box shown in Figure 20-11 appears.

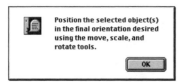 

Figure 20-11: After you select the Generate Sequence command, move, scale, or rotate the 3D object to a new position or size. The Operations menu item remains highlighted to remind you that you are generating a sequence.

Now, move and rotate the object to the final position of the animation. Note that you won't be able to preview the animated sequence. So, if you want to be precise, use any of the Operations ➪ Tranform windows to specify the end position. To create a rotating crosshair, open the Rotate window (Operations ➪ Transform ➪ Rotate) and enter **180** for the Y axis. Click Apply.

Choose Operations ➪ End Sequence to stop the recording process. The Sequence dialog box (see Figure 20-12) automatically opens, and you can specify the number of frames (in the sequence), the file type, and the filename prefix.

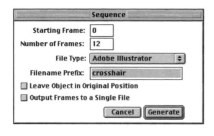

Figure 20-12: Specify the image output settings in the Sequence dialog box.

In order to keep the final Flash file size as small as possible (for optimal transmission over the Web), try to limit the number of frames to as few as possible. Depending on the range of motion and scaling, you may be able to use as few as 5 or

6 frames. For the 180-degree crosshair rotation, a series of 12 frames was generated by Dimensions in the Adobe Illustrator (.AI) format, which Flash can import.

Note You may want to experiment with PICT or BMP file types and use the Trace Bitmap command in Flash to reduce the complexity of the imported bitmaps. It may seem counterintuitive, but small bitmaps in a series are often smaller than their vector equivalents.

Dimensions has a filename prefix property that enables you to specify the name that precedes the numbers in the sequence. For example, if you use "crosshair" as the filename prefix, then the first frame's filename is crosshair0000. You can insert spaces or underscores (for example, "crosshair " or "crosshair_") to separate the number from the prefix.

Tip The Sequence dialog box has two additional options, Leave Object in Original Position and Output Frames to a Single File. The first option, if checked, keeps the object in the center of each frame generated. If it is not checked, then the object's center varies depending on the starting and ending positions. Because you can tween the imported sequence as a movie clip in Flash, you may find this first option very useful, because broad and general movements can be created with a movie clip symbol by applying a motion tween to it.

Click the Generate button, and Dimensions starts processing each frame in the sequence. When it is finished rendering all the frames, you are ready to bring the sequence into Flash.

Bringing a sequence into Flash

With a Flash movie (.FLA) open, create a new layer and import the Dimensions sequence. Refer to the "Importing Poser Sequences in Flash" section in this chapter to see how to contain an imported sequence as a movie clip.

On the CD-ROM Some 3D animations make excellent rollovers for Flash buttons. Refer to the crosshairs_button.swf file in the ch20 folder on the *Flash 4 Bible* CD-ROM for a rollover button example. You can see how this SWF was made from the accompanying file, crosshairs_button.fla. You can also check our Web site at www.theFlashBible.com/ch20 for updates on this subject.

Animating Figures with MetaCreations Poser

MetaCreations Poser 3.0 is a 3D figure generation and animation application. With Poser, you can create lifelike human and animal characters to use in illustrations or animations. Poser 3.0 sports a sophisticated user interface, with dozens of options for every tool and component. In this section, we walk you through the process of making a running mannequin figure that is then imported into Flash. While you need not be an advanced user of Poser to understand this example, you can surely benefit from reading the Tutorial section of the *Poser 3.0 User Guide* (which ships with the Poser software package) prior to starting this example. However, if you don't want to concern yourself with advanced functionality, it's possible to simply read and follow the guidelines in the following paragraphs.

Note   At the time of this writing, MetaCreations was in the midst of developing Poser 4. If you're using Poser 4, check our Web site at www.theflashbible.com for any updates to this section.

Creating a walking figure in Poser

Here's how to create walking motion in Poser:

1. If you open Poser with its default factory settings, a clothed male figure should appear in the center of a 350×350 view window. Using the Translate/Pull tool, position the figure to the upper portion of the 350×350 window. The figure's shadow needs some room to fully display during the walk cycle.

2. With the Translate/Pull too, move the figure to the upper portion of the view window.

3. Next, open the Poser figure and object libraries through the Window ⇨ Libraries command (Shift+Command+B or Shift+Ctrl+B).

4. In this window, select Figures, then Additional Figures, and then Mannequin.

5. Access the Mannequin figure for the Additional Figures library.

6. Click OK to following dialog box. This alert box appears whenever you change the current figure. Do not check the Keep Current Proportions option.

7. Your Poser screen should now resemble Figure 20-13.

8. Open Window ⇨ Walk Designer (Shift+Command+S or Shift+Ctrl+S). In the Walk Designer window, set the Blend Styles Run slider to 52 percent. Click the Walk button to preview the current settings, and then select different angles (¾, side, front, top) to see the walk from varying viewpoints. Click Apply. You'll then be presented with frame settings for the animation. Make sure the End Frame is set to frame 10, and that the Walk in Place option is checked. See Figure 20-14 Click OK, and Poser generates a complete walk cycle with 10 frames.

Figure 20-13: The new mannequin figure on the stage

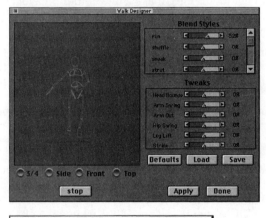

Figure 20-14: The Walk Designer in Poser 3.0 can create full-motion walks for any Poser figure.

9. To preview your figure's new walk, open the Animation Controls window (Shift+Command+ P or Shift+Ctrl+P) and drag the playback head (see Figure 20-15) through each frame. If you press Enter or Return, Poser plays back the entire frame sequence. To stop playback, press Enter or Return.

Playback Head

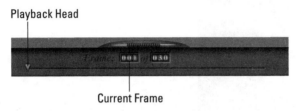

Current Frame

Figure 20-15: Animation Controls

10. *Before* outputting the animation frames, make a new folder on a local drive to store the files. Do this now, because Poser won't give you the option to create a new folder during the save process.

11. Next, to output the animation, go to the Animation menu, and select Make Movie (Command+J or Ctrl+J). Set an end time of eight frames. Note that, because Poser counts time zero as a frame, we'll have a total of nine frames. Furthermore, because Frame 10 is exactly the same as frame 1, we won't need it in Flash. For this example, use Display Settings. This means the exported frames look exactly the same as the figure appears in the workspace of Poser. (You can add more detailed texture and bump maps to figures in Poser, but that's beyond the scope of this tutorial.) Also, if you want smoother-looking edges in the bitmap sequence, make sure the Anti-Alias option is checked. If you're using the Mac version of Poser, you'll want to use PICT files as the Sequence Type instead of QuickTime. On the PC version, you'll want to use BMP or TIF files. Use the TIF format if you need to use an alpha channel. Refer to Figure 20-16 for the correct settings.

Using lower resolutions for flash movies on the Web

Movie:	mannequin	Frame Rate:

- ● Use Movie's frame rate (30)
- ○ Use this frame rate: 30

Sequence Type: PICT files ▼

Resolution: Half ▼
Size: 320 x 320

Quality: Current Display Settings ▼

Antialias: ☑

Time Span:
Start: 0 : 0 : 0 : 0
End: 0 : 0 : 0 : 8
Duration: 0:00:00:09
Frames: 9

Render Settings   Cancel   OK

Specify and end frame of 8

Figure 20-16: Export settings for Poser image sequences

12. Click OK to proceed to the Save dialog box, which prompts you to select a folder and filename for the sequence. Because Poser automatically adds the number extension to your filenames, just type the base filename. For example, typing **mannequin** generates successive filenames beginning with mannequin.0001 on the Mac or mannequin_0001.tif on the PC. Click Save, and Poser renders this little nine-frame animation. Save your Poser project and exit Poser.

Preparing Poser sequences for Flash

It would be nice if we could just directly import our PICT or TIF sequence into Flash, but first a number of small nuisances must be addressed.

To begin with, on the Mac, Flash doesn't seem to like the way Poser creates PICTs — if you're using a PC see the following note. This means that if you import a PICT from Poser directly into Flash, Flash displays the file as a collection of horizontal and vertical lines. Furthermore, Poser creates inverted alpha channels, while Flash expects straight alpha channels, with black indicating hidden areas and white indicating shown areas. (See Chapter 17 for more discussion on alpha channels in Flash.) So, in order to make the Poser files read correctly in Flash, the alpha channels of the Poser PICT files must be inverted and the file format saved correctly. To facilitate this transition, we've created a Photoshop action (located on the CD-ROM) that properly converts a sequence of Poser files into images that Flash understands.

Note   PC Users: The alpha channels of exported TIF sequences are correctly formatted for Flash use. However, Flash can not import TIF files. Therefore, you need to convert the TIF files to the PNG format in Photoshop or another graphics application. The PNG format is the only alpha-channel-enabled, raster-image format that Flash can use. PNG images saved from Photoshop 5 or earlier may appear much darker when imported into Flash. If you have Photoshop 5.5, use the new Save for Web feature to export PNG images with more accurate color.

To load this Photoshop action, first pop the *Flash 4 Bible* CD-ROM into your computer. Then launch Adobe Photoshop (you need version 4 or greater) and open the Actions palette (Window ➪ Show Actions). Make sure that the Actions Palette is *not* set to Button Mode. Then, on the palette's pop-up menu, choose Load Actions. Browse to the Photoshop folder in the ch18 folder on the *Flash 4 Bible* CD-ROM, and choose Flash 4 Actions.atn.

Now choose File ➪ Automate ➪ Batch. In the Set property, choose Flash 4 Actions, and select Poser Alpha Inversion for the Action property. For the Source, choose the folder that you specified for your Poser sequence files. For the Destination, choose Save and Close. Now click OK, and Photoshop fixes the PCT or BMP alpha channels so that Flash recognizes them properly. There's also a Poser Alpha + Image Inversion action that can be used to invert the RGB channels as well as the alpha channels — this is useful for converting Poser's white silhouettes into black ones.

Depending on your Photoshop color profile setup, you may encounter a dialog box which interrupts the automate process. If you are presented with a Missing Profile dialog box (as shown in Figure 20-17), choose Don't Convert. Photoshop continues with the automated processing of your image sequence. Note, however, that, if you receive this message for the first file, you'll keep getting it for every file in the sequence. Just stay with it and repeatedly press Return (on the Mac) or click Don't Convert when the Missing Profile dialog box pops up.

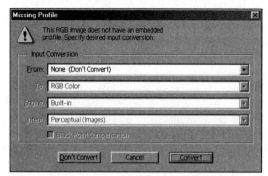

Figure 20-17: Depending on your specific color settings in Photoshop 5, you may receive a Missing Profile alert box when an image without an ICC profile is opened.

If you're using the PC versions of Poser, Flash, and Photoshop, then you can skip to the next section. The Macintosh version of Flash won't recognize the 0001, 0002, or 0003 extension as an image sequence. You need to add a PCT extension to the end of each of your PICT files. This can be a time-consuming task for large sequences, so let the FileMunger shareware application (that is located on the *Flash 4 Bible* CD-ROM) do all the work for you. FileMunger is a great little tool that is used to batch process file creator types, filename extensions, and file date names. Once you've installed the application, run FileMunger, and click the Filename Extensions button on the left (see Figure 20-18). This changes its operating mode to exclusively work with filename extensions.

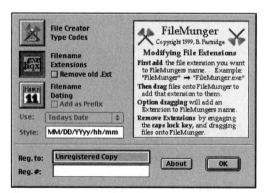

Figure 20-18: Use the Filename Extensions mode of FileMunger to automatically add extension suffixes to a group of files.

Close the FileMunger application, and rename the actual FileMunger application file to FileMunger.pct. This causes FileMunger to work in what is called Filename Extensions mode, meaning that it adds the PCT extension to any file (or group of files) that is dropped on the FileMunger application icon. Now open the folder with the mannequin sequence, select all the files in the window by pressing Command+A, and drag them to the FileMunger application icon (Figure 20-19); FileMunger adds a PCT extension to all your files. Thus, mannequin.0001 is now mannequin.0001.pct. Now the Mac version of Flash recognizes the Poser images as a sequence.

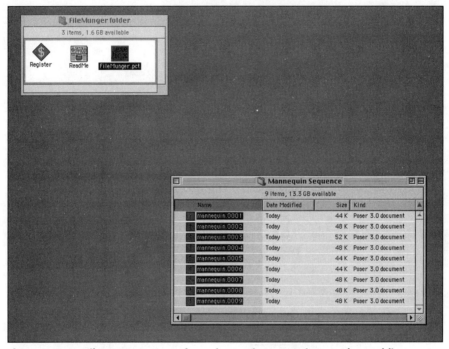

Figure 20-19: FileMunger can perform timesaving operations such as adding extensions to multiple files.

Importing Poser sequences into Flash

Okay, now we can get back to Flash. Open an existing Flash (.FLA) file or create a new one. Make a new symbol (Insert ➪ New Symbol, Command+F8 or Ctrl+F8), and set it to the Movie Clip type. Give it the name **mannequin** or something similar. Automatically, Flash changes the stage to Symbol-Editing mode. Choose File ➪ Import (Command+R or Ctrl+R), browse to the folder containing the Poser sequence, and double-click the first filename in the sequence (such as mannequin. 0001.pct or mannequin_0001.bmp). Now click Import. You should receive an alert box from Flash 4 that asks if you want to import all of the images in the sequence. Click Yes to this dialog box, and Flash imports all the images associated with this sequence. When the import is completed, as indicated by the progress bar, the mannequin symbol has nine frames — and each of these frames is a keyframe.

Next, because Flash auto-aligned the top-left corner of the imported bitmaps to the center of the symbol, we need to change the symbol center to match the center of the bitmaps. Click the Edit Multiple Frames button on the timeline, and drag the End Onion Skin marker to Frame 9. Select all the bitmaps in the symbol by pressing Command+A or Ctrl+A, or by using the Edit ⇨ Select All command. Press Command+K or Ctrl+K to bring up the Align dialog box, set both vertical and horizontal align properties to center, check the Align to Page option, and click OK.

Your movie clip should resemble Figure 20-20.

Onion Skin Markers

Edit Multiple Frames

Figure 20-20: The Mannequin movie clip

Caution   Don't neglect to turn off Edit Multiple Frames so you don't accidentally displace all of these element(s).

Now you need to make a critical decision. Is it better to trace the bitmap files imported from Poser? Or, are there advantages to leaving them as is? If you want to preserve the detail currently displayed by the imported sequence, then tracing the bitmap makes the Flash SWF larger. If you want to minimize detail and can accept a loss of detail in your imported sequence, then use the Modify ⇨ Trace Bitmap command on each frame of the mannequin movie clip symbol, at whatever quality settings you desire. But before you leap to trace those bitmap files, here's a surprising comparison: The mannequin example was exported from Flash as is (with default SWF settings) with a file size of 54.5KB. But the traced bitmap mannequin (using **10** for the Color Threshold, **8** for the Minimum Area, and **Normal** for both Curve Fit and Corners) exported with a file size of 83.6KB!

Note that the traced bitmap version doesn't even look as good as the regular bitmapped version. Granted, we could have used many other procedures in Poser, Photoshop, Freehand, or Streamline to optimize the quality of the bitmap or its converted vector counterpart. The point here, however, is that vector equivalents aren't *always* better than the original bit-for-bit raster graphics. (Here's a related example of a situation where the vector equivalents *would* have been better: a silhouette figure generated in Poser with one solid color fill. Tracing those bitmaps would have yielded better results because the figure has only one color and a relatively simple outline. Remember, for the most part, vector graphics are ideal for illustrations with solid color fields and lines. Raster or bitmap graphics are ideal for continuous tone or photo-quality images.)

Now you have a running mannequin movie clip that can be referenced from your Flash Library and placed anywhere in your Flash movies. Once placed in a scene, this movie clip can be scaled, rotated, or tweened to any position or size.

Exporting Animations from Kinetix 3D Studio Max

Kinetix 3D Studio Max (3DS MAX) is one of the most popular, powerful, and professional 3D modeling and animation programs. The R2.5 release, does not support direct export to Shockwave Flash (.SWF) files. It can, however, export to the EPS vector format. This file format can be imported into Flash, but the file sizes and vector information are usually too weighty for easy Internet transmission. At the time of this writing, Digimation's Illustrate! 4 plug-in is the only one of its kind available for 3D Studio Max which enables the program to export straight to Shockwave Flash files. The following expert tutorial shows you how to customize Illustrate! to deliver optimized Shockwave Flash files.

Note

Illustrate 4! does not convert texture maps or shading into Flash gradients or bitmap fills. For this reason, 3D Studio Max creations with detailed textures and lighting effects do not translate very well when exported via Illustrate!. Ideaworks' plug-in and standalone application called Vectra3D, available in a demo version on the Flash 4 installation CD-ROM, promises to deliver realistic 3D animations and models to Flash movies. While Illustrate! can only be used with the PC-only 3D Studio Max, Vecta3D's standalone application is available for both the Macintosh and Windows platforms. As this is an area of rapid progression, be sure to check out www.theflashbible.com for up-to-date information.

On the CD-ROM

This tutorial requires both 3D Studio MAX and the Illustrate! 4.0 plug-in. The demo version of the Illustrate! 4.0 is included in the ch20 folder on the *Flash 4 Bible* CD-ROM. That's also where you'll find the source file for this tutorial, SunPath_Tutorial.max.

Expert Tutorial: Using Illustrate! to Export Flash Animations from 3D Studio Max by David Gould

Illustrate! 4.0 is a renderer for 3DS MAX that outputs vector artwork directly from 3DS MAX into Flash format. The output includes the object's surface color and transparency as well as the object's lines, which are output with attention to individual thickness, color, and linestyle. It draws lines where surfaces self-intersect and where objects intersect. Billed as the most advanced Toon Shader on the market, it also offers control over the drawing style with individual brushes, paints, and strokes for various types of edges, such as folds, creases, and so on.

Due to the growing interest among Flash developers for ways to include 3D modeling with Flash content, we chose to include this tutorial by David Gould, who created the Illustrate! 4.0 program. In his tutorial, David shows us how to use Illustrate! 4.0 to control frame rates for Flash, to create custom styles, to control transparency, and, also, how to simulate shading with subobject materials. This is a pretty advanced tutorial, as it presumes an understanding of all the applications involved.

Getting started with the Sun Path

First, load the scene, SunPath_Tutorial.max, from the CD-ROM into 3DS MAX. Then click the Play button to view the animation. You'll see a scene of the sun moving slowly across the sky from dawn to dusk, while the dolmens rotate in the foreground. Now, go to frame 40 and click the Render button. You can see how materials have been assigned to the different objects. The sun and the flare have a semi-transparent material, whereas the dolmens have a subobject material. You can also open the Material Editor to look at each of the materials in more detail.

At frame 40, the 3DS MAX render output looks like this.

Frame rate

The first concern before this animation can be output to Flash is to change the frame rate to accommodate the different manner in which Flash animations are played. In Flash, every frame of the animation is drawn in real-time. That's because each Flash frame consists of a series of shapes that must be calculated and then drawn. (Although the standard frame rate for video is 30 fps (frames per second) few machines can play a Flash animation at 30 fps.) So the frame rate must be reduced to ensure smooth playback. To do this in 3DS MAX, click the Time Configuration button. Then, in the Frame Rate section, click the Custom button. Set the rate to 15. Click OK. Now the animation measures 50 frames. Rates of between 10 and 15 are suited to Flash. Which rate you use depends on the complexity of the scene and the output file size.

The Time Configuration dialog box enables you to change the frame rate of the animation.

Creating a rough draft

Next, before rendering the entire animation, it's always advisable to render a rough draft of just the outlines to ensure that everything is going to work properly for the complete (often time consuming) render. To do this, start by clicking the Illustrate! menu item on the main menu bar of 3DS MAX. The Rendering Wizard is now displayed. Click the Shockwave Flash (SWF) radio button and click Next. Accept the default setting of Draft Renderer, and then

Continued

(continued)

click Next. Click the MAX Environment Color radio button and click Next. Click the Cartoon image to change the drawing style. Click Outlines. Click Next. Leave the default output settings as they are, and click Next. Click Finish to save your settings. The Illustrate! window is now displayed. Click the Render button (see the following figure).

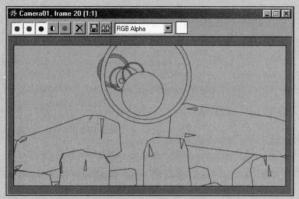

Using the Rendering Wizard of Illustrate!, 3DS MAX can output an outline-only version of the frame.

The scene is displayed in the virtual frame buffer with outlines only. Take a look at the resulting single-frame Flash animation. It shows a single frame with the scene rendered with outlines only. Now, let's create a rough draft rendering of the first half of the animation. Click the Render Scene button. Then, in the Time Output section, set the Range to start at 0 and to end at 25. Finally, click Render. When you look at this Flash animation, you'll see 25 frames of the scene rendered with outlines only. The background color changes as the sun moves across the sky and, towards the end, a lens flare appears.

Creating custom styles

Now we need to create a custom style for both the sun and the lens flare. Here's how: (If the Illustrate! window isn't already open, click the Illustrate! menu item — see the following figure.) Click the Create New button and enter **Surface Only** in the style's name box. Next, open the Surface Only style by clicking the + button displayed to the left of the style's name. Then click the green tick located next to the Edges item — this turns all the edges off. Click the surface Default and, in the Surface drop-down menu, select the predefined surface Flat. This custom style renders the surface of the object with flat diffuse color. The edges won't be drawn.

Next, in the Named Selection Sets, located in the 3DS MAX main toolbar, click both sun and flare to select them. Then, in the Illustrate! window, confirm that the Surface Only style is selected. Click the Assign Style to Selection button. Then, back in the 3DS MAX main toolbar, set the Render Type to Selected so that only the sun and flare render. Click the Render button.

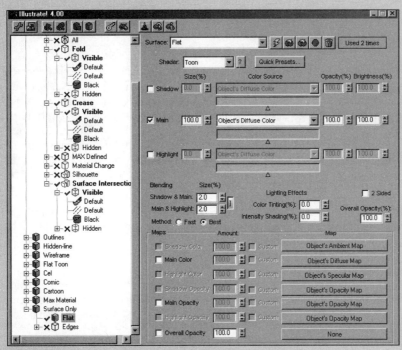

The Illustrate! settings for Surface Only style

When the rendering process is finished, take a look at the resulting Flash animation—the sun and the lens flare are rendered with the style we just assigned. Also, the objects were rendered opaque, whereas the lens flare and sun's corona were rendered semi-transparent.

Now, to create yet another style for the dolmens. Because Illustrate! only supports flat shading of objects, the dolmens have been assigned a subobject material with three different shades of gray in order to simulate dimensional shading. Then the individual faces were assigned gray level material id. The three gray colors were then animated to simulate changes in light so that the shading of the dolmens would appear to change with the rising and setting of the sun. (Open the Material Editor to take a closer look at the stone material and see how this was done.)

Now, to do it: If the Illustrate! window isn't already open, click the Illustrate! menu item to open the Illustrate! window. With a style selected, click the Create New button and type **Dolmen** in the style's name box. Then, open the Dolmen style by clicking the + button displayed to the left of its name. Next, Click the Surface Default. In the Surface drop-down menu, select the predefined surface Flat. Also, click the brush Edges ⇨ Fold ⇨ Visible ⇨ Default. Then, from the Brush drop-down menu, select 1.5 Pixel Circle. Then, click the paint Edges ⇨ Fold ⇨ Visible ⇨ Black. Finally, from the Paint drop-down menu, select Object's Diffuse Darkened.

Continued

(continued)

With these settings the style has been set so that all fold edges are 1.5 pixels thick and are drawn with the darkened diffuse color of the underlying object.

Next, we draw creases with a slightly thinner brush. To do this, click the brush Edges ⇨ Crease ⇨ Visible ⇨ Default. Then, from the Brush drop-down menu, select 1 Pixel Circle. Because the Surface of Intersection doesn't need to be calculated for this scene, it can be turned off. To do this, click the green tick next to the Surface Intersection edge item to turn it off. In the Named Selection Sets located in the 3DS MAX main toolbar, highlight dolmens to select them. Confirm that the Dolmen style is selected in the Illustrate! Window and then click the Assign Style to Selection button. Finally, on the 3DS MAX main toolbar, set the Render Type to Selected so that only the dolmens are rendered; then click the Render button.

When the render is complete, look at the resulting Flash animation: you'll see the dolmens' surface color change with the sun's rising. Notice too that their fold edges are drawn with a darker version of their underlying diffuse color.

Creating the Final Animation

With all of these styles assigned, the final animation can be rendered. Note, however, that the process of rendering parts and pieces of a larger animation to test the individual effects routinely yields the greatest control and the best effects with the least amount of total time. Consequently, it's advisable to take notes of your settings as you proceed toward your final render. With all the settings unchanged from the previous setups, you're ready to render the entire animation. To do this in the 3DS MAX main toolbar, set the Render type to View so that the entire scene renders. Click the Render Scene button, set the Time Output setting to Active Segment, and click the Render button. The resulting Flash animation shows the scene with all of the styles that were previously applied.

The final SWF file animation made with the Illustrate! 4 plug-in

✦   ✦   ✦

Working with QuickTime

This chapter explains how to use QuickTime (QT) media with Flash. Flash 4 expands the definition of desktop video by adding a new track type to QuickTime 4. We explore the integration of QuickTime movies with Flash interactivity, as well as distinguishing the different types of QuickTime movies (Flash, Video, and VR).

QuickTime 4 has introduced a new media track to QuickTime movies: the Flash track. A Flash track is just one of the many multimedia tracks available for use in QuickTime. Flash 4 has the new ability to import QuickTime movies, add Flash content on layers above or below the QuickTime (QT) movies, and re-export the whole product as a QuickTime Flash movie. QuickTime Flash movies are basically the same file type (.MOV file) as other QuickTime movies—QT Flash movies simply have a stored or referenced Shockwave Flash movie (.SWF file).

QuickTime versus Video for Windows

Because QuickTime has the powerful ability to store a combination of multimedia tracks, Flash supports the QuickTime format with its Export and Publish commands. Although PC Flashers can also export Video for Windows files, these files don't support a Flash track. The differences between these two formats are intricate. But before we talk about the intricacies, how do you recognize one from the other? The QuickTime file extension is MOV (from the Macintosh File Type MooV), while the Video for Windows' file extension is AVI (Audio-Video Interleaved format).

Video content is usually delivered in wrapper formats for distribution. Two primary system-level container formats or *wrappers* exist for video content on computer systems today: QuickTime and Video for Windows. Although both can be considered architectures for multimedia content, QuickTime has the most advanced architecture of the two. (Technically, RealSystems' RealPlayer is also a container format for multimedia, but it's only used for delivery — it cannot be used for editing and re-editing material.) Before Windows 95, multimedia developers relied on the QuickTime architecture on the Macintosh to make their multimedia components work together harmoniously. That's because QuickTime for Windows lacked many of the Mac's QuickTime features until the 3.0 release, which finally delivered to Windows the same multi-track interactivity that Mac users had enjoyed from the start. Now, with QuickTime 4, both Windows and Mac versions can store Flash 3 content. This content can be embedded as an interface to control another QuickTime video or audio track, or even as an enhancement to sprite animation.

Caution   Unfortunately, Video for Windows (VfW) wasn't developed along the same lines as QuickTime. Video for Windows is just that — video that's designed to play on Windows machines: It can't contain other media tracks (such as Flash tracks) like QuickTime can. Luckily, newer versions of the Windows Media Player can play QuickTime content, and QuickTime 3.0 (or higher) can play Video for Windows movies, provided that the necessary codecs are installed. Both QuickTime and Video for Windows can read most of the software-based codecs, like Cinepak or Indeo. When you get stuck, usually it's not difficult to translate a QuickTime file to a Video for Windows file using a video-editing application like the PC version of Adobe Premiere, or vice versa with the Mac version.

The only difference between QuickTime files on the Mac and the PC is that movies made on the Macintosh can internally reference media content from either a resource or data fork. Because the two operating systems have different file and directory structures, this referencing system can't be carried over to the PC. Consequently, most Mac movies need to be *flattened* in order to work properly on the PC — *flattening* means that all material referenced in the resource fork of the Mac QuickTime is compiled into one data fork, which is then accessible by all operating systems. Usually, when you are rendering video content on the Mac, you are given an option to flatten (or not flatten) the final movie. A movie can also be flattened with QuickTime Player by selecting Make Movie Self-Contained when you save (or re-save) the movie.

Note   Apple has renamed the MoviePlayer application to QuickTime Player. You need the professional version of QuickTime Player to edit or recompress QuickTime movies. Luckily, you only need to purchase an unlock key code from Apple to transform the regular player into the pro player, as well as download a few extra components using the QuickTime Updater. Use the QuickTime control panel to enter your unlock key. The application name, however, remains QuickTime Player. Even though we refer to QuickTime Player Pro, you won't see the Pro suffix in the application name.

The major limitation of Video for Windows is that it only supports two tracks of multimedia content: video and audio. QuickTime, however, supports multiple media tracks: video, audio, Flash, text, sprite, and timecode tracks. Furthermore, using QuickTime Player, you can set up many options for each movie's track, like pre-loading into memory and enabling high quality. QuickTime 4, which is the latest version, also enables you to create reference movies specifically designed for the varying speeds of Internet connections. Using the free Apple utility, MakeRefMovie, you can create different versions of the same movie with a range of file sizes. Depending on the visitor's QuickTime plug-in settings, the proper movie downloads to the computer. For example, if the connection speed setting of the plug-in is set to ISDN, the visitor receives the ISDN-version of the movie, which is of better quality and — as you've learned in this introduction — also bigger in file size.

Tip   Terran Interactive's Media Cleaner EZ and Pro can take the guesswork out of video compression. It has optimized presets for CD-ROM and Web delivery. Find it at `www.terran.com`.

QuickTime Support in Flash

Flash 4 provides the amazing ability to import QuickTime (QT) movie files into the Library. If you want to synch your Flash movie with a pre-existing QT movie, you can bring the QT movie into a Flash scene and play both movies simultaneously in the authoring environment of Flash. When you're finished, you can export the Flash movie as a QuickTime Flash movie, using either the Export or Publish commands. The result is a QT movie with video, audio, and Flash tracks. At the time of this writing, you need QuickTime 4 to pull off this stunt — with the unfortunate limitation that you can't use any Flash 4-specific actions or functions yet. QuickTime 4 can only interpret Flash 3.0 or earlier actions. This means that any ActionScripting (as described in Part IV of this book) is not recognized. Furthermore, you can't export a Shockwave Flash movie (.SWF file) from Flash 4 with both Flash content and imported QuickTime movies. In order to play QuickTime movies with Flash content, you need to use the QuickTime format (.MOV).

Note   When you import a QuickTime file into Flash, you need to keep your original QuickTime movie file, independent of the Flash (.FLA) file. Flash does not make a copy of the QuickTime file inside the movie. Rather, it links to the external QuickTime movie file for playback and rendering purposes.

A warning for video developers

Flash 4 employs a new method of exporting QuickTime movies. As is shown later in this chapter, you can export two types of QuickTime movies: regular raster-based QTs (called QuickTime Video), or the new QTs with Flash tracks (called QuickTime). The new QuickTime movies (with Flash tracks) can only be played by QuickTime 4 or later. At the time of this writing, most, if not all, video applications on the Mac were not 100-percent compatible with QT4, especially with its new Sound Manager component. Furthermore, using QuickTime 4 with Adobe Premiere 5.1a, Adobe After Effects 4.0 or EditDV 1.5/1.6 may result in degraded playback performance and rendering quality. But then, like being caught between that proverbial rock and hard place, you can't export QuickTimes (with Flash tracks) from Flash 4 without installing QT4. So what does this mean? If you are working on a Mac and you want to use the new QT4 with Flash 4, you probably need to have one computer running QT4 and another running your video editing application (with QT4 or QT3). Otherwise, you need two different startup configurations on your Mac — one with QT4 extensions, and another with QT3 extensions. If you don't like those solutions, the simplest methods for exporting high-quality video from Flash 4 would be: (1) export image sequences only, and (2) refrain from installing QT4 until your video-editing applications fully support it, or (3) export QuickTime Video. (Don't you just love these "upgrade" cycles?) If you work on a PC, then you can install QT4 to utilize Flash-track QuickTime movies and use the Video for Windows (.AVI) format for your video-editing needs, without any conflict between the two.

Note   By the end of 1999, most video applications should be QuickTime 4 compliant. Check the software developer's Web site for upgrades or updates. Also, you need to have the latest version of QuickTime 4 installed (4.01). Run the QuickTime Updater application that is installed with QuickTime 4 to check and update your current version.

Importing QuickTime into Flash

To bring a QT movie into Flash, use the File ⇨ Import command (Command+R or Ctrl+R) and select a QuickTime movie from the ensuing file dialog box. QuickTime movies usually have a QuickTime logo icon and end with the MOV extension, although they sometimes end with QT. Prior to import, make sure you've selected the layer in which you wish to import the QT. It's often a good idea to create a new layer to hold the imported QT. Once you've imported the QT movie, the first frame of the QT movie displays in the current frame of the Flash movie. You also see a new symbol type in the Library window — this is a Movie, not to be confused with a Movie Clip.

The timeline in Flash displays the QT's movie length relative to the duration (in time, NOT frames) of the Flash movie. Note that one second of the Flash movie equals one second of the QT movie: This means that one frame of QT video is NOT equivalent to one frame of a Flash movie. You can see this for yourself. After you have imported a QT, scrub the timeline to preview the QT movie. Stop on any discernable frame, and change the frame rate of the Flash movie via the Modify ⇨ Movie command (Command/Ctrl+M). After you click OK, you notice that the QT movie frame has changed even though the Flash frame marker is still on the same frame. How do you deal with this variability? Usually, if you intend to export the Flash movie as a QuickTime movie with a Flash track, you want to set the frame rate of your Flash movie to match the frame rate of your QT movie. If you have a Flash movie frame rate that's different from the video track of the QuickTime, you may run into slow or jerky playback. QuickTime Flash movies can theoretically have any number of Flash scenes. If you have more than one scene, the QuickTime Player may continue to briefly play any running QT movie from the previous scene. For this reason, you may want to add a few blank buffer frames at the beginning of any transition point (for example, going from one scene to the next).

With regards to movie length, no built-in limitations exist. You can make the scene as long as you wish in order to accommodate any range of interactivity or animation. If you plan to have continuously running Flash and video layers (for example, a Flash animation moving on top of the video track), add enough frames to view the entire length of the QT movie within the Flash timeline. Please see Figures 21-1 and 21-2 for examples.

Figure 21-1: This timeline does not have enough frames to show the entire QT movie — only 15 frames have been assigned to the layer. The Flash movie has a frame rate of 1 fps, and the QT movie is 30 seconds long.

The problem to avoid is this: If you don't add enough frames to accommodate the entire QuickTime movie, then the duration of the Flash movie determines the duration of the video track. This means that your imported QT movie may be arbitrarily cropped or trimmed to the length prescribed in the Flash editor document (.FLA file).

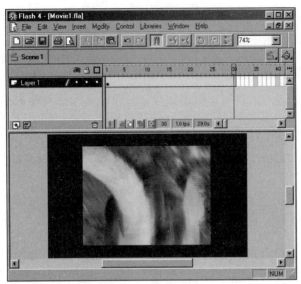

Figure 21-2: This timeline has 30 frames — enough frames to accommodate the entire QT movie.

Combining Flash and QT Movies

Once you've created a Flash movie synched to an imported QT movie, you can export a fully self-contained QuickTime movie that stores both the Flash and imported QT movie. However, you don't need to use Flash to put Flash content into QuickTime movies. If you want to layer Flash movies into pre-existing QuickTime movies, you can import SWF files directly into the QuickTime Player. But you need the latest Player that installs with QuickTime 4 to import Flash material. Prior versions of the QuickTime Player cannot do this.

Creating QuickTime Flash movies

After you've created a Flash movie with an imported QT movie, you can export or publish the entire Flash scene as a self-contained QT Flash movie that can be played with the latest QuickTime Player.

To create a quick and simple QuickTime movie from Flash, choose File ➪ Export Movie (Command+Option+Shift+S or Ctrl+Alt+Shift+S). Browse to a folder where you want to save the QuickTime, type a filename, and click Save (see Figure 21-3). You are then presented with the Export QuickTime dialog box.

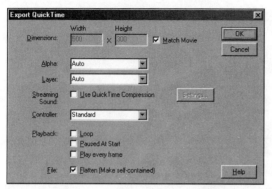

Figure 21-3: For a quick look at a QuickTime Flash version of your Flash document, accept the defaults in the Export QuickTime dialog box.

To check out the quality of the QuickTime movie, open the new QuickTime movie with QuickTime Player.

Caution Be careful with the controller type setting. If you select None, you won't even be able to stop the movie with the space bar once it's started.

While you can use the Export Movie command to produce independent QuickTime movies, the Publish Settings command enables you to create QuickTime movies as well as other linked file formats. Go to the File menu, and choose Publish Settings (Command+Shift+F12 or Ctrl+Shift+F12).

In the Format tab, make sure you have a check next to the QuickTime option, and de-select the others. You notice that each time you check or uncheck an option in the Publish Settings dialog box that the corresponding Settings tab appears or disappears, respectively.

For the purpose of exporting QuickTime, you should only have the Format and QuickTime tabs showing (see Figures 21-4 and 21-5). If Use Default Names is checked, the resulting QuickTime movie has the same name as the FLA file that is currently open in Flash. Otherwise, you can uncheck this option and specify a different name in the text fields next to the corresponding format types. Unfortunately, you can't control the location of the new files that are generated via the Publish command — all files produced via Publish are saved to the same location as the FLA file.

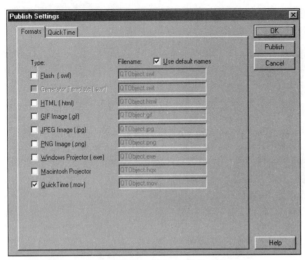

Figure 21-4: The Publish Settings dialog box for QuickTime-only publishing. Click the QuickTime tab to access the movie's properties.

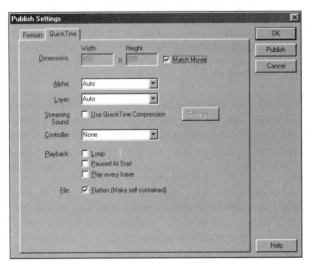

Figure 21-5: Use the Publish Settings' QuickTime tab to control QT movie settings.

Tip   Use the Export Movie command to save QuickTime movies to specific folders or locations.

Dimensions

Although you've probably already set the correct movie size in the Modify ⇨ Movie dialog box to conform to your specific output needs, it's good to note here that you can resize your QuickTime movie with the Dimensions properties to export a movie at alternate dimensions.

Alpha

For the Alpha property, you can decide whether you want the Flash track's background to be transparent or opaque. If want your Flash material to display together with underlying QuickTime video content, choose Alpha-Transparent. If you don't want the underlying QuickTime video to show through the Flash track, choose Copy. The Auto setting makes the Flash background transparent if Flash artwork exists on top of other content. If a QuickTime movie is stacked above the Flash artwork, then Auto makes the Flash background opaque. If you export a QuickTime Flash movie with only Flash artwork, Auto uses an opaque background.

Layer

For the Layer property, you can decide whether you want the Flash track to be layered on top of or below the QuickTime content. If you want the Flash content to play on top of the QuickTime movie, choose Top. If you designed an interface or animation to appear underneath the QT movie, choose Bottom. The Auto setting for the Layer property places the Flash track in front of QuickTime material if Flash artwork appears on top of the QuickTime anywhere in the Flash editor document. If you placed QuickTime movies on top of Flash artwork layers, then Auto places the Flash track behind the video track.

Streaming sound

If you want Flash-enabled sounds to be converted to an additional QuickTime sound track, check the Use QuickTime Compression option for the Streaming Sound property. Any and all sounds that are used in the scenes are recompressed into a separate sound track. This sound track is separate from any other sound tracks that may be present in imported QuickTime movies. The Settings button enables you to define the parameters of the audio compression. You may want to match the audio characteristics of the imported QuickTime movie used in the Flash movie if you choose to use this option. Because this property converts Flash audio into QuickTime audio, you can use any sound compressor that is available to QuickTime. For more sound advice on Flash 4's audio compression settings, refer to Chapters 10, 11, and 12.

Controller

The Controller property determines if a controller (control panel for playback) is shown with the movie in the QuickTime Player application, and if so, what kind of a controller. None disables the display of a control panel, and, subsequently, it is the default setting for the Export Movie command. If you have created your own controller in Flash, you may want to disable the display of the regular QuickTime controller. The Standard option presents the QuickTime movie with the standard QuickTime Player 4 interface, enabling play, pause, frame forward and backward, and volume level, among other controls. The QuickTime VR option displays the specialized control panel for QuickTime panorama or object movies. We discuss QTVR later in the "A Word about QuickTime VR Movies" section of this chapter. To compare the different controllers, see Figures 21-6 through 21-8.

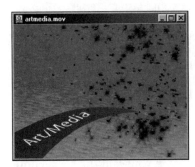

Figure 21-6: A QuickTime movie with no controller. This was made with the Controller property set to None.

Figure 21-7: A QuickTime movie with the standard controller

Figure 21-8: The QuickTime VR controller used with a Flash-enabled QTVR panorama

Playback

The Playback property controls how the movie plays when it's first opened in the QuickTime Player. Check the Loop option if you want to the QuickTime to automatically replay the movie when it's reached the end. Check the Paused at Start option if you don't want the QuickTime movie to automatically start playing as soon as it opens in the QuickTime Player. Note that if any controller (other than None) is specified, the movie is always paused when it loads in the QuickTime Player. The Play Every Frame option, when checked, overrides the frame rate setting to playback every frame contained in the video. Usually, this is not recommended because the QuickTime audio track is silenced.

Note   As of this writing, the Paused at Start option or a Stop Flash action on the first frame does not work if NONE is specified for controller type. Anyone viewing the QuickTime Flash movie must use Get Info in QT Player Pro to access Movie properties and uncheck Auto-Play and resave QT in order for these settings to work. Also, the Play Every Frame option disables playback of any pre-existing QuickTime audio track — but Flash audio still plays.

File

The File property has only one option, Flatten (Make self-contained). Checking this option forces Flash to write one QuickTime movie that contains any and all referenced material. If you imported a 10MB QuickTime movie into Flash and created a few layers of Flash content to work with the QT movie, flattening creates one QuickTime that copies the imported QT movie and Flash material to video, audio, and Flash tracks respectively. If you do not check Flatten, Flash creates a reference QuickTime movie that looks for (and require the presence of) the Flash .SWF file and other QuickTime file(s) on playback. While this reference movie has a very small file size, you need to make sure all the referenced material is readily available for playback. This means that the Format tab of the Publish Settings dialog box should have a checkmark next to Flash (.SWF) as well as QuickTime (.MOV). Furthermore, you may run into linking problems over the Internet due to connection latency or if the referenced files aren't together in one location. For this reason, you may prefer to package everything into one flattened QuickTime movie.

Export Movie or Publish?

Although the Export QuickTime dialog box is identical to the QuickTime tab of the Publish Settings dialog box, one important difference exists. The File property, which controls linking to external files, creates different results with each command.

If Flatten (Make self-contained) is unchecked in the Export QuickTime dialog box, then only the imported QT movie is referenced externally — it is not stored in the new QuickTime Flash movie.

If you check both the Flash (.SWF) and QuickTime (.MOV) options in the Formats tab of the Publish Settings dialog box *and* uncheck the Flatten (Make self-contained) option in the QuickTime tab, then the Publish command creates a QuickTime Flash movie (.MOV file) that links to the .SWF file as well as the original imported QuickTime movie (.MOV). Neither the Flash content or the imported QT movie is stored in the new QuickTime Flash movie — the QuickTime Flash movie, .SWF file and original QuickTime(s) need to be in the same location in order to play.

Click OK to accept your current Publish Settings and return to the Flash scene. Make any final adjustments to your movie. When you're ready to test drive your new Quick-Time movie, you can preview the QuickTime movie by using the Publish Preview menu, and selecting QuickTime. QuickTime Player Pro should automatically start and load the movie. If you like the results, run the File ⇨ Publish command (Shift +F12). Flash saves a QuickTime movie to the same directory where your FLA file has been saved. You can also publish the movie by using the Publish button directly in the Publish Settings dialog box.

Note   For those who want to maximize the built-in functions of QuickTime Player Pro, QuickTime video filters and graphics modes can be applied to Flash tracks.

So far, you've seen how to combine existing QT movies with your Flash content. You don't need to import other QuickTime content into Flash in order to export QuickTime material from Flash. With QuickTime 4, you can create QuickTime movies that are essentially repackaged .SWF files. Using Flash 4, FLA movies can be exported to QuickTime formats. At the time of this writing, QuickTime Player recognizes only Flash 3.0 actions. To export QuickTime Flash movies from Flash 4, follow the same steps described previously without importing any external QuickTime movie files.

Creating QuickTime video with Flash

If you own the Macintosh version of Flash 4, then you can also export QuickTime Video via the Export Movie command. QuickTime Video is raster- or bitmap-based animated movement. Remember, QuickTime Flash movies contain a new Flash media track, which is exactly the same file format as Shockwave Flash (.SWF file). As such, the Flash track uses antialiased vector graphics to store and display information. QuickTime Video, however, uses only raster information—each frame in the movie is described as collection of pixels. This method of storage is much more byte intensive. For this reason, QuickTime Video files are usually several megabytes large, and time-consuming to download over slower Internet connections.

Tip   Why would you want to use QuickTime Video if it creates larger file sizes than QuickTime Flash? Unfortunately, QuickTime Flash movies can only be played with QuickTime 4.0 or greater. If you want to be sure that your QuickTimes can be played with older versions of QuickTime, then the movies need to be QuickTime Video.

In the Mac version of Flash 4, you have the option of creating either QuickTime Video or QuickTime Flash movies. If you want to use your Flash animations in home videos or videotaped presentations, then you need to save Flash movies as QuickTime video movies. These movies can then be edited with your other digitally captured video.

To save a Flash movie as a QuickTime Video movie, choose File ⇨ Export Movie and select QuickTime Video as the Format type. After you specify a file name and a location to save the movie, click Save. Next, you see the Export QuickTime dialog box (Figure 21-9), where you can specify how Flash should rasterize the Flash movie.

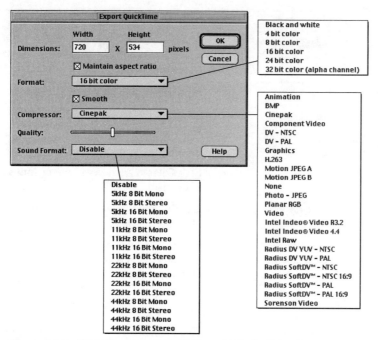

Figure 21-9: With the Export QuickTime (Video) dialog box, you can specify (A) Dimensions, (B) Format, (C) Compressor, (D) Quality, and (E) Sound Format.

Dimensions

This property performs exactly the same way as the Dimensions property of QuickTime Flash movie exports. See our coverage of Publish Settings and QuickTime Flash earlier in this chapter. Because Flash vector can maintain high quality at any size, you can scale the dimensions of the QuickTime Video file to match the requirements of your video project. For example, if you want to use this QuickTime Video with DV format video, then scale the movie dimensions to 720×534.

Cross-Reference See Chapter 22, "Creating Full-Motion Video with Flash," for more detailed information on frame dimensions.

Format

Use the Format property to control the bit-depth of the QuickTime Video movie. For most high-quality video work, use 24-bit or 32-bit color formats. For Web distribution of QuickTime Video movies, lower color formats yield smaller file sizes. Refer to Table 21-1 for a quick breakdown of each color format. If the Smooth option of the Format property is checked, Flash artwork is converted to antialiased bitmap information. Otherwise, curved lines may exhibit the "jaggies"—jagged or staircased steps on curves or gradients.

Table 21-1
QuickTime Video Color Formats

Format	Number of Colors	Description/Use
Black and white	2	Fax-like image quality.
4-bit color	16	Similar to the 16 system colors used by Windows in Safe mode.
8-bit color	256	Indexed Color mode, like GIF.
16-bit color	65,536	High Color in Windows 95/98 or Thousands of Colors on the Mac.
24-bit color	16.7 million	True Color in Windows 95/98 or Millions of Colors on the Mac.
32-bit color	16.7 million + 8-bit alpha channel	Same as 24-bit color; supports 256 levels of transparency.

Compressor

This menu determines which video codec (*compressor-de*compressor) is used for the bitmap frames in the QuickTime Video movie. Because QuickTime Video is more bandwidth-intensive, bitmap information needs to be condensed in some manner. Compressors or codecs reduce the amount of information that needs to be stored for each frame. For general distribution, you may want to use Cinepak or Intel Indeo Video codecs. For high-quality video output for editing or broadcast purposes, use the hardware codec used by your specific video capture card. The next chapter explores codecs more deeply.

Quality

This unmarked slider (which apparently has no units) controls how the compressor selected in the previous menu works. As you drag the slider to the right, less compression is applied to the QuickTime Video, which results in higher-quality video. As you drag the slider to the left, more information is discarded from each frame of video (more compression, lower quality).

Sound format

If your Flash movie contains any audio, then you can choose to convert those audio samples to a QuickTime-compatible audio track. QuickTime can use any major sampling rate (such as 22kHz), bit-depth (such as 8 or 16), or channel (such as mono or stereo). Usually, you won't want to use anything lower than 22kHz 16-bit Stereo for quality audio. If you don't need to use Flash audio in the QuickTime Video file, then choose Disable.

See Chapters 10 and 12 for more information on sampling rates and file formats.

A word about QTVR movies

If you are familiar with QuickTime VR's amazing panorama and object movies, then you should be happy to know that Flash supports QuickTime VR (QTVR) movies as well. Because QTVR movies aren't strict linear playback video movies, you need to keep a few things in mind when you use QTVR movies in Flash. Note that you cannot create QTVR movies from scratch in Flash. You first need to create a QTVR movie with VR equipment and software, like Apple's QuickTime VR Authoring Studio. Flash can then import these movies and add Flash artwork and actions to them.

 The QTVR folder of the ch21 folder on the *Flash 4 Bible* CD-ROM contains sample Flash editor documents (.FLA files) and QuickTime VR movies (.MOV files) to use with this section. Paul Nykamp, a QTVR specialist in Toronto, Canada, provided the QTVR movies. He can be reached at pnykamp@spectranet.ca.

Panoramic movies

QuickTime panoramic movies enable you to view a physical or virtual space by stitching a series of images into a 360-degree view. You navigate the space by clicking and dragging the mouse inside the movie frame. When you import a QTVR panoramic movie (a.k.a. *pano*) into Flash, it only displays the first frame of the QTVR movie on the stage, regardless of the frame marker's position. It's very important to make sure that your timeline's frame span doesn't extend beyond the length of the QTVR movie. Playback beyond the length of the QTVR causes the QTVR to disappear until the Flash frame playback loops back to the starting frame. The best solution, whenever possible, is to limit your timeline to just a few frames (one frame would be ideal), and use movie clips with Tell Target commands to provide longer frame length animations.

 QuickTime VR panos are particularly sensitive to Flash movie frame rates. The default setting of 12 fps may result in incomplete panoramas with missing sections. If a problem occurs, try changing the Flash movie frame rate to 1 fps and re-exporting the QuickTime VR movie.

Due to limitations of the QTVR controller, there's no way to rewind a movie or return to frame 1 of the Flash track. Technically, because each media track has its own timeline of frames, if the Flash track plays beyond the QTVR track, you lose the QTVR movie. You can prevent this from happening by ensuring that you can always view the QTVR's first frame within the Flash authoring environment. Another clue is this: If you go beyond the length of the QTVR movie, the extended area is represented by a striked rectangular box as seen in Figure 21-10.

To export or publish QTVR pano movies, specify the QuickTime VR Controller type in the Export QuickTime dialog box or in the Publish Settings' QuickTime tab.

Figure 21-10: If your Flash movie plays beyond the length of an imported QTVR panorama or object movie, it disappears from the stage and is replaced with a striked box.

Object movies

You can also make QTVR object movies in Flash 4. QTVR object movies let you rotate or spin an object — photographed or 3D-modeled — by dragging the mouse inside the movie frame (see Figure 21-11). You may have seen Apple's QTVR object movies of PowerBook G3s in the QuickTime showcase section of the `www.apple.com/quicktime` Web site. With Flash 4, you can expand the multimedia capabilities of object movies. Adding Flash buttons, audio, and artwork to an object movie can provide a different navigational interface for the object, and provide call-out information to the object movie.

Figure 21-11: QTVR object movies with Flash tracks can have more impact than regular QTVR movies.

Unlike QuickTime pano movies, object movies can be fully viewed within the Flash authoring environment. Each frame of the object movie shows a different viewing angle of the object. Again, like regular QuickTime movies, make sure you add enough frames to view the entire object movie. Keep adding frames until the stage displays the object movie with a striked box. Then, subtract any frames that show the movie as a striked box.

Our tests with object movies have also shown that the frame rate of the Flash movie is a critical setting. Most of our test exports with QTVR object movies played back very poorly — the object's rotation movement was not very smooth. However, when we specified a controller type of NONE and added a Flash button to provide a *play* action, the object movie played back very smoothly.

Tip For Flash-controlled playback of QTVR object movies, you need to add a Go to and Play action to the last frame of the scene, which loops back to the first frame of the scene. However, the QuickTime Player does not recognize a Flash Stop action on the first frame. To start a QTVR Flash movie in a paused state, select the Paused at Start option in the Playback section of the Export QuickTime dialog box or in the QuickTime tab of Publish Settings.

Using Digital Video in Shockwave Flash Movies

Because the strength of Flash lies in its vector animation capabilities, it makes sense that Flash prefers vector-based material. Most Web-site visitors prefer quicker download speeds, and vector animations are much easier to store as small files than raster graphics are. As a result, Flash handles raster-based material with JPEG or lossless (a.k.a. PNG) compression schemes. In the past, Flash didn't let you import digital video files into a Flash movie because they added too much to the file size, which prevented efficient compression and delivery on the Web. So, what do you do if you want to showcase your next blockbuster feature in your Shockwave Flash movie? You compromise. If you want visitors to get a taste (maybe a smell?) of some raster-based animation, it's best to select a short section of the overall movie and extract frames from that selection. In contrast to the next chapter where the process of exporting sequences from Flash movies is discussed, this section describes how to create still image sequences in other applications and bring them into Flash. If you want to accommodate visitors who are willing to wait for larger full-length movies, you can then link the preview in Flash to load the entire QuickTime movie (or QuickTime movie reference), via HTML and the QuickTime plug-in, into its own window or frame. Generally, though, this method of digital video integration into Flash is used for visual effects or just really cool raster content you snagged on video, like water ripples or textures.

New Feature We explained earlier in this chapter the process of creating new QuickTime Flash movies. This is a new alternative to adding Flash content to existing QuickTime movies, and, therefore, distributing Flash and QuickTime content simultaneously on the Web. In this section, we discuss the process of embedding raster material derived from video into a Shockwave Flash (.SWF) file, not a QuickTime Flash (.MOV) file.

This section covers a basic method of converting digital video content into a Flash-friendly sequence of frames. If you want to recreate the movement of original video via the converted vector-based art in Flash, we recommend that you read this section first and then check out WebMonkey's tutorial on Converting Animations to Flash at www.hotwired.com/webmonkey/98/42/index3a.html.

Even though Flash 4 now enables you to place QT movies in a Flash movie, they do not export or link with an SWF file. If you want to embed frames from a QuickTime movie in your Flash movie for playback on the Web, read the rest of the section. If you want to synchronize your Flash animations and interactivity with a QuickTime movie to use in a final QuickTime 4 movie, then refer to "Importing QT into Flash," earlier in this chapter.

Extracting frames from digital video clips

The premise of frame extraction is simple: instead of downloading large video files with Flash content, reduce the video in frame size, rate, and length to something that Flash (and slow Internet connections) can handle.

Although QuickTime video cannot be imported into Flash as one video file (because Flash does not store video files in the current implementation of the .SWF format), Flash does support image sequences in bitmap formats. So, we can convert any video clip into a short sequence of still images that can play as an animation or movie clip in Flash.

The following tutorials/workshops assume that you have some working knowledge of the applications described herein. Also, you must have some existing digital video material; we do not create or edit any video in these tutorials.

We recommend that you have QuickTime 3 or higher installed on your computer, as well as any updates to your video-editing application(s). At the time this book went to press, QuickTime 4 was available for both Windows and the Macintosh. However, as noted previously in this chapter, QT4 was not fully supported by all video-editing applications. Hopefully, by the time this book reaches the bookshelves, many of these issues should have been resolved. Please refer to our Web site at www.theFlashBible.com/ch19 for an index of updates, addenda, and other resources on this subject.

QT Player Pro

You don't need an expensive video-editing application to extract frames from video clips. In fact, you can do it for less than $30! Apple's QuickTime Player Pro (see Figure 21-12) can export any QuickTime movie as a series of individual still frames, which can then be imported to Flash. You need the latest version of the QuickTime software (currently 4.0) to export image sequences.

On the CD-ROM

If you want to use a sample QuickTime movie, choose a QuickTime movie from the ch21 folder on the *Flash 4 Bible* CD-ROM.

Time Display

Playback Head

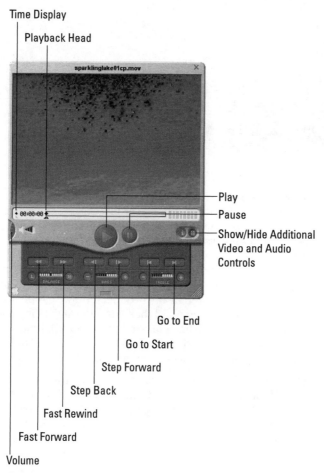

Play

Pause

Show/Hide Additional
Video and Audio
Controls

Go to End

Go to Start

Step Forward

Step Back

Fast Rewind

Fast Forward

Volume

Figure 21-12: The QuickTime 4 Player interface

1. **Making a Selection**: First, decide how much of the QuickTime movie you want to import into Flash. Do this sparingly. Remember that raster animation is heavy on file sizes, and people generally like faster-loading content on Web pages. Restrict your selections to movie clips of very short duration, less than five seconds if possible. If you want the visitor to see more than that, consider linking to the entire QuickTime from the smaller clip that you import into the Flash SWF file.

2. **Define Your Selection**: Use the In and Out markers to define your selection. Unfortunately, QT Player Pro does not show frame numbers in the time code display. As a result, you need to eyeball your selection. You can also use the additional video controls to move through the movie clip frame by frame. The selection is indicated by a gray bar between the In and Out points. Using Movie ⇨ Get Info and selecting Time from the pop-up you can view the timecode of where your selection starts and it's duration. In Figure 21-13, a two-second selection is made from a QuickTime movie clip.

IN Point

OUT Point

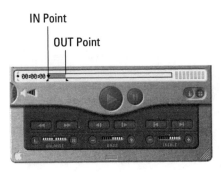

Figure 21-13: Keep your selections as short as possible. Longer selections add substantial weight to the file size of the Flash SWF file.

3. **Trimming the Movie**: After you've defined a selection, you need to delete the rest of the video track. If we don't delete it, QT Player Pro exports the entire movie as an image sequence. Again, we only need the short selection for use in Flash. Hold down the Ctrl and Alt keys (PC) or Command and Option keys (Mac), and click Edit on the QT Player Pro menu bar. Now click Trim. This command discards everything but your selection from the movie clip. (Don't worry about losing this content. As long as you don't re-save your QuickTime movie at this point, your video clip file won't be altered in any way, because we simply want to export this selection as an image sequence and then close the QuickTime movie *without saving.*) After you execute the Trim command, the In and Out markers automatically reset to encompass the entire remaining video, and the QuickTime movie only contains the selection that you defined previously.

4. **Exporting an Image Sequence**: Now you're ready to export the QuickTime as an image sequence. Choose File ➪ Export (Command+E or Ctrl+E), and you see the Save Exported File As dialog box (see Figure 21-14). Select a folder (or create a new one) to store your image sequence, specify a file name and choose Movie to Image Sequence in the Export drop-down menu. Next, click the Options button to define the format settings to be used for the image sequence. You see the Export Image Sequence Settings dialog box. If you are using the PC version of Flash, choose BMP (Windows Bitmap) for the Format property. If you're using the Mac version of Flash, choose the PICT format. For the Frames Per Second property, choose a value from the drop-down menu (or type one) that's appropriate to the length of the clip. For a two-second clip, a value of 4 or 5 is adequate, rendering a total of 8 or 10 frames. Click the Options button to select a bit-depth for the BMP or PICT sequence.

Choose Millions of Colors if you don't want to prematurely limit the color palette used for the image sequence.

Note   The Options dialog box displays the settings applicable for the file format chosen. Some file formats, such as JPEG, enable you to define compression levels in addition to bit-depth.

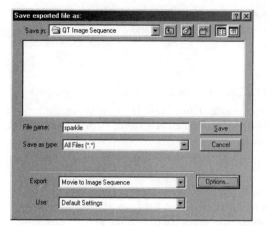
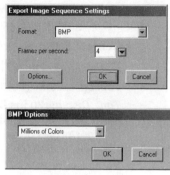

Figure 21-14: In the Save Exported File As dialog box, choose Movie to Image Sequence as the Export type. In the Export Image Sequence Settings dialog box, choose a file type and frame rate for the image sequence. By clicking the Options button of the Export Image Sequence Settings dialog box, you can access the file type-specific settings, such as color depth or compression.

Click OK to the BMP or PCT Options dialog box, and then click OK again on the Export Image Sequence Settings dialog box. Finally, click save on the original Export Image Sequence dialog box to render your image sequence. QT Player Pro adds consecutive numbers to the end of each filename generated in the sequence. Flash can recognize file sequences with this kind of numbering.

Now you have a collection of still images that can be imported into Flash. See "Importing a Sequence into Flash" later in this chapter for instructions.

Adobe Premiere 5.1

Adobe Premiere is a cross-platform video-editing application used by serious hobbyists and professional videographers. Unlike proprietary video systems like Avid, Premiere uses the QuickTime and/or the Video for Windows architecture for processing video. Premiere's functionality extends from creating Web-based video to CD-ROM video to professional broadcast-quality video. You can also use Premiere to generate image sequences from existing projects or movies.

On the CD-ROM

Use the dogs_small.mov QuickTime file on the *Flash 4 Bible* CD-ROM if you need some material for this section.

1. Open Premiere 5.1, and start a new project. If you've left the preferences for Premiere at their defaults, you are automatically presented with a New Project Settings dialog box as soon as Premiere finishes loading.

2. Specify the settings for the new project. See Figure 21-15 for reference. The following table delineates the various settings.

- **General Settings:**

  Editing Mode: QuickTime

  Timebase: 29.97 (For NTSC video. Use 25 for PAL/SECAM video.)

  Time Display: 30 fps Drop-Frame Time Code (For most consumer video material, including mini-DV. Use Non Drop-Frame Time Code for DVCAM or other professional video types.)

- **Video Settings:**

  Compressor: None (Even though you may have used other video compressors (or codecs) for your video footage, the None type configures our export settings correctly for image sequences.)

  Frame Size: 720 × 480 (All DV-captured material is 720×480. Some MJPEG video capture cards, including the Iomega Buz, capture at 720×480 as well. You need to uncheck the 4:3 Aspect box for this frame size. Most MJPEG video capture cards use a 640×480 frame size.)

  Depth: Millions (If you have video that includes an alpha channel or matte, use Millions+.)

  Frame Rate: 29.97 (If you are using PAL/SECAM, use 25. For a thorough explanation of frame rates and timebases, see page 336 of the Premiere 5 User Manual.)

  Quality: 100 percent

  Data Rate: All unchecked

Audio Settings are not available.

Keyframe & Rendering Options has only one setting:

- **Field Settings:** Lower field first (for most DV-captured material. Check your video capture card's user manual to confirm your card's field dominance).

υ

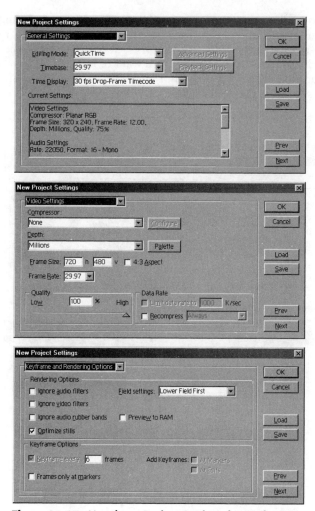

Figure 21-15: Use these Project Settings for DV format video that you want to export as an image sequence.

3. In the Project window, import an existing QuickTime (.MOV) or Video for Windows (.AVI) file. To maintain true cross-platform compatibility, you should use QuickTime movies. To import a movie, double-click in the Project window, and select a file in the following Import dialog box.

4. Next, you need to determine the length of the clip. Double-click the imported movie in the Project window. Premiere loads the clip into the Monitor window (see Figure 21-16). Using the Mark In and Mark Out buttons, set the In and Out points of the clip to reflect the selection you want to bring into Flash. You want to keep the duration of the clip fairly short, around a few seconds. The longer you make the selection, the larger your Flash file.

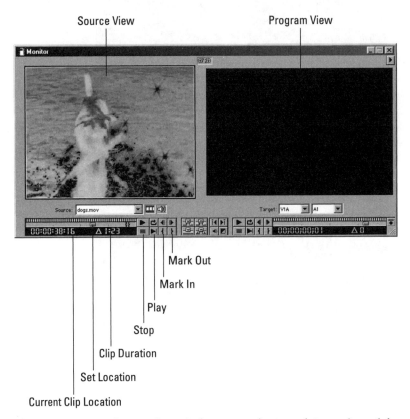

Figure 21-16: Use the Monitor window to set the In and Out points of the movie clip.

5. Put the clip into the Timeline. Open the Timeline window with the Window ➪ Timeline menu item (see Figure 21-17). Set the Time Units pop-up menu to 2 seconds. Click and drag the movie from the Project window onto any Video track in the Timeline window. Make sure you place it at the very beginning of the Timeline, at frame marker 00:00:00:00. If you can't see the clip in the Timeline, you might have to select a smaller time unit, like 2, 4, or 8 frames. If you are not sure that your clip is at the zero point, click and drag the clip in the video track as far left as possible To check this, click the time ruler and drag the edit line to the zero point. Whenever you drag the edit line

along the video in the Timeline, the Monitor window automatically pops
up and plays the video as you drag.

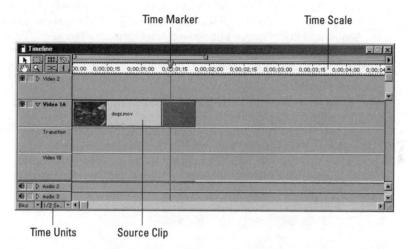

Figure 21-17: Build your video project in the Timeline window. For an image
sequence, put your movie clip on any video track at time 00:00:00:00, which
is at the very beginning (far left) of the time scale.

Note   Do not drag the clip into the Timeline more than once. If you dragged a clip into
the Timeline but don't see it, chances are it's in there somewhere. You can always
check how many times a given clip is used in the Timeline by checking the Video
Usage and Audio Usage columns in the Project window. So far, you should only
have 1 video and 1 audio use of your clip in the Timeline.

6. Now you're ready to export this selection as a sequence of individual images,
   which we can animate in Flash. With either the Monitor or Project window
   highlighted, select File ⇨ Export ⇨ Movie (Command+M or Ctrl+M). In the
   Export Movie dialog box, click the Settings button in the lower-right corner.

7. Specify the export settings. See Figure 21-18 for reference.

   • **General Settings:**

     File Type: PICT Sequence (On the PC, choose Windows BMP Sequence.
     You can also try Animated GIF if you don't mind having the color palette
     of the sequence limited to 256 colors.)

     Range: Entire Project

   • **Video Settings:**

     Compressor: N/A

Depth: Millions (If you have an alpha channel which you wish to also export with each image in the sequence, then select Millions+.)

Frame Size: Use a 4:3 frame aspect ratio (If you want a smaller Flash movie file size and are willing to sacrifice some image quality, shrink the frame size to 320×240 for both DV and MJPEG captured material. Sequences are rendered in square pixel formats. Because DV uses nonsquare pixels, you need to resize the actual frame to achieve the correct aspect ratio. That is, if you have 720×480 captured clips, you need to export 640×480 (or some 4:3 variation) for proper still images.)

Frame Rate: 1–12 fps (The frame rate depends on the length of your clip. If you have a two-second clip, then a setting of 6 fps results in a 12-frame sequence, which is imported into Flash. Higher frame rates equal more individual frames that Flash needs to animate. Basically, you want to obtain a balance between a minimum number of frames and a smooth, believable sense of movement — without the sequence becoming too jerky or jumpy.)

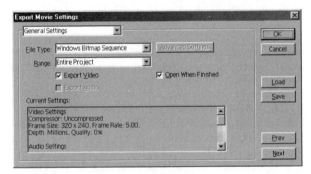

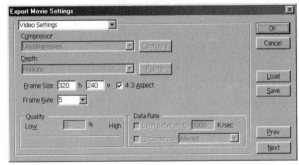

Figure 21-18: Use these settings to export an image sequence that Flash can import.

Audio Settings and Keyframe and Rendering Options are not available.

- **Special Processing:**

  Noise Reduction: None

Better Resize: On if Frame Size in Video Settings is smaller than original frame size

De-Interlace: On

Because the Special Processing dialog box gives you a live preview of each effect, you may want to experiment with different settings. Noise reduction can smooth pixilated edges, while the de-interlace option averages the lower and upper fields for each frame rendering. Otherwise, the field you specified in the New Project settings is used as when rendering the frame. De-interlacing is not recommended if you are scaling down any DV-format video that you want to convert to an image sequence. Meaning, if you're outputting an image sequence at 720×480 (normal DV frame size), then you should turn de-interlace on. If you are outputting at any size smaller than the original interlaced video, then leave the de-interlace option off.

8. After you specify the settings for the export, you should create a new folder or choose an existing folder to store the image sequence. When you name the export, don't worry about adding a number to the file name. Premiere does this automatically. For example, typing **apple_** for the file name directs Premiere to call each frame of the sequence as follow: apple_01, apple_02, apple_03, and so on. In Windows, the appropriate file extension is added as well, such as apple_01.pct.

9. Click OK and Premiere generates a still image sequence from the clip. You're now ready to import the still images into Flash. See "Importing a Sequence into Flash" in this chapter for more details.

Adobe After Effects 4.0

Adobe After Effects is an extremely powerful video compositing tool. You can think of After Effects as Photoshop for video. You can add custom filters and motion control to any graphic or video with After Effects. After Effects comes in two versions: regular (Standard) and professional (Production bundle). The Production Bundle version of After Effects uses the exact same interface as the regular version, but it has superior filters for compositing video. While it's easier to use Premiere or QT Player Pro to extract frames from a movie clip, you can also use After Effects to do it. If you've already constructed a project in After Effects, it's much easier to use it to extract a few frames from a larger project. Otherwise, you need to render the entire project and then go to another application, such as Premiere, to extract those frames from an already-rendered (and possible very large) movie file.

Before we begin the steps to extract frames in After Effects, we briefly discuss the workflow in After Effects. Like Premiere, After Effects uses a Project window that links all your graphics, sounds, and video clips to compositions, or comps. A composition can be thought of as the *real* project container, but you can have more than one composition for a project. In fact, for some killer effects and presentations, comps are often nested within another comp. If you've used After Effects primarily for full-motion video effects, then this section shows you how to repurpose your video content for Flash.

1. Open an existing After Effects project file (.AEP), or create a new project. If you have an existing After Effects project, then open the Time Layout window of the comp you wish to render and skip to Step 5.

2. Import the movie clip which you want to use in Flash, via the File ➪ Import ➪ Footage File command (Ctrl/Command+I). Note the duration and frame size of the clip you have imported

3. Create a new composition (Command+N or Ctrl+N), and conform the settings of the comp to those of the imported movie clip. For example, if the clip's frame size is 320×240 at 15 fps, then make the comp's setting 320×240 at 15 fps.

4. Drag the movie clip from the Project window to the new composition's Time Layout window. If it's not showing, then double-click the composition's name in the Project window. By default, the comp's name is Comp 1. Once you drag the movie clip into the Time Layout window, it shows up as a layer in the composition.

   Now you have to define the work area in After Effects. All extracted frames are drawn from this area. You should keep the length of the work area quite short (a few seconds or less) as each extracted frame adds a lot of weight to the Flash movie.

5. Move the Time Marker in the Time Layout window to the desired *In* point of the composition. The In point is where we start extracting frames. Make sure your Composition window is also open, so you have a visual reference for the Time Marker. If it's not showing, double-clicking the comp's name in the Project window reopens it.

6. In the Time Layout window, click and drag the Work Area Start tab while holding down the Shift key. Drag the tab to the Time Marker's position, and the tab snaps to it.

7. Move the Time Marker to the Out point of the composition, and shift-drag the Work Area End tab to this position (see Figure 21-19).

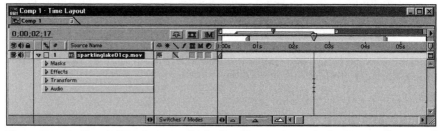

Figure 21-19: Use the Work Area tabs in the Time Layout window to set the In and Out points of the image sequence.

You've now defined the work area in After Effects, and we're ready to render a series of frames from the comp.

8. Choose Composition ⇨ Make Movie (Command+M or Ctrl+M). In the Save Movie dialog box, browse to the folder where you want to store your frames, enter a prefix filename for the frame sequence, such as comp, and click Save. After Effects automatically numbers the sequence by adding _0000, _0001, _0002 . . . to the filename on the PC version, or .0000, .0001, .0002, and so on to the filename on the Mac version. If you're using the PC version of After Effects, you get an automatic AVI extension to the filename. Even though we're rendering frames as individual files, don't worry about the AVI extension. You then see the Render Queue window.

9. Click the underlined Current Settings text field next to Render Settings, and adjust the frame size and rate to match the size you want for your Flash movie (see Figure 21-20). In the following example, a DV format clip at 720×480 is halved in size by choosing Half in the Resolution setting. Choose Work Area Only for the Time Span setting, and note the length of the duration information listed directly beneath this setting. Hopefully, your comp's work area isn't longer than five seconds. For the Frame Rate setting, click the Use this Frame Rate option and type a value that won't overgenerate frames. For a three-second comp, four frames per second will yield 12 frames that can be imported into Flash. Then, click OK to proceed to the next setting dialog box.

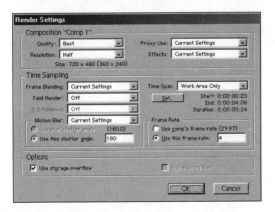

Figure 21-20: Use the Render Settings options to control resolution, time span, and frame rate for image sequences.

10. Click the underlined Lossless text field (or whatever your default may be) next to Output Module. In the Output Module Settings dialog box (see Figure 21-21), choose BMP Sequence (if you're using a PC) or PICT Sequence (if you're using a Mac) from the Output Module, Format setting. Don't change the default settings in the Video section. If you are using nonsquare pixel video like DV, you may want to resize the frame for each still image extracted. For a 360×240 (half-resolution DV) frame size, check the Stretch option and choose Medium, 320×240 in the drop-down menu. Select High for the Stretch Quality. Click OK to proceed to the next step.

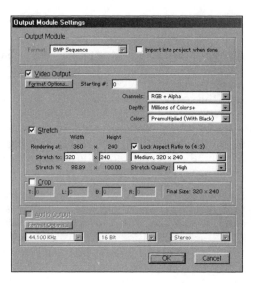

Figure 21-21: The Output Module Settings control the file format, video, stretch, and audio characteristics for a queued composition.

11. Click the underlined filename field next to the Output To setting of the Render Queue window. Make any changes to the filename structure to meet your preferred formatting. On the Mac version of After Effects, you need to add a .PCT extension to the filename. By default, the Mac version outputs a series beginning with Comp 1 Movie.[#####], but Flash won't recognize this as the beginning of a sequence without a .PCT extension. So, you should change the format of the filename to Comp 1 Movie.[#####].pct. Click Save to proceed.

12. When you're ready to render a sequence of frames from After Effects, click the Render button in the Render Queue window. After Effects then generates a series of frames ready to bring into Flash.

Using Audio from Digital Video Movies

If you want to bring the audio portion of this shortened video clip into Flash, then you can choose QuickTime as the Output Module format. Turn off the Video section, and turn on the Audio section with the sampling rate and bit-depth at the settings you want. Then, render the audio-only QT movie, open it in QT Player Pro and export it as a WAV or AIF file. You can then import the WAV or AIF into Flash and synchronize it with the bitmap sequence. You need to use the Stream audio setting in order for the audio to synch with the bitmap sequence. If audio and video synch is a critical issue, you may want to forego the replication of bitmap sequences within SWF movies. Because QuickTime 4 now supports Flash tracks, you can output QuickTime Flash movies that use regular QT movies, complete with video, sound, and Flash tracks.

Importing a sequence into Flash

Once you have created an image sequence from another application, you can import the sequence into Flash as a series of keyframes with bitmaps. Flash can auto-import an entire sequence of numbered stills and place them frame by frame on the Timeline.

Movie clip storage

Rather than import an image sequence directly into a layer within a scene, you can import the sequence into a movie clip symbol. This makes it easier to duplicate an image-sequence animation through the Flash movie in any number of scenes.

1. Create a new Flash (.FLA) file or open an existing one.

2. Create a new symbol of the movie clip type (Insert ⇨ New Symbol), and give it a descriptive name.

3. Choose File ⇨ Import and browse to the folder containing your image sequence. Select the first image of the image sequence, and click OK.

   You are presented with the message box shown in Figure 21-22.

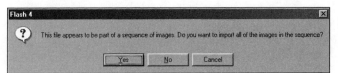

Figure 21-22: Whenever you import a file whose names contains a number, Flash asks you whether you want to import the entire numbered sequence of files.

4. Click Yes in the dialog box shown in Figure 21-22 and Flash automatically imports every image in the numeric sequence.

5. Go back to the stage and drag the movie clip into a scene.

6. Use Tell Target commands to control the movie clip if necessary. For more information on the Tell Target command and other intra-movie interactivity, see Part IV, "Flash Interactivity: Making Things *Happen*."

Optimizing bitmaps

Like any imported bitmap, you can trace each bitmap in the image sequence. Tracing can effectively converts raster information into vector information. Depending on the complexity of the bitmap image, though, the efficiency of tracing can vary wildly. Refer to Chapter 17 for more information on optimizing bitmap images.

Tip

If you plan to trace bitmaps in an imported image sequence, you may want to consider applying an art filter (for example, Extract, Posterize, Solarize) to the original footage in Adobe Premiere or After Effects. Some art filters create more solid areas of color in the image. Therefore, the traced bitmaps in Flash are less complex and result in smaller file sizes.

✦   ✦   ✦

Creating Full-Motion Video with Flash

✦ ✦ ✦ ✦

In This Chapter

A history of digital video

How to prepare Flash movies for video output

Using Flash image sequences in video applications

✦ ✦ ✦ ✦

This chapter explains how to use digital video with Flash. It also shows you how to export high-quality material from Flash to use in your video-editing applications.

High-Quality Video Output from Flash

While Flash is primarily used to create interactive animations and presentations on the Web, you can also generate high-quality output for other media uses. Macromedia began as a company called MacroMind, specializing in frame-by-frame video animation tools for desktop computers. Their flagship product, VideoWorks, eventually became Director, which is still the strongest and most widely used Macromedia product. Like Director, Flash also has some "hidden" video animation capabilities. You can use Flash to create spinning logos for your own corporate, creative, or home videos. Or, you could export those shape morphs — so difficult to create elsewhere — to layer over other video content. As we have seen in the previous section, Flash can output in QuickTime multimedia files. Flash can also generate numbered still sequences for use in other video-editing applications.

In previous Mac versions of Flash, 100 percent video-based QuickTime files could be directly rendered via the Export Movie command. Macromedia has added a more robust solution — based on QuickTime 4 — that exports Flash material directly to a Flash track for use in conjunction with video and audio tracks from other sources. This is wonderful if you want to create QTs for QuickTime 4-enabled applications. At the time of this writing, most Mac and PC applications that use the QuickTime architecture — such as Adobe Premiere and Digital Origin EditDV — cough when they encounter the Flash track on any QuickTime 4 movie. There should be updates available for these applications that will enable them to work 100 percent with QuickTime 4. Please refer to our Web site at `www.theFlashBible.com/Ch19` for an index of updaters, addenda, and other resources on this subject. In the meantime, though, you may have to convert your swanky QT4 movies into QT3 friendly material. We take a look at how to re-render a Flash track to digital video in the "Flattening Flash Tracks in QT Pro" section.

If you're using a PC version of Flash, then you've got a little more flexibility with digital video than Mac users. Both the 3.0 and 4.0 PC versions of Flash can directly render AVI files, ready to insert into your video-editing application. Better yet, the AVI files can store an alpha channel equivalent to the background in Flash. This means you can superimpose a Flash-created AVI on top of another AVI! We'll cover the AVI export process in the "Creating AVI Files on the PC" section.

Note   Because the export process for sequences uses generic vector or raster formats, you lose all interactivity that you have created in Flash. But that's perfectly fine because we're transferring our Flash movie to a linear viewing environment like video — we're simply making something to watch on a television or computer monitor without any involvement from the audience.

In the near future, it's possible that animated material intended for higher bandwidth media such as television or film can be created and generated from Flash. Flash artwork is completely scalable and flexible for just about any media use. Combined with the QuickTime architecture, Flash artwork can be output to DV tape or motion picture film. Granted, Flashers won't be replacing the skilled illustrators and animators at Disney anytime soon, but if you think your project looks good in Flash, you should be able to repurpose that hard work into another format very easily.

A Quick Video Primer

If you're a neophyte to digital video, then you need to know some basic terms and procedures involved with digital video. The following section will be useful if you've never used digital video, or used it without really knowing what you were doing.

A brief history of digital video

In the past, digital video on the desktop computer was almost impossible. It required expensive hardware such as super-fast processors, huge hard drives, video capture boards, and professional-quality video decks and cameras. Beginning at $15,000, such systems were out of reach for most users. But like most technology after it has been around for a while, digital video equipment has become much more affordable for the average user. Although digital video still requires fast and efficient computers to work well, it isn't nearly as expensive anymore. You can get 18GB hard drives for under $500! Since the advent of the DV (Digital Video) format (a.k.a. DVCAM or miniDV), consumer-level video cameras and decks are almost as good as their professional-level counterparts.

The need for space

Why does digital video require so many resources? To begin with, digital video is entirely raster-based. This means that, unlike Flash and other vector file formats, each frame of digital video requires that almost every pixel on the screen is remembered and stored. Vector formats, on the other hand, use mathematical descriptions of objects on the screen and compute their movement very efficiently. The resolution of an average television set is roughly equivalent to a 640×480 resolution at 24-bit color depth on your computer monitor. Mathematically speaking, one frame of digital video at this resolution is nearly 1MB!

$$640 \times 480 \times 3* = 921{,}600 \text{ bytes} = 900\text{KB} = 0.88\text{MB}$$
* Each byte has 8 bits. Therefore, 24 bits is equivalent to 3 bytes.

If that isn't bad enough, consider the fact that one second of video contains 30 frames. That's 26MB for just one second of video! Only the fastest systems and hard drives on the market could deliver such performance. One solution to this performance bottleneck was to compress the data. Thus, most digital video now employs some form of compression (for storage) and decompression (for playback). The short form of this expression is *codec* (*co*mpression and *dec*ompression). You may have already heard of many codecs in use today, but what you probably don't know is that three kinds of codecs exist: software, hardware, and hybrid.

Note

Cinepak, Indeo, RealVideo, and Sorenson are all software-based codecs, meaning that the computer processor has to decompress each frame of compressed video. These differ from hardware-based codecs, such as MJPEG (Motion JPEG, based on the Joint Photographic Experts Group compression scheme), which need video capture cards to compress and decompress each frame of video.

The latest breed of codecs today are hybrids, both software and hardware based, such as the MPEG (Moving Picture Experts Group) and DV codecs. MPEG currently has two versions, MPEG-1 and MPEG-2. Originally, MPEG-1 video needed special hardware to playback, but as computer processors got faster, software-based players could handle the decompression tasks. Today, MPEG-2 is standard for DVD.

DVD, or digital versatile/video disc, is a new storage medium that can handle feature length movies in a snap. DVD should not be confused with DV. DV refers to true Digital Video, in which the source video originates as binary (zeros and ones) data. Furthermore, the general term *digital video* should not be confused with *DV*.

Digital video usually refers to the any video that has been stored as binary data, although it most likely originated from an analog source such as a regular VHS or BetaCam video camera. *DV* refers to video that originated from a digital (a.k.a. *binary*) source and remains digital through any number of edits on a digital system. With the current implementation of DV, using IEEE 1394 (a.k.a. *FireWire*) technology, video is transferred from digital tape to your computer hard drive with virtually no loss of quality. The DV footage is not recompressed unless the image in the footage is changed during editing by adding effects or transitions. But like any digital video, DV still requires a lot of hard drive space — about 2 GB for every 9 minutes.

Note Most operating systems have a maximum file size limit of 2 GB. This means that you cannot have more than 9 minutes of DV-compressed footage in one QuickTime or AVI file. However, you can string many movies together during playback for continuous recording.

Codec, frame size, and frame rate: The keys to manageable video

Before you begin any digital video project you should have a clear understanding of codecs. Most software-based codecs are intended for computer playback and distribution, while hardware-based codecs are intended for capturing and editing original footage to be used for television broadcast or feature films. You can repurpose hardware-based codec video by compressing it with another software-based codec. Most video developers take high-quality video and shrink it, in both frame and file size, to fit onto multimedia CD-ROMs or the Web.

Three variables can be applied to digital video to make it more manageable for most consumer computer systems: frame size, frame rate and compression. Often developers use all three variables to shrink huge 9 GB video projects down to 3 to 5MB, which may lead to undesirable results.

First, let's talk about frame size. Although most professional video uses a 640×480 or greater frame size, you may have noticed that most video on multimedia CD-ROMs only takes up a quarter or less of your entire computer monitor. Most video on the Web or CD-ROMs is rendered at 320×240 resolution, half the resolution of broadcast video. Actually, this is only slightly less than the horizontal line resolution of your VHS recordings.

What about frame rate? You may have also noticed that video on multimedia CD-ROMs often looks a little jerky or choppy. Although this may be due to a slow processor, it's more likely that — in order to cut the file size — the frame rate of the video was reduced. It's not uncommon to find CD-ROM frame rates as low as 12 or 15 fps (frames per second) — about half or the original frame rate of broadcast video. Despite the drop in video quality, the lower frame rates result in much smaller file sizes with fewer frames for the processor to play within each second, which delivers better CD-ROM performance.

Finally, how does compression affect video? You've probably noticed that Web and multimedia CD-ROM video is often blocky looking. This is due to the software-based compression that has been used on the video. Codecs look for areas of the frame that stay consistent over many frames, and then log those areas and drop them from subsequent frames. The result is that no unnecessary repetition of data exists that needs to be continually decompressed. But, depending on the level of compression used, the properties of the codec itself, and the settings used in running that codec, the video varies in quality.

Keeping with the trend of better and faster, digital video continues to improve dramatically. This is well illustrated by the fact that many popular Web sites, such as Apple's QuickTime Web site (`www.QuickTime.com`), now enables visitors to download larger, higher-quality videos (upwards of 15MB) for playback on newer, faster systems.

Playback bottlenecks

Digital video needs to be kept small for two reasons: storage and playback. So far, we have largely discussed storage issues. But playback (or transfer rate) further complicates the creation of digital video. Despite the relatively large capacity of CD-ROMs (650MB) most CD-ROM readers have limited transfer rates of about 600KB/sec. It's important to note that each second of video cannot exceed the transfer rate, otherwise the video will drop frames to keep up with the audio. So if the video is distributed via CD-ROM, this factor results in serious limitations.

Let's look at some of the math involved, under ideal (choppy) playback conditions: If you use 15 fps for compressed video, you are limited to a maximum of roughly 40KB per frame. (Keep in mind, though, that the playback stream usually includes an audio track as well, which that means less than 40KB is available for the video component of each individual frame.

 Cross-Reference For more information on audio formatting and compression, see Chapters 10 and 12.

Unfortunately, the Web still affords less than ideal playback conditions for video. On the Web, transfer rates can be as slow as 500 bytes/sec. On average, a 56K modem downloads around 4KB/sec. The ideal Web video streams to the user while loading the page. If you intend to stream video quickly, you have to keep this very small transfer rate in mind. Large videos simply will not stream! This is why most Web sites offer larger videos as a download file. But you do have an alternative. Later in this section, you can learn how to extract a minimal number of frames in order to simulate digital video motion with Flash, yet keep your Flash files streaming quickly. As modem technologies get faster, though, we'll most likely see bigger and better video delivered across the Web. The ADSL (Asymmetrical Digital Subscriber Line) modem was developed with the MPEG-1 and 2 standards in mind.

It's beyond the scope of this book to fully explain how digital video works. Check out the digital video resources listed in at this book's Web site at `www.theFlashBible.com/ch22`.

Adjusting Flash Movies for Video Output

By default, Flash uses a frame rate of 12 fps for all new movies. Unless you have changed this setting with the Modify ⇨ Movie command (Command +M or Ctrl+M), this is the setting for any Flash movie you have created so far. As mentioned earlier in this chapter, broadcast (NTSC) video needs 30 fps (29.97 fps to be exact) in order for motion to be smooth and fluid. It may be necessary for you to add more blank frames between each of your tweened keyframes to accommodate a faster frame rate. Your 5-second intro to your Web site may have been possible with 70 or fewer frames, but now you're going to need 300 frames for the same amount of time in full-motion video. Flash doesn't support interlacing (or field-ordering) with any export method (see the "What Is Interlacing?" sidebar for explanation of interlacing). As a result, you need twice the number of frames (double the frame rate) used for every second of NTSC video, which would be 59.94 fps to be exact, in order to properly render full-motion video from Flash. It's easier to use 60 fps in Flash, and then conform the rendered sequence to 59.94 fps in the video-editing application.

If you are using the PAL or SECAM video systems, which are video systems used outside of North America, then you'll need to use different frame sizes and frame rates to accurately render Flash content. Use the same methods described here, but adjust any values to fit within PAL or SECAM specifications.

What Is Interlacing?

Most computer monitors are noninterlaced, which means that each "frame" of video is fully displayed with each screen refresh. Most TV sets, though, are interlaced displays, which means that each frame of video consists of two fields, one upper and one lower, and each screen refresh shows one field then the other. Therefore, each second of video contains sixty fields, or thirty frames. Because Flash doesn't export field-ordered sequences, you have to compensate the lack of individual fields by using two Flash frames for every regular frame of video.

If possible, restrict your Flash movie to one scene for video-editing purposes. Flash exports all scenes within a Flash movie into a sequence or QT/AVI movie, which may complicate the editing process later. It's easier to make more Flash movies and render them independent of each other.

Frames stored in movie clips do not export with sequences. Make sure that you have either removed any movie clip symbols, or replaced them with the actual frames contained within the movie clip.

To replace a movie clip symbol with the actual frames contained within it:

1. Open the movie clip in the library, select the frames in the timeline.

2. Copy the frames with the Copy Frames command (Command+Option+C or Ctrl+Alt+C) in the Edit menu.

3. Go back to the Scene and paste the frames with the Paste Frames command (Command+Option+V or Ctrl+Alt+V). Paste the frames on their own layer, so that they won't conflict with any tweens or settings in other layers.

Remember, the exported sequence will not have any interactivity like regular Flash movies. The sequence is simply a collection of still images that will be compiled later in your video-editing application. (So don't mistakenly overwrite or delete your original Flash movie!)

You may also need to adjust your Flash movie's pixel width and height. Depending on the type of video-editing software you are using, this setting needs to be 640×480, 720×534, or something else. Again, use the Modify ➪ Movie command to adjust the size of your Flash movie. You can notice that adjusting pixel sizes of the Flash movie doesn't have the same effect as changing pixel heights or widths of raster-based images. Usually, adjusting pixel sizes will distort or change the shape of elements. With Flash, the movie's pixel size is independent of the pixel sizes of any elements it may contain. You're simply adding or subtracting space to the movie area. If you intend to bring the sequence into other video-editing application such as Premiere and you are outputting with the DV format, a movie size of 720×534 should be used. Why? The DV format uses nonsquare pixels delivering the same 4:3 aspect ratio with 720×480 as other video formats do with only 640×480 square pixels. By using 720×534 movie sizes, the frame can be stretched to fit a 720×480 DV workspace without losing any resolution quality. It's better to adjust the size before you export any material intended for broadcast video delivery (or for transfer to any NTSC recording media), especially with raster formats. Not only does this ensure optimal quality, it could easily lessen the time during video rendering in other applications.

Note   The movie sizes just listed should work just as well for MJPEG video hardware as well as DV hardware. If you use these baseline settings, then you can accommodate either MJPEG or DV specifications in your video-editing application.

Not only do you need to have the proper frame size for high-quality video output, but you also need to be aware of overscanning. TV sets overscan video images, which means that information near the edges of the frame may be cropped and not visible. Because the amount of overscan is inconsistent from TV to TV, some general guidelines have been developed to make sure vital information in the frame is not lost. The crux of the guidelines is simple: Don't put anything important (such as text) near the edges of the frame. Video has two safe zones: title-safe and action-safe. To see these zones on a sample movie in Flash, refer to Figure 22-1.

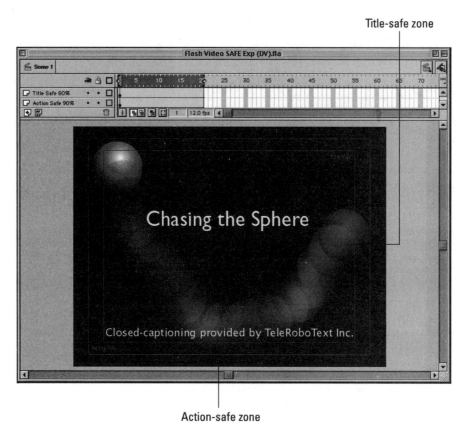

Title-safe zone

Action-safe zone

Figure 22-1: While you're designing for broadcast content in Flash, always be aware of the safe-zone boundaries for NTSC video playback.

The action-safe zone is approximately 90 percent of the 720×534 (or 640×480) frame size we're using in Flash, which calculates into 648×480 (or 576×432). All of your Flash artwork should be contained with the limits of the action-safe zone. The title-safe zone is about 80 percent of the total frame size. For a 720×534 frame size, any text on the Flash stage should fall within the borders of a 576×427 centered frame. With a 640×480 frame size, this centered frame size would be 512×384.

Finally, you may need to adjust the colors and artwork you used in your Flash movie. NTSC video, while technically 24-bit, doesn't display some colors very well. In general, bright and saturated RGB colors tend to bleed on regular TV sets. Here are some guidelines for using broadcast (and WebTV) safe color:

✦ Avoid one-pixel-wide horizontal lines. Because NTSC is interlaced, this line flickers constantly. If you need to use thin lines, try blurring a one-pixel line or simply never use anything less than a 2-pixel stroke width.

✦ Do not use very fine textures as they may flicker and bleed at the edges. Because most NTSC monitors have low-quality resolutions, the fine details are lost anyway.

✦ Avoid using any color that uses any color channel's maximum intensity. Use a NTSC color filter on any bitmap art, such as the NTSC Colors filter in Adobe Photoshop. Full red (R: 255, G: 000, B: 000) displays horribly on TV sets. Replace a full red with R: 181, G: 000, B: 000. Pure white backgrounds should also be avoided, and replaced with R: 235, G: 235, B: 235. Like red, pure white can cause annoying screen flicker, especially if high contrast objects are placed against the white. As a rule of thumb, keep your RGB values within the 16-235 range, instead of 0-255. Although Photoshop's NTSC Colors filter actually allows certain 255 values to be used, you should *only* use these values if they do not occupy large solid areas in the Flash movie.

✦ Use the NTSC & Web Safe color set (ntsc_web_179.act file) on the *Flash 4 Bible* CD-ROM (see Chapter 2, "Flash Color," for more information on importing or switching color sets). Of the 216 Web-safe color palettes, only 179 of them are NTSC/WebTV safe. NTSC TV sets are capable of displaying more colors than that, but if you're used to working with Web palettes, then you may find this optimized palette handy. There's another color set file, ntsc_213_colors.act on the CD-ROM that you can use if you're just taking Flash content to video, which has 213 NTSC-safe colors, converted from the 216 Web-safe colors. Because 35 colors of this set are outside of the Web-safe colors, you should not use this palette for Web and broadcast work.

✦ If you are using video-editing software that allows both color and levels corrections on imported clips, then you might avoid time-consuming adjustments to your Flash movie. After you have generated a Flash sequence and imported the sequence into your video-editing application, restrict the gamut of the sequence clip using the values in the preceding tips.

Tip   In After Effects, use the Broadcast Colors filter to perform NTSC color adjustments on imported sequences or movies. This filter can adjust either luminance or saturation values to bring out-of-gamut colors into the NTSC color gamut. Use caution, however, as reducing the luminance may cause artifacts from MJPEG or DV compression to become more obvious. Reducing saturation is preferred method for using the Broadcast Colors. For more tips on the Broadcast Colors filter, go to this book's Web site at www.theFlashBible.com/ch22.

Refer to Table 22-1 to see how Photoshop's NTSC Colors filter remaps the saturated values of the Web-safe color palette.

Table 22-1 NTSC Color Conversion Chart						
Original Web HEX Value	Original RGB Web Value			Converted RGB NTSC Value		
	R	G	B	R	G	B
FF0033	255	000	051	227	000	045
CC6699	204	051	153	204	102	153
FF00FF	255	000	255	210	000	210
FF00CC	255	000	204	219	000	175
FF0099	255	000	153	226	000	136
FF0066	255	000	102	230	000	092
CC00FF	204	000	255	199	000	248
00CCCC	000	204	204	000	170	170
00FFFF	000	255	255	000	170	170
33FFFF	051	255	255	045	225	225
66FFFF	102	255	255	101	253	253
00CCFF	000	204	255	000	160	201
0099FF	000	153	255	000	147	245
00FFCC	000	255	204	000	178	143
33FFCC	051	255	204	047	237	190
00FF99	000	255	153	000	188	113
33FF99	051	255	153	050	249	150
00CC66	000	204	102	000	193	096
00FF00	000	255	000	000	210	000
00FF33	000	255	051	000	210	042
00FF66	000	255	102	000	198	079
33FF00	051	255	000	047	234	000
66FF00	102	255	000	088	220	000

Original Web HEX Value	Original RGB Web Value			Converted RGB NTSC Value		
	R	**G**	**B**	**R**	**G**	**B**
99FF00	153	255	000	122	203	000
99CC00	153	204	000	142	190	000
FFFF66	255	255	102	252	252	101
CCCC00	204	204	000	170	170	000
CCFF00	204	255	000	148	185	000
FFCC00	255	204	000	191	153	000
CC9900	204	153	000	197	148	000
FF9900	255	153	000	216	130	000
FF6600	255	102	000	248	099	000
FF0000	255	000	000	181	000	000
CC0000	204	000	000	181	000	000

On the CD-ROM

You can find Flash movies (.FLA files) containing grid layers for the safe-zones of NTSC video on the Flash 4 Bible CD-ROM.

Creating Sequences from Flash Movies

A sequence is a series of still images that simulate full-motion video when played back continuously. Think of a sequence as a regular QuickTime or AVI broken down into individual frames. Another analogy would be that of a flipbook made of individual sketches that animate when you thumb through the pages quickly. Flash can export a scene or movie as a series of still images as well, with quite a bit of flexibility.

Because Flash is vector-based, it supports all the major vector formats to use in other applications: EPS 3.0, Illustrator and DXF formats. On the PC version of Flash, you can also export metafile sequences in the WMF and EMF formats. Most likely, all of these vector formats will retain the scalable quality that Flash offers for the Web. Meaning, you can shrink or expand the size of vector formats, displaying equal richness and quality at all sizes. Most vector formats can embed raster content, and any raster content will always have a finite resolution capacity. You will notice degradation on any raster elements if you scale the entire vector graphic beyond its original fixed pixel size.

You can also export a still sequence in raster-based formats such as PICT (Mac only), BMP (PC only), GIF, JPEG or PNG. We can look at the benefits of each format, and the

particular uses each can have. But first, we should look at how to the process of
exporting individual frames works in Flash.

Export process in Flash

Once you have opened your Flash movie, make sure your movie falls within the
guidelines described in the last section. All of these settings are critical for flawless
video playback: 60 frames per second, 640×480 (or greater) movie dimensions,
limitations of scenes and movie clips, and color gamut considerations. When
you're all ready to go, the actual export process is quite simple.

1. Select File ➪ Export Movie (see Figure 22-2).

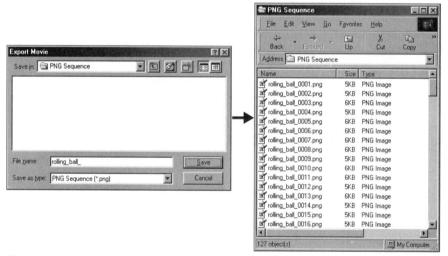

Figure 22-2: When you export a Flash movie as a sequence, Flash generates a still
image (that is, one file) for each frame in the Flash movie.

2. Choose or create the folder in which you wish to store the sequence.

3. Choose the type of file you want Flash to create.

4. Specify a filename, and click Save.

For the highest quality video rendering, you want to use a vector file format for
export. The next section details each file type and its particular uses.

Uses of each sequence format

Flash can export in a variety of file formats, and each one has a particular purpose.
While vector formats allow the most scalability, some Flash artwork does not

display properly in them. Raster formats usually maintain the highest fidelity to Flash artwork, but their file sizes can be rather large.

Vector sequence formats

Use a vector format type for your sequences when you want the highest quality re-rendering in applications such as Adobe After Effects or Premiere (see Table 22-2 for a list of formats supported in Flash). Flash exports vector sequences very quickly, although the sequence files themselves may take longer to re-render in your video-editing application than raster formats. Once you see the smooth edges of vector-rendered sequences, though, you can see that it is worth the wait. Vector formats automatically matte out the Flash background color, and make superimposing Flash material super-easy.

Table 22-2 Flash-Supported Vector Sequence Formats			
Flash Export Format	**File Extension**	**Application Support**	**Comments**
EPS 3.0 Encapsulated PostScript	.EPS	AE*, PR**	Universal vector format recognized by most applications. However, any gradients created in Flash will not export well with this format.
Illustrator Adobe Illustrator	AI	AE*, PR**	Proprietary file .format mainly used by Adobe applications. However, any gradients created in Flash will not export well with this format.
DXF Drawing eXchange Format	.DXF	3S	AutoCAD 2D/3D file format.

Continued

Table 22-2 (continued)			
Flash Export Format	File Extension	Application Support	Comments
WMF/EMF Windows Meta File / Extended Meta File	.WMF.EMF	PR (WMF only)	There's no reason to use these formats over the other vector formats. While some non-Microsoft applications support them, it's not widely used on either Mac or PC systems.

AE = Adobe After Effects

PR = Adobe Premiere

3S = Kinetix 3D Studio MAX

Raster formats

All raster formats can export at variable pixel widths, heights, and resolutions. As long as your Flash movie is in the proper aspect ratio for video (usually 4:3), you can size up your Flash movie on export (see Table 22-3 for a list of formats supported in Flash). This will save time later, during the re-rendering process in the video-editing application. Not all file formats support alpha channels, which are necessary if you intend to superimpose exported Flash material on top of other video material. Refer to Chapter 17 for more detailed information on the options associated with each raster file format.

Table 22-3 Flash-Supported Raster Sequence Formats			
Flash Export Format	File Extension	Application Support	Comments
PICT (Mac only) Picture	.PCT	AE, PR, QT, 3S	Can be used with many PC and all Mac applications. Variable bit-depths and compression settings with support of alpha channels. Supports lossless compression.

Flash Export Format	File Extension	Application Support	Comments
BMP (PC only) Windows Bitmap	.BMP	AE, PR, QT, 3S	Can be used with all PC and some Mac applications. Variable bit-depths and compression settings with support of alpha channels. Supports lossless compression (or is it just uncompressed file info?)
GIF Graphics Interchange File	.GIF	AE, PR, QT, 3S	Limited to a 256-color palette. Not recommended for full-motion NTSC video.
JPEG Joint Photographic Experts Group	.JPG	AE, PR, QT, 3S	Only supports 24-bit RGB color. No alpha channel support. Recommended for full-motion NTSC video, but this format does throw out color information due to its lossy compression method.
PNG Portable Network Graphic	.PNG	AE, QT	Supports variable bit-depth and compression settings with alpha channels. Lossless compression schemes make it an ideal candidate for NTSC video.

AE = Adobe After Effects

PR = Adobe Premiere

QT = Apple QuickTime Player Pro

3S = Kinetix 3D Studio Max

Creating .AVI Files on the PC

If you want a quick-and-dirty 100-percent raster-based video version of your Flash movie and you use the PC version of Flash, then you can export your Flash movie as a Video for Windows (.AVI) file. If you want the best video quality for output to videotape, you should not use this method for rendering video. Flash doesn't support interlaced video, and won't create the smoothest possible video content directly. This export file format is used primarily for digital video intended for computer playback, not NTSC playback.

Note   You can render a Flash movie at twice the frame rate of NTSC video (29.97 × 2 = 59.94 fps) using the necessary codec for your video hardware. If you want to play the AVI through your IEEE-1394 (a.k.a. *Firewire, iLink*) hardware, you need to resize the 720×534 AVI movie to 720×480 in a video-editing application, or by using the Dimensions property of the Export AVI Settings dialog box. Do not change the Flash movie properties via Modify ➪ Movie! DV uses nonsquare pixels, and shapes will be stretched if you use a 720×480 movie size in Flash.

Choose Export Movie from the File menu. Select a folder (or create one) to store the AVI file, type the filename, and click Save. You will then see the Export Windows AVI dialog box, with the following options (see Figure 22-3):

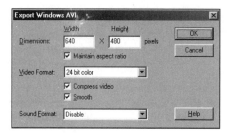

Figure 22-3: Adjust the values of the Windows AVI settings to accommodate your playback needs.

Dimensions

This property enables you to scale your AVI movie. If you wish to scale the movie's width separate from the height, uncheck the Maintain Aspect Ratio box for this property. This may be necessary if you need to accommodate nonsquare pixel formats such as DV or D1.

Video format

The drop-down menu associated with this property enables you to choose a bit-depth for the AVI movie. For serious video work, you'll want to choose 24-bit color or greater.

✦ **8 bit color:** Limits the rendered movie to 256 colors, determined on the fly by Flash.

✦ **16 bit color:** Limits the movie to 65,536 colors, also know as High Color in Windows or Thousands of Colors on the Mac.

✦ **24 bit color:** Enables the movie to use full RGB color (16.7 million colors) Also known as True Color on the PC or Millions of Colors on the Mac.

✦ **32 bit color w/ alpha:** Enables the movie to use full RGB color and store an alpha channel for compositing effects. Not all video codecs can store alpha channel information.

✦ **Compress video:** If this option is checked, then you are given the option to select a video compressor (codec) after you click OK to the Export Windows AVI dialog box. If you do not check this box, Flash generates uncompressed video frames, which can take over 1MB of file space per frame. In general, you do not want to use uncompressed video, as it takes very long to re-render into the hardware codec used by your video setup.

✦ **Smooth:** Using the smooth option antialiases the Flash graphics. This adds more time to the export process, but your AVI file looks much better. If you just want a rough AVI movie, then uncheck Smooth for faster exporting.

Sound format

This drop-down list enables you to specify the audio sampling settings. If you didn't use any audio in your Flash movie, then choose Disable. For a description of each of the sampling rates and bit-depths, please see Chapters 10 and 12.

Video compression

When you've chosen the options you need, click OK. If you specified Compress Video, you'll see the dialog box shown in Figure 22-4:

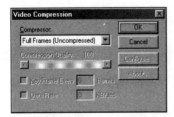

Figure 22-4: Choose the proper video codec for your video output hardware, or select a software-based codec for computer playback and distribution.

In the Video Compression dialog box, you can select a software- or hardware-based codec to use for the AVI movie. By default, Flash chooses Full Frames (Uncompressed). This option is same as de-selecting Compress Video, which forces Flash to render full-frame video. Because you probably want manageable file sizes, choose the codec you need to use for your video hardware. If you want to simply review your Flash work as an AVI movie, use Cinepak or Indeo codecs. Adjust the codec settings as necessary for your needs. Smaller files and lower quality will result from using compression qualities less than 100 percent, the use of keyframes, and data rate limiting. For high-quality rendering using hardware-based codecs, make sure the hardware codec (such as MJPEG or DV) is set to 100-percent compression quality with no keyframes or data-rate limiting. Click OK.

Flash then exports an AVI movie file to the folder you specified earlier. Depending on the length of your Flash movie and the video codec used, the export process could take less than a minute or many hours. Unfortunately, Flash doesn't give you an estimated time for completion like Adobe Premiere or After Effects do. When Flash has finished exporting the file, you can view the video with Windows Media Player, or with the software that your video hardware uses.

Importing Sequences into Video Applications

Now that you've created a sequence or QuickTime movie with Flash's Export or Publish command, you can bring the newly generated material into most video-editing applications. Not all video-editing applications will accept still image sequences and automatically treat them as one movie clip like Adobe Premiere or After Effects do. Just about any video application will accept QuickTime movies. In this section, you see how to prepare either a raster QuickTime movie or an image sequence for video output.

Adobe Premiere 5.1

Adobe Premiere is one of the most popular video-editing applications available for desktop computers. Just about every major video capture card comes with Adobe Premiere (or Premiere LE), and it offers a very intuitive interface for editing video. While not as advanced as Adobe After Effects for visual effects or compositing, it can be used for a variety of tasks, from CD-ROM video to animated GIFs to DV-ready output.

Note   This section assumes that you have a working knowledge of Premiere 5.1 and that you know how to set up a project with optimized settings for your video hardware. If you haven't used Premiere, refer to the Premiere section of "Extracting Frames from Digital Video Clips" earlier in this chapter.

To import a numbered sequence of still images generated from Flash, double-click in the Project window or choose File ➪ Import ➪ File (Ctrl/Command+I). Browse to the folder that contains the image sequence and select the first image in the sequence. Check the box for Numbered Stills underneath the filename field. This option tells Premiere to automatically look for consecutively numbered filenames and treat the group of them as one movie clip.

Caution Premiere cannot recognize 32-bit BMP files with alpha channels. If you want to use a raster image format with an alpha channel, use a PNG image sequence from Flash and use the Photoshop action, Convert to 32-bit alpha TIF on the *Flash 4 Bible* CD-ROM to convert the PNG files into a TIF sequence that Premiere can use. Further instructions can be found in the PNGTOTIF.TXT file, also on the *Flash 4 Bible* CD-ROM.

Click OK, and Premiere will add the image sequence to the Project window as a movie clip. As shown in Figure 22-5, it will display the first frame of the clip as an icon, and include the duration of the clip and its pixel size.

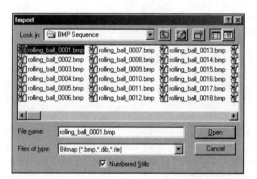

Figure 22-5: The Project window displays useful information about the clip, such as duration and frame size.

If you followed the guidelines in the "Adjusting Movie Properties" section, then you've already anticipated a 59.94 fps playback speed. Because NTSC video uses 29.97, we need to adjust the speed of the imported sequence. Select the clip in the Project window, and choose Clip ➪ Speed (Command+Shift+R or Ctrl+Shift+R). Enter **200** percent for the New Rate setting, as shown in Figure 22-6.

Figure 22-6: Use the New Rate setting to adjust the speed at which Premiere plays the clip. Because Flash does not create interlaced frames, you need to mimic the effect of interlacing by doubling the number of frames in the Flash movie.

Note   If you are using the DV format, you should have made the image sequence from a 720×534-sized Flash movie. Premiere automatically stretches the imported sequence (now a clip) to fill the 720×480 frame size of DV. Because the DV format uses nonsquare pixels, elements in the clip may appear distorted along the horizontal axis. Circles will look like ovals, and squares will look like rectangles. This appearance is normal on computer monitors, which use square pixels. When you play your movie back to tape through the Firewire, i.Link, or IEEE-1394 connection, this distortion will no longer be noticeable.

Drag the imported sequence from the Project window to the Timeline window. Place the clip at the desired insertion point. If you intend to superimpose the image sequence over another video track, place the image sequence clip on the Video 2 track.

Adobe After Effects 4.0

As mentioned in the previous chapter, After Effects is the Photoshop equivalent to video production. After Effects performs with moving images in the same way that Photoshop performs with still images. Although After Effects is a complex program with innumerable settings, you can use it for simple tasks as well.

Using After Effects, you can achieve the highest quality video from your Flash-generated image sequence. That's because After Effects offers subtle controls for video clip and composition settings that deliver crisp, interlaced, frame-accurate video.

After Effects can continuously rasterize any vector content — meaning that After Effects can re-render each vector frame into a raster frame. Most video applications, such as Premiere, rasterize the first frame of a vector image and continue to re-use that first rasterized version for the entire render process.

What does that mean? Simply put, if you have a small vector circle in the first frame of a project that grows larger in subsequent frames, then the circle appears very jagged at the larger sizes. Although both Premiere and After Effects render a Flash-generated image sequence at the same quality, please note the following: If you want to do special effects with just one frame (or still) from a Flash movie (not an entire image sequence), then After Effects does a much better job. Also note that this can be confusing because there are two potential uses of material imported from Flash into either After Effects or Premiere. These are either single frame imports, or multiframe imports. The big point is this: After Effects does a consistent high-quality job with both types, while Premiere only handles the latter type (multi-frame) well.

Caution   While EPS and AI image sequences offer the most scalability for digital video production, Flash poorly translates its gradients into common PostScript-defined colors. As a result, gradients appear as solid color fills in After Effects. If you are using gradients in your Flash artwork, then export the movie as a raster sequence. After Effects can import a PNG sequence, which has superior compression to JPEG.

Please refer to coverage of After Effects earlier in this chapter if you are not familiar with its interface and controls.

To import a sequence into After Effects:

1. Open an existing After Effects project file (.AEP) or create a new project (Command+Option+N or Ctrl+Alt+N).

2. Double-click in the Project window to import the image sequence. In the Open dialog box, browse to the folder containing the image sequence. Select the first file of the sequence (for example, ball_0001.png), and check the Sequence option (such as PNG Sequence, JPEG Sequence, EPS Sequence, and so forth). Click Open.

3. If After Effects detects an alpha channel in the imported file(s), then you receive an Interpret Footage dialog box, as shown in Figure 22-7. You must tell After Effects how to treat the alpha channel. For any image or image sequence with an alpha channel imported from Flash, use the Treat as Straight (Unmatted) setting.

Figure 22-7: After Effects automatically detects the presence of an alpha channel in imported file(s). For alpha channels that Flash creates, use the Treat as Straight (Unmatted) setting.

4. Select the imported sequence (now shown as one footage item) in the Project window, and choose File ➪ Interpret Footage ➪ Main. This time, the Interpret Footage dialog box (see Figure 22-8) displays the complete settings for the selected footage file. In the Frame Rate section, enter the correct frame rate in the Assume this Frame Rate field. If you followed the guidelines earlier in this chapter, then you used a 59.94 fps for your Flash movie. Enter that value here. Also, make sure Square Pixels is selected in the Pixel Aspect Ratio section.

5. Create a new composition via the Composition ➪ New Composition command (Command+N or Ctrl+N). Depending on your video hardware, the settings for a new comp will vary. For the Duration section, enter a value greater than or equal to the length of the imported Flash sequence. See Figure 22-9 for a DV-specific composition.

6. Drag the Flash sequence footage file from the Project window to the Time Layout window.

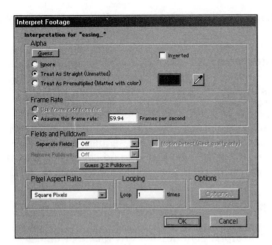

Figure 22-8: In the complete Interpret Footage dialog box, you can set the frame rate and pixel aspect ratio for the Flash image sequence.

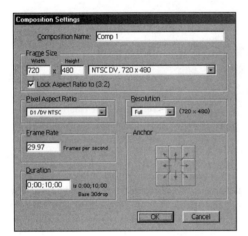

Figure 22-9: Composition settings for DV-format (for example, mini-DV, DVCAM) video

You now have a Flash sequence ready to integrate with other video in After Effects. See the After Effects section in "Extracting Frames from Digital Video Clips" earlier in this chapter for more information on making final movies from After Effects. Use Render Settings and Output Module settings specific for your video hardware.

✦   ✦   ✦

Creating Broadcast-Quality Cartoons

Flash is perfectly capable of creating high-quality cartoons much like those you might see on Nickelodeon, Cartoon Network, or elsewhere. That's because, .with Flash's scalability, video (even film resolution) cartoons are well within its capabilities. Because the subject of creating broadcast cartoons can be extremely complex (and could even fill a book on it's own) we are focusing on fundamental techniques that could start you on the way to becoming the next Tex Avery.

Caution! Large Files Ahead

Because Flash output is usually intended for the Web, Flash file size is usually a dominant concern. But when creating cartoons for broadcast output this concern is thrown to the wind. In cartoon land, you create for digital video output via QuickTime or AVI and these file sizes can be huge. It's common for such projects to expand into the gigabytes, so it's important to have the equipment to handle this kind of work. This means large, fast hard drives and plenty of RAM. The extensive use of bitmaps and full fidelity 16-bit 44kHz stereo audio tracks means that Flash itself requires a great deal of RAM. Your machine should have at least 128MB of RAM with at least 90MB available to Flash. But, even with this configuration, you may — like some hapless cartoon character — paint yourself into a corner and find that you need more RAM in order to render (export raster video) your scene. Also, the time required to perform a render can often take 45 minutes or more. This may cause you to think that the machine has crashed. . . . Sometimes it has, sometimes not. Sometimes, very annoying things can happen. When rendering complex scenes that take a long, long time, it seems that all is proceeding just fine, but then Flash may hiccup and report that it doesn't have enough memory to finish. That's when patience is required. Remember that, although some amazing cartoon animations can be created in Flash, it was engineered to create small, compact files for the Web: Our cartoon use is pushing it far beyond its calling. Remembering this may keep a brick from going through your monitor.

Caution

You may spend many hours working on your animation, so back it up as much and as often as you can! The project file is precious. Make a habit of keeping incremental backups on various disks so that you won't lose everything when disaster strikes (and it will). A good plan here is to make a new copy on a different disk after each major change, rotating through with two or three different disks. This way if Flash eats your project file, you can always go back to the version you saved an hour ago (which should be on a different disk) without losing much time.

The Storyboard

Let's assume that you already have characters and a story (why else would you want to create a cartoon show?) and that you want to build a cartoon based on that small beginning. In this section, we touch on some of the things you need to think about in the storyboard phase. Although it's OK to play around, never start a serious cartoon project without a storyboard. The storyboard is your roadmap, your plan, your menu of things needed, your best friend when things get complicated—without it, you are lost.

On the CD-ROM

You can find a storyboard template on the *Flash 4 Bible* CD-ROM, in the ch23 folder. It's an EPS (storyboardMAC.eps, or storybPC.eps) template form that includes all the essentials of a basic storyboard. Print it out as is, or import it into Freehand, Illustrator, or even Flash and modify it to suit your needs.

First, break up the story into workable cartoon scenes. In creating a broadcast cartoon we'll be using the terminology a bit differently. Long before Flash, cartoonists used the terminology of a scene to describe something quite different than a Flash scene. By scenes we mean a cartoon scene, which is much like a movie or TV scene—not a Flash scene. Remember that cartoons are fast-paced adventures. Most cartoon scenes last less than 30 seconds. A cartoon scene is usually a section of dialogue or action that tells a part of the story. A cartoon scene can generally stand on its own but needs other scenes to complete the story. Because of the length of time required for most cartoon scenes, it would become unruly if we were to rely solely upon Flash's scene function. You'd be scrolling through the timeline forever, just trying to cover a 45-second scene. But, as you'll learn in this section, there's still use for the Flash scene function.

Once you've established your cartoon scenes, break each of these scenes into shots. A shot is a break in camera focus. For example, a soap opera (they are famous for this) may have a scene of dialogue, and the camera will cut back and forth between whoever is talking at the time — which means that one scene may have many shots. Although the art of cinematography is beyond the scope of this book, that is what's involved when deciding shots in a cartoon scene.

Never create an entire cartoon in one Flash project file! Use Flash's scene function for shots. (This may seem confusing at first but the utility of this method will become clear as you work on your masterpiece.) Make a separate Flash file for each story-board scene of your cartoon; then, within each of these Flash files, assign a Flash scene for each of the shots within a storyboard scene. Think of it this way; the Flash project file is the Storyboard Scene, nested within that project file is the Flash Scene, or shot. Although this may seem contrary to the way that you usually work with Flash, but we are trying to reconcile the traditional terminology of cartoon animation with the recent terminology of the Flash program. Besides, the creation of broadcast cartoons isn't an advertised use of Flash.

On the CD-ROM

The Weber cartoon (QuickTime version included on the *Flash 4 Bible* CD-ROM, in the ch23 folder) runs for 6 minutes and contains about 32 shots spread over 13 scenes. The project files (scenes) alone are over 170MB. Loading one 170MB file into Flash is flirting with disaster.

The single most important thing you do in your cartoon is not the drawing but the voices your characters will use: this is what makes the character. Obtaining a voice can be as simple as you speaking into a microphone or as complex as a highly paid professional acting into a microphone. The key here is really not the voice but the emotion put into it. The right mix of unique voice and emotion can be taken into a sound program, such as Peak or even Premiere, and tweaked with the proper plug-ins to render the cartoon sound that you're looking for. Voice effects can always be added digitally, human emotion can't. Here are a few online voice resources:

✦ www.voicecasting.com

✦ www.voice-choice.com

✦ www.voicetraxwest.com

Another important part of the cartoon is the use of sound effects. Try to imagine Tom and Jerry or Road Runner without them. Nothing like a good CLANK, followed by the tweeting of birds, when the old anvil hits Wile E. Coyote's head. Many good sound effects collections are available on CD-ROM and online. These collections, used primarily by radio stations, come on CD-ROM and can easily be imported into the digital realm. One resource for such collections is www.radio-mall.com, which has a range of effects at a broad range of prices; furthermore, most of their collections have Real Audio links, which means that you can audition them online.

Sometimes though, you just can't buy the sound you need. So, when you need that special CLANK, it means it's time to set up the microphone and start tossing anvils at unsuspecting heads. Seriously though, it's not difficult to set up your own little foley stage or sound effects recording area. A good shotgun microphone (highly directional for aiming at sound) and DAT recorder are ideal, although you can get by with less. A tip here; if you have to scrimp, don't pinch pennies on the microphone. A good microphone can make an average capture device sound better than the other way around. The capture device (audio tape, DAT, miniDV, MD, and so on) should be portable, not only in order to get it away from the whirring sound of hard drives and fans but also to enable you to take it on location when needed. Another advantage of a battery-powered portable device is that static from power line voltage won't be a problem. Once you get started and begin playing around, you may be surprised at the sounds you can create with ordinary household objects. Be creative; innovate! Sound effects is an art form unto itself. Although your dinner guests may think you've gone mad as they regard your meditative squeezing of the dish soap bottle, don't worry about it. You know you are right! When amplified, this makes a nice *whoosh*(great for the fast limb movement of that character doing a karate chop.

Backgrounds and Scenery

In Flash, you work in an area that is called the Stage (or Movie) area. For broadcast (or any other kind for that matter) animation it is better to think of it as the viewfinder of a camera. The main difference between this camera and the traditional kind, or even those used in 3D animation, is this: *you can't move it.* So, to give the illusion of camera movement, everything within the view must move. This is not as hard as it might seem due to Flash's ability to use the animated graphic symbols function. A good example is in the Weber cartoon, in the scene where there's a malfunction in the control room and everything is shaking. This effect was created simply by making a graphic symbol of the entire scene of animation that was larger than the camera's view (so that white space wouldn't show at the edges). Then the symbol was placed in the main timeline and every frame was keyframed and moved in a jarring fashion to give the jerking look needed to convey that everything had run amok. This is shown in Figure 23-1.

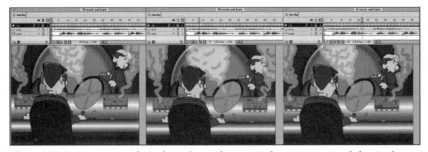

Figure 23-1: Here are a few shots from the control room scene of the Weber cartoon.

Bitmaps

As mentioned previously, when designing with Flash for the Web, the use of raster (bitmap) images should be kept to an absolute minimum. But for broadcast output there's really no limit. Not only can you use as many images as you'd like (within system constraints) but doing so makes a richer, far more attractive finished product. And, unlike with the SWF format, when output as raster video, animations built with such bitmap image intensity always play at the proper frame rate. So move, animate, scale, and rotate them—even play sequences of them. The sky and RAM are the only limits.

New Feature

Flash 4 now has the ability to import raster video, QuickTime, and AVI. When using video output for broadcast you can export to these formats too, but video imported into Flash will not show up when outputting to the SWF format. Unfortunately Flash does not recognize alpha channels embedded in the QuickTime 32-bit animation codec (which supports travelling mattes, or alphas). However you can use mask layers on the video in Flash. Keep in mind that Flash doesn't save the video file within the project file (thank goodness)—it makes a pointer to it instead. This addition brings tremendous functionality to Flash 4 because animations can now be keyed (composited) over (or behind) live video without recompositing in After Effects. To take advantage of this, keep your live video at the same frame rate as the Flash project. Note, however, that Flash only exports the video—audio from the video clip will need to be reapplied in a video editing application. You could, however, bring the video and audio tracks into Flash separately and synchronize them there.

Building layered backgrounds in Flash with Photoshop

Through the use of layers in Photoshop, multi-plane shots are easily accomplished in Flash. Using layers is very important to the organization of the animation. Some shots in Weber employ more than 20 layers to keep things where they need to be. When designing backgrounds (or scenery, to be more precise) keep in mind that, at some point, background elements may need to be foreground. For instance, in the intro of Weber, the sky is always in the background so it is on a layer furthest down in the stack. Unlike the sky, however, the pier, which is also a background object, may sometimes need to be in the foreground to facilitate movement of the character either in front or behind it. Thus, the pier gets a layer (actually a group of layers) of it's own, placed further up in the layer stack, above the sky. When creating such backgrounds, use of Photoshop and alpha channels delivers the most versatility. When using Photoshop for scenery elements it's mandatory to work in layers and save a master file with all layers intact. Then elements can be exported to individual files (with alpha channels) as needed. (Retaining the master layered Photoshop file will give you maximum options later, if edits or changes occur. It can also be used as a resource for subsequent animations, so don't flatten or discard your master layered Photoshop file. Instead, number and archive it!) Why the alpha channels? When translating the Photoshop elements into Flash vector scenery they will automatically mask themselves—so a little pre-planning in Photoshop can save lots of time later on.

Flash mask layers

Whoops! You got to a point where you didn't use layers and now you need a mask. Some situations may be either too complicated or else unforeseeable in the original design. Flash mask layers can come to the rescue. Here's the good news: You can mask (and animate the mask) interactively with the other elements while in flash. The bad news is that you can't feather (soften the edges of) the mask. In the Weber cartoon, an example where masks are used to good effect is the ending, where black circles in as the scene closes.

Long pans

Long pans are a standard device of animated cartoons, as when Fred Flintstone runs through the house and furniture keeps zipping past (that must be one looooong living room — it just keeps goin'). This can be done in Flash in a couple of ways. For landscape backgrounds, it's usually best to first create a very wide bitmap of the landscape and then to motion tween it horizontally, with keyframes for stopping and starting as needed within the tween. If something is either falling or ascending, use a tall bitmap and motion tween vertically. Another solid technique is to create art of the objects that will pan (such as clouds) and then loop them as the background layer, across the view. A good example of this is the chase scene from the Weber cartoon, which is shown in Figure 23-2. To get smooth results when using looping, don't use easing in or out with the tween setup. Also, to maintain constant speed, maintain the exact number of frames between the keyframes. Then, copy the tween by Alt (Option) dragging the selected tween frames to the desired area in the timeline. Repeat copying until you've covered the time needed.

Multi-plane pans

To give it 3D-motion depth during the pan, keep this rule in mind: An object that is further away appears to move slower (than a nearer object) as it moves across the view. This takes some experimenting to get it right but once mastered; this adds a professional touch to your animations. For example, in a 100-frame pan:

✦ The sky moves very slowly, 100 pixels total.

✦ The water moves more quickly, 125 pixels total.

✦ The character on the beach moves more quickly than the water, 150 pixels total.

✦ A parked car in the immediate foreground moves most rapidly, 250 pixels total.

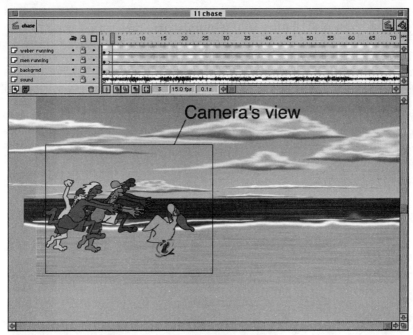

Figure 23-2: The chase scene from the Weber cartoon

Blurring to simulate depth

The multi-plane camera was used in early Disney films to give a feeling of depth in the animation of flat artwork. There was physical space between the individual cels when photographed. By using a short depth of field lens, the artwork that was further away from the lens lost focus slightly. (You may have noticed this in still photography yourself.) If you set up your scenery using bitmaps you can recreate this effect. As shown in Figure 23-3, a good example of this is the pier scene from the Weber cartoon. In Photoshop, it's a simple case of using incrementally higher doses of Gaussian blur on the layers of your scenery that are further way. The further the object is, the more blur that is applied — just be sure that the blur is applied to the alpha channel that Flash will use in compositing. Use this technique as a photographer brings attention to the element in the shot that is in focus. Using it in animation tends to generate the illusion of depth. However, using it in the foreground can also portray various elements such as fog.

Some Cartoon Animation Basics

In the world of film, movies are shot at 24 fps (frames per second) while in video and 3D animation, 30 fps is the norm. But in cartoons 12–15 fps is all that's needed. The cartoon language of motion that we've all learned since childhood has taught our minds to expect this slightly jumpy quality of motion in a cartoon.

As an animator, this is good for you, because 15 fps means half the amount of hand drawing work that 30 fps would require. It also means that you can get your cartoon done within your lifetime and maybe take a day off here and there. Actually, in a lot of scenes as few as three drawings per second can suffice — depending on how well you can express motion with your art, or drawing. The rule of motion here is that things that move quickly take less frames (drawings), while things that move slowly require more frames. This is the main reason you hardly ever see slow motion sequences in cartoons. Broadcast cartoons have lots of fast-paced motion. Fewer drawings are produced more quickly and are less costly. These are very significant factors when battling budgets and deadlines.

Figure 23-3: The opening pier scene from the Weber cartoon

Expressing motion and emotion

The hardest part of animation is expressing motion and emotion. Learn to do this well and it saves you time and makes your work stand out above the rest. One of the best exercises you can do in this respect is to simply watch the world around you as if your eyes were a camera clicking off frames. Videotaping cartoons and advancing through them at single frame speed is also a revealing practice. (If you have digitizing capabilities there's nothing better than capturing a cartoon to your hard drive and then analyzing the results, as you get a more stable frame this way.) If you employ Flash 4's ability to import raster video you can use actual video as your guide and even practice drawing on top of it. While this is good for getting the mechanics of motion down, it's really just a start.

Exaggerate everything! After all, this is what makes it a cartoon. Tex Avery, who we mentioned earlier, created cartoons that revolutionized animation with overblown and hilarious motion. You can read about him at `www.brightlightsfilm.com/22/texavery.html`.

Anticipation

Anticipation is a technique used when the character is about to do something, such as take off running. Before lunging into the sprint, the character slowly backs up, loading all their motion into their feet until their motion reverses and sends them blasting off in the other direction. In a more subtle form, this is shown in Figure 23-4, where Weber takes flight from his perch on the pier.

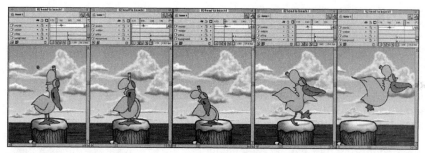

Figure 23-4: Anticipation is used to accentuate Weber's take off

Weight

Keep the weight of things in mind. This helps to making things believable. A feather falls more slowly than the anvil. The feather also eases out (slow down) before landing gently on the ground, while the anvil slams the ground with such force as to make a gashing dent in it. Humor can play a role here by giving extreme weight to things that do not have it (or vice versa), thereby causing a surprise in the viewer's preconceived notion of what should happen: This is the seed of humor.

Overlapping actions

Visualize a jogging Santa Claus, belly bouncing up and down with each step. Because of its weight the belly is still on a downward motion when the rest of the body is being pushed upward by the thrust of the push-off leg. These opposing motions are known as overlapping actions. Another good example of overlapping actions is the scene where Weber is caught by the muscle-man bully and gets his neck wrung. A good example of this is shown in Figure 23-5. Note that, as the bully thrusts forward, Weber's body reacts in the opposite direction . . . only to catch up just in time for the thrust to reverse and go the other way.

Figure 23-5: Overlapping actions are often used to accentuate movement.

Blurring to simulate motion

Blurring is a technique or device that animators use to signify a motion that's moving faster than the frame rate can physically show. In film, this manifests itself as a blurred out of focus subject (due to the subject moving faster than the camera's shutter can capture). You may have already employed this effect in Photoshop, with the motion blur filter. In cartoon animation, blurring is often (and easily) described with blur lines. Blur lines are an approximation of the moving subject utilizing line or brush strokes that trail off in the direction that the subject is coming from. When used properly, this great device can save hours of tedious drawing. A good example of animated motion blur can be seen in Figure 23-6, which shows the opening sequence where the word "Weber" turns into Weber the pelican.

Figure 23-6: Blur lines simulate the effect of motion

Animator's Keys and Inbetweening

Earlier in the book you learned of frame-by-frame and tweening methods to animate in Flash. This section is focused on traditional cartoonist's frame-by-frame techniques together with traditional cartoonist's Key and Inbetween methods to accomplish frame-by-frame animation.

Despite the similarity of terminology, this topic heading does not refer to a menu item in Flash. Rather, it should be noted that the terminology of animation programs such as Flash has derived some of their terminology (and method) from the vintage world of hand-drawn cell animation. Vintage animators used the methods of Keys and Inbetweening to determine what action a character will take in a given shot. It's akin to sketching, but with motion in mind. In this sense, Keys are the highpoints or ultimate positions in a given sequence of motion. Thus in vintage animation:

+ Keys are the pivotal drawings or highlights that determine how the motion will play out.

+ Inbetweens are the fill-in drawings that smooth out the motion.

In Flash, the usual workflow is to set keyframes for a symbol and then to tween the intervening frames, which harnesses the power of the computer to fill the inbetweens. Although this is fine for a many things, it is inadequate for many others. For example, a walk sequence is too subtle and complex to be tweened by a computer. So, let's take a look at the traditional use of keys and inbetweens for generating a simple walk sequence that will start and end according to a natural pace yet generates a walk loop.

Walk cycles (or walk loops)

Earlier in the book, you learned about using Poser to create a walk loop using a 3D model. 3D animation is a wonderful practice and is really coming of age in films such as *Jurassic Park*, *A Bug's Life*, and *Toy Story*. But perhaps you've noticed that a focus on humans is missing from such films. That's because humans are incredibly difficult to animate convincingly in 3D. Why? Because computers are too perfect—too stiff. Human movement is delightfully sloppy—and we are keenly aware of this quality of human movement, both on a conscious and even subconscious level. (Another term for this is body language.) This factor drives the 3D animators nuts when they try to create human characters. Interestingly, these same factors lead to a plus for the 2D hand-drawn animator: because our hands are also sloppy when drawing, we find that there's emotion in the imprecision of a hand-drawn stroke. Which brings us back to keys—keys should be sketched out loosely then refined and inbetweened. Refer to the following diagrams, which express this concept in visual terms.

Notice that these keys are quickly drawn ovals approximating a woman at the highpoints in a walk cycle. This was drawn on a layer in Flash with a light gray pencil. Next, we'll lock that layer and create a new layer on top of it. Then, using the pencil in ink mode with black as our color to ink it in, we'll refine this character to a more finished look, as shown in Figure 23-7. Once we're satisfied with the look, the fast sketch layer can be discarded.

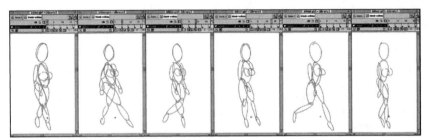

Figure 23-7: Here are some rough finished keys from a walk cycle, prior to playback.

Now, we've set the keys for the finished walk cycle. However, upon playback (although she walks!) it's an extremely jerky and unnatural gait. So where do we start if we want to "fix" the walk? Remember the rule discussed earlier, that the slower the movement the more frames (or drawings) would be needed? A good starting point for a normal walk cycle is about 1.5 seconds or 24 frames at 15 fps. This is timed from when the left foot pushes off the ground until just before it returns to its original position. Why not go back to its original position? Because this would cause two frames to be almost the same and — in a loop — this would introduce a stutter to the walk. (Of course, that might be OK if you're animating a stumbling drunk, but here we want it smooth.) So, depending on the speed that you want the subject to walk, you can determine the amount of inbetweens you need to draw.

Repeaters

You may notice that some blank, nonkeyed frames (repeaters) appear in the timeline. These were used to economize drawing time and also to slow the walk of the character in the previous figure even more. If a speedier walk were called for, we would simply delete these repeater frames. A good basic rule about repeaters is to add no more than one repeater frame between keys — otherwise, the smooth-ness of motion falls apart. If the motion must proceed more slowly, then you have to draw more inbetweens. Fortunately, with Flash onion skinning (ability to see before and after the current time in a dimmed graphic) the addition of a few more inbetweens is not an enormous task. In fact, onion skinning is indispensable for doing inbetweens, and even for setting keys. One pitfall of onion skinning is the tendency to trace what you're seeing. It takes practice to ignore the onion lines and use them as a guide only. You need to remember that the object is to draw frames that have slight, but meaningful differences between them. Although it can mean a lot more drawing, it's well worth it. Because you can use your walk (and running) cycles over and over during the course of your cartoon, you should do them well.

Tip One real timesaver in creating a walk cycle is to isolate the head and animate it separately via layers or grouping. This trick helps to prevent undesirable quivering facial movements that often result from imperfectly traced copies. Similarly, an accessory such as a hat or briefcase can be isolated on a separate layer. Finally, if the character is talking while walking, make a copy of the symbol and eliminate the mouth. Later, the mouth will be added back as a separate animation. We cover this later in the section on lip-synching.

Types of walks

So far, we've covered the mechanics of a walk cycle. But for animators, the great thing about walking — in all its forms — is what it can communicate about the character. We read this body language constantly every day without really thinking about it. We often make judgments about a person's mood, mission, and character based on the way that they carry themselves. Picture the young man or woman, head held high, confidently striding briskly with direction and purpose: They are in control of the situation and can accomplish the task set before them. But if we throw in a little wristwatch checking and awkward arm movements, then that same walk becomes a stressful "I'm late." This late gait suggests a very different story of the person who didn't plan ahead. Or, witness the poor shlub: back hunched, arms dangling at his sides. He moves along, dragging his feet as if they each weigh a thousand pounds. That tells the sad story of a person who's a basket case. Finally, what about a random pace, feet slipping from side to side, sometimes crisscrossing, other times colliding, while the body moves in a stop-and-start fashion as if it were just going along for the ride? Is that someone who couldn't figure out when to leave the bar? Of course, these are extreme examples. Walks are actually very subtle and the basic forms have limitless variations. But if you begin to observe and analyze these details as they occur in everyday life, then you should be able to instill a higher order in your animations. Simply take time to look. It's all there waiting for you to use in your next animation. Then remember; because it's a cartoon, *exaggerate!*

Coloring the Art

Now, to color in the character between the inked lines: In traditional animation, this was the most tedious and time-consuming job of all: endless thousands of cels to be hand painted and dried. Most often, it was sent out to be done by armies of low-paid workers in faraway lands. But with Flash it's a snap! That's because of Flash's wonderful (and sometimes mysterious) gap-jumping fill tool, the Paint Bucket. With Flash, you never run out of paint, and it dries instantly — a real timesaver, to be sure!

The model sheet

Here's a coloring timesaver that you can use for yourself within Flash: Use a fully colored model of your character at the start of a cycle or scene. This then serves as a color model and will be discarded when the cycle or shot is finished. It's very important to keep a model sheet, which is an archive of color models — finished, fully colored characters — to maintain consistent color across the span of the project. (It's also quite useful at the start of future projects.) "Why," you may ask, "is this necessary now that Flash has Color Sets?"

Even though Flash 4 has the ability to save Color Sets it's still difficult to remember which yellow was used on a certain area of the character, especially when ten different yellows exist in the palette. Such a color mistake — even a slight shade off — will cause unsightly flicker upon playback. The Dropper makes no mistakes. So, to develop good animation habits, start a model sheet. When you begin a scene, copy the appropriate color model and paste it into the cycle, setting it off to the side of the active art in the first frame (if needed, ungroup it). Acquire the color you need with the Dropper Tool, and then set about the business of filling.

When filling, we've found that the most efficient method is to go through the entire cycle with one color, filling all objects of that color. Then go back to the beginning and sweep through again, doing the next color. This method saves you the tedium of constantly having to change the Paint Bucket's color, and also minimizes the possibility of mistakes. If some places fill while others don't, you probably need to adjust the Paint Bucket Gap Size Modifier.

Gap problems

At times, however, you can't find the gaps and the Paint Bucket just doesn't work. In this case, keep looking because the gaps are there. But if it just doesn't work, no matter how much you zoom in and click with the Paint Bucket, then you may need to zoom in and use the Arrow tool to close the gap by adjusting a stroke. In a situation where it's not aesthetically pleasing to do that, use the Brush tool (set to the same fill color and to paint fills only) to fill the gaps manually. Perhaps this would be the case on a head and neck situation where you don't want the body connected to it (remember earlier about the advantages of animating the head separately) — you would paint a stroke of fill connecting the inked lines and then fill. This is a great tool, it's a huge timesaver, but a little mysterious at times.

Speed coloring

A good way to speed up the coloring process is to allocate one of the mouse buttons (if you have a programmable mouse) to perform the keyboard shortcut for step forward advancing (which is the > key). If you have a Wacom tablet, then you can allocate a button on the pen to do the same. With a setup like this, you can leave the cursor in pretty much the same place and click-fill, click-advance; click-fill, click-advance . . . and so on.

Temporary backgrounds

Another problem that's easily solved is the process of filling areas with white. If you're like most people, you've accepted the default background color of white — which makes it impossible to distinguish when filling white areas. In this case, it's monstrously helpful to create a very light color that you don't plan to use in the final art, something such as a light grayish puke-pink. While coloring, temporarily change the background color in the Movie Properties Dialog (Modify ➪ Movie) to this "color" for the background of the entire movie. This makes it much easier to see what you're doing when using white as a fill color for objects such as eyeballs, teeth, and clouds. Then, when you're done coloring, you can set the background color back to white.

Flash Tweening

This is about the process known as *Tweening* in Flash. Now that you've created some symbols, such as the walk cycle, here's where you can save a great deal of time making them slink and prance across the view without drawing every tedious frame. The hard hand-drawing work is done, now you can choreograph the character. Because, once you've built a library of various walks, runs, turnarounds, and standstills (a piece of walk cycle that ends with the character just standing still), you can use computer power to help you tell a story. Keep in mind you can always create more symbols of the character as needed — in fact, you can steal from other symbols to create new ones.

Panning

Use the panning techniques discussed earlier in this chapter to get your walking symbol looping, stationary in the middle of the view. Then move the background elements to give the illusion of the camera following alongside the walking character, a sort of dolly. It usually requires a little experimentation to get the motion of the background to match the stride of the step. If the timing isn't correct you may notice that the feet will seem to skate across the ground. To fix this, adjust the speed of the background by either increasing or decreasing the number of frames in the tween of the background. Another trick is to set the walking symbol to start at one end of the view and proceed to the other by tweening the symbol itself. What's really cool is to use a mixture of both. Again, to get it just right, experiment.

Instance swapping

There comes a time when the star of your show must stop walking (or running, or whatever) and reach into his pocket to pull out a hot-rod car and make his getaway. This is where instance swapping comes in. At the end of the tween, create a keyframe on the next frame (the frame immediately following the last keyframe in the tween), and then turn off motion tweening for that keyframe. This causes the symbol to stop at whichever frame the cycle ended on in the timeline. Next, double-click this symbol and, in the ensuing Instance Properties dialog box you'll be presented with a list of all symbols in your project file. Select the one you want to replace it with (in this case the one where he reaches into his pocket) by double-clicking the list item or highlighting it and clicking the Swap Symbol button at the bottom. (Note that you can also choose which frame in the symbol's cycle it will start on. Other choices include limiting it to play once, or just a single frame (still), or to loop.) Also be sure that you've unchecked Syn-chronize Symbols in the motion keyframes properties or your newly chosen instance will not show up (the old one will remain there instead). Now, unless you've drawn all your symbols to perfect scale with each other, this new symbol may not fit exactly. No problem! To fix this, simply enable onion skinning from the main timeline, and set it to show the previous frame (the frame the tween ended on). Now you can align and scale the new symbol to match the ghosted image. We can't begin to tell you how much you'll use this simple instance-swapping func-tion when you create your cartoon. This is one of the unique functions that sets Flash apart from all other cel-type animation programs on the market today. Once you have a modest library of pre-drawn actions the possibilities for combining them are endless.

Motion guides

Although not terribly useful for tweening a walking character, the Flash motion guide function is tops for moving inanimate objects. If your character needs to throw a brick, a straight tween between points and some blur lines will do fine. If he needs to lob that brick over a fence to bonk that pesky neighbor, then the use of motion guides is the ticket. First turn the brick into a graphic symbol if you haven't already. This will make it easier to make changes to the brick later on. Now, simply create a motion guide layer and draw an arc from start to destination. This is best done by drawing a line with the Line tool and then retouching it with the Arrow tool until you have bent it into the desired arc. This method keeps the motion smooth. (To use the Pencil tool to draw the motion guide would create too many points and can cause stuttering in the motion.) Now, although your brick is flying smoothly, something's wrong here. Again, the computer made things too darned smooth. You could insert a few keyframes in the tween and rotate slightly here and there to give it some wobble. But that's still not convincing. You want this brick to mean business! Here's what to do: Because the brick is already a symbol go back to the brick symbol and edit it, adding a few more frames. Don't add more than three or four frames; this will slow it down. At each of these new frames, mess up the brick a little here and there: Differ the perspectives a little from one frame to another. Then, when you go back to your main timeline, the brick should be twitching with vengeance as it sails towards its target.

Lip-Synching

Now, here's the part we've all been waiting for . . . a word from our character. If done properly, lip-synching is where a character can really spring to life. This is accomplished by drawing the various mouth positions that are formed for individual phonemes, which are the basic units of sound that make up a spoken word. Then these phonemes are melded together into morphemes, which are distinct units of a word, such as a syllable. Morphemes are then strung together over the course of a sentence to present the illusion of a talking, animated character. HUH? Phonemes? Morphemes? What the devil are we talking about? Well, it's really not as complicated as all that but it's important to know how a spoken word is made. Most language, although populated with thousands of words, is really made up from around 30–60 distinct sounds, or phonemes. For the purpose of cartooning, these phonemes can be reduced to about 10 basic mouth positions. Perhaps you'll notice, in Figure 23-8, that some of the figures are repeated for more than one sound. Some sounds share roughly the same mouth positions. Although the real world has more subtleties, for cartoons, reliance upon transitions between mouth positions is convincing enough.

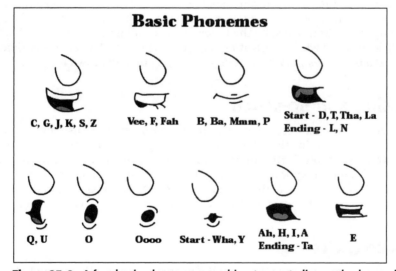

Figure 23-8: A few basic phonemes combine to create lip-synched speech.

Earlier, we suggested that the face in an action (walk) cycle should be drawn without a mouth. That's because this method facilitates the use of layers (in the timeline) for the addition of the lip-synch. To do this, create a layer above the character so that you can freely draw in the mouth positions needed to add lip-synch. It's also very helpful to put the voice track on another separate layer directly beneath the mouth layer. This makes it easy to see the waveform of the sound while you draw — which gives important clues to where and when the sound occurs visually.

New
Feature
Flash 4 now has the ability to scrub the time marker, which means you can now drag the current frame indicator and hear the sound as you drag. The ability to hear the sound (to do this, sound's Sync must be set to Streaming) and see the animation in real time is a definite improvement for lip-synching. This real-time feedback is critical for getting the timing just right. There's nothing worse than being plagued with O.G.M.S. (the Old Godzilla Movie Syndrome), where the mouth doesn't match the sounds coming from it. To use this new feature most effectively, here's a little hint: If you've been following this chapter's advice, then you've probably loaded a ton of moving bitmaps into your scene, which can be a serious hindrance to playback within the Flash authoring environment. You can overcome this drag and get real-time playback at the full-frame rate if you: hide all layers except the mouth layers and turn off antialiasing.

Shape morphing is not for lip-synch

You may be asking, what about shape morphing to save time in lip-synching? Well, shape morphing is a wonderful thing but, for lip-synch, it's more hassle than its worth. That's because your mouth drawings will become very complicated because they consist of lips, tongue, teeth, and facial features. Furthermore, because shape morphing only seems to work predictably on the simplest of shapes out of the box, shape hinting is required. Thus, by the time you've set all hinting (and even hinting heavily still leaves you with a mess at times), you might have had an easier time and obtained a better result (with greater control) if you had drawn it by hand.

Expression and lip-synch

As regards control and expression, it's important to remember to use the full range of expression when drawing the talking mouths. Happy, sad, or confused—these give life to your character. Furthermore, always emphasize mouth movements on those syllables that correspond with spikes of emotion in the voice track. These sections usually have a spike in the waveform that's easily recognized in the voice track. This device helps to convince the viewer that proper sync is happening.

Lip-synch tricks

A few more tricks can help ease the load: When characters talk they do not always have to be looking you square in the face. Try lip-synching the first few words to establish that the character is speaking, and then obscure the character's mouth in some natural way. The character, shown in Figure 23-9 in Weber's intestine, is a good example of this. The head and body bobs with the words being said but the microphone obscures his mouth in a natural way. This saved a bunch of time but did not detract from his purpose in the story line. Here, a bit of design savvy saved a lot of work.

Many animators use a mirror placed nearby and mouth (act out) the words they are trying to draw. This is extremely helpful when learning to do lip-synch. It is also of great help in mastering facial expressions. Just try not to get too wrapped up in drawing every nuance you see. Sometimes less is more. Once you get over feeling a bit foolish about talking to yourself in the mirror you'll be on your way to animating good expressive lip-synched sequences. Another trick that you can use to ease the load is to reuse lip-synch. Do this by copying frames from previous stretches of mouth movements to new locations where the words are the same, and then tweak the copied parts to fit the new dialogue. Still, no magic lip-synch button exists. Even with all these tricks, effective lip-synching is hard work. It's also one of the more tedious tasks in animation, as it demands a great deal of practice to get it right.

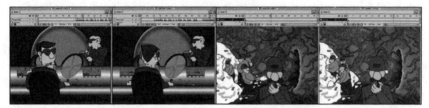

Figure 23-9: Lip-synching tricks include economy of effort, such as having the character begin to speak and then turn away naturally.

Synching with music and sound effects

In the introduction, Weber dances to the theme song, shuffling through a Michael Jackson moonwalk, and then spinning to the scratch of the synth. This really helps to gel things because the action on screen synchs to the sound (music or effect) and helps to draw in the viewer. If you've already succeeded with lip-synching work then this type of synching is easy. All that's going on here is a bit of instance swapping set to the beat of the music. Study your music waveform for visual clues then scrub it for the sound and you're sure to find the exact section where the change in action (instance swap) needs to go. You don't have to make your synch tight to every note. To keep the shot engaging, what matters is that you synch to the highlights, or hard beats.

Adding sound effects is really the fun part. It's easy and highly effective. Either working from your story board, or as you're animating, you'll know where you want to insert a sound effect. For example, when the anvil hits the head, a CLANK is needed there. If the effect you need is on hand, great! Just make sure it has the necessary duration, and then plug it in at the frame where it should start. For broadcast animation you should set the sound sync pop-up to Streaming for the soundtrack exclusively. It's wise to confine your sound effects to a layer or two, as this leads to less confusion and when using two layers allows more than one sound effect to go off at a time.

Finishing Up

When you have a shot done it's often helpful to see it play at full speed. Unfortunately Flash is unable keep up with all of the sounds, bitmaps, and complicated vectors that go into broadcast quality animation. Plus, it's impossible — even with the most macho of processors — to play the shot at full speed, without hiding a bunch of elements. But you're the director of this masterpiece, it's time for dailies, and you need to see it all, baby.

The best way to do this and save disk space is to render (export raster video) of a small 320×240 codec (if working at 640×480) using the standard QuickTime Video compressor on the Mac or the Microsoft Video 1 codec if you're outputting AVI files on a PC. These codecs are for draft purposes only so it may have banding and artifacts from compression . . . but the point here is to generate something so that even a machine that's ill equipped for high-end video output can display the cartoon video easily at full frame rate speed. This method is of great help in revealing those areas of the animation that still need further tweaking and work before going out to the final. The general movement and pace of the shot will make itself known. Look for errors such as unintended jumpiness in frames, color shifts, or inconsistencies between views. Furthermore, your lip-synching efforts will either be a glory to behold or a disaster in need of medical attention. Other things, such as sound clipping (pops in high volume sound) also become apparent here. To put it bluntly, if the preview makes you cringe, then it needs work — if not, you're ready for final output.

Final output

Now, after checking endlessly you're ready for the final video file of the shot to be rendered. Back it up one more time. Then, when you've safely archived your final project file its time to choose the codec that your playback equipment can use and render one out for the tube. Then when you have rendered all your shots at full screen, you can take them into Premiere or After Effects for more detailed editing and tweaking, utilizing all the power that these applications offer. For example, you might want music to play gently in the background across *all* of your scenes. Although this would be impossible to piece together with separate Flash project files, it's a snap in Premiere. Again, the possibilities here are endless.

✦   ✦   ✦

Working with Authoring Applications

Dreamweaver and Director are Macromedia's most
popular authoring solutions for Web and CD-ROM
presentations. As the last chapter to Part V, this chapter
teaches you how to integrate advanced Flash movies,
created from lessons in other sections of this book, into
final production with these two applications.

Flash movies (as .SWF files) have the amazing ability to be
embedded in other applications. The best—and most well
known—example of this is the Flash Player plug-in for Web
browsers. To take more control over the usage of Flash movies
in Web browsers, you can use Macromedia Dreamweaver to
customize plug-in settings. However, the fun doesn't stop
there. You can import Flash SWF files into Macromedia Director.
Director is the premiere multimedia authoring application on
the market. With Director's scripting language Lingo, interactive
commands can be passed between the Flash movie and the
Director movie. In some cases, you can do more with Flash
movies in Director than you can with even the most advanced
ActionScripts in Flash 4 alone.

Caution   You need to know how to export your Flash editor documents (.FLA files) as Flash movies (.SWF files). You may
want to review Chapters 25 and 26 before proceeding with
this chapter.

Integrating SWF Files into Dreamweaver

Although Flash 4's new Publish feature takes a lot of the guesswork out of placing Flash movies on Web pages, you might want to add HTML graphics and text to the page too. Macromedia Dreamweaver has been a huge hit with Web designers — its roundtrip HTML feature keeps your HTML code just the way you like it. Roundtrip HTML refers to Dreamweaver's ability to transfer HTML code back and forth between applications, keeping your preferred formatting intact. In this section, we take a look at the fundamentals of using Flash movies with Dreamweaver and HTML.

Cross-
Reference
For more information on using the Publish feature of Flash 4, see Chapter 25.

Expert Tutorial: Using Dreamweaver 2 with Flash 4 with Flash 4 *by Mark LaBelle*

Mark LaBelle is a Macromedia evangelist — which is a program for avid professional users of Macromedia software (Dreamweaver, Flash, Freehand, Fireworks, Director, and so on). Mark is reputed for his "knack for dredging out problems and providing answers." He's also a regular contributor to several of the sites that host Flash tutorials, most notably www.flashlite.com. *Mark's domain,* www.marklabelle.com, *is the spotlight for Mark LaBelle productions, which specializes in freelance animation, Web design, and logo design. He developed this tutorial to spotlight the synergy of two of his favorite tools, in hopes that it will, "help you on your way to creating dynamic, rich Web content using the most effective HTML tool available." That tool is, of course, Dreamweaver.*

A match made by Macromedia

Macromedia's addition of the new Publish feature to Flash is one of my favorite aspects of the new Flash 4 release. No more Aftershock! The Publish feature has streamlined the process from design to implementation considerably. Moreover, for those who still want to thoroughly harmonize Flash and HTML, Macromedia has delivered flawless integration between the new Dreamweaver 2 and this latest Flash release. In fact, working with Flash files from within an HTML editor couldn't be easier. So, in this tutorial, we show you how simple it is to use Dreamweaver to get your Flash creations out to the Web.

Working with your Flash movie

Once you have created your interactive animation and have exported the file into the SWF format, it's time to put the file into your HTML document. (For more information on exporting a Flash animation to the SWF format, refer to Chapter 25, "Exporting SWF Movies.") To enhance your understanding of this tutorial, you might want to follow each step yourself. To do this, you can use the sample SWF file — named DW740x400.swf — located on the *Flash 4 Bible* CD-ROM in the ch24 folder. Note that the file name contains the dimensions of this Flash file. If your Flash file needs to be positioned in any manner other than centered, this trick helps when you're positioning it in your HTML document.

Let's get started. First, create a new document in Dreamweaver, using File⇨New (Command+N or Ctrl+N). Next, insert the Flash file by selecting Insert⇨Flash, or by using the Object Palette, and clicking the Flash icon, which, as shown in the following figure, is the third from the bottom of the palette. The Select File dialog box will appear. Now, browse the *Flash 4 Bible* CD-ROM to select the DW740x400.swf file from the ch24 folder. (If you're working on another project and have already exported a Flash file to a folder in your hard drive, browse and select that file instead.)

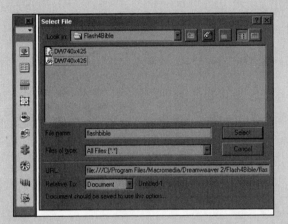

Click the Flash object icon on the Object Palette (left) and the Select File dialog box (right) will appear.

Having selected your Flash SWF file and then clicked Select, you should see a symbol in your Dreamweaver document indicating that this is a Flash movie. As shown in the following figure, this is the ubiquitous Flash icon.

Dreamweaver's Flash object icon

You should also notice that your Flash file now appears in the Dreamweaver Properties Inspector, as shown in the next figure, which displays the properties most commonly used in Dreamweaver. If the Properties Inspector is not visible, access it with Window⇨Properties. If all of the properties are not displayed, click the expand arrow in the lower-right corner to see them. This inspector hosts many options and controls:

✦ **Name:** This field is used to specify a name that can be used to identify the movie or scripting. Enter a name in this field (which is unlabeled) on the far left side of the Property inspector.

Continued

(continued)

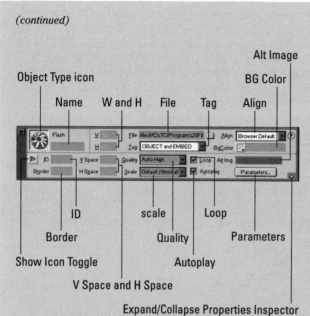

The Dreamweaver Properties Inspector for Flash content

✦ **W and H:** Upon placement of the Flash asset within Dreamweaver, the width and height parameters are automatically filled with the exact dimensions of the SWF, specified in pixels. However, you can change these dimensions and also specify dimensions in the following units: pc (picas), pt (points), in (inches), mm (millimeters), cm (centimeters), or % (percentage of the parent's value). Note that the abbreviations must follow the value without a space: for example, 3mm.

✦ **File:** Specifies the path to the Shockwave movie file. The file location should already appear in this field.

✦ **Tag:** Determines the tags used to identify the Shockwave movie. Although the default value—OBJECT and EMBED—is recommended (To ensure proper plug-in detection, as well as proper playback.), you may choose either tag separately. The OBJECT is the tag defined by Microsoft for ActiveX controls; EMBED is the tag defined by Netscape for plug-ins.

✦ **Align:** Determines how the movie is aligned on the page. The default setting is Browser Default.

✦ **BgColor:** Specifies a background color for the movie. This color appears even when the movie is not playing (both while loading and after playing). This functionality can also be set in Flash 4 with the Modify ⇨ Movie option.

✦ **ID:** Defines the optional ActiveX ID parameter. This parameter is most often used to pass information between ActiveX controls, which is not discussed in this tutorial.

✦ **Borders:** Specifies the width of the optional border around the movie.

✦ **V Space** and **H Space:** Used to specify the number of pixels of space above and below and on both sides of the movie.

✦ **Quality:** Sets the QUALITY parameter for the OBJECT and EMBED tags that run the movie. The choices are Low, Auto Low, Auto High, and High. See the HTML Settings section of Chapter 25 for a full explanation. Dreamweaver does not list Best as an option in the Quality drop-down menu. You can manually type BEST as the value of the QUALITY attribute of the <EMBED> and/or <OBJECT> tag in Dreamweaver's HTML window.

✦ **Scale:** Sets the SCALE parameter for the OBJECT and EMBED tags that run the movie. See the section on scaling in Chapter 25, "Exporting Shockwave Flash Movies," for further explanation.

✦ **Loop:** Makes the movie loop indefinitely.

✦ **Autoplay:** Plays the movie automatically when the page loads. This is the default option, but may be changed to allow for the Control Shockwave or Flash Behaviors in Dreamweaver, which are outside the subject of this tutorial.

✦ **Alt Image:** (OBJECT only) Specifies an image to be displayed if the user's browser does not support ActiveX controls. This is used for Netscape Navigator users who don't have the Flash plug-in.

✦ **Parameters:** This button opens a dialog box in which to enter additional parameters to pass to the Shockwave movie. The Shockwave movie must be authored to receive these parameters, which is also beyond the scope of this tutorial.

Positioning your movie

Using the dimensions 740×400, the sample movie (DW740x400.fla, which is included on the *Flash 4 Bible* CD-ROM) attempts to extend the borders of the movie to the far reaches of the browser window. However, it doesn't necessarily position it in the center of the browser. To achieve the best results, a quick way to center your movie is by simply changing the Width and Height properties in the Property inspector to percentages (%) rather than exact dimensions. Try changing the Width and Height to 100 percent to fill the browser window. You can also use HTML <CENTER></CENTER> tags around the <EMBED> and/or <OBJECT> tags to center a pixel-sized Flash movie on a Web page.

Sometimes, you may observe a slight background difference between the HTML background and the movie background. Using the Background field of Modify ⇨ Page Properties in Dreamweaver to match the color of the Dreamweaver HTML page to that of the Flash movie usually solves this problem. Note, however, that differences between 16-bit and 32-bit display systems may still cause a slight "gutter" around the movie.

Although most Web sites are viewed in full-screen capacity, some users scale their browser to their own desired size, which may adversely impact the aspect ratio (the height and width ratio) of your movie. The scale option enables you to select three options to achieve the desired perspective. These options are:

Continued

(continued)

✦ **showall:** makes the entire movie visible in the specified area. The aspect ratio of the movie is maintained, and no distortion occurs. Borders may appear on two sides of the movie.

✦ **noborder:** forces the movie to fill the specified area. The aspect ratio of the movie is maintained, and no distortion occurs — but portions of the movie may be cropped.

✦ **exactfit:** forces the entire movie to fill the specified area. The aspect ratio of the movie is not maintained, and distortion may occur. For this example, we used the exactfit option to enable users to re-size their windows and still see the entire movie.

Directing the browser to the Flash plug-in

Perhaps one of the greatest timesaving features of using Dreamweaver to publish your Flash movies is Dreamweaver's automatic inclusion of plug-in download locations for both Netscape and Internet Explorer/ActiveX. The following is an example of code that appears in your HTML document — it simultaneously places the Flash movie in your document and also directs the browser to the download location of the Flash Player plug-in if it is not installed.

```
<object
      classid="clsid:D27CDB6E-AE6D-11cf-96B8-444553540000"
codebase=http://download.macromedia.com/pub/shockwave/cabs/flash/
      swflash.cab#3,0,0,0
      width="100%" height="100%">
      <param name="SRC" value="DW740x400.swf">
      <param name="SCALE" value="exactfit">
<embed
      src="DW740x400.swf"
pluginspage="http://www.macromedia.com/shockwave/download/"
      type="application/x-shockwave-flash"
      width="100%" height="100%"
      scale="exactfit">
</embed>
</object>
```

Caution: Dreamweaver still uses the Flash 3.0 ActiveX download location. Change the 3 in the CODEBASE attribute of the `<OBJECT>` tag to 4 to ensure that the Flash 4.0 ActiveX control is downloaded. For more information on the Flash Player plug-in and ActiveX control, see Chapter 27.

Publish or perish?

The last thing to do is to save your Dreamweaver HTML document by selecting File ➪ Save (Command+S or Ctrl + S). Voila, we are done! Dreamweaver and Flash have been so well integrated that using Dreamweaver to publish your Flash movies is easier than ever. Although Flash 4 has developed the publish feature in place of Aftershock, you can use Dreamweaver to achieve the same results. The preceding tutorial has walked you through the basic steps to get your work into an html document. However, when your Flash movie isn't the entire project using Dreamweaver can be a tremendous boon to your productivity and creativity. For example, many designers build sites by integrating an HTML frame with a Flash movie in another frame. If you use Dreamweaver, developing pages with such a scheme is as easy as creating the frames and dropping the movie in.

Animation techniques using layers

One parameter for Flash movies currently only works with the Windows 95/98/NT versions of Internet Explorer 4.0 or higher: window mode. The window mode parameter, wmode, lets the background of a Flash movie drop out, so that HTML or DHTML content can appear in place of the Flash movie background. Because support for this option is not broadly supported, you won't likely find very many Web pages that use it. However, if you want to try it out, it's pretty simple.

First, make sure that your Flash movie is on its own layer — if you want to animate other material behind or in front of the Flash movie. In the Dreamweaver Properties Inspector for Flash movies, click the Parameters button. In the Parameters dialog box, click the + button above the Parameter column. Enter **wmode** in the left column. Click under the Value column, and enter one of the three options:

✦ **Window:** This is the "standard" player interface, in which the Flash movie plays as it would normally, in its own rectangular window on a Web page.

✦ **Opaque:** Use this option if you want the Flash movie to have an opaque background and have DHTML or HTML elements behind the Flash movie.

✦ **Transparent:** This option "knocks out" the Flash background color so that other HTML elements behind the Flash movie shows through. Note that the Flash movie's frame rate and performance may suffer on slower machines when this mode is used, because the Flash movie needs to composite itself over other non-Flash material.

Again, the WMODE parameter is only recognized by 32-bit Windows versions of Internet Explorer 4 or higher. If you are using browser detection on your Web pages, you can divert visitors using these browsers to specialized Flash and DHTML Web pages.

Using SWF Files in Macromedia Director

Director 7.02, Macromedia's flagship product, is the authoring application used to create most of the dazzling multimedia-rich CD-ROMs and, more recently, Shockwave-enhanced Web experiences. Since version 6.5, you could import Flash movies (as .SWF files) via the Flash Asset Xtra. Now, with version 7.02, you can take full control of your SWF movies in Director. Moreover, the latest versions of the Shockwave plug-in automatically install the Flash Asset Xtra on Web browsers. That means that you can count on Shockwave-enabled visitors being able to view your Flash-Director Shockwave content. But why would you want to use Director in combination with Flash in the first place? We'll answer that question next.

 Caution If you want to use Flash 4 SWF files in Director, you must download and install the 7.02 update available for free to registered owners of Director 7. You can find more information by going to the Director Web site at `www.macromedia.com/support/director/downloads.html`.

Benefits and limitations of Flash movies in Director

Flash 4 has been a monumental leap forward for Flash interactivity. With the additional ActionScripting that Flash can now employ, many of the previous Flash-Director scenarios are no longer needed. However, if you're already familiar with Director and Lingo (Director's scripting language), then you may find integrating SWF files into Director projects easier than learning advanced scripting with Actions in Flash 4. The following list reviews some of the benefits and drawbacks of using Flash movies in Director projects.

✦ **Better vector control:** While Director 7 introduced vector shape drawing tools to Director, it doesn't use the same intuitive drawing mechanism that Flash does. Use Flash for any complex vector drawing and animation, and then bring it into your Director project.

✦ **Implement existing projects:** With the ability to use Flash movies in Director, you need not duplicate efforts if material already exists in one format or the other. Meaning, if you've already developed some cool animations in Flash f or your company's Web site, then you can re-use the same Flash SWF files in your Director projects.

✦ **Implement media types not available in Flash:** Director's architecture can be expanded with the use of Macromedia's (or a third party's) Xtras. Even though Flash 4 can import QuickTime movie files, it can only export QuickTime Flash movies — it can't export SWF files that contain QuickTime movies. However, you can import QuickTime movies, as well as many other media types, into Director that can be referenced from Shockwave Director movies. Some audio file formats, such as MP3, AU, and MIDI, are not supported by Flash. Director 7.0 natively supports MP3 and AU import — Flash can only export MP3 sound. With the proper Xtras, you can use MIDI music with your Flash movies in Director.

✦ **Improved audio support:** In versions of Director previous to 7.02, Flash audio could not play simultaneously with Director sound channels. Now, you can control the global property soundMixMedia to mix Flash sounds with Director score sound channels.

✦ **Flash frame rate control:** Ironically, you have more control over a Flash movie's frame rate in Director than you do natively within Flash 4. In Flash, the movie's frame rate is fixed throughout the entire movie — once it is set in the Modify ⇨ Movie dialog box, it cannot be updated or changed during playback. Flash movies also seem to play more smoothly at higher frame rates when played within a Director projector.

✦ **Steeper learning curve with Director:** Director's enhancements come at a price. While Flash was designed with animation in mind, Director has evolved from a frame-by-frame video production application to a powerhouse authoring application. Director's scripting language, Lingo, uses a different model of command and event control than Flash 4 does.

Flash and Director inter-movie activity is a two-way street: you can send events from Flash to Director (via Lingo), or you can control Flash movie playback from Director (via Lingo). The next section shows you how to set up Flash movies to send events to Director.

Creating Director-specific actions in Flash

You can use Flash SWF files in any number of ways with Director. If you simply want to use a Flash animation for graphic content within a Director presentation, you can simply use the same SWF you generated for the Web. Use the Flash Asset Xtra import box (see more in-depth discussion later in this section) to set the parameters of playback — without needing any Lingo. However, if you want Flash actions (in frames or on buttons) to do something in your Director movies, then you need to know how to get Lingo's attention. The drawback to this type of "dual" interactivity is that you need to plan ahead with both your Flash and Director movies. As with any project, you should outline a storyboard before embarking on a task such as this.

Tip   Use a project planner such as Microsoft Organization Chart (included with Microsoft Office) or Kaetron's TopDown (www.kaetron.com) to plan an interactive project. By creating interactive hierarchies and flow-charts (for example, determining which scenes will link to other scenes), you can manage projects with greater ease.

You have three methods to use within the Flash authoring environment, all involving the Get URL action. You can assign any of these methods the same way you would with any other Flash interactivity — attach these actions to buttons, frames, or ActionScript conditions. Note that, if you are not familiar with Director or Lingo, you will need to read this entire section on Director in order to understand what's going on.

Caution If you experience crashes in Director using any of the Get URL commands listed in this section, please see the sidebar "Quirks with Flash Sprites and Lingo 'go' Commands" later in this chapter.

Standard GetURL command

On a Flash button or frame, access the Properties and assign a Get URL action. This is the preferred method of sending information to Director movies because you can deal with the result of the action in Director — you do not need to specify what Director does with the string from Flash. With button actions, Flash 4 automatically creates a default On (Release) action to contain the Get URL action. In the URL setting, create a string to be passed to an event handler in Lingo. In Figure 24-1, a Get URL action is assigned to a frame in Flash. The string ProjectOne is entered in the URL text field. This string, in turn, is received by Lingo.

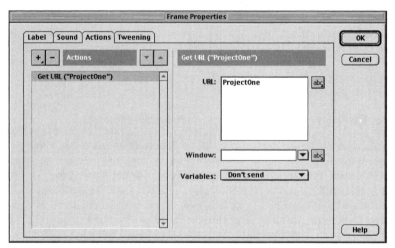

Figure 24-1: You can enter any word or series of characters (that is, a *string*) in the URL field. This string is then passed to Lingo.

In Director, you need to attach a behavior script to the Flash sprite so that the Get URL action and string can be received by Lingo. We'll discuss the actual implementation of this example later in the "Basic Sprite Functions in Director" section. In Figure 24-1, the string ProjectOne was assigned to Get URL. In Director, we could tell Lingo to go to the frame marker called ProjectOne:

```
on getURL me FlashString
   go to frame FlashString
end
```

When the Flash sprite plays in Director and the Get URL action is executed, the ProjectOne value of Get URL is passed as the `FlashString` argument of the Lingo event handler, `on getURL`. Lingo will direct the playback of the Director movie to the frame marker ProjectOne.

Event: command

You can also specify an event: handler in the URL field of the Get URL action. This method is useful if you would like to describe an event that is repeatedly used in Flash, but needs customized settings with each use. For example, if you want to add a mouse click to go to a different Director frame depending on which button was clicked, you could use the following URL in the Get URL action:

```
event: FClick "ProjectOne"
```

In Director, you then write a behavior that would receive the `FClick` event:

```
on FClick me FlashString
  go to frame FlashString
end
```

How is this different from the last example? If you want to have several events in one script that perform different Lingo commands, you need to label each one with a separate event, such as:

```
on FClickButton01 me FlashString
  go to frame FlashString
end

on FClickButton02 me FlashString
  quit
end
```

In the preceding example, we have two defined Flash events, `FClickButton01` and `FclickButton02`, which do different things. If we had used the standard Get URL action, we could only pass the string to one Lingo command.

Tip   With a bit more programming in Lingo, you could pass one argument string to multiple Lingo commands by testing the string with `if then` statements.

Lingo: command

The last Get URL method of sending events to Lingo is the most direct method of communicating with Director movies. In the URL field, a lingo: handler is used to specify a Lingo statement. This is the most inflexible method of sending events to Director — insofar as you cannot do anything in Director to modify or direct the event. For example, if you added the following code to a On(Release), Get URL button event in Flash:

Quirks with Flash Sprites and Lingo "go" Commands

You may experience crashes if you send Flash events to Lingo that make a Director movie go to a frame where the Flash sprite is no longer on the stage. For example, if you start a Director movie with a Flash animation, and you have a frame action on the last frame of the Flash animation that directs playback to a new section of the Director score, the Flash sprite duration needs to be extended all the way to the frame that the Director movie is jumping to. Use a Lingo command such as

```
set the visible of sprite X to FALSE
```

(where X designates the Flash sprite number) to make the Flash sprite invisible on that frame if necessary. If you don't want to extend the sprite to that frame and/or you are jumping to a new movie, see the advanced workarounds at www.macromedia.com/support/director/documents/flash_asset_xtra_go_issue.htm.

```
lingo: quit
```

then the Director movie quits (or the Director projector closes) when that button was clicked.

With lingo: statements in Get URL actions, you do not need to specify any further Lingo in the Director movie, unless you are setting the value of pre-scripted variable or executing a event described in the Director movie script.

Using SWF files in Director

You can import and use Flash movies (.SWF files) into Director just as you would any other cast member. Director controls Flash movies with the Flash Asset Xtra. This section shows you how to import Flash movies and use them in the Director score window. You should already be familiar with the Director authoring environment and basic behavior use.

The Flash Asset Xtra: Importing Flash movies

Since Director 6.5, the Flash Asset Xtra has enabled Flash movies to play within a Director movie. Again, make sure you have the latest 7.02 update installed in order to use Flash 4 movies. If you have Director 6.5, you need to export your Flash movies as Flash 2 movies. Director 7.0.1 supports Flash 3 or earlier movies.

Caution   If you aren't using the latest version of Director (7.0.2), then be extremely careful with the use of Flash audio. In older versions of Director that support Flash movies, Flash audio cannot play simultaneously with Director score sounds. Macromedia's tech notes advise turning sound off when using earlier versions of the Flash Asset Xtra.

To import a Flash movie (.SWF file), do the following:

1. Start a new Director movie (.DIR file) or open an existing movie .

2. Use the File ⇨ Import command (Command+R or Ctrl+R) to select a Flash movie (.SWF file). Double-click the file name in the upper portion of the Import dialog box (see Figure 24-2), or select the file name and choose Add. You can select several files of different types and import them all at once. When you are done adding files, click Import to bring the Flash movie(s) into the internal Cast.

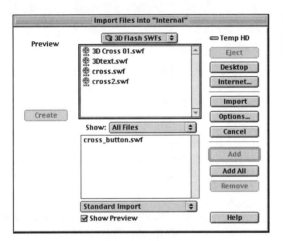

Figure 24-2: You can import several files at once with the Import command.

 You can use any of the SWF files on the *Flash 4 Bible* CD-ROM for this example. For this section, the 3D rotating crosshairs example from Chapter 20 is used. The filename is crosshairs_button.swf, which is located in the ch20 folder on the *Flash 4 Bible* CD-ROM.

3. Open the Cast window (Command+3 or Ctrl+3). Double-click the Flash movie that was imported. This brings up the Flash Asset Properties dialog box (see Figure 24-3). The top section of the dialog box is used to import additional Flash movies (see following Tip), while the lower section sets the playback attributes:

   • **Media:** This setting has two options, Linked and Preload. If you don't want to store a Flash movie within the Director movie, check Link and specify the path to the Flash movie. Unless you want to link to a Flash movie on the Internet, you should store the Flash movie in the Director movie — Flash movies are usually very small due to their vector structure. If Link is checked, then you can also enable Preload. Preloading will force Director to load (or download) the entire SWF file before it starts playing the Flash movie. Otherwise, Director will start playing the Flash movie as soon as it starts to stream the Flash cast member.

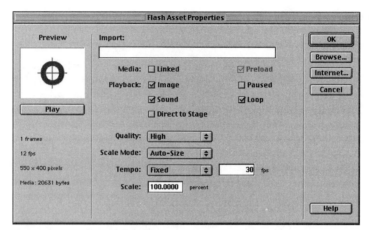

Figure 24-3: The Flash Asset Properties dialog box enables you to specify how the Flash movie functions in the Director movie.

- **Playback:** This setting has five options that control how Director displays the Flash movie. The Image option, checked by default, determines if Director shows the graphic content of a Flash movie. The Sound option determines if Director plays the audio content of a Flash movie. The Direct to Stage option tells Director to give priority to the Flash movie sprite over all other sprites currently on the stage. While this option may enable Flash movies to playback more smoothly, Director ignores any ink effects applied to the sprite (see the "Basic Sprite Functions in Director" section for more information on ink effects), and the Flash movie always displays on top of other sprites. The Paused option is akin to adding a Stop Flash action on the first frame of the Flash movie—you can force Director to display the movie in a paused state. The Loop option enables continuous playback of the Flash movie. If this option is checked, the Flash movie repeats as soon as it reaches the last frame. It continues to repeat while the Flash sprite is present in the Director score, or until it is paused by a Lingo command.

- **Quality:** This setting has a drop-down menu with the exact same settings as the Quality setting in the Flash 4 Publish Settings. By default, this setting is High. For more information on the Quality property of a Flash movie, see Chapter 25.

- **Scale Mode:** By default, this setting uses Auto-Size, which enables Director to automatically resize the Flash movie properties according to the sprite's bounding box on the Director stage. Meaning, if you resize the sprite, then the Flash movie should fit the size of the sprite box. Auto-Size automatically sets the Scale setting to 100 percent. Conversely, No Scale keeps the Flash movie at the size specified by the Scale setting (covered in a moment) and any subsequent resizing of the sprite bounding box may crop the Flash movie. The remaining options, Show All, No Border, and Exact Fit operate the same as the Publish Settings options in Flash 4 (see Chapter 25).

• **Tempo:** Perhaps one of the most powerful setting in the Flash Asset Properties dialog box, Tempo, controls how fast or slow the Flash movie plays in Director scores — irrespective of the Tempo score setting. The Flash Asset Properties' Tempo setting has two options: a drop-down menu and an fps text field. If Normal or Lock-Step is selected, then the fps text field is disabled. Normal plays the Flash movie at the same tempo (or frame rate) as the Director score. Lock-Step plays one Flash movie frame for every Director frame that its sprite occupies (for example, if the Flash movie occupies four frames of the Director score, then only the first four frames of the animation plays back in Director). Fixed Rate enables you to specify a new frame rate for the Flash movie, independent of the original frame rate specified in Flash 4 (via Modify ➪ Movie) or the Director Tempo score setting.

• **Scale:** This setting works hand-in-hand with the Scale Mode setting. If anything other than Auto-Size is selected in Scale Mode, you can specify what percentage of the original Flash movie is used for the Flash sprite. If 50 percent is used for the Scale of 550×400 Flash movie and Exact Fit is chosen in Scale Mode, then it displays at 225×200 in the original placed Flash sprite on the Stage. If you resize the sprite box, then it continues to maintain a 50 percent portion of the sprite box area.

Tip   You can also use the Insert ➪ Media Element ➪ Flash Movie command to import Flash movies via the Flash Asset Properties dialog box. Simply click the Browse button and select a Flash movie (.SWF file). Both the File ➪ Import and Flash Asset Property dialog boxes enable you to enter Internet URLs for the filename path. Forexample, you can type www.theflashbible.com/ ch24/tutorial/crosshairs_button.swf to use the Flash movie used in this example.

After specifying the settings you wish to use for your Flash movie, you can then place the Flash cast member as a sprite on to the Director stage.

SWF files as sprites

In Director, any item that is used in a movie becomes part of a cast, and is referred to as a cast member. When a cast member is placed on the stage, it becomes a sprite. A sprite is an instance of the cast member used in the score. The relationship between a Flash symbol and a symbol instance is similar to the relationship between a Director cast member and its sprite(s).

To place a Flash cast member on the Director stage, simply click and drag its cast member icon from the Internal Cast window to the stage or the Score. If you drag a cast member to the stage (see Figure 24-4), it automatically becomes a sprite on the first sprite channel. If you drag a sprite to the score (see Figure 24-4 also), it is automatically centered on the stage.

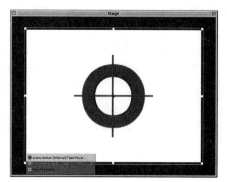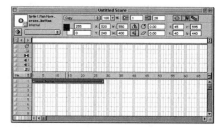

Figure 24-4: A Flash Sprite on the Director stage (left), and a Flash Sprite in the Director score (right)

While Flash sprites perform almost the same as other Director sprites, you should be aware of certain sprite properties before proceeding with Lingo behaviors and Flash sprites. For more information on basic animation features of Director, please consult the *Using Director 7* manual that comes with the Director software.

✦ **Sprite Duration:** Every sprite has a duration in the score. By default, every sprite dragged to the score or stage has a duration of 28 frames. Like digital video and sound sprites, Flash sprites only play for as long as their frame duration allows them. For example, if a Flash movie that is 30 Flash frames long and is assigned a Lock-Step tempo is inserted as a 15-frame Flash sprite in Director, then Director only shows the first half of the Flash movie.

✦ **Sprite Inks:** Of all the inks available to sprites, only Copy, Transparent, and Background Transparent have any noticeable effect on Flash sprites. Copy makes the Flash movie background opaque, in the same color that you specified in the Flash authoring environment. Transparent and Background Transparent (see Figure 24-5) effectively do the same thing. They both render the Flash movie background transparent, so that the Director movie background (and other Director sprites) show through.

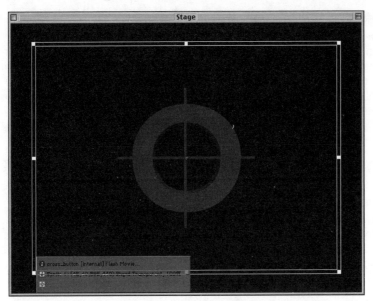

Figure 24-5: With an ink effect of Background Transparent, the white background of the crosshairs_button Flash sprite drops out.

Controlling SWF files with Lingo

Not only can you send events from Flash movies to Director movies, but you can also control Flash movies from Director with Lingo. Over 70 Lingo commands exist that are specific for Flash movie assets in a Director movie. Unfortunately, it is beyond the scope of this book to explore so many different commands. This section teaches you how to alter the size and rotation of Flash sprites. For more Lingo tips and tricks, check out www.theflashbible.com/ch24 for updates to this section.

Tip For a complete listing of the Lingo commands that can be used with Flash movies, see the Macromedia Director support page at www.macromedia.com/support/director/how/d65/tutorial/flashasset/FlashTutorial6.html. At the time of this writing, there wasn't a 7.02 update to this list of Lingo commands. Director 7.02's Lingo can also use getVariable and setVariable, which give you access to any variables inside the Flash 4 movie. Also, Macromedia has expanded the hitTest command (which can be used to detect whether an arbitrary point in the Flash movie is the transparent background area, a normal "fill" area or a Flash button) to include an #editTest return value to detect Flash 4 editable text fields.

Changing the size and rotation of Flash sprites

With the crosshairs_button.swf example used earlier, we can rotate and zoom the Flash movie in Director. Because the crosshairs_button sprite is a Flash button that already plays a 3D rotation sequence, we disable the Flash button by using a Lingo script in the first frame of the score:

```
on enterFrame
   sprite(1).buttonsEnabled = FALSE
end
On exitFrame
   go the frame
end
```

You may notice that we used the new JavaScript-like syntax in Director 7. The sprite(1) line of code refers to the sprite occupying the first sprite channel, which in our example is the crosshairs_button Flash sprite. Adding the .buttonsEnabled property lets Director know what property we want to change with the sprite—in this case, Flash button activity. Setting this property to FALSE means it is being turned off.

Next, add the following behavior script to the Flash sprite:

```
on mouseEnter me
   repeat while sprite(1).rotation < 720
      sprite(1).rotation = sprite(1).rotation + 10
      updateStage
   end repeat
end

on mouseLeave me
   sprite(1).rotation = 0
end
```

This behavior causes the Flash sprite to rotate a full 720 degrees—two revolutions—when the mouse enters the Flash sprite. Here, the .rotation property is called and manipulated. Notice that when the mouse leaves the sprite, the rotation is reset to 0.

To change this to a zooming behavior, simply change the script to the following:

```
on mouseEnter me
   repeat while sprite(1).scale < 800
      sprite(1).scale = sprite(1).scale + 10
      updateStage
   end repeat
end

on mouseLeave me
   sprite(1).scale = 100
end
```

For a super-cool effect, re-enable the Flash button by removing the `on enterFrame` section, containing the `sprite(1).buttonsEnabled` line, from the frame 1 script. Now, as the Flash movie zooms, the button continues to rotate on a 3D axis.

Open the crosshairs_button.dir file in the ch24 folder of the *Flash 4 Bible* CD-ROM to see the rotation and scaling Lingo actions.

Before we get started on this tutorial, please take a moment and have a look at the finished example movie, Flash_Director_Tutorial.dir. You can find it on the *Flash 4 Bible* CD-ROM, in the ch24 folder.

Expert Tutorial: Creating a Flash Catalog in Director
by Chris Honselaar

Chris Honselaar is an educational developer committed to building future-conscious Internet content and enhancing conceptual communications over new media. To implement his ideas, Chris and his partner, Fabian Gort, established a Web design company, HTMWell, which is dedicated to human interaction. As such, HTMWell intends to redefine PR for the net. Reflecting its poly-facetted attitude, HTMWell employs seasoned graphic designers, commercial consultants and utilizes the forefront of Web technology to build Internet solutions that will stand the test of time. You can chat, or chew their eye candy at `www.HTMWell.com`.

Ready to add some Flash to your Director movies? Then let's get our hands dirty on a real-life example of Flash integration. This tutorial will show you how to control Flash movies from Lingo and perform tasks that wouldn't be easily accomplished in Flash 4 alone! Here we build a browseable, zoomable Flash-picture (or product) catalogue, using a history list similar to that of a Web browser. Applying this technique enables us to have browser-like back-and-forward behavior even without playing the movie in a browser. Just for fun, we can also show you how you can easily convert the movie into a full-blown user programmable slide show!

1. Open Director. For this example, we use the default 640×480 pixel Stage. Choose File ➪ Import (Command+R or Ctrl+R), and select the file Tutorial.cst from the *Flash 4 Bible* CD-ROM, as shown in the following figure. Or you can use your own images, if you like! Just insert your own files wherever we use the tutorial cast members.

2. Make sure the playback head is positioned on frame 1. Now clench your teeth and start dragging the 15 thumbnail cast members (imaginatively named Thumb1 through Thumb15) to the stage. Drag the Cast member Navigation Bar to the bottom of the stage. Your stage should now look similar to the second figure that follows. The looks are there, now let's add some interactivity.

Continued

(continued)

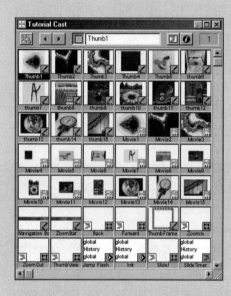

Director Cast window with cast members from the Tutorial.cst file

Director stage with thumbnail bitmaps of the Flash movies

3. We want to link each thumbnail to the corresponding Flash Movie, which is in a separate frame. The behavior cast member "Jump Flash" does exactly this. Now select all thumbnails on the stage, and then drag "Jump Flash" over one of them. Let's have a look at the Lingo, shall we?

```
global History
global HistoryPosition
on mouseUp me
   HistoryPosition = HistoryPosition + 1
   if HistoryPosition > Count(History) then
     Append History, the currentSpriteNum + 30
   else History[HistoryPosition] = the currentSpriteNum + 30
   go to frame(History[HistoryPosition])
end
```

This script does two things: first it adds the number of the current sprite (for example, the thumbnail clicked) to a global list called History. By adding 30 to this number we now have a frame we can jump to, thumbnail 1 referring to frame 31 and so forth. HistoryPosition is a global list index, which indicates at what position in the History list the user is browsing currently. Secondly, the script jumps to the frame number it just added to the list.

4. The script is attached now, but jumps to empty frames. Now we fill them up with some Flash content. Drag the Flash Asset Movie1 (in our cast) to frame 31 in the first channel of the score. Unfortunately Director gives our newly born sprite a standard lifetime of 28 frames. Drag the endframe to the same position as the beginframe, so the whole sprite resides in frame 31. Here's the endurance test: repeat the same procedure for Movie2 through to Movie15, constraining them to frame 32 to 45, respectively.

5. Phew! Well that was actually the hardest part. Now we want a new navigation bar in the Flash frames. Position the playback head on frame 31, and drag Zoom Bar to the stage bottom.

6. Let's wire the buttons! Position the playback head on frame 1. In the Tutorial cast, you find two cast members, Back and Forward. Each is a simply a transparent rectangle that we overlay on to the navigation bar. Drag Back over the left triangle and Forward over the right one. In the Score, extend the sprites Back and Forward to frame 45. Now both navigation bars enable browsing! The Lingo here is relatively straightforward. Consult the "Managing Lists" chapter in the Lingo online help if you need more information. This is the Back behavior:

```
on mouseUp
   if HistoryPosition > 1 then
     HistoryPosition = HistoryPosition - 1
     go to frame(History[HistoryPosition])
   end if
end
```

Continued

(continued)

In this code example, we didn't show the global variables code — it should be included in the actual script. Because it is exactly the same in every script, we didn't list it here. Notice that when the back button is pressed, the Historyposition index is decreased (if it's not already equal to 1). The script then jumps to the frame that was stored at that position. The forward behavior does essentially the same thing, but *increases* the Historyposition.

7. Just throwing a Flash movie on the screen is one thing, but wouldn't you like to zoom in on those details? Three mouse clicks will do: (and some minimalist lingo) Position the playback head on frame 31, showing our second navigation bar. Now drag the Zoom In cast member over the plus picture, and Zoom Out over the minus. Close examination of the script shows a good example of how easy and powerful Flash integration really is. Every click of the ZoomIn button invokes this command:

```
sprite(1).scale = sprite(1).scale + 10
```

Sprite(1) refers to the Flash movie that is currently playing on screen. The scale property determines the viewsize of the movie, within the bounding rectangle of the sprite. ZoomOut decreases the scale accordingly.

8. Wire the button looking suspiciously like a frame on the left of the navigation bar, by dragging ThumbView over it. This script simply jumps to the final frame of the thumbnail view (frame 28).

9. Now let's make our director movie wait for response in all the right places. That is, drag the Hold on Current Frame behavior (in the Navigation part of the Library Palette, Window menu) to frame 28 in the frame channel. Change the number in the Endframe textbox from 28 to 45.

Only one more frame script needs to be attached: the Init behavior, which tells Director to initialize our variables. Drag it to the first frame, again in the frame channel.

10. Pat yourself on the back. You have a working catalogue browser! It won't crush the Internet Explorer competition, but we can now introduce a feature your average Web browser does not offer: a slideshow! The Lingo is a bit more specific here, so please consult the lingo documentation if a command seems esoteric.

11. Position the playback head on frame 1. Let the SlideShow! button fulfill its destiny: drag the Slide! script over it. A click calls this event handler:

```
if count(History) > 0 then
    repeat with index = 2 to 20
```

```
        set the visible of sprite(index) to FALSE
     end repeat
     the timeoutLength = 300
     HistoryPosition = 1
     SlideShow = TRUE
     startTimer
     timeout
  end if
```

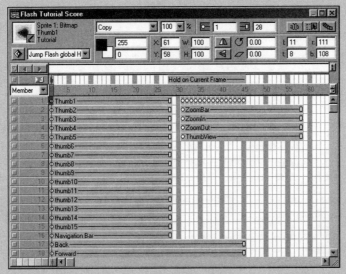

The complete Director score should look like this just before the completion of Step 9.

After a reality check to see if anything exists in the History to show, first the navigation bar and its controls are hidden, by setting the Visible properties of the corresponding sprites to false. Then we initialize Director's timer, which will in turn determine the interval between each picture. When TimeOutLength, which is set to 200 ticks (60 ticks equal a second), is over the handler called `on timeout` is called. This is located in a movie script, which we will discuss in Step 12. The variable SlideShow is set to true, because Director's timer will call ontimeout whenever it wants to, and the handler needs to know if it should slide to the next image or not. Just so the user does not have to wait 3 whole seconds for the slideshow to begin, timeout is called here manually, just for the first picture.

Continued

(continued)

12. The cast member Slide Timer contains the movie script, which handles the slideshow actions.

```
if SlideShow then
    if HistoryPosition <= Count(History) then
        go to frame(History[HistoryPosition])
        HistoryPosition = HistoryPosition + 1
        startTimer
    else
        SlideShow = FALSE
        go to frame(1)
        repeat with index = 2 to 20
            set the visible of sprite(index) to TRUE
        end repeat
    end if
end if
```

When the user has started the slide show, this script enters the frame at the current HistoryPosition, and then increases the position and starts the timer anew. In this way, the slide show iterates through the History from the first to the last position. Finally, it ends the fun by returning to frame 1 and showing all sprites.

13. Just for some icing on the cake, drag the Thumb Frame over each of the thumbnail pictures. (This step is optional).

Finished? Good job. You are now able to use your dear old Flash movies to spice up any Director/Shockwave project! This particular example could be expanded to an electronic shopping cart, or a Flash playlist. Of course you have many more ways to manipulate Flash content, most of which are covered in the Lingo documentation. One distinct advantage to using Flash in Director is having very tight control over frame rate: Flash movies are almost always going to be plain faster if imported in Director!

✦　　✦　　✦

Distributing Flash Movies

After you've created Flash movies that dazzle the eye with morphing shape tweens, soothe the ear with MP3 encoded sound, and interact with mouse movements using ActionScript, you'll need to convert your Flash editor document (.FLA file) to the Flash movie format (.SWF file) so that other people can view the content on a Web browser using the Flash Player plug-in or Active X control. You can also publish your movies as QuickTime 4 movies with Flash tracks (discussed in detail back in Chapter 21), as stand-alone projectors, or as .SWF files that use the stand-alone Flash Player. Standalones are discussed in Chapter 27.

Chapter 25 will walk you through the process of optimizing your Flash movie, testing your movies within Flash, and using the new Flash 4 Publish commands that create pre-formatted HTML documents to display Flash movies. If you prefer to hard code your own HTML, and then jump to Chapter 26, where we'll show you to use <OBJECT> and <EMBED> tags for Flash movies. There, you'll also see how Flash movies can interact with JavaScript and DHTML to change the page attributes on the fly.

Exporting Shockwave Flash Movies

◆ ◆ ◆ ◆

In This Chapter

How to make your
Flash movies more
efficient

Testing modem
speeds with Flash
movies

Using the publish
features to create
instant Flash Web
pages

◆ ◆ ◆ ◆

If you have read the entire book up to this point, then you're probably more than ready to get your Flash movies uploaded to your Web server to share with your visitors. This chapter shows you how to export SWF files from Flash 4 so that your Flash movies can be played with the Flash Player plug-in for Web browsers.

Optimizing Flash Movies

Before you create a SWF file from your Flash editor document (.FLA file), you should read through this section to see if you can optimize your Flash movie. Optimizing can mean finding anything redundant in the final movie — extra points in a line, repeated artwork, and so on. As you should see, symbols are the key to eliminating unnecessary repetition with Flash artwork. Optimizing can also entail the restricted use of bandwidth-heavy items, such as bitmapped artwork or lengthy sound tracks.

Note

With Flash 4, Macromedia has decidedly dropped the term "Shockwave Flash" to refer to SWF files — even though SWF stands for Shockwave Flash. This chapter distinguishes Flash editor documents (.FLA files) from the exported counterpart, Shockwave Flash movies (.SWF files). Don't get confused by the usage of this term.

Simplify artwork

While Flash can do some pretty amazing things with vector shapes and animation, you don't want to overdo it — at least not if you want 28.8-modem users to see your work without too much waiting. Keep the following tips in mind while creating your Flash artwork or reviewing your final production:

✦ Use tweens for animations wherever possible. If you need complicated paths for objects to follow, use a motion guide layer instead of using a series of keyframes: The fewer keyframes, the better.

✦ Custom line types (such as dashed, dotted, ragged, and so on) take up more file space than regular solid lines. Strokes created with the Brush tool also use more memory than lines created with the Pencil tool.

✦ Reduce the number of points and/or lines used to create a shape. In Flash, you can use the Modify ➪ Curves ➪ Optimize command, which will join line segments in an object. Note that you need to ungroup any grouped lines to use this command. The Use Multiple Passes option will optimize the selection to the fullest extent possible.

Cross-Reference

For tips on optimizing vector artwork created outside of Flash, see Chapter 18.

✦ Group shapes and objects where applicable. Grouping objects enables Flash to refer to one item instead of many individual ones.

✦ Gradients are more complex than a solid fill for a computer processor to handle. Try to minimize the number of simultaneous gradients shown in any given frame. Gradients add about 50 more bytes to an SWF's file size than a solid color does.

✦ Don't use many different fonts (typefaces) or font styles (such as Oblique, Bold, Condensed, and so on) in your Flash movies. Most elegant designs use complementary typefaces that occur in the same typeface family, or use a balanced and restricted number of sans serif and serif fonts. Font characters can require a lot of file space, from 81 bytes to over 191 bytes *per character*. Generally, more elaborate serif fonts (such as Garamond) will take up more room per character than sans serif fonts (such as Arial). For text fields, make sure you embed only what is necessary from a font for the given field. For example, if a text field needs to use only lowercase characters of a font for a login or name field, then specify this in the Text Field Properties dialog box for that text field. Ultimately, use device fonts (_sans, _serif, and _typewriter) whenever possible, as they do not need their outlines stored in the SWF file.

✦ Keep bitmap or raster images to a minimum. Flash's strength is its vector-based technology. Animated bitmap sequences inflate your Shockwave Flash file sizes. Unless the content you are creating needs to be photo-realistic (as in a photographer's portfolio), don't use 24-bit color bitmaps.

Cross-Reference

If you want to mimic full-motion video effects in Flash with as little file overhead as possible, see Chapter 21. If you want to optimize bitmaps before you bring them into Flash, see Chapter 17.

Use symbols

Anything in Flash can be turned into a symbol. When the Flash movie is exported as a SWF file, the symbol's contents are stored on the first frame that uses that symbol. Symbol instances are similar to `<A HREF>` tags in HTML: they link data to a given frame, rather than copying or storing it there. Once a symbol's contents are downloaded to the Flash player, it is easily available for any subsequent re-use in the Flash movie. After you've completed a Flash movie, you want to review your Flash production and perform the following optimizations:

✦ If any element is used in more than one keyframe or scene, consider making a symbol out of it. Just about every professional Flash designer uses nested symbols: An element is drawn, made a symbol, and then used in another symbol such as a button or movie clip. Just like groups, symbol instances reduce the resource overhead in SWF files. Unlike groups, symbols need only refer to the original resource in the SWF file rather than storing a new resource for every occurrence of it. You can, however, make a grouped shape or object into a symbol.

✦ If you want to use the same shape in a variety of colors, make that shape a symbol and, for each instance of the symbol, use the Color Effects tab of the Instance Properties dialog box to change the color.

✦ The contents of a symbol are downloaded when the Flash Player encounters the first frame that uses the symbol. Given this, preload any graphics or sound intensive symbol by placing it near the front end of the first scene of the movie. Simply create a symbol instance of the symbol in the first few frames and set its visibility (via Alpha) to 0. If you using this method to preload a movie clip, set the instance's behavior to Graphic instead of Movie Clip — that way, the processor isn't trying to play an invisible movie clip in the background.

You can preload movies into a browser by using the If Frame Loaded action. See Chapter 14 for more information.

Manage the Flash Library

Bitmaps and sound files that have been imported into Flash automatically become items stored in the Flash Library. As later sections of this chapter show you, you can specify the sound quality of audio events and streams in the Export Movie or Publish Settings dialog boxes. However, these settings control the audio quality for the entire movie unless a specific encoding scheme is specified to individual sound clips in the Flash Library. Use the Library to assign specific compression methods to all imported media. For audio, Flash 4's new MP3 encoding provides the best compression to quality ratio available. Specify MP3 compression on as many sounds in the Flash Library as possible

Check out Chapter 7 and Chapter 12 for detailed information regarding compression of Flash media in the Library.

Testing Flash Movies

You have three ways to test your Flash movies: in the authoring environment of Flash 4 using the Test Movie and Scene commands, in a browser using the new Flash 4 Publish Preview command, or in the standalone Flash Player using Shockwave Flash files (.SWF) made with the Export Movie command. You have several reasons why you should test your Flash movie before you transfer Shockwave Flash files to your Web server (or to the intended delivery medium):

✦ Flash editor documents (.FLA files) have much larger file sizes than their Shockwave Flash movie (.SWF files) counterparts. In order to accurately foretell the network bandwidth a Flash movie requires, you need to know how large the final Shockwave Flash movie will be. If the download demand is too overwhelming for your desired Internet connection speed (as with a 28.8 modem), then you can go back and optimize your Flash movie.

✦ The Control ➪ Play command does not give any streaming information. When you use the Test Movie or Scene command, you can view the byte load of each frame, and how long it will take to download the SWF from the Web server.

✦ Movie clip animations and Tell Target commands cannot be previewed using the standard Control ➪ Play command (or the Play button on the Controller).

Tip   You can temporarily preview Movie Clip symbol instances within the Flash authoring environment (for example, the Timeline window) by changing the symbol instance behavior to Graphic instead of Movie Clip. Do this by accessing the symbol's Instance Properties dialog box (right-click or Ctrl+click the symbol on the stage, and select Properties) and selecting Graphic in the Behavior section of the Definition tab.

✦ Most scripting done with new Flash 4 actions, such as Set Property, Set Variable, and Drag Movie Clip, cannot be previewed with the Play command. Enabling Frame Actions or Buttons in the Control menu has no effect with new scripting actions.

✦ Any actions that require the use of remote CGI scripts to load variables and/or values of variables do not work unless the Flash movie is published as a Shockwave Flash movie and loaded into a Web browser. However, load variable commands can import name and value pairs from local text files.

✦ Accurate frame rates cannot be previewed with the Play command. Most complex animations appear jerky, pausing or skipping frames when the Play command is used.

Using the Test Scene or Movie command

You can test your Flash movies directly within the Flash 4 interface by using the Control ➪ Test Movie or Test Scene command. When you choose one of these commands, Flash opens your Flash movie in a new window *as a Shockwave Flash movie*. Even though you are only "testing" a Flash movie, a new SWF file is actually created and stored in the same location as the Flash editor document (.FLA file). For this reason, it is a good idea to always save your Flash editor document before you begin testing it.

Caution   If your movie is currently titled Movie1, Movie2, and so on in the application title bar (at the top of the application window), then it has not been saved yet. Make sure you give your Flash movie a distinctive name before testing it.

Before you use the Test Scene or Movie command, you need to specify the properties of the resulting Shockwave Flash movie. The Test Scene or Movie command uses the specifications outlined in the Publish Settings dialog box to generate SWF files. The Publish Settings dialog box is discussed later in this chapter. For the time being, we can use the Flash 4 default settings to explore the Test Scene and Movie commands.

New Feature   Flash 4 no longer has the Control ➪ Settings command that was available in Flash 3. We have no idea why this was done. At any rate, if you were looking for this quick shortcut to specify Test Movie or Scene settings, look no further. You now have to use Publish Settings.

Test Movie

When you choose Control ➪ Test Movie (Command+Return or Ctrl+Return), Flash 4 generates a SWF file of the entire Flash editor document (.FLA file) that is currently open. If you have more than one Flash movie open, Flash creates a SWF file for the one that is currently in the foreground and/or "focused."

Test Scene

If you are working on a lengthy Flash movie with multiple scenes, you want to test your scenes individually. By using Control ➪ Test Scene (Option+Command+Return or Ctrl+Alt+Return), you can do this. The process of exporting entire movies via Test Movie may require many minutes to complete, whereas exporting one scene will require a significantly smaller amount of time. As is shown in the next section, you can analyze each tested scene (or movie) with the Bandwidth Profiler.

How to use the Bandwidth Profiler

Do you want to know how long it will take for a 28.8 modem to download your Flash movie or scene? How about a 36.6 modem? 56K modem? Even a cable modem? The Bandwidth Profiler enables you to simulate any download speed.

In the ch25 folder of the *Flash 4 Bible* CD-ROM, you can find an FLA file called bandwidth.fla. We'll be using this Flash movie for this section (see Figure 25-1).

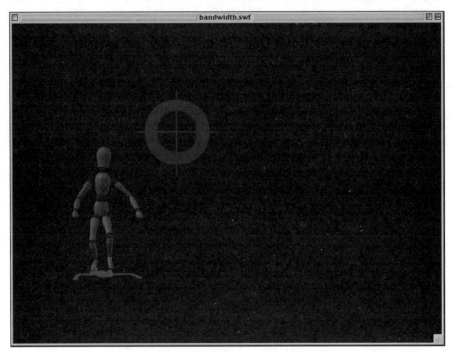

Figure 25-1: This is the bandwidth.fla Flash movie converted into a test SWF file.

To use the Bandwidth Profiler, you first need to create a test movie or scene. When you create an SWF file with the Control ➪ Test Movie or Scene commands, Flash opens the SWF file in its own window.

View menu

The Test Movie or Scene viewing environment changes the View and Control menus. The first four commands in the View menu are the same as the Flash Player plug-in viewing controls:

✦ **100% (Command+1 or Ctrl+1):** This command displays the SWF movie at the original pixel size specified in the Modify ➪ Movie dialog box. For example, if the movie size is 500×300 pixels, it takes up 500×300 pixels on your monitor. If you change the size of the viewing window, the movie may be cropped.

✦ **Show All (Command+3 or Ctrl+3):** This command shrinks or enlarges the Flash movie to fit the current viewing window size.

✦ **Zoom In:** Selecting this option enlarges the Flash movie.

✦ **Zoom Out:** Selecting this option shrinks the Flash movie.

✦ **Bandwidth Profiler:** To view the Bandwidth Profiler in this new window, use View ➪ Bandwidth Profiler (Command+B or Ctrl+B). The SWF movie shrinks to accommodate the Bandwidth Profiler (see Figure 25-2).

  • The left side of the profiler displays three sections: Movie, Settings, and State. Movie indicates the dimensions, frame rate, size (in KB and bytes), duration and preload (in number of frames and seconds).

  • The larger right section of the profiler shows the Timeline header and graph. The lower red line beneath the Timeline header indicates whether a given frame streams in real-time with the current modem speed specified in the Control menu. For a 28.8 modem, any frame above 200 bytes may cause delays in streaming.

  • When the Bandwidth Profiler is enabled, two other commands are available in the View menu: Streaming Graph (Command+G or Ctrl+G) and Frame By Frame Graph (Command+F or Ctrl+F).

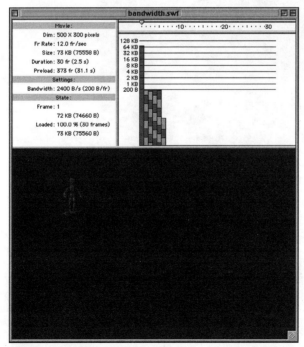

Figure 25-2: The Bandwidth Profiler provides movie-, frame-, and file-size information.

✦ **Streaming Graph:** By default, Flash opens the Bandwidth Profiler in Streaming Graph mode. This mode indicates how the Flash movie streams into a browser (see Figure 25-3). Alternating light and dark gray blocks represent each frame. The size of each block indicates its relative byte size. Remembering what was said earlier in the chapter, a symbol's contents are stored in the first frame that uses it. With the bandwidth.swf example, both bandwidth-intensive symbols (for example, the running bitmapped mannequin and the 3D rotating cross-hairs) occur on the first frame. The remaining frames, 2 through 30, will stream by the time frame 7 is played.

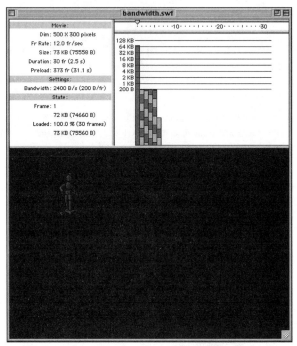

Figure 25-3: The Streaming Graph indicates how a movie will download over a given modem connection.

✦ **Frame-By-Frame Graph:** This second mode available to the Bandwidth Profiler lays each frame side by side under the Timeline header (see Figure 25-4). While the Streaming Graph enables you to see the real-time performance of an SWF movie, the Frame-By-Frame Graph enables you to more easily detect which frames are contributing to streaming delays. If any frame block goes beyond the red line of the graph, then the Flash Player halts playback until the entire frame downloads. In the bandwidth.swf example, frame 1 is the only frame causing a significant delay in streaming. The remaining frames require very little bandwidth — well below the 200 byte maximum per frame limitation of 28.8 modems.

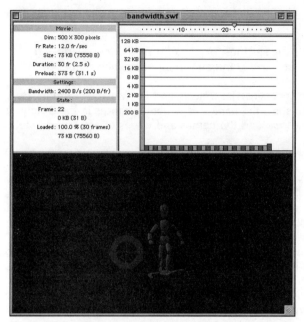

Figure 25-4: The Frame-By-Frame Graph shows you the byte-demand of each frame in the Flash movie.

Control menu

Use the Control menu to play (Return) or rewind (Option+Command+R or Ctrl+Alt+R) the test movie. Rewinding pauses the bandwidth.swf movie on the first frame. Use the Step Forward (>) and Step Backward (<) commands to view the Flash movie frame by frame. If a Flash movie doesn't have a Stop action on the last frame, the Loop command forces the player to infinitely repeat the Flash movie.

The Control menu also features commands that work in tandem with the Streaming and Frame-By-Frame Graphs:

✦ **Show Streaming:** When Show Streaming is enabled, the Bandwidth Profiler emulates the chosen modem speed (also in the Control menu) when playing the Flash movie. The Bandwidth Profiler counts up the bytes downloaded (displayed in the Loaded: subsection of the State heading), and shows the download/play progress via a green bar in the Timeline header.

✦ **14.4, 28.8, 56K:** These settings determine what speed the Bandwidth Profiler uses to calculate estimated download times and frame byte limitations. Notice that these settings use more practical expectations of these modem speeds. For example, a 28.8 modem can theoretically download 3.5 kilobytes by sec (KB/s), but a more realistic download rate for this modem speed is 2.3KB/s.

✦ **User Settings 4, 5 and 6:** These are user-definable speed settings. By default, they are all 2.3KB/s.

✦ **Customize:** To change the settings for any of the modem speeds listed previously, use the Customize command to input the new value(s).

Note   The Control menu also contains List Objects and List Variables commands. List Objects can be used to show the names of symbol instances in the Output window, while List Variables displays the names and values of any currently loaded variables.

Using the size report

Flash also lets you view a text file summary of movie elements, frames, and fonts called a size report. In addition to viewing frame-by-frame graphs of a Flash movie with the Bandwidth Profiler, you can inspect this size report for other "hidden" byte additions such as font character outlines. This report can only be generated when using the Export Movie or Publish commands.

On the   A sample size report, called bandwidth_report.txt, is included in the ch25 folder of
CD-ROM   the *Flash 4 Bible* CD-ROM.

Publishing Your Flash Movies

After you've made a dazzling Flash movie complete with motion tweens, 3D simulations and ActionScripted interactivity, you need to make the Flash movie usable for the intended delivery medium — the Web, a CD-ROM (or floppy disk!), a QuickTime movie or a template for Macromedia Generator, to name a few. As we mentioned in the introduction to this book, you need the Flash 4 application to open FLA files. Because the majority of your intended audience won't have the full Flash 4 application, you need to export or publish your FLA movie in a format that your audience can use.

A Word about the Export Movie Command

Even though Flash 4 has incredibly streamlined the process of creating SWF movies with the Publish commands (discussed in the next section), it is worth mentioning that the File ⇨ Export Movie command provides the most direct route to creating a simple SWF file. While the Publish command is the quickest way to create HTML-ready Flash movies, the Export Movie command can be used to create updated SWF files that have already been placed in HTML documents, or Flash movies that you intend to import into Macromedia Director movies (see Chapter 24).

You can convert your Flash movie (.FLA) files (also known as Flash editor documents) to Shockwave Flash movie (.SWF) files by using either the File ⇨ Export Movie or File ⇨ Publish/Publish Settings commands. The latter command is Flash 4's brand-new Publish feature that replaces Aftershock, the standalone HTML-formatting application that shipped with Flash 2 and 3. The Publish feature offers many more options than Aftershock did. Previously, turning your Flash movies into Shockwave Flash movies (embedded in preformatted HTML) was a two-step process: First, export the Flash SWF file using the Export Movie command, and then open Aftershock, a separate application, to specify HTML specifications for placing the SWF file on a Web page. Now, you can specify just about all file format properties in one step using the File ⇨ Publish Settings command. Once you've entered the settings, the File ⇨ Publish command exports any and all file formats with your specified parameters in one step—all within the Flash 4 application.

Cross-Reference The Export Movie command is discussed throughout the book. For more information on exporting still images in raster/bitmap formats, see Chapter 17. To export vector formats, see Chapter 18. To export QuickTime or AVI files, see Chapters 21 and 22.

Three commands are available with the Publish feature: Publish Settings, Publish Preview, and Publish. Each of these commands is discussed in the following sections.

Publish Settings

The Publish Settings command (File ⇨ Publish Settings) is used to determine which file formats are exported when the File ⇨ Publish command is invoked. By default, Flash 4 ships with Publish Settings that will export a Shockwave Flash (.SWF) file and an HTML file with the proper markup tags to utilize the Flash plug-in. If you want to customize the settings of the exported file types, you should familiarize yourself with the Publish Settings before you attempt to use the Publish command.

Selecting formats

Select File ⇨ Publish Settings to access the Publish Settings dialog box, which is nearly identical for both PC and Mac. The dialog box opens to the Formats tab, which has check boxes to select the formats in which your Flash movie will be published (see Figure 25-5). For each Type that is checked, a tab appears in the Publish Settings dialog box. Click each type's tab to specify settings to control the particulars of the movie or file that will be generated in that format.

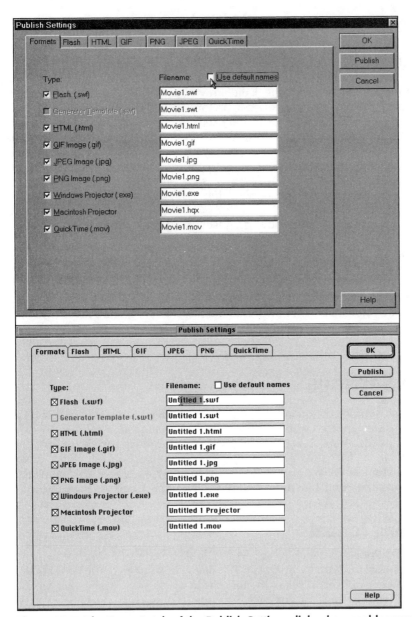

Figure 25-5: The Formats tab of the Publish Settings dialog box enables you to select the published file formats and to use default or custom names for these published files.

The Use Default Names check box either enables or disables default names (disabled means that the Filename entry boxes will be unavailable or grayed out). For example, if your movie is named intro.fla, then, if Use default names is selected, this is the base from which the names are generated in publishing. Thus, intro.swf, intro.html, intro.gif, and so on would result.

Using the Flash settings

The primary and default publishing format of Flash 4 movies is the Shockwave Flash (.SWF) format. Only SWF movies retain full support for Flash 4 actions and animations.

Here are your options:

✦ **Load Order:** This option determines how Flash will draw the first frame of the Flash movie as it is downloaded to the plug-in or player. When Bottom Up (default) is chosen, the layers load in ascending order: The lowest layer displays first, then the second lowest, and so on, until all of the layers for the first frame have been displayed. When Top Down is selected, the layers load in descending order: The top-most layer displays first, then the layer underneath it, and so on. Again, this option only affects the display of the first frame of a Flash movie. If the content of the first frame is downloaded or streamed quickly, you probably shouldn't notice the Load Order's effect.

✦ **Generate size report:** As discussed earlier in this chapter, the size report for a Flash movie can be very useful in pinpointing problematic bandwidth-intensive elements, such as font characters. When this option is checked, the Publish command exports a SimpleText (Mac) or TXT file (PC) to view separately in a text editor application.

✦ **Protect from import:** This option will safeguard your Flash SWF files on the Internet. When enabled, the SWF file cannot be imported back into the Flash 4 authoring environment, or altered in any way. Note that this option, when enabled, will *not* prevent Director 7.0.2 from importing and using SWF files. Also, hacking utilities called *swiffers* can break into any SWF file and extract artwork, sounds and ActionScripted code. Did you know that even Notepad can open SWF files and see variable names and values of those variables? For this reason, you should always use CGI scripts to "check" password entries in Flash movies, rather internal ActionScripted password checking. Don't store sensitive information such as passwords in your source files!

✦ **Omit Trace Actions:** When this option is selected, the Flash player ignores any trace actions used in Flash ActionScripting. Trace actions will open the Flash Output window for debugging purposes. In general, if you used Trace actions, you will want to omit them from the final SWF file—they can't be viewed in the Flash Player anyway.

✦ **JPEG Quality:** This slider and text field option specifies the level of JPEG compression applied to bitmapped artwork in the Flash movie. The value can be any value between (and including) 0 to 100. Higher values apply less compression and preserve more information of the original bitmap, whereas lower values apply more compression and keep less information. The value entered here applies to all bitmaps that enable the Use Document Default Quality option, found in the Bitmap Properties dialog box for each bitmap in the Flash Library. Unlike the audio settings discussed in a moment, no "override" option exists to disregard settings in the Flash Library.

✦ **Audio Stream:** This option displays the current audio compression scheme for Stream audio. By clicking the Set button (see Figure 25-6), you can control the compression applied to any sounds that use the "Stream" Sync setting in the Sound tab of the Frame Properties dialog box. Like the JPEQ Quality option discussed previously, this compression value is applied to any Stream sounds that use the Default compression in the Export Settings section of each audio file's Sound Properties dialog box in the Flash Library. See Chapter 11 for more information on using Stream sounds, and Chapters 10 and 12 for more information on audio compression schemes.

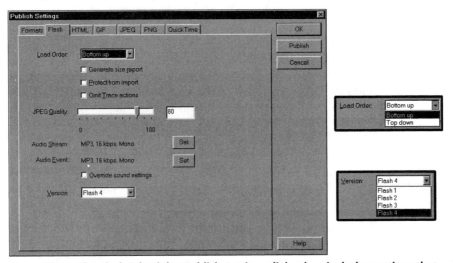

Figure 25-6: The Flash tab of the Publish Settings dialog box includes settings that control the many particulars of a movie published in the Flash format.

✦ **Audio Event:** This setting behaves exactly the same as the Audio Stream option, except that this compression setting applies to Default compression-enabled Event sounds. See Chapter 11 for more information on Event sounds.

New Feature

As discussed in Part III, Flash 4 has added MP3 audio encoding schemes to SWF movies. Use this compression type when you want maximum high-fidelity music with the smallest file size. This does not mean you cannot achieve smaller file sizes with other encodings. Rather, MP3 has one of the best quality-to-file size ratios available.

✦ **Override sound settings:** If you want the settings for Audio Stream and Audio Event to apply to all Stream and Event sounds, respectively, and disregard any unique compression schemes specified in the Flash Library, then check this option. This is useful for creating multiple SWF versions of the Flash movie (hi-fi, lo-fi, and so on) and enabling the Web visitor to decide which one to download. See Figure 25-7.

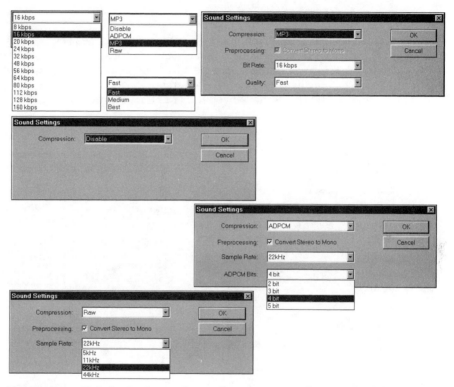

Figure 25-7: Click the Set button for Audio Stream or Audio Event and the Sound Settings dialog box appears.

✦ **Version:** This drop-down menu provides the option to publish movies in any of the Flash SWF formats. To ensure complete compatibility with all of the new Flash 4 features, select Flash 4. Flash 1 and 2 support only basic anima-tion and interactive functions. Flash 3 will support just about all animation and artwork created in Flash 4, but doesn't recognize any of the new Actions, editable text fields (such as form elements), or MP3 audio available in the Flash 4 SWF format. If in doubt, you should test your choice of version in the Flash Player.

When you are finished entering the settings for the SWF movie, you can proceed to other file type settings in the Publish Settings dialog box. Or, you can click OK to go back to the authoring environment of Flash 4 so that you can use the newly entered settings in the Test Movie or Scene environment. You can also export an SWF file (and other file formats currently selected in Publish Settings) by clicking the Publish button.

Using the HTML settings

HTML is the language in which the layout of most Web pages is written. The HTML tab of the Publish Settings dialog box has a number of settings that control the way in which Flash will publish a movie into a complete Web page with the HTML format. As you may have guessed, the Aftershock options (from the separate utility that shipped with Flash 3) have been integrated into this area of Publish Settings. See Figure 25-8.

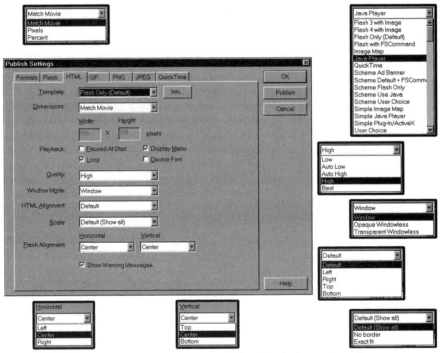

Figure 25-8: The HTML settings tab controls flexible Flash movie options—you can change this options without permanently affecting the Flash SWF movie.

✦ **Template:** Perhaps the most important (and versatile) feature of all Publish Settings, the Template setting enables you to select a predefined set of HTML tags to display your Flash movies. To view the description of each template, click the Info button to the right of the drop-down list (shown in Figure 25-8). All templates use the same options listed in the HTML dialog box — the template simply places the values of those settings into HTML tags scripted in the template. You can also create your own custom templates for your own unique implementation of Flash movies. See the *Flash 4 Bible* Web site at www.theFlashBible.com/ch25 for more information on creating your own templates for Flash 4. See Figure 25-9.

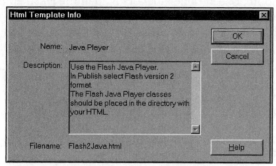

Figure 25-9: Clicking the Info button shown in Figure 25-8 summons a brief description of the HTML template that has been specified in the Template drop-down list.

Tip

You can view the "source" of each template in the HTML folder of the Flash 4 application folder. Although these template files have.html extensions, use Notepad (PC) or SimpleText (Mac) to view the files. All of the preinstalled templates include HTML tags to create an entire Web page, complete with <HEAD>, <TITLE>, and <BODY> tags.

- **Flash 3 with Image:** This template adds the necessary JavaScript to detect if the Flash Player plug-in (version 3) is installed. You need to specify a version 3 SWF file in the Version option of the Flash tab in Publish Settings, as well as a GIF or JPEG image (check either file type in the Formats tab in Publish Settings). See the section on GIF or JPEG image export later in this chapter for more information.

- **Flash 4 with Image:** Same as Flash 3 with Image, except that the JavaScript detects if version 4 of the Flash Player plug-in is installed, and you need to specify a version 4 SWF file in the Publish Settings' Flash tab.

- **Flash Only (Default):** This template simply inserts the <OBJECT> and <EMBED> tags for the Flash movie. It does not perform any browser or plug-in detection.

- **Flash with FSCommand:** Use this template if you are using the `FSCommand` action in your Flash movies to communicate with JavaScript in the HTML page. The `FSCommand` is discussed in the next chapter. The necessary `<OBJECT>` and `<EMBED>` tags from the Flash Only (Default) template are also included.

- **Image Map:** This template does not use or display any SWF movie. Rather, it uses a GIF, JPEG, or PNG image (as specified in the Publish Settings' Format tab) as a client-side image map, via an `<IMG>` tag with a `USEMAP` attribute. Use a frame label of #map in the Flash editor document (.FLA file) to designate which frame is used as the map image. See "Using the GIF Settings" later in this chapter for more details.

- **Java Player:** Instead of using the Flash Player or an image map, this template creates the necessary `<APPLET>` tags to utilize the Flash Java Player. To use this player, you must select the Publish Settings' Flash tab and specify a version 2 SWF format. The Flash Java Player needs to access Java class files (found in the Players folder of the Flash 4 application folder). Make sure you have uploaded the class files to your Web server. You may need to add a `CODEBASE=[URL of class files]` to the `<APPLET>` tag created by this template.

- **QuickTime:** This template creates an `<EMBED>` tag to display QuickTime Flash movies. You need to enable the QuickTime file type in the Publish Settings' Format tab. A QuickTime Flash movie is a new type of Quick-Time movie, playable with QuickTime 4 or higher. Currently, QuickTime 4 can only recognize Flash 3 features. Select the Flash tab in Publish Settings to export version 3 SWF files. Note that, depending on the options selected in the QuickTime tab of Publish Settings, the Flash movie may or may not be stored within the QuickTime movie file. See Chapter 21, "Working with QuickTime," for more information.

- **User Choice:** Often the scripter's testing tool, this template creates a HTML document with Flash 4 plug-in detection and a JavaScript cookie that enables you to choose three loading options for the Flash SWF file: automatic plug-in detection, standard plug-in usage (via direct non-JavaScript written `<OBJECT>` or `<EMBED>` tags), or substitute image (for example, GIF, JPEG, or PNG).

✦ **Dimensions:** This setting controls the `WIDTH` and `HEIGHT` values of the `<OBJECT>` and `<EMBED>` tags. Note that the dimension settings here do not change the original SWF movie. They simply create the viewport through which your Flash movie is viewed on the Web page. The way that the Flash movie "fits" into this viewport is determined with the Scale option (discussed later). Three input areas exist: a drop-down menu and two text fields for `WIDTH` and `HEIGHT`.

- **Match Movie:** If you want to keep the same WIDTH and HEIGHT that you specified in the Modify ⇨ Movie dialog box, then use this option in the drop-down menu.

- **Pixels:** You can change the viewing size (in pixel units) of the Flash movie window by selecting this option and entering new values in the Width and Height text fields.

- **Percent:** By far one of the most popular options with Flash movies, Percent scales the movie to the size of the browser window — or a portion of it. Using a value of 100 on both Width and Height expands the Flash movie to fit the entire browser window.

- **Width and Height:** Enter the values for the Flash movie width and height here. If Match Movie is selected, you shouldn't be able to enter any values. The unit of measurement is determined by selecting either Pixels or Percent from the drop-down menu.

✦ **Playback:** These options control how the Flash movie plays when it is downloaded to the browser. Each of these options has an <OBJECT> and <EMBED> attribute if you want to control them outside of Publish Settings. Note that these attributes are not viewable within the Publish Settings dialog box — you'll need to load the published HTML document into a text editor to see the attributes.

- **Paused at Start:** This is equivalent to adding a Stop action on the first frame of the first scene in the Flash movie. By default, this option is off — movies play as soon as they stream into the player. A button with a Play action can start the movie, or the Play command can be executed from the Flash Player shortcut menu (by right-clicking or Ctrl-clicking the movie). *Attribute:* PLAY=TRUE or FALSE. If PLAY=TRUE, then the movie will play as soon as it is loaded.

- **Loop:** This option causes the Flash movie to repeat an infinite number of times. By default, this option is on. If it is not checked, the Flash movie stops on the last frame unless some other ActionScripted event is initiated on the last frame. *Attribute:* LOOP=TRUE or FALSE.

- **Display Menu:** This option controls whether the person viewing the Flash movie in the Flash Player environment can access the shortcut menu via a right-click (PC) or Ctrl-click (Mac) anywhere within the movie area. If this option is checked, then the visitor can select Zoom In/Out, 100%, Show All, High Quality, Play, Loop, Rewind, Forward, and Back from the menu. If this option is not checked, then the visitor can only select About Flash Player from the menu. *Attribute:* MENU=TRUE or FALSE.

- **Device Font:** This option only applies to Flash movie played in the Windows version of the Flash Player. When enabled, this option replaces fonts that are not installed on the Player's system with antialiased system fonts. *Attribute:* DEVICEFONT=TRUE or FALSE.

✦ **Quality:** This menu determines how the Flash artwork in a movie will render. While it would be ideal to play all Flash movies at high quality, slower processors may not be able to redraw antialiased artwork and keep up with the frame rate.

- **Low:** This setting forces the Flash Player to turn off antialiasing (smooth edges) completely. On slower processors, this may improve playback performance. *Attribute:* QUALITY=LOW.

- **Auto Low:** This setting starts in Low quality mode (no antialiasing), but will switch to High quality if the computer's processor can handle the playback speed. *Attribute:* QUALITY=AUTOLOW.

- **Auto High:** This setting is the opposite of Auto Low. The Flash Player starts playing the movie in High quality mode, but, if the processor cannot handle the playback demands, then it switches to Low quality mode. For most Web sites, this is the optimal setting to use because it favors higher quality first. *Attribute:* QUALITY=AUTOHIGH.

- **High:** When this setting is used, the Flash Player gives preference to the visual display of the movie. All vector artwork is antialiased. Bitmaps are smoothed unless they are contained within an animation sequence such as a motion tween. By default, this setting is selected in the HTML tab of the Publish Settings dialog box. *Attribute:* QUALITY=HIGH.

- **Best:** This mode does everything that High quality does, with the addition of smoothing all bitmaps — regardless of whether they are in motion tweens. This mode is the most processor-intensive. *Attribute:* QUALITY=BEST.

✦ **Window Mode:** As discussed in "Animation Techniques Using Layers" section of Chapter 24, the Window Mode setting only works with the Flash ActiveX control. Therefore, it only applies to 32-bit Windows versions of Internet Explorer. If you intend to deliver to this browser, then you can animate Flash content on top of DHTML content. Refer to Chapter 24 for more information. *Attribute:* WMODE=WINDOW or OPAQUE or TRANSPARENT.

✦ **HTML Alignment:** This setting works much like the ALIGN attribute of <IMG> tags in HTML documents — but it's used with the ALIGN attribute of the <OBJECT> and <EMBED> tags for the Flash movie. Note that these settings may not have any effect when used within a table cell (<TD> tag) or a DHTML layer (<DIV> or <LAYER> tag).

- **Default:** This option horizontally centers the Flash movie in the browser window. If the browser window is smaller than a Flash movie that uses a Pixel or Match Movie dimensions setting (see Dimensions setting earlier in this section), then the Flash movie will be cropped.

- **Left, Right, Top, and Bottom:** These options align the Flash movie along the left, right, top, or bottom edge of the browser window, respectively.

✦ **Scale:** This setting works in tandem with the Dimensions setting discussed earlier in this section, and determines how the Flash movie displays on the HTML page. Just as big screen movies must be cropped to fit the aspect ratio of a TV screen, Flash movies may need to be modified to fit the area prescribed by the Dimensions setting.

- **Default (Show all):** This option fits the entire Flash movie into the area defined by the Dimensions setting without distorting the original aspect ratio of the Flash movie. However, borders may appear on two sides of the Flash movie. For example, if a 300×300 pixel window is specified in Dimensions and the Flash movie has an aspect ratio of 1.33:1 (for example, 400×300 pixels), then a border fills the remaining areas on top of and below the Flash movie. This is similar to a "letterboxed" effect on wide-screen video rentals. *Attribute:* SCALE=SHOWALL.

- **No border:** This option forces the Flash movie to fill the area defined by the Dimensions setting without leaving borders. The Flash movie's aspect ratio is not distorted or stretched. However, this may crop two sides of the Flash movie. Using the same example from Show All, the left and right sides of the Flash movie are cropped when No Border is selected. *Attribute:* SCALE=NOBORDER.

- **Exact fit:** This option stretches a Flash movie to fill the entire area defined by the Dimensions setting. Using the same example from Show All, the 400×300 Flash movie is scrunched to fit a 300×300 window. If the original movie showed a perfect circle, it now appears as an oval. *Attribute:* SCALE=EXACTFIT.

✦ **Flash Alignment:** This setting adjusts the SALIGN attribute of the <OBJECT> and <EMBED> tags for the Flash movie. In contrast to the HTML Alignment setting, Flash Alignment works in conjunction with the Scale and Dimensions settings and determines how a Flash movie is aligned within the Player window.

- **Horizontal:** These options, Left, Center, and Right, determine if the Flash movie is horizontally aligned to the left, center or right of the Dimensions area, respectively. Using the same example from the Scale setting, a 400×300 pixel Flash movie (fit into a 300×300 Dimension window with SCALE=NOBORDER) with a Flash Horizontal Alignment setting of Left crops only the right side of the Flash movie.

- **Vertical:** These options, Top, Center, and Bottom, determine if the Flash movie is vertically aligned to the top, center, or bottom of the Dimensions area, respectively. If the previous example used a Show All Scale setting and had a Flash Vertical Alignment setting of Top, then the border only occurs below the bottom edge of the Flash movie.

✦ **Show Warning Messages:** This useful feature alerts you to errors during the actual Publish process. For example, if you selected the Image Map template and didn't specify a static GIF, JPEG, or PNG file in the Formats tab, then Flash returns an error. By default, this option is enabled. If it is disabled, then Flash suppresses any warnings during the Publish process.

Using the GIF settings

The GIF (Graphics Interchange File) format, developed by CompuServe, defined the first generation of Web graphics, and is still quite popular today, despite its 256-color limitation. In the context of the Flash Publish Settings, the GIF format is used to export a static or animated image that can be used in place of the Flash movie if the Flash Player or plug-in is not installed. While the Flash and HTML tabs are specific to Flash movie display and playback, the settings of the GIF tab control the characteristics of a GIF animation (or still image) which Flash will publish. See Figure 25-10.

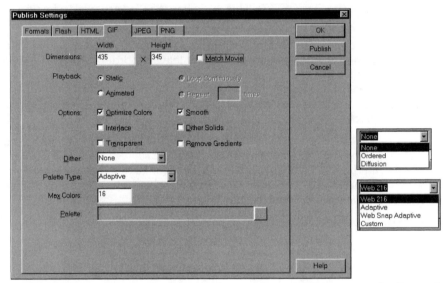

Figure 25-10: Every subtle aspect of a GIF animation or still image can be finessed with these settings of the GIF tab of the Publish Settings dialog box.

✦ **Dimensions:** This setting has three options: Width, Height, and Match Movie. As you might surmise, Width and Height control the dimensions of the GIF image. These fields are enabled only when the Match Movie check box is unchecked. With Match Movie checked, the dimensions of the GIF match those of the Flash Movie that is being published. Unlike the Width and Height settings for a Flash movie (with default Scale options), changing the Width and Height of a GIF image distorts the aspect ratio.

✦ **Playback:** These radio buttons control what type of GIF image is created, and how it plays (if Animated is chosen).

   • **Static:** If this button is selected, then Flash exports the first frame of the Flash movie as a single still image in the GIF format. If you want to use a different frame other than the first frame, use a frame label of #Static on the desired frame. Alternatively, you could use the File ➪ Export Image command to export a GIF image from whatever frame the Current Frame Indicator is positioned over.

- **Animated:** If this button is selected, then Flash exports the entire Flash movie as animated GIF file (in the GIF89a format). If you don't want to export the entire movie as an animated GIF (indeed, a GIF file for a Flash movie with over 100 frames would be most likely too large to download easily over the Web), you can designate a range of frames to export. Use a frame label of #First on the beginning frame of a given range of frames. Next, add a frame label of #Last to the ending frame of the desired sequence of frames. Flash actually does a pretty good at optimizing animated GIFs by only saving areas that change over time in each frame — instead of the entire frame.

- **Loop Continuously:** When the Animated radio button is selected, you can specify that the animated GIF repeats an infinite number of times by selecting the Loop Continuously radio button.

- **Repeat __ times:** This option can be used to set up an animated that repeats a given number of times. If you don't want the animated GIF to repeat continuously, then enter the number of repetitions here.

✦ **Options:** The options in the Options settings control the creation of the GIF's color table and how the GIF is displayed by the browser.

- **Optimize Colors:** When you are using any palette type other than Adaptive, this option removes any colors preexisting in the Web 216 or custom palettes that are not used by the GIF image. Enabling this option can only save you precious bytes used in file overhead — it has no effect on the actual quality of the image. Most images do not use all 216 colors of the Web palette. For example, a black and white picture can only use between three and ten colors from the 216 palette.

- **Interlace:** This option makes the GIF image download in incrementing resolutions. As the image downloads, the image becomes sharper with each successive "scan." Use of this option is usually personal preference. Some people like to use it for image maps that can provide basic navigation information before the entire image downloads.

- **Smooth:** This option antialiases the Flash artwork as it exports to the GIF image. Text may look better when it is antialiased, but may want to test this option for your particular use. If you need to make a transparent GIF, then smoothing may produce unsightly edges.

- **Dither Solids:** This option determines if solid areas of color (such as fills) are dithered. In this context, this type of dithering would create a two-color pattern to mimic a solid color that doesn't occur in the GIF's color palette. See the discussion of dithering later in this section.

- **Remove Gradients:** Flash gradients do not translate or display very well in 256 or less colors. Use this option to convert all Flash gradients to solid colors. The solid color is determined by the first color prescribed in the gradient. Unless you developed your gradients with this effect in mind, this option may produce undesirable results.

✦ **Transparent:** This setting controls the appearance of the Flash movie background, as well as any Flash artwork that uses alpha settings. Because GIF images only support one level of transparency (that is, the transparent area can not be antialiased), you need to exercise caution when using this setting. The Threshold option is only available if Alpha is selected.

- **Opaque:** This option produces a GIF image with a solid background.

  The image has a rectangular shape.

- **Transparent:** This option makes the Flash movie background appear transparent. If the Smooth option in the Options setting is enabled, then Flash artwork may display halos over the background HTML color.

- **Alpha and Threshold:** When the Alpha option is selected in the drop-down menu, you can control at what alpha level Flash artwork becomes transparent by entering a value in the Threshold text field. For example, if you enter **128**, then all alphas at 50 percent become completely transparent. If you are considering an animated GIF that has Flash artwork fading in or out, then you probably want to use the Opaque transparent option. If Alpha and Threshold were used, then the fade effect would be lost.

✦ **Dither:** Dithering is the process of emulating a color by juxtaposing two colors in a pattern arrangement. Because GIF images are limited to 256 colors (or less), dithering can often produce better-looking images for continuous tone artwork such as gradients. However, Flash's dithering seems to work best with the Web 216 palette. Dithering can increase the file size of a GIF image.

- **None:** This option does not apply any dithering to the GIF image.

- **Ordered:** This option applies an intermediate level of dithering with minimal file size overhead.

- **Diffusion:** This option applies the best level of dithering to the GIF image, but with larger file size overhead. Diffusion dithering only has a noticeable effect when the Web 216 palette is chosen in Palette Type.

✦ **Palette Type:** As mentioned earlier in this section, GIF images are limited to 256 or less colors. However, this grouping of 256 is arbitrary: Any set of 256 (or less) colors can be used for a given GIF image. This setting enables you to select predefined sets of colors to use on the GIF image. See Chapter 2 for more information on the Web color palette.

- **Web 216:** When this option is selected, the GIF image only uses colors from the limited 216 Web color palette. For most Flash artwork, this should produce acceptable results. However, it may not render Flash gradients or photographic bitmaps very well.

- **Adaptive:** With this option selected, Flash creates a unique set of 256 colors (or fewer, if specified in the Max Colors setting) for the GIF image. However, these adapted colors fall outside of the Web-safe color palette. File sizes for adaptive GIFs are larger than Web 216 GIFs, unless few colors are chosen in the Max Colors setting. Adaptive GIFs look much better than Web 216 GIFs, but may not display very well with 8-bit video cards and monitors.

- **Web Snap Adaptive:** This option tries to give the GIF image the best of both worlds. Flash converts any colors close to the 216 Web palette to Web-safe colors and uses adaptive colors for the rest. This palette produces better results than the Adaptive palette for older display systems that used 8-bit video cards.

- **Custom:** When this option is selected, you can specify a palette that uses the .ACT file format to be used as the GIF image's palette. Macromedia Fireworks and Adobe Photoshop can export color palettes (or color look-up tables) as ACT files.

In the Mac version of Flash 4, the Adaptive palette is hardly adaptive. Our tests revealed that Flash did not apply dithering to published GIFs that used any of the dithering options — every test image appeared blotchy and undithered. However, when the same frame was exported as a GIF image using the File ⇨ Export Image command (with GIF as the file type), Flash did produce GIF images with true adaptive palettes. On the PC version of Flash 4, the same frame published (or exported) as a GIF image with no problems — the Adaptive palette rendered a photographic bitmap very nicely.

✦ **Max Colors:** With this setting, you can specify exactly how many colors are in the GIF's color table. This numeric entry field is only enabled when Adaptive or Web Snap Adaptive is selected in the Palette Type drop-down menu.

✦ **Palette:** This text field and "..." browse button are only enabled when Custom is selected in the Palette Type drop-down menu. When enabled, this dialog box is used to locate and load a palette file from the hard drive.

Using the JPEG settings

The JPEG (Joint Photographic Experts Group) format is just as popular as the GIF format on the Web. Unlike GIF images, though, JPEG images can use much more than 256 colors. In fact, JPEG files must be 24-bit color (or full-color RGB) images. While GIF files use lossless compression (within the actual file itself), JPEG images use lossy compression, which means that color information is discarded in order to save file space. However, JPEG compression is very good. Even at its lowest quality settings, JPEG images can preserve quite a bit of detail in photographic images.

Another significant difference between GIF and JPEG is the fact that GIF images do not require nearly as much memory (for equivalent image dimensions) as JPEG images do. You need to remember that JPEG images "uncompress" when they are downloaded to your computer. While the file sizes may be small initially, they still open as full-color images in the computer's memory. For example, even though you may get the file size of a 400×300 pixel JPEG image down to 10KB, it still requires nearly 352KB in memory when it is opened or displayed.

Flash publishes the first frame of the Flash movie as the JPEG image, unless a #Static frame label is given to another frame in the Flash movie. The limited settings of the JPEG tab of the Publish Settings dialog box (see Figure 25-11) control the few variables of this still photo-quality image format:

✦ **Dimensions:** This setting behaves the same as the GIF Dimensions setting. Width and Height control the dimensions of the movie. But these fields are enabled only when the Match Movie check box is unchecked. With Match Movie checked, the dimensions of the JPEG match those of the Flash Movie.

✦ **Quality:** This slider and text field work exactly the same way as the JPEG Quality setting in the Flash tab of Publish Settings. Higher values apply less compression and result in better quality, but create images with larger file sizes.

✦ **Progressive:** This option is similar to the Interlaced option for GIF images. When enabled, the JPEG image loads in successive scans, becoming sharper with each pass.

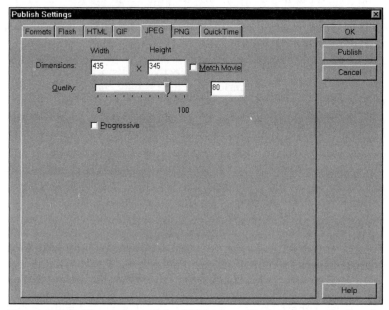

Figure 25-11: The settings of the JPEG tab are limited due to the fact that JPEGs are still images with relatively few variables to be addressed.

Using the PNG settings

The PNG (Portable Network Graphic) format is another still image format. It was developed quite recently and is an improvement over both the GIF and JPEG formats in several ways. Much like JPEG, it is excellent for transmission of photographic quality images. The primary advantages of PNG are variable bit-depths (images can be 256 colors or millions of colors), multi-level transparency, and lossless compression. However, most browsers do not offer full support for all PNG options without some kind of additional plug-in. When in doubt, test your PNG images in your preferred browser.

Caution   Flash 4's PNG export or publish settings do not reflect the full range of PNG options available. PNG can support transparency in both 8-bit and 24-bit flavors, but Flash only enables transparency in "24-bit with Alpha" images.

The settings of the PNG tab control the characteristics of the PNG image which Flash will publish (see Figure 25-12).

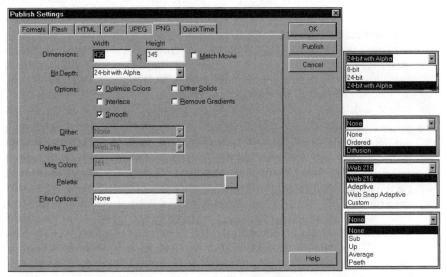

Figure 25-12: The settings found on the PNG tab closely resemble those on the GIF tab. It was engineered to have many of the advantages of both the GIF and JPEG formats.

The PNG tab options are as follows:

✦ **Dimensions:** This setting works just like the GIF and JPEG equivalents. When Match Movie is checked, you cannot alter the Width and Height of the PNG image.

✦ **Bit Depth:** This setting controls how many colors are created in the PNG image:

- **8-bit:** In this mode, the PNG image has a maximum color palette of 256 colors, similar to the palette function of GIF images. When this option is selected, the Options, Dither, Palette Type, Max Colors, and Palette settings can be altered.

- **24-bit:** When this option is selected, the PNG image can display any of the 16.7 million RGB colors. This option produces larger files than 8-bit PNG images, but renders the Flash artwork most faithfully.

- **24-bit with Alpha:** This option adds another 8-bit channel to the 24-bit PNG image for multi-level transparency support. This means that Flash will treat the Flash movie background as a transparent area, so that information behind the PNG image (such as HTML background colors) shows through. Note that, with proper browser support, PNG can render antialiased edges on top of other elements, such as HTML background images!

✦ **Options:** These options behave exactly the same as the equivalent GIF Publish Settings.

✦ **Dither, Palette Type, Max Colors and Palette:** These settings work exactly the same as the equivalent GIF Publish Settings. Because PNG images can be either 8- or 24-bit, these options are only apply to 8-bit PNG images. If anything other than 8-bit is selected in the Bit Depth setting, then these options are disabled. Please refer to the previous section for more information.

✦ **Filter Options:** This drop-down menu controls what type of compression sampling or algorithm the PNG image uses. Note that this does not apply an art or graphic "filter effect" like filters in Adobe Photoshop, nor does it throw away any image information—all filters are lossless. It simply enables you to be the judge of what kind of compression to use on the image. You need to experiment with each of these filters on your Flash movie image to find the best filter-to-file size combination. Technically, the filters do not actually look at the pixel data. Rather, they look at the byte data of each pixel. Results vary depending on the image content, but here are some guidelines to keep in mind:

- **None:** When this option is selected, no filtering is applied to the image. When no filter is applied, you usually have unnecessarily large file sizes.

- **Sub:** This filter works best on images that have repeated information along the horizontal axis. For example, the stripes of a horizontal American flag filter nicely with the "sub" filter.

- **Up:** The opposite of the "sub" filter, this filter works by looking for repeated information along the vertical axis. The stripes of a vertical American flag filter well with the "up" filter.

- **Average:** Use this option when a mixture of vertical and horizontal information exists. When in doubt, try this filter first.

- **Path:** This filter works like an advanced "average" filter. When in doubt, try this filter after you have experimented with the "average" filter.

Note Unlike Adobe Photoshop, Flash 4 doesn't offer an "adaptive" PNG filter. While "adaptive" is not a real PNG filter (according to the PNG Specification), in Photoshop, it finds the filter that works best with the content of the image.

Creating Windows and Macintosh projectors

The process of creating and using Flash standalone projectors is described in Chapter 27, "Using Players and Projectors."

Using the QuickTime settings

Now that QuickTime 4 includes built-in support for Flash tracks and SWF files, you may want to publish QuickTime 4 movies (.MOV files) in addition to your Shockwave Flash movies (.SWF files). The QuickTime publish settings are discussed at length in Chapter 21. If you want to enable QuickTime movie output via the Publish command, make sure it is selected in the Formats tab of the Publish Settings dialog box.

Publish Preview and Publish Commands

After you have entered the file format types and specifications for each in the Publish Settings dialog box, you can proceed to preview and publish the file types you selected.

Using Publish Preview

The Publish Preview submenu (accessible from File ➪ Publish Preview) lists all the file types currently enabled in the Publish Settings dialog box. By default, HTML is the first file type available for preview. In general, the first item enabled in the Formats tab of Publish Settings should be the first item in the submenu, and can be executed by pressing F12. Selecting a file type in the Publish Preview menu launches your preferred browser and inserts the selected file type(s) into the browser window.

Note When you use Publish Preview, Flash 4 actually creates real files in the same location as the saved Flash movie. In a sense, previewing is the same as running the Publish command, except that Publish Preview will save you the steps of opening the browser and loading the files manually.

Using Publish

When you want Flash to export the file type(s) selected in the Publish Settings, choose File ⇨ Publish (Shift+F12). Flash creates the new files wherever the Flash movie was last saved. If you have selected an HTML template in the HTML tab of Publish Settings, then you may receive a warning or error message if any other necessary files were not specified. That's it! After you've tested the files for the delivery browser and/or platforms of your choice, you can upload the files to your Web server.

✦   ✦   ✦

Structuring Flash Content

◆   ◆   ◆   ◆

In This Chapter

How to add Flash movies with raw HTML

Filling the entire browser window with a Flash movie

How to use JavaScript with Flash movies

◆   ◆   ◆   ◆

If you're not one for automated HTML production using templates, then this chapter is for you. This chapter teaches you the in's and out's of the `<OBJECT>` and `<EMBED>` tags, as well as some secrets to using `<FRAMESET>` tags to display Flash movies. At the end of this chapter, you should see how Flash movies can interact with JavaScript and DHTML.

Writing Markup for Flash Movies

In Chapter 25, you learned how to use the new Publish feature, which included automated HTML templates. These templates created the necessary HTML tags to display Flash movies on Web pages. This section discusses the use of Flash movies in your hand-written HTML documents. You can also use this knowledge to alter HTML documents created by the Publish feature.

Using the `<OBJECT>` and `<EMBED>` tags

Two tags can be used to place Flash movies on a Web page (such as an HTML document): `<OBJECT>` and `<EMBED>`. Each tag works pretty much like the other, with some slight differences in attribute names and organization. Keep in mind that, if both sets of tags are included with the HTML, only one set of tags is actually read by the browser depending on which browser is used to view the Web page. Without these tags, Flash movies cannot be displayed with other HTML elements, such as images and text.

Tip   You can, however, directly link to SWF files as an alternative method for displaying Flash content. That method, however, precludes the use of parameters to control the look and playback of the Flash movie—it would be the same as loading the SWF movie straight into the standalone Flash Player. See Colin Moock's tutorial later in this chapter for more information on direct linking.

The <OBJECT> tag

Microsoft Internet Explorer uses this tag exclusively to enable the Flash ActiveX control. When the Flash 4 Only (Default) HTML template is used in Publish Settings, the HTML document that is published uses the <OBJECT> tag in the following way:

```
A. <OBJECT
B.      classid="clsid:D27CDB6E-AE6D-11cf-96B8-444553540000"
C.      codebase="http://active.macromedia.com/flash2/cabs/¬
swflash.cab#version=4,0,0,0"
D.      ID=home
E.      WIDTH=550
HEIGHT=400>
F.      <PARAM NAME=movie VALUE="home.swf">
G.      <PARAM NAME=quality VALUE=high>
H.      <PARAM NAME=bgcolor VALUE=#FFFFFF>
I.*     <PARAM NAME=scale VALUE=noborder>
J.*     <PARAM NAME=play VALUE=false>
K. </OBJECT>
```

* Not a default setting of the Flash 4 Only HTML template.

A. <OBJECT: This is the opening tag containing the ID code and locations of the ActiveX control for Flash. Note that this opening tag includes the attributes lettered B through E.

B. classid: This lengthy string is the unique ActiveX identification code. If you are inserting the <OBJECT> tag by hand in a text editor, make sure you copy this ID string exactly.

C. codebase: Like the codebase attribute of Java <APPLET> tags, this attribute of the <OBJECT> tag specifies the location of the ActiveX control installer as a URL. Notice that the #version=4,0,0,0 portion of the URL indicates that the Flash Player version 4 should be used. If the visitor doesn't have the ActiveX control already installed, then Internet Explorer automatically downloads the control from this URL.

D. ID: This attribute of the <OBJECT> tag assigns a JavaScript identifier to the Flash movie, so that it can be controlled by HTML JavaScript functions. By default, this attribute's value is the name of the actual of SWF file, without the SWF. Each element on an HTML page should have a unique ID or NAME attribute. The NAME attribute will be discussed in the next section.

E. `WIDTH` **and** `HEIGHT>`: These attributes control the actual width and height of the Flash movie, as it appears on the Web page. If no unit of measurement is specified, then these values are in pixels. If the % character is added to the end of each value, then the attribute adjusts the Flash movie to the corresponding percent of the browser window. For example, if 100% was the value for both `WIDTH` and `HEIGHT`, then the Flash movie fills the entire browser, except for the browser gutter. See Colin Moock's tutorial later in this chapter to learn how to minimize this gutter thickness.

F. `<PARAM NAME=movie VALUE="home.swf">`: This is the first set of `<PARAM>` subtags within the `<OBJECT></OBJECT>` tags. Each parameter tag has a unique `NAME=` setting, not to be confused with JavaScript `NAME`'s or `ID`'s. This parameter's `NAME` setting `movie` specifies the filename of the Shockwave Flash movie as the `VALUE` attribute.

G. `<PARAM NAME=quality VALUE=high>`: This parameter has a NAME attribute-setting quality that controls how the Flash movie's artwork renders within the browser window. The VALUE can be `low`, `autolow`, `autohigh`, `high`, or `best`. Most Flash movies on the Web use the `autohigh` value, as this forces the Flash Player to try rendering the movie elements antialiased. If the processor of the machine can't keep up with the Flash movie using antialiased elements, then it turns off antialiasing by switching to a `low` quality. For a full description of each of the `quality` settings, please refer to the section "Using the HTML Settings" in Chapter 25.

H. `<PARAM NAME=bgcolor VALUE=#FFFFFF>`: This last parameter name, `bgcolor`, controls the background color of the Flash movie. If you published an HTML document via the Publish command, then the `VALUE` is automatically set to the background color specified by the Modify ⇨ Movie command in Flash 4. However, you can override the Movie setting by entering a different value in this parameter tag. Note that this parameter, like all HTML tags and attributes concerning color, uses hexadecimal code to describe the color. For more information on color, see Chapter 2.

I. `<PARAM NAME=scale VALUE=noborder>`: This optional parameter controls how the Flash movie scales in the window defined by the `WIDTH` and `HEIGHT` attributes of the opening `<OBJECT>` tag. Its value can be `showall`, `noborder`, or `exactfit`. If this entire subtag is omitted, then the Flash Player treats the movie as if the `showall` default setting was specified. The `showall` setting fits the Flash movie within the boundaries of the `WIDTH` and `HEIGHT` dimensions without any distortion to the original aspect ratio of the Flash movie. Again, refer to "Using the HTML Settings" section of Chapter 25 for a complete description of the `scale` settings and how they work within the dimensions of a Flash movie.

J. `<PARAM NAME=play VALUE=false>`: This optional parameter tells the Flash Player whether or not it should start playing the Flash movie as it downloads. If the `VALUE` equals `FALSE`, the Flash movie loads in a "paused" state, just as if a "stop" action was placed on the first frame. If the `VALUE` equals `TRUE`, Flash starts playing the movie as soon as it starts to stream into the browser.

K. `</OBJECT>`: This is the closing tag for the starting `<OBJECT>` tag. As is shown later in this chapter, you can put other HTML tags between the last `<PARAM>` tag and the closing `</OBJECT>` tag for non-ActiveX-enabled browsers, such as Netscape. Because Internet Explorer is the only browser that currently recognizes `<OBJECT>` tags, other browsers simply skip the `<OBJECT>` tag (as well as its `<PARAM>` tags) and only read the tags between the last `<PARAM>` and `</OBJECT>` tags.

Tip

The `<OBJECT>` tag can use other parameter tag names such as `WMODE`. This parameter only works on 32-bit versions of Windows 95/98/NT Internet Explorer. See the end of the Dreamweaver section in Chapter 24 for more information regarding its use.

The `<EMBED>` tag

Netscape Navigator uses the `<EMBED>` tag to display nonbrowser native file formats which require a plug-in, such as Apple QuickTime or Macromedia Shockwave Flash and Director.

```
A.  <EMBED
B.        src="home.swf"
C.        quality=high
D.        scale=noborder
E.        play=false
F.        bgcolor=#FFFFFF
G.        WIDTH=550
HEIGHT=400
H.        swLiveConnect=false
I.        TYPE="application/x-shockwave-flash"
J.        PLUGINSPAGE="http://www.macromedia.com/shockwave/¬
download/index.cgi?P1_Prod_Version=ShockwaveFlash">
K.  </EMBED>
```

A. `<EMBED`: This is the opening `<EMBED>` tag. Note that lines B through H are attributes of the opening `<EMBED>` tag, which is why you won't see the `>`character at the end of line A.

B. `src`: This stands for "source," and indicates the filename of the Shockwave Flash movie. This attribute of `<EMBED>` works exactly like the `<PARAM NAME=movie VALUE="home.swf">` subtag of the `<OBJECT>` tag.

C. `quality`: This attribute controls how the Flash movie's artwork will display in the browser window. Like the equivalent `<PARAM NAME=quality>` subtag of the `<OBJECT>` tag, its value can be `low`, `autolow`, `autohigh`, `high`, or `best`.

D. `scale`: This attribute of `<EMBED>` controls how the Flash movie fits within the browser window and/or the dimensions specified by `WIDTH` and `HEIGHT` (F). Its value can be `showall` (default if attribute is omitted), `noborder`, or `exactfit`.

E. `play`: This attribute controls the playback of the Flash movie. If set to `FALSE`, the Flash movie does not automatically play until a Flash action tells the movie to play (such as a Flash button or frame action). If set to `TRUE`, then the Flash movie plays as soon as it starts to stream into the browser.

F. `bgcolor`: This setting controls the Flash movie's background color. Again, this attribute behaves identically to the equivalent `<PARAM>` subtag of the `<OBJECT>` tag. See that tag's description in the previous section.

G. `WIDTH` **and** `HEIGHT`: These attributes control the dimensions of the Flash movie as it appears on the Web page. Refer to the `WIDTH` and `HEIGHT` descriptions of the `<OBJECT>` tag for more information.

H. `swLiveConnect`: This is one attribute that you can't find in the `<OBJECT>` tag. This unique tag enables Netscape's LiveConnect feature, which enables plug-ins and Java applets to communicate with JavaScript. By default, this attribute is set to `false`. If it is enabled (for example, the attribute is set to `true`), the Web page may experience a short delay during loading. The latest versions of Netscape don't start the Java engine during a browsing session until a Web page containing a Java applet (or a Java-enabled plug-in such as Shockwave Flash) is loaded. Unless you use FS Commands in your Flash movies, it's best to leave these attribute set to `false`.

I. `TYPE="application/x-shockwave-flash"`: This attribute tells Netscape what MIME (Multipurpose Internet Mail Extension) content-type the embedded file is. Each file type (.TIF, .JPG, .GIF, .DOC, .TXT, and so on) has a unique MIME content-type header, describing what its content is. For Shockwave Flash movies, the content-type is `application/x-shockwave-flash`. Any program (or operating system) that uses files over the Internet handles MIME content-types according to a reference chart that links each MIME content-type to its appropriate parent application or plug-in. Without this attribute, Netscape may not understand what type of file the Flash movie is. As a result, it may display the broken plug-in icon when the Flash movie downloads to the browser.

J. `PLUGINSPAGE`: Literally "plug-in's page," this attribute tells Netscape where to go to find the appropriate plug-in installer if it doesn't have the Flash plug-in already installed. Note that this is not equivalent to a JavaScript-enabled auto-installer. It simply redirects the browser to the URL of the Web page where the appropriate software can be downloaded.

K. `</EMBED>`: This is the closing tag for the original `<EMBED>` tag in line A. Some older or text-based browsers such as Lynx are incapable of displaying `<EMBED>` tags. You can insert alternate HTML (such as a static or animated GIF with the `<IMG>` tag) between the `<EMBED>` `</EMBED>` tags for these browsers.

Caution

You may be surprised to learn that all versions of Internet Explorer (IE) for the Macintosh cannot read `<OBJECT>` tags. Rather, IE for Mac uses a Netscape plug-in emulator to read `<EMBED>` tags. However, this emulator does not interpret all `<EMBED>` tags with the same level of support as Netscape. As a result, the swLiveConnect attribute does not function on IE for Mac browsers. This means that FS Commands are not supported on these browsers.

Expert Tutorial: Filling the Browser Window Using the `<FRAMESET>` Tag *by Colin Moock*

Originally a painter and a writer, Colin Moock became involved with Web design in 1994 (when the latest technological breakthrough was colored table cells and the only applications for Web design were freeware). Having produced sites and online content for Sony, Nortel, Air Canada, and The Movie Network, Colin began experimenting with Flash to produce animated shorts for his eclectic Web site, www.moock.org. *His Levi's Canada HotSpot—an animated Flash tavern—won recognition in Applied Arts, and was a Shocked Site of the Day in January 1998. Now Colin pushes pixels for Toronto-based interactive agency ICE, Integrated Communications and Entertainment (www.iceinc.com). His latest Flash project is the design of the interactive module of McClelland & Stewart's,* The Canadian Encyclopedia 1999 *CD-ROM. This expert tutorial is one of several contributions by Colin to the* Flash 4 Bible *(he's the primary contributor to Part IV of this book). Colin's other instructional writing on Flash is posted at* www.moock.org/webdesign/flash/.

Filling the gap

Many Flash designers have experienced the problem that Flash movies don't default to fill the entire viewing space of a browser window. This results in wasted screen space, or what's worse, an unsightly gutter, or gap, between the edge of the Flash movie and the edges of the browser.

In the following figure, the browser on the left sports an unsightly white gutter around a Flash Movie. On the right, the same movie is displayed with a minimal gutter around a framed Flash Movie. For designers who prefer the effect shown on the right, two options work with most browsers. One solution depends on the use of frames, and is therefore limited to frames-capable browsers. The other solution requires that the Flash Player plug-in be detected prior to serving pages built with this method—so it's not appropriate for a splash page.

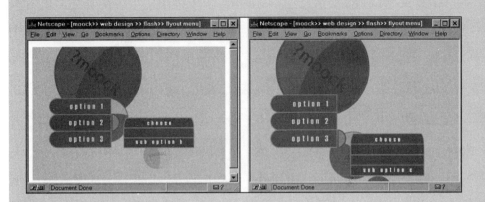

Single-frame frameset

With the attributes a frameset set correctly, framed Flash content can stretch to within 1 or 2 pixels (depending on the browser) of the edge of the browser window. To do this, first make the page (yourmovie.html) in which your movie is embedded. Then when embedding the movie, set the width, height, and scale for the desired effect. The SCALE parameter has three options:

✦ **HEIGHT="100%" WIDTH="100%" SCALE="EXACTFIT":** This combination forces every edge of your movie to the edge of the browser, and distorts your movie to fit the aspect ratio (proportion of height to width) of the browser.

✦ **HEIGHT="100%" WIDTH="100%" SCALE="SHOWALL":** This combination fits the width or height of your movie to the smaller of either the width or height of the browser. Your movie is not cropped or skewed to fit the browser window, but there are borders on either the top and bottom or right and left of your movie.

✦ **HEIGHT="100%" WIDTH="100%" SCALE="NOBORDER":** This combination adjusts either the height or width of your movie to the larger of either the width or height of the browser. When the dimensions of your movie do not match the dimensions of the browser, your movie is cropped on either the top and bottom or on both sides.

Your embedded movie code will look something like this:

```
<OBJECT
CLASSID="clsid:D27CDB6E-AE6D-11cf-96B8-444553540000"
WIDTH="100%"
HEIGHT="100%"
CODEBASE="http://active.macromedia.com/flash3/cabs/">
<PARAM NAME="MOVIE" VALUE="moviename.swf">
<PARAM NAME="PLAY" VALUE="true">
<PARAM NAME="LOOP" VALUE="true">
<PARAM NAME="QUALITY" VALUE="high">
<PARAM NAME="SCALE" VALUE="SHOWALL">
```

Continued

(continued)

```
<EMBED
SRC="yourmovie.swf"
WIDTH="100%"
HEIGHT="100%"
PLAY="true"
LOOP="true"
QUALITY="high"
SCALE="SHOWALL"

PLUGINSPAGE="http://www.macromedia.com/shockwave/download/index.
cgi?P1_Prod_Version=ShockwaveFlash">
</EMBED>
</OBJECT>
```

Now you're ready to make the single frame frameset. Actually, it's a two-frame frameset, but you only use one of the frames for displaying your page. The first frame is allotted 100 percent of the browser area, and the second frame is allotted "*" (meaning whatever is left, which is nothing). The SRC of the first frame of the frameset will be the page (yourmovie.html) with your Flash Movie, while the SRC of the second frame will be an empty HTML page with a matching BGCOLOR. Then real trick is to specify the attributes of the frameset and frames so that the Flash movie will extend to the edges of the browser. Here's an example of code with the correct settings:

```
<HTML><HEAD><TITLE>Your Flash Movie Title</TITLE></HEAD>

<FRAMESET ROWS="100%,*" FRAMESPACING="0" FRAMEBORDER="NO"
BORDER="0">
<FRAME NAME="top" SRC="yourmovie.html" FRAMEBORDER="0" BORDER="0"
MARGINWIDTH="0" MARGINHEIGHT="0" SCROLLING="NO">
<FRAME NAME="hidden" SRC="empty.html" FRAMEBORDER="0" BORDER="0"
MARGINWIDTH="0" MARGINHEIGHT="0" SCROLLING="NO">

</FRAMESET></HTML>
```

Notes:

✦ As an attribute of <FRAMESET>, FRAMEBORDER is either true or false, but as an attribute of <FRAME>, FRAMEBORDER is a pixel value for setting the width of the space between the browser edge and the page content.

✦ On <FRAMESET>, BORDER refers to the number of pixels between frames, while on <FRAME>, BORDER is simply a now-obsolete version of FRAMEBORDER.

✦ The SCROLLING attribute must be set to NO, otherwise, if the content is not larger than the browser window, a gap will appear on the right and bottom of the frame where the scrollbars would normally appear.

As a final option, to reduce the gutter as much as possible in Internet Explorer 4 and Netscape Communicator 4, you can set the margin values on the movie page (yourmovie.html). To accomplish this, Netscape 4 or higher uses `MARGINHEIGHT` and `MARGINWIDTH`, while Internet Explorer 4 or higher uses `TOPMARGIN`, `BOTTOMMARGIN`, `LEFTMARGIN`, and `RIGHTMARGIN`. So, to accommodate both browsers, use these values:

```
<BODY MARGINWIDTH="0" MARGINHEIGHT="0" LEFTMARGIN="0"
RIGHTMARGIN="0" TOPMARGIN="0" BOTTOMMARGIN="0">
```

Directly linking to the Flash movie (.SWF file)

An alternate method to the single-frame frameset described previously is to link directly to the Flash Movie and let the browser display it inline. So, if your movie mymovie.swf is normally embedded in mymovie.html, then:

```
<A HREF="mymovie.html">View my movie</A>
```

would be changed to:

```
<A HREF="mymovieSWF">View my movie</A>
```

This method is easier to implement than the frames method, but should only be used after Flash has been successfully detected, because the browser won't have access to any of the HTML instructions that would normally tell it where to get the plug-in if the plug-in is not present. Thus, this method should not be used for a splash page.

If you use the Direct Link method, it's also important to remember to set the QUALITY of your movie to "high" from inside your movie using the Toggle High Quality action (Flash 3+ only). To do this, go to your first keyframe, select frame properties, click the actions tab, and then add a Toggle High Quality action as seen in the following figure.

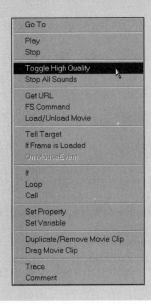

Using Flash Movies with JavaScript and DHTML

The new ActionScripting features in Flash 4 have greatly increased the range of interactive and dynamic possibilities for Flash movies on the Web. In previous releases of Flash, Flash movies could only interact with external HTML or scripts through the FS Command action. This meant mapping commands and variables to JavaScript, which, in turn, passed information to the document object model of DHTML, Java applets, or CGI scripts. Now that Flash movies can directly send and receive data to server-side CGI scripts, just about anything can be done within the Flash movie. However, if you want to directly communicate with the Web browser or the HTML document, you need to use FS Commands or Get URL actions with javascript: statements. Because all JavaScript-capable browsers do not support these methods, we're limiting our discussion to FS Commands and JavaScript-controllable Flash movie properties.

A word of caution to Web developers

This section covers FS Commands, which, when used in Flash movies on Web pages, are only supported by a handful of browsers. Currently, not one version of Internet Explorer for Macintosh (up to version 4.5) can interpret FS Commands (see the Caution note in "The <EMBED> Tag" section earlier in this chapter). Only Netscape 3.0 (or higher) offers cross-platform support for FS Commands. Internet Explorer 3 (or higher) for Windows 95/98/NT also support FS Commands. Our coverage of the FS Command assumes you have basic knowledge of JavaScript and Flash ActionScript. If you don't know how to add Actions to frames or buttons, please read Chapter 13. If you don't know JavaScript, you can still follow the steps to the tutorials and create a fully functional Flash-JavaScript movie. However, because this isn't a book on JavaScript, we won't explain how JavaScript syntax or functions work.

How Flash movies work with JavaScript

As mentioned earlier, Flash has an action called `FS Command`. FS Commands are used to send a command (and an optional argument string) from a Flash movie to its hosting environment (such as a Web browser or standalone Flash Player). What does this mean for interactivity? The FS Command offers the ability to have any Flash event (button or frame actions) initiate an event in JavaScript. While this may not sound too exciting, you can use FS Commands to trigger anything that you would have used Javascript alone to do in the past, such as updating HTML-form text fields, changing the visibility of HTML elements, or switching HTML background colors on the fly. Most Flash-to-JavaScript interactivity works best with dynamic HTML (DHTML) browsers, such as Netscape 4 or higher and Internet Explorer 4 or higher. We take a look at these effects in the next section.

Flash movie communication with JavaScript is not a one-way street. You can also monitor and control Flash movies with JavaScript. Just as JavaScript treats an HTML document as an object and its elements as properties of that object, JavaScript treats Flash movies as it would any other element on a Web page. Therefore, you can use JavaScript functions and HTML hyperlinks (<A HREF> tags) to control Flash movie playback. At the end of this chapter, we show you how to make an HTML form menu that can jump to various scenes of a Flash movie.

Note In order for JavaScript to receive Flash FS Commands, you need to make sure the attribute swLiveConnect for the <EMBED> tag is set to TRUE. By default, most Flash HTML templates have this settings set to FALSE.

Changing HTML attributes

In this section, we show you how to dynamically change the BGCOLOR attribute of the <BODY> tag with a FS Command from a Flash movie while it is playing in the browser window. In fact, we change the background color a few times. Then, once that has been accomplished, we show you how to update the text field of a <FORM> tag to display what percent of the Flash movie has been loaded.

On the CD-ROM Open the Flash editor document countdown.fla located in the ch26 folder of the *Flash 4 Bible* CD-ROM. This is quite a large .FLA file (over 14MB) as it uses many imported bitmap images and sounds to demonstrate slow-loading movie. If you are using the Mac version of Flash 4, you may want to increase the memory allocation for the Flash 4 application file to 64MB or higher.

Adding FS Commands to a Flash movie

Open the countdown.fla Flash movie from the *Flash 4 Bible* CD-ROM, and use Control ➪ Test Movie to play the Shockwave Flash version. You should notice that the filmstrip countdown fades to white, and then to near-black, and then back to its original gray color. This countdown contains to loop until the entire first scene has loaded into the Flash Player. When the first scene has loaded, playback will skip to a movie clip of two dogs (in "negative") and a title sequence. There's more to the Flash movie, but for now, that's all we need to deal with.

Our goal for this section of the tutorial is to add FS Command frame actions to specific keyframes in the countdown.fla Flash demonstration movie. When the Flash Player plays the frame with the FS Command action, the Player sends a command and argument string to JavaScript. JavaScript then calls a function that changes the background color to the value specified in the argument string of the FS Command (see Figure 26-1). To be more exact, you will add an FS Command to the frames where the color fades to white, black, and gray. When the Flash movie changes to these colors, so will the HTML background colors.

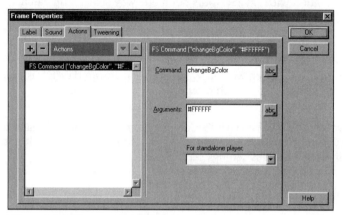

Figure 26-1: Frame 16: FS Command of `changeBgColor` **with an** argument of #FFFFFF (the hexadecimal code for the color white)

Here's the process:

1. On frame 16 of the "Introduction" scene, double-click the keyframe for the Countdown layer. Click the Actions tab of the Frame Properties dialog box, and add a FS Command action from the + pop-up menu. In the Command text box, type `changeBgColor`. In the Arguments text box, type #FFFFFF. The command `changeBgColor` is mapped to a JavaScript function called `changeBgColor` later in this tutorial. The argument string #FFFFFF is passed to that function, changing the HTML background color to white.

2. On frame 20, add another FS Command action to the keyframe of the Countdown layer. Again, insert `changeBgColor` in the Command text box. In the Arguments text box, type #333333. This argument changes the HTML background color to a dark gray.

3. On frame 21 of the Countdown layer, follow the same instructions for Step 2, except use #9E9E9E for the argument string. This changes the HTML background color to the same color as the Flash movie countdown graphic.

4. On frame 66 of the Countdown layer, add another `changeBgColor` FS Command action to the empty keyframe. This time, use an argument string of #000000, which changes the HTML background color to black.

5. Now that we've added a few FS Commands, let's try them out in the browser. Save the countdown.fla Flash movie to a folder on your hard drive, and open the Publish Settings dialog box (for more information on Publish Settings, refer to Chapter 25). In the HTML tab, select the template Flash with FS Command. Click OK to close the Publish Settings dialog box. Select the File ➪ Publish command to export the Flash SWF movie and HTML document.

Next, we look at the automated JavaScript code that the HTML template created. While the basic code structure has been set up, we need to make some alterations and additions to the JavaScript in order for our FS Commands to work.

Note You may have noticed that some FS Commands have already been entered on other keyframes of the countdown.fla movie. These have been placed to ensure that the background color stays consistent with other settings, regardless of where playback occurs.

Enabling JavaScript for Flash movies

Although the Flash with FS Command template does a lot of the JavaScripting for you, it doesn't automatically map out the commands and arguments (args) to JavaScript-defined functions. In this section, we'll add the necessary JavaScript to make the FS Commands work in the browser. What follows is the JavaScript code that Flash 4 generates.

Note Any numbered line of code marked with an asterisk (*) is custom JavaScript code that Flash 4 does not create.

```
1. <SCRIPT LANGUAGE=JavaScript>
2. <!--
3. var InternetExplorer = ¬
navigator.appName.indexOf("Microsoft") != -1;
4.*     var stringFlash = "";
5. // Handle all the FSCommand messages in a Flash movie
6.      function countdown_DoFSCommand(command,args){
7.             var countdownObj = InternetExplorer ¬
? countdown : document.countdown;
8.*            stringFlash = stringFlash + args;
9.*            if(command=="changeBgColor"){
               changeBgColor();
               }
       }
10.*    function changeBgColor(){
11.*           document.bgColor = stringFlash;
12.*           stringFlash = "";
       }
13. // Hook for Internet Explorer
       if (navigator.appName &&
              navigator.appName.indexOf("Microsoft") != -1 &&
              navigator.userAgent.indexOf("Windows") != -1 &&
              navigator.userAgent.indexOf("Windows 3.1") == -1)
              {
       document.write('<SCRIPT LANGUAGE=VBScript\> \n');
       document.write('on error resume next \n');
   document.write('Sub countdown_FSCommand(ByVal command,¬
ByVal args)\n');
document.write('  call countdown_DoFSCommand(command,¬
args)\n');
       document.write('end sub\n');
       document.write('</SCRIPT\> \n');
```

```
     }
    //-->
14. </SCRIPT>
```

The following is a line-by-line explanation of the code:

1. This HTML tag initializes the JavaScript code.

2. This string of characters is standard HTML comment code. By adding this after the opening `<SCRIPT>` tag, non-JavaScript browsers ignore the code. If this string wasn't included, text-based browsers such as Lynx might display JavaScript code as HTML text.

3. This variable simply condenses the JavaScript code that detects Internet Explorer into a single term, `InternetExplorer`.

4. We added this line of code to declare a variable called `stringFlash`. Its value is set to nothing by putting two straight quote characters together. This variable is necessary for FS Command arguments to pass cleanly into JavaScript functions on both Netscape and Internet Explorer.

5. This is comment code added by the Macromedia team to let us know that the following JavaScript code is designed to catch the FS Commands from a Flash movie.

6. This is the initial JavaScript function that works exclusively with Flash FS Commands. The function's name is the value of the `NAME` attribute of the `<EMBED>` tag (or the value of the `ID` attribute of the `<OBJECT>` tag) followed by a underscore and `DoFSCommand(command,args){`. In this sample, the Flash movie `NAME` is `countdown`. Notice that the command and arguments that were specified in Flash are passed to this function as `(command,args)`, respectively.

7. This is a handy optional variable that the Flash with FS Command template created. Strangely, it is not necessary unless you need to refer to the differing document object models between Internet Explorer and Netscape. Instead of testing for either browser, you can insert the countdownObj variable in your own JavaScript code. For this example, though, it is not needed.

8. This code makes the `stringFlash` variable called in line 4 equal to the argument string (`args`) from the Flash FS Command. Because stringFlash was equal to nothing (""), `stringFlash` is now exactly the same as the original argument string. This isn't necessary for Internet Explorer, but Netscape doesn't recognize arguments straight from Flash without it.

9. This compares the passed command string from the Flash FS Command to the string `changeBgColor`. If they're the same, then JavaScript executes the code contained within the `if` statement. Because we only made one unique command in Flash for this sample, we only have to map the Flash FS Command `changeBgColor` to the JavaScript function `changeBgColor()`.

10. This is where the function `changeBgColor()` is defined. Remember that line 9 maps the Flash FS Command `changeBgColor` to this JavaScript function.

11. This line of code passes the variable `stringFlash` to the `document. bgColor` property, which controls the HTML background color. When the Flash FS Command sends the command `changeBgColor`, the JavaScript `changeBgcolor()` function is invoked, which passes the argument string from the Flash FS Command to `document.bgColor`.

12. This resets the variable `stringFlash` back to nothing ("\"\""), so that future invocations of the FS Command don't use the same argument from the previous execution.

13. This section of code detects the presence of Internet Explorer for Windows and maps the JavaScript functions to VBScript (which is used exclusively by Windows-only versions of Internet Explorer).

14. The closing `</SCRIPT>` tag ends this portion of JavaScript code.

Caution　For some reason, the Flash with FS Command template omits the `NAME` attribute for the `<EMBED>` tag. Make sure you add this attribute to the `<EMBED>` tag. Set its value equal to the name of the Flash SWF movie, without the SWF file extension. For example, in the sample used for this section, the `<EMBED>` tag should have a `NAME` attribute equal to countdown.

That's it! Once you've manually added the custom lines of JavaScript code, you can load the HTML document into either Internet Explorer or Netscape (see the caveats mentioned at the beginning of this section). When the Flash Player comes to the frames with FS Commands, the HTML background should change along with the Flash movie. Next, we add a `<FORM>` element that displays the percentage of the Flash movie that has loaded into the browser window.

On the CD-ROM　You can find the completed version of the countdown.fla movie on the *Flash 4 Bible* CD-ROM. It is called countdown_complete.fla and is located in the ch26 folder. You will also find countdown_completeSWF and a fully JavaScripted HTML document called countdown_complete.html. The JavaScript and HTML reflect the usage of the countdown_complete filename.

Using the PercentLoaded() method

JavaScript can control several Flash movie properties. It's beyond the scope of this book to describe each JavaScript method for Flash movies. If you want to see a complete list of Flash JavaScript methods, see the Macromedia Flash tech support page:

```
http://www.macromedia.com/support/flash/how/subjects/¬
scriptingwithflash/scriptingwithflash04.html
```

In this section, we'll use the `PercentLoaded()` method to display the Flash movie's loading progress update a text field of a `<FORM>` element. First, we add the necessary FS Command to the Flash movie. HTML `<FORM>` elements, and then we add the appropriate JavaScript.

1. Open the countdown.fla movie that you used in the previous section. There should already be an empty keyframe present on frame 1 of the Titles layer. Add a `FS Command` action to this keyframe. Insert `PercentLoaded` in the Command field. This command has no arguments. Add the same FS Command to the keyframes on frames 10, 20, 30, 40, 50, 60 and 67 of the Titles layer. Export a Flash 4 SWF movie called countdown.swf with the File ⇨ Export Movie command. Make sure you place the new SWF file in the same folder as the HTML document we were using in the previous section.

2. In a text editor such as Notepad or SimpleText, open the HTML document showing the countdown.swf Flash movie.

3. Add the following HTML after the `<OBJECT>` and `<EMBED>` tags:

```
<FORM METHOD="post" ACTION="" NAME="flashPercent"
STYLE="display:show">
  <INPUT TYPE="text" NAME="textfield" SIZE="5" STYLE =
"display:show">
</FORM>
```

The code in Step 3 uses two `NAME` attributes so that JavaScript can recognize them. Also, the DHTML `STYLE` attribute assigns a `display:show` value to the both the `<FORM>` and `<INPUT>` tags.

Caution

Netscape 4's implementation of the document object model (DOM) doesn't allow styles to be updated on the fly unless the page is reformatted (for example, the window is resized by the user). It could be possible to write more JavaScript code that would insert JavaScript styles for the `<FORM>` elements, but that's beyond the scope of this section.

4. Now we need to map the `PercentLoaded` FS Command to a JavaScript function. Add the following JavaScript to the `if` statement(s) in the `function countdown_DoFSCommand` of the HTML document:

```
if(command=="percentLoaded"){
        moviePercentLoaded();
}
```

5. Add the following JavaScript after the `function changeBgColor()` section. This function tells the browser to update the `<FORM>` text field with the percent of the Flash movie currently loaded. When the value is greater than or equal to 99, then the text field reads 100% and disappears after two seconds. As mentioned earlier, Netscape is unable to change the `style` of the `<FORM>` elements on-the-fly.

```
function moviePercentLoaded(){
    var m = InternetExplorer ? countdown_complete : ¬
document.countdown_complete;
    var Percent = m.PercentLoaded();
    var temp = 0;
    if(Percent >= 99 ){
        document.flashPercent.textfield.value="100 %";
        if (navigator.appName.indexOf("Microsoft") != -1){
            setTimeout("document.flashPercent.¬
textfield.style.display = 'none'",2000);
            setTimeout("document.flashPercent.style.¬
display = 'none'",2000);
        }
    }
    else {
        temp = Percent;
        document.flashPercent.textfield.value = temp + " %"
;
    }
}
```

6. Save the HTML document and load it into a browser. If you run into errors, check your JavaScript syntax carefully. A misplaced ; or } can set off the entire script. If you continue to run into errors, compare your document to the countdown_complete.html document on the *Flash 4 Bible* CD-ROM.

Okay, that wasn't the easiest task in the world, and, admittedly, the effects might not have been as spectacular as you may have thought. However, now that you know the basics of Flash and JavaScript interactivity, you can take your Flash movie interactivity one step further. Check out `www.theflashbible.com/ch26` for updates to this section, as well as further tips on FS Commands in Flash.

✦   ✦   ✦

Using Players and Projectors

◆ ◆ ◆ ◆

In This Chapter

Using the Standalone
Player or Projector

How FS Commands
control a Projector

Understanding the
Flash Player plug-in

◆ ◆ ◆ ◆

This last chapter explores alternative means of distributing your Flash movies, as self-contained executable applications for CD-ROMs or floppy disks. Also, we look at the broad support available for the Flash Player plug-in for Web browsers.

The Flash Standalone Player and Projector

The Flash Standalone Player and Projector let you take your Flash right off the Web and onto the desktop without having to worry whether users have the plug-in. In fact, you don't even need to worry about them having browsers! Standalone Players and Projectors have similar properties and limitations, although they're slightly different.

> ✦ **Standalone Player:** This is an executable player that comes with Flash. You can open any SWF file in this player. The Standalone Player can be found in the Macromedia/Flash 4/Players directory where you installed Flash 4.

> ✦ **Projector:** A Projector is an executable copy of your movie that doesn't need an additional player or plug-in to be viewed. It's essentially a movie contained within the Standalone Player. The Projector is ideal for distribution of Flash applications on floppy disks or CD-ROM's. Figure 27-1 shows a Flash movie played as a Projector.

Figure 27-1: This movie is being played as a Projector.

For the sake of simplicity, we refer to both Projectors and movies played in the Standalone Player as "standalones" in this discussion. Because both the Projector and Standalone Player have the same properties and limitations, you can apply everything discussed here to either one you choose to use.

Creating a projector

When you have finished producing a Flash movie, it's fairly simple to turn it into a projector. You have two ways to create a self-contained projector. Turning your Flash movies into self-contained projectors typically adds 316KB to the final file size.

New Feature

In previous versions of Flash, you were limited to creating projectors for the platform you were using. Flash 4 adds the ability to produce both Mac and Windows projectors from either version of Flash. Note that the Macintosh version of Flash 4 can directly create Windows executable files (.EXE files), while the Windows version of Flash creates Macintosh projectors that are automatically compressed as BinHex files (.HQX files).

Method 1: Using the Publish command

1. Select File ⇨ Publish Settings from the main menu.

2. When the Publish Settings dialog box opens, select the Formats tab and then check the projector formats. Publish both Windows and Macintosh projectors using this method. Figure 27-2 shows the Publish Settings dialog box with the appropriate formats selected.

3. Press the Publish button in the Publish Settings dialog box, and your Flash movie will be published in all of the formats (for example, .SWF, .GIF, .JPEG, and projector formats) specified with Publish Settings.

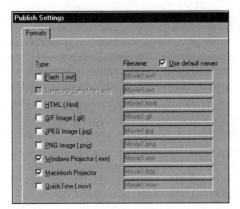

Figure 27-2: Select the projector formats in the Publish Settings dialog box.

Method 2: Using the Standalone Flash Player

1. Export your movie using File ➪ Export Movie from the main menu.

2. Open the exported Shockwave Flash movie (.SWF file) in the Standalone Player.

3. Choose File ➪ Create Projector from the Standalone Player menu, as shown in Figure 27-3.

Figure 27-3: Choose File ➪ Create Projector from the Standalone Player menu.

4. When the Save As dialog box opens, name the Projector and save it.

Tip

If your movie is set to play at full screen (see FS Commands later in this chapter), press the Escape key to make the Standalone Player menu appear. If the movie is set to play without the menu, you should use the Publish method—there's no shortcut key to create the Projector.

Distribution and licensing

Distribution of standalone projectors or the Flash Player is free. You don't have to buy a license to distribute the Standalone Player or Projector. However, according to Macromedia, you need to follow the "Made with Macromedia" guidelines for distributed Flash Players and projectors. Among other things, you need to include the "Made with Macromedia" logo on your product's packaging and credits screen. The run-time license agreement and Macromedia logos can be downloaded from the Macromedia Web site. For more information, check out `www.macromedia.com/support/programs/mwm`.

Distribution on CD-ROM or floppy disk

Flash has become increasingly popular for use on multimedia CD-ROMs, especially as embedded SWF files in larger Macromedia Director projectors. Standalones can be used as front-ends for installations, splash screens for other programs, or even as complete applications. When you combine the good looks of a Flash interface with a few FS Commands (see "FS Commands" in the next section), some simple scripting (BAT and AppleScript), and put them together on a CD-ROM that's programmed to start automatically on insertion, you have a first-class product.

Because Flash movies can be very small (even when packaged as a projector), you can fit interactive multimedia presentations on 3.5-inch 1.44MB floppy disks! This is truly revolutionary, as floppy disks can be copied very easily on any system with a floppy drive — you don't need a CD recorder to distribute your Flash movies in promotional mailers to clients.

Refer to the chapter27.html document located in the ch27 folder of the *Flash 4 Bible* CD-ROM for URL links to information on using scripting (BAT and AppleScript) with Flash standalones. You can also find instructions about creating CD-ROMs that start automatically on insertion.

FS Commands

FS Commands can be used to provide greater functionality to your standalones. These actions can turn a simple Flash movie into something spectacular! When combined with additional scripting and executables, you can make fully functional applications. Table 27-1 lists FS Commands for standalones.

When a FS Command action is added in the Frame Properties or Instance Properties dialog box, you can access standalone specific commands from a drop-down menu (see Figure 27-4). Refer to Chapter 13 for more information on adding actions to Flash frames or buttons.

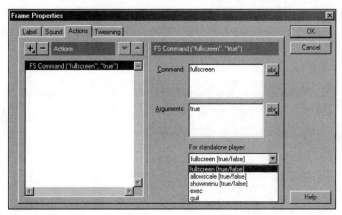

Figure 27-4: Flash 4 adds a convenient drop-down menu for FS Commands specific to the standalone Flash Player or projector.

Be sure to look at the chapter27.html document in the ch27 folder of the *Flash 4 Bible* CD-ROM for more information on using FS Commands.

Table 27-1		
FS Commands for Standalones		
FS Command	**Arguments**	**Function**
FullScreen	True/False	True sets the standalone to full-screen mode, without a menu. False sets it to the size specified by the Movie Properties.
AllowScale	True/False	Allows for scaling of the movie. False sets the movie to the size specified by the Movie Properties. This doesn't actually keep the standalone from being resized, it only the keeps the movie inside of it from being scaled.
ShowMenu	True/False	Toggles the menu bar and the right-click/control-click menu. True enables them, False turns them both off.
Exec	Path to executable (BAT, COM, EXE, and so on)	Opens an executable from within the standalone player. The application opens in front of the projector.
Quit		Closes the standalone.

On the CD-ROM
The source file for this tutorial, which is located in the ch27 folder of the *Flash 4 Bible* CD-ROM, contains three examples that use the Get URL action in a standalone projector.

Expert Tutorial:
Opening Web Pages from Standalone Projectors
by Chrissy Rey

Chrissy Rey is an energetic young woman from the suburbs of Washington, D.C.. She graduated from the University of Maryland in 1995, with a degree in Zoology. During her final year of study, she discovered the Web. After a couple of brief stints in her field of study (as a zookeeper aide, and an animal technician) she veered away from Zoology to pursue the Web full-time, working as both a freelance contractor (evenings) and as a full-time developer (days). In her spare time she runs FlashLite (www.flashlite.net), *which she established to post tutorials and tips on the use of Flash. In response to her work at FlashLite, we invited Chrissy to contribute material for this book—Part II is substantially based on her contributions. In addition, she developed this tutorial.*

One of the great improvements delivered with Flash 4 is the ease with which an external URL can be opened from the Standalone Projector. You'd surely appreciate this if you, too, labored endlessly with Flash 3, trying to find a way to open Web pages from the Standalone Projector . . . only to learn that there was no easy solution. (Furthermore, if you threw cross-platform compatibility needs into the mix, you had to spend considerable time writing BAT files and AppleScripts to get everything to work.) Happily, Flash 4 has solved this problem, and it's as simple as adding a Get URL action to your movie—in fact that's exactly what we're going to do here.

1. Create your movie as you normally would.

2. When you get to the button or keyframe where you want to open a Web page, simply use the Get URL action, with the URL value set to the local HTML file or Web site that you'd like to open.

   You can also use the Get URL action to create an e-mail link from the standalone. Just type the e-mail address preceded by mailto: in the URL box (for example, mailto:userID@domain.com). You don't need to worry about the Window settings when using Get URL action in the standalone. Each time the action is called, it will open the URL in the user's default browser. The Variables setting is only important if your standalone will be communicating with a back-end script.

3. Export the movie and open it in the standalone, or publish the movie as a projector. Test your actions to see how nicely they work.

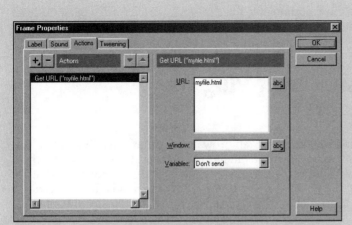

In the Frame Properties or Instance Properties dialog box, you can add a Get URL action that opens a Web page in the default browser.

Unfortunately this method doesn't let you open anything but HTML files. In order to open other file types, you still need to use the FS Command "Exec" in conjunction with a BAT file, AppleScript, or another trick to open these files. Refer to the section on FS Commands, earlier in this chapter, for more information on standalone specific commands.

Standalone Limitations and Solutions

When you distribute your Flash movies as standalones, you may think that you won't have to worry about streaming and download. As a consequence, standalones are often made considerably larger than a typical Flash movie—which can be a mistake! Very large movies (1MB or more) may not play on slower computers. Remember that Flash requires the computer processor to compute all of those vector calculations. When you try to give a slower computer 1MB worth of Flash at once, it may not be able to handle it.

Tip   One way to get around this limitation is to break your movies into several smaller movies. You can use the Load Movie/Unload Movie actions to open and close other movies within the original movie. You should use these actions in your standalones.

You should also test your movies on a variety of computers, especially if you plan to put a lot of money into distributing them on CD-ROM. Some processors handle the movies better than others and you often have to decide which processor you want to target as the lowest common denominator.

On the
CD-ROM

Refer to chapter27.html document in the ch27 folder of the *Flash 4 Bible* CD-ROM for more information about standalone limitations and solutions.

Using the Flash Player Plug-In for Web Browsers

Flash 4 movies can only be played in Web browsers that have the Shockwave Flash Player plug-in installed. Macromedia has made huge strides in making the plug-in prepackaged with recent Web browsers and operating system installation programs, eliminating the need for users to manually download and install the plug-in themselves. Unfortunately, the Flash 4 version of the plug-in will only be included in future releases of Web browsers and operating systems. Remember that the Flash 3 Player plug-in *can* play Flash 4 movies — however, any new features in Flash 4 movies will not be available (such as form fields, new actions, MP3 sound, and so on).

Note

For up-to-date information on the Flash Player plug-in, see Macromedia's download page at www.macromedia.com/shockwave/download/alternates.

Supported operating systems

Since Flash 3, Macromedia has greatly expanded its platform support for the Flash Player plug-in, to be used with Netscape-compatible browsers. At the time of this writing, you can download players for Windows 95/98/NT, Windows 3.1, Mac PPC, Mac 68k, Sun Solaris, and Linux x86. At the Macromedia User Conference in May 1999, the Flash Player was demonstrated on a Palm Pilot! While this was an "unofficial" player that is not publicly available (for example, it was a "proof of concept" demo), Macromedia has proven that Flash graphics can be ported to a variety of GUIs (graphical user interface) or operating systems.

Supported browsers

The Flash Player plug-in works best with Netscape and Internet Explorer browsers. Any browser that is compliant with Netscape Navigator 2.0's plug-in specification or Internet Explorer's ActiveX technology can support the Flash Player plug-in or ActiveX control. Note that Mac versions of Internet Explorer use a Netscape plug-in emulator to use the Flash Player plug-in rather than an ActiveX control.

For AOL subscribers, any version of AOL's 3.0 or 4.0 browsers (except for the earliest 3.0 release that used a non-Microsoft Internet Explorer shell) will support Shockwave plug-ins.

Caution   The Flash action FSCommand, which can be used to communicate with JavaScript, will only work with certain browser versions. Currently, all versions of Internet Explorer on the Macintosh do not support the FSCommand action. Netscape 3.01 or greater (on both Macintosh and Windows) or Internet Explorer 3.0 or greater for Windows 95/98/NT is necessary for FSCommand implementation.

Plug-in and Flash movie distribution on the Web

Anyone can download the Flash Player plug-in for free at the Macromedia Web site. You can direct visitors at your Web sites to Macromedia's Shockwave download page, www.macromedia.com/shockwave/download/index.cgi?P1_Prod_Version=ShockwaveFlash. In fact, according to Macromedia's licensing agreement, if you're publishing Shockwave movies on your Web site, you need to display the "Get Shockwave" logo on your Web site. This logo should link to Macromedia's download page, just listed. However, you need to license the right to distribute any Shockwave plug-in installer from Macromedia. For more details on licensing, see www.macromedia.com/shockwave.

Plug-in installation

In Chapter 25, we discuss the new Publish feature of Flash 4 and the use of preformatted HTML templates to deliver your Flash movies to your Web site. The template and/or hand-written HTML that you use for your Flash-enabled Web pages determines the degree of difficulty your visitors will have upon loading a Flash movie. Because Web browsers vary so drastically between operating systems (for example, Internet Explorer for the Mac behaves very differently from Internet Explorer for Windows), make all attempts to make the plug-in process as invisible as possible. The following are the possible outcomes of each HTML template that Flash 4 uses:

✦ **Flash Only (Default):** This template doesn't use any JavaScript detection for the Flash Player plug-in. It simply places the <OBJECT> and <EMBED> tags for the Flash movie into an HTML document. The CODEBASE attribute of <OBJECT> will direct Internet Explorer for Windows to the download location of the Flash ActiveX control. This process should be relatively straightforward for Windows users. For visitors using Netscape 3.0 or greater (on any platform), the PLUGINSPAGE attribute of <EMBED> provides the browser with the plug-in location, and prompts the visitor to go there.

✦ **Flash 4 with Image:** This template inserts an <OBJECT> tag for Internet Explorer (just as the Flash Only template will) and JavaScript detection code for the presence of the Netscape plug-in. When a Netscape browser loads the HTML page, JavaScript checks for version 4 of the Flash Player plug-in. If the plug-in is installed, then JavaScript writes the proper <EMBED> tag and attributes for the Flash movie. If the plug-in is not installed, then JavaScript writes HTML code for a static GIF image.

✦ **Flash 3 with Image:** This template uses the same HTML code as the "Flash 4 with Image" template, except that it checks for version 3 of the Flash Player plug-in. Note that the Flash 3 format should be selected in the Flash tab of the Publish Settings.

✦ **Flash with FSCommand:** This template does not employ any JavaScript plug-in detection. The JavaScript inserted by this template is solely for the Flash action, FSCommand.

✦ **Java Player:** This HTML template will use an ⟨APPLET⟩ tag with ⟨PARAM⟩ subtags to employ the Flash Player Java edition. It does not use ⟨OBJECT⟩ or ⟨EMBED⟩ tags. See the next section for more information.

✦ **QuickTime:** This template will create an HTML document containing the ⟨EMBED⟩ tag information to display a QuickTime Flash movie — a .MOV file, not a SWF file. The QuickTime Player is discussed in the next section.

Unfortunately, you can never predict with any certainty how visitors will encounter a Flash plug-in installation. Most of the automated HTML coding from earlier versions of Flash and/or Aftershock may make an "upgrade" installation very difficult for Web visitors. For example, if an HTML document uses JavaScript to detect the Flash Player version 3 plug-in and the visitor's browser is using the version 4 plug-in, the browser may return a "false" value for the plug-in and direct the visitor to a non-Flash page. The older JavaScript code doesn't know that the Flash 4 plug-in is perfectly able to play older Flash movies. If you have created Web pages and Flash movies with previous versions of Flash, see Macromedia's tech note at www.macromedia.com/support/flash/ts/documents/flash4_detection.htm for more information on updating JavaScript code to detect Flash Player version 4.

Tip

If you are using scripting to detect the Flash Player plug-in, check out Macromedia's tech note at www.macromedia.com/support/flash/ts/documents/browser_detection_of_flash.htm. This Web page provides information regarding which browsers can employ detection for plug-ins or ActiveX controls.

Plug-in setup on Internet Explorer for Mac

You may experience difficulties with the auto-installation of the Flash Player plug-in with Internet Explorer for Macintosh (IE Mac). IE Mac does not use the Flash ActiveX control like Internet Explorer on Windows. Rather, it uses a Netscape plug-in emulator so that plug-ins developed for the Macintosh version of Netscape can be used interchangeably with IE Mac.

For some reason, the Shockwave Flash movie file type (and MIME type) doesn't always properly register itself in the IE Mac preferences. This means that when a Web page containing Shockwave Flash movies (.SWF files) is loaded into the browser, the movie may not appear — it will be replaced with a "broken" plug-in icon. However, it's not too difficult to setup the Flash movie file type in the IE Mac preferences. Before you work through the following steps, make sure that you have run the Shockwave Installer from the Macromedia Web site. The installer copies the Shockwave Flash plug-into the Plug-ins folder of the Internet Explorer application folder.

1. Open Internet Explorer and choose Edit ⇨ Preferences. In the Receiving Files category in the left column of the Internet Explorer Preferences dialog box, highlight the File Helpers subcategory (see Figure 27-5).

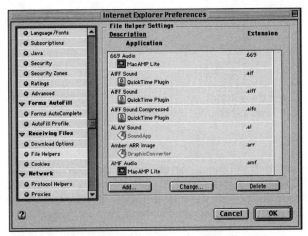

Figure 27-5: The File Helpers list displays the current plug-ins and application handlers from Web content and downloaded files.

2. Scroll through the File Helpers list, and look for a Shockwave Flash or Flash movie listing with a SWF file extension. If you find a Shockwave Flash entry (NOT Shockwave Director), highlight the entry and click Change. If you can't change a Shockwave Flash entry, click the Add button.

3. In the Edit File Helper dialog box, change or enter the settings shown in Figure 27-6. Most importantly, make sure you specify SWF as the Extension, application/x-shockwave-flash as the MIME type, SWFL as the File Type and SWF2 as the File Creator. In the Handling section, choose View with Plug-in, click the Browse button, and find the Shockwave Flash NP-PPC or Shockwave Flash NP-64K plug-in file in the Plug-Ins folder of the Internet Explorer application folder. When your settings are identical to Figure 27-6, click OK.

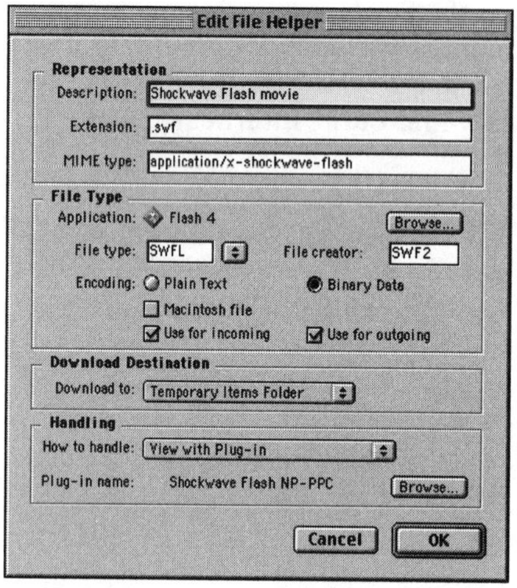

Figure 27-6: You can adjust the settings for any file type in the Edit File Helper dialog box.

Now that you've set up the Preferences correctly for Flash playback, quit Internet Explorer and restart the application. Direct the browser to a Flash-enabled Web site to view a Flash movie, or drag a SWF file into the browser window. Internet Explorer should now be able to display and play the Flash movie.

Alternative Flash-Content Players

While Flash 4 movies play back best with Macromedia's Flash Player plug-in (or standalone player), Macromedia has developed Java class files (available in the Flash application folder) so that Java-enabled Web browsers can play Flash movies. Macromedia has also teamed up with Real Systems and Apple to enable Flash content in RealPlayer and the QuickTime Player, respectively. By enabling Flash content in other players, Macromedia is promoting the acceptance of Flash as the de-facto vector standard for Web graphics. Moreover, with so many alternatives for Flash playback, it is more likely that your Web visitors can see your Flash content.

Flash Player Java edition

You can use the Java Player HTML template to enable the Flash Player Java edition in Web browsers. This player will work on any Java-compatible Web browser. However, you need to do a bit of work to make sure that the Flash class files are available on your Web server. The Java Player HTML template inserts the following `<APPLET>` and `<PARAM>` tags into a Web document:

```
<APPLET CODE=Flash.class ARCHIVE=Flash.jar WIDTH=550
HEIGHT=400>
<PARAM NAME=cabbase VALUE="Flash.cab">
<PARAM NAME="movie VALUE="home.swf">
<PARAM NAME=quality VALUE=high>
<PARAM NAME=bgcolor VALUE=#FFFFFF>
</APPLET>
```

You may need to adjust the `CODE` and `ARCHIVE` paths to indicate where the class files are located relative to the HTML document. You can find the Java class files (as well as Netscape .JAR and Internet Explorer .CAB files) in the Flash Player Java Edition folder, located inside the Players folder of the Flash 4 application folder. Upload the CLASS, JAR and CAB files to a folder located on your Web server.

Tip   You may have noticed another folder called FlashSmall inside the Flash Player Java Edition folder. The class files inside of the FlashSmall can be used instead of the regular CLASS, JAR, and CAB files if your Flash movie does not contain any bitmaps or sounds. The FlashSmall class files are smaller and easier for visitors to download. You'll need to change any reference to Flash.xxx files in the `<APPLET>` and `<PARAM>` tags to FlashSmall.xxx (for example, Flash.class should be changed to FlashSmall.class).

You can only use Flash 2 format SWF files with the Java Player. To export Flash 2 movies, select Flash 2 in the Version setting of the Publish Settings' Flash tab. Flash 2 movies can not use many of the features available to Flash 3 and 4 movies, which include:

✦ Alpha channel effects (transparent colors)

✦ Shape tweening

✦ Mask layers

✦ Movie clip symbols

✦ Many Flash actions such as `Tell Target`, `If`, `Set Property`, `Set Variable`, and so forth.

RealPlayer 5.0 with Flash playback

With a little effort, you can repackage your Flash SWF movies as RealFlash presentations over the Web. Web visitors can use the RealPlayer G2 to play RealFlash, RealAudio, or RealVideo (among a long list of Real Systems media types) content. RealPlayer movies stream from a RealServer (special server software running concurrently with Web server software) into the RealPlayer plug-in (Netscape) or ActiveX control (Internet Explorer).

This section will briefly explore the uses and functionality of RealPlayer with Flash playback. For detailed information on converting Flash content and audio to the Real format, check out `www.real.com/devzone/library/stream/flash/`. You can download the Real Flash Kit for either Mac or Windows (which includes an excellent tutorial Acrobat PDF) and the Real Encoder. Both utilities are available for free.

The following six steps provide an overview of RealFlash content creation. The PDF file in the Real Flash kit explains how to perform the following process in much more detail.

1. Create a Flash movie that is synched to a Stream event audio track, using an imported WAV or AIF sound file. See Chapter 11 for more information on Streamed audio.

2. Export a SWF file from Flash with all audio events disabled.

3. Export an AVI (Video for Windows) or MOV (QuickTime Video) file from Flash. You can extract and convert the audio portion of the exported AVI or MOV file to the RealAudio format using the free Real Encoder utility or RealPublisher. Either application creates a RealMedia (RM) file that works with RealPlayer.

4. Create a text-based metafile (using Notepad or SimpleText) that specifies the location of each RealMedia file, including the SWF file from Flash. The pnm protocol is specified to invoke the RealServer software — do not use http. Join the Flash file name and RealMedia file name with a + operator in the URL: `pnm://www.yourserver.com/realmedia/flashmovie.swf+audio.rm`.

5. Save this text metafile as a RAM or RPM file. Use the RAM extension to play the content in a separate RealPlayer window, or RPM to play the content within the browser window.

6. In the HTML code of your Web page, insert `<OBJECT>` and `<EMBED>` tags directing the browser to the .RAM or .RPM file.

RealPlayer can only recognize Flash 2–formatted movies (for example, .SWF files). When you create Flash movies that are intended for RealPlayer delivery, you need to adhere to the same restrictions as prescribed in the Java Player section. You should limit Flash actions to those listed in Table 27-2.

Table 27-2
Flash Actions that are Compatible with RealPlayer

Flash Action	Translated to RealPlayer As	Description
Play	Play	Starts the movie.
Stop	Pause	Halts playback until another button or action initiates a Play command.
Go To	Seek	This action jumps playback to a different section of the Flash movie. Because Real files are buffered, you may experience delays to load new portions of the movie.
Get URL	(Intercepted by browser as URL link)	This action loads a new Web page into the browser window. Because such an action leaves the RealPlayer interface, reserve the use of this action for the end of a Flash movie.

Why would you use RealPlayer to view Flash movies instead of the Flash Player plug-in? Admittedly, the restrictions for Flash content may dissuade you from publishing RealFlash content on your Web pages. However, if you offer other RealMedia downloads from your Web site, you may want to provide RealFlash presentations as well. Because Flash 4 exports MP3 audio, the reliance for high-quality streaming RealAudio is not as strong as it was with Flash 2 or 3 movies.

QuickTime Player

Apple introduced playback support for Flash movies with QuickTime 4. Better yet, Macromedia included QuickTime Flash export options with Flash 4. A QuickTime Flash movie (.MOV file) is essentially a Flash SWF file packaged as a QuickTime media type.

Cross-Reference The QuickTime architecture and QuickTime Flash format are discussed at length in Chapter 21. The QuickTime HTML template is discussed in Chapter 25.

You can use the QuickTime HTML template in Publish Settings to create an instant Web page that utilizes the QuickTime Player plug-in. It uses the <EMBED> tag to prescribe the name, width, height, and plug-in download location:

```
<EMBED
  SRC="flashmovie.mov"
  WIDTH=550 HEIGHT=400
  BGCOLOR="#FFFFFF" BORDER="0"
PLUGINSPAGE="http://www.apple.com/quicktime/download/">
</EMBED>
```

At the time of this writing, QuickTime 4 can only support Flash 3 graphics and actions. Remember that Flash 4 has only added new interactive components such as ActionScript to the Flash milieu—all Flash graphics, including mask layers and movie clips, are supported by the QuickTime Player. For interactivity, you should limit yourself to the actions prescribed in the RealPlayer section. Flash movies can act as a timeline navigator for other QuickTime media, such as video or audio.

 Tip   Check out Apple's QuickTime Sprites overview page at `www.apple.com/ quicktime/overview/sprites.html` **for a demo of QuickTime Flash.**

✦   ✦   ✦

Using the CD-ROM

The CD-ROM included with this book aids you with many examples and tutorials, including the following:

◆ Trial versions of all the Extensis plug-ins and applications (including Portofolio, Mask Pro and PhotoTools), all of the BoxTop plug-ins (including ColorSafe, GIFmation and ImageVice).

◆ Limited-edition version of Paul Mendigochea's FlashMail CGI script. Note that this script requires that PHP be installed on your Web server. You can download the PHP source code at www.php.net.

◆ Just about every .FLA and .SWF file that is discussed in the book, including those used in Expert Tutorials.

◆ QuickTime movies and QTVR panorama and object movies. Many thanks to Paul Nykamp from Focus VR for the QTVR samples.

Installing and Using Plug-Ins and Applications

In the "software" folder of the CD-ROM, you'll find the trial versions of the BoxTop and Extensis plug-ins and applications.

On a Macintosh, go to the specific application's folder and double-click the installation file. Then follow the installer's instructions to proceed.

On a PC, go to the specific application's folder and either unzip the installation .ZIP file or double-click the installation .EXE file.

Installing and Using FlashMail

To use Paul Mendigochea's FlashMail CGI script (the .php3 file), you'll need to download and install the PHP engine on your Web server. You may need the assistance and permission of the system administrator of your Internet service provider (ISP) or Internet presence provider (IPP) in order to install PHP. Once it is installed, upload the FlashMail CGI script file, flashmail.php3, to a directory or folder that is accessible by PHP. You may need to edit the first line of the script to indicate the path to the PHP files on your server.

Once you have PHP installed, you should be able to follow Paul's Expert Tutorial in Chapter 15 to create a FlashMail form in your Flash movies. For updates and revisions to FlashMail, see Paul's Flash CGI Web site at www.flashcgi.com.

✦   ✦   ✦

Author and Contributor Contact Information

Authors

Robert Reinhardt
rob@theFlashBible.com
www.o-n-s-i-t-e.com/
1706 North Stanley Avenue, Apt. 6
Los Angeles, CA 90046

Jon Warren Lentz
jon@theFlashBible.com
www.uncom.com
2718 Socorro Lane
Carlsbad CA 92009

Contributors, Technical Editors

Justin Jamieson
Co-Pilot, mediumLarge
justin@mediumlarge.com
www.mediumLarge.com
19 Elm Grove Avenue, Studio 2
Toronto, ON, Canada M6K 2H9

Paul Mendigochea [a.k.a. "Pablo"]
pablo@digitology.com
www.flasher.net/flashpad.html
545 East Orange Grove, Apt. P
Burbank, CA 91501

Colin Moock
fritz@iceinc.com
colin_moock@iceinc.com
www.moock.org
92 Walmer Road, Apt. #3
Toronto, ON, Canada M5R 2X7

Chrissy Rey
artemisian@erols.com
www.flashlite.net
4817 Blackfoot Road
College Park, MD 20740

Bill Turner
Turnertoons Productions
kar2nist@turnertoons.com
www.turnertoons.com
2124 Algeria Street NE
Palm Bay, FL 32905

Guest Tutorialists

Manuel Clement [a.k.a. ManoOne]
manoone@bwave.com
MANO1 Digital Visions
www.manoone.com

David Gould
3D artist and programmer
davidgould@davidgould.com
www.davidgould.com
P.O. Box 706, Burleigh Heads
QLD. 4220. Australia

Christiaan Luitzen Honselaar
Educational programmer
c.l.honselaar@bioledu.rug.nl
www.HTMWell.com
Rummerinkhof 12
9751 SL Haren, Netherlands

Mike Jones
mikej@flashgen.com
www.flashgen.com
www.spookyandthebandit.com
12 Theobalds Road
London, England WC1X 8P

Mark LaBelle
Macromedia Evangelist
mlabelle28@yahoo.com
www.marklabelle.com
1030 Palm Avenue
Wildwood, FL 34785

Larry Larsen
Macromedia Evangelist
777@greenjem.com
www.greenjem.com

Dorian Nisinson
Design Director, Flash Central
dorian@bway.net
www.bway.net/~dorian
233 West 77th Street
New York, NY 10024

Todd Purgason
Creative Director
JUXT Interactive
858 Production Place
Newport Beach, CA 92663

Anders F. Rönnblom
Editor-in-Chief
EFX Art and Design [formerly known as *Mac Art & Design*]
macartdesign@matchbox.se
www.efxmag.com
Roslagsgatan 11
113 55 Stockholm, Sweden

✦ ✦ ✦

Index

continued

continued

continued

continued

continued

continued

IDG Books Worldwide, Inc.
End–User License Agreement

READ THIS. You should carefully read these terms and conditions before opening the software packet(s) included with this book ("Book"). This is a license agreement ("Agreement") between you and IDG Books Worldwide, Inc. ("IDGB"). By opening the accompanying software packet(s), you acknowledge that you have read and accept the following terms and conditions. If you do not agree and do not want to be bound by such terms and conditions, promptly return the Book and the unopened software packet(s) to the place you obtained them for a full refund.

1. **License Grant.** IDGB grants to you (either an individual or entity) a nonexclusive license to use one copy of the enclosed software program(s) (collectively, the "Software") solely for your own personal or business purposes on a single computer (whether a standard computer or a workstation component of a multiuser network). The Software is in use on a computer when it is loaded into temporary memory (RAM) or installed into permanent memory (hard disk, CD-ROM, or other storage device). IDGB reserves all rights not expressly granted herein.

2. **Ownership.** IDGB is the owner of all right, title, and interest, including copyright, in and to the compilation of the Software recorded on the disk(s) or CD-ROM ("Software Media"). Copyright to the individual programs recorded on the Software Media is owned by the author or other authorized copyright owner of each program. Ownership of the Software and all proprietary rights relating thereto remain with IDGB and its licensers.

3. **Restrictions On Use and Transfer.**

   (a) You may only (i) make one copy of the Software for backup or archival purposes, or (ii) transfer the Software to a single hard disk, provided that you keep the original for backup or archival purposes. You may not (i) rent or lease the Software, (ii) copy or reproduce the Software through a LAN or other network system or through any computer subscriber system or bulletin–board system, or (iii) modify, adapt, or create derivative works based on the Software.

   (b) You may not reverse engineer, decompile, or disassemble the Software. You may transfer the Software and user documentation on a permanent basis, provided that the transferee agrees to accept the terms and conditions of this Agreement and you retain no copies. If the Software is an update or has been updated, any transfer must include the most recent update and all prior versions.

4. **Restrictions on Use of Individual Programs.** You must follow the individual requirements and restrictions detailed for each individual program in Appendix A of this Book. These limitations are also contained in the individual license

agreements recorded on the Software Media. These limitations may include a requirement that after using the program for a specified period of time, the user must pay a registration fee or discontinue use. By opening the Software packet(s), you will be agreeing to abide by the licenses and restrictions for these individual programs that are detailed in Appendix A and on the Software Media. None of the material on this Software Media or listed in this Book may ever be redistributed, in original or modified form, for commercial purposes.

5. Limited Warranty.

(a) IDGB warrants that the Software and Software Media are free from defects in materials and workmanship under normal use for a period of sixty (60) days from the date of purchase of this Book. If IDGB receives notification within the warranty period of defects in materials or workmanship, IDGB will replace the defective Software Media.

(b) **IDGB AND THE AUTHORS OF THE BOOK DISCLAIM ALL OTHER WARRANTIES, EXPRESS OR IMPLIED, INCLUDING WITHOUT LIMITATION IMPLIED WARRANTIES OF MERCHANTABILITY AND FITNESS FOR A PARTICULAR PURPOSE, WITH RESPECT TO THE SOFTWARE, THE PROGRAMS, THE SOURCE CODE CONTAINED THEREIN, AND/OR THE TECHNIQUES DESCRIBED IN THIS BOOK. IDGB DOES NOT WARRANT THAT THE FUNCTIONS CONTAINED IN THE SOFTWARE WILL MEET YOUR REQUIREMENTS OR THAT THE OPERATION OF THE SOFTWARE WILL BE ERROR FREE.**

(c) This limited warranty gives you specific legal rights, and you may have other rights that vary from jurisdiction to jurisdiction.

6. Remedies.

(a) IDGB's entire liability and your exclusive remedy for defects in materials and workmanship shall be limited to replacement of the Software Media, which may be returned to IDGB with a copy of your receipt at the following address: Software Media Fulfillment Department, Attn.: *Flash 4 Bible*, IDG Books Worldwide, Inc., 10475 Crosspoint Blvd., Indianapolis, IN 46256, or call 1-800-762-2974. Please allow three to four weeks for delivery. This Limited Warranty is void if failure of the Software Media has resulted from accident, abuse, or misapplication. Any replacement Software Media will be warranted for the remainder of the original warranty period or thirty (30) days, whichever is longer.

(b) In no event shall IDGB or the authors be liable for any damages whatsoever (including without limitation damages for loss of business profits, business interruption, loss of business information, or any other pecuniary loss) arising from the use of or inability to use the Book or the Software, even if IDGB has been advised of the possibility of such damages.

(c) Because some jurisdictions do not allow the exclusion or limitation of liability for consequential or incidental damages, the above limitation or exclusion may not apply to you.

7. **U.S. Government Restricted Rights.** Use, duplication, or disclosure of the Software by the U.S. Government is subject to restrictions stated in paragraph (c)(1)(ii) of the Rights in Technical Data and Computer Software clause of DFARS 252.227-7013, and in subparagraphs (a) through (d) of the Commercial Computer — Restricted Rights clause at FAR 52.227-19, and in similar clauses in the NASA FAR supplement, when applicable.

8. **General.** This Agreement constitutes the entire understanding of the parties and revokes and supersedes all prior agreements, oral or written, between them and may not be modified or amended except in a writing signed by both parties hereto that specifically refers to this Agreement. This Agreement shall take precedence over any other documents that may be in conflict herewith. If any one or more provisions contained in this Agreement are held by any court or tribunal to be invalid, illegal, or otherwise unenforceable, each and every other provision shall remain in full force and effect.

my2cents.idgbooks.com

Register This Book — And Win!

Visit **http://my2cents.idgbooks.com** to register this book and we'll automatically enter you in our fantastic monthly prize giveaway. It's also your opportunity to give us feedback: let us know what you thought of this book and how you would like to see other topics covered.

Discover IDG Books Online!

The IDG Books Online Web site is your online resource for tackling technology — at home and at the office. Frequently updated, the IDG Books Online Web site features exclusive software, insider information, online books, and live events!

10 Productive & Career-Enhancing Things You Can Do at www.idgbooks.com

- Nab source code for your own programming projects.

- Download software.

- Read Web exclusives: special articles and book excerpts by IDG Books Worldwide authors.

- Take advantage of resources to help you advance your career as a Novell or Microsoft professional.

- Buy IDG Books Worldwide titles or find a convenient bookstore that carries them.

- Register your book and win a prize.

- Chat live online with authors.

- Sign up for regular e-mail updates about our latest books.

- Suggest a book you'd like to read or write.

- Give us your 2¢ about our books and about our Web site.

You say you're not on the Web yet? It's easy to get started with IDG Books' *Discover the Internet*, available at local retailers everywhere.

CD-ROM Installation Instructions

The *Flash 4 Bible* CD-ROM is packed with tutorials, plug-ins, and examples from almost all of the FLA and SWF files that are discussed on the book. You'll find all kinds of useful things so you can easily learn — and master! — Flash 4.

The CD-ROM that accompanies this book can be used on both Windows and Macintosh Systems. To make sure that your computer can run the CD-ROM, please check the system requirements that are found on the back of the book.

For more information on installing and using the programs on the CD-ROM, please read Appendix A.